DEADLINE DISASTER

© Michael Wynn Jones 1976
All rights reserved.
First published in Great Britain in 1976 by
David & Charles (Publishers) Limited
Newton Abbot, Devon
First published in the United States in 1976 by
Henry Regnery Company
180 North Michigan Avenue, Chicago, Illinois 60601
Printed in the United States of America
Library of Congress Catalog Card Number: 76-6273
International Standard Book Number: 0-8092-8033-7(cloth)
0-8092-7985-1(paper)

Designed and produced in England by
London Editions Limited
30 Uxbridge Road London W12 8ND

DEADLINE DISASTER

a newspaper history

Michael Wynn Jones

Henry Regnery Company
Chicago

Acknowledgements
My grateful thanks are due to the
Superintendent and staff of the British
Newspaper Library at Colindale, to John Frost
for selections from his collection, to Penny
Ayles for her devoted research, and, of course,
to the reporters and photographers of all the
newspapers included in this book without
whom it would not have been possible.

Contents

7 The Press and Disasters

10 Headlines 1870–1900

13 Out of the Ashes
The Chicago Fire 1871

17 Tragedy over the Tay
Tay Bridge Disaster 1879

20 A Trick of Fate
Sunderland Panic 1883

22 A City Paralysed
New York Blizzard 1888

24 The Day the Dam Broke
Johnstown Flood 1889

28 A Cause for War
The Sinking of the *Maine* 1898

32 The Death of Galveston
Galveston Flood 1900

36 Headlines 1900–1920

39 Island Holocaust
Eruption of Mt Pelée 1902

44 Last Drama at the Iroquois
Chicago Theatre Fire 1903

47 The End of an Excursion
The Sinking of the *General Slocum* 1904

50 A God-forsaken Mess
The San Francisco Earthquake 1906

55 Too Much Stress
The Quebec Bridge Collapse 1907

57 The Earthquake at Messina 1908

58 Maiden Voyage
The Sinking of the *Titanic* 1912

63 The Death of a Valley
Senghenydd Mine Disaster 1913

66 Fog of Misunderstanding
The Sinking of the *Empress of Ireland* 1914

70 In the Front Line
The Quintinshill Rail Crash 1915

72 Lethal Cargo
The Halifax Explosion 1917

74 The Unstoppable Virus
The Flu Epidemic 1918

76 Headlines 1920–1939

79 Out of the Blue
The *R.38* Crash 1921

81 The Darkest Day
Tokyo 1923

86 The Murphysboro Tornado 1925

88 The Broken Giant
The *Shenandoah* Crash 1925

90 Race against Time
The Sinking of the *S.4* 1927

93 Women and Children First
The Sinking of the *Vestris* 1928

95 A Sacrifice to Improvidence
The *R.101* Crash 1930

101 The Earthquake at Hawkes Bay 1931

103 The Deciding Factor
The *Akron* and the *Macon* 1933 and 1935

106 The *Morro Castle* Mystery
New Jersey 1934

110 The Gresford Colliery Disaster 1934

112 The Final Spectacular
Crystal Palace Fire 1936

114 The Advancing Crest
Ohio Valley Floods 1937

117 Fire in the Sky
The *Hindenburg* Crash 1937

122 A Freak of Nature
New England Hurricane 1938

124 Forty-eight Hours on the *Thetis*
The Sinking of the *Thetis* 1939

128 Headlines 1939–1960

131 Black Friday
The Bush Fires of Victoria 1939

133 The Fire at the Coconut Grove 1942

135 The Panic at Bolton Wanderers 1946

136 The Texas City Explosions 1947

138 Death Dive
Farnborough Air Crash 1952

141 The Ransom of Progress
The Comet Disasters 1953–4

145 Invasion by Sea
North Sea Floods 1953

150 The Christmas Eve Rail Crash
Tangiwai, New Zealand 1953

152 The Rough Law of Sport
Le Mans Disaster 1955

154 The Day a Team Died
The Munich Air Crash 1958

158 Headlines 1960–1976

161 The Last Avalanche
Vaiont Dam Disaster 1963

163 The Fire on the *Lakonia* 1963

164 The Sinking of the *Thresher* 1963

167 The Black Mountain
The Aberfan Disaster 1966

171 Lost Heritage
The Florence Floods 1966

174 Oil on Troubled Waters
The Sinking of the *Torrey Canyon* 1967

178 The Apollo Fire 1967

179 The Sinking of the *Wahine* 1968

180 An Improper Balance
The Yarra Bridge Collapse 1970

182 What Happened at Ibrox?
The Glasgow Panic 1971

184 Paris Air Show Disaster 1973

185 The D.C. 10 Crash at Ermenonville 1974

187 The Destruction of Darwin 1974

188 The Udine Earthquake 1976

191 Index

Introduction

The Press and Disasters

To say that newspapers thrive on disasters is to say as much about the reading public, I suspect, as about the papers themselves. The appearance of the first recognizable, regular English-language newspaper (the *Oxford Gazette*) coincided with—indeed was partly occasioned by—two of the greatest disasters Britain ever experienced: the Plague and the Fire of London. The *Gazette*'s early columns were virtually monopolized by chilling accounts of these dread visitations and daily lists of casualty-figures. And since that time the Press has never knowingly allowed an important disaster to escape its attentions (except when official restraints have been placed upon it). But just as the birth of the *Gazette* was in direct response to the hunger of the refugee Court at Oxford for news from the dying capital, so today the apparently obsessive emphasis given to modern calamities in our newspapers still reflects the public's own preoccupation with death and disaster—as witnessed for instance, by the queues that formed in the streets of New York and London, waiting for a new edition of news of the Titanic.

One might speculate, perhaps, on why the public is so fascinated by headlines of disaster; why it congregates at the scene of a tragedy; or why it flocks in its thousands to film-epics of earthquake, inferno, or disintegrating airship. There are doubtless deep-seated reasons, but the question itself has never unduly exercised the Press: it has simply responded to this human characteristic without any qualms—some might even say, with relish. Their function, as the newspapers see it, is to give a responsible but not necessarily unemotional account of the event, to ascertain where help is needed and in what form (and in many cases to help get it there), and to investigate the causes of a disaster, exposing if necessary any culpability and helping to safeguard that such a disaster is not repeated (assuming that Man has any control over this aspect of the situation).

Arguments about Press treatment of disasters over the years have rarely disputed the newspapers' role, rather they have criticized the way that role has been interpreted. Journalists have frequently been accused of sensationalizing stories (presumably to attract more sales). It is not an argument to be lightly dismissed; undoubtedly there are instances where relatively minor occurrences have been blown up out of proportion. And there can be no excuse for the kind of one-sided coverage presented by some sections of the New York Press when the Maine sank in 1898 (which is dealt with in later pages). However it's difficult to see how very many of the disasters dealt with in this book could have been over-estimated: they *were* terrible and shocking, and it would have done no-one a service to minimize them. Of course, in the immediate aftermath of a tragedy the main sources of information are survivors or eyewitnesses—who may well be themselves in a state of shock—and the reporter on the spot who will, not unreasonably, wish to communicate his own personal sense of horror and outrage. His technical ability to do so will vary considerably.

This aspect of 'sensationalism' is purely subjective, and will invariably invite criticism. Equally, what the public actually expects from its first-hand narratives of disaster has changed considerably in the 100 years covered by this book. The Victorians seem to have had an impelling urge to romanticize calamity (not view it through rose-coloured spectacles, rather to invest it with epic qualities) and the papers happily accommodated them, with their oratorical prose, lamentable dirges and reprints of moralistic sermons. Nowadays we require rather more precise, factual accounts—partly because we can make our own interpretations when we see the television pictures, and partly because in an over-populated and increasingly technological age that offers a far greater *potential* for disaster, we are less inclined to see these things romantically.

One factor that the arrival of reporters from rival news-agencies or newspaper chains does introduce is the edge of competition. This may indeed have the excellent result of inducing individual correspondents to make keener efforts to overcome the often awesome difficulties involved in 'getting the story': transport to the scene of a disaster, and communication out of it, are nearly always disrupted or non-existent. With the possible exception of war-reporting no other kind of assignment can stretch the resources and initiative of a newspaper so much as a disaster, and in this respect it may be said that the Press has acquitted itself honourably over the years. Competition, on the other hand, can sometimes lead to less desirable manifestations—for example, the traffic in 'numbers'. Certain forms of catastrophe (earthquakes or hurricanes, let's say) seem to induce the belief that the greater the death-toll, the more newsworthy the story is—and from that springs the pressure to 'find' more casualties than your competitor. Within three days—and in what was essentially an information vacuum—newspaper reports of the deaths in the 1923 Tokyo earthquake rose from 10,000 to half a million to one million (the real figure was somewhere in the region of 150,000).

To be fair, this failing has to be seen in the context of the confusion and chaos surrounding such events—and also the reporter at the scene of a disaster is often regarded as a parasite by rescuers and rescued alike (photographers had their cameras smashed by distraught victims of the Galveston flood in 1900 and it still happened sixty-six years later at Aberfan). There exists a strong, and perfectly reasonable, belief that suffering is private, that personal loss should not be shared with the general public. This is an inherent anomaly in the role of the reporter covering a disaster: when is he only doing his job, and when is he intruding? It is a question that has never been satisfactorily resolved, by the Press itself, by the public, or by the numerous official inquiries that have sat to consider the matter. It is open to so many interpretations—when Matt Busby was photographed in his oxygen tent after the 1958 air crash at Munich, opinions on this 'intrusion into privacy' were sharply and, so far as one can see, evenly divided.

But having considered some of the brickbats that are heaved at the Press from time to time, there are bouquets to hand out, too. One of the characteristic features of many disasters is that the victims are isolated from the outside world, whether it is the island of Martinique after the 1902 eruption of Mount Pelée or the inhabitants of Louisville marooned by the 1935 floodwaters of the Ohio. Until the world knows what has happened, and the magnitude of it, no aid can be forthcoming. Florence in 1966 (see page 171) is a prime example of the danger of underestimating both the threat and the effects of a disaster. The function of the Press on such occasions is to communicate a sense of urgency, which authorities are sometimes reluctant to show. For the most part newspapers have done this exceedingly well, and have very often taken the lead in raising funds for the relief of victims.

In this, and in their zeal to investigate and to apportion blame, papers are often seen to be taking the side of the sufferers against 'authority'—whatever that might appropriately be (the Fire Inspection Department after the appalling Iroquois theatre fire in 1903, the shipowners after the Vestris disaster in 1928, the Italian Government after the Florence floods, and so on). If there is a danger of this becoming 'trial by Press', as for instance the British Government claimed when a gag was imposed on Fleet Street after its attacks on the Coal Board over the Aberfan tragedy, it is surely better to live with this danger than to risk the perpetuation of official negligence, lack of humanity, or irresponsibility.

The disasters selected in this book are intended to be representative, rather than exhaustive. Magnitude has not been a criterion for inclusion. Indeed I have found it almost impossible actually to define what constitutes a 'disaster'. In Tokyo 150,000 died: after the wreck of the Torrey Canyon only one man died. But they were both disasters—and described as such unanimously by the newspapers. At the same time I did not once find the word applied to the Flu Epidemic of 1918, which killed an estimated fifteen million!

1870-1900

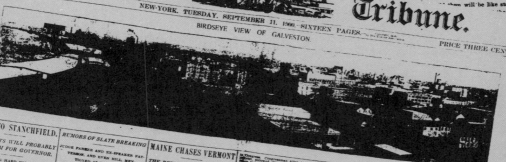

New-York Tribune.

VOL. XLIX.....No. 15,541.   NEW-YORK, MONDAY, JUNE 3, 1889.—TEN PAGES.

CHASED BY A GUNBOAT.

FIRED ON BY LEGITIME'S CANNON.

THE STORY OF THE CAROLINE MILLER'S ESCAPE

FORMING A GREAT SALT COMPANY.

WHAT MESSRS. BURGER AND

TWO BODIES FOUND IN THE RUINS.

THE BODY OF A YOUNG MAN OF GOOD FOUND AT A STATEN ISLAND HOT

THE ANNAPOLIS POSTOFFICE ROBBED.

REGISTERED LETTERS FOR AN AUSTRIAN SHIP STOLEN.

THE BOSTON MAY NOT GO TO HAYTI.

THERE MAY ... AD.

Hundred Bodies Have Been Taken Out to Sea in Barges.

But Putrid Carcasses Are Beginning to Poison the Air and Endanger Health.

Thousands of Persons Injured and Many Are Dying from Their Wounds.

The First Relief Boat Reaches the Island and Soon Distributes Its Provisions to the Starving.

TIFYING THE DEAD.

DISSOLUTION.

But New York in the Way of Life, Not Death.

ALL HER ENERGIES REVIVE.

Cars Running Again in Flowing Streets and Commerce and Industry Disdaining Gondolas.

SOMETHING TO LIVE UPON, TOO.

Babies and Lovers of Milk Punch the Greatest Sufferers So Far.

THE DEAD AS WELL AS THE QUICK.

A Way to the Cemeteries and Christian Burial Almost Assured.

SAFE AT LAST IN ALTOONA.

SCORES OF PASSENGERS ESCAPE THE HORRORS OF THE CONEMAUGH DISASTER.

THREE EXPRESS TRAINS CAUGHT IN THE FLOOD REACH ALTOONA—WHO THE

New-York Tribune.

VOL. LX—No. 19,658.   NEW-YORK, TUESDAY, SEPTEMBER 11, 1900.—SIXTEEN PAGES.   PRICE THREE CENTS.

BIRDSEYE VIEW OF GALVESTON.

GALVESTON IN RUINS.

Awful Ravages of Storm and Flood in Texas.

ESTIMATES OF DEAD IN THOUSANDS.

STICK TO STANCHFIELD.

DEMOCRATS WILL PROBABLY NAME HIM FOR GOVERNOR.

RUMORS OF SLATE BREAKING

JUDGE PARKER AND EX-SPEAKER PATTERSON, AND EVEN BILL, MENTIONED AS DEMOCRATIC POSSIBILITIES.

MAINE CHASES VERMONT

THE REPUBLICAN PLURALITY WILL PROBABLY BE 30,000.

MR. MANLEY, OF THE STATE COMMITTEE, SUMS UP THE FEATURES OF THE DAY'S VICTORY.

NO RAMAPO, SAYS ODELL.

CANDIDATE PLEDGES HIMSELF FOR CITY OWNERSHIP OF WATER.

FIRE AND DEATH IN CHICAGO.

The Most Disastrous Conflagration That Ever Occurred in America—Over One Third of the City in Ruins—Map of the Destroyed City.

LAKE MICHIGAN

THE FASTEST YACHT IN ENGLISH WATERS.

CLOVER IN THE PRIX DU JOCKEY CLUB

MRS. MAYBRICK TOO ILL TO

A C. P. TRAIN CROSS

A CALAMITY TH

THE DEATH

Further Deta

The Aftermat

San Francisco Chronicle.

SAN FRANCISCO, CAL., WEDNESDAY, JUNE 5, 1889.

-York

NEW-YORK, SUNDAY, JUNE 2, 1889.—TWENTY PAGES.

Tribune.

PRICE FIVE CENTS.

WORK OF THE CONFERENCE.

EVERYTHING DEMANDED BY AMERICA
PRACTICALLY CONCEDED.

WAITING INSTRUCTION FROM WASHINGTON TO
SIGN THE SAMOAN TREATY—GERMAN
IRRITATION AT THE DELAY.

Copyright, 1889: By the New-York Associated Press.
Berlin, June 1.—After the seventh plenary sitting of the Samoan Conference, held on Wednesday last, the American Commission was in a position to cable Secretary Blaine the definitive acceptance by the German and English definitive amendments of the Washington proposals limiting the German indemnity and Samoan rights to levy import duties and some of Mr. Blaine's amendments relating to the internal Samoan policy.

ALL WARNINGS UNHEEDED.

THE DELUGE WAS EXPECTED.

AT LEAST TWELVE HUNDRED LIVES LOST.

FROM EARLY MORNING PEOPLE WERE URGED
TO FLEE—THE WALL OF THE RESERVOIR
KNOWN TO BE WEAKENED—FLAMES
ADDED TO THE HORROR OF THE
FLOOD—ONLY A FEW HOUSES LEFT
OUT OF THE THOUSANDS THAT
STOOD IN THE CONEMAUGH
RIVER VALLEY.

Pittsburg, June 1.—The number of lives lost in the flood, which swept almost every living creature out of the Conemaugh River v...

A SCENE OF DESOLATION.

WHAT DAWN REVEALED AT NEW-FLORENCE.

BODIES OF THE DROWNED SCATTERED DOWN
THE VALLEY—ACCOUNTS FROM THOSE
WHO SAW THE FLOODS.

New-Florence, Penn., June 1.—The gray morning light does not seem to show hope or mitigation of the awful fears of the night. New-Florence is four-teen miles from the scene of desolation.

CHICAGO AND CHRISTIANITY.

The Tongue of Fire Eloquent in
the Pulpits of the Land.

PATHETIC TALK AND PRACTICAL GIVING.

The Furnaces of Want and the
Lamp of Prosperity.

The Chicago Conflagration an
Anachronism in History.

An American Herculaneum
or Pompeii.

Noble Generosity and the Sympathy
of Christian Hearts.

THE WAYS OF PROVIDENCE INTERPRETED.

God Restraining the Pride and the Covetous-
ness of the Nation.

The Moral Power of Society
Illustrated.

Dr. Bellows on the Moral Ashes of
New York and the Burned
Ashes of Chicago.

"THE GOSPEL" IN CHRIST CHURCH PULPIT.

Practicalness of the Principles of Christ's
Kingdom Shown in the Na-
tional Contributions.

The Conflagration Has Refined and
Purified Humanity.

WHAT THE CATHOLIC CHURCH HAS LOST.

An Appeal for Aid from Two
Chicago Catholic Clergymen.

Organization of the Churches
for Relief.

The Heart of the World Touched
Thankfulness Unto God and
Love for Mankind.

A STUDY FOR MEN AND ANGELS.

The Silver Lining on the Chicago Cloud.

TERRIBLE CALAMITY
AT SUNDERLAND.

MESSAGE FROM THE QUEEN.

THE
CAUSE OF THE DISASTER
IMPORTANT STATEMENTS:

CORONERS' INQUESTS:

IDENTIFICATION OF THE BODIES.

PAINFUL INCIDENTS:

PROPOSED MEMORIAL:

MEETING OF THE INHABITANTS.

TWELVE THOUSAND.

Victims of the Great
Flood.

Estimates of the Loss of
Life.

Responsibility for the Terrible
Disaster.

Recovery and Burial of the
Bodies.

Governor Beaver Appeals for Aid—
Many Thousands of Dollars
Contributed.

The exact number of people who perished in the...

AFTER THE FLOOD.

Fixing the Blame for the
Disaster.

Burial of Hundreds of the
Victims.

Robbery of the Dead and Looting
of Houses.

Epidemics of Pneumonia and
Fever Feared.

The President Makes an Appeal
for Aid—The Relief Fund
Reaches Half a Million.

NO. 230.

SIXTEEN PAGES.—IN TWO PARTS.

WEDNESDAY, SEPTEMBER 12, 1900.

LL WILL REACH FIVE THOUSAND.

the Calamity at Galveston Add to Its Horror.

Terrible Than the Terrors of the Midnight Storm

1870–1900

Out of the Ashes
The Chicago Fire 1871

Tragedy over the Tay
Tay Bridge Disaster 1879

A Trick of Fate
Sunderland Panic 1883

A City Paralysed
New York Blizzard 1888

The Day the Dam Broke
Johnstown Flood 1889

A Cause for War
The Sinking of the *Maine* 1898

The Death of Galveston
Galveston Flood 1900

Out of the Ashes
The Chicago Fire 1871

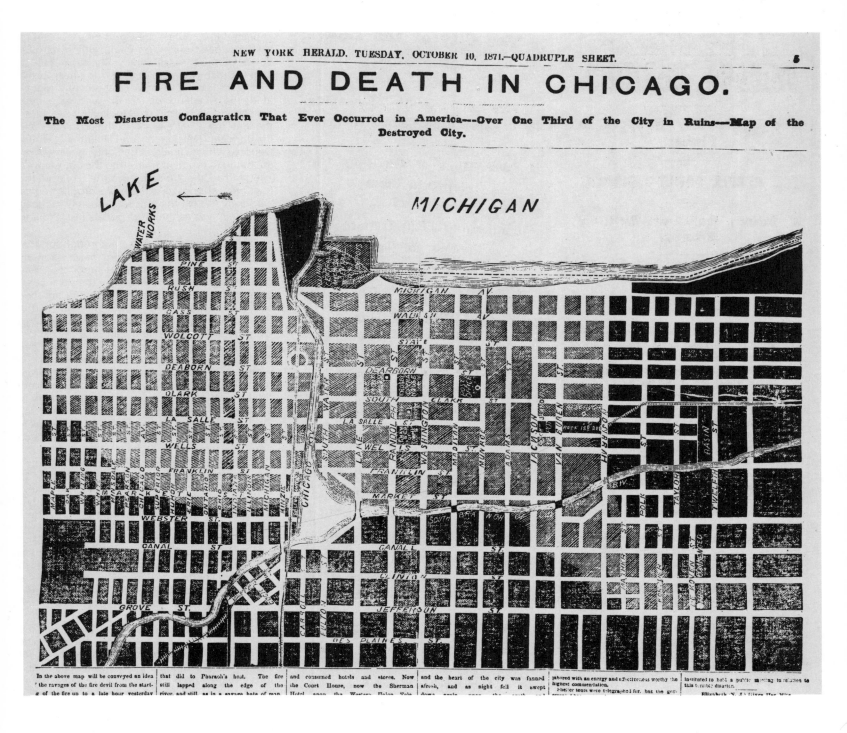

FIRE AND DEATH IN CHICAGO.

The Most Disastrous Conflagration That Ever Occurred in America---Over One Third of the City in Ruins---Map of the Destroyed City.

For two days the wind had been blowing from the south-west, bone-dry and unrelenting. It travelled across the prairies of Illinois parched by six weeks of summer drought, over the Garden City where men sweated their day out in huge airless grain elevators, and on into the tinderbox forests of Michigan. People's tempers were short, that autumn in Chicago, but so they were every October till the rain came and at least this year there was some consolation in the way business was booming: a record harvest, the stockyards at full stretch, even the lumbermen were looking less surly than usual.

The fire that broke out in a planing-shop just north of Van Buren Street, about 10 o'clock on the night of Saturday 7th, caused few people much anxiety. There was a wake in progress near the Adams Street bridge and when the flames spread the mourners, with one accord, fled to leave the corpse to be prematurely cremated. But the Chicago fire brigade was well thought of, and well equipped with hydrants and hoses: its prompt exertions only went to

prove what most men believed—that the city was well nigh fire-proof. The night sky had been dramatically illuminated by the conflagration which had consumed some sixteen acres, but when the next morning the faithful assembled for Matins the smouldering embers only testified to the Almighty's goodwill towards the better-off citizens whose mansions had not been in the slightest danger.

That evening (the 8th) on the corner of Dekoven and Jefferson streets a party was in progress. Mrs Leary, the landlady, had taken to her bed with a 'sore foot' but in her front room the McLaughlins were welcoming a distant cousin from Ireland with oysters and a few tunes on the fiddle. Mrs McLaughlin swore 'before God, this day' she never cooked anything, and only half a gallon of beer was drunk by the whole company. The first they knew of the fire was seeing the barn, where Mrs Leary kept her cow, ablaze beyond redemption. Someone, clearly, had knocked over a kerosene lamp in the stable and set the straw alight, Who, no-one knew,

nor ever did find out.

It was fifteen minutes before the engines arrived, and by then sparks had set the whole area ablaze. This time the firemen, exhausted by their efforts a few hours earlier, were helpless in the face of the inferno: the nearest hydrant proved to be a mile away, and the one hose that was operative soon gave up. Aghast, they watched the flames mow a path due north-east, feeding hungrily on the wooden buildings and lumber piles. Now, if ever, was the moment for decisive action but, strangely, no-one yet thought of alerting the mayor or local troops. Anyone who saw the reflection of the blaze naturally assumed it was the remnants of Saturday's fire; yet by 1.45am bulletins were reaching New York of 'the most awful night in the annals of the city'. The last edition of the *New York World* went to press with the news that the whole of Chicago was wrapped in flames.

Prophetically this was true: but in reality it was not yet the case. There was still hope that

THE WORLD: NEW YORK, OCTOBER 9, 1871.

POSTSCRIPT.

4:30 o'clock A.M.

CHICAGO BURNING.

The Whole City Wrapped in Flames.

THE PEOPLE PANIC-STRICKEN.

A Steady Rain of Burning Brands.

HUNDREDS OF LIVES LOST,

&c.,   &c.,   &c.

CHICAGO, October 9.—1:45 A. M.—To-night is the most awful in the annals of the city. The fire, which commenced at 10 P. M., has already swept over a space of at least three times as large as that of last night, and is still rushing on with greater fury than has marked any stage of its progress.

The engines appear almost powerless.

Fire-Marshall Williams has just telegraphed to Milwaukee for all steamers they can spare.

The conflagration has already devastated at least twenty blocks, mostly composed of smaller class dwellings inhabited by poor people. Not less than three hundred buildings have been entirely destroyed, and more than that number of families rendered homeless.

The wind is blowing almost a gale from the south, and showers of sparks and burning brands are sweeping over the city, threatening destruction on every hand.

The tower of the Court-house caught fire from flying brands, but was extinguished by the watchman of the tower.

No description can give an adequate idea of the terrible scene. The fire started in a row of two-story wooden tenements on Decloven street, between Jefferson and Clinton, and, as was the case last night, spread with terrible rapidity. Before a single engine could get on the road half the block was in flames and burning furiously.

The entire department were soon on the ground and at work. For a time it seemed probable they would succeed in confining it to four or five blocks. The wind was blowing fresh when the fire started, increased to a gale, and suddenly the flames seemed to spread in every direction, becoming beyond the control of the fire department.

LATER.

CHICAGO, October 9—2 A. M.—The fire is still raging with increased fury, and has spread almost with the velocity of the wind, and has now reached West Monroe street, a distance of more than a mile from where it started, and covers a breadth of nearly half a mile, reaching from the river to Jefferson street. The district already burned embraces an immense number of lumber-yards and the freight depots of the Chicago and St. Louis, and Pittsburg, Fort Wayne, and Chicago Railroads.

The property already destroyed counts up many millions of dollars, and perhaps half is not told.

The task of arresting the flames now seems five-fold greater than an hour ago, and no one dare venture the opinion as to when or where it will stop.

NEW YORK HERALD, OCTOBER 10, 1871.

DESOLATED CHICAGO!

The City of the Lakes in Ruins.

Fire and Death Sweeping Everything Before Them.

Four Miles of the City Enveloped in Flames.

One Hundred and Fifty Thousand People Houseless and Homeless.

Fearful Loss of Life Apprehended

Scores of People Lost in the Sea of Fire.

Hundreds of Families Fleeing Before the Waves of Conflagration.

Blocks of Buildings Blown Up to Stay the Progress of Destruction.

VAIN ARE THE EFFORTS OF MAN!

From Fifty to One Hundred Millions of Property Said To Be Burned.

All the Churches, Hotels, Theatres, Banks, Railway Depots, Telegraph Offices, Newspaper Offices, Gas Works, Public Buildings and Shipping in Ashes.

The Great Water Works Probably Gone Too.

Impossible to Estimate the Total Loss.

CRY OF THE SUFFERERS FOR HELP

Noble Response from All Parts of the Union.

Cincinnati, St. Louis, Milkaukee and All the Cities of the East and West Contributing

the holocaust could be contained at the south branch of the Chicago River, and in the feeble light of dawn citizens struggled desperately to close the swing bridges. It was futile—the inexorable gale simply bounced the flames onto the opposite bank, and the whole of the city's business centre lay at their mercy. By midday on the Monday (the 9th) the city centre was a furnace: churches, banks, hotels and theatres simply melted in the heat. Great landmarks disappeared in minutes: the Court House, even as its bells tolled peal after peal, ringing its own death-knell; the splendid Sherman House Hotel; Crosby's Opera House, the finest in the land; McVicker's Theatre, only recently renovated; the Academy of Design with its superb collection of paintings; Hooley's little bijou theatre; the Chamber of Commerce; and the magnificent Michigan and Illinois Central Depots (whose directors had only recently won the battle to run their trains into the city centre). The staff of the *Chicago Tribune*—one of the buildings supposed to be fire-proof, battled heroically to save the offices but barely escaped with their lives as the huge girders buckled and shattered.

The scenes in the streets throughout that fateful Monday almost defied description by even the most imaginative of reporters. Their problems were compounded by the disappearance of the telegraph offices, one after another, in the flames, until finally only one remained in the suburbs to tell the world of the agony of Chicago; how a horse-and-cart (in a city packed with them) fetched first $100, then $1000, then could not be purchased for any money in the world. How women crowded into Lincoln Park for safety gave birth to still-born babies. How fifteen frantic refugees had sought sanctuary in a blacksmith's shop only to be 'burnt to a crisp'. Or how, with summary justice, looters were being strung up on lamp posts by incensed householders.

One paper, the *New York Herald*, devoted one extravagant column to a lurid account of the evacuation of Reynold's Block, the business premises of more than 200 of the city's prostitutes: how, in the emergency, they were obliged 'to expose their nakedness to the eyes of thousands' (and their clients with them) and how 'intoxicated lewds' had to be manhandled out of danger by their hysterical mistresses. In the next column the paper castigated 'the supineness of the authorities' who had neglected to detonate sufficient buildings to stem the progress of the fire.

Only after one more night of terror did 'the fiend of hell' consider itself sated, though some of the ruins smouldered on for weeks. For several days estimates of the casualties in the press veered from the speculative (one thousand) to the fantastic (ten thousand), but by the end of the week most authorities seemed to agree that some 200 men, women and children had perished and that 200,000 had been made homeless. The cost of the fire, finally set down at $190 million, left everyone gasping: those fire insurance companies who, at the beginning of the week, were 'vigorously asserting their determination to pay every dollar as rapidly as possible' went just as rapidly bankrupt. But the material response from other cities was overwhelming and a tribute, in all fairness, to the efforts of the press to mobilize relief. Boston, Pittsburgh and Philadelphia all sent more than $250,000 each, and St Louis, Baltimore and Cincinnati not much less.

Indeed the emotional impact of the tragedy on the nation was meticulously documented by the papers. Lugubrious laments and heroic couplets flowed into their offices—and were printed in rows more or less uncritically. One of the better efforts, from the *New York Evening Post*, began:

> O bird with a crimson wing
>   And a brand in thy glowing beak,
> Why did'st thou flutter o'er seas to bring
>   A woe that we dare not speak?

THE WORLD: NEW YORK, OCTOBER 10, 1871.

POSTSCRIPT.

5 o'clock A.M.

DOOMED.

The Last Words from the Burning City.

ALL HOPE ABANDONED

The Fire Spreading in Every Direction.

TELEGRAPHIC COMMUNICATION CEASES,
&c.,   &c.,   &c.

ASSOCIATED PRESS OFFICE,
NEW YORK, October 10—4 A. M.

No press despatches have been received from Chicago later than 6 P. M. The last despatch was sent circuitously by way of St. Louis and Cincinnati, and reached us four hours after it left Chicago.

The agent of the Associated Press at Cincinnati reports that private advices from Chicago were received in the early part of the night announcing that the fire had been checked, but he was unable to get confirmation of the good news, as the wires were not working to Chicago, and up to 3 A. M. communication had not been restored. The "private advices" referred to may have been simply a repetition of the report in the 6 P. M. despatch from Chicago, which represented that the flames were checked at 1 P. M. in the southern district of the city by the blowing up of buildings under the direction of General Sheridan.

But since that hour a service despatch was sent from the Western Union Telegraph office at Buffalo at 11 o'clock P. M. to the general office of the company in New York stating that the following had been received from Chicago [no time given]:

Fire rapidly spreading. The telegraph company has been driven from its temporary office. The whole city is doomed to go. The wind has changed, and is blowing the fire in all directions.

Since the above report was received nothing has been heard from Chicago, and the telegraph office here reports that no telegraphic communication whatever has been had with the city.

Losses of the Hartford Insurance Companies.
HARTFORD, Conn., October 9.—The fire insurance companies of Hartford have not yet attempted to make a definite estimate of their losses; but, doubtless, the aggregate will be several millions. The directors and other officers of all the leading companies vigorously assert their determination to pay every dollar as rapidly as possible, and they have already begun their arrangements to that effect.

The life insurance companies have many millions loaned upon real estate security in Chicago, but as their rule is to require that the land shall more than secure the debt, they apprehend no loss.

Relief for Chicago.
The officers of the Great Western and Michigan Central Railroads also announce that they will transport free of charge, from Suspension Bridge to Chicago, all supplies addressed to the Mayor of Chicago, contributed for the relief of the sufferers from the great fire.
CINCINNATI IN EARNEST.

NEW YORK HERALD. OCTOBER 11, 1871.

CHICAGO.

The Frightful Conflagration Quenched at Last.

Rain and Gunpowder to the Rescue.

Graphic Accounts of the Origin and Expansion of the Fire, the Terror of the People and the Sufferings of the Shelterless.

Five Hundred Lives Lost—Twelve Thousand Houses Burned—Three Hundred Millions in Property Destroyed.

INHUMAN INCENDIARIES CAUGHT.

The Men-Wolves Hanged to Lampposts or Shot.

THE BOY'S FATAL KEROSENE LAMP.

Resistless Speed of the Fire—The Roar of the Flames—The Storm of Burning Brands.

The Hurricane Helping the Conflagration.

Maddened Flight of One Hundred Thousand People—Heartrending Scenes.

Drunken Men and Boys Falling Victims to the Fire.

Miles of Wooden Pavement Burning—A Literal Sea of Flames.

PROMINENT CITIZENS KILLED.

Fears of Pillage---1,500 Special Police and 500 Troops on Guard.

Encamped on the Prairie---Births, Deaths, Wakefulness, Cold, Thirst

---

NEW YORK HERALD. OCTOBER 15, 1871.

THE DESOLATE CITY.

Additional Accounts of Suffering and Death.

ROBBERY, RAPINE AND FAMINE.

A Night in Lincoln Park---Birth of Three Children in the Open Air.

FEEDING OF THE MULTITUDE.

The Demi-Monde Escaping from Reynolds' Block.

A SCENE OF TERROR.

Drunken Harlots Make the Air Resound with Curses.

A FEAST OF DEATH.

The Fire Runs Through a German Burying Ground and Consumes the Vaults Filled with Dead Bodies.

Tombs Overturned and Graves Burned.

ORDER RESTORED.

Cause of the Fire and Estimated Loss.

THE FUTURE OF CHICAGO.

OUR MAP OF CHICAGO.

The map of Chicago in our present number is, we believe, the most correct and faithful one that has yet been issued. No trouble has been spared in getting it up in the most perfect manner possible, it having been drawn under the supervision of a gentleman, a resident of Chicago, well acquainted with the topography of the city. He was in the city all through the conflagration, and therefore is in a position to vouch for the accuracy of our representation of the burned district. A few explanatory remarks relative to the map will not be out of place. At first sight, on looking at it, one would suppose that the extent of territory the fire covered had been greatly exaggerated, but a closer inspection will show that this is not the case. A large part of the city, as presented in the map, consists merely of suburbs and streets in the prospective, with houses scattered at wide intervals from each other. The burned part, it is scarcely necessary

An illustration from the book *The Great Conflagration: Chicago*, published in 1871 and
written by James Sheahan and George Upton,
Associate Editors of the *Chicago Daily Tribune*

Some journalists even felt constrained to break into verse themselves, like Bret Harte of the *Overland Monthly:*

Blackened and pleading, helpless, panting, prone

On the charred fragments of her shattered throne

Lies she who stood but yesterday alone.

The *New York Herald* went to great pains to reproduce a dozen Sunday sermons on the subject. Some churchmen, inevitably, saw the disaster as a divine commentary on the moral disgraces of 1871; one found 'nineteenth century boasting of its telegraphs, its railroads, its triumphs of steam . . . nauseating to men of good sense'. Another, the aptly-named Dr Bellows, gleefully drew his parallels between the burned ashes of Chicago and 'the moral ashes of New York'. But others were content to see in the imminent re-birth of Chicago a paradigm of the Resurrection.

And no better illustration of the city's un-diminished spirit could be found than in the determination of the Chicago newspapers themselves. Although burned out of their premises the *Tribune*, the *Post*, and the *Evening Journal* all succeeded in producing editions on the second day of the fire. The *Chicago Tribune's* first editorial was as inspiring as had been its owner Joseph Medill's energy in organizing relief. 'CHEER UP!' it was headed, and went on: 'In the midst of a calamity, without parallel in the world's history, looking upon the ashes of thirty years' accumulation, the people of this once beautiful city have resolved that

CHICAGO SHALL RISE AGAIN

And individuals reflected this indomitable optimism: the editor of the *Evening Post* was observed by a reporter spitting on a brick 'to see if they were cool enough to clear out and build

over again'. Another citizen was observed lugging around a marble mantle. It was all, he said, that he possessed in the world but he was going to see if he could find another, and build a house to fit them.

Amid all this new-found enthusiasm, the voices of recrimination were drowned. True, there were post-mortems and some ludicrous theorizings—one report attempted unsuccessfully to demonstrate that the city had been fatally constructed of 'petroleum-bearing stone' while one correspondent to the *New York Evening Post* hypothesized that the wind itself had been 'electrified'. Well, Chicago could leave all the scientifics to others: she preferred to believe, with the *Missouri Republican* 'That she is absolutely ruined or permanently disabled is a sheer impossibility which no sensible person will for a moment credit'.

Tragedy over the Tay

Tay Bridge Disaster 1879

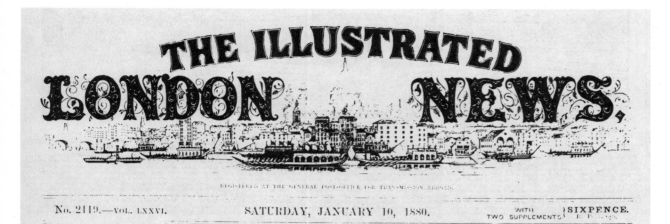

THE ILLUSTRATED LONDON NEWS.

REGISTERED AT THE GENERAL POST-OFFICE FOR TRANSMISSION ABROAD.

No. 2119.—VOL. LXXVI.   SATURDAY, JANUARY 10, 1880.   WITH TWO SUPPLEMENTS   SIXPENCE.

THE TAY BRIDGE DISASTER: VIEW OF THE BROKEN BRIDGE FROM THE NORTH END.—SEE PAGE 27.

REYNOLDS'S NEWSPAPER, SUNDAY, JANUARY 4, 1880.

FRIGHTFUL DISASTER.

A RAILWAY BRIDGE BLOWN DOWN.

FALL OF A TRAIN INTO THE RIVER.

EVERY PERSON IN IT DROWNED.

GREAT LOSS OF LIFE.

The following are particulars of the most appalling railway disaster that has ever happened in the United Kingdom. On Sunday night the train from Edinburgh, in passing across the Tay bridge, fell into the water, and all were drowned. Not a soul in the ill-fated train has survived to give even the merest hint as to how the accident happened, and the final results of any inquiry, however searching, will hardly be more than conjecture. The only ray of comfort which has been vouchsafed is the official assertion that the accident has not been so serious in its results as was first stated to be the case. From 200 and 300, which was the first official announcement, the manager of the North British Railway Company now states that there were only about seventy-five passengers in the train, this computation having been arrived at from the number of tickets at St. Fort Station, the ticket platform on the south side of Tay bridge. When, however, it is considered that there were many children unpaid for in the train and several season ticket passengers, of whom the officials at St. Fort Station have no definite record, it must be seen that the loss of life will greatly exceed this number. Taking these with the railway employés, the loss of life can scarcely be estimated at below 100 souls. The particulars which have transpired since the disaster occurred, although having little bearing on the disaster itself, have been eagerly sought for by the sorrow-stricken Scots on the banks of the Tay. It appears that the ill-fated train, which consisted of four third-class carriages, one first-class, one second-class carriage, guard's brake, and engine, left Edinburgh on Sunday afternoon at 4.15, stopping, as is usual with many Sunday trains, at nearly all wayside stations. On arrival at St. Fort, the last station before reaching the Tay-bridge, the train was found to be five minutes late, and here the tickets were collected. The train again moved on its journey, and those on the banks

TAY BRIDGE.

There had not been a night like it for years. The gale roared out unresisted to the North Sea, whipping off the chimney-pots of Dundee and lashing the waters of the Firth of Tay into a frenzy. A man could scarcely walk in the teeth of such a wind—as James Lawson discovered as he left his home in Dundee with a friend at about 7.00 in the evening of Sunday 28 December. The Edinburgh train was almost due in, but the two men were curious whether it would even be allowed over the Tay Bridge. They decided to walk to the signal-box at the north end of the bridge to find out. Others had had the same idea: there was a shivering crowd clustered round the box. Yes, the signalman said, the Edinburgh train had been signalled to him at nine minutes past seven from St Fort on the other side of the Firth. It had entered the bridge at fourteen minutes past. Some of the crowd confirmed that they had seen lights from the train as it approached the first spans.

The great Tay Bridge, eighty-five spans of it, nearly two miles long, had been opened in September 1877. Queen Victoria had travelled across it in her private train en route to Balmoral, and shortly afterwards had knighted its designer, Thomas Bouch. It had taken seven years to build, and its great lattice-work of girders (some weighing nearly 200 tons) was a testament to the grand vision of Thomas Bouch, who had proved that a work of engineering could be a thing of beauty as well.

At the signal-box the little crowd waited, their apprehension turning to anxiety. After a while Lawson ran to Tay Bridge station to alert the station-master, James Smith. So fierce was the gale funnelling itself between the shores that to walk on the bridge was almost suicide, but by clinging desperately to the metal rail Smith inched his way into the darkness. He could just make out the beginning of the high central section that carried the track over the navigable part of the Firth—then what he saw filled him with horror. A black, gaping void.

The news spread through Dundee like a fire, and soon fearful crowds were thronging the station and the esplanade. A ferry-boat was commandeered in a hopeless search for survivors. At ten o'clock a telegram arrived from Broughty, reporting that several mail-bags had been washed up on the shore there: anyone on the Edinburgh train who might have survived that 100-foot fall—the searchers were forced to conclude—would have been washed far out to sea by then. Other eye-witnesses began arriving at the station, having struggled through the storm to say they had seen 'a comet-like stream of fiery sparks' blaze on the centre of the bridge, then extinguish itself in an instant.

With daybreak and a lessening of the storm a despairing search was made by divers around the broken piers, but the only melancholy trophy they returned with was a first-class oilskin mat, and the news that the train lay on its side some thirty feet from the bridge. There were no bodies to be found at all. Indeed it was only after a count of tickets was made at St Fort station that it was established that eighty people had been aboard—not including children (who needed no ticket) and anyone who might have been carrying a season-ticket.

The tragedy immediately became the sensation of Victorian Britain. Not only was it by far the worst railway accident in history, there was the added shock that one of the great monuments of a nation of bridge-builders had vanished ignominiously. Sir Thomas Bouch's first reaction, according to *Reynolds News*, was to declare that the train had been blown off the rails—the 'fiery sparks' that witnesses had seen were the result of the train scraping against the girders. He was adamant that had the train not been derailed the disaster would not have occurred. *Reynolds* treated his view with the utmost scepticism, pointing out that the train was known to have been travelling at only three miles an hour! The *Morning Post*, while reserving judgement on the condition of the bridge, considered 'we have learned enough to satisfy us that the railway officials on both sides of the river manifested a lamentable want of prudence in not arresting the train on the south side of the river .

That—both from the point of view of salvaging Bouch's reputation and on the question of compensation—was the key question. Were the builders to blame, or the railway? The *Pall Mall Gazette* did its best to sort out the issues: 'On the one hand it is said that the disaster was the result of unforeseen causes . . . what our own lawyers call "the Act of God".' That is to say, the gale was of such unprecedented force that it could not reasonably have been anticipated. 'On the other hand' the paper went on, 'we have the argument that negligence is proved by the most practical and positive of all evidence: that the fall of the bridge shows ipso facto that it was unable to stand the strain which was put upon it when the train was signalled on.'

The *Standard* had no doubts about the elements: 'The gale or hurricane which swept along the valley of the Tay on Sunday night will be repeated again and again in the course of years, and under like circumstances there will be the same catastrophe.' And indeed there were many of the older locals who claimed to recall storms thereabouts of equal, even greater, severity. A highly significant correspondence, which had been published in the local *Dundee Advertiser* in 1870 (when Bouch's plans were

under discussion) was poignantly resurrected and given wide publicity. A certain Patrick Matthew had denounced Bouch's aesthetic structure at the time. 'It is not our usual strong gales of wind that such a rainbow bridge as that proposed must sustain, but the very strongest winter tempests that are found to occur every few years' he had argued.

It was a warning Bouch would have done well to heed. At the Inquiry it was discovered that the engineer had neglected to take lateral pressures into account in his calculations—and that on a site where such pressures could be the highest in the country! It was also remarked that another of Bouch's artistic designs, a viaduct near Consett, might have suffered a similar fate had not Robert Stephenson examined the finished bridge and ordered it to be strengthened. Worse still, when Bouch's plans for the proposed bridge over the Firth of Forth were examined, it was found that he had envisaged an edifice capable of withstanding wind pressure of only ten pounds per square foot— less than a tenth of what would have been required!

Bouch was ruined, but at least another Tay Bridge had been avoided. Characteristically the Victorians refused to forget the tragedy altogether—enshrining it like a precious object in ballad and folk-lore, legend and melodrama, though of all the contemporary effusions that found their way into print it is, perversely, the ludicrous lines of McGonegal that have survived best:

Oh! Ill-fated Bridge of the Silv'ry Tay
I must now conclude my lay
By telling the world fearlessly without the
    least dismay,
That your central girders would not have
    given way,
At least many sensible men do say,
Had they been supported on each side
    with buttresses,
At least many sensible men confesses,
For the stronger we our houses do build,
The less chance we have of being killed.

Illustrated London News 10 January 1880

A Trick of Fate
Sunderland Panic 1883

THE NEWCASTLE
DAILY JOURNAL,
JUNE 18, 1883.

TERRIBLE
CALAMITY
AT SUNDERLAND.

PANIC AT THE VICTORIA
HALL.

186 CHILDREN KILLED
AND MANY INJURED.

HARROWING SCENES.

STATEMENTS BY EYE-WITNESSES.

PERSONAL NARRATIVES
OF THE DISASTER.

IDENTIFICATION OF THE BODIES

LIST OF THE KILLED.

HOW THE DISASTER
OCCURRED.

TERRIBLE SPECTACLE IN
THE BUILDING.

PULPIT REFERENCES TO THE
CALAMITY.

Sunderland was on Saturday afternoon the scene of the most terrible calamity which has occurred in this country since the loss of the steamer Princess Alice on the river Thames, and the number of the victims, their tender years, and the fearful nature of their deaths probably exceed anything of the kind which has been recorded. One hundred and eighty-six children, who had been enjoying an entertainment in a large building known as the Victoria Hall, were either suffocated or crushed to death, and the circumstances of their deaths and the discovery of their bodies are of the most heart rending description. The calamity seems to have been occasioned by the unchecked and undisciplined rush of over one thousand children towards the means of exit, and the result was that scores became jammed into a position in which they could not breathe and from which they could not escape. Their struggles but added to the horror and panic, the condition of the bodies testifying to the fearful but futile efforts which the children had made to escape being buried beneath the weight of their struggling companions. The

The Fays, Miss Annie and Mr Alexander Fay (from the Tynemouth Aquarium, Conjuring, Talking Waxworks, Living Marionettes, The Great Ghost Illusion, etc) were giving a Grand Day Performance for Children at the Victoria Hall, Sunderland on the afternoon of Saturday 16 June 1883. That their show was very nearly a sell-out was a tribute to the zeal with which their manager had toured all the local schools, distributing tickets (to be paid for at the door, price 1d). Well over 2,000 children had turned up, so many in fact that even after the body of the hall had been filled there still remained more than a thousand of them to be accommodated in the gallery. Children's treats were a rare occurrence in Sunderland—and, the posters promised, there were prizes: 'Every child entering the room will stand a chance of receiving a Handsome Present, Books, Toys, Etc.'

As it turned out, the prizes were not distributed as the children *entered* the hall at all, but just before they were due to leave after the performance. The means of distribution was simple: the performers threw them into the audience, leaving selection to nature. Not unnaturally those children in the gallery—aged from four to fourteen—soon perceived that they were well out of range and more than likely to miss out on the presents entirely. As if by common consent a stampede began to reach the floor of the hall, down a flight of stairs, along a passage, down another flight of stairs . . .

At the bottom of the second flight stood a pair of swing doors. Not an ordinary pair of swing doors, but ones which by a cunning contrivance could be opened some twenty inches then automatically locked themselves by means of bolts which dropped into a slot in the floor. It was an arrangement designed to allow paying customers in one by one, and so avoid a melee in which unscrupulous folk might slip in free.

It was up against these doors that the swirling, pushing mass of some 400 children came in their headlong flight. Even if they had understood the intricate nature of the barrier ahead of them, the crush was far too great to have allowed them through singly. Within seconds the leading children were jammed inextricably against the doors, tighter and tighter as the hundreds pressed on them from behind. Then children began to fall down the stairs, and more fell on top of them, then more. The screams alerted the hall's door-keeper, who had the presence of mind to rush to open a door on the higher landing, and siphon off part of the rout. But he was minutes too late: the stairway was an indescribable mountain of flailing limbs above, and who dared think what beneath?

Rescuers who rushed in from the street found many children so tightly wedged they could not even be moved for some time, and with every minute's sickening delay more children died. In all, 190 lost their lives, and many more were barely brought round from unconsciousness. As the word spread round the town parents besieged the hall, begging for news. Scarcely a street in Sunderland was unscathed by the appalling tragedy.

And elsewhere, as the *Daily Telegraph* confirmed, 'a thrill of universal and heartfelt pity will pass through the land at the shocking intelligence.' That paper was unwilling to apportion blame, but the *Standard* was immediately struck by 'the deplorable blunder' of allowing eleven hundred children to be packed into a gallery without adult supervision. The

Daily News was even more outspoken. To have allowed such doors in such a position was 'reprehensible, almost iniquitous, folly'. The question arose, how did the doors (which, of course *could* have been opened wide) come to be only partially open? The *Standard* quoted the evidence of the hall-keeper, to the effect that an agent of the performers had deliberately half-closed them when he heard the rush down the stairs—an accusation that was vigorously denied, though confirmed by evidence given to a local paper, the *Newcastle Journal*, by one of the surviving children. This thirteen-year-old boy claimed that a man had been standing at the foot of the stairs, with a box of prizes ready to hand out. 'There was a lot coming down with a rush . . . The man with the prizes said "This'll never do". He pulled the door, and he shut it just so that one could get out at a time. He put the bolt down with his foot.' The children never stood a chance of receiving a Handsome Present.

THE ILLUSTRATED LONDON NEWS.

No. 2305.—VOL. LXXXII.   SATURDAY, JUNE 23, 1883.   WITH TWO SUPPLEMENTS   SIXPENCE.

STAGE OF VICTORIA HALL, FROM THE GALLERY.

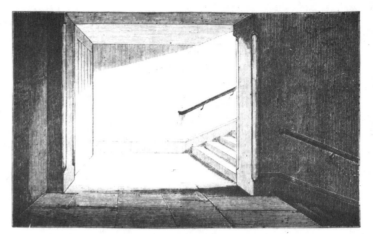

DOORWAY, SHOWING THE DOOR WIDE OPEN.

EXTERIOR OF VICTORIA HALL.

TOP OF THE STAIRS LEADING TO THE DOORWAY.

STAIRCASE AND DOORWAY WHERE THE CATASTROPHE HAPPENED.

THE TERRIBLE DISASTER AT SUNDERLAND: TWO HUNDRED CHILDREN CRUSHED TO DEATH.—SEE PAGE 635.

A City Paralysed

New York Blizzard 1888

A STRUGGLE TO ANSWER A FIRE-ALARM DURING THE NEW YORK BLIZZARD.—Drawn by T. DE THULSTRUP.

'With men and women dying in her ghostly streets, New York saw day breaking through the wild clouds yesterday morning. Nature had overwhelmed the metropolis and citizens were found dead in the mighty snow drifts. White, frozen hands sticking up out of the billowed and furrowed wastes testified to the unspeakable power that had desolated the city.' Thus dramatically the *New York Herald* began its report of the great New York blizzard of March 1888. Not a newspaper known for its understatement, the *Herald* on this occasion was doing no more than justice to a strange, and momentarily terrible, phenomenon. Jules Verne himself could scarcely have devised a more macabre setting than that huge city isolated from without and utterly paralysed within.

The white hurricane that visited New York at midnight on Monday 12 March raged for two days and nights, piling snow into grotesque mountains till Wall Street resembled an Alaskan canyon. In sub-zero temperatures the first morning braver souls attempted to get the city moving, but the roads were mostly impassable and cab drivers refused even to begin a journey for less than $50. A few elevated trains did get under way, then froze into immobility, stranding their helpless passengers high above the ground —until the more enterprising locals fetched ladders and permitted them to descend for twenty-five cents a time. But most people elected to stay at home that morning—often to find themselves literally imprisoned in snow by the evening.

In the course of the day the situation rapidly deteriorated. The unremitting 70mph gales uprooted trees and smashed ferry-boats to pieces; seventy-five trains en route for New York found themselves trapped impotently in drifts; one by one the telegraph wires out of the city snapped, until operators were obliged to cable London to find out what was happening in Boston. By nightfall the city was firmly under siege by snow, and all through the night the tragic reports came in. A frozen corpse had been discovered outside a police station—the man had fainted there and never recovered consciousness. A bread-roundsman, who had insisted on attempting his round, had died of exposure on top of his cart. The frozen body of a woman was dug out on the steps of a restaurant . . . The *New York Herald* estimated more than a score died in the blizzard that night, quite apart from the unknown dead inside unapproachable buildings.

On Tuesday New York was at a standstill, nothing came in, nothing went out. The dead lay unburied in undertakers' back rooms, horses deserted by their cabmen collapsed and died on the streets. Food and coal were being sold at black-market prices: a small fortune could not buy milk. A strange form of graffito humour began to appear on the deserted streets: 'Snow for Sale—Come early and avoid the Rush' and 'Keep off the Grass'. How long New York could have kept its sense of humour under the same circumstances (what with a stranger from Texas snorting 'you call this a blizzard!') was fortunately not put to the test. On Wednesday the wind dropped, the snow settled and the mercury rose. Within hours the streets were scintillating with rows of bonfires, lit to expose the tramlines, and Broadway became jammed with thousands 'come to see the sights'. Like blood to frost-bitten hands, circulation returned painfully and slowly to the city, but by the end of the week the harshest legacy of 'King Blizzard', according to the *Herald*, appeared to be the dubious condensed milk the survivors were having to put into their milk punch. 'Milk' said the headline, 'Babies pining for it and even Seasoned Topers languishing.'

NEW YORK HERALD, MARCH 13, 1888.

SNOWBOUND.

New York's Mighty Pulse Almost Stilled by a Terrible Storm.

RAGI'G WIND AND BLINDING DRIFT.

The City's Busiest Thoroughfares Turned Into Scenes of Winter Desolation.

TRAVEL AND BUSINESS PARALYZED.

Only One "L" Road Attempts to Run and the Horse Cars Give Up Altogether.

TELEGRAPH AND TELEPHONE WIRES DOWN.

Ferryboats Struggling with the Storm and Trains Snowed Up in the Country.

PUBLIC OFFICES AT A STANDSTILL.

Courts of Justice Closed, the Post Office Idle and the Fire Department in Suspense.

PEDESTRIANS' MISFORTUNES.

NEW YORK HERALD, MARCH 14, 1888.

THE BURIED CITY

New York's Dreadful Sepulture Under Masses of Snow.

A NIGHT OF DEVASTATION.

How the Tempest Howled and Raged Through the Dark Wilderness of Streets.

PERISHING MEN AND WOMEN

Wanderers Found Dead in Snowdrifts and Families Driven Into the Storm by Fire.

AND THE TEMPERATURE BELOW ZERO.

Harper's Weekly 24 March 1888

The Day the Dam Broke
Johnstown Flood 1889

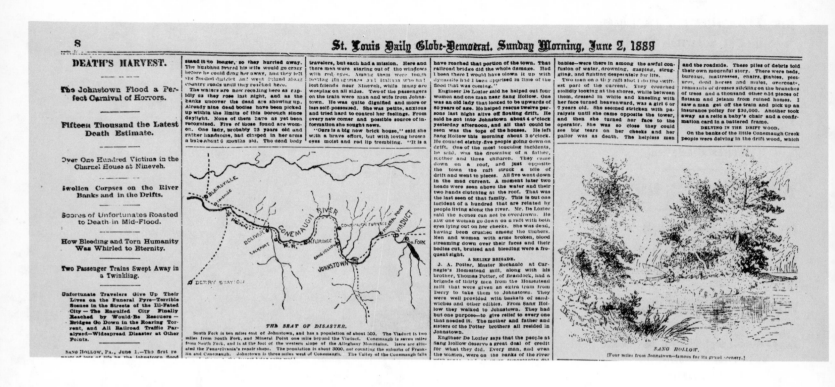

THE SEAT OF DISASTER.

SANG HOLLOW.
[Four miles from Johnstown—famous for its grand scenery.]

The South Fork Fishing and Hunting Club was a highly desirable, and highly exclusive, haven. Only the very richest families from Pittsburgh could qualify for membership of this summer retreat high in the Alleghenies, with its club-house and private cottages lining the picturesque waters of the South Fork Reservoir. The lake and its 100-foot high dam had originally been built in the 1840s to provide water for the Pittsburgh-Johnstown canal, in the days when the superior way to travel between the two towns was on a complex interlocking system of horse-drawn trains and canal barges. The advent of steam engines had rendered the reservoir redundant within a couple of years of its completion: but it still stood—now the property of some wealthy Pittsburgh business-men—well-stocked with fish and ringing to the happy sounds of boating-parties on cool evenings.

It presented a marked and often envied contrast to the scene further down the valley of the Little Conemaugh River. Here lay Johnstown at the heart of a growing industrial complex, a crowded vista of foundries, blast-furnaces, rolling-mills and marshalling-yards. The rising fortunes of Johnstown and its satellites of Franklin, Conemaugh, Cambria City and Morrel-ville, were solidly based on the Cambria Iron Company, the Gautier wireworks and the Pennsylvania Railroad. Most of the area's 18,000 inhabitants, a characteristic pot-pourri of a dozen European races, worked for one or other of these giants. Life was prosperous enough in Johnstown, but if there was one recurring irritation to life there—apart from the ever-present smoke—it was the floods.

Almost every year the Conemaugh, and its tributary the Stonycreek, seemed to siphon off all the spring rains from the great watershed behind them and spill it into the streets and houses, shops and factories. Carpet-moving and furniture-piling were annual events. And then there was The Dam. Twenty million tons of water poised more than 400 feet above Johnstown. It was a favourite joke thereabouts, to shout 'the dam is going—run for your lives': it was guaranteed to raise a laugh, for there were few who seriously thought that gigantic

mass of earth, slate and stone would crumble for many years yet. But there were a few who had their doubts: after its engineers had inspected the dam and found that its flood-gates were kept permanently shut (to preserve the fish) and that large portions of it were definitely suspect, the Cambria Iron Company made repeated representations to the South Fork Fishing and Hunting Club to get the dam repaired. The officers of that club declined, however, to waste their money on what they considered to be a perfectly sound structure.

On 30 and 31 May 1889 that confidence was put to the test. The downpour turned into deluge, waterspouts hissed among the mountains, streams turned into torrents. The waters of the dam began to rise steadily, inches at first, then three feet in as many hours. In Johnstown the old familiar routine got under way, as the Conemaugh began to lick the doorsteps. It was at times like this that folk looked anxiously up at the hills that hid the dam: had they seen that by 11.30 on the morning of the 31st the flood-waters had already reached the crest of the dam, and that ominous jets were even then shooting through the earthworks, they might have taken more seriously the whispered warnings to take to the hills.

At 3.10 in the afternoon the accumulating pressures proved irresistible: a 300-foot section of the dam wall suddenly melted away. A sheer face of water forty feet high hurled itself down the valley with pent-up fury. Trees, farms, and bridges were all tossed about in the maelstrom like playthings: the village of South Fork was overwhelmed, Mineral Point was swept from the face of the earth. On it rushed devouring East Conemaugh, swallowing up a stranded express-train and most of its passengers. At Woodvale, further on, most people were overcome before they had time even to reach their doors. The hideous din of boiler explosions and the hissing extinction of furnaces announced the tide's arrival at the Gautier wireworks. At exactly 4.10pm the waters descended on Johnstown.

By then the moving dam was more like a moving mountain of thousands of tons of iron and wood, stone—and human beings. This

monstrous battering-ram smashed through the town, before splitting itself in two parts: one careering down the main channel of the Conemaugh, the other veering off down the Stonycreek. One of the few structures to withstand the onslaught was the great Stone Bridge where debris piled up, complete houses mounting one another into an evil mountain, an unhappy chance that was to have fatal results.

Down-river, at Sang Hollow, New Florence, and Ninevah, local inhabitants were dimly beginning to comprehend the nature of the disaster that was happening just a few miles away, as scores of dead bodies were swept past their thresholds. Those in the path of the flood who survived did so by a freak, by clinging for their lives to rooftops and being washed down into less turbulent waters. Many others, though, were watched horrified from the bank as they slipped from their perches and disappeared into the brown scum. The worst fate was reserved for those who, the prey of the waters, were driven helplessly towards the Sargasso of mounting debris at Stone Bridge. It was estimated that it covered some thirty acres when, as some live coals from a wrecked house ignited a floating petroleum car, it burst into flames. Hundreds managed to extricate themselves from the pyre in time; but hundreds more failed. 'A thousand persons were struggling in the ruins and imploring for God's sake to release them' the *New York Sun* quoted a witness of the tragedy. 'Frantic husbands and fathers stood at the edge of the furnace that was slowly heating to a cherry red and incinerating human victims.'

Column upon column of equally pitiful stories were to appear in the papers in the days that followed. But the problem the first evening for the Press was to obtain any news at all. Johnstown was totally cut off from the world, the nearest information available coming from railway officials at Sang Hollow (where the energy of the flood had begun to spend itself). The reports on 1 June were largely guesswork, bare facts gleaned from fugitives and totally deficient in geography. But at least the estimates of the dead erred on the conservative side: 800 to 1,000 was the most popular figure.

NEW ORLEANS, JUNE 1, 1889.

FRIGHTFUL

Collapse of the South Fork, Pa., Reservoir.

An Enormous Lake on the Line of the Pensylvania Railroad.

Destruction of Johnstown, South Fork and Other Villages.

Between 800 and 1000 Lives Estimated to Have Been Lost.

The Inhabitants Caught in the Frightful Rush of Water

And Swept Away Beyond the Reach of Human Aid.

All Rivers in West Virginia and Pennsylvania Rising Rapidly.

Several of the Larger Cities Already Under Water, and Millions of Dollars of Damage Done.

DERRY, Pa., May 31.—A flood of death swept down the Allegheny mountains this afternoon and to-night, almost the entire city of Johnstown is swimming about in the rushing, angry tide. Dead bodies are floating about in every direction, and almost every piece of movable timber is carrying from the doomed city a corpse of humanity drifting with the raging waters, God knows where.

The disaster overtook Johnstown about

6 O'CLOCK THIS EVENING.

As the train bearing the special correspondents sped eastward the reports at each stop grew more appalling. At Derry a group of railway officials were gathered, who had come from Bolivar, the end of the passable portion of the road westward. They had seen but a small portion of the awful flood, but enough to imagine the rest.

Down through the pack saddle came the rushing waters. The wooded heights of the Alleghenies looked down in solemn wonder at the scene of the most terrible destruction that ever struck the romantic valley of the Connemaugh. The water was rising, when the men left at 6 o'clock, at the rate of

FIVE FEET AN HOUR.

Clinging to improvised rafts, constructed in the death battle from floating boards and timbers, were agonized men, women and children, their heartrending shrieks for help striking horror to the breasts of the onlookers. Their cries were of no avail. Car-

JUNE 3, 1889.

THOUSANDS PERISHED.

FURTHER DETAILS OF FRIDAY'S AWFUL CALAMITY.

AN ADDED HORROR OF FIRE

HUNDREDS OF PEOPLE BURNED UP WITH THE WRECKAGE.

TELEGRAMS DIRECT FROM JOHNSTOWN

THE LOSS OF LIFE ESTIMATED AT 8000 TO 10,000.

SCENES OF DESOLATION AND WOE

JOHNSTOWN AND HER SISTER TOWNS ANNIHILATED.

PREPARING TO BURY THE DEAD

TWO THOUSAND COFFINS SENT ON FROM PITTSBURG.

THUGS ROBBING DEAD BODIES

SIX OF THE RUFFIANS CAUGHT AND LYNCHED.

GENERAL HASTINGS TAKES CHARGE

RELIEF ARRIVING AND HOSPITAL WORK BEGUN.

REPAIRING THE RAILRAOD LINES.

THROUGH TRAVEL LIKELY TO BE STOPPED FOR SOME TIME.

NEWS FROM DELAYED TRAINS

[SPECIAL TO THE PUBLIC LEDGER.]

JOHNSTOWN, Pa., June 2.—I have just come from Johnstown proper, over a rope bridge which was completed this afternoon. I reached there at 5 o'clock last night, and tell only what I did see and do know.

The mighty wave that rushed through the Conemaugh Valley on Friday evening cut a swath of death 13 miles long. In its way lay one of the most thickly populated centres of the Keystone State, and within a few minutes from the time the dam at Lake Conemaugh broke houses were rolling over one another in a mad whirl, as they were carried by the seething waters down the gorge between the endless hills.

At Johnstown the whole centre of the city was cut, as if a mammoth scythe had passed over the land. At that place was a large stone bridge of the Pennsylvania Railroad Company, one of the strongest that the company owns. The Conemaugh river is crossed by it at an angle. Into this angle houses, trees and fences that came down the left side of the river rushed, and were piled one on top of another until the arches under the bridge

ST. LOUIS, JUNE 5, 1889.

A GIGANTIC BURIAL.

Dead Bodies Everywhere In and About Johnstown.

Unidentified Victims Laid Away Without Mourners and Without Tears.

Hundreds Roasted Above the Bridge Who Will Never Be Recognized.

The Monster Funeral Pyre Still Sullenly Consuming Its Prey.

Meanwhile the Ghastly Harvest of the Dead Goes On.

Pneumonia Breaks Out Among the Refugees On Prospect Hill.

Acres of Debris and Death Which Threaten a Pestilence.

Wails of Anguish From the Hospitals—Men Who Have to Be Their Own Undertakers, Pall Bearers and Grave Diggers — What the Registry Offices Show—The Death Roll —Relief Measures.

JOHNSTOWN, PA., June 4.—Four days have elapsed since the Angel of Death swept through the Valley of the Conemaugh. For thirty-six hours without intermission the fire engines have played upon the smoking ruins above the bridge, but the flames that break out afresh at frequent intervals in this floating field of ruins seem to defy the subduing force of water. Nearly 2000 men are employed in different parts of the valley clearing up the ruins and prosecuting diligent search for the undiscovered dead. Their investigations are not without fruitful results, for the bodies of the dead and charred victims of flood and fire are discovered with undiminished frequency. It becomes hourly more and more apparent that not a single vestige will ever be recognized of hundreds that were roasted in the flames above the bridge. Since the last sentence was penned, a party of searchers unearthed a charred and unsightly mass from the smoldering debris within 30 yards in front of the Associated Press headquarters. Unused to such frightful discoveries, the leader of the gang pronounced the remains to be a blackened log, and it required the authoritative verdict of a physician to demonstrate that the ghastly discovery was the charred remains of a human being. Only the trunk remained, and that was roasted beyond all semblance to flesh. Five minutes' search revealed fragments of a skull that at once disintegrated of its own weight when exposed to air, no single piece being larger than a half dollar, and the whole resembling the remnants of shattered charcoal. Within an hour a half dozen discoveries in no way less horrifying than this ghastly find were made by searchers as they raked with sticks and hooks in the smoking ruins. So difficult is it at times to determine whether the remains are those of human beings, that it is apparent that hundreds must be fairly burned to ashes. Thus the number that have found a last resting-

The next day the figure had leaped to 5,000 or 6,000, based entirely on the situation at New Florence since, as the *New York Tribune* had the grace to admit: 'So far as is known at this hour no newspaper man has yet entered Johnstown, or even floated over the roofs of the remaining houses.' The following day, without much further evidence, casualties were put at 10,000 (most papers), 12,000 (*San Francisco Chronicle*) or even 15,000 (*The World*).

The frustrating absence of hard fact goaded editors into all manners of speculation. At first the *New York Times* suggested a waterspout had caused the flood, the *Evening Post* a gas-main explosion. But certainly it was a gruelling assignment for the reporters that converged from all over America on the stricken valley. Rail lines were blocked fourteen miles from Johnstown, virtually all roads were impassable, and swollen rivers had to be crossed by improvised bosun's chairs. And when they did reach the scene of utter desolation, there were few means of getting the story out. By this time the slimy floodwaters were receding, exposing with every few feet a new misery. 'As the banks uncover the dead are seen' telegraphed the *Tribune* reporter. 'One woman, probably twenty-five years old with rather handsome features, had clasped in her arms a babe about six months old . . .' 'One walks across a desolate sea of mud in which there are interred the remains of many human bodies', the *Associated Press* correspondent wrote. 'A person who has never seen the city can hardly imagine the houses ever stood where they did.' Already he noted with distaste that morbid sightseers had struggled in from nearby towns and that some of the more unruly survivors had requisitioned floating whisky barrels and got roaring drunk.

In their efforts to communicate to the outside world the profound horror of the situation, some of the 'specials' ransacked their stocks of allegory beyond belief. One attempt has long been part of the mythology of American journalism: the reporter who began his dispatch, 'God looked down from the hills surrounding Johnstown today on an awesome scene of destruction . . .' To which his editor cabled back: 'Forget flood. Interview God'. But if that story is probably apochryphal, the repeated accounts of looting and desecration have an air of consensus about them that is equally suspect. Hungarians —those swarthy un-American villains—were the most popular scapegoats. 'Lying upon the shore a party of 13 Hungarians came upon the dead and mangled body of a woman, upon whose person there were a number of trinkets of jewellery and two diamonds' gasped the *Philadelphia Public Ledger*. 'In their eagerness to secure the plunder the Hungarians got into a squabble, during which one of the number severed the finger upon which were the rings . . .' Pursued by outraged farmers, apparently, nine of the brutes escaped though four of them were driven into the river and their death 'including the atrocious monster whose inhuman act has been described.' This and other Hungarian stories, with more refinements of detail, found their way onto front pages all over the country.

Interviewing survivors the Press soon came to the conclusion that many had died through their apathy. 'More lives have been lost because of foolish incredulity than from ignorance of the danger' the *St Louis Globe-Democrat* suggested. 'The foundations of the dam were considered to be shaky last spring, and many increasing leakages were reported from time to time . . . Those who heeded [warnings] early in the day were looked upon as cowards, and many jeers were uttered by lips that are now cold among the rank grass beside the river.' More rational examination after the event showed that the papers' passionate estimates of the dead had been fantasy: the true figure was in the region of 2,200. But not even their sternest critics could deny that they had failed to convey the desperation of Johnstown's plight to the world, or that the millions of dollars and material aid that flowed into the town were largely due to their efforts.

Inevitably the reporters soon turned their attention to the owners of the lake, the South Fork Fishing and Hunting Club. For days after the flood officials at the club house lived in dread of a rumoured gang of dynamiters bent on razing the club, as their own homes had been, but nothing happened. Virtually under siege from the Press, members maintained a tight-lipped silence. Only by persevering did *The World* extract from one of them the opinion that the ultimate cause of the disaster had been the unprecedented storms in the mountains, a whim of nature over which even rich businessmen had no control. To this day no-one has officially—by Inquiry or law-suit—proved that gentleman wrong.

A Cause for War
The Sinking of the Maine 1898

The USS *Maine* was an unlucky ship from the very beginning. No sooner was she in commission than it was discovered that she drew three feet more water forward than aft, and her armour-plating at the water-line was more of a hazard than a defence against the enemy. In 1897 she was caught in a storm off North Carolina and six of her crew were lost overboard. Two months later she was found to be leaking, and had to be returned to dry dock. Nevertheless, in February 1898, when she was ordered to her station in Havana harbour, she was rightly regarded as one of the brightest stars in America's rapidly-growing naval constellation.

Even for a battleship bristling with guns and stuffed to the hull with torpedoes, Havana was an uncomfortable place to be. For three years Cuba had been in the throes of one of its periodic revolts against its Spanish overlords, and in particular against the legendary brutality of General ('Butcher') Weyler. Riots in Havana occurred almost daily, and the *Maine*'s mission was to stand as watchdog for the interests of the numerous American citizens living there and to offer instant protection should the need arise. There were newspapers, notably *The World*, who saw this manoeuvre as gunboat diplomacy on behalf of the oppressed Cubans but for nearly three weeks the *Maine* remained quietly, if hardly unobtrusively, at anchor. Then at 9.45 in the evening of 15 February a terrific explosion rocked the waterfront. Observers on the shore saw a pall of black smoke lying over the *Maine*, and a column of flame shoot up from her bows. Within moments fire seemed to have enveloped the ship as she crumpled into the water, a pile of wreckage. In all, 250 officers and men of the *Maine* were killed.

The World scooped all its rivals in publishing news of the disaster, by the simple expedient of having its cable composed and transmitted in Spanish, thus avoiding interminable wrangles over translation in the Spanish censor's office. And as it predicted, public reaction to the news was outraged—since in the absence of reliable information, it was uncritically assumed that the explosion was the result of 'an infernal machine' detonated by 'enemy agents'.

To understand this impetuous assumption the *Maine*'s tragedy has to be seen in the context of America's ripening overseas ambitions. For some years powerful interests in the United States had hungered for expansion abroad, an appetite sharpened by the awareness of their country's growing economic influence, and since 1896 their attention had been focussed on Cuba in particular, where the grip of the Spanish imperialists looked ready to be prized away. It would probably mean war, but after decades of isolation war was not an unromantic notion to the mass of the public. Certainly it appealed to a section of the press then engaged in a frantic circulation struggle. The chief contestants in the New York arena, both hovering near the million-mark, were Joseph Pulitzer's *World* and Randolph Hearst's *Journal*, and their tactical weapons consisted for the most part of scandal and sensation.

Along with the *New York Sun*, these papers had for two years prior to the *Maine*'s arrival in Havana been assiduous in exposing Spain's evil designs upon American interests and her frequent 'massacres' of the native Cuban population (real or imagined). The *Journal* even went so far as to intervene on its own account—smuggling a beautiful 'innocent' rebel maiden out of a Cuban jail (and taking her to shake hands with President M'Kinley), then intercepting and publishing a private letter from the Spanish ambassador to Madrid in which he had made certain injudicious references to the President. But none of these constituted a justifiable cause for armed intervention. The sinking of the *Maine*, on the other hand, was a heaven-sent opportunity. Provided, of course, it wasn't an accident.

The *Journal*, from the moment the news broke, had no doubts at all about that. 'Des-

$50,000 REWARD.—WHO DESTROYED THE MAINE?—$50,000 REWARD.

The Journal will give $50,000 for information, furnished to it exclusively, that will convict the person or persons who sank the Maine.

EDITION FOR GREATER NEW YORK.
NEW YORK JOURNAL
AND ADVERTISER.

The Journal will give $50,000 for information, furnished to it exclusively, that will convict the person or persons who sank the Maine.

NO. 5,572.   Copyright, 1898, by W. R. Hearst.—NEW YORK, THURSDAY, FEBRUARY 17, 1898.—16 PAGES.   PRICE ONE CENT in Greater New York and Jersey City.   Elsewhere, TWO CENTS.

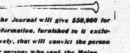

DESTRUCTION OF THE WAR SHIP MAINE WAS THE WORK OF AN ENEMY.

$50,000!

$50,000 REWARD!
For the Detection of the Perpetrator of the Maine Outrage!

The New York Journal hereby offers a reward of $50,000 CASH for information FURNISHED TO IT EXCLUSIVELY, which shall lead to the detection and conviction of the person, persons or government criminally responsible for the explosions which resulted in the destruction, at Havana, of the United States war ship Maine and the loss of 258 lives of American sailors.

The $50,000 CASH offered for the above information is on deposit with Wells, Fargo & Co.

No one is barred, be he the humble but misguided seaman eking out a few miserable dollars by acting as a spy, or the attache of a government secret service, plotting, by any devilish means, to revenge fancied insults or cripple menacing countries.

This offer has been cabled to Europe and will be made public in every capital of the Continent and in London this morning.

The Journal believes that any man who can be bought to commit murder can also be bought to betray his comrades. **FOR THE PERPETRATOR OF THIS OUTRAGE HAD ACCOMPLICES.**

W. R. HEARST.

Assistant Secretary Roosevelt Convinced the Explosion of the War Ship Was Not an Accident.

—

The Journal Offers $50,000 Reward for the Conviction of the Criminals Who Sent 258 American Sailors to Their Death. Naval Officers Unanimous That the Ship Was Destroyed on Purpose.

$50,000!

$50,000 REWARD!
For the Detection of the Perpetrator of the Maine Outrage!

The New York Journal hereby offers a reward of $50,000 CASH for information FURNISHED TO IT EXCLUSIVELY, which shall lead to the detection and conviction of the person, persons or government criminally responsible for the explosions which resulted in the destruction, at Havana, of the United States war ship Maine and the loss of 258 lives of American sailors.

The $50,000 CASH offered for the above information is on deposit with Wells, Fargo & Co.

No one is barred, be he the humble, but misguided, seaman, eking out a few miserable dollars by acting as a spy, or the attache of a government secret service, plotting, by any devilish means, to revenge fancied insults or cripple menacing countries.

This offer has been cabled to Europe and will be made public in every capital of the Continent and in London this morning.

The Journal believes that any man who can be bought to commit murder can also be bought to betray his comrades. **FOR THE PERPETRATOR OF THIS OUTRAGE HAD ACCOMPLICES.**

W. R. HEARST.

POWDER MAGAZINE

NAVAL OFFICERS THINK THE MAINE WAS DESTROYED BY A SPANISH MINE.

George Eugene Bryson, the Journal's special correspondent at Havana, cables that it is the secret opinion of many Spaniards in the Cuban capital that the Maine was destroyed and 258 of her men killed by means of a submarine mine, or fixed torpedo. This is the opinion of several American naval authorities. The Spaniards, it is believed, arranged to have the Maine anchored over one of the harbor mines. Wires connected the mine with a powder magazine, and it is thought the explosion was caused by sending an electric current through the wire. If this can be proven, the brutal nature of the Spaniards will be shown by the fact that they waited to spring the mine until after all the men had retired for the night. The Maltese cross in the picture shows where the mine may have been fired.

Hidden Mine or a Sunken Torpedo Believed to Have Been the Weapon Used Against the American Man-of-War---Officers and Men Tell Thrilling Stories of Being Blown Into the Air Amid a Mass of Shattered Steel and Exploding Shells---Survivors Brought to Key West Scout the Idea of Accident---Spanish Officials Protest Too Much---Our Cabinet Orders a Searching Inquiry---Journal Sends Divers to Havana to Report Upon the Condition of the Wreck. Was the Vessel Anchored Over a Mine?

BY CAPTAIN E. L. ZALINSKI, U. S. A.

(Captain Zalinski is the inventor of the famous dynamite gun, which would be the principal factor in our coast defence in case of war.)

Assistant Secretary of the Navy Theodore Roosevelt says he is convinced that the destruction of the Maine in Havana Harbor was not an accident. The Journal offers a reward of $50,000 for exclusive evidence that will convict the person, persons or Government criminally responsible for the destruction of the American battle ship and the death of 258 of its crew.

The suspicion that the Maine was deliberately blown up grows stronger every hour. Not a single fact to the contrary has been produced.

Captain Sigsbee, of the Maine, and Consul-General Lee both urge that public opinion be suspended until they have completed their investigation.

truction of the Warship Maine was the Work of an Enemy' ran its headline on the 17th, with a drawing of a spiky-looking mine floating beneath the battleship to convince the sceptical. It also offered $50,000 to whoever could unmask the villain who had done it! *The World* the same day did at least have the grace to add a question-mark to its headline: 'Maine Explosion caused by Bomb or Torpedo?' The ship's commander, Cpt Sigsbee, was reported to be in doubt about what had caused it. On the other hand one Dr Pendleton, recently arrived from Havana, swore he had overheard a plot there to blow up the battleship. In view of this revelation it must have been disappointing, the next day, to gather expert opinion from all round the world and to find it unanimous in supposing the explosion to be entirely accidental. The British naval expert, Lord Charles Beresford, even offered a comprehensive explanation of how it might have happened considering the vast amount of high explosives the *Maine* carried.

No matter, plenty of politicians in the United States were convinced there was dirty work afoot—not least among them Theodore Roosevelt, Assistant Secretary of the Navy, who dearly wanted an early opportunity to pit his new squadrons against the Spanish fleet. From all quarters, political, commercial and journalistic, immense pressure was now building up on President M'Kinley to take the initiative. In an effort to cool the situation M'Kinley announced a Court of Inquiry to investigate the disaster and—just so his actions could not be misconstrued—issued a press statement to the effect that it was his belief 'the Maine was blown up as the result of an accident, and he hopes the Court will develop that fact.' The most pacific newspapers, like the *New York Tribune*, wel-

comed his responsible attitude: *The World* and the *Journal*, though, declined to wait upon the tedious deliberations of a Court.

For its own part *The World* announced its own 'commission' of experts to examine the relics of the *Maine*. The *Journal* even announced that divers had already inspected the wreck and found incontrovertible proof of treachery (in fact divers had *not* inspected the ship, only searched for victims). A similar report somehow got to the ears of the British Press, followed closely by an appeal from *Reuters* that it be suppressed. It made no difference, the papers printed both the report and the account of the attempt to suppress it, the *St James's Gazette* adding 'President M'Kinley is afraid of the consequences of this startling information leaking out.' The *Journal* then disclosed a secret cable from Cpt Sigsbee to the Secretary of the Navy claiming that vessel had not been blown up by accident. History has produced not one jot of evidence to support the existence of this mysterious 'cable'.

Other papers were getting faintly embarrassed and decidedly troubled at the antics of their colleagues. Growled the *New York Evening Post*: 'during the present war crisis, the newspapers' lying with a view of promoting the outbreak of war, has excited the disgust and reprobation of all intelligent people.' *The World* was unrepentant: as soon as its 'commission' returned with predictable findings it devoted its entire front page to 'Fifty Physical Proofs that Maine was blown up by a Mine or a Torpedo.' There weren't, literally, fifty proofs—indeed the burden of the evidence appeared to rest on the flimsy suggestion that such havoc as was obviously wrought could not have been caused by the amount of explosive material known to have been aboard the ship, and on the slightly

more substantial point that the twisted shape of the metalwork indicated an external rather than an internal explosion. The conclusions of the official inquiry were very similar, as it turned out, though the Court refused to lay any blame at Spain's door (sadly for the *Journal* which had declared well in advance of the report that the Court's verdict was 'Spain is Guilty').

The circulation of both *The World* and the *Journal* had now leapt far beyond a million, and their jingoist fever had percolated deep into the public consciousness. The President was rapidly becoming confronted with a situation from which there was no escape. Briefly and without conviction he attempted to negotiate with Spain for Cuba's independence, but such were the forces arrayed against him that even when Spain agreed to virtually all his demands he could no longer publicly resist the tide of war. On 24 April, with no dissenting voices, Congress passed the resolution that a state of war existed between the United States and the Kingdom of Spain.

The sinking of the *Maine* cannot be said to have been the exclusive cause of a war that would very likely have happened anyway, but it was an important catalyst in the political chain reaction that led to the final eruption. Yet *was* it sabotage? A great many more maritime explosions have occurred since the *Maine*, and a great deal more information has been gathered about the strange effects of such disasters. It is one of the ironies of history that today an expert presented with the same evidence available to the *Journal*, *The World*'s 'commission', the Court of Inquiry, and even Theodore Roosevelt, would undoubtedly come to the conclusion that the *Maine* had been carrying unstable explosives and had simply blown herself up.

The Press Publish-
ew York World. }   NEW YORK, FRIDAY, FEBRUARY 18, 1898.   ..   PRICE {

MIDNIGHT OPINION FROM THE PRESIDENT.

His Latest Information Leads Him to Believe "that the Maine Was Blown Up as the Result of an Accident," and He Hopes the Court of Inquiry Will Develop that Fact."

IF THE "DISASTER WAS NOT ACCIDENTAL PROMPT AND DECISIVE STEPS WILL BE TAKEN."

(By Telegraph from a Staff Correspondent of The World.)

Washington, D. C., Feb. 17.—In view of the "war alarms" throughout the country, The World is authorized to make the following statement, which represents the views of President McKinley a little before midnight:

"Based upon information now in his possession, the President believes that the Maine was blown up as the result of an accident, and he hopes the Court of Inquiry will develop that fact. If it is found that the disaster was not an accident, prompt and decisive steps will be taken in the premises.

"The finding of the Naval Court will develop the cause, and until that is submitted nothing will be done."

The World

OVER ONE MILLION TWO HUNDRED THOUSAND *EVERY* DAY.

THE CIRCULATION OF THE JOURNAL SATURDAY WAS **1,220,618**

ALL FREE COPIES, EXCHANGES, SAMPLES AND WASTE DEDUCTED.

WAR EXTRA

NIGHT SPECIAL. AN AMERICAN PAPER FOR AMERICANS.

NEW YORK JOURNAL

NO. 5,639—P. M.   NEW YORK, MONDAY, APRIL 25, 1898.   PRICE ONE CENT.

CONGRESS DECLARES WAR

ASSERTS HOSTILITIES BEGAN ON APRIL 21.

Washington, April 25.—Both houses of Congress this afternoon, at the request of President McKinley, passed the following bill, declaring that war existed between Spain and the United States since April 21, the date on which Minister Woodford was dismissed by the Spanish Government:

"A bill declaring that war exists between the United States of America and the kingdom of Spain.

"Be it Resolved, By the Senate and House of Representatives of the United States of America in Congress assembled,

"First—That war be, and the same is hereby declared to exist, and that war has existed since the twenty-first day of April, A. D., 1898, including said day, between the United States of America and the kingdom of Spain.

"Second—That the President of the United States be, and he hereby is directed and empowered to use the entire land and naval forces of the United States, and to call into the actual service of the United States the militia of the several States, to such extent as may be necessary to carry this act into effect."

The bill was at once sent to President McKinley.

It was passed by the House early in the afternoon, as the reply to a message from President McKinley. The Senate debated it for a couple of hours in executive session.

Many Senators urged that the date when the war began be not mentioned in the bill.

Mr. Turpie also advocated an amendment in recognizing the independence of the Republic of Cuba, but it was defeated.

PRESIDENT ASKS FOR DECLARATION OF WAR.

President McKinley sent to Congress at noon to-day a message requesting that both Houses make formal declaration of the existence of a state of war.

The message was accompanied by copies of the correspondence relating to the breaking off by Spain of all diplomatic negotiations and the proclamations by the President of a blockade and his call for troops.

Large and expectant crowds listened to the reading of the message in both Houses. The message was immediately referred by the lower House to the Committee on Foreign Affairs, and in the Senate to the Committee on Foreign Relations.

Senator Allen, of Nebraska, introduced a resolution in the Senate at 12:20, declaring that a state of war exists between the United States and Spain. The resolution was referred to the Committee on Foreign Relations, which went into session at once to consider the President's message.

In the House, Representative Adams, Chairman of the Committee on Foreign Affairs, at 1:19, reported a bill in conformity with the President's message. It was put upon its passage within two minutes and passed without a dissenting voice. Applause followed the Speaker's announcement of the vote.

TEXT OF THE PRESIDENT'S MESSAGE.

The message is as follows:

"To the Senate and House of Representatives:

"I transmit to the Congress for its consideration and appropriate action copies of correspondence recently had with the representative of Spain in the United States, with the United States Minister at Madrid, and, through the latter, with the Government of Spain, showing the action taken under the joint resolution approved April 20, 1898.

"Upon communicating to the Spanish Minister in Washington the demand which it

Continued on Second Page.

LEVY FOR TROOPS MADE ON THE STATES

New York Called Upon for Twelve Regiments of Infantry and Two Troops of Cavalry.

Washington, April 25.—The War Department late this afternoon issued a call upon Governors of States for troops, as follows:

ALABAMA—Two regiments infantry and one battalion.
ARKANSAS—Two regiments infantry.
CALIFORNIA—Two regiments infantry, two battalions; four heavy batteries.
CONNECTICUT—One regiment infantry, two light batteries, one heavy battery.
COLORADO—One regiment infantry, one battery.
FLORIDA—One regiment infantry.
GEORGIA—Two regiments infantry, two light batteries.
ILLINOIS—Seven regiments infantry, one troop cavalry.
INDIANA—Four regiments infantry, two light batteries.
IOWA—Two regiments infantry, two light batteries.
KANSAS—Three regiments infantry.
KENTUCKY—Three regiments infantry and two cavalry.
LOUISIANA—Two regiments infantry.
MAINE—One regiment infantry, one heavy battery.
MARYLAND—One regiment infantry, four heavy batteries.
MASSACHUSETTS—Four regiments infantry, four heavy batteries.
MICHIGAN—Four regiments infantry.
MINNESOTA—Three regiments infantry.
MISSISSIPPI—Two regiments infantry.
MISSOURI—Five regiments infantry, one light battery.
MONTANA—One regiment infantry.
NEBRASKA—Two regiments infantry.
NEW HAMPSHIRE—One regiment infantry.
NEW JERSEY—Three regiments infantry.
NEW YORK—Twelve regiments infantry, two troops cavalry.
NORTH CAROLINA—Two regiments infantry, one heavy battery.
OHIO—Six regiments infantry, four light batteries, two squads cavalry.
OREGON—One regiment infantry.
PENNSYLVANIA—Ten regiments infantry, four heavy batteries.
RHODE ISLAND—One regiment infantry.
SOUTH CAROLINA—One regiment infantry, one light battery, one heavy battery.
TENNESSEE—Three regiments infantry.
TEXAS—Three regiments infantry, one cavalry.
UTAH—One troop cavalry, two light batteries.
VERMONT—One regiment infantry.
VIRGINIA—Three regiments infantry.
WASHINGTON—One regiment infantry.
WEST VIRGINIA—One regiment infantry.
WISCONSIN—Three regiments infantry.
WYOMING—One light battery, one troop cavalry.
DISTRICT OF COLUMBIA—One battalion infantry.
NORTH DAKOTA—Five troops cavalry.
SOUTH DAKOTA—Seven troops cavalry.
IDAHO—Two troops cavalry.
NEVADA—One troop cavalry.
ARIZONA—Two troops cavalry.
NEW MEXICO—Four troops cavalry.
OKLAHOMA—One troop cavalry.

PREFERENCE GIVEN TO MILITIA.

The telegram to the Governors, after mentioning the quota, says:

"It is the wish of the President that the regiments of the National Guard or State militia be used as far as their

EXTRA

NO. 11 LATEST NEWS

REED AND HOBART

SIGN WAR DECLARATION

WASHINGTON, APRIL 25.—THE BILL PASSED BY BOTH HOUSES THIS AFTERNOON DECLARING THAT WAR WITH SPAIN HAS EXISTED SINCE APRIL 21 WAS SIGNED BY SPEAKER REED AT 4.50 P. M.

VICE-PRESIDENT HOBART SIGNED IT AT 4.55 P. M., AND IT WAS AT ONCE FORWARDED TO PRESIDENT McKINLEY.

NEW YORK-WASHINGTON GAME POSTPONED—RAIN. BROOKLYN-BALTIMORE GAME POSTPONED—WET GROUNDS.

WINNERS AT AQUEDUCT.

FIRST RACE—Tabouret, Arban, Zanone.
SECOND RACE—Peace, Coquette, Crown.
THIRD RACE—Arsenal I., Auckland, Bluebeard.
FOURTH RACE—The Merchant, Don't Care, Tabouret.
FIFTH RACE—Ben Ronald, King T., Long Acre.

numbers will permit, for the reason that they are armed, equipped and drilled."

The Secretary also asks the Governors to telegraph at once what equipments, ammunition, arms, blankets, tents, etc., are on hand and what are needed; and also when the troops will be ready for muster into the United States service.

This will be followed by a letter of detail to be sent out to-morrow.

The Death of Galveston

Galveston Flood 1900

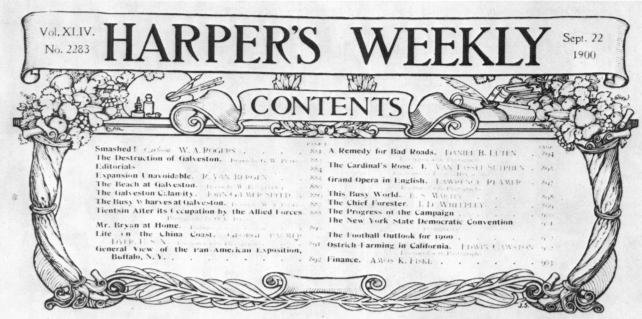

Vol. XLIV.
No. 2283

HARPER'S WEEKLY

Sept. 22
1900

CONTENTS

Smashed! *Cartoon.* W. A. ROGERS 881
The Destruction of Galveston. *Drawn by* G. W. Peters 883
Editorials 884
Expansion Unavoidable. R. VAN BERGEN . . 885
The Beach at Galveston. *Drawn by* W. Glackens 886
The Galveston Calamity. JOHN GILMER SPEED . 886
The Busy Wharves at Galveston. *Drawn by* W. J. Glackens 887
Tientsin After its Occupation by the Allied Forces 888
    Photograph by J. H. Bass.
Mr. Bryan at Home. 891
Life on the China Coast. GILBERT PALMER
    DYER, U. S. N 891
General View of the Pan-American Exposition,
    Buffalo, N. Y. 892

A Remedy for Bad Roads. DANIEL B. LUTEN . 894
    Illustrated with Photographs.
The Cardinal's Rose. L. VAN TASSEL SUTPHEN . 895
    Illustrated.
Grand Opera in English. LAWRENCE REAMER . 897
    Illustrated with Photographs.
This Busy World. E. S. MARTIN 898
The Chief Forester. J. D. WHELPLEY . . . 899
The Progress of the Campaign 900
The New York State Democratic Convention . 901
    Photographs.
The Football Outlook for 1900 902
Ostrich-Farming in California. EDWIN CAWSTON 902
    Illustrated with Photographs.
Finance. AMOS K. FISKE 903

THE DESTRUCTION OF GALVESTON.

DRAWN BY G. W. PETERS FROM TELEGRAPHIC REPORTS

The Galveston Daily News.

59TH YEAR—NO 173.   GALVESTON, TEXAS, THURSDAY,- SEPTEMBER 13, 1900   ESTABLISHED 1842

STORY OF THE GREAT DISASTER AT GALVESTON

Loss of Life Is Estimated at Between 4000 and 5000---Not a Single Individual Escaped Property Loss---The Total Property Loss From Fifteen to Twenty Million Dollars.

Galveston, at the turn of the century, was a striking testament to the booming success of the American economy, a bustling sea-port on the Gulf of Mexico of wharves and cotton warehouses and grain elevators, of tidy square buildings and geometric streets. Built on an island in the heart of Galveston Bay, you approached it from the north by ferry, or from the west by the Southern Pacific, Santa Fe or Galveston & Houston Railroads whose bridge spanned the waters of the bay. The sea was Galveston's life, and its relaxation—in contrast to the busy quayside the southern shore of Galveston was lined with pleasant beach chalets, the great Olympia pleasure gardens, and the impressive bathing pavilion known as The Pagoda. The sea was also its death.

In the first days of September 1900, somewhere in the doldrums near the Cape Verde islands a hurricane was brewing. At first a breeze, then a wind, then a spiralling gale, it set off for the coast of Texas, dispatching a familiar storm-swell across the ocean ahead of it. By Saturday 8 September, accompanied by torrential rains, the foaming sea had already eaten into parts of the city and flooded it to a depth of three feet, bringing all work to a standstill by ten o'clock. Then the hurricane descended, lashing the sea to further frenzies and scything down anything in its path. The demonic combination of wind and sea was irresistible: Galveston collapsed against their onslaughts.

For a whole day the city suffered alone, all communication with the rest of the world hopeless. On Sunday the floods which had covered virtually the whole island (in parts to a depth of over ten feet) receded almost, it seemed, as suddenly as they had come. Behind them they left a scene of horror unparalleled in the United States to this day. Descriptions brought out by the first refugees from the city almost defied belief. Among the first to reach the outside world was a journalist, Richard Spillane, a correspondent for *Associated Press*: he had been officially detailed by the Mayor of Galveston to make for Houston as soon as he could—to give the world an unvarnished account of the disaster, and plead for aid. Here is part of his story as it appeared in the *New York Tribune* (though it differed little in other papers).

'The wreck of Galveston was brought about by a tempest so terrible that no words can adequately describe its intensity, and by a flood which turned the city into a raging sea. The Weather Bureau records show that the wind attained a velocity of 84 miles an hour when the measuring instrument blew away, so it is impossible to tell what was the maximum. While the storm in the Gulf piled the water up on the beach side of the city, the north wind piled the water from the bay on the bay part of the city . . . The winds were rising constantly and it rained in torrents. The wind was so fierce that the rain cut like a knife. By 3 o'clock the waters of the bay and Gulf met, and by dark the entire city was submerged. The flooding of the electric light plant and the gas plants left the city in darkness. To go up the streets was to court death. The wind was then at cyclonic velocity: roofs, cisterns, portions of buildings, telegraph poles and walls were falling, and the noise of the wind and the crashing of the buildings were terrifying in the extreme. The wind and the waters rose steadily from dark until 1.40 o'clock Sunday morning. During all this time the people of Galveston were like rats in traps. The highest portion of the city was four to five feet under water, while in the great majority of cases the streets were submerged to a depth of ten feet. To leave a house was to drown. To remain was to court death in the wreckage. Such a night of agony has seldom been equalled by people in modern times.'

After the floodwaters had gone down, he went on, survivors cautiously set out to survey their once flourishing city. They were greeted with 'the most horrible sights imaginable . . . the whole of the beach front on the Gulf was stripped of every vestige of habitation, the dwellings, the great bathing establishments and every structure having been either carried out to sea or its ruins piled in a pyramid far into the town, according to the vagaries of the tempest. The first hurried glance over the city showed that the largest structures, supposed to be the most substantially built, suffered the most. The Orphans' Home fell like a pack of cards. How many dead children and refugees are in the ruins cannot be ascertained. Of the sick in St Mary's Infirmary only eight are known to be saved. The Ball High School is but an empty shell, crushed and broken. Every church in the city, with one or two exceptions, is in ruins. At the forts nearly all the soldiers are reported dead . . . the bay front is in ruins, nothing but the wreckage of the great warehouses remain . . . The flood left a slime about one inch deep over the whole city, and unless fast progress is made in burying corpses and carcasses of animals there is danger of pestilence.'

Horrific though Spillane's account was, it was a conservative one, for he estimated fatalities to be only about 1,000. The confused days that followed in Galveston revealed beyond any shadow of doubt that at least five to six thousand had died. 'The last days of Pompeii were not as terrible as the last days of Galveston' exclaimed the *New York Herald* correspondent, one of the first to reach the island. 'Hell is the only word that fittingly describes Galveston's scene today . . .' The sheer logistic problem of disposing of bodies forced the authorities to order them to be piled into barges by the hundred and dumped at sea, or else to be incinerated in huge bonfires along the beach without any attempt at identification. This caused a storm of protest from relatives, but as the *Herald* reporter said 'abhorrent as this may appear to the sanctified sentiments pertaining to religious burial and the proper identification of the remains, there is a higher necessity which must assert itself in the best interests of the living.'

Under strict martial law Galveston forced itself into action—though not without understandable tensions. A feud between the mayor and the police chief resulted in a move to depose the mayor, and on a less elevated plane pent-up emotions were freely vented upon anyone who did not appear to be fulfilling a useful function. 'People with cameras are especially the object of attack,' complained the *New Orleans Daily Picayune*, 'and many of the picture machines have been taken away from their owners and smashed, the men who had them being compelled to go to work as day-labourers. Newspaper men are not treated in that way exactly, but nearly!' And of course the 'ghouls' made their customary appearance in print. 'Negro looters held high carnival' said the *New York Herald*. 'Thrice we saw negroes burglarising and once a shot was fired from ambush. It whizzed past our ears. Life is cheap in Galveston. The awful presence of widespread death to rich and poor has made men callous, and a shooting or a killing attracts little attention.' As at Johnstown minorities served admirably as scapegoats—though some of the justifications sounded a little hollow. 'This latent animalism has been covered over by a thin incrustation of civilisation which conceals and confines man's real nature within bounds' pontificated the *Memphis Commercial*. 'The thinner the veneering of civilisation the easier it is destroyed and the sooner does the savage appear. Hence it is easy to believe the negroes are the chief sinners because they are the least civilised'. It didn't apparently occur to the *Commercial* to make any comparison with the white men who, even at that moment, were merrily slaughtering one another in the midst of the Pennsylvania coal strikes.

But if disaster exposes the darker side of human nature in some, in others it also reveals a heroic aspect. Galveston did not despair. Within a week bridges had been repaired, and inside a month temporary wharves had been built and business began flowing in once more. Help poured in from every state in the Union,

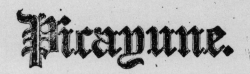

The Daily Picayune.

VOL. LXIV.   NEW ORLEANS, THURSDAY, SEPTEMBER 13, 1900.—FOURTEEN PAGES.—IN TWO PARTS.   NO. 231.

BRINGING ORDER OUT OF CHAOS IN GALVESTON.

Stupendous Task Undertaken by the Authorities Assisted by the State and Federal Governments Partially Accomplished.

Prompt and Drastic Measures Teach the Lawless Elements to Respect the Living and the Dead.

FOR GOD'S SAKE, HELP!

Memphis, Tenn., Sept. 12.—The following telegram was received at the Cotton Exchange this forenoon with reference to the money to be raised at the citizens' meeting here this afternoon:

"Galveston, Tex., Sept 12.—Wire money collected at the meeting. Send disinfectants and food for man and beast. Situation horrible. Can't describe it. For God's sake, help us!

"J. H. STEELE, Chairman.

"RABBI COHEN.

"W. J. McMAHON.

"B. B. MURRAY."

THE DEAD.

Galveston, Tex., Sept. 12.—Following are additional names of the dead:
Mrs. Maria Lewis, colored.
Mrs. Anderson.
Miss Mattie Anderson.
Bradley family.
Bonham family.
Mr. and Mrs. George Falkenhagen.
Mrs. H. Clem Ruhn and two children.
Willie Ivy.
Mrs. James Holland.
Mr. and Mrs. H. Lockman.
Sam Williams, colored.
Mrs. Nathan Moore.
Julius Everget.
D. B. Ross.
Chas. Ross.
Mrs. Erita Prether.
—— Engelhart.
Mrs. W. J. Johnston and two children.
Mrs. John Holland.

Jordan Trezevant.
Mrs. Turner.
Mrs. C. C. Williams, colored.
Prof. Weiss.
Sella Seraline.
Mr. Jones and child.
Mrs. Zweigel and two daughters.
Mrs. Gaule and child.
Mrs. Mary Pierson.
Alice Pierson.
Frank Pierson.
Mrs. Nelson and daughter.
Mrs. Johnson.
—— Friedman, wife and son.
Mr. and Mrs. Dempsey.
Mrs. Mary Burnett.
Mrs. J. E. Toothaker.
Miss Etta Toothaker.
Wm. Miller, wife, son-in-law, daughter and five children.
Lucia Miner.
H. E. Ehdemann.
Chas. Darby.

Mayor Jones Creates a Sensation by Deposing the Militia Commander.

The Sea Gives Up Its Dead and Causes a Change in the Mode of Burials.

Estimates of the Loss of Life Now Run as High as Ten Thousand.

Relief Pouring in and Its Distribution is Being Systematized—Plenty of Fresh Water

---

THE COMMITTEE'S THANKS.

Galveston, Tex., Sept 12.—To the Associated Press: We are receiving numerous telegrams of condolence and offers of assistance. As the telegraph wires are burdened, we beg the Associated Press to communicate this response to all:

Nearby cities are supplying, and will supply, sufficient food, clothing, etc., for immediate needs. Cities farther away can serve us best by sending money. Checks should be made payable to John Sealey, chairman finance committee. All supplies should come to W. A. McVitie, chairman relief committee. We have 25,000 people to clothe and feed for many weeks, and to furnish with household goods. Most of these are homeless, and the others will require money to make their wrecked residences habitable. From this the world will understand how much money we will need.

This committee will from time to time report our needs with more particularity. We refer to dispatches of this date by Major R. G. Lowe, which the committee fully indorses. All communications will please accept this answer in lieu of direct response, and be assured of the heartfelt gratitude of the entire population.

W. C. JONES, Mayor.

M. LASKER.

J. D. SKINNER.

O. H. McMASTER.

R. G. LOWE.

CLARENCE OUSLEY.

Committee.

---

armory and swore satisfactorily that they | Late in the afternoon Adjutant General

---

VOL. LXIV.   NEW ORLEANS, TUESDAY, SEPTEMBER 11, 1900.—SIXTEEN PAGES.—IN TWO PARTS.   NO. 229.

A SCENE OF DEVASTATION AND RUIN.

WIND AND WAVE CAUSED RUIN AT GALVESTON.

City Still Cut Off and in a Terrible State for All Necessities.

The Loss of Life Is Estimated from 1000 to 1500 Souls.

Governor Sayers Places His Estimate at the Former Figure.

Loss on Property is Thought to be $20,000,000, at Least.

Governor Asks for Aid From the Government and States, Not in Vain.

Relief Promised from Various States and Cities and the National Government.

Horrors of the Storm Increased by Lack of Drinking Water.

A VIEW AT THE WHARVES.

Mrs. Clarence Howth.
Mr. and Mrs. Schuler and five children.
Mrs. Motter and two daughters.
Mrs. David Wakelee.
C. B. Fix.
W. F. Fisher and wife, two children, two sisters-in-law and a niece.
John F. Gorn and two children.
Mr. and Mrs. A. J. Compton.
Mrs. Hughes.
Mr. and Mrs. John F. Broecker and two children.
—— Hobeck and son.
Mother-in-law and sister-in-law of Wm. Thompson, of the fire department.
Thos. Webster, Sr., secretary of grain inspector of this port, and family of four.
Mrs. J. R. Correll and family.
"Frances," a well known ————, re-

Captain R. H. Peck, city engineer, wife and five children.
Mrs. J. W. Munn, Sr.
Mrs. Chas. Walter and three children.
Mrs. Barbon.
Edward Webster and two sisters.
Mr. J. H. Harris.
Mrs. Rebecca Harris.
Barney Kelly.
Willie Kelly.
Allin Bessie Questerr.
Mrs. Harris, colored.
Joe Schwartzbach.
Mrs. M. Quester, little son and daughter.
J. F. Roll, wife and four children.
Joe Hughes.
Mrs. Katie Evans and tw. children.
Kate and Fannie.

weather bureau. Dr. Cline and his brother, Joe Cline, and three children drifted about in the raging torrents for three hours on a roughly-constructed raft. They were all bruised and cut from their struggles with flying debris.

Loss May Be 1500.

Houston, Tex., Sept. 10.—The first reports of the appalling disaster which has stricken the city of Galveston do not seem to have been magnified. Communication was had with the island city to-day by boat, and reports received there indicate that the death list will at least 1000, and perhaps more, lives being lost within a few hours. Imagine strong men, awe-struck so that they absolutely realized their perfect impotence in the face of danger and are compelled to see their dependent relatives, the weak wife, sister or mother, and the helpless children swept away by the raging, seething torrent. All is yet confusion; everyone is looking over his own situation or

and cities, and early this morning trains with food supplies and other articles left the city by the Santa Fe and International and Great Northern. The Lawrence was chartered to take a supply of provisions, but got down only as far as Hill street bridge. The bridge would not turn, so the Lawrence could not proceed further, and it was determined to secure a tug from the Direct Navigation Company. To all intents and purposes Galveston still lies prostrate and entirely cut off from all communication with the outside world. The bridges which connects the island with the main land are gone, the boats are, with the exception of a few little pleasure boats, all lost, so that people can get neither in nor out. Telegraph and telephone wires lie flat and useless.

In order to send relief a thorough system must be inaugurated. For some time yet it will require every boat procurable to convey supplies into the city, as there is neither food nor water obtainable, and the latter is particularly necessary. It might be the part of wisdom to request New Orleans to dispatch a ship load of water at once to Galveston. Houston could and would supply everything needed to assist her sister city in the hour of distress, but unfortunately the boats to carry the water are not obtainable. There has been very little news from Galveston since last night.

Mr. Richard Spillane, who came up this morning for the purpose of sending off dispatches to the outside world, is confined to his room, in a hot fever from the effects of the strain he underwent during that awful Saturday night last.

In speaking of the catastrophe he said:

"Conditions in Galveston cannot be exaggerated. Never was there such a storm as that that has befallen the city. Think of at least 1000, and perhaps more, lives

life anew. They have lost their all. Homes are wrecked, business houses damaged and stocks of goods ruined by the high waters which invaded the principal stores of the city. The docks, wharves, elevators, public utilities are all obliterated and must renew. It is simply a scene of unparalleled ruin and desolation, and we appeal to the outside world for aid until we can re-establish ourselves and get on our feet again.

Between Houston and Virginia Point the country presents a woebegone appearance, and at all the towns which are witnessed which appeal to the sympathy of those wending by on the trains. Houses are unroofed, some are lying prone on their side, while one is at Webster lying on its top. No news of any definite nature as to casualty list of life can be reported. It must have been severe, as buildings and their contents were, in many instances, blown completely away or collapsed in such shape that the inmates could not possibly escape injury or death. The prairie is covered deep with water and a great deal of live stock has been lost.

Manager Vaughan, of the Western Union, expects soon to have telegraphic communication with Galveston over its lines restored. A gang of 150 men is

VIEWS OF DEVASTATION WROUGHT IN STRICKEN CITY OF GALVESTON

[From Photographs Taken for the HERALD.]

"RUINS OF HOUSES"

SCENE ON POST OFFICE ST.
FIRST BUILDING, HARMONY CLUB
BUILDING IN DISTANCE, MASONIC TEMPLE

BURYING THE DEAD AT SPOTS WHERE FOUND.

NEW YORK IN DANGER, SAYS SENATOR HANNA

Republican Chairman Tells Chicago Business Men Bryan May Carry This and Other Eastern States Unless McKinley's Friends Are Aroused from Apathy.

DECLARES CROKER WILL CONTROL FEDERAL PATRONAGE

This To Be His Reward if He Carries New York and Bryan Is Elected While Democrats Are Working Hard to Capture Other Doubtful States.

STRIKERS DECLARE 112,000 ARE IDLE IN ANTHRACITE REGION

Scarcely a Pick Raised in the Lackawanna and Wyoming Districts, but Many Men Refuse to Obey the Call in Lehigh and Schuylkill.

MITCHELL REJECTS MEDIATION AT MARKLE MINES

President of the Union Fails to Meet Company's Offer to Submit to Rulings of Archbishop Ryan as Arbitrator, and Will

but it was the determination and resilience of the Texans themselves that triumphed ultimately—a spirit characterized by the city's own *Galveston News*, which picked itself out of the mud and three days after the flood was urging all and sundry to 'build'. 'It is a time for courage of the highest order' it exhorted, 'when men and women show the stuff that is in them. We shall convince the world we have the spirit to overcome misfortune and rebuild our homes!'

The World.

"Circulation Books Open to All."   "Circulation Books Open to All."

The Real Employment Agency. | 7,166 Help Wants were printed in The World last week. The next highest New York newspaper printed 2,877, or away less than half.

The Resort-Seekers' Guide.

VOL. XLIV., NO. 15,640.   Copyright, 1904, by the Press Publishing Company, New York World.   NEW YORK, THURSDAY, JUNE 16, 1904.   PRICE ONE CENT in Greater New York and Jersey City. TWO CENTS outside of Greater New York and Jersey City.

IDENTIFIED   EXCURSION BOAT IN FLAMES AND ... PRYING ONLY ... CAPTAIN.

1900-1920

700 LIVES LOST WH... EXCURSION BOAT

The Daily M...

THE MORNING JOURNAL WITH THE SECOND LARGEST NE...

No. 1,620.   WEDNESDAY, JANUARY 6, 1909.

THE TERRIBLE EARTHQUAKE IN MESSINA: K... SORROW IN THE PRESENCE OF DE...

DOCTOR ON EMPRESS WAS GOING TO CLAIM HIS FIANCEE AS BRIDE

Mrs. W. E. Paton Wires Brother She is None the Worse for Thrilling Experience—Mother of One Passenger Not Expected to Live.

OF WELL-KNOWN ...REAL PEOPLE ON BOARD LOST STEAMER

Word Received That Mr. and Mrs. C. D. Tylee, and G. W. S. Henderson Saved—Mrs. W. E. Paton, of Sherbrooke, and J. L. Black, of Ottawa, Also Reported Rescued — Those Whose Names Were on the List.

MRS. GALLAGHER AND SON.

J. D. TAYLOR.

"Enough Life-Boats For All," Is Statement Of C. P. R.

...MES, TUESDAY, FEBRUARY 11, 1919.

INFLUENZA AGAIN.
LESS VIRULENT ATTACKS.

...EAPER BEER.
...ORDER FOR FEB. 24.
OF MAXIMUM PRICES.

SINN FEIN AND RACING.
A RED CROSS MEETING STOPPED
DUBLIN, Feb. 10.

1900–1920

Island Holocaust
Eruption of Mt Pelée 1902

Last Drama at the Iroquois
Chicago Theatre Fire 1903

The End of an Excursion
The Sinking of the *General Slocum* 1904

A God-forsaken Mess
The San Francisco Earthquake 1906

Too Much Stress
The Quebec Bridge Collapse 1907

The Earthquake at Messina 1908

Maiden Voyage
The Sinking of the *Titanic* 1912

The Death of a Valley
Senghenydd Mine Disaster 1913

Fog of Misunderstanding
The Sinking of the *Empress of Ireland* 1914

In the Front Line
The Quintinshill Rail Crash 1915

Lethal Cargo
The Halifax Explosion 1917

The Unstoppable Virus
The Flu Epidemic 1918

Island Holocaust
Eruption of Mt Pelée 1902

FORTY THOUSAND LIVES LOST IN THE GREAT DISASTER IN MARTINIQUE; CITY OF ST. PIERRE DESTROYED AND EIGHTEEN VESSELS LOST IN PORT

ST. PIERRE, FROM THE MOUNTAIN
COPYRIGHT 1898 BY J. MURRAY JORDAN

HARBOR OF ST PIERRE
COPYRIGHT 1898 BY J MURRAY JORDAN

Death List Exceeds That of Any Other Calamity in the History of the Western Hemisphere.

ERUPTION OF MONT PELEE THE CAUSE

Consul Ayme, at Guadeloupe, Cables That Only Twenty Persons in St. Pierre Were Saved.

TOTAL POPULATION THERE ABOUT 25,000

Cable Communication Broken and Full Details Will Be Delayed.

VIEW OF ST PIERRE SHOWING THE VOLCANO OF MONT PELEE

PHOTOS COPYRIGHT 1898 BY J. MURRAY JORDAN. PHILA. PA.

French and Danish War Vessels Have Gone to Render Relief to the Survivors. in the Fated Island.

THE GOVERNOR IS AMONG THE DEAD

American Consul at Martinique, Thomas Prentis, Is Believed To Be Lost.

VOLCANIC ACTION IN OTHER ISLANDS

Sonfriere, in St. Vincent's Island, Also Active and May Cause Disaster.

FORTY THOUSAND HUMAN LIVES ARE BELIEVED TO HAVE BEEN LOST BY VOLCANIC ERUPTIONS IN THE FRENCH WEST INDIES.

St. Pierre, the principal city of Martinique, the gem of the Windward Islands, has been blotted out under a storm of fire and avalanches of molten rock and ashes.

With a population of upward of twenty-five thousand persons, the city has been totally destroyed, and the survivors are reported to number less than two score, nearly all of them burned, wounded and suffering awful tortures.

Loss of life in Morne Rouge and other neighboring towns and parishes, it is feared, will swell the death list to the appalling total of forty thousand.

No such calamity has been chronicled in recent times. For anything approximating a parallel in horror and in the extent of the disaster one must hark back to the fate of the cities of the plain or to the doom of Herculaneum and Pompeii. Even under that historic outpouring from Vesuvius the loss of life was probably not so great as that which occurred on Thursday in the sun kissed little island of the Caribbean.

Mount Pelee, a great volcano, long ago believed to be extinct, suddenly awoke from the sleep of many years. Out of the mouth of the treacherous crater, around which nestled the summer villas and the pretty homes of the wealthier of the French West Indian residents, suddenly belched smoke and flame. Then, like the discharge from a Titanic gun, the whole crest of the mountain leaped thousands of feet into the air, and from the awful caldron's mouth poured down rivers of fire, swallowing up everything that lay in their path to the sea.

Torrents of red hot ashes buried the country round about for miles, covering it as the blizzard blankets the earth in January. Groves, orchards, towns and city burst into flame under the shower of death, and even the shipping in the roadstead of St. Pierre had no time to up anchor and get to sea.

The Roraima, of the Quebec line, which sailed from New York

peditions are being sent out from St. Thomas, Santa Lucia and San Juan, Puerto Rico.

Volcano Poured Flaming Gas and Cinders on St. Pierre for Hours

From Eight o'Clock in the Morning Until One o'Clock in the Afternoon the Town Was a Bed of Fire.

[FROM THE HERALD'S SPECIAL CORRESPONDENT.]

St. Thomas, D. W. I., Friday.

AN eruption of the Mont Pelee volcano destroyed by flaming gas and cinders the beautiful town of St. Pierre, Martinique, yesterday morning. From eight o'clock in the morning until one o'clock in the afternoon St. Pierre was a mass of fire.

During the intervening hours a torrent of red hot cinders poured

The French cruiser Suchet was in the port when the disaster took place. Her officers went ashore to give relief, but were unable to render much assistance, except to rescue about thirty persons.

Great heaps of bodies were seen on the blazing wharves. It was impossible for the Suchet's officers to penetrate the town.

Although the Mont Pelee volcano had been emitting ashes and smoke at intervals for several days, the residents of St. Pierre did not apprehend any great eruption.

When the volcano became active after a silence of half a century, the inhabitants were startled and became panic stricken. But fears began to subside after a few days.

Then came the destruction of the Guerin factories, near Martinique, and the loss of about one hundred and fifty lives. The panic in the town was renewed, but the population began to recover just as the final catastrophe took place.

The inhabitants of St. Pierre perished through their bravery and devotion to their town and homes.

Captain Freeman, of the British steamship Roddam, which was at St. Pierre at the time of the holocaust, and which brought the news to St. Lucia, is in a critical condition in a hospital at St. Lucia.

All of the Roddam's officers and engineers are dead or dying. Most of the crew perished. The supercargo, Campbell, and ten men jumped overboard and lost their lives.

A vessel which arrived at Dominica to-day reports that she was compelled to run from St. Vincent because of the volcanic eruption on that island on Wednesday afternoon.

This vessel was off Martinique yesterday morning, about eight o'clock, when the eruption of Mont Pelee occurred.

Those on board the vessel say there was a tremendous explosion of the mountain, and a great cloud of fire seemed to sweep down upon the city and all the territory around it, leaving no chance for escape for its citizens.

Shipping lying off St. Pierre was also

MAY 9, 1902.

EVENING NEWS
AND EVENING MAIL,

LATE EDITION.

ANOTHER POMPEII

The Destruction of St. Pierre Confirmed.

THE TOWN ENGULFED

Official Report Made to the French Government.

ONLY 30 SURVIVORS.

A Mass of Volcanic Fire Descended on the Town at 8 o'clock in the Morning.

Official confirmation has been received at two o'clock this afternoon of the appalling catastrophe, which the *Times* announced this morning in the following three line cablegram from its correspondent at St. Thomas, in the Danish West Indies.

"St. Pierre and its inhabitants and all the shipping have been totally destroyed by a volcano."

The St. Pierre referred to in this telegram is the town of that name in the French island of Martinique. Though not the capital, St. Pierre is the most important town in the island.

Its population is estimated at 20,000 souls, and it is moreover a busy centre of trade and shipping, with a splendid harbour.

The victims of the disaster must therefore be numbered by many thousands, which constitute it one of the most appalling volcano disasters in the history of the world.

The volcano which has wrought this havoc is Mount Pélée, a mountain that rises on the north-west side of the island to a height of 4,429ft., and dominates the town and harbour of St. Pierre. Its slopes have been cultivated to a height of over 2,000ft.

The confirmation of the first reports is conveyed in the following official telegram to the French Government.

PARIS, Friday.—The Minister of Marine has received from the commander of the

MAY 12, 1902.

GRAVER NEWS.

COLOSSAL ERUPTION OF LA SOUFRIERE.

ST. VINCENT'S PERIL.

BRITISH TOWNS UNDER A RAIN OF STONES.

THE ST. PIERRE HORROR.

GHASTLY STORIES OF THE GREAT DISASTER.

RENEWED ERUPTION.

IMPOSSIBLE TO APPROACH

TERRIFYING SPECTACLES.

OUR SPECIAL CABLES.

To-day's news with respect to the disaster in the West Indies is more ominous than ever.

No language is sufficient to describe the appalling disaster which has happened. In Martinique, St. Pierre has been visited and found to be a heap of ruins and dead bodies, but Mount Pelée is still in active eruption and threatening the entire country side. In fact, the whole north of the island is still inaccessible.

Unfortunately there is no reassuring news from St. Vincent. The island is still cut off from human communication, and the volcano La Soufrière is raging with such intensity that it is deluging the entire country with ashes and producing the appearance of a fog of cinders. Enormous damage has been done, but probably only a very small proportion of it is yet known.

THE LAST DAYS OF ST. PIERRE.

HOW THE DISASTER CAME UPON THE TOWN.

(From Our Own Correspondent.)

ST. LUCIA, Sunday, May 11.

'It is a sublimely awful demonstration of the majestic violence of Nature' meditated the *New York World* when the first news of the utter destruction of St Pierre on the island of Martinique reached the outside world, 'of the latent forces that repose in her bosom and, once set in motion, are utterly beyond the control of man and laugh to scorn his title as the lord of creation.' Granted man was no match for a volcano, however, the fatalistic attitude of the citizens of St Pierre to the cataclysm that threatened to overwhelm them for weeks in the spring of 1902 went far deeper than a simple acceptance of man's vulnerability. No clearer signs that doomsday was about to descend could have been given them, yet hardly a soul stirred himself to make the self-evident decision —quit St Pierre.

St Pierre in 1902 was a thriving colonial port on the French island of Martinique, prettier and certainly gayer than the island's administrative capital, Fort de France. All around it on the rich lava-soil exotic plants burgeoned, and orchards and sugar plantations flourished on the lower slopes of Mont Pelée, which towered more than 4,500 feet above the town. It was a very pleasant place to live—as a rule. But since the middle of April the dormant giant in their back-garden had been rumbling deep in the earth's bowels. Mont Pelée had been asleep, well, for more than fifty years to the best of anyone's knowledge. He was so familiar and the lake that filled his crater was so placid, that most of the inhabitants simply smiled indulgently at the giant tossing in his sleep. Even the thick films of ash he deposited over the countryside (and the town) at the beginning of May, even the vapour trails that clouded out the sun during the day and the flashes that illuminated the night sky apparently failed to excite anything more than curiosity. The thick, choking smell of sulphur that permeated the whole area was seemingly regarded as only an irritation.

No stranger example of this obdurate blindness in St Pierre was to be found than in the columns of the town's daily paper, *Les Colonies*. Day after day it assured its readers that there was no cause for concern, and denounced those few prudent individuals who were beginning to talk of a general evacuation or else had packed up, bag and baggage, and headed for Fort de France on the other side of the island. True, the paper had a political motive: the island elections were due in a few days, and it suited *Les Colonies* very well to accuse the Radicals and their negro leader of stirring up a panic—but even its crowing confidence palled on 5 May. That day the elements gave their clearest warning: tremors shook the earth, sucked back the sea and hurled it against St Pierre (drowning dozens of people), a sulphureous shroud descended, and floods of boiling mud snaked down the mountainside—one of them obliterating the Guerin sugar factory with all its hands.

That should have been enough to make *Les Colonies* reconsider its stance, but the same day an official 'commission' which had supposedly examined the volcano reported that there was 'nothing in the activity of Pelée that warrants a departure from St Pierre.' The newspaper returned the next day to its favourite theme, and the inhabitants (though many of them thoroughly frightened) stayed firmly put.

What happened at St Pierre on the morning of 8 May was not known to the reading public in Europe or America for two days, after fugitive ships which had witnessed the bursting of the mountain from the high sea made it back to Fort de France. In London *The Times* received a terse three-line cablegram from its correspondent in the West Indies: 'St Pierre and its inhabitants and all the shipping have been totally destroyed by a volcano.' In New York the *Associated Press* estimated forty thousand people had perished. At first there was considerable confusion as to precisely where the tragedy had taken place, since another volcano, La Soufrière on the British island of St Lucia,

FIRST RELIEF EXPEDITION PENETRATING ST. PIERRE FINDS AN AWFUL SCENE OF DEATH AND DESOLATION--- STARVATION THREATENS THE STRICKEN REFUGEES

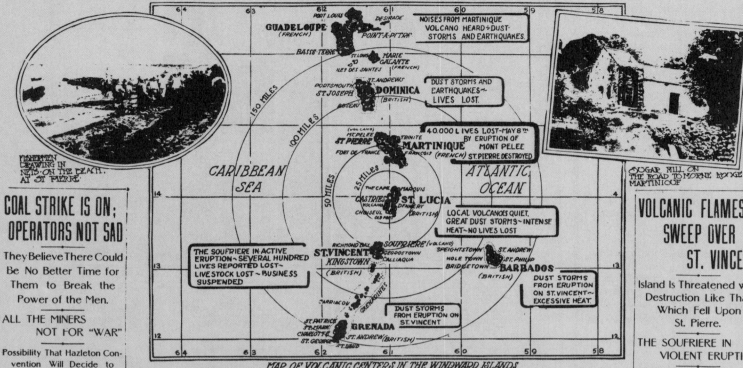

MAP OF VOLCANIC CENTERS IN THE WINDWARD ISLANDS

COAL STRIKE IS ON; OPERATORS NOT SAD

They Believe There Could Be No Better Time for Them to Break the Power of the Men.

ALL THE MINERS NOT FOR "WAR"

Possibility That Hazleton Convention Will Decide to Postpone the Conflict.

INFLUENCE OF THE CLERGY

Bishop and Priests Advise Workers To Be Cool and Not Bring on Clash with Employers.

SCRANTON, Pa., Sunday.—Not a pound of coal will be taken to-day from the 337 anthracite coal mines. Not one of the 147,000 men and boys who are affected by the temporary strike order will go to work. There will be gloom and idleness in many towns and in many homes.

It will rest with the Hazleton Convention, which meets Wednesday, to say whether the men return to work or whether capital and labor engage in a struggle which may be one of the greatest in recent times.

While there seems to be a radical difference of opinion among mine workers about the advisability of a strike at this juncture, the mine operators appear unanimous in their desire to have the men quit work. So strong has the miners' union suddenly become in the anthracite field that it is only a question of time when the supreme test of strength must be made.

Such to Senator Hanna.

Conditions differ radically from those prevailing in October, 1900, when the last strike was settled and the union obtained great prestige through a substantial victory. Politics was then paramount. There was a Presidential campaign in progress, and Senator Hanna was able to induce J. Pierpont Morgan to agree to concessions for the sake of the republican party.

Senator Hanna has been interested in an even greater extent this year, but the operators have refused to listen to him. The president of one of the great coal carrying railroads has not hesitated to say publicly that he resented the interference of politicians, and he would like to teach the lesson to them that they must not meddle with his affairs. In the event of a strike, George F. Baer, president of the Reading road, would probably act as commander of the joint forces of the operators, and Senator Hanna's chances of making him weaken seem small.

There is a significant difference between the attitude of the operators at present and their methods before the strike of 1900. Two years ago the superintendents and the "bosses" were calling aside the Irish and "foreign" miners individually, urging them to remain firm and promising them good contracts and steady employment if they would refuse to join the strikers. Now the "bosses" are listless, apparently indifferent whether the men stay or leave, ready to meet the fight if it must come and asking for no favors. The shrewdest leaders of the labor union realize this and hesitate about calling a strike which must involve great hardship for their followers, with the possibility of defeat in the end.

Opposition to Mitchell.

In the sessions of the joint executive committees, which have just closed their work here by ordering a temporary suspension of labor and a convention to meet in Hazleton on Wednesday, there were two distinct factions, one clamoring for an immediate strike, the other, led by John Mitchell, in favor of temporizing and a reference back to the men most vitally affected. T. D. Nichols, president of the local union, with headquarters here, showed great strength in his opposition to Mr. Mitchell, the national president. At almost the last moment Mr. Mitchell issued a statement to the effect that

[CONTINUED ON PAGE SIX.]

THE HERALD HAS SENT A DESPATCH AND RELIEF VESSEL TO MARTINIQUE AND ST. VINCENT

OFFICIAL advices and cable despatches from the HERALD'S correspondents fully confirm the worst reports of the terrible catastrophe which has befallen the inhabitants of the islands of Martinique and St. Vincent. Harrowing tales of suffering are reported by all correspondents, and it is evident that unless prompt and intelligent relief is at once afforded the list of dead will be much greater.

When the news of the disaster was first received the HERALD, together with the leading newspapers of the country, which compose its news syndicate, chartered a fast vessel to transport correspondents, artists and photographers to St. Pierre. This vessel is now at sea under orders to touch at San Juan, Puerto Rico, for orders. The HERALD, by means of this vessel, will undertake to forward any relief that the charitably disposed may care to offer.

Cash contributions will be received by the HERALD and transmitted by cable to San Juan, where the money will be expended for supplies most needed, under the supervision of the United States authorities. These supplies will then be taken by the HERALD's ship and delivered to the local relief committee.

Subscriptions received at the HERALD office up to Wednesday night will be transmitted to San Juan in time to be used to the best advantage.

Relief Workers in St. Pierre Find Bodies in Lifelike Positions, so Sudden Was Death

Piles of Dead in the Vicinity of the Cathedral Also Show the Rush to Obtain Sanctuary and Refuge—Storehouses Containing Provisions Are Destroyed—Martinique Depends on the Charity of the World to Prevent a Famine.

[FROM THE HERALD'S SPECIAL CORRESPONDENT.]
(Copyright, 1902, by the New York Herald Company.)

CASTRIES, ST. LUCIA, W. I., Sunday

THE first relief parties have ventured into the streets of St. Pierre. It was not expected that survivors would be found, and so there has been no disappointment at the mournful reports that have been returned.

All of the earlier stories of the disaster worked by Mont Pelee have been verified. THE DESTRUCTION OF THE CITY IS COMPLETE. Not a building remains standing. The desolation is appalling.

Piles of dead in the vicinity of the site of the Cathedral tell a story of the attempt to find sanctuary and refuge in the great structure of worship. Men and women, panic stricken at the cataclysm, turned in the moment of their despair to the Cathedral and were apparently overcome before they could reach its doors.

RELIEF PARTIES ARE IN GREAT DANGER.

So far the search has been hindered by the fires that are still raging, and the investigators are in great danger. Mont Pelee is active, but the eruption is subsiding. In St. Pierre every form of life has apparently been destroyed. It will be impossible to penetrate to the centre of the ruins for several days.

From the positions of the bodies is formed that many were overcome almost before they realized the extent of the peril. Many of the bodies are in lifelike positions, as though death had come with a breath, as indeed may have been the case.

Many of the bodies are so burned as to make identification impossible, but in other cases the opposite is the case. Some have been identified by the searching parties, which are all under military control and are conducted under orders.

Scenes in St. Pierre are heartrending. Steps have been taken to prevent disease from resulting from the disaster. Burial parties are working night and day, but it is impossible that the dead can be cared for as their friends would wish.

MILITARY RULE ESTABLISHED IN ST. PIERRE.

Military rule is established in the town to prevent vandals from working. Such property as has not been destroyed will be protected. ONE OF THE GREAT MISFORTUNES ARISES FROM THE FACT THAT THE STOREHOUSES OF PROVISIONS HAVE BEEN SWEPT OUT OF EXISTENCE.

Martinique must depend upon the charity of the world to prevent a famine. ALREADY FOOD IS EXHAUSTED at Fort de France, which has been overrun by refugees from the country.

Appeals have been sent to the neighboring islands for assistance and food may come in to-morrow. Meantime the few provision stores are under close guard by the soldiers.

IN THE COUNTRY THERE IS NO FOOD AND IT IS BELIEVED THAT THOUSANDS ARE STARVING. As soon as food can be obtained relief parties will be sent out from Fort de France.

LOSS OF THE CABLE STEAMSHIP GRAPPLER CONFIRMED

Wife of the Steward on the Lost Steamer Roraima Will Wait Two Weeks to Hear from Him.

[FROM THE HERALD'S SPECIAL CORRESPONDENT.]

St. Thomas, B. W. I., Sunday.—Confirmation has been brought by the Korona of the Quebec steamship line of the destruction near the harbor of St. Pierre of the cable ship Grappler.

Captain Borchart, the mates, Calcutt, Boyce and Holland; the engineers, Marshall, Broome, Torrey and Young; the electrician, Murphy; the purser, Meges; the carpenter, Smart, and the crew of forty, all perished.

VOLCANIC FLAMES SWEEP OVER ST. VINCENT

Island Is Threatened with Destruction Like That Which Fell Upon St. Pierre.

THE SOUFRIERE IN VIOLENT ERUPTION

Northern Coast Enveloped in Smoke and Ships Dare Not Venture Near.

KINGSTOWN REPORTED SAFE

Country Round About Is Under Constant Bombardment of Stones and Cinders.

[FROM THE HERALD'S SPECIAL CORRESPONDENT.]
(Copyright, 1902, by the New York Herald Company.)

Castries, St. Lucia, W. I., Sunday.

ST. VINCENT is still threatened with the destruction which fell upon St. Pierre.

The Soufriere is still in violent eruption. Terrific detonations follow one another so closely that they form one incessant rumble.

Great columns of steam, smoke and ashes shoot into the air so high that no eye can see where they break. These are lighted up by tongues of flame that frequently spread out over the country, carrying death to every living thing.

Country Under Bombardment.

For many miles to the southward of the Soufriere the country is under constant bombardment. Large stones fall from the darkened skies, adding to the destruction worked by the heat and the clouds of ashes.

It is impossible to estimate the loss of life, but it is already so great as to be appalling, and the death list is constantly increasing. EARLY REPORTS PLACED THE LOSS OF LIFE IN ST. VINCENT AT MORE THAN FOUR HUNDRED, AND THAT ESTIMATE MUST NOW BE FAR BELOW THE REAL TOTAL.

Flames are literally sweeping the entire northern end of St. Vincent. A great area has been isolated by a flow of lava, which has reached across the island. The clouds of smoke overcast the skies in every direction, and ships dare not venture near the coast.

Kingstown Reported Safe.

Kingstown is reported as safe this morning by a steamer that has just arrived here. The city does not seem to be threatened with destruction, though pebbles and ashes fall without ceasing, keeping the inhabitants within doors. Cinders was also in eruption. But when the *Associated Press* dispatch boat returned to Fort de France with an appalling pen-picture of the ruin beneath Mt Pelée, any doubts vanished. In the harbour it found 'the water filled with swollen bodies and masses of debris from the wrecked vessels and the town. Flocks of scavanger birds swarmed over the water. The harbour was infested with sharks attracted by the dead bodies . . .' In the town (the report continued) 'not one house was left intact. Vivid heaps of mud, ashes and volcanic stones were seen on every side. The streets could hardly be traced . . . men, women and children were mingled in one awful mass, arms and legs protruding as the helpless beings fell in the last struggles of death's agony . . . Great trees with roots upward and scorched by fire were strewn in every direction. From under one large stone the arm of a white woman protruded. Most notable was the utter silence, and the awful, overpowering stench from the thousands of dead.'

The first landing-parties could scarcely believe the evidence of their eyes. Some 30,000 people had been wiped out in a matter of seconds: many of them were found in perfectly natural postures, as if unaware of the fate that had overtaken them—like the petrified bodies excavated at Pompeii (after the eruption of Vesuvius in 79AD). But unlike the citizens of Pompeii, these bodies had not been swamped by lava but had been engulfed by the shrivelling heat of the volcano's gases and ash particles. One survivor from the steamship *Roraima* (which, anchored in the roadsteads, had caught the fringe of the enveloping deadly cloud) described it as 'a horrid, fiery, choking whirlwind' that blistered and asphyxiated anyone it touched.

Each newspaper had some extra horror to add to the catalogue of tragedy. The *Daily Mail* correspondent reported that 8,000 charred corpses had been discovered inside the ruins of the cathedral. The *New York Herald* quoted a survivor from one of the ships who testified he had been thrown into the water which 'was almost hot enough to parboil me'. The *New York Journal* noted that a French cable repair ship reported that one part of the ocean bed had sunk some 2,700 feet. In the area of the customs-house, the *Daily Picayune* declared, 'corpses were found lying in all kinds of attitudes, showing that the victims had met death as if by a lightning stroke . . . Curiously enough the features of the dead were generally calm and reposeful, although in some cases terrible fright and agony were depicted.'

It seemed as if literally no-one in St Pierre itself could have survived. Yet, incredibly, at least two did: one, a shoemaker named Leon Comprere-Leandre, though frightfully burned, escaped suffocation by taking refuge in his cellar in time. The other became almost a legend. He was a negro called Raoul Sartout who had been in prison at the moment of the explosion, fortunately for him an underground dungeon. He, too, might have died if his feeble cries for help had not been heard by a French marine four days later. He was pulled out of his underground cell on the verge of death.

Mont Pelée had not done with St Pierre yet. Even as burial (or rather incinerating) parties moved into the skeleton of the town it continued to shower down its superheated cinders, and semi-darkness persisted over the whole countryside. Twelve days after the explosion the whole island was racked by an earthquake, persuading thousands, who fled to neighbouring St Lucia and Gaudeloupe, that their erstwhile home was about to disappear beneath the ocean. It didn't, though it was very nearly swamped by well-intentioned aid instead. Provisions and supplies poured into Fort de France from all quarters. But the obvious fact had been overlooked—the only town that might have needed help had been wiped off the face of the earth. Fearing that Martinique's economy was being seriously undermined by the mountain of

The World.
"Circulation Books Open to All."   "Circulation Books Open to All."
NEW YORK, TUESDAY, MAY 27, 1902.   PRICE

BIG BEAR BIT OFF LITTLE TOMMY'S LEG.

HUMBERTS' VALET CAUGHT BY POLICE?

Man Arrested in Jersey City Supposed to be Swindlers' Servant.

THE ONLY MAN WHO LIVED THROUGH ST. PIERRE'S HURRICANE OF FIRE, AND THE ONLY ONE WHO FLED, THE TOWN ON DAY OF THE DISASTER.

FERDINAND CLERE,
Who Alone Heeded Pelee's Warning Blasts, and Fled with His Family to a Morne Rouge Village on Morning of the Eruption.

ROUL SARTOUT,
Sole Survivor of the St. Pierre Disaster—This Dungeon Prisoner Was the Only Man Out of a Population of 30,000 to Live Through Mont Pelée's Hurricane of Fire.

FERDINAND CLERE TELLS HOW ST. PIERRE WAS LOST.
Rich Planter Fled With Family an Hour Before Eruption—Explosion as Witnessed from Morne Rouge, on Mountain Side.

COLLEGE SPORT ENDS IN DROWNING.
University of Vermont Freshman Chased by Sophs Jumps Overboard.

STORY OF ROUL SARTOUT, ST. PIERRE'S ONLY SURVIVOR.
Had He Not Been in a Dungeon Underground He, Too, Would Have Perished—For Four Days the Only Living Being in St. Pierre.

material goods piling up in unaffected Fort de France the *New York Herald* reporter pleaded that *no* more be sent. 'The relief business has been greatly overdone' he cabled his paper. 'I assure you that if the relief movement is not curbed *at once* this island will be pauperised!'

Double Page
St. Pierre Eruption
Photographs
Pages 8 and 9

Double Page
St. Pierre Eruption
Photographs
Pages 8 and 9

The World.

"Circulation Books Open to All."   "Circulation Books Open to All."

VOL. XLII. NO. 14,884.   ★   Copyright, 1902, by the Press Publishing Company, New York World.   NEW YORK, THURSDAY, MAY 22, 1902.   PRICE { ONE CENT in Greater New York and Jersey City. { TWO CENTS outside of Greater New York and Jersey City and on trains.

FIRST PHOTOGRAPHS OF SCENES IN THE RUINED CITY OF ST. PIERRE.

(The Photographs on This and Succeeding Pages of To-Day's World Were Taken Specially for The World on Sunday, May 11, the Third Day After the Destruction of the City, and the First Day It Was Possible to Enter.)

[Pictures Specially Copyrighted May 21, 1902, by the Press Publishing Company—Reproduction Forbidden.]

KEY TO PICTURES.

1—STREET SCENE in the heart of St. Pierre. Bodies of sixteen human beings, old and young, lie huddled in ghastly confusion. Evidently each one fell dead where he stood. No bones or skulls was fractured by falling timber, so it is plain that these people came out after the fire blast only to be suffocated or asphyxiated by noxious gases.

2—HERE is where the first body was found by the English rescue party from Barbados. It is lying upon its left side, the hands clinched and the knees drawn up. Apparently the man remained in the house until the blast of fire from the volcano had passed, then ran out and was strangled in the rush of sulphur fumes.

3—THIS is a view along the southern shore of the city of St. Pierre, showing houses, trees, telegraph poles and brick and stone from strong buildings swept together by the blast from the volcano, as sawdust is swept by a broom. Volcanic dust lies thick over everything. There are many bodies hidden under the debris.

Last Drama at the Iroquois

Chicago Theatre Fire 1903

Chicago Sunday Tribune 27 December 1903

'In the Pale Moonlight' the voices on stage began to sing. That was the cue for comedian Eddie Foy to get ready for his popular 'elephant' turn, one of the high spots in the musical extravaganza *Mr Bluebeard*. That afternoon, Wednesday 30 December, the Iroquois Theater was packed for the first matinee after Christmas, row upon row of gleeful children's faces (and their mothers) gazing in wonder at the dizzying changes of sumptuous scenery, and waiting in breathless anticipation for the famous 'aerial ballet' everyone in town was talking about. In the five weeks it had been open the Iroquois had already established itself as one of Chicago's best-appointed and successful theatres. So what if the builders were still at work between performances putting the finishing touches? The money was rolling in.

'In the Pale Moonlight'. That was also the cue for stagehand Cummings to change the calcium flood from white to blue, for a touch of authentic moonlight. As he adjusted the lamp, it sparked: the spark caught the edge of a muslin fly, setting it ablaze instantaneously. Scene-shifters rushed to attack the flames with brooms, forgetting the brand-new extinguishers in the wings. They were too late. The singers faltered as a large piece of blazing muslin descended to the stage. The audience gasped in horror. Eddie Foy saw what had happened and made a decision: half made-up, he rushed on-stage and shouted to the audience not to be afraid. 'Don't panic, and there'll be no trouble.' As if to confound his well-meaning advice at that moment a shower of fiery debris landed all round him. The oil-painted scenery was already burning like a torch. As if hyp-

notized the audience stared at the tongues of fire licking along the red velvet curtain, and gaped as the cumbersome (and much-publicized) asbestos safety-curtain lumbered slowly down from the roof.

Suddenly, it stopped: backstage hands tugged and swore at its ropes and wheels, but it would not budge. Twenty-five feet from the ground it had stuck solid, and in doing so created a fatal draught that bellowed the flames deep into the auditorium. 'Just then the shrill cry of some woman caused the women and children to rise to their feet, filled with a sudden and uncontrollable terror' a survivor told the *Chicago Daily Tribune* afterwards. 'In another instant the rush for the door began. The roar of hundreds in the balcony was soon deadened by the cries for aid from those who were hemmed in by the struggling mass.' Many of those in the balcony, nearly nine hundred, never stood a chance: the billowing flames from the stage reached out upwards at them, asphyxiating some as they sat. Others stampeded for the exits, only to find many of them locked. Yet others burst through the doors and out onto fire-escape balconies—only to find themselves staring into space. The fire-escapes had not yet been built, but it was impossible to turn back against the crush of people behind them. Dozens were sent hurtling into the void.

On the ground floor pandemonium reigned. Hundreds fought to get through the claustrophobic corridors into the open air, trampling others to death on their way. In some passageways firemen later found bodies piled four high. At the back of the stage a crowd of chorus girls, high up in the wings waiting their cue for the 'aerial ballet', found themselves cut off on all sides by the advancing flames. Only the courage of a liftboy who coolly took his lift up to the roof saved them. They were the lucky ones: out of 1,300 people in the theatre that afternoon, no less than 587 died and many more were seriously burned.

When one of the theatre's owners, J. Fred Zimmerman, was informed of the fire by a *Philadelphia Inquirer* reporter, he at first refused to credit it. 'Nonsense' he was quoted as saying. 'Why, the theatre has only just been opened. It is fireproof.' Assured that the fire really had occurred, he insisted 'there was no means of preventing a fire in a theatre that was not used in the construction of the Iroquois . . . no expense was spared to prevent the possibility of an accident.' Which led the *Inquirer* to assume 'it will probably be found that most of the loss of life was due to the maddened stampede of people who had ceased for the moment to be reasoning and responsible beings.' But the next day some rapid investigations by the *Chicago Tribune* indicated there was far more to it than that. Some very disturbing facts were uncovered. The vaunted asbestos curtain proved to be of the cheapest material possible. 'The theatre wanted a cheap curtain' said the firm that supplied it. 'It got it.' And anyway the stagehand who should have operated it when the disaster struck turned out not to have been in the theatre at the time. There was evidence that a number of city ordinances had been broken or overlooked: many of the street doors were locked, and some of the fire-exits had not even been finished. There was no sprinkler system installed, and a fire-alarm had never been considered. The theatre was overcrowded at the time, and most of its decorative fabric was instantly combustible.

Yet the Iroquois on the day of its grand

opening had possessed all the necessary certificates showing it complied with the letter of the law. Clearly a few pockets had been lined up at City Hall. 'Is this official nonfeasance or just ordinary "graft"?' the *New York Times* wanted to know. 'Laws are of very little value if those hired and paid to see after their enforcement content themselves with being kindly blind.' The *Kansas City Star* was less circumspect in its comment: 'Investigation has demonstrated in Chicago that the function of municipal government in this country is largely the persistent violation of public ordinances.' The Iroquois tragedy led directly to a tightening-up of fire regulations throughout the country to see if existing laws were being obeyed. 'Doubtless a good many people have been so frightened by the Chicago catastrophe' thought the *Pittsburgh Gazette*, 'that they are disposed to stay away from the theatres. If so their impulse is without reason. The theatres are all safer now than they were the first of last week.' No less confident was the *New York Herald*: 'It is not conceivable that such a catastrophe as that at the Iroquois could occur in this city.' No doubt it came as somewhat of a shock to both papers to learn that, after inspection, half the theatres in Chicago and New York had to be closed down.

Chicago Daily Tribune

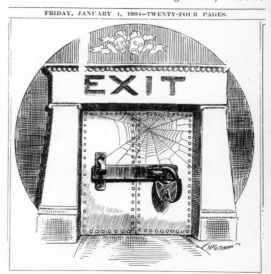

FRIDAY, JANUARY 1, 1904—TWENTY-FOUR PAGES.

The Chicago Daily Tribune.

VOLUME LXII.—NO. 313.   THURSDAY, DECEMBER 31, 1903—SIXTEEN PAGES.   PRICE TWO CENTS.

IROQUOIS THEATER FIRE REAPS AWFUL HARVEST OF DEATH; WOMEN AND CHILDREN BURNED, SUFFOCATED, AND CRUSHED.

RECORD OF THE DISASTER.

The Dead	550
The Injured	350
Identified Dead	100
Reported Missing	250

IN THE ALLEY OF DEATH AND MUTILATION.
JUMPING FROM THE FIRE ESCAPES TO ESCAPE THE FLAMES.

BODIES AT MORGUES.

Rolston	102
Jordan	149
Gavin	35
John Carroll	21
J. W. Buffum	32
County	17
Sheldon	47
Perrigo	19
Boydston	8
Ryan	10
S. E. Cleveland	8
Total	520

Five hundred and sixty-two lives were destroyed by fire in the Iroquois theater in the fifteen minutes between 3:15 and 3:30 o'clock yesterday afternoon. Over 350 persons were injured. Of the dead, less than 100 were identified last night.

Of the unidentified nearly all were so badly burned that recognition was impossible. Only by trinkets and burned scraps of wearing apparel will the bodies of hundreds be made known to their families.

March from Deadhouse to Deadhouse.

All night long a horror chained but resolutely persistent throng of those whose friends and relatives were numbered among the missing lifted blanket after blanket in the search of fear through the morgues of the city.

Not since the fire of 1871, when 250 were killed, has Chicago been smitten by such a universal tragedy; never has it received a blow so instantaneously shocking.

This frightful thing was over before the city knew that it happened; the news in its wild spread left paralysis behind.

"Bluebeard" was being performed in the theater. An audience not only of unusual size but of unusual composition was listening to it. It was the matinee audience of the midholiday season.

Children and Women the Victims.

Only once in a year could such an audience have gathered; only once in all the twelvemonth could so many children have been collected within the walls of the theater.

And on this one occasion the sacrifice to flame was demanded. There were men in the audience; there were men in the men on side of the curtain. There were women, too.

Fire Curtain a Delusion.

Between audience and performers was the curtain line, down which an asbestos fire curtain should have fallen a second after the alarm was given, confining the fire to the stage.

The curtain never fell.

Why Curtain Failed to Work.

The only thing plain last night was that the asbestos curtain did not fall. The flyman of the theater, Charles Johnson, said that for some time past it had been the practice at the theater to have the curtain high at night so as to permit a good view for the aerial ballet.

Absent from All Important Post.

All Hope Lost for Gallery.

Some Exits Are Closed.

Theatrical People All Escape.

Dead Piled Six Feet Deep.

Bridge the Alley with Planks.

Little Girl First Across.

Die with Safety in Sight.

"Anybody Alive Here?" No Answer.

Not a Moan Is Heard.

In Death They Save Others.

No Alarm Box at Theater.

Few in Balcony Escaped.

SCENES IN THE CHARNEL HOUSE AFTER REMOVAL OF THE DEAD.

IN THE FIRST BALCONY.

THE DEATH TRAP IN THE TOP GALLERY.

AT THE HEAD OF THE STAIRS, FIRST BALCONY.

RUIN ON THE STAGE.

LIVES DRAGGED INTO MAELSTROM

Hundreds of Bodies Are Found Piled High in the Dread Stairway Angles.

ONLY A FEW ARE SAVED.

Ghouls at Work Amid Scenes of Horror in Ruins of "Handsomest Theater."

On the heels of the firemen came the police, intent on the work of rescue. Chief O'Neill and Assistant Chief Schuettler ordered captains from a dozen stations to bring their men, and then they rushed to the theater and led the police up the stairs to the landing outside the east entrance to the first balcony.

The firemen, rushing blindly up the stairs in the dense pall of smoke, had found their path suddenly blocked by a wall of dead eight or ten feet high. They discovered many persons alive and carried them to safety. Other firemen crawled over the mass of dead and dragged their boon into the theater to fight back the flames that seemed to be crawling nearer to turn the fatal landing into a funeral pyre.

dead and tore rings from the fingers. In the blackness of the theater they could work unobserved, but it was not long before the police had discovered their presence and made war on them.

The police had barred every one from the theater except newspaper reporters and a few others entitled to enter, but when the blankets were sent from the stores volunteers were called to carry them in. The thieves seized the opportunity and entered the place of death in the guise of messengers of mercy, but once inside the theater and hidden by the pall of smoke they turned into fiends. The first intimation of their presence was when a boyish looking young man carrying a single blanket crawled boldly over the pile of dead at the fatal angle and pushed past the police.

"The firemen sent me in with the blanket," he shouted.

Forces Way Past Police.

Chief O'Neill caught him by the arm, but the man wriggled loose and pushed towards the interior of the theater, shifting that the blanket was needed by the firemen.

"Get out," roared the chief, who was struggling to dig down through the heap of dead to where the moaning told that some one yet lived. "Men, throw that boy out of here. He's a thief." A policeman seized the man and pushed him downstairs. A moment later Chief O'Neill straightened up.

"Men," he said, "that man was here to rob the dead. You who are not needed here hurry through the theater and put out everybody not entitled to remain."

Strip Rings from Fingers.

The police jumped to their work. A fireman crawling on his hands and knees in the smoke saw a figure that he thought at first was that of a victim of the fire. As he drew nearer it arose and disappeared in the gloom. The fireman found a body on the floor where he had seen the man. After the body of the woman had been carried out it was seen that

Cross Shows Where The Fire Started.

M. LEIBERT. Painter Who Threw Bridge Across From N.W. Building To Theater.

View Of Interior Showing Ruined Boxes.

Part Of Stage And Dressing Rooms.

ALL THE WORLD JOINS IN SORROW

President Roosevelt, Prince Henry of Prussia, and Foreign Officials Sympathize.

MANY CITIES IN MOURNING

Governors, Mayors, and Civic Bodies Telegraph, Offering Aid and Condolence.

Carter H. Harrison, Mayor: In common with all our people throughout this land I extend through you to the people of Chicago my deepest sympathy in the terrible catastrophe which has befallen them.
THEODORE ROOSEVELT.

Messages of condolence poured in upon Mayor Harrison yesterday from cities in both the United States and foreign countries. One of the first expressions of sympathy was that from President Roosevelt. It

City board of trade extends to the members of the Chicago board of trade and the citizens of Chicago their deepest sympathy.
E. D. BIGELOW, Secretary.

The secretary of the Duluth organization sent this message:

The Duluth board of trade will adjourn at 12 o'clock as an expression of sympathy to Chicago's bereavement by yesterday's calamity.

New Orleans—News of the terrible catastrophe in your midst is a shock to our entire community, and the members of the New Orleans board of trade join me in extending heartfelt sympathy in this great calamity.
HENRY LA FAYE, President.

George S. Broomhall, Liverpool board of trade: I and many members of the trade offer deep sympathy and sincere condolence to your city for the awful loss of life by fire.

TRAGEDY TOLD IN TELEGRAMS.

Savanna, Ill., Young Woman and Her Two Sisters Are Among the Fire Victims.

Savanna, Ill., Dec. 31.—Miss Mary Harbaugh, 6415 Harvard avenue, Chicago. Is report of Harriet's death true? Wire answer.
F. S. GREENLEAF.

Chicago, Dec. 31.—F. S. Greenleaf, Savanna, Ill.: Harriet unconscious at Samaritan hospital. Rose at St. Luke's. Mary dead.
MRS. WARNER.

The above telegram explain, as vividly as few words can, the suspense and anguish experienced by friends and relatives of persons visiting in the city.

Miss Harriet Harbaugh, a school teacher of Savanna, Ill., was spending the holidays with her sister, Mary Harbaugh, of 6415 Harvard avenue, a kindergarten teacher in the O'Toole school. They went to meet a married sister residing in Oak Park, and the three proceeded to the theater.

Mary, to whom the telegram was ad-

The End of an Excursion
The Sinking of the General Slocum 1904

The World.

"Circulation Books Open to All."   "Circulation Books Open to All."

The Real Employment Agency. 7,166 Help Wants were printed in The World last week. The next highest New York newspaper printed 2,877, or away less than half.

The Resort-Seekers' Guide. The World printed 1,505 separate Summer Resort advertisements last week—430 more than any other New York city newspaper.

VOL. XLIV. NO. 15,640.   Copyright, 1904, by the Press Publishing Company, New York World.   NEW YORK, THURSDAY, JUNE 16, 1904.   PRICE {ONE CENT in Greater New York and Jersey City. TWO CENTS outside of Greater New York and Jersey City and on trains.

Weather Forecast: SHOWERS.   Weather Forecast: SHOWERS.

IDENTIFIED DEAD.

A.

ABENDSCHEIN, MARY, twenty-four years old, No. 22 East Eighteenth street; identified by brother, George, at the Morgue.
ALBRECHT, SELMA, No. 212 East Tenth street, identified by husband and the Morgue.
ANSELL, LOUISA, Mrs., twenty-eight, No. 109 East Fourth street; identified by her husband, Eugene. Their two children are still missing.

B.

BALLMER, MARY, thirty-five years old, No. 123 First avenue; identified by her husband, Joseph.
BALLMER —, girl, six years old, identified by her father, Joseph.
BRUNNING, J. I.; address, Produce Exchange.
BAURLE, MARGHERETTA, thirty-five, No. 432 Sixth street; identified by her husband, Frederick.
BERKHART, MRS. ANNIE E., address unknown.
BURNS, FRED, ten years, No. 22 St. Mark's place.
BURNS, HENRY, six years, No. 22 St. Mark's place.
BRINING, MRS. ANNIE, forty-three years old, No. 75 East Twelfth street.
BACHMAN, MARGARET, seven months, of No. 1934 Third avenue, identified by father, H. Z. Bachman, at the Morgue.
BALZER, CATHERINE, thirty-two, No. 32 Avenue B; identified at the Morgue by George Balzer, same address.
BECK, CHRISTINA, fifty, No. 21 Avenue A; identified at Morgue by son.
BEHRENS, MRS. AUGUSTA, No. 17, Garden street; identified by husband at Morgue.
BERG, MRS. LENA, forty-six, No. 158 Goerck street; identified by husband at Morgue.
BIRMINGHAM, KATHERINE, seventy-two, of No. 19 Mangin street; identified by brother, Michael Dillon, at Morgue.
BORGER, FLORENCE, three years, of No. 310 Putnam avenue, Brooklyn; identified by father, William, at Alexander Avenue Station.
ROZENHAHN, EMILY, thirty-eight, of No. 120 First avenue, identified by brother, Bernard, at Morgue.
BROWN, ALFONSO, No. 702 Fifth street, identified by James Roth, of same address, at Morgue.
BUCHARDT, MRS. ANNA ELIZA, sixty-nine, of No. 141 East Third street; identified by son-in-law, Jacob Schwartz, at the Morgue.
BURFIEND, JOHN J., ten months, of No. 303 West One Hundred and Sixth street, identified by father, J. H. K. Burfiend, at the Alexander Avenue Station.

C.

CLOW, MARY, thirty-five years, of No. 54 East Seventh street, identified by husband, Alfred, at Alexander Avenue Station.
CORDES, MRS. METTA, fifty-one, of No. 437 East Sixteenth street, identified by son John at Alexander Avenue Station.
CROFINE, LILLIE, Mrs. No. 205 Avenue A.

D.

DENGLER, ADOLPH, Jr., three years, No. 122 Seventh street, identified by father, Adolph, at Alexander Avenue Station.
DEPPERT, AGNES, sixty-two, of No. 238 Sixth street, identified by neighbor at Alexander Avenue Station.
DICKER, THEODORA, three years, of No. 1030 East One Hundred and Seventy-eighth street, identified by father, Frank, at the Morgue.
DONHIUM, Mrs., of No. 61 Third street, identified at the Morgue.
DREWS, CATHERINE, Mrs., sixty-eight, of No. 116 East Fourth street, identified by son Herbert at the Morgue.
DIEHL, CATHARINE, Mrs., fifty-eight, No. 255 Courtlandt avenue, Bronx, identified by husband, at Morgue.
DOORHOFFER, two children, No. 122 Avenue A.

E.

ENGELMAN, Mrs. LOUISE, twenty-eight years old, of No. 423 East Twelfth street; identified by husband at Morgue.
EICHOFF, WILLIAM, thirty years old, of No. 108 Second avenue; identified by George Bates, of the same address, at the Morgue.

F.

FRITZ, Mrs. ALMA, twenty-five years, of No. 1235 Park avenue, wife of George Fritz, collector for Lippmann's brewery; identified at the Morgue.
FROLICH, MRS. CHARLES, address unknown.
GIESER, KATE, twenty-five years, no address given, identified by husband, Henry, collector for Lippmann's Brewery, at Alexander Avenue Station.
FLEISCHER, HENRY, fourteen years, No. 82 East Thirteenth street.
FICKBOHM, MRS. MARIE, forty years old, No. 31 Avenue B; identified by her husband, Peter J. Fickbohm.

G.

GAGE, GRACE, sixteen years, No. 26 Fifth street, identified by brother, Henry, at the Morgue.
GALLAGHER, AGNES, ten months.
GREUBEN, EMMA, thirty-nine years, No. 430 East Seventeenth street, identified by John L. Distler, nephew.
GOETZ, ALBERT, twenty-five years, No. 40 First avenue, identified by Edward Foetz at Morgue.
GOETZ, CATHERINE, twenty-eight years, No. 59 First avenue, identified by husband, Edward, at the Morgue.
GRAFING, LILLIE, twenty-eight years, No. 308 Avenue A, identified by father at the Morgue.
GRANNER, Miss LOUISE, twenty-two years, No. 106 University place.
GRANEFIRE, LILLIAN, No. 296 Avenue A.

H.

HERSEL, WILHELMINA, fifty-three, No. 322 East One Hundred and Forty-seventh street.
HERDT, MARY, fifty-three, No. 611 Columbus avenue.
HECKERT, ANNIE K., eleven, No. 63 Avenue A.
HERMAN, GEORGE, thirteen months, No. 439 Third avenue, identified by his father, Henry Herman.
HENDERSEN, BARBARA, thirty, No. 298 West One Hundred and Twenty-fifth street; identified by Miss Pauline Steiger (questionable).
HOELDER, MARY, seventy-nine, No. 63 Avenue A identified by daughter-in-law.
HERL, GEORGE, fourteen, of No. 25 Fifth avenue; identified by father at the Morgue.
HOLLER, MRS. BARBARA, No. 13 Sixth street.
HEINZBERGER, Mrs., forty-five, No. 61 Columbus avenue; identified by daughter, Mrs. Louise Buffo, of No. 82 West Ninetieth street, at the Alexander Avenue Station.
HOFFMANN, Mrs. ELIZABETH, identified by letter on body at Morgue. Address not given.
HOFFMAN, Mrs. SOFIA, sixty...

H.

No. 72 Second street; identified by son, Frederick, at the Morgue.
HURWAY, JOHANNA, thirty-eight, of No. 321 East Ninth street; identified by brother, William Beck, at the Morgue.

I.

IDEN, GRACE, six years, of No. 109 Fourth street, identified by brother Henry at the Morgue.

K.

KLEIN, DENNA, forty years, No. 18 Avenue A, died at Lincoln Hospital.
KRAMER, MRS. —, janitress, No. 23 First avenue.
KEPPLER, IRENE, twelve years old, First avenue, between Twelfth and Thirteenth streets.
KESSLER, BABETTE, forty-five years, No. 506 East Fifth street.
KLATTHWAAR, KATHARINE, fifty-six years, No. 98 Fifth street.
KLATTER, KATHERINE, fifty-six years, No. 98 Fifth street.
KOEHLER, HENRY, forty years, No. 315 East Thirteenth street.
KLINGER, MRS. EVA, identified by papers and bank books in her bustle.
KALB, MAGDALONE, seventy-two years, of No. 742 West Two Hundred and First street, identified by son Albert at the Morgue.

L.

LANN, AMELIA, forty, widow; identified by Kate Muller, of No. 203 Avenue C, at the Alexander Avenue Station.
LUDWIG, GEORGE, 6 years, No. 613 East Seventeenth street.
LUTJENS, MRS. KATE, of No. 196 Clymer street, Brooklyn; identified by husband August, at the Morgue.
LULLMAN, CARRIE, twenty-four years, No. 100 University place.

M.

MAYER, MRS. LOUISE, No. 130 East Seventeenth street.
MESWCK, MRS. KARL, No. 508 Robbins avenue.
MILBORNE, WILLIAM, No. 443 West Fifty-sixth street.
MULLER, MRS. ANNA, thirty-one, No. 16 Seventh street, identified by son, Jacob.
MEYER, KATE or ELIZABETH, forty, No. 9 Avenue A.
MANHEIM, MAMIE, thirty-six, of No. 54 Seventh street; identified by husband, Henry, at the Morgue.
MAY, CHARLOTTE, fifty-one, of No. 590 East Sixteenth street; identified by son Charles at the Morgue.
MEHLEIN, MRS. MINNIE, thirty-eight, of No. 616 Fifth street; identified by husband, Otto, at the Morgue.
MILLER, MRS. MARTHA, No. 29 St. Mark's place.

O.

OCHS, —, died at Lebanon Hospital.
OLFETH, ANNIE, forty-five years, of No. 330 Sixth street; identified by husband, Carl, at the Morgue.

P.

PULLMAN, WILLIAM H., of No. 327 East Eighteenth street, treasurer of church supper.
POTTEBAUM, HERMAN, of No. 61 St. Mark's place.

R.

RHEINGER, META, Mrs., thirty-nine, No. 47 St. Mark's Place.
ROTH, LENA, seventeen, of No. 198 Fifth street; identified by her father, James, at the morgue.
ROTH, JOSEPHINE, Mrs., of No. 198 Fifth street; identified by her husband, at the morgue.
RYAN, MAMIE, five years, No. 145 East Fifteenth street.

S.

SCHWARTZ, LOUISA A., No. 203 East Thirty-eighth street.
SCHNEIDER, A. T., address unknown.
STROPL, CATHARINE, No. 128 East Sixth st.
SCHMID, KATHERINE, sixty-seven, of No. 435 East Ninth street; identified by son Charles at the morgue.
SCHNITZLER, TINA, Mrs., identified by her husband, Patrolman Edward Schnitzler, of the East One Hundred and Fourth Street Station, at the morgue.
SCHWARTZ, LOUISA, Mrs., forty-three, of No. 145 Third street; identified by her husband, Jacob, at the morgue.
SIERICHS, LETTA, thirty-eight, of No. 473 East Twelfth street; identified by her husband, William, at the morgue.
SMITH, MARY, Mrs. thirty-five, of No. 76 Seventh street; identified by her cousin, Charles Stock, of No. 142 Seventh street, at the morgue.
STOEHR, SUSIE, of No. 348 Sixth street; identified by husband, William, at the morgue.
STRINZ, MRS. AUGUST, fifty-two, No. 10 First avenue; identified by son, Paul, at the morgue.
SMITH, MISS MARTHA, eighteen years, No. 204 East Thirteenth street; identified by her.
SCHAEFER, KATE, six years, No. 202 East Thirteenth street.
SCHRUMPF, MRS. LIZZIE, forty-eight years old, No. 28 Avenue B, identified by her husband, Jacob Schrumpf.
SPRINZ, MRS. AUGUSTA, forty-six years old, No. 10 First avenue; identified by her son, Paul.

T.

TOTTEBAUM, HERMAN, of No. 61 St. Mark's place; identified by brother Charles at the Morgue.

U.

UNGER, KATE, forty-eight years, No. 39 Avenue A.

V.

VOLLMER, MARY, thirty-five, No. 128 First avenue (by husband Joseph).

W.

WALTER, ELIZABETH, sixty-seven, of No. 334 Sixth street. Identified by son Philip at the morgue.
WIEDEMAN, CAROLINE, fifty, of No. 79 East Houston street; identified at the morgue.
WUBBER, MRS. CAROLINE, No. 218 East Ninth street.
WEAVER, ESTHER, No. 204 East Ninth street.

MISSING.

ADDICKS, Amelia; seventy-five years old.
ADDICKS, John; sixteen years old.
ADDICKS, Mary; nine years old.
ADDICKS, Annie; seven years old.
ADDICKS, Ernest; five years old.
ADDICKS, Martha, ten years old.
ALBRECHT, Mrs. Joseph; forty years old.

BAGLEY, Mrs. Mary; forty-one years old; No. 489 West One Hundred and Thirtieth street.
BAGLEY, Lizzie, eleven years old; daughter of Mary.
BALLNER, Joseph, sixteen; No. 139 First avenue.
BALLNER, Minnie, eight; No. 139 First avenue.
BERGE, Mrs. Ellen; Goerck and East Third streets.
BENECKE, Mrs. William C.; No. 433 East Seventeenth street.
BENECKE, Miss Mamie, seventy-eight; No. 433 East Seventeenth street.
BOEGER, Mrs. Susan, wife of William A. Boeger, No. 39 Putnam avenue, Brooklyn.
BECK, Mrs. Christina, fifty-six, wife of John Beck, No. 323 East Ninth street.
BUCK, —, child of George Buck.
BUCK, —, child of George Buck.
BEHRENS, ALICE, fifteen years old; No. 127 Garden street, Hoboken.

EXCURSION BOAT IN FLAMES AND CARRYING ONLY THE DEAD, PASSES ON TO SINK: HER CAPTAIN.

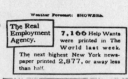

The BURNING of the GENERAL SLOCUM SCENE as SHE PASSED NORTH BROTHER ISLAND From a SKETCH by an EYE WITNESS

CAPTAIN'S VAN SCHAICK

President Roosevelt Wires His Sympathy.

The Rev. George C. F. Haas, the pastor of the church, received the following message of sympathy last night from President Roosevelt:

To the Rev. George C. F. Haas, St. Mark's German Lutheran Church:

Accept my profound sympathy for yourself, your church and your people.

THEODORE ROOSEVELT.

700 LIVES LOST WHEN EXCURSION BOAT BURNS IN HELL GATE AND SINKS.

Steamer General Slocum, Loaded with Sunday School Party of St. Mark's Church, Bursts Into Flame, and Women and Children Leap Into River---Scenes of Horror on Board As Panic-Stricken Passengers Fight for Life.

BOAT IS FINALLY BEACHED ON NORTH BROTHER ISLAND.

Many Gallant Rescues of the Drowning Made There—Bodies Brought Back to the Morgue Fill It to Overflowing—Divers Work All Night Taking Victims From the Wreck—Thrilling Stories of the Disaster Told by Survivors—1400 Persons Aboard the Steamer.

Probably 700 lives were lost when the steamer General Slocum, loaded down with an excursion party of about 1,400 persons from the St. Mark's Lutheran Church, took fire in Hell Gate yesterday morning, and was sunk near North Brother Island. Most of the victims were women and children. Capt. Van Schaick, of the Gen. Slocum, and five of his crew have been arrested.

Scenes of Horror When Steamer Burned.

It was a spectacle of horror beyond words to express—a great vessel all in flames, sweeping forward in the sunlight, within sight of the crowded city, while her helpless, screaming hundreds were roasted alive or swallowed up in the waves—women and children with their hair and clothing on fire; crazed mothers casting their babies overboard or leaping with them to certain death; wailing children and old men trampled under foot or crowded over into the water—and the burning steamboat, her whistle roaring for assistance, speeding on for the shore of North Brother Island, with a trail of ghastly faces and clutching hands in the tide behind her—gray-haired mothers and tender infants going down to death together.

The captain of the steamer has been arrested; there are stories of rotten life-preservers and of life-preservers placed out of reach, of the failure of the crew to fight the fire, and of the captain's mistake in not heading for the nearest land; but few know exactly what happened in that terrible scene of suffering and death, for many of the survivors are practically insane, and hundreds of others are in the hospitals.

It was a few minutes before 10 A. M. when the General Slocum left the recreation pier at the foot of East Third street with the Sunday-school scholars and members of the congregation of St. Mark's German Lutheran Church, on Sixth street, between First and Second avenues.

The General Slocum arrived at the pier at 8.20 o'clock. She had been tied up the previous night at the foot of West Fiftieth street, and had left the dock there at 7 A. M. For over an hour and a half the holiday-makers had trooped aboard the boat.

Hundreds of them had met near the church earlier in the morning and with the Rev. George C. F. Haas, the pastor of St. Mark's, at their head, had marched to the pier, the children waving flags and the mothers carrying lunch-baskets full of good things. The band was on the after-deck of the boat playing merry tunes, and from every flagstaff on the General Slocum streamed gayly colored bunting. The sun shone brightly, and the crisp, cool air gave a splendid promise of a happy day for the church people.

982 Tickets Were Sold.

When the lines were at last cast off and the go-ahead bell rang in the engine-room, one of the deck hands went up to the pilot house and reported to the captain, William Van Schaick, that 982 tickets had been taken in at the gang-plank. This represented the adult passengers and the children over nine and ten years of age. In addition to these, it was estimated that there were about 360 babies and young children who did not require tickets. There were also on board the ship's regular crew of twenty-three men, the employees of the caterer, numbering about fifteen men, and the members of the band, numbering ten. In all, it was estimated that there were almost 1,350 people on the boat.

At a fifteen-knot clip the Gen. Slocum steamed up the East River, it being the plan of her captain to reach Locust Grove, Long Island, the destination of the excursionists, shortly after the noon hour.

When the boat reached a point opposite Ninety-seventh street several of the crew who were on the lower deck saw puffs of smoke coming through the seams in the flooring immediately above what is called the second cabin. The forward part of the hold of the Gen. Slocum was divided in this way. In the extreme bow was the forecastle. Immediately aft the forecastle is what is called a second cabin. In the second cabin was a dynamo, the electric appliances and a number of stores, including the ships' lamps and the oil used to fill them. Nobody was in the second cabin so far as could be learned, when the fire started. The negro porter, Walter Payne, who had charge of the lamps, said that he had attended to the lamps early in the morning, and that he was confident nobody was in the second cabin.

Passengers on Upper Decks.

Nearly all of the excursionists were on the two upper decks at the time the first puffs of smoke were seen. The band had taken up a position on the middle deck and most of the excursionists were sitting around it. A large number of the children were on the top, or hurricane, deck. There were two policemen on the boat who had been detailed to take care of the crowd—Charles Kelk and Abel R. Vantassel, both of the Forty-second, or Harbor Police Precinct.

A few minutes after the boat had got off the deck a number of the children began to romp on the hurricane deck, and one of the band's crew asked Patrolman Kelk to go up there and keep them in order. Kelk went up on the upper deck.

For some reason the fact was not communicated immediately to Capt. Van Schaick. Some of the deck hands went below and ran into the furnace, believing they could easily extinguish the fire. They found the place a furnace.

Some of the dead lights had been left open and through these the wind had fanned an insignificant fire-draught into a blaze that could not be conquered. When the

(Continued on Third Page.)

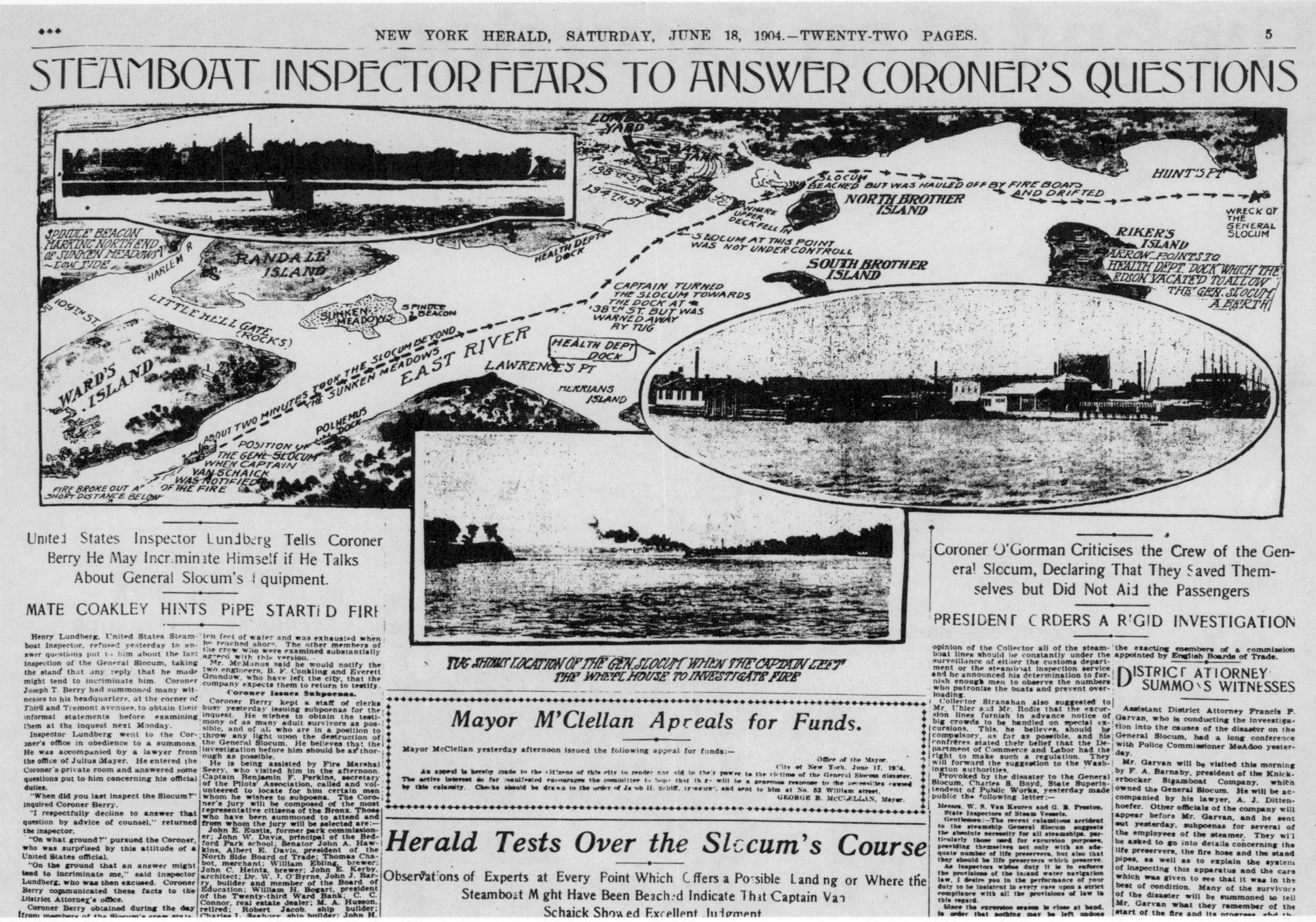

NEW YORK HERALD, SATURDAY, JUNE 18, 1904.—TWENTY-TWO PAGES. 5

STEAMBOAT INSPECTOR FEARS TO ANSWER CORONER'S QUESTIONS

TUG SHOWS LOCATION OF THE GEN. SLOCUM WHEN THE CAPTAIN LEFT THE WHEEL HOUSE TO INVESTIGATE FIRE

United States Inspector Lundberg Tells Coroner Berry He May Incriminate Himself if He Talks About General Slocum's Equipment.

MATE COAKLEY HINTS PIPE STARTED FIRE

Henry Lundberg, United States Steamboat Inspector, refused yesterday to answer questions put to him about the last inspection of the General Slocum, taking the stand that any reply that he made might tend to incriminate him. Coroner Joseph T. Berry had summoned many witnesses to his headquarters, at the corner of Third and Tremont avenues, to obtain their informal statements before examining them at the inquest next Monday.

Inspector Lundberg went to the Coroner's office in obedience to a summons. He was accompanied by a lawyer from the office of Julius Mayer. He entered the Coroner's private room and answered some questions put to him concerning his official duties.

"When did you last inspect the Slocum?" inquired Coroner Berry.

"I respectfully decline to answer that question by advice of counsel," returned the inspector.

"On what ground?" pursued the Coroner, who was surprised by this attitude of a United States official.

"On the ground that an answer might tend to incriminate me," said Inspector Lundberg, who was then excused. Coroner Berry communicated these facts to the District Attorney's office.

Coroner Berry obtained during the day from members of the Slocum's crew state-

ten feet of water and was exhausted when he reached shore. The other members of the crew who were examined substantially agreed with this version.

Mr. McManus said he would notify the two engineers, B. F. Conkling and Everett Grandow, who have left the city, that the company expects them to return to testify.

Coroner Issues Subpoenas.

Coroner Berry kept a staff of clerks busy yesterday issuing subpoenas for the inquest. He wishes to obtain the testimony of as many adult survivors as possible, and of all who are in a position to throw any light upon the destruction of the General Slocum. He believes that the investigation before him should be as thorough as possible.

He is being assisted by Fire Marshal Seery, who visited him in the afternoon. Captain Benjamin F. Perkins, secretary of the Pilots' Association, called and volunteered to locate for him certain men whom he wishes to subpoena. The Coroner's jury will be composed of the most representative citizens of the Bronx. Those who have been summoned to attend and from whom the jury will be selected are:—

John E. Eustis, former park commissioner; John W. Davis, principal of the Bedford Park school; Senator John A. Hawkins, Albert E. Davis, president of the North Side Board of Trade; Thomas Chabot, merchant; William Ebling, brewer; John C. Heintz, brewer; John E. Kerby, architect; Dr. W. J. O'Byrne, John J. Barry, builder and member of the Board of Education; William H. Bogart, president of the Twenty-third Ward Bank; C. C. Connor, real estate dealer; M. A. Husson, retired; Robert Jacob, ship builder; Charles L. Seabury, ship builder; John H.

Mayor M'Clellan Appeals for Funds.

Mayor McClellan yesterday afternoon issued the following appeal for funds:—

Office of the Mayor,
City of New York, June 17, 1904.

An appeal is hereby made to the citizens of this city to render any aid in their power to the victims of the General Slocum disaster. The active interest so far manifested encourages the committee to hope that there will be a generous response to the necessities caused by this calamity. Checks should be drawn to the order of Jacob H. Schiff, treasurer, and sent to him at No. 52 William street.

GEORGE B. McCLELLAN, Mayor.

Herald Tests Over the Slocum's Course

Observations of Experts at Every Point Which Offers a Possible Landing or Where the Steamboat Might Have Been Beached Indicate That Captain Van Schaick Showed Excellent Judgment

Coroner O'Gorman Criticises the Crew of the General Slocum, Declaring That They Saved Themselves but Did Not Aid the Passengers

PRESIDENT ORDERS A RIGID INVESTIGATION

opinion of the Collector all of the steamboat lines should be constantly under the surveillance of either the customs department or the steamboat inspection service and he announced his determination to furnish enough men to observe the numbers who patronize the boats and prevent overloading.

Collector Stranahan also suggested to Mr. Uhler and Mr. Rodie that the excursion lines furnish in advance notice of big crowds to be handled on special excursions. This, he believes, should be compulsory, as far as possible, and his confrères stated their belief that the Department of Commerce and Labor had the right to make such a regulation. They will forward the suggestion to the Washington authorities.

Provoked by the disaster to the General Slocum, Charles S. Boyd, State Superintendent of Public Works, yesterday made public the following letter:—

Messrs. W. S. Van Keuren and G. B. Preston, State Inspectors of Steam Vessels.

Gentlemen:—The recent calamitous accident to the steamship General Slocum suggests the absolute necessity for all steamships, particularly those used for excursion purposes, providing themselves not only with an adequate number of life preservers, but also that they should be life preservers which preserve.

As inspectors whose duty it is to enforce the provisions of the inland water navigation law, I desire you in the performance of your duty to be insistent in every case upon a strict compliance with all the provisions of law in this regard.

Since the excursion season is close at hand, in order that nothing may be left undone

the exacting members of a commission appointed by English Boards of Trade.

DISTRICT ATTORNEY SUMMONS WITNESSES

Assistant District Attorney Francis P. Garvan, who is conducting the investigation into the causes of the disaster on the General Slocum, had a long conference with Police Commissioner McAdoo yesterday.

Mr. Garvan will be visited this morning by F. A. Barnaby, president of the Knickerbocker Steamboat Company, which owned the General Slocum. He will be accompanied by his lawyer, A. J. Dittenhoefer. Other officials of the company will appear before Mr. Garvan, and he sent out yesterday, subpoenas for several of the employees of the steamer. They will be asked to go into details concerning the life preservers, the fire hose and the stand pipes, as well as to explain the system of inspecting this apparatus and the care which was given to see that it was in the best of condition. Many of the survivors of the disaster will be summoned to tell Mr. Garvan what they remember of the start of the fire and its progress, and the

Wednesday 15 June 1904, was the day of the Sunday School outing for the children of Saint Mark's Lutheran on Sixth Street, New York. The bright sunshine augured well for the picnic planned on Long Island: the procession down to the pier on East Third Street was an excited one, the children waving flags, their mothers toting bulging hampers. There at the water's edge stood their excursion boat, the *General Slocum*, bannered and buntinged, with a band on the after-deck already striking up popular melodies. There was some delay getting all the boisterous congregation aboard, 1,300 of them, but shortly before midday the Slocum was paddling away merrily up the East River.

The steamer was just passing opposite 97th Street when some of the crew on the lower deck noticed puffs of smoke seeping through the boards from a cabin where electrical appliances, lamps and oil were stowed. They did not, apparently, inform the captain immediately, thinking they could deal with the outbreak themselves. By the time they reached the cabin, it was a furnace, and all efforts at extinguishing the flames were foiled by rotting hoses and unyielding pumps. At fifteen knots the speed of the boat served to fan the flames greedily through the dry wooden superstructure, so that as the vessel passed into the channel known locally as Hell Gate watchers on the shore could clearly see the tongues of fire leaping towards the hurricane deck, where moments before hundreds of youngsters had been romping about.

In helpless horror they watched the floating pyre sail past Sunken Meadow, and on into the distance. Now there was utter bedlam aboard, mothers searching desperately for their children, some snatching at life-preservers that crumbled in their hands, others throwing themselves over the side—only to be churned to death by the huge paddle-blades. And still the *Slocum* sailed on—until it reached North Brother Island in mid-river, where Captain Van Schaick finally succeeded in beaching her. At that moment the hurricane deck collapsed into the inferno.

New York was stunned that such a catastrophe could have happened within sight of the city. The sheer weight of casualties—and most of them children—paralysed the imagination. The final yet inconclusive assessment was 1,021 dead.

'Few know exactly what happened in that terrible scene of suffering and death' reported the *New York World* the next day, 'for many of the survivors are practically insane and hundreds of others are in the hospitals.' But gradually an astonishing story emerged that smacked at best of criminal inefficiency, at worst of outright corruption. Why had the captain (who was arrested the moment he reached land) not driven the boat ashore earlier, for instance on Sunken Meadow? His initial defence was that by the time the fire had got out of control his nearest landfall had been North Brother Island. To check out his story the *New York Herald* sailed its own boat up-river following the course of the ill-fated voyage, and decided there might be something in it. But then Captain Van Schaick announced that he *had* intended to beach on Sunken Meadow but the engine room had not carried out his instructions. 'Whether the captain of the vessel erred in judgment in steering for the Island will be determined' declared the *Pittsburg Gazette*. 'But in any case that was not his most serious error. He should never have taken out his boat with that sort of load without an abundance of life-preservers in easy reach of all.'

Ah, but there were over 3,000 life-preservers on the boat, all easily accessible, retorted the Knickerbocker Steamboat Company who owned the *General Slocum*. What was more—whatever condition survivors complained they might have been in—they had all been inspected and passed by the Inspection Service. Which was not an argument that endeared the owners to the *New York Tribune*: 'There should be no tenderness for men who did not realise their obligations and followed custom without thinking; or for men, if such there are, who dismissed their own well-founded doubts and scruples when they came into possession of a perfunctory offical license.' The local inspector made a statement to *The World* emphasizing that the previous month he had counted every one of the boat's life-preservers and found them 'in good condition'—which made strange reading to those survivors who insisted they had seen inspection seals on some life-preservers dated 1891 (the year the *Slocum* went into service) and on others the name *Edwin Forrest* (a boat that had been out of commission for at least ten years).

Clearly something was deeply amiss in the Inspection Service, a conviction fortified by a startlingly frank interview given to the *Washington Post* by the service's head, General Uhler. He virtually admitted that, in the past at least, there had been corruption and political interference in the service: 'The evil has existed for years' he said. 'When fines have been imposed for the violation of the law the offenders have brought political influence to bear to secure a reduction or remission of the penalty. Under such a system the law becomes worse than a dead letter.' Whether this was a case of brutal honesty or an effort to divert the issue into the political arena, the subsequent federal inquiry laid the disaster firmly at the Inspection Service's door. The *General Slocum* had been carrying—probably for years—disgracefully inadequate life-saving and fire-fighting equipment. The real wonder, as one out-of-town paper exclaimed, was that this horror was so long in coming.

Three inspectors were fired, and a thorough examination of the whole service was ordained by the President. Some papers felt even this did not go to the heart of the problem. This awful

Weather Forecast: SHOWERS

Record-Breaking Days.

The World printed **1,206** Business Opportunities advertisements the first 15 days of this month.

NO OTHER NEW YORK NEWSPAPER PRINTED SO MANY.

The World.

"Circulation Books Open to All."   "Circulation Books Open to All."

Weather Forecast: SHOWERS

Record-Breaking Days.

The World printed **967** For Sale advertisements the first 15 days of this month. :: :: ::

NO OTHER NEW YORK NEWSPAPER PRINTED SO MANY.

VOL. XLIV., NO. 15,641.   ★   Copyright, 1904, by the Press Publishing Company, New York World.   NEW YORK, FRIDAY, JUNE 17, 1904.   · ·   PRICE {ONE CENT in Greater New York and Jersey City. / TWO CENTS outside of Greater New York and Jersey City and on trains.}

SIGHTSEERS' AUTO KILLS MAN ON BROADWAY.

Merry Party, Including Several Women and Children, Are Shocked by Tragic End of a Day's Outing.

FLED FROM HUGE CAR AS BODY LAY BENEATH.

Commissioner McAdoo Sees Accident in Front of Hoffman House and Gives Aid.

THE SAD SEARCH FOR LOVED ONES AMONG THE MANY HUNDREDS OF CORPSES IN THE MORGUE.

INTERIOR of the MORGUE showing RELATIVES IDENTIFYING VICTIMS.

RICH DIRECTORS OF LINE MUST EXPLAIN KILLING OF HELPLESS HUNDREDS

Bodies of 532 Dead Have Been Recovered and Total Loss May be 700— Committee to Raise Big Fund for the Survivors.

POLITICIANS MEDDLE WITH THE INSPECTION SERVICE

Chief Inspector Uhler, in Washington, Declares They Have Obstructed the Enforcement of Laws—Members of the Board of Inspectors Here to Really Investigate Themselves.

Dead recovered	532
Missing or unaccounted for	350
Injured in hospitals	49
Identified dead	427
Unidentified dead	105

NIECE OF CROKER WEDS GERMAN BARON

Were on a Trolley Outing When They Decided to Get Married.

"VERY MUCH ALIVE," SAYS MISS DAYTON.

Has Advertisement Printed Denying Unkind Rumor that She Had Died.

LIVE BABY BOY IS WASHED ASHORE.

Pretty Child, Whose Parents Are Unknown, Plays About Hospital Floor.

Additional List of Dead that Have Been Identified.

catastrophe and many similar tragedies' remarked the *Kansas City Star*, 'stand as a shocking arraignment of the tendency of New York to place the care of property above the care for human life, and to exalt commercialism above humanity.' Which was a sentiment that could have been echoed in many other places in many other circumstances for years to come.

A God-forsaken Mess
The San Francisco Earthquake 1906

HARPER'S WEEKLY

JOURNAL OF CIVILIZATION

New York, Saturday, May 5, 1906

Copyright, 1906, by Harper & Brothers. All rights reserved.

Drawn by Arthur Lewis

THE HEART OF THE RUINS

This drawing, by Mr. Arthur Lewis, the artist, who lived in San Francisco, shows the centre of San Francisco's business section during the fire. The view is eastward from the junction of Market, Kearny, Geary, and Third Streets. Here the fire reaped its fullest harvest

From the the Ferries to Van Ness
   you're a Godforsaken mess;
But the damndest finest ruins—
   nothin' more or nothin' less.

For sheer unquenchable optimism it's hard to beat a San Franciscan. That verse, printed on cards and distributed to survivors in the debris of the 1906 earthquake, could well stand as the city's epitaph, an epitome of the spirit that had resurrected San Francisco from the rubble of a dozen fires or earthquakes within half a century. It is difficult to imagine a more beautiful setting for a great metropolis—or a more unsuitable one, sitting firmly astride a massive flaw in the earth's crust—the San Andreas Fault—and within shaking distance of another, the Hayward Fault. These geological caprices are liable, at any time and without a by-your-leave, to shudder the city to its very foundations. It has been happening since the dawn of time, and it will assuredly happen again.

In 1906 San Francisco still betrayed its cosmopolitan origins—bigger, richer, more substantial of course than the shanty-town that had mushroomed in the wake of the '49 gold-fever, but no less lusty and materialist. The millionaires' mansions on Nob Hill, the fabulous luxuries of the Palace Hotel, the classical 'earthquake-proof' City Hall, these tokens of respectability coexisted tolerably alongside the lurid delights of the Barbary Coast ('that sink of moral pollution' as the *San Francisco Call* described it) and the debauched mysteries of Chinatown. On Tuesday 17 April, however, the night belonged to the smarter echelons of San Francisco society: the Metropolitan Opera Company from New York was playing *Carmen* at the Opera House, with the great Caruso as Don Jose. As befitted so august a cultural event the city glittered with smart dinner-parties that

evening, and the streets scintillated with elegant ballgowns.

By 5.00am the next morning only the most dedicated of the revellers would still be up and about. For the most part the city's 450,000 inhabitants were fast asleep when, at twelve minutes past, a sudden convulsion gripped the earth, creating waves along the street that remoulded the tramlines like plastic, contorting buildings till they disintegrated like matchwood. Deep fissures opened in the ground, and vast chunks of masonry plunged onto the roads. Those who were awakened found their walls buckling and swaying, their furniture dancing a macabre dance, as if in a dream. Those who did not awake were dead and buried—like forty guests at the Valencia St Hotel—beneath a mountain of wreckage, or crushed—like the city's fire chief and his family—by falling chimney pieces.

The first spasm lasted (if anyone was counting) thirty seconds. A silent breathing space of ten seconds was all the rampant earth needed to launch itself into an even more spiteful tremor, lasting twenty-five. The work the first 'quake had begun was finished off by the second: the crumbling columns of the City Hall collapsed, leaving only the dome aloft on a skeleton of girders, whole blocks in the poor Mission area were levelled instantaneously. Within moments the streets were thronged with frantic crowds, many in nightdresses, a few even in the starched shirt and tails that had graced the opera some hours earlier—they would probably not have recognized Signor Caruso now, as he sat disconsolately on his suitcase on the steps of the Palace Hotel (having first trumpeted a few well-chosen notes out of his bedroom window, he said later, to check that the tremors had not affected his vocal cords).

If shock and then relief that it was over were

the predominant emotions, new fears were soon to take their place. Smoke that signalled latent fires within the debris in more than fifty places inside the hour had blossomed into outright conflagrations. Unchecked, the flames began hungrily to devour the ruined jigsaw of wooden terraces, replenishing themselves at broken gas-mains. Without the direction of their now-dead chief, fire teams hustled their engines to the nearest hydrants—only to find to their horror they would only yield the merest trickle. San Francisco was utterly without water: the supply-pipes had been laid right across the path of the Fault.

In an effort to contain the growing holocaust to one side of the city's main thoroughfare, Market Street, the desperate firemen began to dynamite whole streets with the hope of creating strategic firebreaks. Their first attempts succeeded only in creating haphazard areas of wanton destruction, that helped rather than hindered the flames. In other parts of the city, too, unthinking survivors lit open-air fires (some of them for breakfast, like the 'ham-and-eggs' fire that devastated acres in the Van Ness Avenue district). By midday the greater part of the city-centre was a vortex of fire, as one landmark after another was engulfed—the Palace Hotel, the magnificent *Call* skyscraper, the Opera House . . .

All but one of the San Francisco papers were burned out of their premises. The *Call*, the *Chronicle* and the *Examiner* forgot their rivalries and contrived to get out an impromptu joint edition from the offices of the nearby *Oakland Tribune* the day after the earthquake. Only by laboriously printing on a hand-press out in the suburbs did the *Daily News* manage to publish an edition on that historic day, though (no doubt in the heat of the moment) its headlines were decidedly alarmist: 'Hundreds Dead!' it

ENTIRE CITY OF SAN FRANCISCO IN DANGER OF BEING ANNIHILATED

Big Business Buildings Already Consumed by Fire and Dynamite---30,000 Smaller Structures Swept Out and Remainder Are Doomed

PANIC-STRICKEN PEOPLE FLEE

SAN FRANCISCO, April 18.—This city lies in smouldering ruins and total annihilation seems to be its fate. The magnificent business district lying between the water's edge and Tenth street and even still farther west is destroyed, and there is scarcely any hope of saving but a few of the magnificent skyscrapers that have been erected during the last ten years.

Thirty thousand houses were either partially or wholly destroyed by earthquake, and the subsequent fire which started in 100 different places simultaneously has swept the city from one end to the other. Hundreds of buildings are burning without any effort being made to check the fire. By tonight it is estimated that there will

of the fire and all the intervening streets are practically under martial law

Mayor Schmitz to prevent disorder ordered all of the saloons closed. There were but few cases of theft reported.

The Call building is already destroyed utterly and 1 is probable that the Examiner building and the Chronicle building will also be destroyed.

The Emporium is reduced to ashes as is the Flood building. The magnificent new store of Hale Brothers was dynamited in an effort to stop the progress of the flames which burned with the same uncontrollable intensity that was manifested in the Baltimore fire.

CITY HALL GONE.

The City Hall is a grand mass of ruins.

broken by the earthquake during the early progress of the fire nothing could be done to stay the hungry blaze.

BUILDINGS DYNAMITED.

More than 100 buildings were dynamited with hope that the fire could be kept within a certain district.

In the business district, at Sansome and Bush streets, the flames are supposed to be under control. Twenty buildings were dynamited in this district.

One of the particularly sad features of the catastrophe was the drowning of a score or more persons in the Mission. Apparently the earthquake was more violent at this point than anywhere else in the city. Depressions of ten feet were made.

MAINS BROKEN.

BIG FIRE IN MISSION

SAN FRANCISCO, April 18. —A great fire is raging in the Mission district and is utterly beyond control. Before night, it is estimated, that in this particular section of the city 50,000 persons will be homeless.

EMPORIUM IN RUINS

SAN FRANCISCO, April 18. —The Emporium is a mass of ruins, with nothing but the walls of this magnificent store standing. The buildings immediately adjoining it are doomed to destruction.

FATEFUL BUILDING

SAN FRANCISCO, April 18.—The scene at the Mechanics' pavilion during the early hours of the morning and up until noon, when all the injured and dead were removed, because of the threatened destruction of the building by fire, was one of indescribable sadness. Sisters, brothers, wives and sweethearts searched eagerly for some missing dear ones. Thousands of persons hurriedly

THEATERS RUINED

All of San Francisco's best playhouses, including the Majestic, Columbia and Grand Opera House, are a mass of ruins. The earthquake demolished them for all practical purposes, and at the

THE NEW YORK HERALD.

NEW YORK, THURSDAY, APRIL 19, 1906.—TWENTY-SIX PAGES.—[COPYRIGHT, 1906, BY THE NEW YORK HERALD COMPANY.]

EARTHQUAKE AND FIRE DEVASTATE SAN FRANCISCO, 1,000 LIVES LOST, $100,000,000 IS THE PROPERTY LOSS

Birdseye View of San Francisco Showing Extent of Principal Burned District
Dotted lines surround burned district.

Flames, Unchecked, Sweep the City, Mint Ablaze, Big Hotels in Ruins

Water System Destroyed by Earthquake and Despite Use of Dynamite in an Endeavor to Check Fire It Has Passed Beyond Control

Families, Asleep, Crushed as Earthquake Destroys; Big Pavilion a Morgue

Thousand Persons Injured and Still More Thousands Rendered Homeless by Shocks That Drive

---

cried. 'City Seems Doomed.' Only one telegraph line out of the vanishing city remained: consequently first reports of the devastation reached the outside world largely from elements of the growing exodus of refugees across the Bay. Early accounts at Oakland reflected the conflicting emotions of the evacuees who had fled the wall of fire. 'No Hope Left' thought the hybrid *Call-Chronicle-Examiner.* 'Citizens are Forced to Fight Flames at Point of Revolver' reported the *Oakland Tribune.*

Inevitably the news that percolated across the nation was highly coloured: a panic-stricken flight was in progress, martial law had been declared, San Francisco was being annihilated. In reality, many San Franciscans refused to desert their beloved city (as later photographs, showing families sitting down to alfresco suppers against a backdrop of blazing buildings, proved). Nor was martial law ever required—though the army did take over on Wednesday and in an excess of zeal to prevent looting undoubtedly gunned down some innocent householders. But whether San Francisco really was to be 'annihilated' remained an open question for the three days the fires raged. A stand along wealthy Van Ness Avenue was determined on, and one by one the palatial homes of the rich fell before the dynamite. It was a worthy sacrifice, though in the event the conflagration died at the foot of Telegraph Hill partly from exhaustion, partly from the merciful rains that broke on the Saturday.

At last San Francisco could count the cost. Four square miles of the city had been razed to the ground, some 28,000 houses destroyed, $500 million-worth of property incinerated or demolished. The human loss could never be

more than guessed at—though in all likelihood it was nearer to five hundred than the thousand many papers reported. The Press after its initial flurry of sensation made considerable amends, not only by strenuous fund-raising but also by offering its advertisement columns free for tracing relatives, and its telegraphic facilities for sending personal messages.

One burning issue that followed in the aftermath of the disaster was whether the army had, in fact, abused its license to kill during those terrible three days. 'Misery laden Victims are Freed from Fear of Death by Bullets of Soldiers' was the *New York Herald's* cynical verdict after the emergency was over. Other papers, such as the *Troy Times*, had no doubts where the military's duty had lain. 'In the midst of the ruins of a mighty city' it insisted, 'with havoc, death, conflagration and demoralisation upon every side the army came upon the scene and enforced law, order and the rights of property. Ghouls were restrained or shot and crime checked with splendid celerity.' The other question, of course, was would San Francisco rise again? The *Seattle Post-Intelligencer* (which no doubt had hopes that its own city might now become the major centre of West Coast commerce) warned that 'in such a locality the damages from an earthquake would always be much greater in proportion to its severity than in other places where there was a more solid foundation.'

Sound advice, but San Franciscans would have been more inclined to agree with the *Chicago Record* that 'anyone who had viewed its magnificent harbour will agree that it is a gift of nature to the whole continent.' It was an academic debate anyway, for the work of

reconstruction was already under way even before the final flames guttered out—as if to fulfil the *Buffalo Commercial's* patriotic prophecy: 'Here a new, stronger and better city— not the conglomerate, half-foreign, bizarre old San Francisco but a new, modern American San Francisco—will arise from the ashes as if by magic in five years.'

Seventh Edition

20 PAGES TODAY

"FIRST IN EVERYTHING."

ST. LOUIS POST-DISPATCH

ONLY ST. LOUIS EVENING NEWSPAPER WITH ASSOCIATED PRESS DISPATCHES.

VOL. 58. NO. 240. ST. LOUIS, WEDNESDAY EVENING, APRIL 18, 1906. PRICE (In St. Louis, One Cent. Outside St. Louis, Two Cents.

Seventh Edition

FOURTH EXTRA

SAN FRANCISCO BURNING UP!

Earthquake Topples Down Hundreds of Buildings, Killing or Injuring 1500 Persons; Tidal Wave Sweeps Water Front.

Fifty Blocks of Buildings Are Destroyed

Structures Are Dynamited to Check the Flames!

$7,000,000 City Hall Is a Crumbling Ruin!

Great Wave Tosses Shipping Into the City!

Receding, It Carries Many to Their Death!

SPECIAL TO THE POST-DISPATCH.

SAN FRANCISCO, April 18. --With the entire north section of the city in ruins and with the flames leaping from building to building in all directions, San Francisco seems doomed.

Unless the wind shifts to the west and blows the flames towards the bay, nothing can prevent the destruction of the city. The Fire Department, working frantically without water, is dynamiting building after building in the path of the flames, but the wind is carrying a roaring river of fire across each gap and it appears impossible to check the conflagation.

One by one the finest structures in the business section are being reduced to wreckage. Every building surrounding the Palace Hotel is in flames. Fire is eating its way into the 16-story building of San Francisco Call, a morning paper, and the rear section of the 11-story Monadnock Building has collapsed, spreading the fire in all directions.

The Postal Telegraph Co. is preparing to vacate its building. and this will shut off all telegraphic communication with the outside world.

The death list is added to every moment. Aside from those

Newspaper Square, Showing Buildings of Call, Examiner and Chronicle

LOOKING UP MARKET STREET TO THE CLAUS SPRECKLES BUILDING, IN WHICH IS THE DAILY CALL.
Copyrighted by R. L. Ragley.   Courtesy of Keystone View Co.

SAN FRANCISCO'S $7,000,000 CITY HALL.

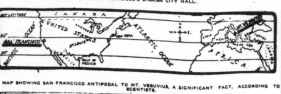

MAP SHOWING SAN FRANCISCO ANTIPODAL TO MT. VESUVIUS, A SIGNIFICANT FACT, ACCORDING TO SCIENTISTS.

that lost their lives nearly 1500 are injured, it is estimated. It is utterly impossible to care for the wounded as they should be.

and many are lying in the streets breathing their last, with the people in their madness unable to get them to places of

IDENTIFIED DEAD AT SAN FRANCISCO.

The following persons are known to have lost their lives in the San Francisco disaster:

POLICEMAN FENNER, killed while fighting fire.

POLICE SERGEANT BUNKER, killed when Central fire house collapsed.

KNOWN DESTRUCTION AT SAN FRANCISCO.

Following is a partial list of the damage wrought by the earthquake and subsequent fires in San Francisco:

CITY HALL, a $7,000,000 structure, totally destroyed.

PUBLIC LIBRARY, a handsome edifice donated to the city by former Mayor James D. Phelan, destroyed.

ARMORY BUILDING, a skyscraper, wiped out by fire.

WESTERN UNION TELEGRAPH BUILDING, wrecked.

ASSOCIATED PRESS BUILDING, wrecked.

NEW YORK LIFE INSURANCE BUILDING, wrecked.

THE EXAMINER (newspaper) BUILDING, damaged; vacated.

THE CHRONICLE (newspaper) BUILDING, damaged; vacated.

THE CALL (newspaper) BUILDING, burning; vacated.

POSTAL TELEGRAPH CO. BUILDING, partially wrecked.

PALACE HOTEL, one of the finest hotel structures in the world, rendered uninhabitable.

GRAND HOTEL, uninhabitable.

OCCIDENTAL HOTEL, uninhabitable.

THE LICK HOUSE, uninhabitable.

VALENCIA HOTEL, total wreck.

KINGSLEY LODGING HOUSE, total wreck.

GRAND AND CRYSTAL THEATERS destroyed.

WINCHESTER HOUSE, destroyed.

ARONSON HOUSE, destroyed.

GRAND OPERA HOUSE, finest theater in the city; badly damaged.

CENTRAL FIRE HOUSE, destroyed.

Many other fire houses partially wrecked.

MAJESTIC THEATER, in ruins.

RIALTO BUILDING, destroyed.

PACIFIC STATES TELEPHONE CO. BUILDING, destroyed.

NATOMA BUILDING, destroyed.

MUTUAL LIFE INSURANCE CO. BUILDING, destroyed.

EASTERN VISITORS IN CITY UNINJURED.

The agent of the Associated Press wires to the Post-Dispatch this comforting message:

"SAN FRANCISCO, April 18.-- For the benefit of Eastern people who have friends visiting in San Francisco it is safe to say that they have not been injured.

CLOUDS AND SOUTH WINDS

CARDINALS 6
CHICAGO 3
McCLOSKEY CERTAINLY WAS A "FIGHTn' MAN

It's the same thing over again.... some clouds but no probability of rain and if northerly winds. The official forecast:

"Partly cloudy Wednesday night and Thursday; cooler by Thursday night. Southerly winds."

Showers are reported from Texas, Colorado, Utah, Wyoming but in other sections it is fair. East of the Rocky Mountain region there is a general rise in temperature, but in the Northwest it is getting cooler. Nothing indicates that there will be any general unsettled weather here.

City Under Martial Law; Citizens Flee to Country!

Hundreds Are Crushed By the Falling Walls!

Magnificent Palace Hotel Is Burning

Street Car and Ferry Service Has Ceased!

Succession of Shocks Every Few Moments!

safety.

Men, women and children with broken limbs can be seen vainly trying to reach medical aid. Physicians from Oakland, Berkeley, Alameda and San Rafael have arrived on the scene and are doing good work in caring for the injured.

With no water to fight the flames and the town being gradually consumed and the moaning and cries of the injured, the city has been thrown into a panic.

The awful scenes of dead bodies lying around on the streets have caused widespread horror. The Waterworks is destroyed.

SAN FRANCISCO, April 18. 10:15 a. m.--There has just been another shock, which intensified the panic. People have started to rush into the streets, but the shock was of short duration and alarm subsided.

The gas works, south of Market street, has blown up and an immense fire rages in that vicinity.

The fire in the vicinity of the Palace and Grand hotels is rapidly approaching these buildings and from present indications they will fall prey to the flames within half an hour.

Weather Forecast: FAIR.

An Industrious Incubator!
3,968 WORLD WANTS YESTERDAY
1,511 **907**

WATCH WORLD WANTS WORK WONDERS WHILE YOU WAIT.

The  World.

"Circulation Books Open to All."   "Circulation Books Open to All."

"His Fortune."
A Story in a Picture.
FREE
With Next Sunday's World.
ANOTHER CHARLES DANA GIBSON DRAWING.

VOL. XLVI. NO. 16,313.   Copyright, 1906, by the Press Publishing Company, New York World.   NEW YORK, FRIDAY, APRIL 20, 1906.   PRICE ONE CENT In Greater New York and Jersey City. TWO CENTS outside of Greater New York and Jersey City and on trains.

GENERAL VIEW OF THE RANGE OF THE EARTHQUAKE AND VIEWS AND BUILDINGS IN THE PRINCIPAL TOWNS.

FIRES YET RAGING LAY ALMOST ALL THE CITY OF SAN FRANCISCO IN ASHES.

Flames Sweep Into the Wealthy Residence District, Destroying the Magnificent Mansions on Nob Hill, but It Is Believed the Worst Has Now Been Seen.

GREATEST DANGER THREATENING IS FROM THE LACK OF PROVISIONS.

Miles of Houses Dynamited in an Attempt to Check the Fire—300,000 Persons Made Homeless — Property Damage Estimated at $250,000,000—Hosts Camp in the Parks and Unoccupied Districts, and Many Flee the City—Loss of Life May Exceed 1,000.

The situation at 3 A. M. to-day is as follows:

1. San Francisco is a heap of ashes.
2. The property loss is placed at from $250,000,000 to $300,000,000.
3. A conservative estimate places the loss of life at 1,000, but this number may be increased. In fact, the present estimate is mere guesswork.
4. More than twenty cities and towns other than San Francisco have been destroyed in part or in whole.
5. The property loss in outside places is estimated at $30,000,000.
6. The loss of life in outside places is estimated at 800.
7. The people made homeless exceed 300,000.
8. The only public or semi-public building standing in San Francisco is the United States Mint.
9. A slight tremor shook the Pacific coast yesterday from San Francisco to Los Angeles without doing great damage.
10. Measures for relief were undertaken by the nation, States and cities. More than $3,000,000 was raised.

(Special to The World.)

SAN FRANCISCO, April 19.—While the entire business section of this city is in ashes, and the best part of the residence district destroyed, the belief grew strong to-night that the worst had been seen. The fires that had devastated the city were believed to be burning themselves out.

Three distinct areas of fire were still raging at 10 P. M., but they were growing feebler. One was in the territory that extends from Nob Hill easterly toward the water front. It was travelling slowly northerly toward the Telegraph Hill section, and it was thought would die out from lack of material, or be turned toward the extreme water front.

The second centre was in the Mission district. Here the fire had reached Eighteenth street, but was making little headway toward the hillsides to the west, where thousands of people were camped.

The Most Dangerous Fire.

The third and most dangerous fire was that threatening the western part of the city. This was a continuation of the Nob Hill fire. It was wedge shape, with the apex pointing toward the west. This was the blaze against which the firemen bent their greatest efforts. Dynamite was used for back firing, but not with marked success.

Many blocks will be blown up, and the hope was strong that this fire might be checked.

The greatest danger now menacing the 300,000 homeless people is the lack of provisions. The water supply is also scant. It was announced to-night, however, that to-morrow there would begin a daily delivery of 10,000,000 gallons of water.

To-night, for the first time since the earthquake, direct telegraphic communication was re-established between San Francisco and the outside world. By the most energetic efforts in the face of great obstacles, the Postal Telegraph Company succeeded in restoring one of its shattered lines, and its managers were hopeful of bringing back its service to normal in a day or two.

The fire spread everywhere to-day, borne by an ever-changing wind. The section of the city west of Van Ness avenue, which contains the homes of the wealthy, was fired at 6 o'clock to-night. The district was soon surrounded by flames and could not be saved.

From noon until 6 o'clock soldiers, police and firemen demolished the splendid homes on the easterly side of the broad avenue with dynamite and black powder.

They carried the devastation for a distance of one mile, under orders from Mayor Schmitz and the Council and Gen. Funston.

Buildings were still toppling under the dynamite when the flames leaped across the area of destruction, and the district that a million dollars' worth of property had been destroyed to save was doomed.

300,000 Are Now Homeless.

The Deputy Chief of the San Francisco Fire Department got out the following bulletin:

"At 7.30 to-night the fire was still under headway, gathering force

---

PANIC IN LOS ANGELES FOLLOWS TWO SLIGHT EARTHQUAKE SHOCKS.

Men, Women and Children Ran to the Parks Fearing the Buildings Would Fall—Business Abandoned and the City in Anxiety Fearing Fate That Befell San Francisco.

(Special to The World.)

LOS ANGELES, Cal., April 19.—Two slight shocks of earthquake were felt here soon after noon to-day. Tall buildings swayed a little, windows rattled and chandeliers moved. No damage was done. At any other time little attention would have been paid to such a disturbance, but owing to the San Francisco disaster people became terror-stricken and for one hour the city was in a panic.

The shocks came about six minutes apart and lasted only a few seconds. They were followed by occasional very faint tremors that died away after an hour.

So great is the fright that business was suspended generally for the remainder of the day. In every home to-night there is fear and trembling. Many people are remaining out of doors, apprehending a renewal of the shocks during the night.

Fled In a Wild Panic.

When the quaking began at noon hour large crowds were gathered around bulletin-boards eagerly reading the news from San Francisco. As the ground trembled beneath their feet they were paralyzed with terror for a moment. Then panic seized the throng. Men, women and children ran aimlessly about, fearing that tall buildings would fall on them. From stores, office buildings, factories and homes thousands more fled toward open spaces and parks.

When it was found that the earth had quieted and no damage had been done there was a cautious return. Every nerve of the city is on edge, and the slightest disturbance would be the signal for another panic.

G. E. Franklin, head of the United States Weather Bureau in this city, in his report of the earthquake, ten minutes after it occurred, said:

"There was nothing at all unusual in the shock. It was of hardly sufficient

(Continued on Third Page.)

More Than $3,000,000 Raised Yesterday for Relief Fund.

More than $3,000,000 cash was raised throughout the nation yesterday for the San Francisco sufferers. The principal contributors in this city and elsewhere were:

John D. Rockefeller	100,000
New York Stock Exchange	100,000
Clarence H. Mackay	100,000
Lackenburg, Thalmann & Co., the United Railways Investment Company. Patrick Calhoun, Sydney Shepard, and Ford, Bacon & Davis	20,000
M. Guggenheim's Sons	25,000
J. P. Morgan & Co.	25,000
Carnegie Hero Fund	25,000
Morris K. Jesup	25,000
Brown Bros. & Co.	10,000
August Belmont	10,000
J. & W. Seligman & Co.	10,000
J. Henry Smith	10,000
H. E. Huntington	10,000
H. C. Otis	10,000
Representative Nicholas Longworth	250
Robbins Dry Goods Company	2,500
Members of local councils of Knights of Columbus	25,000
F. M. Rothschild & Sons, London, through August Belmont & Co.	25,000
Mrs. Phoebe Hearst	50,000
Mrs. Collis P. Huntington	25,000
W. R. Hearst	25,000
Charles M. Schwab	25,000
Grover J. Gould	5,000
North British and Mercantile Insurance Company	10,000
Mrs. John W. Mackay	5,000
B. H. Macy & Co.	5,000
A. Carfield	5,000
Consolidated Stock and Petroleum Exchange	2,500
Pike, Fabyan & Co.	1,000
Cornelius N. Bliss	1,000
Charles Stewart Smith	1,000
New York National Exchange Bank	5,000
Kuhn, Nichols & Co.	5,000
Wolf Bros. & Co.	500
H. Harris	1,000
Dowager Duchess of Marlborough, formerly Miss Hammersley	1,000
Arion Ridder	1,000
Enoch Morgan's Sons	1,000
Astaetic City	1,000
Percent Lebrudy through the French Ambassador	1,000
Vice-President Charles W. Fairbanks	2,500

SOUTHERN PACIFIC TRAINS RUNNING.

The Southern Pacific Railroad Company received information at its New York offices yesterday afternoon that trains were running from San Francisco south down the peninsula toward San Jose. Refugees were being handled as speedily as possible.

The company's station at Third and Townsend streets, San Francisco, while damaged, was not destroyed, and was being used as a terminus.

A despatch from Sacramento said that the Southern Pacific repaired its tracks and telegraph lines south of San Francisco yesterday and resumed traffic in the afternoon between Sacramento and Oakland.

Disaster Cost 1,845 Lives and $283,180,000 in Property.

In the following list of California cities, towns and villages blighted by earthquake and fire the casualties and damages reported as to each are estimated from the most conservative reports:

City, Town or Village.	Population.	Damage.	Casualties.
San Francisco	345,000	$250,000,000	1,000 +
Oakland	70,000	500,000	5 +
Alameda	17,000	400,000	?
San Jose	35,000	3,000,000	50 +
Agnew (State Hospital for Insane)	800	400,000	275 +
Palo Alto (Stanford University)	5,000	5,000,000	3 +
Salinas	3,000	2,000,000	None
Napa	5,500	250,000	?
Hollister	1,900	200,000	?
Vallejo	8,000	40,000	?
Sacramento	30,000	25,000	?
Redwood City	1,800	30,000	?
Port Richmond (Terminal of Santa Fe RR.)	400	?	?
Suisun	1,000	50,000	?
Santa Rosa	7,000	800,000	500 +
Watsonville	3,000	70,000	?
Monterey	2,500	25,000	8
Loma Prieta	300	?	4 +
Stockton	18,000	40,000	?
Brawley	500	100,000	?
Santa Cruz	7,000	150,000	Conflict'g
Gilroy	2,500	100,000	?
*Healdsburg	1,900	Reports conflicting.	
*Cloverdale	1,000	Reports conflicting.	
*Geyserville	500	Reports conflicting.	
*Hopland	600	Reports conflicting.	
*Ukiah (State Hospital for Insane here)	2,000	Reports conflicting.	
Totals		$283,180,000	1,845 +

*Indicates probable greater loss of life.
*Note.—The last five towns are reported wiped out; $20,000,000 would not cover property loss.

Too Much Stress
The Quebec Bridge Collapse 1907

Insure your business by advertising in the "TELEGRAPH"

The hope of this vertiser is realized everytime in the "TELEGRAPH"

THE DAILY TELEGRAPH.

NO. 206   QUEBEC, FRIDAY, AUGUST 30 1907   ONE CENT.

QUEBEC BRIDGE FALLS INTO RIVER

Carrying Over Three Score of Persons to Death in the Crash and Causing a Loss of About $3,000,000

National Calamity Caused by Collapse of the Total Steel Superstructure of the South Shore

Number of dead, about 65.
Loss roughly estimated at about $3,000,000.
Time of accident 5.40 p.m.
Collapsed portion about 1,200 feet in length.
Probable cause of accident—Steel work, as piers are intact.

Carrying about seventy souls with it, the whole south shore steel superstructure of the Quebec Bridge, between eleven and twelve hundred feet, representing a cost of about $3,000,000, crumbled and fell into the river about 5.30 p.m. yesterday, and now lies there—a part of it above water—a massive heap of twisted and tangled steel.

Only about ten of the whole number of people on the bridge at the time of the terrible catastrophe were saved from death, and one at least of these will die, so that the total number of victims will be sixty at least, it is said, and may be even more, the number not being definitely known until the roll is called.

LIKE AN EARTHQUAKE SHOCK

Crashing down into the river, the falling debris shook the ground for miles around, St. Romuald, New Liverpool, Sillery, Cap Rouge, and other small places nearby, shivering as if an earthquake had occurred, and

WHO THE MANY VICTIMS ARE

Most of those who met death in the calamity were structural workers, though Chief Engineer Birks, of the Phoenix Bridge Co., was among the number, he being out on the structure with Foreman Yanson, Whaly and Ioaine, all going down. While many of the workmen were from the United States, there were also a number of people from St. Romuald, New Liverpool and other places along the south shore and a number of Caughnawaga Indians.

The names of the dead or missing cannot be learned yet, but it is known that among the number were

ALBERT WILSON, St. Romuald.
J. THEBERGE, St. Romuald.
J. PROULX, New Liverpool.
ANGUS LEAF, Caughnawaga.
NAP. LACHANCE, Caughnawaga.
G. BEAUDRY, St. Romuald.
ENGINEER BIRKS, Philadelphia
FOREMAN YAN

The Piers Still Remain Intact - Channel may Be Blocked and Bridge Completion Delayed Some Years

CAUSED SOME HEART-RENDING SCENES

The grief of some of the wives and relatives of the victims was heartrending. Several women whose husbands, brothers or sons were, had rushed to the scene. One woman became hysterical and it was with difficulty she was removed from the scene. At St. Romuald the crying of the women was pitiful to hear. This was especially the case

---

QUEBEC TELEGRAPH

Quebec's Only English Evening Newspaper

EVENING   EDITION

WEATHER PROBS
Moderate to fresh southeast to southwest winds, a few scattered showers, but mostly fair.

QUEBEC TEMPERATURE
Yesterday's readings Maximum, 61; minimum, 46; during the night, 43; to-day, 67.

MONDAY EVENING, SEPTEMBER 11, 1916

VOL. XLI, NO. 215

8 PAGES   PRICE: ONE CENT

QUEBEC BRIDGE AGAIN SCENE OF CATASTROPHE

CENTRE SPAN OF THE QUEBEC BRIDGE UNACCOUNTABLY COLLAPSES, AND LIVES ARE LOST

Another Catastrophe Marks the Building of a Great Structure—Floating of Span Into Position Was Successfully Carried Out Until Fatal Moment, Which Caused The Loss of a Number of Workingmen Engaged in Important Work.

WIDESPREAD SYMPATHY FOR FAMILIES OF VICTIMS

GERMAN INTENSITY PROVED FUTILE WITH BRITISH

Battle for the Ridge of Ginchy Redoubled in Fury But British Withstood Onslaught—Hun Trenches Destroyed Over a Four Mile Stretch

Mr Ulric Barthe, the secretary of the Quebec Bridge Company, had good reason to be proud. For years they had planned a great bridge across the St Lawrence, and his voice had been one of those most influential in getting the enormous project started. Now, on 29 August 1907, the dream was nearing reality. The new Quebec bridge would be one of the modern wonders of the world, its main span of 1,800 feet making it the greatest suspension bridge ever built. That afternoon he was taking a few friends to the river to inspect the work: they drove out onto the great anchor pier and looked in wonder at the magnificent arch curving gracefully up till it towered some 160 feet above the water. Work was at full stretch, ninety-two men swarming over the girders—a few Americans, but for the most part the labourers were local Caughnawagi Indians, excellent workers (apart from the seven who had quit the site at lunchtime after a dispute with the foreman). As Barthe's party drove back off the bridge, an engine loaded with iron pulled onto the pier. It was nearly half-past six.

Barthe and his friends had hardly reached the road when they heard a spine-chilling crack. They turned in horror to see the far end of the soaring half-arch slowly bending. Then with a crash so loud the inhabitants of Quebec thought there was an earthquake, the entire fabric collapsed into the water.

Eight of the workmen were picked up by boat, alive, within a few minutes. The rest were either drowned or pinned helplessly by the huge girders. The tragedy was compounded (in the words of the *Montreal Gazette*) 'by the fact that there are a number of wounded men pinned in the wreckage near the shore. Their groans and shrieks can be plainly heard by the anxious crowds who are waiting at the water's edge, but nothing so far can be done to rescue them or relieve their sufferings in the slightest degree. There are no searchlights available and by the feeble light of lanterns it is impossible to even locate the sufferers, so that for the present nothing can be done but to leave them to their fate.' Their fate was to be overwhelmed by the rising tide of the river.

It was manifestly clear, from the beginning, that the bridge had contained some inherent design fault. Within a day of the disaster the *Montreal Daily Star* was reporting: 'the current view is that the responsibility will fall on the Phoenix Bridge Company.' They were the contractors from Pennsylvania and specialists in the work, and it was their consulting engineer, a Mr Theodore Cooper, who had approved the design. He was soon tracked down in New York, and admitted that illness had prevented him from even visiting the site for two years! The *Daily Star* also recalled that the Phoenix Bridge Company had also had the contract for the New York and Ottawa railway bridge some years before. That, too, had collapsed.

Then a very curious fact emerged. On the day before the disaster Mr Cooper had apparently sent a cable, ordering all work on the bridge to be stopped. According to the *Daily Star* an inspector had told the consulting engineer 'things did not look well for the bridge. He thought it ought to be looked into immediately.' That telegram, however, never reached Quebec.

At first it was supposed that this was due to a telegraphers' strike. But the next day the *Quebec Daily Telegraph* revealed that Mr Cooper had in fact sent the message ('Do not place any more load on Quebec Bridge at present: better look into it at once') not to the site, but to the company's office in Phoenixville. When it arrived the Chief Engineer was out: he returned shortly after five o'clock on the 29th. The matter was being discussed at the moment the bridge gave way.

The *Montreal Gazette*'s editorial was very charitable under the circumstances. The structure was intended to be one of the greatest of its kind in the world. It has attracted the attention of engineers everywhere . . . There will be some pity for the designers whose work has failed so badly . . .' The Royal Commission set up to investigate the disaster and which reported six months later was more uncompromising. It found the cause in the failure of the lower chords in the anchor arm, adding this failure 'was due to their defective design, not to abnormal weather conditions or accident . . . the failure cannot be attributed directly to any other cause than the errors of judgement on the part of the [company's] engineers.'

What was more, it went on, there was no practical way of bracing or reinforcing the structure as it stood. 'A bridge of the adopted span which would unquestionably be safe can be built, but in the present state of professional knowledge a considerably larger amount of metal would have to be used.' The Commission added there had been inefficient supervision of all parts of the work, and *that* had been the responsibility of the Quebec Bridge Company.

Any further work by that company was out of the question—it had already spent $4 million on the bridge and was financially precarious. The Dominion Government agreed to take over its liabilities and proceed with a new bridge—this time armed with a whole battery of engineers. Once again, after new studies and designs, a vast cantilever construction began to rear over the St Lawrence. Work progressed painfully slowly—if without any serious mishap—until the autumn of 1916. On 11 September, even before it was light, tens of thousands of spectators had assembled on the banks to witness the final act in the epic drama—the hoisting of the final span into position to complete the bridge. They watched the tugs arrive, cheered as the span was placed delicately under the cantilevers, then began to wander home as the hydraulic jacks imperceptibly levered it into place: the task was all but accomplished.

Afterwards one spectator was reported as saying: 'I was looking at it one moment. Then I turned around for a few seconds . . . when I looked again it was gone.' The 5,600 tons of iron had proved too much for the lifting girder, and the great span plunged down into the waters. Relieved of the weight, the supporting cantilevers whipped back and forth, smashing platforms and hurtling men into the river. Nine of them were never seen again.

For a few moments there was panic, when it was feared the entire construction would disintegrate, as it had in 1907. But this time, the calculations proved sounder, the trembling edifice calmed—and held. Two days later the papers were confidently declaring the surviving sections to be as solid as rock. 'There is no doubt' said the *Montreal Gazette* 'but that the cause was the breaking of the steel bearing casting supporting the span . . . the casting that failed was not part of the permanent structure.' 'Just a piece of bad luck' the Chief of the Engineering Board summed it up. Which would have served very well as an epitaph for the ill-omened Quebec Bridge: by the time a new central span had been cast, it had become the most expensive bridge in the world, in human lives as well as money.

The Earthquake at Messina 1908

Like San Francisco two years before, the great sea port of Messina in Sicily had enjoyed a grand opera gala on the eve of its earthquake (in this instance, *Aida*). When the twenty-five second tremor struck the town, at 5.20 in the morning of 28 December 1908, here too you might have seen tail-coated men and tiaraed ladies fleeing the ruins. But there all resemblance ended: Messina was neither physically nor psychologically so well-equipped to deal with disaster, despite its appalling history of earthquakes. Ninety-eight per cent of the ornate but crudely-constructed buildings in the city collapsed, including the ancient cathedral: the narrow streets were death-traps even for those who managed to escape their crumbling homes: the harbour, where thousands of survivors gathered in flight, was overwhelmed by an enormous tidal wave that followed in the wake of the shock. A deathly film of dust settled over the dead and living alike, as if to emphasize the mental paralysis that took hold of those who were spared: indeed the only form of organization discernable in the immediate aftermath was the systematic looting by ruthless gangs of bandits. Only the arrival of sailors and marines from ships in the area, Russian, British, German and French, succeeded in restoring morale and order before the city was stripped clean. As it was, it had lost (at a cautious estimate) 50,000 of its citizens.

The Daily Mirror

THE MORNING JOURNAL WITH THE SECOND LARGEST NET SALE.

No. 2,645.	Registered at the G.P.O. as a Newspaper.	TUESDAY, APRIL 16, 1912	One Halfpenny.

DISASTER TO THE TITANIC: WORLD'S LARGEST LINER SINKS AFTER COLLIDING WITH AN ICEBERG DURING HER MAIDEN VOYAGE.

Disaster has overtaken the great steamer Titanic, the world's largest and most luxuriously appointed vessel. The liner, which was the latest addition to the White Star fleet, left Southampton last Wednesday on her maiden voyage to New York, and was in the vicinity of the Newfoundland banks, to the south of Cape Race, when she struck an iceberg, an ever-present peril in those latitudes at this time of the year, and, after her passengers had been saved—sank. "Wireless" again demonstrated its immense value, assistance being summoned by this means. Above, the mighty vessel is seen leaving Southampton on Wednesday.—(D.M.P.)

HOW MENTAL TRAINING WILL MAKE MONEY FOR YOU. See page 5.

Daily Herald

THE LABOUR DAILY NEWSPAPER.

HOW MENTAL TRAINING WILL MAKE MONEY FOR YOU. See page 5.

NO. 2.   APRIL 16, 1912.   ONE HALFPENNY.

TITANIC FOUNDERS.

SENSATIONAL ICEBERG COLLISION

GREAT LOSS OF LIFE.

WOMEN AND CHILDREN SAVE

2.19 a.m. The Liverpool correspondent of the Exchange Company telegraphs:—

TITANIC FOUNDERS. FEARED LOSS OF LIFE.

The same correspondent telephones early this morning that the officers of the W Line at Liverpool have just received official intimation fr the liner "Olympic liner "Titanic" has foundered.

The same message states that many passengers and members of the crew have Confirmatory details are anxiously awaited and friends of passengers are makin enquiries at the White Star offices, for unfortunately the wording of the informati gives ground for the fear that there has been a serious loss of life.

This contradicts the statement of the Exchange Telegraph Company's Montpondent who cabled at 7.57 p.m. that

"It is now confirmed that the passengers of the "Titanic" have been safely transhipped to the Allan liner "Parisian" and the Cunarder "Carpathia."

2.40 a.m.—Survivors aboard "Carpathia," and a marconigram received from the Cape Race Wireless station a few minutes before 2.30 a.m. reports that the Cunard liner "Carpathia" reached the scene of the disaster of the "Titanic" at daybreak to find only boats and wreckage.

The "Titanic" foundered about 2.20 a.m. in 41-16 N. 50-4 W.

The boats were accounted for, and about 675 souls were saved, including crew and passengers, the latter being nearly all women and children.

The Leyland liner, "Californian," is remaining at the scene of the disaster, and is making further search.

The "Carpathia" is returning to New York with survivors. (via Marconi.)

The maiden trip of the White Star Line's mammoth steamship, the "Titanic," has been rendered unexpectedly sensational by a disastrous mid-ocean collision with an iceberg. Following the emergency call of "S.O.S." at once sent out through the night over a radius of 1,000 miles of sea, upwards bearing toward the di already come to her as herself, meanwhile, 1,500 passengers and m the Allan liner "Pari "Carpathia," is being "Virginian" towards is reported by telegra different quarters to b ward, experts declare th constructed as to be p view was strikin hour last night in a w by Mr. and Mrs. G. A Godalming, from their operator on the "Tit for Halifax," runs this ance; "practically unsi

How the New

The first news of the Reuter's Montreal corre a wireless communicatio morning from the Allan li day out from Halifax, w "Titanic" had collided w 500 miles south-east of Ne calling for help. The accid 3.20 a.m. The messages from w., and longitude 41/46// which was at that time abo the "Titanic," signalled h proceed at once to the scene assistance, and within h "Olympic" and the "Baltic within 200 miles of her si ported to be in direct comm and heading for the scene of "Baltic," curiously enough, ship to answer the famous "by Jack Binns from the stricken "Republic.

"**Virginian" to the Rescue.**

For a time the wildest rumours were afloat. The "Titanic" was sinking with all hands on board, wireless communication was severed, the small fleet of liners who were heading towards the "wreck" would be too late. For by this time the "Mauretania," the "Cincinnati," the "Parisian," the "Carpathia," and the German ships "Amerika," "Prinz Friedrich Wilhelm," and "Prinz Adalbert" had all been hailed at various points on the trans-Atlantic course, and were hurrying towards the distressed signals off the Nfwfoundland Banks. By the afternoon, however, there came reassuring despatches from all quarters. At 5.20 a.m. the messages from the "Titanic's" wireless ceased suddenly, the "Virginian's" operator noticing a blur and then one abrupt stop with considerable noise. Much was made of this fact, and crowds besieged the steamship offices in Montreal and New York till at last the news came through that the "Titanic" was slowly moving towards Halifax on her own steam, while the "Virginian" was

standing by ready to give assista "Parisian" and the "Carpathi the scene; twenty boatloads of p reported to be safely transhipp former and the remainder tak Cunarder, while to accelerate "Virginian" paid out tow line fallen monarch along to the p sion of her sensational maiden tr

An Unsinkable S

The most cheering news of th testimony of Mr. A. S. Frank of the International Mercan Shipping Combine which con Star Line, that the "Ti unsinkable ship. The impac must have struck the iceberg a smaller ship, or one con fashioned lines, beyond a do ments in the "Titanic's" b they may fill separately, are sealed from the rest of th design by which the hull h is in accordance with M Wolff's very latest pate against shipwreck by collisi

Well-known N

According to telegram night the fallen "Titac

THE LEOMINSTER TRAGEDY

Curious Evidence by Clergyman in Murder Cha ge.

Samuel Henry, of More on Lodge, Eye, clerk in Holy Orders, who is charged with the wilful murder of his wife and attempted suicide, was yesterday brought up at Leominster. The pri will be remembered, recently fired a House of Commons.

BLUE JACKET DROWNED.

Lieut.-Commander Commended For Gallant Conduct.

Mr. C. B. Harris, the County Coroner, held an inquest at Chatham yesterday afternoon on the death of James Galloway, a young blue jacket of the destroyer "Vulture." The deceased fell overboard nearly a month ago, and his body was not recovered until Sunday last.

verdict of "accidentally

SOCIALIST UNITY

Inaugural Meeting of British Socialist Party.

STIRRING SPEECHES

At the London Opera House.

The British Socialist Party held their inaugural meeting at the London Opera House Mr. H. M. Hyndman, who pre

---

50 POINTS FOR HOME RULE.

From Bookstalls, or The Publisher, "The Daily News," Bouverie Street, London, and 63, Deansgate, Manchester.

PRICE 1d.   BY POST 1½d.

The Daily

D.N. 20,625.   LONDON & MANCHESTER. WEDNESDAY,

TITANIC DEATH-ROLL OVER 1,300.

Liner Lying Two Miles Deep Beneath the Atlantic.

868 SAVED ON THE CARPATHIA

"Help! Help! Hurry! Hurry!"

WIRELESS OPERATOR'S LAST PATHETIC CRY FOR RESCUE.

Two miles deep in t the great li

nearly six hours until the Carpathia ended their heartbreaking emotion.

No explanation has yet been given of the contradictory Marconigrams which flooded New York from Halifax yesterday and buoyed up with hope the White Star officials long after they had received the fear of a horrible loss of 1,800 lives.

Every message so far has been wireless, and has come from some steamship officer or land station operator who has picked up ethergrams emitted from the keyboards of the Carpathia, Olympic, Parisian, Virginian, Baltic, or Californian, and intercepted in their mysterious passage through the air.

The tremendous anxiety of relatives of the Titanic's 1,400 passengers to ascertain the names of survivors has found expression in the greatest avalanche of Marconigrams ever despatched off the Atlantic coast.

Siasconset, Glace Bay, and Cape Race are flooded with messages for the Carpathia, the Cunard

WERE THERE BOATS ENOUGH?

BOARD OF TRADE RULES OBSERVED

BUT OUT OF DATE.

POSSIBLE CAUSE OF HUGE LOSS OF LIFE.

Much comment has been excited, both in this country and America that the que

---

THE DAILY NEWS. SATURDAY. APRIL 20. 1912.

NO TRACE OF PANIC.

LONDON MASTER'S STORY.

"ANY MORE LADIES?"

LAST SCENE VIEWED FROM THE BOATS.

APPALLING CRIES AS SHIP DISAPPEARED.

NEW YORK, April 19.

"A slight jar. The engines stopped. I went on deck in my dressing gown, and found only a few people there who had come up in the same way to inquire why we had stopped, but there was no sort of anxiety in the mind of anyone."

Thus did Mr. Beesley, of London, lately a science master at Dulwich College, commence his description of the disaster to Reuter's Special Correspon

Adams, Italian
Quatorze, Gee
Modern Dutch

CORR

No. 14. which had filled rapidly with men, and was coming down on us in a way that threatened to submerge our boat.

"'Stop lowering 14,' our crew shouted, and the crew of No. 14, now only 20 feet above, cried out the same. But down she came until a stoker and I reached up and touched the bottom of the swinging boat above our heads.

"The next drop would have brought her on our heads. Just before she dropped another stoker sprang to the ropes with his knife open in his hand 'One,' I heard him say, and then 'Two,' as the knife cut through the pulley rope.

"The next moment the exhaust stream carried us clear, while boat No. 14 dropped into the water, taking the space we had occupied a moment before. Our gunwales were almost touching. We drifted away easily, and when our oars were got out we headed directly away from the ship.

STOKER IN COMMAND.

"The crew seemed to me to be mostly cooks. They sat in their white jackets two to an oar, with a stoker at the tiller. There was a certain amount of shouting from one end of the boat to the other, and the discussion as to which way we should go was finally decided by our electing as captain the stoker who was steering, and by all agreeing to obey his orders.

"He set to work at once to get into touch with the other boats, call on upon them and get word of

27	
698	1,293
	900
	2,193
Known survivors	868
Missing	1,325

Some famous people figure in the list of survivors; many more—among them Colonel Astor, the multimillionaire, and Mr. W. T. Stead, the brilliant journalist—are among the missing

HOPE ABANDONED.

Unsuccessful Search for Survivors.

(From Our Own Correspondent.)

NEW YORK, Tuesday Night.

Gradually the story of the Titanic disaster is being pieced together, but not a word has been received direct from the survivors, of whom there are between 800 and 870 on board the Car

"23 KNOTS THE SPEED,"

THOUGH NEARNESS TO ICEBERGS KNOWN.

WHY BULKHEADS WERE INEFFECTIVE

NEW YORK, Friday.

The "New York World" publishes a complete story of the disaster written by a staff correspondent, Carlos F. Hurd, who chanced to be a passenger on board the Carpathia. Mr. Hurd writes as follows:—

"The facts which I have established by inquiries on the Carpathia positively as they could be established in view of the silence of the few surviving officers are that the Titanic's officers knew several hours before the crash of the possible nearness of icebergs; that the Titanic's speed was nearly 23 knots; that speed was not slackened; that the accommodation of the lifeboats of the Titanic was not sufficient to accommodate much more than one-third of the passengers, to say nothing of the crew.

"The bulkhead system, though it was

repetition of the Titanic's last cry of distress given forth by John Geo. Phillips, the young English wireless operator, who doubtless died at his post. He kept stabbing his signal until the ocean lanes were full of vessels babbling to the distressed liner.

"Help! Help! Hurry! Hurry!" was calling two hours, the Virginian catching his last blurred cry at 12.17

SUCKED DOWN WITH THE LINER.

Marvellous Escape of the Last Man Saved.

NEW YORK, April 19.

Of all the recitals of personal adventure in the Titanic disaster that of Colonel Gracie, of the United States Army, who jumped from the topmost deck of the Titanic when she sank and was sucked down with her, is the most extraordinary. He was the sole survivor after the wave that swept the liner just before the final plunge. Colonel Gracie, on reaching the surface again, swam until he found a cork and canvas raft, and then helped to rescue others. He gives the exact time of the sinking of the Titanic at 2.22 a.m., which was the hour at which his watch was stopped by his leap into the sea.

"After sinking with the ship," he said, "it appeared to me as if I was propelled by some great force through the water. I struck out with all my strength for the surface. I got to the air again after a time, which seemed to me to be unending. There was nothing in sight save the boat dotted with ice and strewn with large masses of — for age. Dying men and were  when the ship sank flattered to show whether it was lack of time or some other natural or material difficulty in the way of meeting such an emergency that sent two-thirds of the Titanic's human freight to the fathomless depths.

"But it more quently shown by the proportion of women to men among the survivors, only 79 men so far having been reported as aboard the Carpathia out of a total of 248 souls whose names are as yet to hand. The wireless messages have told how in the darkness their crews had to guide the boats with the greatest caution to prevent their being jammed by the ice or overturned by the swirling flow, or that heated heavily laden craft became widely separated from each other.

"There followed hours of heart-breaking anguish before daylight came and the first faint tones of the searching Carpathia's siren came and then the dense fog.

"Even then their anxiety was not at an end, for the Carpathia proceeded cautiously, sounding her fog-whistle almost continuously, until one after another she picked up the scattered lifeboats.

"No other ship was in the neighbourhood of the disaster, and

THE LORD MAYOR'S FUND.

OVER £40,000 LAST NIGHT.

NOBLE RESPONSE BY CITY FIRMS.

The Lord Mayor's Fund at the Mansion House for the relief of the Titanic sufferers amounted up to last night to over £40,000. Amongst the contributors were:—

H.R.H. Princess Louise (Duchess of Argyll)	£100
Lord Michelham	1,050
Members of the Baltic	846
Mr. W. A. Horn	525
Messrs. Willis and Faber	500
Swiss Bankverein	500
Canadian Pacific Railway	500
Messrs. Robert Fleming and Co.	500
Messrs. B. Nivison and Co.	500
Mr. Walter Morrison	250
Sir Ernest Cassel	262 10
Messrs. F. Ruth and Co.	250
Messrs. Balli Bros.	250
Messrs. Fruhling and Goschen	250
Mr. Jas. Buchanan	250
Messrs. J. Buchanan & Co. (Ltd.)	250
Messrs. Bessler, Waechter, and Co. (Ltd.)	250
The Alliance Assurance Co. (Ltd.)	250
Messrs. Myers and Robertson	250
The Hon. W. F. D. Smith	250
Sir Julius Werther	250
London and South Western Bank	250
	210

some 500 souls have been saved? The Titanic only in an evening contemporary last night that there were sufficient boats for twice the number of passengers carried. This, unfortunately, is not the case. There were, it is stated, in all sixteen boats—fourteen lifeboats and two cutters, which carry some 500 souls; but sixteen boats would account for those saved from the wreck. In addition, the Titanic was provided with the usual collapsible rafts and minor means of life-saving. Of the value of these I shall know more when the full facts are to hand.

"Perhaps the saddest thing about this inexpressibly tragic catastrophe is that though the Titanic had only sixteen lifeboats, the gear with which she was fitted provided for forty-eight, or three times as many as she carried. There is no suggestion that the company failed to comply with the regulations of the Board of Trade; indeed, they did more than the Board of Trade demands. The Board of Trade requires that vessels of 10,000 tons and upwards must have sufficient lifeboats with a cubic capacity of 5,500. The Titanic registered 45,000 tons, and, under the regulation sixteen lifeboats. At the same time, the company, as it was not bound to do, increased the cubic capacity of the boats from 5,500 required, carried the regulation sixteen lifeboats. On 21st November last Mr. Bottomley asked a question of the Pre

The *Titanic* disaster has come down in history as a drama, epic in scale and almost classical in development. Even its name was borrowed from mythology, and its fate contained all the classic elements of formal Greek tragedy: the godlike assumptions of mortals, the blind disregard of omens, the nemesis in mid-Atlantic, the chorus of woe and recriminations, the expiation of death and heroism. But this cocoon of romance woven round the event by later generations disguises what was basically a story of sheer folly and, sometimes, selfishness. The legend of the millionaire's wife who chose to die with her husband lives on, eclipsing the memory of the steerage passengers who were locked below to prevent them scrambling for the boat deck. Posterity (rightly) remembers the ship's orchestra gamely playing 'Nearer My God To Thee' as the liner sunk beneath the waves. How many recall the half-empty lifeboats which refused to turn back to pick up drowning passengers?

There was every reason for Britain to be proud of the *Titanic* when she sailed out of Southampton on 10 April 1912, on her maiden voyage to New York. Nearly 900 feet long and weighing 66,000 tons, she was divided into sixteen watertight compartments—a much-vaunted feature of her revolutionary design that inspired many people, the Press included, to pronounce her unsinkable. In her public rooms no expense had been spared, a restaurant in the style of Louis XVI, a Parisian boulevard cafe, Jacobean reception room, squash court, swimming pool, Turkish bath. Coal fires burned in the first-class suites which at £870 a passage were strictly for American millionaires. Even the third-class, since no transatlantic shipping line could hope to stay in business without the swelling flood of immigrants to the New World, had its smoking-room and lounge. In all, 2,603 people could be conveyed across the ocean at best in unimagined luxury, at least in unprecedented comfort.

On 10 April the *Titanic* was sailing just over half-full, with 1,316 passengers—which was in retrospect a blessing since her sixteen lifeboats could accommodate only 1,178 (and even that was considerably in excess of the British Board of Trade requirements). Still, who believed they were more than a formality? Or who questioned the absence of a boat-drill?

For four days the liner ploughed peacefully through the Atlantic, a glittering round of cocktail parties, tea-dances and full-dress dinners. On Sunday 14 April, when the ship's powerful transmitter established contact with Cape Race, passengers began to avail themselves of the still-fresh novelty of sending messages to friends on shore telling them their estimated time of arrival. It was a busy day for the Marconi operators, Phillips and Bride, in the radio room for reports from other ships were also coming in, from the *Caronia*, the *Baltic* and others, warning of ice-floes in the area. It was unusual, though not unheard-of, for the ice to be so far south at that time of the year. But Captain Smith and all his senior officers had had years of experience with icebergs: they did what they had always done—continued to run at full speed and kept their eyes skinned. You could spot a berg normally at three to four miles; even at night the reflected light off the ice made it visible, and with a good swell there were always small breakers to warn you.

But that Sunday night, alas, was abnormal. The elements conspired to mock the seafarers' lore: the ocean was calmer than a mill-pond, the moon-less sky was midnight black. And the iceberg when it loomed 500 yards ahead was the dreaded 'black iceberg' (that is, one that

Daily Graphic 20 April 1912

had recently capsized, its exposed underpart not yet turned white). The *Titanic* bulldozed into it at 22 knots, tearing a 300-foot wound in her hull. The passengers, those who even felt the slight shudder, thought no more of it: but Captain Smith, observing the water broaching first one, then two, three, four and the fatal fifth watertight compartment, knew within minutes his ship was doomed.

It was 11.40pm. A few minutes after midnight the Captain instructed Phillips to call for assistance. A few more minutes, the boat now listing noticeably to starboard, and the captain reappeared in the radio room. 'What are you sending', he asked. 'CQD' (the international call for assistance) answered Phillips. 'Try SOS' suggested Bride. 'It's the new call, and it may be your last chance to send it.' They all laughed, but it was the only time that night. Phillips's signals were heard incredulously by a dozen ships over a radius of several hundred miles, then as the awful truth was confirmed they turned about and headed for 41.46N, 50.14W. On the Newfoundland coast the Marconi station at Cape Race heard them too, passed the stunning news on to Cape Ray, whence it reached the White Star office in New York and shortly afterwards *Associated Press*.

At 1.00 in the morning (New York time) the bombshell dropped on the newspaper offices, first that the *Titanic* had hit an iceberg, soon after, that it was sinking by the head. Then the messages ceased. Most New York papers categorically refused to believe the report that she was going down, which appeared to them in blatant contradiction of all that was known about the liner's unsinkability. They reassured themselves that the lines of communication had been tenuous and confused, and played safe by printing only the collision story. Only the *New York Times* had the nerve to draw the inevitable conclusion from the *Titanic*'s radio silence: its final edition informed the world that the unsinkable *had* sunk. It was a courageous stroke, based on no more evidence than was available to the rest of the Press. The *New York Sun*, after all, had flatly refuted such a proposition. Nor when day came was there any further enlightenment—the White Star Line doggedly denied that the pride of its fleet could sink, and the babel of wireless messages that crackled out of the air all morning appeared, on balance, to justify its view.

One report stated that the *Carpathia* was standing by the stricken liner to render any necessary assistance. Another that the *Titanic* was being towed in to Halifax. Yet another—which found its way into the *Evening Star*'s front-page headline—that 'All Saved from Titanic After Collision.' In London, too, chaos reigned as Fleet Street on the 16th printed every rumour and counter-rumour indiscriminately. Front pages that morning were masterpieces of utter confusion: yes, the *Titanic* was sinking—though yes, it was unsinkable: all passengers were reported safe, but then so was a great loss of life. The *Daily Herald* was not alone in giving prominence to a mysterious telegram received by Phillips's parents in Godalming, to the effect that the liner was under tow. 'Practically unsinkable. Don't Worry' ran this unexplained message of filial affection.

By lunchtime in New York, White Star had admitted their boat had gone down. By teatime they were prepared to concede that many had perished. At long last some firm news, desperate though it was, was coming in: from the *Carpathia* was flashed the tidings that she had picked up some 800 survivors from the lifeboats, and from the *Virginian* that she had arrived too late. Finally the Press, like *The Star* was forced to acknowledge that 'another human illusion has proved to be in vain.'

Soon it became clear that only the *Carpathia* had managed to pick up survivors, and that any account of the tragedy must be obtained from that ship which was heading for New York. In

LONDON,
APRIL 16, 1912.
STOP-PRESS NEWS.

TITANIC SINKS.

New York, Monday, April 15. The Titanic sank at 2.20 this morning.

No lives were lost.—Reuter.

MANY LIVES LOST.

New York, Monday, April 15 The White Star officials now admit that many lives have been lost. —Reuter.

675 SURVIVORS.

New York, Monday, April 15 (8.45 p.m.) The following despatch has been rereceived from Cape Race:—

The steamer Olympic reports that the steamer Carpathia reached the Titanic's position at daybreak, but found boats and wreckage only.

She reported that the Titanic foundered about 2.20 a.m. in Lat. 41., Deg. 16 mins., Long 50, Deg. 14 mins. The message adds:—

All the Titanic's boats are accounted for. About 675 souls have been saved of the crew and passengers. The latter are nearly all women and children.

The Leyland liner California is remaining and searching the vicinity of the disaster. The Carpathia is returning to New York with the survivors.

OFFICIAL STATEMENT.

New York, Monday, April 15. 8.20 p.m.

The following statement has been given out by the White Star officials:—

"Captain Haddock, of the Olympic, sends a wireless message that the Titanic sank at 2.20 a.m. Monday, after all the passengers and crew had been lowered into lifeboats and transferred to the Virginian.

"The steamer Carpathia, with several hundred passengers from the Titanic, is now on her way to New York."—Reuter.

"GO AHEAD."

"Express" Correspondent.

Montreal, Monday, April 15. The first news of the disaster to the Titanic was received in Montreal.

It came in a wireless message to the Allan Line headquarters from Captain Gamble, of the Virginian, bound from Halifax with the English mails, stating that he had received a distress appeal from the Titanic, announcing that she had been in collision with an iceberg.

"Am going to her assistance," added Captain Gamble. "Go ahead," replied the Allan Line.

The last message received here states that the Virginian has the Titanic in tow, and is attempting to reach Halifax.

Daily Express

APRIL 22, 1912.

"ALL SAFE ON THE TITANIC!"

EXPLANATION OF THE FALSE MESSAGES BY WIRELESS.

MYSTERY SOLVED.

VITAL QUERY LOST BY TAPPERS.

"TANKS" INTERPRETED AS "TITANIC."

TIME PROBLEM.

The mystery of the wireless messages which led the world to hope that the accident to the Titanic was not so disastrous as it proved to be was cleared up by Captain Haddock, of the Olympic, at Southampton yesterday, in a statement made to a special representative of the "Express."

He declared that at 10.23 .... Mon....

Daily Express

the event, that proved bewilderingly difficult. Under a hail of Press inquiries the *Carpathia*'s wireless operator reluctantly confirmed that the millionaire John Jacob Astor (who had been returning from a honeymoon in Europe) was not among the saved; then he announced he would provide a list of survivors—which he did with infuriating laboriousness—but that was all. The story of the decade would have to wait until the ship docked, on the 18th.

Meanwhile the newspapers were free to indulge their wildest speculations, based on the ever-lengthening list of casualties. Millionaires Guggenheim, Widener and Straus were missing. So was the President's military aide, Major Butt; the painter Francis Millet, and the old crusading journalist, W. T. Stead, once editor of the *Pall Mall Gazette*. Indignantly it was noted that the President of White Star, Bruce Ismay, had contrived to get himself saved. 'So long as there was a soul that could be saved' opined the *Evening Post*, 'the obligation lay upon Mr. Ismay that that one person and not he should have been in the boat.' Other papers expressed their disgust in far less gentlemanly terms, notably Randolph Hearst's *New York American* which also (foreshadowing its proprietor's declared preference for Germany in the coming conflict) had some harsh abuse to pour upon British ships and seamanship.

Tens of thousands packed the dockside when the *Carpathia* berthed in New York on the evening of the 18th, but once again in the scramble for 'exclusives' the resourceful *New York Times* (with the aid of Signor Marconi himself) scooped the pool by signing up the one surviving wireless operator, Bride. The next morning the public read of those last pathetic minutes before the transmitter went dead, of Phillips in his lifejacket tapping away to the end, and of the unscrupulous seaman who attempted to steal that life-jacket: 'The man was slipping the belt off Phillips's back. I remembered in a flash how I had to fix that life belt in place because he was too busy to do it . . . I suddenly felt a passion not to let that man die a decent sailor's death. I wished he might have stretched rope or walked a plank. I did my duty. I hope I finished him. I don't know. We left him on the cabin floor and he was not moving . . .'

Some passengers, like schoolmaster Laurence Beesley, had already prepared their narratives on the journey back in the *Carpathia*. Here is how his account of the *Titanic*'s last moments appeared in the *Daily News*. 'She slowly tilted straight on end, with the stern vertically upwards. As she did so the lights in the cabins which had not flickered for a moment since we left, died out, flashed once more, then went out altogether . . . It was certainly for some minutes that we watched at least 150 feet of the *Titanic* towering up above the level of the sea, looming black against the sky. Then, with a quiet slanting dive, she disappeared beneath the waters. Then there fell on our ears the most appalling noise that human being ever heard—the cries of hundreds of our fellow beings struggling in the icy water, crying for help with a cry that we knew could not be answered.'

Other nuggets were mined by other papers, both factual and fanciful: how Benjamin Guggenheim and his valet had re-appeared on deck in full evening dress, to meet their end suitably attired: how frantic passengers had fought their way into lifeboats with guns, threatening to shoot anyone who stood in their way: how Captain Smith had last been seen rescuing a baby then was dragged down into the deep. One survivor, a Colonel Gracie, recounted how thirty of them had swum to an upturned raft which had begun to sink beneath their weight, and as others had been turned away from the raft they had cried out "Good luck! God bless you!"' *The World*, which had chanced to have a staff correspondent aboard the *Carpathia* as a passenger, made much of his account of how 'a rush of steerage men towards the boats was checked by the officers with revolvers in their hands.' *Reuters* were clearly less than happy about reports of an officer of the bridge shooting himself in shame: 'If anyone committed suicide—which is still doubtful' the agency declared, 'it is agreed that it was probably Mr Murdoch (First Officer) and not Captain Smith.'

The depths of the disaster were now apparent, 1,503 out of 2,201 aboard the *Titanic* had gone down with her. Worse still, it was clear that there had been a shameful class discrimination against third-class passengers. Whereas only four women and children in the first-class had failed to make the lifeboats (and three of those by choice) over a hundred—or half—of the third-class women and children had died. This discrimination, unhappily, was extended to the boards of inquiry that were set up both in America and Britain: few third-class survivors were even called to the hearings. The whole American Inquiry, indeed, had the British Press hopping mad—in particular its chairman Senator Smith whose lack of nautical knowledge proved spectacular. 'While Mr Smith puts his farcical questions, and flashlights are flared that photographers may get pictures of the witnesses, while outside the American Press retails the latest lie, the latest slander about British seamen, honest Americans will feel shame that not merely the White Star Line, but American civilization itself is on trial' growled the *Morning Post*. The American papers responded later by castigating the British Inquiry as a 'whitewash'.

Some good came out of the accusations and counter-accusations. The antedeluvian Board of Trade regulations were speedily changed, so that ever since all ships have carried sufficient lifeboats for all aboard. And the 'accepted' practice of steering full tilt through icefields (to save company time and coal) was finally exposed for the dangerous habit it was. But one puzzle neither inquiry ever got to the bottom of: a mysterious boat had been seen by numerous *Titanic* survivors on the skyline at the time of the tragedy. That boat never moved to their aid, nor was it ever satisfactorily identified. In an interview with the *Boston American* (for which he was paid $500) a seaman from the SS *Californian* claimed that she had been laid up in loose ice within sight of the stricken liner, and that his captain and officers had even seen the *Titanic*'s distress rockets. The captain, Stanley Lord, admitted hearing of rockets from members of the watch but denied to his dying day that the *Californian* was remotely within sight, or even reach, of the *Titanic* that fateful night.

THE SCENE ROUND THE FATEFUL BOARD AT SOUTHAMPTON.

The board erected by the White Star Company outside their Southampton offices was watched all day yesterday by the crowd of grief stricken wives and other relatives of the Titanic's crew. One list of members of the crew known to be on the Carpathia was posted, but it only contained about half a dozen names.

285

The Death of a Valley

Senghenydd Mine Disaster 1913

LLOYD'S WEEKLY NEWS.   OCT. 19, 1913.

THE APPALLING PIT DISASTER IN SOUTH WALES.

General view of the Universal Colliery, Senghenydd, including the shafts of the York and Lancaster Pits.

ERNEST
COFFIN
SENGHENYDD
OCT. 15. 1.30 A.M.

"Lloyd's News" special artist watched the rescuers carrying away the eighteen miners found alive on Wednesday morning. "Who is that?" was the cry as each stretcher was gently carried past the sorrowing crowd. He depicts the scene at the pit-brow in the gloom shortly after midnight.

Anxious wives with their children waiting patiently for news of their entombed husbands. The agony and suspense were terrible, yet they waited from dawn till sunset, and from sunset until morning, hoping to the last.

WESTERN MAIL. OCTOBER 16. 1913.

NO HOPE FOR MEN BELOW.

FEARED DEATH-ROLL OF 422 AT SENGHENYDD.

DANGEROUS RESCUE OPERATIONS.

WESTERN MAIL. OCTOBER 18. 1913.

MORE DEAD BODIES REACHED

THE SENGHENYDD PIT FIRE MASTERED.

A FALL FORTY YARDS IN LENGTH.

APPALLING TRIALS OF PARTIES IN BURNING AREA.

HEAT WHICH NEARLY DROVE THEM BACK

MORE ROYAL SUBSCRIPTIONS TO RELIEF FUNDS.

'I have been present at many a colliery disaster in the North of England and South Wales' the *Lloyd's News* correspondent began his report. 'I have seen strong men perish in desperate rescue work; women overwhelmed with grief as the breadwinners of their humble homes were carried one after another with affecting solemnity from the pit shaft and laid for identification, shockingly charred and mutilated. But of all scenes of appalling tragedy witnessed by journalists the disaster at the Universal Colliery, Senghenydd, is the most terrible.' Somewhere beneath the self-conscious melodrama of that reporter's prose, there is a ring of hardbitten realism. Each new pit disaster always seems to be an echo of the last: the visible images are frighteningly familiar—the anxious, stoic crowd at the pithead, the blackened and haggard faces of returning rescue parties, the ebbing-away of hope.

Wales, as he said, had long lived with crippling calamity. Many a miner still recalled the agonies of Ebbw Vale, Penygraig, Abersychan, Bridgend, and Pontypridd within their own lifetime—five tragedies that had claimed almost a thousand of their colleagues between them: five among countless others. Senghenydd, a characteristically grimy mining village in the otherwise green and beautiful Vale of Aber, had known the long hours of despair too: in 1901 an underground explosion had entombed eighty-two of its men, and only one had been got out alive. Most mining families, early on a Tuesday morning 14 October 1913, knew instinctively what had happened when a muffled roar from the pitshaft shook their houses to the foundations. The dense pall of black smoke and the scene of desolation at the shaft confirmed their worst fears.

Nine hundred men were down the mine when the explosion occurred—the day shift had started two hours earlier. For the women crowding nervously around the wreckage there was no way of knowing how many—if any—of them had survived: the pit-cage had been hurled high into the air, the shaft itself was a mass of smoking rubble. The only conceivable access to the devastated tunnels was through the adjoining York pithead, and there volunteers from neighbouring valleys queued silently waiting their turn to descend into the inferno. The pitiful condition of rescue teams returning to the surface testified to the deadly state of the workings below: some were fainting or blinded, others were quite unconscious. The main galleries were blocked in one part by an uncontrollable fire whose heat alone defied all efforts to get near it: in another section huge falls made progress impossible—and everywhere lurked the imminent danger of lethal gas fumes.

Seemingly oblivious to the heat scorching their hands and faces, rescuers hacked away desperately at obstructions throughout the day. Their reward came on the east side of the main tunnel, where 500 of the trapped men had assembled in the darkness. Many were terribly burned, and others collapsed and died on reaching the surface, but this first breakthrough raised high hopes that the same miracle had happened on the west side.

But who could know? In one gallery that had offered some hope of a way through, a canary (the miner's trusty gas-detector) had suddenly expired—warning the rescuers to flee for their lives. Experts believed there might be an 'air bridge' somewhere along the main gallery: it was at all events the men's only hope of survival, and a straw of comfort for those on vigil up above. At one o'clock on the Wednesday morning, came another gleam of hope when a small party of twenty-one men were discovered alive, but barely, on the Pretoria level (built during the Boer war the Universal mine was liberally endowed with reminders of South Africa).

It was, as it happened, the last triumph of the rescue operations. Now already scores of dead were being hauled to the surface—some had been found overcome by the fumes within a few yards of fresh air. Throughout Wednesday and into Thursday the fire raged unabated, surrendering only a few mean feet at a time and often threatening to burst into fresh areas. It burnt still on Friday, when all hope for more than 300 men still unaccounted for was abandoned (except by incurable optimists like Keir Hardie, who descended the pit and pronounced that all was not yet lost).

The pithead nevertheless continued to buzz with rumour and counter-rumour, all meticulously catalogued by the army of reporters encamped there. 'Voices' and 'knocking' in distant recesses of the mine were reported one day, only to be denied the next. The ghostly figure of a beckoning miner, allegedly witnessed by several rescuers, made a brief appearance in the columns of some papers. But, in truth, by the end of the week little remained for the papers but to count the cost of the wholesale destruction: over half Senghenydd's brass band, famed at the Crystal Palace for its excellence, was gone and from one Chapel, the entire male congregation. One poor woman was bereft of her whole household at a stroke—her husband, four sons, two brothers and a brother-in-law. The dignity of the mourners profoundly impressed newsmen, as much as the behaviour of the 'vulgarly curious' disgusted them. 'A well-dressed young bounder on a motor-bicycle' wrote one of them, 'went racketing past one funeral procession, making no pretence even to cover his head, and tooting his motor-horn as though to bid the dead move aside.' Nor, apparently did the reporter's tolerance extend to forms of communication less hallowed than his own: 'As the dead bodies were brought up from the pit . . . they were met first by the vicar of Abertridwr, and next by the cinematograph operator openly grinding the handle of his machine. Such is modernity!'

A final total of 439 miners died at Senghenydd. It was—and remains to this day—the worst mine disaster in British history. There followed, inevitably, a prolonged debate in the press, revolving for the most part on whether the extraordinary death-roll need have been so high—if (as the Court of Inquiry suggested) the water-supply had not been less than adequate, or if (as a local member of Parliament complained) there had not been fifteen hours' hesitation in sending rescuers down a suspect shaft that had proved in the event to be quite safe. The consensus of opinion was that the explosion had been caused by an electrical spark from some signalling equipment. If that was so—and there was no-one alive to confirm or deny it—it was a needless and tragic waste of life: warnings of such a contingency had been widely circulated, following an explosion in a neighbouring mine just the year before from precisely the same cause.

PICTURES OF YESTERDAY'S APPALLING COLLIERY DISASTER AT SENGHENYDD.

GENERAL VIEW OF THE COLLIERY WHERE THE DISASTER OCCURRED.   [Western Mail photo.

CROWD AT THE PIT-HEAD WAITING ANXIOUSLY FOR NEWS.   [Western Mail photo.

A NEARER VIEW OF THE SHATTERED PIT-HEAD.   [W. T. P.

RESCUE WORKERS FROM THE BURNING MINE.   [W. T. P.

THE PIT-SHAFT UNDER WHICH THE EXPLOSION OCCURRED, SHOWING THE BROKEN ROOF.
[Western Mail photo.

The man Waldron, who was talking to the banksman when the explosion occurred. The banksman was instantly killed; Waldron escaped.   [Marion.

TESTING THE AMBULANCE TO BE USED FOR CONVEYANCE OF THE WOUNDED.   [Western Mail photo.

BRINGING UP THE BODIES.   [Western Mail photo.

Fog of Misunderstanding

The Sinking of the Empress of Ireland 1914

If there was one lesson Canadian Pacific had taken to heart after the dire tragedy of the *Titanic* two years before, it was to ensure that all *their* splendid fleet of liners carried enough lifeboats for everyone aboard, crew and passengers. Fate, unfortunately, is no respecter of company regulations. The *Titanic* proved you cannot make a ship unsinkable: the terrible loss of the *Empress of Ireland*, pride of the Canadian Pacific Line, showed equally you cannot make human beings infallible either, no matter how many lifeboats there are aboard.

Since many of the facts of the disaster were bitterly disputed after the event, it is best to start with those that were not. In the early hours of Friday 29 May 1914, in the middle of the St Lawrence, the *Empress of Ireland*, Liverpool-bound from Quebec, was rammed by the Norwegian collier *Storstad* approximately amidships. It was extremely foggy. Into the gash left by the collision the water rushed in— and then through the open watertight doors— with such speed that the liner developed an immediate list and had sunk within twenty minutes. Most of the 1,050 passengers and many of the crew of 400 were still asleep. There was barely time for them to escape from their cabins, let alone launch any of the lifeboats: 1,011 were drowned.

So much for the bare and incontestable facts. The controversy revolved around the utterly conflicting versions of the two captains, concerning the circumstances preceding and immediately following the collision. Captain Kendall of the *Empress* claimed that his ship lay 'dead in the water' at the moment of impact since his engines had been running full speed astern for several minutes. The *Storstad*, he

went on, had been going ahead too fast for the weather conditions, but what was worse, instead of obeying his injunction not to back out after the collision (so that the hole could have remained 'plugged') the collier had immediately reversed engines and disappeared. On the *Storstad* Captain Andersen's account maintained that the *Empress* was still moving when the ships met, and that the movement of the larger vessel had swung him round making disengagement unavoidable. Far from going too fast, he added, the *Storstad*'s headway had been almost checked at the moment of the crash.

That was not the impression formed by the newspapers after a few investigations among the crew of the *Storstad*. In spite of stern injunctions not to talk of the disaster, the third officer admitted the engines had been reversed *after* the impact. And another officer later confessed to putting the helm hard aport just before the collision—in flagrant breach of the rules about changing course in fog. Faced with an almost hopeless case at the Inquiry on 16 June, the *Storstad*'s counsel, attempted to prove that the *Empress of Ireland*'s steering had been faulty and that three hours before the disaster she had nearly run down another ship. But the Court would have none of it. Captain Andersen was held solely to blame.

The news of the disaster, both in Canada and Britain, revived painfully familiar memories. As with the *Titanic* newspapers rushed out special editions for an insatiable public haunting the news-stands— the *Quebec Daily Telegraph* published all through the day and well into the night. In London the first reports were as confused and misleading as on that previous fateful day: the *Empress* had hit an iceberg, was

Reuters' earliest information, then it had collided with a steamer called the *Hanover* which had also sunk. As more reliable cables arrived the capital was stunned by the depth of the tragedy. Survivors spoke of frenzied struggles up almost vertical passageways in the minutes before the *Empress* sunk, of drowning people carried off into the fog, of crashing funnels and exploding boilers. The body of Laurence Irving, identifiable only from his signet ring, was washed up the next day—his clutched hand still held part of his wife's clothing. The body of the well-known big-game hunter, Sir Henry Seton-Karr, was unrecognisable. Out of 176 Salvation Army delegates who had set out in the *Empress*, to attend a convention in England, only twenty-two were left alive. One woman was discovered wandering, naked and incoherent, on the shore near Rimouski three days after the tragedy: her long ordeal, floating on a piece of wreckage, had driven her out of her mind.

A small monument on the bank of the St Lawrence marking where some of the victims were buried, is the only visible reminder of the tragedy. The great liner herself still lies embedded in the mud some fifteen fathoms down, having defied all efforts to discover why she sank so quickly after her holing. One contributory factor —that the *Storstad*'s ice-strengthened bows were vertical, thus piercing the *Empress* below the waterline—was universally recognized and in due course led to the more general acceptance of overhanging bows.

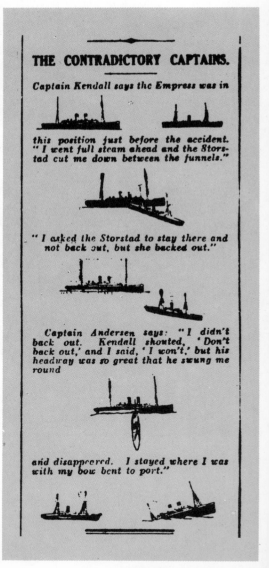

ADVERTISING-ISMS.

The declared policy of a business man or of a firm has a far wider acceptance when set forth by sensible studied advertising.

The Montreal Daily Star.

CIRCULATION OF THE STAR
Last Week's Daily.. 537,180
Last Week's Weekly 132,992
Total.. 670,172

VOL. XLVI., NO. 126 | The Weather: FINE; WARM. | MONTREAL, FRIDAY, MAY 29, 1914. | PRICE ONE CENT.

Of 350 Survivors from Empress 12 Were Women. Over 1000 Lost

Twenty-two of Those Rescued Died after Reaching Shore -- Collier Rammed Big Empress of Ireland while latter was stopped in Dense Fog. She Sank in 10 Minutes.

Lady Evelyn and Eureka Rushed to Scene, Latter Reaching Location of Collision 25 minutes after it occurred--Captain Kendall Saved from wreckage. Latest Details of Catastrophe.

DIAGRAM SHOWING WHERE THE COLLISION OCCURRED AND THE LOST EMPRESS OF IRELAND

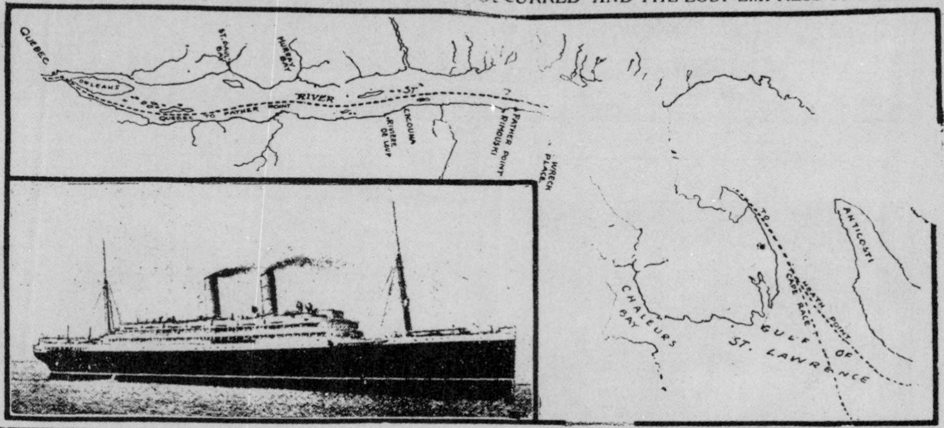

Special to The Montreal Star.

Rimouski, May 29.—Of the 350 survivors of the Empress of Ireland who were landed here this morning, 22 have since died from injuries and shocking exposure.

Of the 350, only 12 were women.

"The Storstad is proceeding slowly towards Quebec. She took a pilot on board at Father Point. Her bows are low down in the water, and she is in a very damaged condition.

"The C. G. S. Eureka was the first steamer to reach the scene of the accident, the Lady Evelyn arriving shortly afterwards. Both steamers rendered great assistance."

Father Point Despatch Reports 337 People Saved in All—Many Bodies Are Recovered.

Special Marconigram to The Montreal Star.

Father Point, Que., May 29.—The Empress sank ten minutes after her collision with the collier Storstad and immediately after she had Marconied out the "Save our ship." Mr. White, the Marconi telegrapher here, instantly notified all the Government steamers in view, and the Eureka, Captain Belanger, was the first to get away, she having her steam up. She must have reached the scene about forty-five minutes after the disaster.

The Lady Evelyn had to get up steam, and also rushed to assist.

When daylight broke, I saw on the grey horizon, with the aid of a telescope, a collier, the two Government steamers and nine lifeboats all around the same spot.

Shortly after the Eureka came by with 32 survivors and several bodies. Later, the Lady Evelyn, with Captain Kendall and more; and later still, the Storstad, with a few more and some bodies. All were landed at the Rimouski Wharf, to which place the scene has now been shifted. About 337 were saved in all. I cannot possibly cope with all queries received from all parts of the world.

"(Signed), J. McWILLIAMS, Operator.

Marconi Operator Tells Story of Sinking Of Liner in Brief Despatch This Morning

Rimouski, Que., May 29.—The Marconi Company's operator here supplies the following account of the sinking of the steamer Empress of Ireland in the early hours of this morning, after a collision with the Norwegian collier Storstad, in which it is believed one thousand lives were lost, three hundred and fifty passengers being saved:—

"The Empress of Ireland was rammed this morning at 1.45 by the Storstad, twenty miles out from Father Point. The Empress sank within ten minutes.

"The S.O.S. signal sent out was received at Father Point, and the Government steamers Eureka and Lady Evelyn were despatched to the distressed vessel's assistance. The Empress of Ireland listed and was unable to get most of the boats out.

"Captain Kendall was saved, being picked up on some wreckage by No. 3 lifeboat fully thirty minutes after his ship had foundered.

"Both wireless operators, assistant pursers, chief engineer and chief steward were saved. Chief officer and purser are amongst the missing."

The Captain was found on the wreckage by lifeboat No. 3 after the ship foundered.

E. Hayes, Assistant Purser, is also saved.

The SS. Empress of Ireland left Quebec yesterday afternoon with nine hundred and ninety passengers and a crew of 432 officers and men on board, bound for Liverpool.

The scene immediately after the collision baffles description. The shrieks of passengers rudely awakened from their slumbers, the hoarse cries of the captain and officers, and the wailing of women, mingled with the rushing of the waters of the Gulf.

There was hardly any time in which to launch boats. Only the most meagre details are available at this hour. Four hundred and twenty passengers are believed to have been saved, but it is feared that all the remaining 1,002 have found a grave in the murky waters of the Gulf.

The S.O.S. signal was sent out by the wireless operator of the Empress at once, and reached the Government steamers, Lady Evelyn and the Eureka, which were at the wharf at this place. They immediately steamed full speed to the scene of the disaster.

The Empress of Ireland was in command of Lieut. Kendall, R.N.R., who commanded the Montrose when Crippen was captured. He is among those saved. Other officers of the ill-fated liner were: M. R. Steede, Chief Engineer; W. Sampson, Chief Engineer; A. B. McDonald, R.N.R., Purser; J. F. Grant, M.D., Surgeon; A. W. Gaade, Chief Steward.

The Norwegian steamer collier Storstad passed inward at 6.40 A.M., with her bow badly driven in, but is proceeding slowly to Quebec under her own steam.

CITY STUNNED BY NEWS OF DISASTER; ANXIOUS ENQUIRIES ARE MADE

Only one official statement was issued by the C.P.R. until 1.30 to-day. This was the wire from Captain Kendall announcing the collision, and stating that the ship had gone. There was a meagre list of some of those who had been saved, but this referred mostly to members of the crew. Another list was expected momentarily.

The official statement is as follows:—

"Empress of Ireland was stopped off Father Point in the fog. She was struck amidships by the collier Storstad. Ship gone."

"(Signed) CAPT. KENDALL, R.N.R."

The first news of the disaster reached Montreal at about 3 a.m. this morning, and Capt. Walsh, who had gone home on the previous day, suffering from ptomaine poisoning, was telephoned for and, despite his condition, lost no time in getting down to the office to arrange for the prompt receipt of reliable information from Father Point. There is only one operator at Father Point, Mr. McWilliams, of the I.C.R., who is also the agent for the C.P.R. He it was who sent the first tidings to Montreal.

The C. P. R. offices were early the centre of a small knot of people who tried to secure assurances where there could be at that early hour, nothing but doubt. There was nothing to do but wait, and so the little group, with faces already showing the marks of anxiety, talked in whispers and felt the hours tugging as they crept by.

At the Passenger Department office in the Dominion Express Building, also, there were many, many enquiries, and the answer always came, as the worried enquirer asked if such a person were saved, that as yet "nothing definite" could be given out.

As the morning wore on Geo. Ham, Mr. Foster, Mr. Gibbon, Mr. Annabel, and others of the chief officials of the C.P.R., got into consultation.

At 5.30 this morning a special train left for Rimouski to be on hand for the use of the passengers.

Anxious inquirers at the C. P. R. offices this morning were: C. F. Gaunt, whose daughter, Miss Gaunt, was on board the Empress; A. C. Johnston, of Mappin and Webb, St. Catherine street, one of whose directors, A. G. Maginnis, with Mr. and Mrs. Adie, the former a Birmingham manufacturer.

Both Mr. Gaunt and Mr. Johnston arranged to leave for Quebec by special train to-day, where they should arrive at least an hour or two in advance of the first contingent saved from the wreck who are not expected to reach Quebec until 8 or 8.30 this evening.

FAMILIES ON BOARD.

The first inquirers for survivors this morning were David Jacks and Albert Parrish, who were returning

(Continued on Page Three.)

THE SURVIVORS

The following list was issued by the C.P.R. this afternoon as that of the names of persons known to be saved:

B.

Blyth, Miss.
Boile, R.
Bantala.
Brown, Wm.
Burt, C. L.
Byrne, John.
Backford, Miss
Brennan, R.
Burouse, W. T.
Banfort, Marconi Operator.

C

Camepe.
Court, Miss.
Copplin, George.
Colbaeba, A.
Coombes, C., pantryman.
Clandon.
Clark, Charles.

D.

Davis, W., Toronto.
Duckworth, M. D.
Dandy, J. P., Manitoba.
Donovan, G.
Dorts, John.
Davies, Peter.
Davies, John
Darcy.
Doolix.

E.

Erginger, W.
Elgbish, A.
Evanson, Arthur.
Ellis, Alec.
Elliott, A. Baker.

F.

Faverstone, Mrs.
Fedor.
Flair, Roy.
Front.
Fitzpatrick, John.
Feneday, Arthur.
Fanton, Manchester.
Fugemp, William.
Foster.
Ferguson, A. C.

G.

Gray, A.
Grey.
Gibson, John.
Greveri, Alec.
Gard, J.
Gaade, A. W., chief steward.
Gratwick.
Grant, Dr. J. F., ship's surgeon.

H.

Hayes, First Asst. Purser.
Henderson, G., Montreal.
Hughes.
Henralain, W.
Hobinski, C.
Helm, S. F., Bugler.
Hampter, W.
Heller, W.
Holt, R., Steward.
Hughes, Hugh.
Harbanen.
Haron, P.

J.

J. Johnstone.

K.

Kohl, Miss Grace.
Kendall, Capt.
Kohl, Miss.
Koromas, Michael.
Kingscott, —.

L.

Lyon, Chena.
Lee, Miss.
Lowler, Hebert.
Lommi.
Laski, K.

M

Measurs, Wm., Salvation Army Bandsman.
Mere.
Misite.
Metcalfe, G. J.
McCone, J.
McDonald, C. P.
McWilliams, H.
McDougall G. or MacDougall.
McCrudy, Thomas.
Malte.
Moreland.
Murphy, O. S.

N

Noseal.
Novek.

O.

Owen, W. T.

P

Potvert.

Q.

Quinn, William.

R.

Rioulente.
Rin, John.
Roberts, W.
Rowen, William, Steward.
Romaruh, John.
Renne.
Rudley, A., Bo'sun's Mate.
Reginald, A.

S.

Starr, baker.
Smith, C. H.
Smith, H. H.
Samuelson, C.
Shannon, E.
Sims, John.
Spencer, C. S.
Smith, J.
Smith, J.
Suzzera, Adam.
Sims, Jubainer.
Simmonds, Mrs. R., London.
Spedden.
Samson (chief engineer).
Swan.
Sprague, T. (Q.M.).
Sapeke.
Salio, J.
Savoin.

T.

Tock.
Thorne.
Tiddell.

V.

Vell, J. (Boy).

W.

Walinski
Weyke
Williams, O.
White, J. B.
Weinrauch, Mrs. B., Montreal
White, Steward
Williams, J.
Williams, A.

Z.

Zuh, H.

THE SPECIFICATIONS OF SUNKEN EMPRESS

While Lloyd's Register contains no mention of the value of the Empress of Ireland, or the amount the insurance on her, it contains the following specifications of the vessel:

She was a steel, twin-screw steamer, rated 100A1, which applies only to the best steel and a certain class of iron vessels. She was equipped with wireless and submarine signalling apparatus, and was built in 1906 by Fairfield & Company, of Glasgow, for the Canadian Pacific Railway.

Her port of registry was Liverpool, England, and the official number and designation 123792, HGLB. Her registered tonnage was 14,191.

No figures as to value or insurance could be got at Capt. Walsh's office, and Mr. Dunlop, the C. P. R.'s claims adjuster and insurance expert, was out of town.

GREAT ANXIETY IN LONDON

Canadian Associated Press.

London, May 29.—The greatest consternation is shown here over the news of the Empress of Ireland disaster. The streets are aflame with newspaper bills announcing that the liner has sunk. Reporters are clamoring at the Canadian Pacific offices

(Continued on Page Three.)

WIRELESS OPERATOR DESCRIBES SCENES OF MIDNIGHT DEATH

Officers Had No Time to Awaken Passengers or Launch Lifeboats—Empress Sank in Fourteen Minutes — Survivors Were Almost Naked—Some Were Wounded When Rescued.

Special by Wireless to The Montreal Star.

Father Point, P. Q., May 29.—"The Empress of Ireland passed and landed her pilot here at 1.30 this morning. There was a haze at the time. At 1.50 a.m. I was awakened by an "S.O.S." ring on my door bell and rushing down, was informed by a Marconi operator that the Empress of Ireland was sinking, having been struck by some vessel. In undress I started to help. No other signal could be got from the doomed vessel. She had no time to give another, as she sank ten minutes after being struck.

"Mr. Whiteside, manager of the Marconi station, rendered effective service by notifying the Government steamer Eureka at Father Point wharf, and the Yady Evelyn at Rimouski wharf.

"Captain J. B. Belanger, of the Eureka, immediately rushed to the scene, and Captain Pouliot, with the Lady Evelyn, followed later, his ship being three miles further away.

"Meanwhile daylight broke and early scanning the horizon with a telescope I saw the two government steamers nine life boats and a collier in the vicinity, going here and there. About 3 a.m. the Eureka arrived at Father Point wharf with 32 survivors, and several poor drowned bodies; also several of the survivors who had been wounded.

"The scene on the Eureka was most distressing, the survivors walking around their dear shipmates stretched out in their last sleep. The Eureka was advised to go to Rimouski wharf with all on board, and the Canadian Pacific Railway agent, Mr. Webber, who was here, having just got off the ill-fated vessel, with the pilot, engaged all the cabs he could find and telephoned for all medical assistance. As the company's agent here, I advised all the survivors that their cables and telegrams to their families would be paid by the C.P.R.

SURVIVORS ALMOST NAKED.

"The Lady Evelyn passed into Rimouki wharf about four a.m. with some more survivors and bodies. Among the survivors was Captain Kendall, Commander of the ill-fated ship, who was picked up by a lifeboat from the wreckage after the ship had gone down.

"Most of the survivors were almost naked in the cold morning with the temperature at 35, and white frost on the ground.

"At 6.10 the Norwegian collier, Storstad, coal laden from Sydney, N.S., for Montreal, came along slowly, when her bow was seen smashed in. It became known that she was the vessel that had struck the Empress of Ireland the fatal blow. The Storstad was not too much damaged to allow her to proceed to Quebec under her own steam, but before proceeding she landed a few survivors and some dead bodies, which were taken off by the steamer Eureka and Lady Evelyn, and landed on the Rimouki wharf.

"The Empress foundered in a depth of seventeen fathoms, about ten miles below Father Point. There was not sufficient time to launch all the life-boats. The two Marconi operators were among the saved. Their signalling was the means of very quickly bringing assistance to the victims.

"The survivors number about 337, and is a small portion of the passengers and crew. A thousand are missing. Boats are still searching the locality.

"(Signed) J. McWILLIAMS."

EXTRA EDITIONS UNTIL FULL DETAILS ARE RECEIVED

The Star will continue to publish extra editions until the complete details of the Empress disaster have been told. Four special correspondents of The Star Staff will send fresh descriptions of the wreck and interview the survivors. A photographer and an artist were also on the special train chartered by The Star this morning.

The Sinking of the Empress of Ireland

CAPTAIN KENDALL

Waiting for news—a scene outside the London offices of the C.P.R. yesterday afternoon.

The Marconi station at Father Point and portraits of Mr. Edward Bamford (on left), and Mr. Ronald Ferguson, Marconi operators in the sunken liner.

"Daily Mail" photograph of the crowd scanning the passenger list outside the C.P.R. London offices-yesterday.

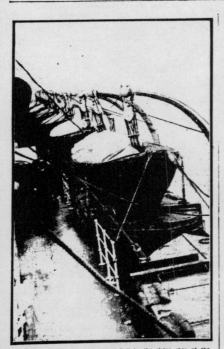

The boat deck of the Empress of Britain, the sister ship of the sunken liner, which sailed from Liverpool yesterday. One of the boats on the right does not appear in the picture.

The ill-fated liner leaving Liverpool with the Duke and Duchess of Connaught in October ..... , when the Duke went out as Governor-General.

A game of shovel board on board the Empress of Ireland, and the flag at half mast on the roof of the West End offices of the C.P.R.

EXTRA
10.30 A.M.

THE DAILY TELEGRAPH

EXTRA
10.30 A.M.

VOL. XXXIX, NO. 127   QUEBEC, FRIDAY EVENING, MAY 29, 1914   PRICE ONE CENT

R.M.S. EMPRESS IRELAND GOES DOWN WITH NEARLY 1,000 PEOPLE

Queen of St. Lawrence Route Collided With Black Diamond Collier Storstad off Father Point at 2. A. M. To-day and Sank Quickly---Left Quebec Port Yesterday Afteroon at 4 O'clock

R.M.S. EMPRESS OF IRELAND LEAVING PORT OF QUEBEC YESTER-DAY AFTERNOON

350 SURVIVORS LANDED AT RIMOUSKI

The C. P. R. Liner Empress of Ireland sank last night thirty miles off Father Point after a collision with a collier with, it is reported 1000 people on board. The collision took place at two o'clock this morning and the first announcement of the disaster came from the Marconi station at Father Point, which had received word that the Empress was sinking.

The big liner sent out the S. Q. S. call which was picked up by the government steamer Eureka and the Mail tender Lady Grey, which immediately rushed to the rescue of the sinking ship.

The number lost on board is now stated to be 870.

The Marconi station at Father Point kept in communication with the Empress for sometime, when wireless messages suddenly ceased. Those on the wharf at Father Point discerned life boats as day was breaking and a coal steamer, which believed to have been in collision with the Empress was standing by.

135 PASSENGERS LANDED AT RIMOUSKI

About 135 passengers and crew were landed at Rimouski.

SANK IN TEN MINUTES

Reports early said the Empress sank within ten minutes.

CAPTAIN KENDALL'S MESSAGE

Montreal.—The first official account of the disaster to the Empress of Ireland came from Captain Kendall, who sent a wireless to Captain Walsh, Marine Supt. of the C. P. R. here as follows:

"Empress of Ireland stopped by dense fog, struck amidships in vital spot by collier Storstad."

ROUSED PEOPLE FROM BEDS

A number of the passengers were hastily roused from their beds and rushed into the boats.

Captain Kendall, who won renown as the man who first detected Crippen, the murder, on the Montfort, and who was in command of the Empress, was said to be among those picked up by the lifeboats.

NEARLY 1500 PEOPLE ON BOARD

The Empress, which left Quebec last night for Liverpol, carried 77 first class, 206 second and 594 third class Passengers. Among them are the actors Laurence Irving and Mrs Irving, who had just completed a tour of Canada, and Sir Henry Seton-Kerr, the well known big game sportman. The ship also carried a large portion of Salvation Army delegates to a conference in London. The crew numbered over 500.

Rimouski. May 29. — At present three hundred and fifty passengers have been landed at Rimouski, and others are to follow. When the first S. O. S. call was received from the Empress of Ireland at 1.45 this morning, the operator on the doomed vessel said she was sinking fast. The Government steamers Evelyn and Eureka were at once rushed to the scene of the disaster.

But the ship had gone down before the ships arrived.

Repeated attempts were made to get the Empress by wireless but nothing which was read from her beyond the communication that the Storstad had rammed her in a vital spot and that she was going down rapidly and that the weather was clear.

COULD'NT GET OUT ALL LIFEBOATS

The Empress listed quickly when struck and was unable to get most of the boats out.

CAPTAIN SAVED-PICKED UP BY LIFE BOAT

"Captain Kendall was saved, being picked up on some wreckage by No. 3 life boat fully thirty minutes after his ship had foundered.

OTHER OFFICERS SANK

Both wireless operators, assistant pursers, chief engineer and chief steward were saved.

CHIEF OFFICER AND PURSER MISSING

Chief officer and purser are amongst the missing."

SPECIAL TRAIN FOR SURVIVORS

INCOMPLETE LIST OF SURVIVORS

(By Special Leased Wire.)

Rimouski, Que., May 29.- Mr. Dunbar, the Marconi operator of the Eureka, reports the following incomplete list of survivors at Rimouski:—Parkinson; R. Holt, bedroom steward; W. Bowen, steward; Mrs. Radley, Coombs, pantry man; A. Reginald, Moreland, White, Greye, James, Williams, assistant steward; E. Foster, A. Elliott, baker; A. C. Ferguson, S. E. Simon, Nostal, Dodiz, Speddon, Noysk, A. W. Grade, chief engineer; S. Sampson, Swan, J. K. A. Possibly, tenth engineer; T. Bradwick, sailor; S. Murphy, T. Borah, reported quartermaster; Duckworth, electrician; J. Sabo, Sapete, Donovan, A. Williams, H. Clarkson, T. Hanon, Charles Clarke, K. Laski, Savein, King, Scott, Haes, assistant purser; J. W. Langley, Merrit, B.C.; Miss M. E. Langley, Vancouver; Mr. and Mrs. and Master Law, Calgary; Mr. J. Lennon, Winnipeg; Miss A. Liston, London, Eng.; A. Metier, Indianapolis; A. McAlpine, Montreal; Mrs. Charles Moir, Toronto; Mr. J. Morgan, Winnipeg; Mr. Wm. Morgan, Winnipeg.

Only one woman, Mrs. Simon, is among those picked up by the Eureka. The greater number are members of the crew and third class passengers.

A list of those saved by the steamer Eureka is as follows:—Banford, Mare. Parkinson, R. Holt, bedroom steward; Wrowen, Alex. Rathey, boat's mate; C. Coombs, pantry; H. Reginald Morland, White, Greye, Jos. Williams, E. Foster, A. Elliott Baker, A. C. Ferguson, Mrs. R. Sims, Nesod Dodix, Speddon Noysk, Gadde, C. S. Sampson, Swan A. Johnson, Gratwick, O. S. Murphy, Q.M.; T. Sprague Boats; Duckworth, etc., J. Satis, Save, L. E. Donovan, A. Williams, H. Clandon, P. Haran, Chas. R. Clark, first saloon, London; Kluskielkluski, Savin Kinegscott. Captain Kendall on Lady Evelyn with two Marconi operators.

THE TWO VESSELS

The Empress of Ireland was a vessel of 14,191 tons and was built by the Fairfield Company, Ltd., at Glasgow in 1906. She carried a full wireless equipment and was a twin screw boat.

The Storstad, with which the Empress collided, weighs 6,028 tons. She was built by the Armstrong, Whitworth Company at Newcastle in 1910 and is owned by the Atkies Maritime, of Christiania, Norway. She is a single screw steamer and was laden with coal.

CABIN PASSENGERR ON BOARD

The saloon passenger list of the Empress of Ireland is:—

MR. J. R. ABERCROMBIE. Vancouver,
P. J. ADIE, MRS. ADIE, Birmingham.
A. B. ANDERSON, London.
MR. P. C. AVERDICK, Manchester.
CP. BARLOW. MRS. BARLOW

L. A. GOSSELIN, Montreal.
W. D. GRAHAM, MRS. GRAHAM, Hong Kong, China.
MRS. D. T. HAILEY, Montreal.
G. W. S. HENDERSON, Vancouver.
W. HIRXHEIMER, Montreal.
MRS. C. HOLLOWAY, Quebec.
F. W. HOWES, Birmingham.
L. A. HYAMSON, London.
LAURENCE IRVING, London.
SIR HENRY SETON KERR, London.
LIONEL KENT, Montreal.
MISS GRACE KOHL, Montreal.
LIONEL KENT, Montreal.

SS. STORSTAD NOW EN ROUTE FOR QUEBEC

Has Some Survivors and Bodies of Victims on Board

(By Special Leased Wire.)

Father Point, Que., May 29.—The Norwegian steamer Storstad, with which the Empress of Ireland collided, passed inward at 6.30 a.m., with her bow badly driven in, but is proceeding slowly to Quebec under her own steam. She has 360 survivors and dead bodies from the ill-fated Empress of Ireland, which she is placing on the Government steamers Eureka and Lady Evelyn, to be landed at Rimouski wharf.

The Empress sank in nineteen fathoms of water.

The disaster recalls the accident which happened to the sister ship of the ill-fated vessel, the Empress of Britain, which two years ago rammed and sank the collier Helvetia in almost the same spot that the collision took place this morning.

"GOD BE WITH YOU TILL WE MEET AGAIN"-

The Empress of Ireland sailed from here yesterday afternoon with more than twelve hundred on board. As she steamed away the brass band of a party of the Salvation Army, who arrived on a special train from Toronto and are going in a big Salvation Army gathering in London, played the hymn, "God be with you until we meet again," which makes the setting of the awful tragedy a parallel with that of the heroic band on the ill-fated Titanic.

SECOND CABIN PASSENGERS ON BOARD

MISS JENNIE NEWTON, Antler, N.D.
MISS OSTENDER, England.
JOHN PATTERSON, ROBERT PATTERSON, MISS S. PATTERSON, Calgary.
J. PATRICK, Toronto.
W. H. PERRY, Peterboro.
H. AND MRS. PATTERSON, Winnipeg.
MISSES A. AND M. PRIESTLY, Edmonton.
GEORGE PRIOR, Winnipeg.
MISS W. M. FUARTLEY, Vancouver.
JOHN REILLY, Hamilton.
W. J. RICHARDSON, AND MRS. RICHARDSON, Vancouver.
GEORGE C. RICHARDS AND MRS. RICHARDS, Terre Haute, Wisconsin.
S. J. SAMPSON. Guelph.
MISS SCHONGUTT, Montreal.
JOHN SCOTT, Mortlach, Sask.
MRS. W. MOUNSEY, Chicago.
MRS. T. MUTALL, Vancouver.
MISS NUTALL, also INFANT MUTTALL, Winnipeg.
MISS A. S. MASSAFREY, Winnipeg.
MISS W. ATKIN, Prince Albert.
MISS D. BALCOMB, Vancouver.
MISS A. BALES, Toronto.
MRS. W. BARBOUR, MISS FLORENCE BARBOUR, MISS EVELYN BARBOUR, Silverton, B.C.
MR. ALFRED BARKER.
MISS BESSIE BAWDEN, MISS FLORENCE BAWDEN, Peterboro.
MISS MARY BARTER, Toronto.
MR. EDWARD BEALE, London.
MISS E. BERRY, Vancouver, B.C.
HENRY BIRKETT, Garstairs, Alb.
G. D. BISHOP, Vancouver.
MISS I. BLACKHURST, Paris, Ont.
J. W. AND MRS. BLACK, Ottawa.
MISS EDITH BOCH, MR. REINHOLDT BOCH, Rochester, Minn.
MRS. F. E. BOYNTON, St. Thomas, Ont.
J. M. FINLEY, Liverpool.
MRS. JOHN FISHER, Chicago.

ONE QUEBEC LADY ON BOARD VESSEL

It is believed Mrs. C. Holloway, widow of the late C. Holloway, was the only Quebec person on board the Empress of Ireland.

Mrs. Holloway is a sister of Mr. G. S. Oliver, of Oliver and Coolican.

No word has been received yet as to Mrs. Holloway's fate.

QUEBEC'S HARBOR MASTER A FORMER COMMANDER

The ss. Empress of Ireland, in charge of Captain Kendall, was until quite recently in charge of Captain Murray, appointed Harbor Master of Quebec this spring.

1640 PEOPLE ON BOARD

(By Special Leased Wire)

Montreal, May 29.—The Empress of Ireland carried a crew of 650 officers and men, making with the passengers a total of 1640 people on board.

QUEBEC FLAGS AT HALF MAST

The citizens of Quebec are requested to fly all flags at half mast in token of our deep sympathy with the awful disaster to the ss. Empress of Ireland, and the great loss of life.

ALEX. BUNTHRONE, Santa Barbara, Cal.
MR. E. AND MRS. E. BYRNE AND MISS G. BYRNE, Brisbane, Australia.
A. E. CAUGHEY AND MRS. CAUGHEY. Ottawa.

In the Front Line

The Quintinshill Rail Crash 1915

Frank Scott was something of a celebrity at his local Carlisle railway depot. He had driven the royal trains of no less than three British monarchs, Victoria, Edward VII and George V. That morning however, 22 May 1915, he was engaged on less glamorous but no less patriotic work—driving a troop train to Liverpool. On board were 500 officers and men of the 7th Royal Scots, bound for the war in the Dardanelles. At 6.43, on his way south, Scott's train was signalled to pass through Quintinshill, a remote junction near the border village of Gretna (in more peaceful times well-known as a haven for eloping couples). As he approached the junction on a slight right-hand curve, Scott might have made out (through the road bridge ahead of him) a stationary goods train on the left-hand siding—nothing to make him lose speed. As the track straightened out, though, he could not have failed to see another train facing him. It was on his line!

At that point less than 300 yards separated the two trains, less than ten seconds, neither time nor distance to brake a train on a down-gradient. The troop train thundered into the stationary train, wreaking appalling havoc: the wooden carriages where the soldiers huddled tight, eight to a compartment, were splintered like matchwood and hurled into the air. The two engines, locked together as an indistinguishable mass of crushed metal, ground to a halt fifty yards further down the line, spilling over onto the northbound track. What happened then, as some of the stunned soldiers crawled out of their nightmare and attempted to extricate their trapped comrades, *The Scotsman* graphically described: 'Concentrated on their great task few of the survivors were in a position to see another dreadful disaster rolling down upon them. Suddenly there came an appalling sequel. Through the fearful tangle of wreckage and injured and dead, and into the striving heroes of the stricken remnant of the two companies there ripped the northbound express, double-engined and running late. Never was there such a disaster nor such a scene on a British railway.'

Nor has there been since, fortunately. The express train ploughed the wreckage up into a grotesque mountain, which erupted into flame as gas cylinders for the light fixtures exploded. Those not killed by the double impact were consumed in the holocaust that burned for twenty-four hours after. Two people died in the almost empty local train, seven in the express. But in the troop train: 'When the work of rescuing was over, the uninjured survivors of the half-battalion of the Royal Scots were assembled, and that the 7th Battalion had been terribly stricken was revealed when no more than 67 responded to their names out of nearly 500 men . . .' The roll-call revealed 211 soldiers killed and more than 230 injured. It was, as one veteran observed, worse than anything he had ever seen in the trenches.

And the cause of it all had been, quite simply, human error. The signalman, James Tinsley, had *forgotten* the local train parked on the main line when he cleared the troop train to pass through. Normally the local would have been shunted onto one of the loop lines on either side of the main line, to allow the express to overtake it. But on this particular day, Whit Saturday, the loop lines both contained goods trains.

The mystery was *how* Tinsley could have forgotten the existence of the local train, puffing and hissing within sight of his signal-box: he had only ten minutes earlier got off it himself to begin his day's shift (to save himself a long walk from Gretna he had an unofficial—and illegal—arrangement with his mate George Meakin that he would catch the local and begin his shift half-an-hour late, and George would cover for him by making all log entries after 6.00 on a separate piece of paper). Perhaps he was too engrossed in writing up the log in his own hand—yet there, staring him in the face in black-and-white, was the written testimony of impending disaster! The same mental paralysis seems to have affected others. Meakin, still in the box but deep in the morning papers, failed to notice his replacement accepting the fatal troop train. The fireman of the local, whose duty it had been to confirm that the signals were duly protecting his train, failed to note that the vital 'safety-collar' was not on the signal-lever. Both Tinsley and Meakin were tried and sentenced for culpable homicide, though released after a year and severe nervous breakdowns.

The newspapers generally played down the full horror of this unprecedented disaster, bowing to the official consensus that such morale-shakers in the midst of war were not in the national interest. And as for the remnants of the 7th Battalion, those passed medically fit were immediately shipped off for active service. Most of them were soon to die in another disaster of human error, Gallipoli.

Daily Mail 24 May 1915

THE TROOP TRAIN DISASTER IN PICTURE & DIAGRAM.

ENGINES OF EXPRESS TRAIN

Down Line from Glasgow

Troop train, coming south, collided head on with local train

Local train, going north, crossed from down to up line to allow express to pass

Goods train (also damaged) occupying siding

Express train, going north, collided with wreckage of the two other trains

Up line, from Carlisle and London

SIGNAL BOX

WRECKAGE OF TROOP & LOCAL TRAINS

The worst railway disaster in Great Britain or the United States occurred about two miles from Gretna Green, near Carlisle, on Saturday morning. Here is a photograph showing the scene after the accident and a diagram illustrating how the collision happened.

£1,000

THIS ISSUE OF THE "DAILY GRAPHIC" CARRIES A FREE INSURANCE OF £1,000
UNDERTAKEN BY THE OCEAN ACCIDENT & GUARANTEE CORPORATION, Ltd. (See p. 16)

LONDON EDITION

The DAILY GRAPHIC
ONE PENNY

LONDON: MONDAY, MAY 24, 1915.

No. 7943. Vol. CII.

Registered as a Newspaper.

PEACE HATH ITS HORRORS AS WELL AS WAR.

Hitherto we have enjoyed an almost miraculous immunity from railway accidents in the transport of hundreds of thousands of troops, a fact which is eloquent of the highly efficient and careful manner in which the railway companies have worked in conjunction with the War Office. But that splendid record has now been marred by the appalling disaster of Saturday morning of the troop train of the 7th Battalion Royal Scots, resulting in upwards of 150 killed and over 300 injured. The scene of the catastrophe was not far from the Gretna of famous memory. The troop train dashed into a local train. The north-bound Scottish express came up at full speed and plunged into the debris, which soon became a mound of raging fire. Amid the heart-rending scenes the surviving soldiers preserved heroic discipline, rendering priceless services in rescuing the injured. 1. The colliding engines. 2. The roll call of the Royal Scots after the injured had been removed.

Lethal Cargo
The Halifax Explosion 1917

In the winter of 1917 the people of Halifax, Nova Scotia, had been at war with Germany for three years. But while they might read with pride in the papers how their boys were helping to capture Passchendale Ridge (wherever that was), the war impinged on their lives most noticeably when the great convoys assembled in the harbour, before steaming for Europe and the U-boat infested Atlantic. The first week in December yet another convoy waited at Halifax, gathering its fold from all parts of the eastern seaboard.

It was an ideal assembly-point for the big ships, deep and wide. Only one spot in the channel—where it narrowed to half a mile between Dartmouth and Richmond—called for intricate navigation. At 9.00 in the morning of 6 December two ships were steaming into these narrows: one, the *Imo*, a cargo-boat loaded with Red Cross supplies for the trenches, was outward-bound. The other, the *Mont Blanc*, carried a deadly consignment of explosives—a forward hold of picric acid, two after-holds jammed with 3,000 tons of TNT, and a deck-cargo of benzine.

No rational explanation was ever found as to why these two vessels, both at half-speed, should have collided in good visibility and calm waters. According to the testimony of the *Mont Blanc*'s pilot, there was a fatal misunderstanding of the *Imo*'s signals and intentions. By the time the *Imo*'s engines went into reverse a collision was inevitable: it came at the very place where the barrels of benzine were stowed. Within minutes the *Mont Blanc* was uncontrollably ablaze and its crew—knowing the Armageddon that was only moments away when the fire reached the TNT—were rowing frantically for the nearest land.

The explosion that annihilated the great part of the city at its breakfast was seen and heard more than fifty miles away. More than two square miles, two-thirds of the city, was levelled by the blast—homes and churches, schools where children were getting ready for class, factories where the day's shift was beginning, streets and stations where people were hurrying to work. 'Houses were simply indistinguishable masses where they had not been devoured by the flames that rise and fall, that roared and seethed and made the place like a smelting oven' the *Montreal Daily Star* described the scene. On top of the havoc of fire and blast, a fifteen-foot tidal wave had swept across the basin, drowning people near the shore and crushing buildings on the waterfront.

First reports of the tragedy put the death-toll at hundreds, but then as the larger buildings were uncovered (200 bodies of children were found in one school alone) the estimates leaped to a thousand, then two thousand. But then the snow began to fall, turning the grim scene into a lunar waste but, more important, concealing the injured from the rescue parties and medical teams that were rushed to Halifax. No accurate estimate of the numbers of the dead was ever possible (the coroner ordered 4,000 coffins, it is said) but it is certain that at least 8,000 people were injured—many of them blinded—and 3,000 homes were destroyed. 'The war has touched Halifax' the *Star* lamented. 'Where only a few hours ago the most prosperous city in Canada stood secure in her own defences, unafraid and almost apathetic, there are now heaps of ruins . . . The crash came as suddenly and unexpectedly as the Zeppelin bombs have fallen upon undefended English towns and the effect has been the same.' It was no consolation to the inhabitants of Halifax in their distress, but at least four times as many had been killed by a single explosion as fell victim to all the Zeppelin bombs of the First World War that day, the day the war touched Halifax.

THE NET CIRCULATION OF THE GLOBE DURING NOVEMBER, 1917, WAS 2,210,965, A DAILY AVERAGE OF 85,037

The Globe.

THE WEATHER: Probabilities — Fair and cold.
The sun rises at 7.27 a.m. and sets at 4.41 p.m.
THE MARKETS: New York irregular and generally unchanged. Canadian markets steady. Winnipeg December oats closed ½c lower at [illegible]. Chicago December corn closed ½c higher at $1.25.

VOL. LXXIV. NUMBER [illegible]. TORONTO, FRIDAY, DECEMBER 7, 1917—TWENTY PAGES. PRICE TWO CENTS.

HALIFAX DEAD MAY BE 2,000

HALIFAX, N.S., Dec. 6—Chief of Police Hanrahan to-night estimates that the dead from the explosion on a munition ship and subsequent fire, destroying a large section of the north end of the city, may reach two thousand. Another estimate says over two thousand. Twenty-five teams loaded with bodies have arrived at one of the morgues.

CITY SHATTERED BY EXPLOSION

Halifax Half in Ruins as Munitions Ship Blows Up

COLLISION IN HARBOR

Whole Streets Wrecked and Hundreds Killed by Fire and Debris.

(Canadian Press Despatch.)

HALIFAX, Dec. 7.—(Friday).—It is now estimated the dead will exceed two thousand.

Halifax, Dec. 6.—As the result of a terrific explosion aboard the munition ship Mont Blanc in Halifax harbor this morning, a large part of the north end of the city and along the waterfront is in ruins and the loss of life is appalling. Early estimates place the number of dead at between eight hundred and one thousand, but late to-night the Chief of Police placed the killed at possibly 2,000. On one ship alone, forty persons were killed. Thousands have been injured. The property damage is enormous, and there is scarcely a window left in a building in the city.

Among the dead are the Fire Chief and his deputy. They were hurled to death when a fire engine exploded. Fire followed the explosion and this added to the greatest catastrophe in the history of the city.

Business Suspended.

All business has been suspended and armed guards of soldiers and sailors are patrolling the city. Not a street car is moving, and part of the city is in darkness. All the hospitals and many private houses are filled with injured.

The offices of the railway station, Arena rink, military gymnasium, sugar refinery and elevator collapsed, and injured scores of persons.

The munition ship was bound from New York for Bedford Basin, when she collided with a Belgian relief ship bound for sea.

Explosion Shakes Whole City.

Following the collision, the explosion occurred, and in less than a minute the whole city was shaken from its foundation. Thousands rushed for the open, and some of the little children in the schools became panic-stricken. On every street could be seen adults and children, with blood streaming from their wounds, rushing to the nearest doctor's office. The work of rescue was greatly impeded by the piles of debris in the devastated area.

Great Areas in Ruins.

A part of the town of Dartmouth is also in ruins.

ALONG THE WATERFRONT OF THE STRICKEN CITY.

All the buildings shown in the right-hand section of the picture are more or less badly damaged. These buildings include the naval machine shops, stores, Naval Academy and barracks, and the sectional freight shed in the lower right-hand corner. On the left are small torpedo boat and launch houses, which were probably also damaged. The explosion took place at Pier 8, beyond the extreme right-hand limit shown in the picture.

Toronto Promises Her Full Assistance

After a meeting with the civic heads yesterday afternoon regarding the Halifax disaster, Mayor Church wired Mayor Martin of Halifax as follows:

"Please accept Toronto's deepest sympathy in terrible calamity. Advise us forthwith what assistance and aid we can give you. We are at your service, and will despatch any aid necessary by special train. Do not fail to call upon us. Toronto's heart goes out to you."

Nearly all the buildings in the dockyard are in ruins.

Practically all the north end of the city has been laid waste.

The destruction extends from North street railway station, as far north as Africville, to Bedford Basin, and covers about two square miles.

The buildings which were not destroyed by the explosion were laid waste by the fire that followed.

Thousands Homeless.

Thousands of persons have been rendered homeless. The Academy of Music and many other public buildings have been thrown open to house the homeless.

Five hundred tents have been erected on the Common, and these will be occupied by the troops, who have given up their barracks to house the homeless women and children.

Temporary hospitals and morgues have been opened in the school houses in the western section of the city. The doctors and nurses worked heroically in rendering aid to the injured.

Fate of the Vessels.

The collision which occurred between the two steamers took place near the point of the harbor known as Pier Eight, and was between a French munition ship, the Mont Blanc, and an unnamed Belgian relief ship.

The Mont Blanc lies in the Narrows, shattered, while the Belgian relief boat is beached on the Dartmouth side of the harbor, near what is known as Tuft's Cove.

Explosion Comes Like Bolt From Blue

At nine o'clock the city was enjoying its usual period of calm and the streets were crowded with people wending their way to work, little thinking of that which in a few minutes was to befall them.

Suddenly, like a bolt from the blue, there came an explosion. From one end of the city to the other glass fell, and people were lifted from the sidewalks and thrown flat into the streets. In the down-town offices, just beginning to hum with the usual day's activities, clerks and heads alike cowered under the shower of falling glass and plaster which fell about them.

The collision was a terrific one, the munition boat being pierced on the port side almost to the engine-room. The relief vessel, which was practically uninjured, kept going ahead with the wounded craft, and when the fire was seen to break aboard her, backed away, and the crew started to abandon her.

Houses Crumpled Up.

The Mont Blanc drifted away, a burning wreck, while the relief boat beached near Tuft's Cove on the Dartmouth side of the harbor. Seventeen minutes after the collision the explosion occurred. Under the force of the explosion houses crumpled like decks of cards, while the unfortunate residents were swept to death in the debris.

In the main portion of the city, where the buildings are more or less of stone or concrete construction, the damage was confined to the blowing in of windows, and the injuries sustained by the citizens were in the main due to the cuts from flying glass. Proceeding south to the extreme end of the city the same thing was observed.

Like Town in Flanders.

In the west end and northwest end the damage was more extensive, and the walls of houses were in places blown to atoms, and the plaster and laths strewn on the streets more like a small section of Flanders than a town or city of Canada.

The main damage, however, was done in the north end of the city, known as Richmond, which was opposite the point of the vessels' collision. Here the damage is so extensive as to be totally beyond the field of description. Street after street is in ruins and flames swept over the district.

In this section many of the larger buildings are a mouldering heap of ruins and the ordinary frame houses are a mere heap of shattered, flattened ruins.

Automobiles scurried here and there in this section of the city, each bearing a blanket-clad burden which told only too plainly of serious injuries, or in many cases death.

The hospitals, each and everyone with admirable order, were rendering aid, and in the military hospitals the soldiers who were on guard duty were being hurried in odd twisted heaps and blackened, powder-stained faces to the wards for relief.

Confusion Over Whistles Blamed for Disaster

(Canadian Press Despatch.)

HALIFAX, Dec. 6.—Pilot Frank Mackie, who was on the munition ship, declares that the accident was due to a confusion of whistles, sounded by the Belgian relief steamer.

In addition to her cargo of munitions, the Mont Blanc carried a deckload of benzine, and this caught fire, following the explosion.

The Captain of the Mont Blanc ordered his crew to take to the boats. The men hastily left the ship in two boats and rowed for the Halifax side of the harbor, which they reached in safety.

The men ran for refuge, as they felt that an explosion was inevitable. Twenty minutes later the explosion occurred, and the men were hurled flat on the ground.

Halifax Calls For Country's Aid

(Canadian Press Despatch.)

HALIFAX, Dec. 6.—A committee of citizens was formed to-day and assistance from all outside points is asked. Things most needed at once are glass, tar paper, beaverboard, putty, bedding and blankets. The glass in practically two sides of every building in Halifax and within five miles of the city and Dartmouth has been demolished.

The Mayors of every town in the Province have been communicated with to rush these things to Halifax.

Terror-stricken People Throng the Streets

Five minutes after the explosion occurred the streets were filled with a terror-stricken mob of people, all trying to make their way as best they might to the outskirts in order to get out of the range of what they thought to be a German raid.

Women rushed in terror-stricken mobs through the streets, many of them with children clasped to their breasts. In their eyes was a look of terror as they struggled in mobs through the streets with blood-stained faces and endeavored to get anywhere from the falling masonry and crumbling walls.

Torn and Wrecked Bodies.

By the wire and lath-littered roadsides as they were passed there could be seen the remains of what had once been human beings, now sadly torn and wrecked, but beyond realization of what had occurred.

Here and there by a cracked and shattered telegraph pole was the cloth-wrapped body of a tiny tot scarred and twisted in the force of the horrible explosion which had withered all in its path.

Women See Homes Burn.

By the side of many of the burning ruins were women who watched with horror the flames as they consumed the houses, which in many instances held the bodies of loved ones. With dry eyes they watched their homes perish in the flames, and as others passed with inquiries as to whether they could render any aid they shook their heads in a dazed manner, and turned their gaze once more to the funeral pyre on all those whom they held dear.

Ontario Offers Help to Halifax

Sir William Hearst, Premier of Ontario, last night wired to Premier Murray of Nova Scotia as follows:

"On behalf of the people of Ontario I extend hearty sympathy to the sufferers from the Halifax disaster. Please suggest how this Province can most usefully help."

A somewhat similar message was sent to Sir Robert Borden.

A Sad Case.

Among the hundreds who were killed by the explosion was one particularly sad case of a Canadian Government employee named MacDonald, who, on rushing to his home after the explosion, found that all his family, consisting of his wife and four children, had perished. Before him on the roadway were the mangled remains of his little two-year-old child, who had met death while playing on the roadside.

Many of those composing the crews of ships in the harbor were killed and injured. The damage along the water front is very serious.

On one steamer, the Picton, it is reported that thirty-three of the crew of forty-two have been killed. Many bodies of seamen have been picked up in the harbor and rescue parties are working among the ruins of buildings removing bodies of the dead.

The munition ship, after the crew left her, veered in towards the Halifax side of the harbor, and the city received the full force of the explosion.

Pitiable Scenes in the Schools.

The rescuers, who were early on the scene, say that the sights in the public schools at the north end of the city were pitiable. They found the bodies of dozens of little chil-

(Continued on Page 4, Col. 3.)

SPLENDID HELP FROM OUR ALLY

Relief Trains From Boston and Portland Despatched to Halifax

EVERY AID OFFERED

(Canadian Press Despatches.)

Boston, Dec. 6. — A. C. Ratshesky of the Public Service Committee heads the party sent by the State of Massachusetts to the aid of Halifax.

Gov. McCall sent the following letter to the Mayor of Halifax, to be delivered in person by Mr. Ratshesky:

"I am sending A. C. Ratshesky of the Massachusetts Public Safety Committee, immediately to your city, with a corps of our best State surgeons and nurses, in the belief that they may be of service to you in this hour of need. I need hardly say to you that we have the strongest affection for the people of your city, and that we are anxious to do everything possible for their assistance at this time. Kindly express to the people of your city the very deep sympathy of the people of the Commonwealth of Massachusetts, and assure them that we are ready to answer any call that they may make upon us. Massachusetts stands ready to go to the limit in rendering every assistance you may be in need of.

"Won't you please call upon Mr. Ratshesky for every help you need? The Commonwealth of Massachusetts will stand back of Mr. Ratshesky in every way. Realizing the time is of utmost importance, we have despatched the train."

Lieut.-Col. William Brooks, Acting Surgeon of the State Guard, was placed in charge of the unit of surgeons and nurses.

Relief Train From Boston.

Officials of the Boston & Maine, the Maine Central, and the Canadian Railroads, promptly made all arrangements to put the train through in record time. The War Department was asked to use its wireless to inform the Mayor of Halifax that the relief train was coming. The train consists of two baggage cars, two sleepers and a buffet car.

The decision to send the relief party was made at the meeting of the Public Safety Committee and officers of the State Guard, called by Governor McCall. President James H. Hustis of the Boston & Maine Railroad told the committee that he would have the train ready by 10 p.m. Chairman Victor Heath of the Boston Public Safety Committee promised the co-operation of the city authorities. He said the Boston Committee had funds which could be drawn upon.

On motion by Bernard J. Rothwell, former President of the Chamber of Commerce, the meeting went on record as ready to back by popular subscription any expenditures that might be found necessary in the relief work.

Quick Aid From Maine.

Augusta, Maine, Dec. 6. — Governor Milliken to-day sent the following telegram to the Lieutenant-Governor of Nova Scotia and Mayor of Halifax:

"I extend to you the deepest sympathy of the people of Maine in the terrible disaster that has stricken Halifax. Any help Maine can give is yours."

Five carloads of supplies, including additional telegraph material, groceries and dry goods, left Portland to-night by special train for Halifax.

THE NEWS OF THE DAY

CONTENTS.

Detailed weather report on page 1.
1. War Summary (continued from page 1). British withdrawal around Cambrai.
3. Bishop Fallon favors Union Government.
4. Stories and incidents of Halifax disaster (continued from page 1).
5. Making issues on Pacific coast.
6. Editorial.
7. Central Appeal Judge rules for farm exemptions. Menace of the sub.
8-9. Toronto news. Legal Intelligence.
10. What women are doing.
11. Say Dewart charges are false.
12. Italians forced back; lose 11,000 men.
13. Official Canadian casualty lists.
14. Sporting news.
15. Guelph Stock Show. Armistice on Russian front.
16-17. Financial and commercial.
18. U. S. hope of Italian. Navigation news. Condensed advertisements (continued).
19. Condensed advertisements.
20. Eaton's advertisement.

BRITISH AND FOREIGN.

Eleven enemy airplanes were brought down by the French.

The British House of Commons has decided to disfranchise the conscientious objectors.

Lord Robert Cecil stated in the British Commons that an allied reply to the Vatican was unnecessary.

THE DOMINION.

Mr. Justice Duff, Central Appeal Judge, has made a ruling on a test case of exemption of a farmer.

Hon. Thos. H. Johnson, Attorney-General of Manitoba, made a strong speech in the interests of Union Government to his Icelandic compatriots at Lundar.

William Bennett, a returned soldier, was found guilty of murdering Bruce Leitch, the successful soldier suitor of the girl he loved, at Sand Point on the 16th July last, and sentenced to be hanged.

Bishop Fallon, Roman Catholic Bishop of London, and Bishop Williams, Anglican Bishop of Huron, made strong statements in support of the Union Government. Bishop Clark of Niagara Diocese (Anglican) will issue a pastoral to be read in the churches Sunday, supporting the Government.

LT. HITCHON PROBABLY BLINDED.

Brantford, Dec. 6.—(Special.)—Word was received here to-day that Lieut. W. W. Hitchon, who left Toronto with the 205th Battalion, has been so badly wounded that he would probably lose the sight of both his eyes. He received a piece of shrapnel which blinded one eye, and this affected the other. He was also severely wounded in the legs and arm. Before his departure he was wedded to Miss Edna Verity, daughter of Mr. W. J. Verity of the Verity Plow Co.

Time for Appeal Extended One Day

Mr. W. G. Thurston, K.C., Acting County Crown Attorney, last night announced that his Honor Judge Coatsworth, Chairman of the Board of Appeals, had been advised by the authorities at Ottawa that the time for appeals, which closed last night, had been extended to midnight to-night.

LATEST BULLETINS OF DISASTER

Following are the latest bulletins from Halifax concerning yesterday's great disaster, received early this morning:

Two men were killed and a number of the crew of the H.M.C.S. Niobe were injured.

All the churches in the city were damaged, the glass being blown out and the interiors wrecked.

There is not a whole pane of glass left in the newspaper offices. The presses are filled with broken glass, and the typesetting machine cannot be operated on account of the gas being cut off.

No estimate can be made of the property damage to-night.

All the guests in the hotels of the city are safe. Some of them were cut by flying glass, but all escaped serious injury.

Among the known dead are: William McPatridge, merchant; Chief of the Fire Department, Edward Condon; William Brunt, Deputy Fire Chief, and Captain Peter Broderick of the Fire Department; John Roymane, reporter on The Morning Chronicle; Mrs. W. J. Sweatman and son, wife of Rev. W. J. Sweatman of the Kaye Street Methodist Church. Dr. Murdock Chisholm is also reported dead.

Convent Girls Escape.

St. John, Dec. 6.—(Special.)—Word has just been received here that the pupils of the Mount Saint Vincent Convent Girls' Fining School at Halifax escaped without injury, and are on a special train bound for St. John.

All the guests at the city hotels escaped without serious injury.

St. John has been quickly organized for relief. The Mayor and a committee of four are going to render assistance. Twenty-five thousand blankets ordered by the Provincial Government are going forward by to-night's train.

ANXIETY FOR KINGSTON SOLDIERS.

Kingston, Dec. 6.—(Special.)—There is anxiety here as to the fate of the Kingston members of the infantry and artillery drafts which are still in Halifax. Five of the artillery officers are understood to have been staying in the King Edward Hotel, opposite the I. C. R. station. The men of the draft were probably in the upper part of the city.

ANOTHER ESTIMATE OF DEATH LIST

Hon. J. D. Reid, Minister of Railways, who was in Toronto yesterday, received despatches which indicated that the death roll in Halifax would reach 1,000, but stated that this was only an estimate.

PREVIOUS DISASTERS

April 14, 1912—Steamer Titanic, wrecked by collision with iceberg. Estimated 1,503 lives lost.

May 29, 1914—Steamer Empress of Ireland, wrecked by collision with steamer Storstad. Estimated 1,024 lives lost.

May 7, 1915—Steamer Lusitania, torpedoed by German submarine. Lives lost, 1,198.

May 31, 1889—Johnstown wiped out by flood. Over 2,000 lives lost.

Sept. 8, 1900—Galveston, Texas, wiped out by flood. Over 5,000 lives lost.

May 8, 1902—Eruption of Mount Pelee, wiped out St. Pierre, Martinique. Estimated 30,000 lives lost.

June 15, 1904—Steamboat General Slocum took fire going through Hell Gate, East River, New York. Over 1,000 lives lost.

April 18, 1906—Earthquake at San Francisco, $150,000,000, 28,080 buildings and several hundred lives lost.

Aug. 17, 1906—Earthquake at Valparaiso, Chile. Six hundred lives lost.

Dec. 28, 1908—Earthquake destroyed city of Messina; 77,283 lives lost.

TO-DAY'S WAR SUMMARY

ITALY'S DEFENCE IS ONCE MORE BEING SUBJECTED TO A SEVERE TEST. The enemy's second hammer-stroke, this time in the mountainous region of the north, is being delivered with terrific force. The German War Office yesterday claimed the capture of eleven thousand prisoners and over sixty guns in the storming of strong positions in the Meletta region, on the Asiago Plateau. The Italians admit withdrawal of their line from the slopes south of Monte Castelgomberto to the Foza Spur. General Diaz reports that the Austro-German command attempted to take this position in the rear, but was forced to abandon this for a frontal attack, which the defenders resisted stubbornly, giving up their lines only after inflicting heavy losses on the attackers, and their new line has been well prepared. The War Office at Rome announces that a powerful enemy effort in the Upper Brenta Valley was repulsed with heavy losses.

* * * * *

IT IS CERTAIN THAT THE INVADERS WILL CONTINUE TO HAMMER the line hard in Northern Italy. One despatch yesterday stated that fresh Austro-German divisions from the French and

(Continued on Page 2, Cols. 2 and 3.)

The Unstoppable Virus
The Flu Epidemic 1918

New York Times 24 October 1918

SOME SCENES OF RED CROSS ACTIVITY YESTERDAY AS THE APEX OF THE FIGHT AGAINST INFLUENZA WAS being reached. At the left a police officer, James Fogarty, is shown in an unusual posture. He is sitting down while Mrs. Genevieve Murray is making him look like his hereditary enemy—the highwayman. Mrs. E. P. Stimpson and Mrs. Leone Phelps, leaders of Red Cross work, assigning "mothers" to care for stricken families, are shown in the lower picture. Mrs. Eugene H. Folsom (standing) and her Red Cross girls are caught in the picture to the right, in the midst of a busy day, making masks.

RED CROSS WORKERS SUCCEED IN MEETING HEAVY CALLS FOR AID IN BATTLE ON INFLUENZA

Women of Mother Kind Still Urgently Needed for Service in Stricken Homes; Mask Profiteers Scored; Street Expectoration to Be Severely Punished

OPEN AIR AND VACCINE WILL FIGHT DISEASE

300,000 Cases in State Are Feared Unless Patients Kept in Uncovered Hospitals

"Unless more drastic precautionary measures are taken and open-air hospitals generally established, the number of influenza cases in California will increase to 300,000," Dr. George E. Ebright, president of the State

It would be a mistake to think that the biggest disasters necessarily qualify for the biggest headlines. Catastrophe on a world-wide scale can assume many insidious forms that defy the newsmen's concept of 'news'. Famine, unhappily, is a case in point. Death by degrees can be overwhelming whole countries without any visible concern from the press—not from lack of humanity, but from the timeless, placeless nature of the tragedy that mocks the 'instant' apparatus of modern news-gathering.

Epidemics—at least in their global form as pandemics—give rise to a similar paradox. By the time the full scope and virulence of a disease is understood, it has already become almost an accepted fact of everyday life. It is no longer headlines. A study of the course of the Spanish Influenza epidemic of 1918—statistically the worst disaster of the twentieth century, perhaps of all time—shows very clearly how this can happen. The facts contained here are only those published at the time in *The Times* and *New York Times*, but they were found only rarely on the front pages, more often in correspondence, editorials, and obscure feature pages.

On 21 June 1918, there was a small front page report in the *New York Times* about 'a

mysterious sickness now prevalent in Spain' which 'came from Germany and will doubtless soon reach other countries.' It was caused, apparently, by undernourishment and the enormous quantity of turnips the Germans were having to eat. 'The workmen at Essen especially' said a witness 'are dying by hundreds although no-one hears of it.' A few days later it was identified as a form of influenza, and was said to be 'weakening the German army.' Just to be on the safe side, the *New York Times* reported on 3 July, passengers arriving from Spain were being fumigated before landing. 'Passengers said it was supposed in Spain that the germs of the influenza had been brought by the strong winter winds from the battlefields of France.'

Meanwhile in Britain, according to *The Times*, the disease had already reached Birmingham. On 4 July, 'reports from all parts of the United Kingdom show that the influenza epidemic is spreading.' Two days later 'a somewhat serious situation has arisen.' Chemists had run out of quinine and cinnamon—two supposed cures. However a letter to *The Times* offered hope of an alternative: 'the specific is simple. It is to take snuff which arrests and stays the insidious bacillus with great effect . . . I may add that when journeying on the other

side of the border I not only took snuff, but had it on the table across which I was able to interview the victims of la grippe with impunity.'

In spite of the Registrar General's report on 18 July, that the death-roll in London from influenza had risen to 287 in a week, only a dedicated searcher after news would have found these nuggets. In New York too no-one was unduly worried when a Norwegian steamship arrived in July with ten people patently displaying symptoms of Spanish influenza. In August Dr Copeland, NY Health Commissioner, was said by the *New York Times* to be emphatic there was not the slightest danger of an epidemic in the city. 'You haven't heard of our doughboys getting it, have you?' he added. 'You bet you haven't and you won't.'

And he was still as cheerily optimistic on 4 October, even as the *New York Times* announced: 'Grippe now sweeping 43 States. Drastic steps taken throughout nation to check epidemic.' These included the closure of theatres in Washington, and in Chicago the arrest not only of anyone 'violating the spitting ordinance' but of anyone 'found coughing or sneezing without using a handkerchief.' On 13 October Dr Copeland, admitting there was an unusual amount of illness among teachers, refused to close schools and saw no reason to put a ban on public assemblages; but '4,930 new cases in the city', reported the *New York Times.*

There now arose the suspicion that in New York the situation was being deliberately played down. A former Health Commissioner, Dr Goldwater, spoke out: 'Conditions are much worse than the public has any idea . . . I believe there are far more cases of influenza in this city than the reports of the Health Department show.' In Baltimore the emergency had caught the undertakers by storm: they complained that 'families of the victims sought expensive coffins, the supply of which was exhausted. The mayor issued a statement calling on the people to be content with simple funerals.'

By the middle of October news was reaching both *The Times* and *New York Times* of critical conditions all over the world. On 10 October: 'The scenes in Cape Town are unprecedented . . . in the poorer quarters terrible distress prevails.' On 18 October: 'In Tangiers natives petitioned that the filthy state of their roads renders them impassable for the funerals of the many victims of the epidemic.' On 19 October: 'Canada in grip of epidemic—163 die from influenza in Montreal in one day' while in Sierra Leone 'the deaths average 1,000 a week . . . and chimpanzees and monkeys who are very weak in the chest are dying like flies.' On 22 October: 'Colombo: influenza has been raging in Ceylon for the past week.'

Now *The Times* needed no foreign correspondents to assess the seriousness of the epidemic. At home, figures showed that over 4,000 people had died of the disease in Britain in the third week of October: literally scores of victims were collapsing in the London streets. On the 28th *The Times* published a long and important leading article of 'The Mystery of Influenza', which sensibly swept away many of the fanciful notions of its cause and provenance. It ended with some hard words: 'We pride ourselves upon our progressive civilisation, and yet those in high place refuse to create the most paramount of necessities—a Ministry of Health. Had there been such a Ministry the visitation from which we are suffering today might not have found us absolutely unprepared. We had ample warning from Spain . . . No warnings were issued, no watch was kept, no adequate steps were taken. It is now too late . . .'

Indeed it was. By November over 3,000 a week were dying in Greater London alone. *The Times* was most impressed by what authorities in America were doing, even Dr Copeland (who by now had been moved to impose restrictions on hours of business and recreation to avoid overcrowding). It noted that in San Francisco the compulsory wearing of masks had stopped the outbreak in nine days.

As news of American advances at the Front poured in ('Why not forthwith call the present scourge of influenza The German Plague? Why give it the name of a respectable nation such as Spain?'—letter to the *New York Times*), the news at home worsened. 'Influenza deaths exceed war losses' reported the *New York Times* ominously in November, and produced some sketchy statistics from forty-six cities which appeared to show that at least a quarter of a million people in America had died from the epidemic in the months of September and November. *The Times* in December also produced some random figures, which made barely credible reading: an estimated six million deaths —three million in India alone. It estimated that if the disease lasted as long as the Great War it would account for five times as many casualties. 'The visits of the raiding Gothas to London were but as a summer shower compared with the deluge of germs we have just received.' 'Never since the Black Death has such a plague swept over the face of the earth. Nor perhaps' it added, 'has a plague been more stoically accepted.'

There really wasn't any alternative, in fact.

Beyond the fact that it appeared to be a bacteriological strain similar to one that spread in 1890 ('Russian' influenza), doctors were baffled. Vaccines were urged and searched for, without effect. Wholesale disinfection (though doubtless helping with other diseases) was tried and ridiculed. The best advice seemed to be to spot a sufferer early and isolate the infection. 'The person who coughs or sneezes discharges a spray more deadly than bullets or poison gas . . .' announced the now-active Dr Copeland.

By the beginning of January 1919 the rate of new cases in both London and New York had dropped so dramatically that many expressed their conviction that the epidemic had run its course. It hadn't. As *The Times* had warned, as early as October, there was bound to be a new wave of infection. It came at the end of January with renewed vigour partly, *The Times* claimed, through 'the use of unsterilized cups and glasses in clubs, public bars, restaurants, tea-rooms, cafes . . .' But on both sides of the Atlantic, as milder weather set in, this new outburst of fever was claiming fewer lives: the total for the whole of Britain in the second week of March 1919 was just 3,000— a fact that inspired *The Times* to declare 'this wave of the influenza epidemic has now ended.'

Of course, in other parts of the world winter was just starting. In April Australia began to know the ravages of the ubiquitous virus: within ten weeks Sydney alone buried 2,890 victims, and the *Melbourne Argus* was accusing the authorities of disguising the true dimensions of the outbreak in the city. The fact was that even when after a year the pandemic had spent itself, no-one could do anything but guess wildly at the overall damage caused. In Britain the number of deaths was later put at 150,000 —a nice round figure—and 15 million was suggested for the whole world. However hypothetical, it was a figure that quite eclipsed the total war-fatalities of 1914-18.

SPANISH INFLUENZA MUCH LIKE GRIPPE

Malady Found Not Dangerous Unless Neglected, When Pneumonia May Develop —Its History and Symptoms

EARLY last May dispatches from Madrid told of a mysterious malady which was raging through Spain in the form and of the character of the grippe. Not long after, a similar epidemic took hold in Switzerland and penetrated simultaneously in mild and isolated forms into France, England, and Norway. Early in August this disease, carried from Europe in ocean liners and transports, began to make its appearances in this country, and within the past two weeks the occurrences of the malady in the civilian population and among the soldiers in the cantonments have increased so greatly in number that Government, State, and municipal health bureaus are now mobilizing all their forces to combat what they recognize to

During the Punic wars, the Carthaginian Army was said to have been reduced by smallpox, and Hamilcar was forced thereby to raise the siege of Syracuse. In the year 165, the Roman legions before Seleucia were thinned by a similar scourge, the disease following the banners of the conqueror and conquered and spreading to Rome itself, where it worked havoc under the name of "Antonin's Plague." The Black Death which swept over Europe in the fourteenth century attacked the army of the Black Prince and forced him to abandon the siege of Calais. Syphilis at the end of the fifteenth century spread through the army of Charles VIII, invader of Naples, decimating it after the battle of Fornuovo.

Since the seventeenth century the

decided at Washington that such a step would not check the spread of influenza. Outbreaks of Spanish influenza at five additional training camps were reported on Friday by Surgeon General Gorgas, making a total number of cases up to noon on Friday 9,313, with 11 deaths. Of these Camp Devens had the greatest number, 6,583; Camp Lee, 1,211, and Camp Upton, 602. Other camps reporting were Camp Gordon, Ga., 138; Camp Syracuse, N. Y., 64; Camp Humphreys, Va., 56; Camp Merritt, N. J., 182. and Camp Lewis, Wash., 11.

Reports received at Washington from European countries indicate that 20 per cent. of the population has been affected this Summer by Spanish influenza, for which reason General Rupert Blue

EXPERTS DISAGREE ON EPIDEMIC HERE

Dr. Goldwater Asserts Situation is Serious with Lack of Nurses and Hospital Beds.

DR. COPELAND DENIES IT

Increase of Only Three New Cases in City, He Reports—Arranges for Federal Aid.

OLD VISITOR, SAYS DR. DOTY

He Sees No Reason for Fearing Scourge—Cleanliness the Chief Preventive.

Dr. Royal S. Copeland, the Health Commissioner, and Dr. S. S. Goldwater, Director of Mt. Sinai Hospital and former Health Commissioner, disagreed sharply yesterday concerning conditions in this city in the matter of hospital facilities for caring for Spanish influenza and pneumonia patients.

Dr. Goldwater is of the opinion that conditions are far worse than the public is aware and that unless help comes from the Government, should the epidemic spread, there will be danger that many will suffer for lack of care. Dr. Copeland, taking the contrary view, called Dr. Goldwater's statement his "weekly letter to the public," and said the former Health Commissioner was taking the provincial view "bounded by the walls of Mt. Sinai Hospital."

EXTRA **FIRST PICTURES** EXTRA

Taken at Hindenburg Tragedy Scene

San Francisco Chronicle
Home-Owned Newspaper

...CISCO, CAL., FRIDAY, MAY 7, 1937 — DAILY 5 CENTS, SUNDAY 10 CENTS.

...HUGE ZEP EXPLODES

HINDENBURG DESTROYED, 33 D...

Photodrama

At the exact moment the Hindenburg exploded at Lakehurst last night an Associated Press staff photographer had his camera focussed on the mammoth dirigible and captured one of the most remarkable news photos ever taken.

Here is that picture:
The Zeppelin exploded with a terrific ro... the airsc...

THE WEATHER
Today: ... little change in ... temperature ...

COMPARATIVE TEMPERATURES

	High	Low		High	Low
San Francisco	56	49	Denver	70	48

Herald Tribune
NEW YORK — FRIDAY, MAY 7, 1937
LATE CITY EDITION

Hindenburg Explodes at Lakehurst, 34 Die; Dirigible, Landing, Falls 500 Feet in Flames

63 Survive in Plunge Of Burning Zeppelin

World's Largest Airship Shattered as She Approaches Mooring Mast at End of Season's First Flight

Static Electricity Theory Is Advanced as a Cause

Commander Pruss and Captain Lehmann Save Latter Believed Dying; Ground Crew in Peril Heat Drives Rescuers Back From Ship

The German dirigible Hindenburg, largest airship ever destroyed by explosion and fire at 7:25 o'clock last night...

Horror Dazes Field Crowd Unable to Aid

Allen, Herald Tribune Aviation Editor, Pictures Spectacle He Sees as 'Most Terrible' of Air

Storms Kept Ship Drifting 3 Hours

Air Station a Madhouse of Activity as Trucks and Ambulances Race Out to Succor Victims

By C. B. Allen

LAKEHURST, N. J., May 6...

---

186 Dead, 39... 333 Survive...

Victims Fight Raging Seas On Rafts, Logs

The Morro Castle B...

Crowds Seek Kin; Confusion Reigns

Cars Pack Highways as Ambulances and Guards Speed to Aid Injured

---

The Courier-Mail
GREATEST DAILY SALE IN QUEENSLAND
BRISBANE, MONDAY, JANUARY 16, 1939

BUSH FIRE TOLL RISES

LOSSES IN 4 STATES

RAIN CLOSES DREADFUL WEEK IN VIC.

One of 17 Found Alive

99.8 DEG. IN CITY: SMOKE FROM MACKAY TO BORDER

AIR FORCE LEADE... EXCHANGE...

Mr. Lyons Answ... Board's Commen...

ROME TALKS Chamberlain Optimistic

Financial Supplement In This Issue

FUND BEGUN QUICKLY HERE
Red Cross Chapter on Way to Raising Flood Relief Quota

Crowd Vi...

LAKEHURST, N. J., May 6 (AP)—Germany's great silver Hindenburg, the world's largest dirigible, was ripped apart by an explosion tonight that sent her crumpling to the naval landing field a flaming wreck with horrible death to about a third of those aboard.

Dies in Wife's Arms Just as Help Arrives

HITLER STUNNED B...

BERLIN, May 7 (Friday)... stunned by the news. He refused...

Known Dead

AIRSHIP DRIVEN TOO LOW BY STORM

BALLAST NOT ...OWN OUT

...ROL LEVERS ...HAT WERE UNUSED

...-ENGINED ?

an Air Expert ...endure strains far greater ...e would be theoretically ...withstand in navigation, ...believed to be disaster-

...appear that wh... ...her while ...singly

OFFICERS AND CREW OF THE R101.—An official photo.
J. Binks (10), S. Church (13), V. Savory (14), W. Radcliffe...
...men without numbers are thos...

150,000 DEAD IN TOKYO.

...EVASTATED JAPAN.

...OHAMA AND NAVAL BASE
TOTALLY ...ESTROYED

BLAZING CAPITAL

FEARS FOR THE SAFETY OF BRITISH RESIDENTS

...a maxi-
...eet.
...xtra lift of
...r 172

...EW YORK

...DAY, SEPTEMBER 9, 1934

Tribune

Section One

LATE CITY EDITION

...ious DISASTERS

...zeppelin LZ5 destroyed by
...in LZ6 destroyed by
...in LZ7 destroyed by
...l LZ8 destroyed by
...two naval Zeppelins
destroyed; 8 killed in one, 13 in
the other.
1917—Five Zeppelins destroyed by
storm during raid.
1921—British airship R38 broke up
in the air; 44 killed.
1922—Italian ship Roma caught fire
in air; 34 killed.
1923—French ship Dixmude lost;
...killed.
...Shenandoah de-
... killed. ...to

DID "RED" PLOTTERS FIRE MORRO CASTLE?

ACTING CAPTAIN'S DISCLOSURES

SECOND ATTEMPT AT INCENDIARISM

WHOOPEE PARTIES

Girls Probably Burned In Their Beds

CHIEF-OFFICER WILLIAM F. WARMS, ACTING CAPTAIN OF
THE ILL-FATED AMERICAN CRUISING LINER ...
CASTLE, MADE SENSATIONAL DISCLOSURES YESTER...
...THE OPENING OF THE OFFICIAL INQUIRY INTO ...
...WHICH LED TO SUCH HEAVY LOSS OF LIFE IN THE ...
SATURDAY.

He believed the fire was the work of in
"Somebody put something in the locker where i
was discovered," he said. "Power failed. I co
my ship."

He spoke, too, of a previous attempt to set the line
fire on her outward voyage to Havana. The police ar
Havana declare that a Communist was responsible.

Mr. Warms disclosed that the heavy loss of life was probably
due to the drinking parties among the passengers. It was impossible to get some of them from their cabins, he said, and many girls
must have been burned to death in their beds.

GAME WITH LIGHTED CIGARETTES

LORD THOMS...

Brilliant Soldier, Great ...

By William Leach, M.P.
(Under-Secretary for Air in the
first Labour Government)

I AM almost too horrified and full
of grief to write.
That my friend "C. B." is no more
seems too evil news to be true.
Brigadier-General Christopher Bird-
wood Thomson, later to become peer of
the realm, polished, handsome, tall and
slim, a supremely confident man, was of
a type uncommon in the ranks of
Labour.
His distinguished military career led
...to fields which are not productive

LORD

Born i...
Entered
Fought
Brevet-...
War—1900
General
Chief of...
-19...

Miss Jenny Lee To Be Engaged

TO MR. ANEU... BEVAN, M.P.

SPECIAL DAILY MAIL

IT the engagement of
Aneurin Bevan Socialist M.P.
...bbw Vale, and Miss Jennie
...formerly Socialist M.P. for N...
Lanark, is shortly to be announ...
...'ee two aren't members wh...
...cols a Mem... of Parliament in 19...
...be age of 25 has no attractive po...
...it's and great ability as a ...

...is her ...ist in 1931 ...
...'er has ...cded about at her time to...
...ning in the United States. She int...
...to return to that country in the ...
...of another lecture tour.
...a Sammouth University she ear...
...a degree for her academic progr...
...een forced to settle she took her
...gree in Art with honours; but remai...
...at the University to take her LL. B.
...fore she believed to be the fir...
...'kire woman to receive the ful...

CAPTAIN KEPT PERIL SECRET, VESTRIS SAID, 'NOTHING NEW' 5 HOURS BEFORE THE S O S

VOLTAIRE CALLS UNHEEDED

Wireless Logs Show No
Response Even After
Serious Cargo Shift.

Then
caus... SHIP FAILED TO NOTIFY LINE

But Made Frantic Calls for Help,
Urging Speed, After First
Distress Signal.

ONE VESSEL 35 MILES OFF

Records Show Italian Freighter
Heard the S O S, but
Made No Rescues.

...LAY

gas fires over-
...der immediately
... have promised
...s will be so busy
...es that with the best
will in the ...
...everyone cannot be
attended to at once.

...is Liner Morro Castle Burns; ...of Heroic Rescues Off Jersey

...nes, and Passengers Fleeing in Lifeboat

3 Relief Ships Bring Many Injured Here

Charred Hulk Beached After Flames,
Origin a Mystery, Sweep Liner,
Trapping Passengers in Sleep

Tourists, in Panic, Feared To Enter Boats, Crew Says

Disaster Occurs in Storm Off Asbury P...
Captain, Heart Victim, Lies Dead
Bodies Strew Jersey Beache...
Morgue Set Up

The liner Morro C...
Havana to New Yo...
burned before th...
Park wit...
wreck...

GRAVE WEAKNESSES IN AIRSHIP PROJECTS

...structor's Prophecy of Three ...Ago Against R101 Type of ...Lighter-Than-Air Vessel

MEN MAY LOSE THEIR LIVES

...e years since the following striking prophecy was made by
...anner (formerly of the Royal Corps of Naval Constructors),
...sing the Institute of Marine Engineering concerning such

...f the technical design of the new airships is faulty—if it is
...upon faulty deductions as to the stresses to be met with in
...R101 and R100—40 men or more will probably lose their
...dy air conditions on the trial trip.
...on or soon after I have come to the conclusion that there are very grave
..."And I have come to the conclusion that there are very grave
...ses in the airship projects on which the Air Ministry is
...ding money."

...ERT'S WARNING

POLITICAL EFFECTS

Changes in the Ministry and
Criticism Likely

...Mishap May Be Turned
...a Serious One

...Into...or.

From Tottenham Ct. Road Tube Station.

WHEN AND WHERE WAS R101 DAMAGED?

Inquiry as to What Preceded
Hydrogen Blaze

WRECKAGE MILES AWAY

R101'S CHEERY SEND-OFF

Why No Woman Was In the Airship

VILLAGE OF TEARS

Where Dirigible Dropped Sprays
of White Heather

MAN who FORETOLD DISASTER to R101

Reasons Why He Expected the New Attempt at Air Conquest to Fail

MR. E. F. SPANNER

MANY theories are put forward to
account for the wreck of R101, and
considerable importance attaches to
criticisms which have been made by the
well-known naval architect, Mr. Edward F.
Spanner.
He has frequently expressed grave
doubts regarding the safety and commercial
value of giant airships.
In his books he has emphasised with
dramatic accour... what he described with
we know that the passenger load is a live
phrase of fabric and goldbeater's skin
one, capable of inclining the vessel three
or four degrees on either side of the
vertical, and capable also of varying the
pitch of the airship three degrees of w...
...sengers.

would be increased—roughly as the square
of the comparative speeds.

Losing Lift.

Dealing further with this assertion that
an airship would rarely be able to fly without
being pitched either up or down, due to a
discrepancy between load and lift, Mr.
Spanner says:—
"Suppose we neglect external influences entirely, that is, neglect all up-
draughts, storms, and so on, and even assume
that there is no super-heating, we know
that fuel and food will be consumed; we
know that the gasbags will continually
lose lift by reason of the unavoidable
passage of hydrogen through the dia-
phragm of fabric...

"Each and every one of these internal
influences, particularly the latter, will be
helping to keep busy the man operating
the elevator controls and tending to
upset steady axial flight conditions.
"To my mind the problem of maintaining
steady axial flight with R100 and R101 in
steady air conditions is going to prove one
of great difficulty."

Loss of Efficiency.

Spanner said that stability in flight, Mr.
...expected from the fact that these new ships might be
tended to be driven at high speeds, and
from the fact that the control surfaces would
require to be very large.
"This latter circumstance would result in
considerable loss of efficiency when the
ships were flying pitched up or down as
...us before we ...
...the ground. Then ca...
which merely stunned me, ...
violent shock."

Another eye-witness said that he
watched R101 from an attic window.
"The airship," he said, "was flying
with a sideways movement as if seeking a suitable place to land. Suddenly,
the airship's nose dipped deeply, and
the whole structure rushed downwards."

In a chapter on stability in flight, Mr.
...

CAVALRY MAN

...vapidly to in...
...sucess. He...

...ountiful in ...
...-the well-b...
...won the Ki...
...s win ...
...speech ...
...hour.

...nap

...denly

...lds are
... command
...mediately.

...VOLTAIRE ...

SERIOUS CARGO SHIFT

PASSENGERS IN BED

SILENCE—THEN DISASTER

LOG OF THE LAST VOYAGE OF R101

...ASSENGERS smoked final
...cigar and have now gone to ...

...s an extract from the log of
...oomed airship. The following
...e messages sent out from the
...he left Cardington:—

Over London—Moderate rain, base
... cloud, 1,500 feet. Wind 240
... Strength 25 m.p.h. Course now
...r Paris.

...ssing French coast near Hastings.—It
... hard and there is a strong south-
...ly wind. Cloud base is at 1,500
...ffer a good get-away from the
...g-tower at 6.36 the airship
...Bedford before settling a course
...was set for London at 6.54. En-
...nning well and cruising speed a...
...2 knots. Reached London at ...
...then set course for Paris, gradu-
...reasing height so as to avoid ...

...ssing French coast at Point de
...tin.
...degrees. Strength 35 m.p.h.
...ition now 15 miles south-west
...ile.
...up to this time 33 knots, wind
...38 m.p.h. Height 1,500 feet.
...xcellent supper, distinguished ...
...smoked a final cigar, and ...
...ed the French coast, have now ...

...roydon)—Thanks for valuable ...
...Will not require your further ...
...night. (In spite of this mes-
...croydon operator remained on ...

...received a message asking
... In reply Croydon gave the
... one kilometre (five-eighths
...orth of Beauvais ...

...received at Croydon that
...aerodrome that GFAW ...
...taken fire.

CAVALRYMAN

CRITICISM FROM CARDINGTON

From Our Special Correspondent.
CARDINGTON, Sunday.
Last night the people here bravely
waved goodbye to R 101 when she
slipped into the night.

To-day there is scarcely one that does
not mourn husband, son or close friend.

All day groups have stood outside the
entrance to the Air Ministry's station
for news of the injured. From time...

FIGHT FOR LIFE.

...PPED MAN TEARS AT ...ABRIC WITH TEETH.

...Page One.

...ns were crushed to ...
...nat, in his opinion, was ...
...disaster.
...said.
...heavy from England ...
...uring rain all the way.
...ir more and more ...

LONDON'S LAST GLIMPSE.

It was towards half-past nine on
Saturday night when London had
her last sight of R 101.
At that hour (writes a correspondent) she passed over the extreme
south-eastern suburbs, in driving

"She Is Done For."

"I was roused from sleep a few
minutes before 2 o'clock by the noise
of the airship's engines," he said.
"It was an extraordinary noise,
which awoke my wife and children,
too. We had the sensation that a
tremendous thunderstorm had just
broken a hundred yards over our
heads. My house was shaken to its
foundations, and I jumped out of bed,
opened a window and saw the dirigible
passing over my garden.

round to the other side of the ship,
where we found four or five others.
We dashed, shouting, into the flames,
doing everything we could to find our
companions.
"We were burned and exhausted as
the gondolas began to crash down,
sending millions of blazing sparks into
the air. Finally, we saw lights coming
towards us, and motorists rushed up
and gave us their help."
Mr. George Darling, a former Leeds

GRAVEN SHORT?

...VEN SHORT?

1920–1939

Out of the Blue
The *R.38* Crash 1921

The Darkest Day
Tokyo 1923

The Murphysboro Tornado 1925

The Broken Giant
The *Shenandoah* Crash 1925

Race against Time
The Sinking of the *S.4* 1927

Women and Children First
The Sinking of the *Vestris* 1928

A Sacrifice to Improvidence
The *R.101* Crash 1930

The Earthquake at Hawkes Bay 1931

The Deciding Factor
The *Akron* and the *Macon* 1933 and 1935

The *Morro Castle* Mystery
New Jersey 1934

The Gresford Colliery Disaster 1934

The Final Spectacular
Crystal Palace Fire 1936

The Advancing Crest
Ohio Valley Floods 1937

Fire in the Sky
The *Hindenburg* Crash 1937

A Freak of Nature
New England Hurricane 1938

Forty-eight Hours on the *Thetis*
The Sinking of the *Thetis* 1939

Out of the Blue

The R.38 Crash 1921

THE DAILY MIRROR, Friday, August 26, 1921.

PICTURES OF R 38'S DOOM: SEE PAGES 6, 7, AND 12

The Daily Mirror

NET SALE NEARLY TWICE THAT OF ANY OTHER DAILY PICTURE NEWSPAPER

No. 5,560. | Registered at the G.P.O. as a Newspaper. | FRIDAY, AUGUST 26, 1921 | One Penny.

HOPELESS DAWN BREAKS OVER AIRMEN'S RIVER GRAVE

All the night Mrs. Steele (left) and Mrs. Julius, two English-women married to American airmen, watched and waited on the quay at Hull hoping in vain to hear good news of their husbands, who are believed to have been killed.

The stern of the mighty hull of the R 38 floating half an hour after the disaster. Already hundreds of helpers were swarming about the wreck in daring attempts at rescue work.

As the dawn broke eerily over the twisted remains of the world's biggest airship floating in the Humber, relief parties continued their night-long search for survivors.

Although earlier reports of the terrible disaster to the R.38 gave hope of there being other survivors of the forty-nine passengers aboard the giant air liner, it is now definitely established that all but five perished when the airship broke her back and, following a terrific explosion, dropped, a mass of flaming wreckage, into the Humber. Flight-

Lieut. A. H. Wann, the British officer who was in charge when disaster overtook the magnificent craft, states that the R.38 had been sailing beautifully and had slowed down from sixty to fifty knots when, just over Hull, there was a crash, followed by a fearful explosion, which, in his opinion, must have killed many of the crew.

R38 FALLS IN FLAMES: 5 SAVED OUT OF 49 ABOARD

Giant Airship Destroyed at Hull During Trials Prior to Atlantic Flight.

BREAKS IN TWO AND CRASHES INTO HUMBER

A terrible disaster befel the airship R 38 last night. She burst into flames over Hull and fell a total wreck in the River Humber.

Of the forty-nine persons aboard—thirty-two Britons and seventeen Americans—only the following five are reported by the Air Ministry as saved :—

Lieutenant A. W. Wann, in charge of airship (in hospital, injured, but not dangerously) ; A.C. E. W. Davis (in hospital, injured) ; Corporal W. P. Potter and T. O. Walker (uninjured) ; Mr. Bateman, of the N.P. Laboratory. Walker is the only American saved.

The 44 others, including Air-Commodore Maitland, are missing.

Two terrific explosions rent the air as the giant ship broke in halves and fell. Some of those on board escaped by parachutes.

Dr. Jayne, Bishop of Chester, who has died at Oswestry, at the age of seventy-six.

Miss Bleibtrey (U.S.) claims the record for women's 200yds. swimming race in 75ft. tank.

FULL LIST OF THE 49 ABOARD AIRSHIP.

Commodore Maitland Who Flew Atlantic Missing.

AIRSHIP'S LAST TALK TO AERODROME.

Tragic End to Voyage of Thirty-Five Hours.

NIGHT OF TRIALS.

Big Dirigible That U.S. Was Going to Buy.

The story of the last tragic flight of the airship is told in the following communique from the Air Ministry last night :—

The airship left Howden Airship Base at 7.10 a.m. on Tuesday for her fourth trial under the command of Flight-Lieutenant A. H. Wann. She reported her position at various times throughout the day, and proceeded to carry out different tests which had been arranged before.

As an offensive weapon of war Count Zeppelin's airships had a rather more psychological than practical impact. Huge sinister shadows in the sky, they may have looked like the Avenging Angel, but in practice these lumbering leviathans of the sky proved mortally vulnerable. The bombs they mysteriously shed over Goole or the Norfolk Broads paled into insignificance set against the fiery death-traps they became at the hands of the Royal Flying Corps. All the same, there was no denying their peacetime potential, their carrying-power and endless mileage; accordingly, the Government sanctioned a cautious programme of development.

Its foresight was rewarded in July 1919, when the *R.34* triumphantly buffeted its way across the Atlantic and back. And no doubt this pioneering feat would have mesmerized the press too, had not Alcock and Brown scooped up the *Daily Mail*'s £10,000 prize by flying the ocean in a heavier-than-air craft just a fortnight earlier. Thus overshadowed, airship building limped forward: the *R.35* was never begun, the *R.37* never finished, and the *R.36* after a few moments of glory as a 'traffic-spotter' was permanently grounded after an accident.

All the hopes of the lighter-than-air enthusiasts rested then on the *R.38*, completed in 1921 and destined for export to the US Navy. It was the biggest airship ever built, with a volume of over 2.5 million cu.ft, and a theoretical top speed of 70mph.

It was to test her speed that *R.38* took off from Howden on 23 August under the command of Fl. Lt. Wann. Aboard were twenty-eight Britons including the Ministry's Director of Airships, Air Commodore Maitland, the future US crew of seventeen, the ship's designer (Commander Campbell) and four men from the National Physical Laboratory. That day she behaved impeccably, only to find her destination, Pulham, fog-bound. An uncomfortable night shrouded in a blanket of fog was spent over the North Sea, but the dawn came safely and the captain elected to proceed with the trials. By 5.20 that afternoon *R.38* was over Hull, and performing her circular manoeuvres perfectly.

Exactly what happened then was a matter of some dispute among the citizens of Hull, who were staring up from the streets. Certainly there was an enormous explosion, heard 'like an earthquake' twenty-five miles away. But some witnesses told the *Daily Mirror* she 'emerged from the clouds burning like a rag, then disintegrated' before plunging into the dark waters of the Humber. More reliably, others testified that the monster broke in half first, then exploded as the gas hissed away. It was, they all agreed, 'a miracle that the ship didn't crash on the town', for she had been heading directly for the centre when the explosion occurred. In some papers the captain was credited with a remarkable feat —that of actually speeding up the burning hulk to clear inhabited land! Only five of the forty-nine aboard survived. By next morning all that was left for the photographers was a charred skeleton half-submerged in the estuary.

Of course the consuming question was *why* had the machine broken its back in mid-air? Only one paper, the *Daily News*, recalled an interesting item in the previous Sunday's *Observer*, reporting on *R.38*'s earlier trial. There had been, the paper noted, a definite tendency for the airframe to buckle, and the ship had bumped heavily on landing. 'For some reason' the report ended, 'the defect in the R.38 had been kept secret for four or five weeks.' Strangely, this astonishing piece of information was not followed up by a single newspaper, not even the *Observer* in its next issue. The Press, on the contrary, seemed far more concerned with promoting the virtues of lighter-than-air travel. 'We believe,' said the *Daily News*, 'that an impartial examination will show the claim made for the airship of greater stability and safety to be true.' The *Daily Telegraph* was even more emphatic: 'the development of the airship is essential to the consolidation of the Empire. And we do not believe that in this country the hopes which reside in the airship will be regarded as having been buried in the pathetic wreck of R.38 which now lies in the river Humber'.

Sadly for the *Telegraph* that is precisely what did happen. All airship projects in Britain were summarily cancelled. And reading the grim news from abroad over the next few years, of the disintegration of Italy's pride, the *Roma*, the total disappearance of the French ship *Dixmude*, the sudden fracture of the US *Shenandoah* in mid-air—the public would have heartily agreed with the decision.

The Darkest Day
Tokyo 1923

San Francisco Chronicle
LEADING NEWSPAPER of the PACIFIC COAST — REG.U.S.PAT.OFF.

WEATHER
FAIR

FOUNDED 1865 — VOL. CXXIII. NO. 50   C   SAN FRANCISCO, MONDAY, SEPTEMBER 3, 1923 — TWENTY-FOUR PAGES   DAILY 5 CENTS, SUNDAY 10 CENTS: DAILY AND SUNDAY PER MONTH, 95c.

100,000 PERISH

NAGASAKI, Sept. 2 (by the Associated Press).—It is feared that the casualties in Tokyo will exceed even those of the great disaster of 1856, when more than 100,000 were killed in Yeddo alone. A number of volcanoes are reported active.
Several more earth shocks were felt at Yokohama at 1 o'clock Sunday afternoon.
Tokyo is still burning and explosions there are frequent. Only those with food may enter the city.
At Hakone, a famous mountain resort, it is said to be easier to count the living than the dead.

Allied Forces of Death Reap Fearful Harvest

Mountainous Tidal Waves Wipe Peninsula Community Out of Existence; Toll Grows: Historic Capital of Nippon in Ruins: Famine Stalks

SHANGHAI, Sept. 3 (by the Associated Press).---Bulletins received here from Japan report that 100,000 persons perished in Tokyo and Yokohama alone in Saturday's earthquake and fire. The bulletins said fires in the Tokyo arsenal caused explosions, destroying the arsenal and the adjoining printing bureau, killing several thousand persons. The Nichi Nichi was the only newspaper in Tokyo to escape destruction. The Japanese community here is grief stricken.

The most serious damage was done to the tract covering the Yamanote district, including the Tokyo wards of Honjo, Fukagawa, Akusaka, Shitaya, Nihombashi and Kanda, where hardly a single structure was left standing.

At Ito, on the Idzu peninsula, more than 500 houses were washed away by tidal waves. Six hundred persons are said to have perished when the railway tunnel at Sasako, the largest in Japan, collapsed.

The British light cruiser Dispatch, the only foreign vessel at Shanghai, sailed at 4 o'clock this morning for Yokohama, expecting to arrive in eighteen hours.

Thousands are without water and food. The famed twelve-story tower of Asakusa was demolished. Among the larger buildings destroyed were the Mitsugoshi department store, the Imperial Theater, the Marunouchi building and the Imperial Hotel.

When the Kaijo and Marunouchi buildings collapsed there were thousands of casualties. Many lofty buildings that lined the street opposite the Tokyo Central Railway station were burned, although the main building of the station remained intact.

In Yokohama the fire following the earthquake started in the Bund (the foreign section), and spread first through Benten and Isezaki streets, wiping out the business district. Tens of thousands of guests in the mountain resorts of the Hakone district, many of whom were foreigners, were panic-stricken. There were repeated quakes at Mount Hakone, and the town of Atana, in this district, was demolished. Six or seven thousand persons perished.

S. F. Girl on Ship Due in Yokohama

SHANGHAI, Sept. 3 (by the Associated Press.—The Canadian Pacific liner Empress of Australia, which sailed from this port for Yokohama August 27, carried three Americans on her passenger list. They were Miss Mary Ellison of San Francisco and E. C. Allan and G. E. Taylor of Shanghai. The vessel was due to arrive in Yokohama last Saturday, the day of the earthquake and tidal wave. No news has been received from the ship up to early today.

British Extend Their Sympathy to Japan

HONGKONG, Sept. 3 (by the Associated Press.—Sir Reginald Edward Stubbs, governor of the colony of Hongkong, today conveyed to the Japanese consul-general for the great disaster that Japan had suffered.

Santa Cruz Man Dies From Heart Failure

Special Dispatch to The Chronicle.

SANTA CRUZ, Sept. 2.—Ed Hanlon, about 70 years old, was found in his cabin yesterday, where he had been dead for at least two weeks. J. J. Odgar, a neighbor, forced his way into the cabin and found Hanlon dead in his bed. The coroner's jury found a verdict of death from heart disease.

Anxiety Felt Here for U.S.Shipmen in Japan

With the toll of life taken by earthquake and fire mounting hourly in the stricken city of Yokohama, much anxiety is felt for the safety of W. A. Campbell, former general manager of the Pacific Mail Steamship Company and his assistant, James Farley. The offices of the Pacific Mail are located in the heart of the business section of Yokohama.

Three Officials of U.S. Court and Families Are Missing in Yokohama Zone

Mrs. Leonard G. Husar as she appeared on the transport leaving San Francisco recently for Shanghai, where she became the bride of the U. S. District Attorney there. Grave fear is felt for her safety.

Anxiety Felt for Judge Lobingier, Associates, and Wives in Japan

SHANGHAI, Sept. 3 (by the Associated Press.)—Fears are entertained here for the safety of Judge Charles Lobingier of the United States Court for China, his wife, United States District Attorney Leonard Husar, his wife, and United States Marshal Thurston Porter, all of whom are believed to be in Yokohama.

They left for Yokohama recently after a term of court at Harbin. Porter went to Yokohama to greet his fiancee, Miss Louise McCoubrey. They were planning to marry in Japan.

Judge Charles Sumner Lobingier has, for about 20 years old, was one of the best known jurists in the Orient. He has served on the Shanghai bench since 1914, and before that was judge of the court of First Instance in the Philippines for ten years.

Going to the Philippines from Nebraska in 1904, he was active in reforming the island primary courts, held the first justice of the peace assembly in the archipelago and subsequently conducted schools of instruction for native magistrates. He was chairman of the preliminary committee to codify the Philippine laws in 1907.

(Continued on page 3, column 2)

Many San Franciscans In Midst of Orient Quake

Among the 1500 citizens of the United States living in the foreign colonies of Tokyo and Yokohama, in the districts where casualties and wainage was reported heaviest, are eighty San Franciscans. In addition to these, registered and engaged in business there, are many tourists from California. It is believed scores of other United States citizens, either registered permanently or visiting in the stricken cities are among the dead and suffering. The San Franciscans whose names appear in the official registry of the Empire are:

Mr. and Mrs. Marcus Harlow, Yokohama. Harlow is a member of the United States Shipping Board.

W. R. Lynch, Yokohama. Lynch is also a member of the Shipping Board.

Mrs. Earl Ransom and family, Yokohama. Ransom is attending the University of California at Berkeley.

Mr. and Mrs. W. R. Devin, Yokohama.

Three members of the Klinger family, Tokyo. Harry Klinger is registered at the Whitcomb Hotel here. Klingen's mother is court costumer at Tokyo.

Mrs. William Scott and family, Yokohama. Scott is in San Francisco on a business mission.

Miss Josephine Cook, Yokohama.

Miss Mullins, Yokohama. A sister of Miss Mullins resides in Berkeley.

Miss J. Nanley, Yokohama.

A. Kasfner, Yokohama.

M. Frank, Yokohama. Mrs. Frank is in San Francisco.

Miss Josephine Laffin, Yokohama.

Mr. and Mrs. E. Lord, Yokohama.

Mr. and Mrs. E. J. King and two children, Yokohama.

Mr. and Mrs. Herbert Hall, Yokohama.

W. W. Baer, Tokyo.

A. E. Bennett, Tokyo. Manager of the Grand Hotel, Tokyo. Bennett's daughter is living in San Francisco.

Roger (Dinty) Moore, Tokyo. Assistant manager of the Grand Hotel, Tokyo. Moore's family is in San Francisco.

Mrs. D. H. Wainright, Tokyo. Wainright is at present in Oakland.

(Continued on Page 2, Column 3)

Japan Stricken by Fire, Quake; Cities in Ruins

Tokyo Populace Flees Before Flames Spreading Desolation and Death; City Under Martial Law; Yokohama Foreign Section Escapes Disaster

LONDON, Sept. 2.---The foreign section of Yokohama, which is situated high on a hill, escaped destruction, according to an Osaka dispatch to the Daily Express.

Martial law in Tokyo, which is without an adequate supply of food.

Not a single house standing in the cities of Yokosura and Kamajura, as the result of a tidal wave.

Flames sweeping through eight of the leading wards of Tokyo and inhabitants fleeing to other sections of the city.

All six bridges spanning the Sumita river in Tokyo destroyed, crippling communication.

These startling developments are contained in an epitome of the destruction wrought by earthquake, fire and tidal wave in Japan since Saturday, as flashed across the Pacific last night by the lone operator of Station JAA at Tomioka and received here by the Radio Corporation of America.

In brief sentences, the Japanese operator at the lonely station—the same man who voluntarily stepped into the breech on Saturday when the cables were "out"—and flashed the news of the disaster—reported additional information.

Tokyo now is under martial law and, with the military in control, nobody is admitted to the city unless they have their own provisions. A railroad man from Tokyo estimated the casualties in that city at 100,000.

The fire following the earthquake broke out in more than twenty places and spread over the wards of Honjo, Fukagawa, Asakusa, Nihombashi, Akasaki, Kojimachi and Shiba. The Nihombashi ward apparently suffered the most, being reported as "practically annihilated" by the wireless operator.

The message contained the
(Continued on Page 3, Column 5)

Japanese Cities Are in Ruins and Streets Strewn With the Dead

PEKING, Sept. 2.—Wireless dispatches reaching here today tell of possibly the greatest disaster in the history of the world, following tremendous earthquakes and subsequent tidal waves which have caused widespread death and desolation throughout Japan.

The fragmentary messages tell of thousands of dead lying in the streets of Tokyo and Yokohama. All the important buildings of Tokyo have been demolished or consumed by fires, Yokohama is in ashes. Many other cities have been hit equally as hard.

The death list is mounting hourly. Those who escaped the disaster are without food or water. The number who lost their lives in other cities is still unknown.

No word has been received from the more than 1000 American residents of Japan.

Martial law has been declared in Tokyo.

The United States warship Huron is proceeding to the stricken area bearing a corps of physicians, nurses and medical supplies.

The first earth shock that hit Tokyo toppled practically every big building. These in turn crushed smaller ones, piling mountains of wreckage. Fire broke out immediately, resulting in a vast conflagration. Bridges across the Tokyo canal were destroyed by fire, preventing the escape of thousands of panic-stricken people who perished. The business sections of
(Continued on Page 3, Column 1)

Tokyo buildings completely destroyed were the two largest department stores, Mitsukoshi and Shirokiya; the army arsenal, military academy, metropolitan police headquarters, Imperial Theater, the home office of the finance department of

ITALIAN FORCES OCCUPY MORE GREEK ISLANDS

The Daily Mirror

NET SALE MUCH THE LARGEST OF ANY DAILY PICTURE NEWSPAPER

No. 6,187.   Registered at the G.P.O. as a Newspaper   MONDAY, SEPTEMBER 3, 1923   One Penny.

HAVOC OF GREATEST EARTHQUAKE IN HISTORY

Mount Fujiyama, around which many towns have been destroyed.
The Crown Prince of Japan.

The Ginza, the Bond-street of Tokio, capital of Japan.

The ruins of Yokohama after the great fire of 1919. The present outbreak, of even greater intensity, has left the city again a mass of smouldering ruins.

Japan is in the throes of what is described as the worst earthquake disaster in her history. Yokohama has been devastated by fire following earthquake shocks, and Tokio is wrecked. Fires are spreading over an area of 300 miles. The toll of dead was added to by a tidal wave and is known to be a terrible one, though, owing to the destruction of all means of communication, details are still lacking. Yokohama alone has 10,000 dead. Further tremors are at frequent occurrence. Other pictures on pages 8 and 9.

One thing all earthquakes have in common, and that is that the clocks stop. In Tokyo on 1 September 1923 the clock on the Meteorological Institute stopped at two minutes to noon. At that moment the streets of the city were crowded with shoppers and workers hurrying to lunch: in the houses women were lighting up their little charcoal burners for the midday break. The life of the city, that humid morning, was reaching its crescendo when the shock began—at first with deceptive gentleness, then after perhaps five or six seconds with growing fury. For four minutes the earth heaved and tossed before subsiding once more into undulations, then stillness. Over two hundred more shivers of the ground were to occur during what remained of that dark day, but in the horror of what followed, few of these new convulsions were even noticed.

For thousands of years the area around what had once been the old imperial capital of Edo had been densely populated: in 1923 Tokyo and its port of Yokohama embraced more than 2.5 million people. Once its houses, even its public buildings, had been constructed with paper-thin walls—in deference not only to the climate but also to the giant catfish that slept in the ocean (earthquakes, in Japanese mythology, were unmistakable signs of this submarine beast waking up). But since Japan had roused itself from its medieval isolation after the Meiji 'restoration' half a century before, its passion for all things Western had extended to

bricks and mortar. Indeed Tokyo's very latest architectural wonder, the new Imperial Hotel designed by the American architect Frank Lloyd Wright, incorporated some highly un-Japanese ideas, such as sunken concrete piles and wedge-shaped walls.

Tokyo had suffered recurrent earthquakes, but no serious loss of life, since 1885 when 6,700 had died in the ruins—but there were those (including Japan's leading seismologist) in the early 1920s who were predicting an imminent catastrophe in the Tokyo region that would surpass anything this land of earthquakes had ever known. Even as the first vibrations arrived on 1 September, it was manifest that this prophesied terror had come: within seconds the city's highest building, the twelve-storey Asakusa Tower, had crashed in a heap of rubble, reportedly killing hundreds. On the coast the Tokyo express train, just pulling into a station, was swept over the cliff into the sea taking 600 to their deaths.

Statistics were soon to lose their meaning in this vulnerable concentration of humanity, yet the casualties directly attributable to the tremors themselves were utterly eclipsed by their sequels —the inevitable tidal wave, some 35 feet high, that struck Atami and nearby coastal towns; the subsequent epidemics that killed nearly 4,000; and the fires . . . Fuelled by the hundreds of domestic blazes that had started at the height of the earthquake, the central areas of Tokyo became one huge holocaust by mid-afternoon.

Small cyclones developed, sucking in blazing debris and carrying it into new territories. Even in large open spaces where tens of thousands had instinctively fled to escape falling roofs and encroaching flames, these fiery cyclones brought death. The most virulent of them all came to life on the lower reaches of the Sumida River and advanced inexorably across the city: its deadly path coincided with one of Tokyo's biggest open spaces, the grounds of the Clothing Depot where 40,000 refugees were huddled together. It took perhaps a few minutes to traverse the area—when it passed every single one of those inside was dead, burnt or asphyxiated where they stood!

Virtually every important building in central Tokyo, shrines, temples, churches, ancient monuments, modern commercial centres, was destroyed: over 350,000 houses were razed to the ground, making three-quarters of the population homeless. So far beyond the scope of imagination was this wholesale destruction that rumours spread, almost as fast as the fires, that they had been deliberately started. Suspicion fell at once on an unpopular minority, the Koreans (Korea was at that time still part of the Japanese Empire), and a savage persecution was unleashed against anyone who was, or looked, remotely Korean. Only by the intervention of the police and a declaration of martial law were these outrages diminished— but not before several hundred 'Koreans' had been lynched, stabbed or otherwise disposed of. Nor did it prevent a persistent whisper that a huge army of Koreans was massing outside Tokyo to march on the ruined city to pillage it.

At Yokohama—though the city was much smaller than Tokyo—the casualties were proportionately higher. Less than one person in ten survived the disaster unaffected by death, injury or the loss of their home: the city was to all intents and purposes obliterated. Panic in its narrow streets was compounded by the maze of canals that criss-crossed the area. Most bridges had been demolished by the first tremors, and those who attempted to flee the city by barge found themselves trapped between converging conflagrations, or else drowned. In the port section, where most of the more substantial buildings were, the death-toll was highest and escape by boat across the bay was cut off for many when the waters of the harbour were ignited by oil escaping from burning refineries.

In spite of all this, it was from Yokohama that the first news reached the rest of the world. The city's police chief, himself injured by falling masonry, had struggled out to a Japanese freighter in the harbour and commandeered its radio. Having failed, not surprisingly, to elicit any response from Tokyo, he then tried to raise Osaka. This message was intercepted by a transmitting station at Iwaki, 150 miles to the northeast, where the radio operator took it upon himself to send out a dramatic paraphrase of what he had heard: 'Conflagration subsequent to severe earthquake at Yokohama at noon today. Whole city practically ablaze with numerous casualties. All traffic stopped!' His faint signal was picked up in San Francisco, and passed immediately to *Associated Press*. Inevitably those papers able to publish the news at once, therefore, made no mention of any disaster in Tokyo. Even when more reports, via Shanghai, filtered out later the Press found itself utterly at a loss. There was no way to establish contact with resident correspondents in Tokyo (it took the first one nearly three days to get an eyewitness account out over the wires), and the tantalizing scraps of information available could scarcely command the kind of space such a story merited. For several days newspapers all over the world got by on reasonable guesswork and photographs depicting earlier Japanese calamities (of which there were many in the files, ranging from typhoons to floods).

Estimates of the dead began at 10,000 and, in some papers, quickly reached a million.

Daily News

150,000 DEAD IN TOKYO.

DEVASTATED JAPAN.

YOKOHAMA AND NAVAL BASE TOTALLY DESTROYED.

BLAZING CAPITAL.

FEARS FOR THE SAFETY OF BRITISH RESIDENTS.

The Japanese Consulate at Liverpool yesterday afternoon received the following cable from Tokyo:—

Yokohama, Kamakura and Yokosuka naval base totally destroyed.

Eight districts out of fifteen in Tokyo are partially destroyed. Fires are not under control in some districts.

All the bridges over the River Sumida, which runs through Tokyo, have been carried away by the tidal flood. The Island of Koshima, which is 30 miles away from Tokyo, is erupting.

The above is the first official news from Tokyo of the great Japanese earthquake disaster. The estimated death roll in the two chief cities affected is now reported as follows:—

TOKYO	...	150,000
YOKOHAMA	...	100,000

If these figures are correct the total death roll must be vastly more than the 250,000 indicated, as many other towns and villages have been destroyed.

Much anxiety is felt concerning the fate of British residents in Japan, and no news of them has been received in London yesterday. Forty foreigners are reported killed at Hakone.

HUGE DEATH-ROLL.

PRINCE AND PRINCESS KILLED.

OSAKA, Monday.

The Minister of Marine estimates that the fatalities resulting from the earthquake catastrophe have reached 150,000 in Tokyo alone.

At Hakone a representative of the "Osaka Jiji Shimpo" came across a number of foreign refugees, who were penniless and without food, and some were suffering from injuries.

They stated that about forty foreigners had perished there.—Reuter.

THE DEAD PRINCE

NAGASAKI, Monday.

The Nagoya Railway Bureau has received a report that Prince Matsukata has died at Karuisawa (which is destroyed) as the result of injuries received in the earthquake.—Reuter.

[Prince Matsukata was a marquis last year, when he was created a Prince on resigning the post of Lord Keeper of the Imperial Seal. He was one of the Genro, or "Elder Statesmen," and was Premier in 1901 and in 1896-98. He was born in 1840, and was created Count in 1884, and Marquis in 1907.]

SAN FRANCISCO, Monday.—It is reported that Prince Yamashina and Princess Yamashina are among the killed.—Central News.

FLIGHT OVER RUINS.

OSAKA, Monday.

The aeroplane of the Nagoya Division has arrived in report from Lieutenant Ishida, who flew for some time over Tokyo and the stricken district yesterday and states that the Imperial Palace is safe, and that only partial damage was done to it.

Not a single house could be seen in Amakusa and Yokosuka.

The airman says it was difficult to fly over the city at a good observing height owing to the intensity of the flames and the suffocating smoke.

The latest estimate of the casualties at Yokohama alone exceeds 100,000. Odowara has been washed away by a tidal wave.

An officer of the London Maru, who landed at Yokohama, reports that dead bodies are scattered everywhere.—Reuter.

BURNING TOKYO.

MORE EARTH SHOCKS AT YOKOHAMA.

NAGASAKI, Monday.

TOKYO is still burning, and the offices of the Bank of Japan are reported to have been demolished yesterday.

It is impossible to estimate the number of earthquake casualties in all the districts affected, but it is feared that the casualties in Tokyo are over 100,000.

It is reported that the Fuji spinning mills near Mount Fuji collapsed, and that 8,000 operatives perished.

A number of volcanoes are stated to be in active eruption.

There were several more shocks at Yokohama at one o'clock to-day.

Nobody is permitted to enter Tokyo unless they have with them a sufficient supply of food for their own needs.—Reuter.

ARSENAL EXPLODES.

Thousands of Deaths in a Tokyo Disaster.

SHANGHAI, Sunday.

The fire in Tokyo caused the arsenal adjoining the printing bureau to explode. It was entirely destroyed, and there were several thousand casualties as the result of the explosion.

The most serious damage done was in the Tamaoote district. In the Nihonbashi and Kanda wards of the capital there is scarcely a single structure left standing. Thousands of people are without water or food.

The Kaijo building at Marunouchi collapsed, causing thousands of casualties. The buildings that lined the streets opposite the Tokyo central railway station have been burned, although the main building remained intact.

CAPITAL TO BE MOVED?

Starving People Catch Carp in Park.

The following are some minor incidents of the Japanese disaster.

The damaged Imperial Palace, Tokyo, is being used to house refugees.

Martial law and the Emergency Commandeering Act are to be promulgated.

The Prime Regent is taking a leading part in the work of relief, and refuses to rest.

While Tokyo Burned.

While Tokyo burned Count Yamamoto, the new Premier, hurries on the formation of his Cabinet.

Eno-Shima, one of the sacred islands, and a popular holiday resort, is submerged.

Starving refugees have been catching carp for food in a pond in a Tokyo park.

Saved by Bamboo Grove.

All the lighthouses in the Bay of Tokyo have been rendered useless.

At Hakone, the famous mountain resort, it is said to be easier to count the living than the dead.

Prince Satomi, who was staying at Gotenba, which was destroyed, escaped to a bamboo grove and was saved.

News by Air.

Two newspapers, the "Asahi Shimbun" and the "Mainichi Shimbun," are sending reporters from Nagasaki to Tokyo by aeroplane.

The capital may be temporarily transferred to Kyoto or Osaka owing to the damage in Tokyo.

[Further earthquake news on Page Three.

ON OTHER PAGES.

Page
Russian Trade Openings ...
Trade Union Congress ...
The Woman Abroad ...
Motor-Car Highwaymen ...
Wrangel Island Proclamation ...
Books and Authors ...
Motoring ...
Winter Work Plans ...

FLEEING BEFORE THE TERROR
This photograph, taken on the occasion of the last great earthquake and fire in Tokyo, shows refugees thronging the streets with their household goods. Other earthquake pictures will be found on the Back Page.

2,000 BRITISH IN TOKYO.

GREAT ANXIETY AS TO THEIR FATE.

British official circles are still without news regarding the 2,000 British subjects in Tokyo, including the diplomatic and consular staffs there, and those at Yokohama.

Great anxiety is felt as to their fate, and urgent telegrams have been sent to Kobe, but no reply has yet been received.

The Japanese Embassy in London has been out of touch with Japan since Friday, and has no news of British residents.

As far as British residents generally are concerned the Embassy is inclined to be optimistic, as the most of them, like the missionaries, are probably on holiday in the hills.

MISSIONARIES SAFE.

"Unharmed earthquake—Barclay."

This laconic message was received by cablegram by the Church Missionary Society yesterday. It was dated from Karuisawa, a mountain holiday resort 85 miles from Tokyo.

The Church Missionary Society has two clergymen and their wives and two single ladies resident at Tokyo. The Society also has a clergyman at Yokohama.

As it is customary for them to go into the mountains at this time of year for a holiday it is assumed that the short message refers to all the missionaries, of which the Society has 35 in Japan.

The "Daily News" Rome correspondent telegraphs that the staff of the Italian Embassy at Tokyo is safe.

BRITISH RELIEF.

Probable Expedition and Action with Powers.

The British Government has not yet received official details of the calamity which has fallen upon the Japanese nation.

There is a possibility that, as soon as the exact situation is more fully apprehended, a relief expedition will be organised with official assistance.

It is being strongly urged in some quarters that Great Britain ought to send at once what ships are available to the zone of the disaster, and that she should initiate co-operative action by the Powers to carry succour to the stricken cities.

The Japan Society and the Japanese Association, London, have opened a joint fund for the relief of distress caused by the earthquake in Japan. Donations may be sent to the hon. treasurer, Japan Society, 22, Russell-square, W.C.1, and to the hon. treasurer, Nihonjin-kwai (Japanese Association), 3, Cavendish-square, W.1.

HEROES OF THE ARCTIC.

DESPERATE DASH TO SIBERIA.

FOOD SHORTAGE.

ESKIMO WOMAN'S STORY OF WRANGEL TRAGEDY.

In the long thrilling cable printed below Mr. Harold Noice, Commander of the relief party, tells the full story of the tragic Wrangel expedition of 1921 and the sad meeting with Ada Blackjack, the devoted Eskimo woman who nursed Lorne Knight for four months until his death last June.

Owing to food shortage, Crawford, Galle, and Maurer left the camp in January of this year for a desperate last hope dash to Siberia.

Nothing has been heard of them since Mr. Noice says: "I do not believe they had one chance in a thousand of getting through."

From HAROLD NOICE, Commander of the Wrangel Island Relief Expedition.

[SPECIAL CABLE TO THE "DAILY NEWS."]

NOME (Alaska), Sept. 2.

IN the early morning of August 20 we reached the vicinity of Doubtful Harbour, Wrangel, after a long battle with the ice floes.

At 8 a.m. I saw something moving on the beach, and soon could see the slight figure of a woman coming down to the water's edge.

It was Ada Blackjack, the seamstress of the expedition. We steered close inshore and anchored. I jumped into the skiff and paddled ashore. As we neared the beach Ada started out in the shallow water to meet us. I sprang out and shook her hand.

For a moment neither spoke. Then she said: "Where is Crawford and Galle and Maurer?"

SOBBED LIKE A LITTLE GIRL.

I told her I had just arrived from Nome expecting to find them on Wrangel Island. She choked down a sob and said: "There is nobody here but me. I am all alone. Knight—he died on June 22."

Then Ada, a queer, frightened note in her voice, said: "I want to go back to my mother. Will you take me back to Nome?"

When I assured her that most certainly we would a bright light came into her eyes. The strange dazed expression left her face. She just stood and looked at me and then she tottered forward and, as I caught her in my arms, commenced to sob like a little girl.

I lifted her into the skiff, brought her aboard the Donaldson, took her down into the cabin and gave her hot coffee and food.

ESKIMO WOMAN'S STORY.

After the first shock had passed me told the sad story of the expedition. Briefly, it is as follows:—

The expedition, which landed on Wrangel on September 16, lived on the beach at the first camp four miles east of Doubtful Harbour in tents covered with snow blocks. In the first year game was plentiful in the autumn, and the party killed numbers of Polar bears, but because of insufficient snow for sledging a large amount was eaten by foxes and bears before it could be hauled into camp.

By November 16 the meat was all gone. Then they started to cook their own provisions for the dogs. They were just able to get a bare living in the first year, and by the spring had little food except polar bread. They killed that year about forty seals.

In the spring and succeeding autumn there were large herds of walrus about the island, but because they had no boats they could not kill any.

(CONTINUED ON PAGE SIX.)

BIG FIRE AT SUTTON.

150 HOMELESS AFTER TIMBER BLAZE.

REMARKABLE SCENES OF PANIC.

From Our Special Correspondent.

SUTTON (Surrey), Monday Night.

A street of houses in the poor part of Sutton was threatened with destruction to-night in the worst fire that has occurred in the town for 40 years. Damage is estimated at £15,000 was done.

About 150 people were homeless for the night. They were accommodated in the Parish Hall and Municipal Public Hall. The Crown-road School, with places for 1,000 children, caught alight, and the flames were rapidly gaining a hold when the wind veered round and the danger was over.

At one time there were grave fears for the gas works, about 200 yards away, owing to the sparks carried by the wind. The fire was discovered at 6.30 p.m. in the timber yard belonging to Messrs. Wakeford and Co., timber importers and builders' merchants, and the Leyton Timber Company, in Haddon-road.

Extraordinary scenes were witnessed. While the fire raged, and burnt out the wood-yard, people in the surrounding streets threw their furniture into the roadway, and neighbours aided peoples' homes and whether they liked it or not threw their furniture out also.

SUPPOSED CAUSE.

The fire began either in or around the engine room in Wakeford's timber yard, it is supposed through a boiler bursting. There was a flare-up instantly, and clouds of thick, pungent smoke rolled out of the engine-room and smothered the surrounding streets.

The flames leapt at the stacks of wood and burnt them up, an onlooker told me to-night, "as quickly as a match burns your fingers." A hundred yards from the outbreak was Haddon-road. It was here that the worst scare occurred. What happened is best told in the words of Mr. Anthony, of Haddon-road.

"I had just finished my tea," he said, "when I noticed the fire. Some people rushed down the side entry and into the kitchen, very excited and shouting. Before I knew where I was they were picking up my furniture, and carrying it out. Then I heard some smashing in the front. The frame of the bay window had been smashed in, and my furniture was being pitched into the street as fast as possible."

Captain Day, president of the Sutton British Legion, organised an army of workers, who helped the firemen to break down fences and wooden buildings around the houses to prevent the fire spreading. Pigeons and chickens perished in the flames, but many were set free, and a number of horses were also saved.

DEATH FROM SHOCK.

Mr. C. Mortiboy, an elderly man, of Marshalls-road, near by, saw his house on the rise of fire, and rushing out into the High-street collapsed on the pavement. He was dead when picked up, presumably having died of shock. A woman and her young baby were taken from their bed at a house in Haddon-road, and in the confusion in Chandlers-alley was also rescued.

One cottage was destroyed, but the splendid work of the fire brigade and voluntary workers saved the other dwellings. The boy scouts did splendid work, and of the other Haddon-road was destroyed.

The prompt measures taken by the professional and amateur fire fighters prevented the fire spreading to the shops in High-street, which at one time it was thought nothing could possibly save. This involved a considerable amount of structural damage. The fire was under control at 8 p.m.

OUTBREAK AT MITCHAM.

A serious fire occurred at the Free Insurance scheme, insures the household furniture and personal effects of all registered readers, up to £250 in amount, against loss or damage by fire. SIGN THE FORMS.

A serious fire occurred at a large piggery and stables on the Gorringe Park Estate, Mitcham, last night. A large number of pigs and horses were removed from buildings when the outbreak seemed true spreading. Owing to the fire which was at the same time at Sutton, the fire brigade were taxed to the utmost.

LEAGUE UNITY.

"Fearless and Resolute Action" on Italy's Defiance.

FRANCE SUPPORTS BRITAIN.

From Our Diplomatic Correspondent,
H. WILSON HARRIS.

GENEVA, Monday.

THE Italian Greek situation has taken a distinct turn for the better so far as Geneva is concerned, as the result of the decision of the French Government to support the contention which the British delegates have strongly urged—that the whole question must be handled by the League here, and not by the Council of Ambassadors at Paris.

Instructions to this effect were received by the French delegation this morning, and the establishment of Franco-British solidarity on this fundamental principle may well prove to be a turning point in the whole controversy.

LEAGUE UNITED.

This development is particularly important in that Italy's easiest way of evading League action—a way which the French Government has assiduously recommended to her, and which Signor Salandra endeavoured to take at Saturday's Council meeting—is to plead that the matter must remain in the hands of the Ambassadors' Conference.

France's declaration of League jurisdiction does not, of course, clear every obstacle from the path, but it does remove one serious cause for anxiety. Unless there is some new modification of the French position the League will now proceed to its difficult task as a united body.

Absurd reports emanated from somewhere that among the Council members only Lord R. Cecil and M. Branting were opposed to Italy. In point of fact, so far as I can discover, every State represented here is of one mind—not to denounce Italy as such, but to insist on fearless and resolute action against a State which openly violates engagements it has undertaken under the Covenant.

The Little Entente is solid on this

NO HASTY ACTION.

This does not mean that swift or dramatic action by the League is to be expected. Rather the contrary. The French, in particular, feel that matters must be allowed to move a little slowly in order to give the Italian feeling time to subside, and there is no disposition in British quarters to question the wisdom of that course.

It is recognised that Signor Mussolini has placed himself in a position from which graceful retreat is not easy, but he can, I think, be assured that the

CHILD VICTIMS OF CORFU.

The first authentic news from Corfu, given by Colonel Lowe, of the American Near East Relief organisation.

Page Three.

League Council will do nothing to accentuate his difficulties gratuitously. Everything, or nearly, depends on whether they abandon scrupulously from further acts of aggression. If she does not the League must act without a moment's hesitation, and there is now a sufficiently clear demonstration of unity of resolve to satisfy the belief that the necessary action will be forthcoming.

As things stand the Council intends to meet to-morrow afternoon, but as Signor Gaurani, the Italian delegate, who left for Rome on Saturday mid-

(CONTINUED ON PAGE THREE.)

San Francisco Chronicle
LEADING NEWSPAPER OF THE PACIFIC COAST
REG. U.S. PAT. OFF.
FOUNDED 1865 — VOL. CXXIII, NO. 51 — SAN FRANCISCO, TUESDAY, SEPTEMBER 4, 1923 — TWENTY-SIX PAGES — DAILY 5 CENTS, SUNDAY 10 CENTS: DAILY AND SUNDAY PER MONTH, $1.15

FAIR WEATHER

RIOTS RAGING IN TOKYO; QUAKE DEATHS MOUNT

Famous Nippon Island and Two Villages Swept Away By Tremendous Tidal Wave

Thousands Trampled to Death in Mad Rush, Many Burned; Rich and Titled Suffer With Poor in Greatest Calamity of Modern Times

(By Associated Press)

Food riots have broken out in Tokyo, according to a radiogram received last night by the Radio Corporation from Iwaki station, 155 miles from Tokyo. Gendarmerie are reported in these advices to have exercised the most strenuous measures to surpress the disorder, even attacking the rioters with their swords.

A number of Koreans were in the mob, the advices said. The advices confirmed earlier reports of a great fire in Yokohama and an estimate that there had been at least 100,000 casualties there. The fires, the message said, were caused by or followed by the explosion of oil storage tanks in the city, where reserves of fuel oil for the merchant and naval marine were kept.

The advices also confirmed earlier reports of the submergence of the island of Enoshima, "Picture Island," one of Japan's most beautiful spots. This island, the message said, was swept away by a tidal wave, as were also Honomuku and Isoko, villages in the vicinity of Enoshima.

Many Europeans, visitors and residents of that section, are missing.

OSAKA, Sept. 3 (by the Associated Press).—The Minister of Marine today estimated the fatalities from the earthquake and fire in Tokyo alone at 150,000.

MANY FOREIGNERS BELIEVED AMONG VICTIMS

It is reported that Viscount Takahashi, former Premier, and twenty other leading members of the Seiyukai or government party were killed on Saturday while holding a conference.

A representative of the Osaka Jiji Shimpo met a number of destitute foreigners at Hakone, who stated that about forty foreigners had perished there.

Almost the whole of Tokyo and Yokohama have been destroyed by earthquake, followed by fire, and the loss of life now is estimated at from 120,000 to 200,000 or more.

Two hunrded thousand houses have been burned down in the two cities.

Water mains have been broken and food supplies destroyed by the fire so that the people are near starvation and suffering much from thirst.

It is reported, but not confirmed, that the section of Tokyo where most of its foreign population resided, is not greatly damaged.

Martial law has been proclaimed and no one is allowed to enter the stricken districts at the capital, although thousands whose friends or relatives resided there have gathered about the city seeking entrance that they may at least find the bodies of their loved ones.

MILITARY FORCES TO CONTROL SITUATION

Military and naval forces have been gathered at the imperial villa at Nikko for use in controlling the situation, and other forces are on duty in Tokyo itself.

The air is filled with wildest rumors, including one that the new Premier, Count Yamamoto, was assassinated within a few hours after formation of his cabinet.

The reason for the rapid spread of the fire, which took such an awful toll in Tokyo, came to light today when it was learned that the pipes conveying gas for lighting and heating purposes throughout the city were broken by the earthquake, which shook and twisted the ground almost unbelievably.

(Continued on Page 5, Column 3)

Late News of Nippon Horror Told in Brief

LATEST reports from the Japanese disaster show:

The known death list is nearing 200,000 and may far exceed that number.

The island Enoshima, one of the scenic wonders of Japan and two villages swept away by a tidal wave.

Food roits break out in Tokyo. Troops are hastening to the city.

Yokohama is virtually wiped out. Human bodied feed the flames as they rage through the city.

Thousands of refugees who seek safety on vessels perish when the ships are swallowed by tidal waves.

In Tokyo eight of the fifteen wards are in ruins with an estimated death list of more than 100,000.

A volcano is emitting smoke at Oshima.

Odawara is swept away by a tidal wave.

Viscount Takahashi, former premier, and twenty members of the government party killed when fire breaks out in a conference hall.

Martial law proclaimed in Tokyo.

Nothing definite known of the fate of the embassies and legations at Tokyo although it is rumored that the American embassy has been destroyed.

While the emporer and empress are reported safe, Prince Ramashina and Princess Kaya are said to be dead.

S. F. Liner Safe, Cablegram Says

The Toyo Kisen Kaisha steamer Korea Maru is safe in the harbor of Yokohama with 2000 refugees on board, according to a cablegram received at the company's offices here today from its agents in Kobe. Communications of all kinds have been reopened up to Numza, eighty-five miles west of Tokyo, the cablegram said.

The Korea was in the harbor throughout the beginning of the disaster period, and was at once made available for relief purposes. She was to have sailed for San Francisco yesterday, but the sailing has been indefinitely postponed.

The cablegram said that Tokyo and Yokohama "have been destroyed."

Mexican, U. S. Envoys Present Credentials

WASHINGTON, Sept. 3.—Manuel C. Tellez, charge d'affaires of the Mexican embassy here presented his credentials to Acting Secretary Phillips today, thus finally restoring full international relations between the two governments. At the same time George T. Summerlin, charge of the American embassy in Mexico City, presented his credentials to the Mexican Foreign Office

ALL AVAILABLE U.S. SHIPS SENT TO JAPAN'S AID

Asiatic Fleet Rushed to Stricken Area With Food and Medical Supplies

COOLIDGE ISSUES CALL

President Urges Contributions for Red Cross Relief Work

The War Department has sent cable instructions to Manila for the army transports Meiggs and Merritt to proceed to Yokohama with food and medical supplies, tentage, bedding and cots.

PEKING, Sept. 3.—Six United States destroyers left the port of Dairen for Yokohama this afternoon, carrying a number of doctors and a large quantity of supplies to aid the earthquake victims in the stricken city. The flagship Huron of the Asiatic fleet picked up Admiral Anderson at Chefoo and has proceeded to Japan. The Japanese Legation here issued a statement to the effect that the Foreign Office at Tokyo had burned. No other authentic news has been received here from the stricken area, although it is rumored that there are 10,000 dead in Yokohama.

By ARTHUR S. HENNING

Special by Leased Wire to The Chronicle

WASHINGTON, Sept. 3.—America took the lead today in relief of stricken Japan.

While all the available ships, food and relief workers at the command of the United States in the Far East were being rushed to Yokohama, President Coolidge issued an appeal to the American people for contributions to a great relief fund, and the American Red Cross appropriated $110,000 from its reserve fund for immediate expenditure on the scene.

Contributions of any amounts individuals, corporations or organizations desire to make will be received by local Red Cross chapters or by the national headquarters of the Red Cross in Washington. It is expected that a fund of millions of dollars will be subscribed by the American people.

Coolidge Appeals to People for Funds

In his appeal to the people, President Coolidge dwelt on the appalling character of the disaster, and while giving assurance that every assistance possible will be rendered by the executive branch of the Government, he said he was moved by the magnitude of the suffering in Japan to solicit aid from the public. The need of such aid, the President pronounced urgent. He recommended that contributions be sent to the Red Cross headquarters here or to local Red Cross chapters for transmission to Japan.

The Red Cross headquarters here announced the steps it has taken for immediate relief in the following statement:

American Red Cross Gives Out Statement

"The American Red Cross has opened the national fund for the relief of the victims of the Japanese earthquake horror, with a contribution of $100,000. In addition, it has appropriated from its reserve fund $10,000 for the assistance of Americans caught in the disaster zone.

"Supplementing these appropriations for relief work, which will be forwarded, together with contributions from the public made, in re-

(Continued on Page 4, Column 2)

Radio Tells Stirring, Halting Story of Worst Catastrophe in History

Nippon's Capital City in Grip of Hunger-Maddened Mobs; Hundreds, Trapped 'Neath Debris, Are Cremated by Flames

A gripping, vivid story of Japan's condition, as the island nation battles for its life amid ruined cities, desolated towns and villages, stalked by the invisible presence of approaching famine, was contained in a radio dispatch from Tomioka, received here last night by the Radio Corporation of America.

"We want details—give us facts!"

This was the request that spanned the Pacific from the American coast early yesterday. All day the world waited. When evening came, Tomioka broke its silence. Haltingly, as the Japanese was translated into English, the story came through—shocking an entire globe with the stark horror of the picture painted in the cryptic utterances of the radio code.

Hunger-Maddened Mobs Range Tokyo Streets

Tokyo, according to the message, is witnessing terrible scenes of mob violence, as hunger-maddened mobs range the streets hunting for food. Hand-to-hand battles are taking place everywhere.

Gendarmes, armed with naked blades, are trying to restore order. Mobs of Koreans, hated enemies of Japan, are foraging like wild animals. Upon these, the gendarmes are concentrating their attention, trying to curb the battle lust that is born of dire necessity.

At Yokohama, huge oil tanks exploded with a roar that overshadowed the grinding echoes of the terrible earthquake. The whole city seemed to burst into flames from a score of points. Only the Bluff, the hilltop occupied by foreigners, escaped.

Yokohama casualties are estimated at 100,000. Dead are everywhere, some piled in heaps, others lying where they fell. Victims were trapped beneath piles of brick and fallen timbers.

Three Seaboard Towns Washed Out of Existence

Outside of Yokohama three seaboard towns are entirely washed away. They are Enoshima, Hommoku and Isoka—engulfed by the giant tidal wave that followed the earth shocks and blotted thriving marine communities from existence with a mountain of water. In these towns many Europeans are missing—lost with hundreds of others living there.

Bonin island, beauty spot off the coast of Japan, has sunk into the sea, leaving no traces of its presence but heaps of wreckage floating on the surface. Oshima Idzu also is submerged—sunken with the other.

(Continued on Page 5, Column 1)

Disaster Is Held Commercial Boon

The destruction of Tokyo and Yokohama is viewed as a great commercial blessing by Professor Y. S. Kuno of the department of Oriental languages at the University of California.

"The great loss of life and misery caused by the catastrophe is deplorable, but in the long run, the earthquake and fire will prove of inestimable benefit to the empire," declared Dr. Kuno yesterday.

[illegible] commercial growth was handicapped because the people in the ancient cities were huddled together without modern sanitation or street improvements, to the detriment of business.

"With the burning of the antique houses and the razing of old institutions, an excellent opportunity is presented for the rebuilding of the cities in a modernized way," Kuno said.

"The disaster will also prevent the breach in the Japanese Cabinet, which might otherwise have been caused, following the death of Prime Minister Kato. A Cabinet united by adversity will for the next few years devote its entire attention to the rebuilding of the empire. The catastrophe will in no way damage the potential military or naval power of Japan," Kuno concluded.

Pope Pius Sends His Sympathy to Tokyo

ROME, Sept. 3 (by the Associated Press).—Pope Pius has sent through the Apostolic delegate in Tokyo profound condolence to the Japanese Imperial family and the Government and people of Japan.

Aid Campaign to Be Launched Here

Immediately upon learning of the extent of the disaster in Japan, all Japanese-American organizations in San Francisco called a joint meeting yesterday afternoon in the Japanese consulate and prepared to launch a campaign to secure funds to alleviate the suffering in their homeland.

The meeting was presided over by I. Shibata, Vice-Consul General, who has been in charge of the San Francisco office in the absence of U. Oyama, Consul-General.

Among the bodies represented were the Japanese Benevolent Society, Japanese Red Cross Society, Japanese Women's Patriotic Society, Japanese Association, Japanese Salvation Army, the Japanese America News and the New World, the last two Japanese-language newspapers published in San Francisco.

A relief committee to direct the campaign was organized and Vice-Consul Shibata selected as chairman.

James King Steele, editor of "Japan," urged that all nations and creeds join in extending aid to the stricken people of Tokyo, Yokohama and the other disaster-visited cities.

"We citizens of San Francisco," said Steele, "can appreciate the calamity that has befallen Japan. It is a terrible happening and all the relief organizations of the world must come to the assistance of the homeless and bereft Japanese."

FEDERAL JUDGE VAN FLEET IS TAKEN BY DEATH

Presiding Justice of U. S. District Court in S. F. Expires After Stroke

IS STRICKEN SUDDENLY

End Comes Following Two and One-Half Days of Unconsciousness

Federal Judge William C. Van Fleet, presiding member of the bench of the United States District Court here, died at his home, 2020 Pacific avenue, at 1:30 yesterday afternoon, after a brief illness.

After holding court last Friday, apparently in the best of health, the noted jurist suffered a stroke of cerebral hemorrhage at the dinner table at his home that evening.

Death Comes After Cerebral Attack

He lapsed into an immediate coma at that time, from which he never emerged. The best efforts of attending physicians were unavailing, and death came after two and a half days of unconsciousness.

The death of Judge Van Fleet comes as a shock to his fellow jurists and those with whom he came into constant contact at the Federal building here.

Throughout the past weeks, Judge Van Fleet has been sitting daily in charge of criminal cases here. As usual he occupied the bench Friday, hearing various pleas and sentencing a number of confessed criminals.

Saturday his absence at the court was explained by reports of his illness. Judge John Partridge occupied Judge Van Fleet's place on the bench that morning.

Funeral to Be Private, Time Not Yet Set

The funeral, according to his own oft-repeated request, will be private. The time has not yet been set.

The dead Judge leaves aside from the widow, four sons: Carey and Alan C., San Francisco attorneys; William, engineer in Seattle, and Clark, an electrician at Santa Rosa.

(Continued on Page 10, Column 3.)

THE DAILY GRAPHIC

Sudden Death of Viscount Morley : Special Memoir.

DAILY GRAPHIC

No. 10,535.   ♦   Registered as a Newspaper   MONDAY, SEPTEMBER 24, 1923.   ONE PENNY

FIRST PICTURES OF DISASTER TO U.S. DESTROYERS.

An unprecedented photograph of American destroyers which were flung on the rocks of Santa Barbara, California, while racing to the help of the Cuba, a Pacific liner. Seven of them being drowned in their bunks. | destroyers were caught in a tidal wave which followed the Japanese earthquake, and to add to their terrible ordeal a dense fog prevailed. Twenty-five men lost their lives, some

A group of the survivors. Some are asleep in their blankets. Inset: A. Peterson, of the destroyer Young, who swam to the Chauncey and brought a lifeline back to his ship.

Passengers in a lifeboat from the wrecked liner Cuba were picked up by the American destroyer Reno, which escaped the disaster, and took them into port.

Weird, half-understood stories readily found column-space: Mount Fuji had erupted (it hadn't); an island in Sagami Bay had disappeared beneath the waves (nor had that); or the new Prime Minister had been assassinated by a frantic mob (he hadn't). Among the many ambiguities created by the lack of information was the story that Lloyd Wright's magnificent Imperial Hotel had collapsed. Informed of this news by a Los Angeles reporter, the architect refused to believe it and optimistically cabled his sponsor in Tokyo for confirmation. Days later he received his reply: his hotel had remained unscathed amid the desolation, and had provided invaluable sanctuary for hundreds of foreign refugees (it seemed that Tokyo was full of Imperial Hotels, most of which *had* collapsed).

The final death-toll was roughly estimated at 150,000 for the whole area, and the sections consumed by fire amounted to some seven square miles in Tokyo and another three in Yokohama. Correspondents, when they finally managed to penetrate the chaos, found the surviving population desperate for lack of water —main supplies were non-existent and nearly all the wells in Tokyo had been filled in some years earlier on Government orders (so that its brand-new water system should not run at a

loss). Appeals for aid were swiftly launched in the Press—especially in San Francisco where memories of a similar fate were still alive and where even Mr Hearst's chain of papers (usually so virulent about the Yellow Peril) were asserting that 'the sense of racial distinction sinks into insignificance' in the face of such appalling acts of nature. Tokyo recovered and reconstructed itself, if not on the Utopian lines envisaged by some ministers at the time, then at least with the impressive speed and dedication that characterizes the Japanese worker today. One unalterable consequence of the earthquake, however, was the astonishing change in the underwater topography of Sagami Bay which appeared in places to have sunk or been elevated by hundreds of feet. Even on the coast of California strange things appeared to have happened, providing an odd epilogue to the earthquake. On the night of 1 September— through the mysterious confusion of conflicting currents and shifting landscapes—within a few miles of Santa Barbara a veritable armada of ships went down. The warship *Texas* collided with a freighter, the *Steel Seafarer*; the liner S.S. *Cuba* ran aground; and no less than seven U.S. destroyers ploughed, one after another, into the rocks of Point Arguello.

The Murphysboro Tornado 1925

The twister that was born at 1.0 o'clock on 18 March 1925 near Annapolis, Mo., and died in the early evening outside Elizabeth, Ind., was the most spiteful ever to descend upon the Mid-West. In its brief and virulent career it cut a swathe of destruction 300 miles long and in places up to twenty miles wide through three States. The townships of southern Illinois suffered worst, where the tornado reached its peak and struck in mid-afternoon while schools and factories were still crowded. 'Men and women glanced at the sky and thought a storm was coming', said the *Chicago Daily Tribune*. 'They hardly had time to fasten the windows, call in the children or run for shelter before it came. And such an arrival! A slashing bitter rain, a rain of boards and shingles, tree-tops and automobile parts, bits of human clothing, sheet iron, whirling glass, books, toys . . .' Five minutes over each community was all the twister needed to complete its havoc. At Murphysboro, Ill., the largest town on its pre-destined route, two hundred died as three miles of buildings were mown down including a schoolhouse which collapsed on all its inmates. Whole blocks disappeared at the mining town of West Frankfort and the world's second largest coal-mine was wrecked. At Princeton, Ind., the great Heinz pickle factory was razed to the ground, and a hundred were left dead in the town itself. Smaller communities were obliterated from the face of the earth: Griffin where barely fifty inhabitants escaped injury, Gorham, McLeansboro and Parrish. But no more tragic demonstration of the arbitrary viciousness of the storm was to be found than at Desoto, Ill., a village of not more than 700 folk and barely half a mile from end to end. Here the tornado chose to come closest to the ground, its arc of destruction narrowed to half a mile. It landed with mathematical precision upon Desoto, ripping up everything above ground and killing 120. Yet, outside the limits of the village, not so much as a blade of grass was disturbed.

CHICAGO DAILY TRIBUNE: FRIDAY, MARCH 20, 1925.

Murphysboro and West Frankfort Feel Full Force of Storm in Which Nearly 1,000 Lost Their Lives

[TRIBUNE Photo.]

RUINS OF MURPHYSBORO, ONE OF THE CITIES IN SOUTHERN ILLINOIS WHICH FELT THE FULL FORCE OF THE TORNADO IN WHICH 823 WERE KILLED AND MORE THAN THREE TIMES AS MANY INJURED. This picture gives a general view of the ruins of the homes and business houses in the Jackson county seat where the loss of life was great. The city was in the direct path of the storm, which started in Missouri and then swept through southern Illinois and southern Indiana. The loss of life caused by the storm is still not definitely known, but there is no reason to believe that earlier reports were exaggerated.

[TRIBUNE Photo.]

MANY FAMILIES IN SIMILAR PLIGHT IN WEST FRANKFORT. R. M. Davidson and his family in their ruined home in the Franklin county mining town. Scores of similar scenes could be observed yesterday in West Frankfort.

[TRIBUNE Photo.]

ILLINOIS NATIONAL GUARD ON DUTY IN DEVASTATED CITY. This view of part of the district shows a member of the 130th infantry doing sentry duty to prevent plunderers from entering ruins.

[TRIBUNE Photo.]

ALL THAT WAS LEFT OF A BUILDING BLOCK. This picture was taken at the corner of 17th and Walnut streets in the center of the business district.

Average net paid circulation of
THE CHICAGO TRIBUNE
February, 1925

Daily · · · 631,291
Sunday · 1,065,422

VOLUME LXXXIV.—NO. 67 C
[REG. U.S. PAT. OFFICE. COPYRIGHT 1925
BY THE CHICAGO TRIBUNE.]

Chicago Daily Tribune

THE WORLD'S GREATEST NEWSPAPER

THURSDAY, MARCH 19, 1925.—36 PAGES THIS PAPER CONSISTS OF TWO SECTIONS—SECTION ONE

** PRICE TWO CENTS IN CHICAGO AND SUBURBS ELSEWHERE THREE CENTS

FINAL EDITION

830 DEAD IN TORNADO

First Pictures of Desolation in Wake of the Storm Taken from Airplane and F...

BIRDSEYE VIEW OF WEST FRANKFORT, ILL., FRANKLIN COUNTY MINING TOWN IN WHICH MORE THAN 100 PERISHED. This picture and others on this pa... taken from a Tribune airplane which left Chicago yesterday morning, hovered over the devastated district for a time and then returned to the city before sunset. The journey in... was almost 700 miles with only two stops—at Rantoul field going and coming. A companion plane carried a reporter for The Tribune who landed last night at Princeton, Ind., from... ...told the story of what he had observed.

[TRIBUNE Photo.]

STORM CAUSES HAVOC ACROSS THE INDIANA STATE LINE. This picture was taken in the yards of the Southern Railway company at Princeton, Ind., by a Tribune staff photographer. Princeton suffered severely from the cyclone.

[TRIBUNE Photo.]

[TRIBUNE Photo.]

PRINCETON, IND., FACTORY DESTROYED BY WEDNESDAY'S TORNADO. Interior view of one of the principal plants in the southern Indiana town. The roof was torn off the building and the brick walls caved in by the force of the wind.

ANOTHER PICTURE OF THE DEVASTATION IN WEST FRAN... The freaks of the storm are well illustrated by this picture. It will be noti... which were destroyed, making the ruins of the mining town resemble an... is shown in one corner of it.

FORCE OF WIND BLOWS HEAVILY LADEN FREIGHT TRA... plane, shows the tremendous force of the wind which was able to coil... sembled a giant snake.

CHICAGO PURSE OPENS TO HELP STORM VICTIMS

When news was received of the widespread damage and loss of life consequent on the storm that swept through southern Illinois and Indiana, The Tribune established a relief fund. The Tribune company opened it with an initial contribution of $1,000.

Later Mayor Dever asked The Tribune to collect a fund in the name of the people of Chicago. He also asked this newspaper to announce that all resources of the city were at the disposal of the state officials for relief work.

The contributions to the fund now stand:

The Tribune	$1,000
Evanston Post, American Legion	100
Leo Ginsburg	50
R. C. Pogge	25
Miss Carrie B. Neely	25
Lieut. A. C. Christensen	25
Better Brew Products Company	5
Charles Buchanan	25
Richard Henry Little	25
L. J. Leahy	10
Total	$1,255

The Tribune will receive and acknowledge contributions to the relief fund, forwarding them to the American Red Cross.

The publisher of the Casper, Wyo., Herald wired THE TRIBUNE to draw on him for $50 for the tornado relief fund.

LATEST REPORTS GIVING LIST OF WIND'S VICTIMS

The latest list of casualties of yesterday's storm, with the towns listed in the order in which they were struck, follows:

	Dead.	Injured.
Annapolis, Mo.		50
Biehle, Mo.	2	
Altenburg, Mo.	10	20
Cape Girardeau, Mo.	1	10
Gorin, Ill.	12	50
Murphysboro, Ill.	200	50
Gorham, Ill.		300
De Soto, Ill.	7	300
Royalton, Ill.	140	100
Bush, Ill.	3	60
Hurst, Ill.	5	40
West Frankfort, Ill.	6	830
Benton, Ill.	100	50
Logan, Ill.		2
Parrish, Ill.	3	70
Thompsonville, Ill.	7	
McLeansboro, Ill.	6	40
Carmi, Ill.	17	80
Near Carmi	7	25
Crossville, Ill.	1	
Griffin, Ind.	50	10
Owensville, Ind.	75	75
Princeton, Ind.	25	100
Poseyville, Ind.	100	100
Elizabeth, Ind.	3	20
		12
Totals	829	2,574

Heavy winds, probably part of the same storm which swept Illinois, struck parts of Kentucky. Eight were killed and fifty injured.

Late in the night the storm had reached eastern Ohio, but its strength was diminishing rapidly. It struck Portsmouth, uprooting trees and breaking windows, but no heavy damage resulted.

Another terrific storm swept over parts of Tennessee and Alabama. Twenty-three were killed and scores injured in Sumner county, Tenn. One was killed at Littleville, Ala.

FIERCE BLAST SWEEPS CITY; TRAFFIC DELAYED

Telegraph wires were blown down, traffic was blocked, and windows were broken in many sections of the city by a thirty mile an hour storm, accompanied by rain, sleet, and snow, which swept in from the north last night.

At least one automobile accident was attributed to the storm. Stephen Ivanter, 22, 822 South Wabash avenue, was injured by a delivery truck when the driver, Joseph Shapiro, blinded by the snow and wind, ran him down at State and 13th streets.

Traffic in Throop street near Eleanor street was stopped for an hour when a trolley wire was blown down. Telegraph wires were blown down at 95th street and Exchange avenue and at 93d street and South Chicago avenue. Trains over the Oak Park elevated railroad had to be rerouted for more than two hours last night when a circuit was burned out, disabling the Lake street bridge.

ILLINOIS TOWNS RAZED BY STORM 3 STATES HIT

Children Die When Schools Collapse.

[By the Associated Press.]

A tornado tore through southern Illinois late yesterday afternoon, lashing eastern Missouri, and then caused considerable damage in Indiana before it died out.

A total of 3,714 persons were killed or injured, according to estimates available last night.

Communications with the storm swept regions were difficult, and it is feared the list of victims will grow as the rural districts are heard from.

830 Die; 2,884 Hurt.

Estimates which came in through various sources with ever increasing totals placed the total dead at 830 and the injured at 2,884 before midnight last night.

The destruction of property was enormous, several towns being almost entirely wiped out.

Such populous places as West Frankfort, Ill., and Murphysboro, Ill., lost whole blocks of buildings.

In the town of Parrish, which has only 300 inhabitants, 7 were killed and 52 injured.

School Falls on 245.

At Murphysboro, where the dead totaled 200, a schoolhouse was blown down over the heads of 245 pupils.

At De Soto, Ill., estimates placed the dead at 140 and the injured at 300 out of a total population of 703.

A schoolhouse at De Soto was razed and only three of the 250 occupants escaped unhurt, while 88 bodies already have been taken from the ruins.

Heavy Losses in Indiana.

Indiana suffered almost as much as Illinois. Princeton reported 100 dead and twice as many injured. The latest tabulation at Griffin placed the dead at seventy-five and as many more hurt.

Owensville also reported seventy-five dead when the wives came up late at night, and probably 100 injured. Poseyville had a loss of five dead and a score hurt.

Buildings Carried Far.

In some places, where the wind struck hardest, whole buildings were moved from their foundation, a grain elevator at De Soto having been carried intact some forty feet.

The storm was not so severe in Missouri, but it laid waste a number of towns and many farms before it jumped the Mississippi river into Illinois.

There the tornado was at the height of its fury for miles as it careened from Murphysboro to Parrish. It rose above the tree tops for a considerable distance, but lapped the earth again just west of the Indiana line, creating more damage at Carmi.

As it passed into Indiana the tornado lifted slightly again, split into two sections, and swept northeast and southeast through Princeton, Griffin, Owensville, and Poseyville.

Relief Work Starts Soon.

Relief was almost as quick in its action as were the ruins of the storm elements in destroying so much property and so many lives.

Relief trains bearing doctors,

The Broken Giant

The Shenandoah Crash 1925

The World

VOL. LXVI. NO. 23,390—DAILY. ★   Copyright (New York World) Press Publishing Company, 1925.   NEW YORK, FRIDAY, SEPTEMBER 4, 1925.   Entered as Second-Class Matter Post Office, New York, N. Y.   •• THREE CENTS WITHIN 100-MILE RADIUS

OFFICIAL WEATHER FORECAST
Partly cloudy to-day; fair to-morrow; not much change in temperature; moderate west winds to-day.
TEMPERATURE YESTERDAY
Highest 73, 10 A. M.; lowest 67, 7.30 A. M.

SHENANDOAH DESTROYED BY STORM OVER OHIO; COMMANDER LANSDOWNE AND 13 OF CREW DEAD; POLITICS FORCED FLIGHT, SAYS LEADER'S WIDOW

Smith Assails Hearst, Insists He's the Issue

Asks If Democratic Party Here Is To Follow an Alien Leader Lacking Morals---Declares He Hasn't Even Right to Vote. Turns Guns on Hylan.

SMITH "ALIBI AL," HEARST'S ANSWER

Governor's K. K. K. Issue False, Truckles to Wall Street, Publisher Retorts

ADMITS HE'S NO DEMOCRAT

Assails Party and Its Leaders —Talks of Jails

The World's Real Estate Ads Sell Property Worth $1,150,000.00

Poison King Boris By Bacilli in Food

THE FLYING FISH IN ACTION—Views of the Shenandoah as She Left Lakehurst Home on Last Trip and As She Poised Between the Woolworth and Pulitzer Buildings on One of Her Several Visits to New York

The SHENANDOAH LEAVING LAKEHURST
By World Staff Photographer

The SHENANDOAH BETWEEN the PULITZER and WOOLWORTH BUILDINGS.

FIND WIDOW DEAD IN LOOTED ROOMS

Caller Leads Way to Scene of Strange Tragedy of Mrs. Carthart

SHERIFF IS SLAIN IN COURT IN FEUD

Mountaineer Officer Shot by Deputy From Another County in Chattanooga

Flight Ordered Over Protest, Is Charged

Skipper Had Foretold Just Such Disaster In Service Manual

SHENANDOAH VICTIMS AND HOME ADDRESSES

THE DEAD

Lieut. Commander Zachary Lansdowne, Greenville, O., Commander of the Shenandoah.
Lieut. Commander Louis Hancock, Austin, Tex., Executive Officer.
Lieut. J. B. Lawrence, St. Paul, Minn., watch officer.
Lieut. A. R. Houghton, Allston, Mass., watch officer.
Lieut. E. W. Sheppard, Washington, D. C., engineer officer.
George C. Schnitzer, Tuckerton, N. J., chief radio man.
James A. Moore Jr., Savannah, Ga., aviation machinist's mate.
Everett F. Allen, Omaha, Neb., aviation chief rigger.
Ralph T. Joffray, St. Louis, Mo., aviation rigger.
Bartholomew O'Sullivan, Lowell, Mass., aviation machinist's mate, first class.
William H. Spratley, Venice, Ill., machinist's mate, first class.
Charles H. Broome, Toms River, N. J., aviation machinist's mate, first class.
Celestino Mazuco, Murray Hill, N. J., aviation machinist's mate.
James W. Cullinan, Binghamton, N. Y., aviation pilot.

THE INJURED

John F. McCarthy, Freehold, N. J., aviation chief rigger, suffered fractured pelvis and internal injuries; condition critical.
Raymond Cole, Lima, O., chief gunner, slight injuries.

SURVIVORS

DIRIGIBLE RIPPED APART CRASHES MILE TO EARTH

Pride of Navy Strewn Over Ohio Farms After Thundersquall at 5 A. M.—Eight Bodies Fall in Farmer's Garden

NO STRUCTURAL DEFECTS IN SHIP; SUDDEN STORM IS OVERWHELMING

Dirigible Reported at 1.45 Over Wheeling; Next Word Was "I'm Losing My Seat"— Souvenir Hunters on Scene—Legion Forms Cordon About Wreckage

By Peter Vischer
Staff Correspondent of The World

CAMBRIDGE, O., Sept. 3.—The Shenandoah is wrecked. The giant dirigible, product of American aeronautical genius and skill, pride of the United States Navy, was cracked and broken and smashed to the ground near here early to-day in angry winds.

Fourteen of her crew, including Lieut. Commander Zachary Lansdowne, her commander, were killed and two were injured.

Daughter of the Stars was her name, in Indian— Shenandoah. She was romantic from the start, a sleek and silvery beauty with the power to draw a host of adoring admirers wherever she went. But unlike the other stars of the firmament, her glittering career was short and tragic. America's first airship emerged from her hangar at Lakehurst in September 1923 just plain *ZR.1*, but her appearance on Broadway where she stopped the traffic as she flew over, and on Capitol Hill where Congressmen craned their necks to catch a glimpse of her, clearly required of her a more evocative image. Her flying visit to St Louis was rapturously acclaimed: her tour of Boston was a triumph. It was proposed—and decreed—that the following year she would make her international début by crossing the North Pole!

In January, however, this grandiose scheme was almost nipped in the bud: a particularly severe gale tore the airship away from her mooring mast and hoisted her off on an unscheduled flight. Two of her gas-bags were ripped apart; only brilliant manoeuvring by the skeleton crew aboard kept her in one piece, and only the fact that she was filled with non-flammable helium averted a fatal conflagration. The Polar expedition was postponed, but to prove to her public that she was far from written-off a spectacular transcontinental voyage from New Jersey to San Diago and back was undertaken in the fall. It was a magnificent comeback: creeping low through the mountain passes, the *Shenandoah* covered 9,317 miles in under twenty days.

After her exertions she was rested—to allow her precious helium to be transferred to her sister-ship, the *Los Angeles*. But the summer of 1925 found her back in commission, with a taxing schedule of guest-appearances at a succession of state fairs in the Mid-West, St Louis then on to Minneapolis and Detroit. On Thursday 3 September she was en route, somewhere in the neighbourhood of Ava, Ohio, trying to make headway against a vicious wind that cut her ground-speed to practically nil. Suddenly the coxswain reported he could do nothing to stop the ship gaining height—she was being sucked into the heavens at more than 200 feet a minute. Momentarily, with the crew struggling to keep her bow at eighteen degrees, she levelled off at 3,000 feet then pitched into her crazy ascent faster than ever. A massive release of helium calmed her at 6,000 feet, only to plunge her earthwards with equal abruptness.

Over 4,000 lb. of ballast was immediately shipped overboard, to no effect. Then as the crew prepared to jettison fuel tanks yet another capricious up-current of air sent her spinning. Caught in a whirlpool of turbulence the *Shenandoah* lurched to an angle of thirty degrees and, strained beyond her endurance, snapped clean in half with a spine-chilling crashing of metal. Three engineers, who had the misfortune to be standing precisely at the point of fracture, were thrown out. Seconds later, as the stern section ballooned its way to earth, the control car (with eight men inside, including the captain, Commander Lansdowne) convulsively tore itself away and plummetted into the night. Two more cars, engine gondolas, also broke away taking three men with them before the free-floating carcass carried the twenty-two men still clinging to it to a relatively gentle landing.

The bow section, where Lt. Commander Rosendahl and six others discovered themselves staring out into nothing, suddenly stampeded into space, an uncontrollable gas-container. At 10,000 feet desperate broaching of the gas valves succeeded in halting its ascension. By a miracle of manipulation—a combination of valving and hurling out anything heavy enough to qualify as ballast—the seven men contrived to bring their strange craft to earth, two hours later.

Daily Mail 4 September 1925

WRECK OF THE NAVY DIRIGIBLE SHENANDOAH TOLD IN PICTURES

REMARKABLE VIEW OF THE MAIN AFTER-PORTION OF ILL-FATED SHENANDOAH, TAKEN FROM AIRPLANE AT AVA, O., A FEW HOURS AFTER GIANT SHIP WAS TORN APART IN STORM—It was in this section—the stern—that twenty-two officers and men were carried to the ground in safety, the fall being checked somewhat by the amount of helium remaining in the uninjured gas bags. Photograph shows wreckage surrounded by automobiles and hundreds of spectators who flocked to scene when disaster became known
Copyright, 1925, Acme Newspictures

Race Against Time

The Sinking of the S.4 1927

For three years the Coast Guard destroyer *Paulding* had been patrolling the waters of Cape Cod in the never-ending game of cat-and-mouse with the rum-runners. Prohibition enforcement was a thankless job most of the time, ninety-nine parts routine and one part excitement, if you were lucky. It was on a perfectly routine patrol that the *Paulding* was cruising about a mile off Provincetown, in the mid-afternoon on 17 December 1927, when the officer of the watch spotted a stick-like object in water ahead. 'I thought it was a fish stick, a marker which fishermen use for their nets' he explained later to reporters. 'I shifted the helm because I did not want to get this supposed stick jammed in our screw. Next I saw part of a submarine's conning tower. Then the crash came. The submarine turned over and sank bow first at an angle of 45 degrees within a few minutes.'

The submarine was the *S.4* sister-ship of the *S.51* which had also been rammed just over a year before off Rhode Island, with the loss of thirty-three lives. Observers on the shore confirmed that the submarine had surfaced directly in the path of the *Paulding,* and that the destroyer had had no time to take evasive action. The speed with which the *S.4* sunk in 100 feet of water offered little hope for the survival of the forty-five

officers and men aboard, and the fruitless efforts of the *S.8* that evening to establish contact by means of a submarine bell held out still less. By midnight, at least, Coast Guard boats dragging the sea-bed had located what they supposed was the hull of the crippled submarine and succeeded in getting a line attached to it.

At daybreak the first diver went down. His report eighty minutes later was received with mixed feelings: the superstructure of the sub was a mass of wreckage. The conning tower had been sliced in half, the control-room and the crew's quarters were smashed to pieces. There could be no hope for anyone who had been in either at the time of the crash. However he was convinced he had heard faint taps inside the forward compartment, the torpedo room. A little later another diver, armed with a hammer, descended and confirmed there was indeed life aboard. Slowly and painfully he battered out a morse-code conversation on the sub's hull. 'Is the gas bad?' he asked. Then through the darkness came the reply: 'No, but the air is. How long will you be now?' 'How many are there?' the diver asked. 'Six, please hurry.' 'Will you be long?' the trapped men desperately wanted to know. 'We are doing everything possible' was the only reply he could give.

Even at that moment compressed air was

being pumped from the rescue ship *Falcon* into the *S.4*'s ballast tanks in the hope that the lightened submarine would up-end itself. If that did not work, there were huge pontoons being towed to the scene from New York, to attempt to lift the vessel bodily (or even, it was seriously suggested, just the front section where the survivors were imprisoned). Admiral Brumby, in charge of the operation, was cheerily optimistic: it would be 'a simple task' to raise the *S.4*, he thought. The problem was time—even using the oxygen flasks that were known to be stored in the torpedo room, the men had only forty hours' supply of air at best. But then again, although it had never been attempted before, it should prove possible to get food and oxygen to them through the torpedo tubes. That night the nation—now thoroughly caught up in the drama being played out in the Atlantic—slept a little easier.

But out on the Atlantic that night, it was a nightmare. The air in the ballast tanks was not having the slightest effect—the mud held its prey like a huge clamp. A diver who went down to inspect progress got into serious difficulties and barely escaped with his life. The pontoons were taking an unconscionable time to arrive (in fact, one of them had gone aground). Worst of all was the rapidly accelerating gale that had already whipped up a dangerous swell. By dawn

90

THE WEATHER
Today: Cloudy, continued cold; fresh northwest winds.
To-morrow: Cloudy and cold
Tuesday's Temperatures—Max. 32; Min. 24
Detailed weather report on Page 13

NEW YORK
Herald Tribune

LATE CITY EDITION

Vol. LXXXVII No. 29,618   (Copyright, 1927, New York Tribune Inc.)   MONDAY, DECEMBER 19, 1927   * * * *   TWO CENTS In Greater New York | THREE CENTS Within 200 Miles | FOUR CENTS Elsewhere

Men Alive in S-4; Diver Hears 6 Tapping: "Hurry"; Air Pumped to Put Craft on End and Free Survivors

Tammany Aid Seen as Final Defense Hope For Connolly

Queens President Expected to Use Force on Tiger if Plea of Administration Responsibility Fails

Scudder to Disclose Inquiry Plan To-day

Steuer Also May Announce Whether He Can Take Charge of Defense in the State's Investigation

Maurice E. Connolly, President of the Borough of Queens, will plead that if the Queens taxpayers have been put through his sewer contracts, is alone not responsible, since all contracts under question were approved by representatives of the Finance Department and the Board of Estimate. This in the opinion of friends of Mr. Connolly yesterday, will be his defense against charges that from $6,000,000 to $8,000,000 of the $16,000,000 Jamaica sewer contracts alone were needlessly expended.

Shrewdness Acknowledged

Representatives of both the Department of Finance and the Board of Estimate already have admitted that those departments shared in the responsibility of certification of pay vouchers for the sewer work. Mr. Connolly is admittedly one of the shrewdest political generals in the city. By his strategy he has kept his boroughs apart from the Tammany organization and in crucial campaign moments he has been able to say, "See me," before Queens stood. In political circles yesterday it was predicted that Mr. Connolly would use every ounce of pressure he could bring out of the joint responsibility of the Department of Finance and the Board of Estimate, of which Mayor Walker is head, to whip the municipal government and Tammany Hall into line for his defense.

Representatives of both the Finance Department and the Board of Estimate have already defended the Queens sewer contracts, in so far as their responsibility for their approval was concerned.

Charles H. Graham, chief engineer of the Finance Department, on the witness stand before Commissioner of Accounts Higgins last Friday, testified

85,000th Baby Born At N. Y. Child Hospital

Enough babies have been born at the New York Nursery and Child's Hospital, 161 West Sixty-first Street, to populate a city as large as Evansville, Ind. or larger than "Savannah, Ga., or Troy, N. Y., John Howard Jr., superintendent, said yesterday in announcing the birth of the 85,000th baby at the institution. The hospital is 104 years old.

2 Suspects Held For Murder of Kidnaped Girl

Indianian Held in Nevada, College Graduate in Los Angeles for Slaying of Banker's Abducted Child

By The Associated Press

LAS VEGAS, Nev., Dec. 18.—Lewis D. Wyatt was taken from the Red Feather stage here to-night by Los Angeles detectives seeking the kidnaper and slayer of Marian Parker. He was held for questioning, fingerprinting and photographing in the Clark County jail here.

Wyatt, said the California officers, was too stocky to answer fully the description of the man wanted in the Parker case. He talked freely and offered to return to Los Angeles for further. He declared that he paid for his ticket on the stage line from Los Angeles to Terre Haute, Ind., with three gold back $20 bills, which money was telegraphed from the East.

[The money paid by Perry M. Parker for the ransom of his daughter was in $20 Treasury notes, corresponding in style to those described by Wyatt, but officers said their serial numbers did not check with the numbers on Wyatt's currency.]

Wyatt said that he had an Army service record and while in Los Angeles had stopped at the Lennox Hotel. His fingerprints will be sent to Los Angeles to-morrow morning by Western express airplane.

Asked Wife to Send Money

TERRE HAUTE, Ind., Dec. 18 (AP).—Lewis D. Wyatt formerly was employed as a lumber salesman at Terre Haute. His wife, who lives here, could not be located to-night. Wyatt left the employ of the lumber company last spring, it was learned, and went to Los Angeles. A week ago he wrote her seeking a job and money with which to come home for the Christmas holidays. Whether such money was sent him could not be determined.

University Man Held

LOS ANGELES, Dec. 18.—Following the discovery to-day of the remaining

Crowds Cheer Lindbergh at 2 Bullfights

Nervous at First, He Sees 8 Dispatched, One by Ex-Ring Hero Paying Him a Special Tribute

He Doesn't Applaud; Morrow Is Absent

92,000 Laborites Parade for Envoys; Flyer Receives Ovation at Show

By Jack Starr-Hunt
By Cable to the Herald Tribune
Copyright, 1927, New York Tribune Inc.

MEXICO CITY, Dec. 18.—Colonel Charles A. Lindbergh witnessed two bullfights to-day. This morning at a private rodeo he saw a demonstration of the art by Rodolfo Gaeno, who was Mexico's foremost bullfighter until his retirement two years ago. Gaeno returned to the ring to-day as a tribute to the trans-Atlantic flyer, giving a personal demonstration this morning and sitting at the side of the young American this afternoon at the regular Sunday afternoon performance held in the great Coliseum of Mexico City.

Despite some sixty protests cabled by individuals and humane societies, Lindbergh was honor guest this morning at a program arranged by the National Charro Association in an arena on the outskirts of the city. Lassoing, riding, "bull-dogging" and steer-throwing were also demonstrated.

Watches Parade of 92,000

After the morning bullfight Lindbergh witnessed a parade of 92,000 members of the Mexico Regional Federation of Labor offered as a friendly gesture to the flyer. Ambassador Dwight W. Morrow witnessed the parade but did not attend either of the bullfights.

Gaeno's entrance into the bull ring this morning would be his last, he declared, and he killed one bull, the first of eight slain during the day, as a personal tribute to Lindbergh. The second bull was the victim of General Gomes Velasco, chief of the Mexico Traffic Department and an amateur matador. Ambassador Morrow defended Lindbergh's attendance at the bullfights, declaring that it was the flyer's personal affair and the courteous thing to do in a friendly country whose national sport is bullfighting. Ambassador Morrow attended neither bullfight himself.

The afternoon performance was attended by 28,000 persons, only a few of whom came to see the fights. Among those present were President Calles, General Obregon, Luis Morones and

Navy Auxiliary Ships Standing Guard Over the Sunken S-4

Herald Tribune Telephotograph—Acme
A yellow buoy marks the spot where the submarine, sunk in a collision on Saturday, lies on the ocean floor in 102 feet of water. A mile away be seen the shores of Cape Cod.

Tax Along New Subways Asked By Untermyer

Tells Berry Benefited Property Should Pay Share to Keep 5-Cent Fare; Taxpayer Hearing To-morrow

In a letter to Comptroller Charles W. Berry written yesterday, Samuel Untermyer, special counsel for the Transit Commission, voiced his opposition to the latest plan of Chairman John H. Delaney for saving the five-cent fare through short term bond issues, and advocated the original plan of Mr. Delaney, which called for assessing part of the cost of new subways on property owners along the routes.

Mr. Untermyer did not mention the plan of Mr. Delaney by name, but declared that he was opposed to building the subways entirely with bonds.

Seen as Administration Views

In view of the working agreement that has united the special counsel for the Transit Commission and Mr. Delaney and Mayor Walker, who recently took an unsuccessful appeal from Justice Wasservogel's decision striking the $13,000,000 item for short-term subway bonds from the budget, some of those who have been following the recent

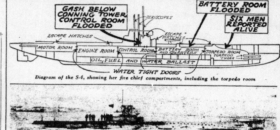

GASH BELOW CONNING TOWER CONTROL ROOM FLOODED

ESCAPE HATCHES

MOTOR ROOM

ENGINE ROOM CONTROL ROOM

OIL, FUEL, AND WATER BALLAST

WATER TIGHT DOORS

PERISCOPES

ESCAPE HATCHES

BATTERY ROOM FLOODED

SIX MEN REPORTED ALIVE

TORPEDO ROOM TUBES

Diagram of the S-4, showing her five chief compartments, including the torpedo room

$400,000,000 Extra Dividends Await Investors

Five Million Stockholders, Associated Press Estimates, Will Get Record Christmas Distribution

At least $400,000,000 will be distributed by American industrial and business corporations to about 5,000,000 stockholders at Christmas in the form of extra dividends. It is estimated to-day by The Associated Press.

Mate Rescues Diver Held in S-4 Wreckage

NEW LONDON, Conn., Dec. 18 (AP).—L. S. Michael, one of the navy divers who went down 102 feet in the ocean to examine the sunken S-4, had a narrow escape from death when his lines became entangled in the wreckage, a radio message revealed to-night. Michael was hooking up the floor of one of the S-4 compartments when his lines fouled and he was unable to clear them. Thomas Eadie, the first diver to detect signs of life in the S-4, again descended and extricated his com-

Cheering News Speeds Rescue Work by Navy

Entire Department From Wilbur Down Concentrates on Task as Word Comes of Finding Six Men Alive

From the Herald Tribune Washington Bureau

WASHINGTON, Dec. 18.—Definite news that at least six members of the crew of the ill-fated S-4 are alive reached Washington to-night and stirred the entire Navy Department to

Rescue Work Hastened to Beat 40-Hour Limit of Life

Clear Signals in Code Received From Forward Compartment, Fainter Reply Comes from Rear

Some Probably Dead In Smashed Tower

'All Lost in Battery Room' First Survey Indicates; Pontoons To Be Used if the Pneumatic Lift Fails

By Francis D. Walton
A Staff Correspondent

PROVINCETOWN, Mass., Dec. 18.—From the deck of the United States submarine S-4, which was rammed and sunk with forty-five officers and men aboard by the Coast Guard destroyer Paulding yesterday afternoon and now lies in 101 feet of water on the ocean side of this harbor, there came the message late this afternoon:

"There's life aboard."

Later in the day a diver with a hammer communicated with those in the forward compartment, tapping on the hull with questions in Continental code and receiving replies from within.

"Six Here; Please Hurry"

"Is the gas bad?" was his first query.

"No," came the response, "but the air is. How long will you be now?"

"How many are there?" inquired the diver with his hammer.

"There are six. Please hurry."

At the end of the conversation the imprisoned men reverted again to their first question, the one which occupies all their thoughts:

"Will you be long now?"

"We are doing everything possible," returned the diver.

Conning Tower Split

The first message from the men aboard the submarine, that there was life there, was telephoned to the submarine tender Falcon by Thomas Eadie, chief torpedo mate, veteran deep-sea diver and the outstanding hero in the release of the

Tuesday Edition

Vol. LXXXVII No. 29,619   (Copyright, 1927, New York Tribune Inc.)   TUESDAY, DECEMBER 20, 1927   * * * *   TWO CENTS In Greater New York | THREE CENTS Within 200 Miles | FOUR CENTS Elsewhere

Gale Blocks Rescuers as 6 in S-4 Use Last Oxygen; Food and Air Flasks to Go in Torpedo Tubes To-day

Steuer Urges Halt to City's Sewer Inquiry

Lawyer Tells Walker That Use of Officials as Witnesses Hampers Connolly in Preparing Defense

Decision Referred To Justice Scudder

Queens President Receives Charges and Will Face Them 'Now or Any Time'

Max D. Steuer, asked by Maurice E. Connolly, President of Queens Borough, to serve as his counsel in the forthcoming state investigation into Queens affairs, wrote yesterday to Mayor Walker urging that he order both Commissioner of Accounts James A. Higgins and the Board of Assessors to dig no further into the Queens situation until after Justice Townsend Scudder, representing Governor Smith, shall have completed his investigation.

Mr. Steuer contended that the constant use as witnesses before the Commissioner of Accounts and the Board of Assessors of engineers and others whose help Mr. Connolly may need in preparing his defense would greatly embarrass Mr. Connolly.

Messenger Delivers Letter

So anxious was Mr. Steuer to have all hearings stopped at once that he sent his letter to the Mayor by messenger and requested that the Mayor answer by the same messenger, saying

Deny Hoover's War Absence Bans '28 Race

Friends Hold He Kept U. S. Home While Aiding Belgians and Is Eligible Under 14-Year Clause

Resent New Attack On His Americanism

Constitutional Experts Answer Charge Relief Work Expatriated Him

From the Herald Tribune Washington Bureau

WASHINGTON, Dec. 19.—Friends of Herbert Hoover are prepared to meet the question of his constitutional eligibility for the Presidency with a joint statement signed by five or six leading constitutional authorities which will show that he maintained a residence in the United States for more than fourteen years.

This statement has been drafted in anticipation of a revival of the old issue as to the Secretary's foreign residence during two years of the World War period. The Federal Constitution requires residence "within the United States" for at least fourteen years on the part of the man who takes the oath as President.

Kept U. S. Residence During War Work

The Hoover authorities will admit that he was absent from this country for the better part of two years during 1914 and 1916, engaged in Belgian relief work, but will show that he never gave up his American residence.

Steel-Girt Torpedo Room Where Six Men of the S-4 Were Still Tapping for Aid at Dusk Yesterday

Henry Miller photos

Forward end of chamber showing the closed torpedo tubes through which, it was hoped, air might be sent to the imprisoned men   *Aft end of the room. In the center is the door which leads to the battery room, now flooded and which was shut and clamped after the crash*

Is There Hope? Men Signal as Lines Fail and Pontoons Lag

Divers Helpless on Top With Storm Growing and Captives Go Unanswered; Hull Is Sinking in Mud

Taps Grow Fainter; Zero Hour Nearing

6 P. M. To-night Set as Time When Suffocation Will Begin; No Chance to Lift Wreck for Days

By Francis D. Walton
A Staff Correspondent

PROVINCETOWN, Mass., Dec. 19.—Signals rapped out in international code and faintly heard by an oscillating sound detector aboard the United States submarine S-8, indicated to-night that six men still lived in the torpedo compartment of their sister submersible, the S-4, which was sunk by the destroyer Paulding outside the harbor out of this port on Saturday.

The signals were heard throughout the day, growing fainter as a new night, the third since the submarine sank, came accompanied by a raging gale from the west and made all res-

Woman Held as Kidnap Suspect; Murder Evidence Found in House

Clews to Murder of Los Angeles Child Discovered in Mystery Dwelling; Slayer's Car Also Found; City Plans to Raise $100,000 Reward

Mrs. Lindbergh At St. Louis on Mexican Flight

Delighted With Trip From Detroit in Huge Plane as

Wilbur Despairs of Saving Men Waiting Suffocation Underseas

Scant Hope Held at Washington That Those Still Alive Can Be Reached Before Gas Overcomes Them; Foreign Governments Send Sympathy

all operations had been suspended to await a break in the storm. It never came. All day the rescue squadron rode it, frustrated and with sinking hearts. 'The scene of the disaster is as bleak and chilling as the fate that creeps on the imprisoned men with every lungful of air that each takes in their steel cylinder', the *New York Herald Tribune* described those long, impotent hours. 'Late today saw an agonizing message throbbed through the oscillating signal system. It revealed that the oxygen bottles in the submarine torpedo room were exhausted and pleaded in hammered dots and dashes for air to be sent through the torpedo tube. The men inside believe it can. The helpless men outside know that it can't.' No diver could even attempt to go down in this weather, and to add to the pathos every pitiful plea from inside the hull could be picked up by the *S.8* lying nearby. 'Is there any hope?' came a message as night began to fall up above. There was no way of telling them that hope was fading as fast as the daylight.

The bitterness of frustration among those who waited on shore began to take over anxiety. 'Why can't they draw a circle of heavy ships around the spot and then flood the place with oil. They've got all the men they need and they've got the money. It ain't right to fiddle about this way with the boys only 102 feet under water' complained one old sea salt to reporters. The father of one of the trapped men couldn't understand what another boat had been doing in that charted submarine lane. 'I never was a believer in prohibition' he declared angrily. 'Now look what they've done with their piddling rum-chasing.' And at the Navy Depart-

ment in Washington officials were getting edgy. 'Do something!' was the peremptory order sent out to Admiral Brumby.

But there was nothing he could do. The last message heard from the *S.4* consisted of seven indecipherable taps, at eleven o'clock on the morning of the fourth day. That afternoon, with the storm girding itself for an even greater offensive, the armada of rescue ships turned back to port in a thin despairing line. The next day the *Baltimore News* published an account of a telephone conversation between the Navy and the wife of the commander of the *S.4*. 'Why' she wanted to know 'was the *Paulding* allowed to patrol in an area set aside for submarine manoeuvres?' The Navy didn't know. 'Why was the *S.4* allowed to make a deep sea dive with no salvage vessels at hand?' she went on. It was not deemed practicable that salvage vessels be present every time a submarine submerged. 'Then why' she persisted 'didn't the Navy Department have pontoons at hand?' Because operations were conducted along the entire Atlantic seaboard, and the Navy Department was unable to predict when or where these accidents would occur. Finally, 'Why was Provincetown with its cold stormy waters selected as the scene of the manoeuvres' she asked. That was because of its proximity to its base at Portsmouth navy yard. She was not criticizing the Navy, she told the *Baltimore News*, but would feel more reconciled to his death if given satisfactory answers. 'I wouldn't want to think they were murdered' she explained.

7 Taps at 5:25 P.M. Stir Faint Hope of Life on S-4;
Rescue Fleet, Helpless in Gale, Sees Its Battle Lost

Calles Rides Sky as Guest Of Lindbergh

Mexican President Thrills at First Air Trip Over Capital in Cabin Plane; Obregon Enjoys a Spin

Morrow, Army Men Praise Pilot's Skill

Craft 'Flies Self,' Aviator Shows Newspaper Men; Reviews Future Officers

By Jack Starr-Hunt
By Cable to the Herald Tribune

MEXICO CITY, Dec. 20.—President Calles had his first flight in an airplane this morning, piloted by Colonel Charles A. Lindbergh who, on one of the pleasantest days of his visit to Mexico had a good time in bearing aloft, besides the President, the other of the two most influential men in the Republic, former President Alvaro Obregon, the sole remaining candidate for re-election...

Emory R. Buckner

6 Airport Sites Here Picked by Hoover Board

Include Governors Island, Brooklyn, Queens, Bronx, Jamaica Bay, Newark and Hackensack Meadows

Plans calling for the utilization of 2,800 acres for the development of six airports in the New York–New Jersey area, including one each in Governors Island, were submitted yesterday by the Fact Finding Committee selected from the two states in August at the request of Secretary Hoover of the Department of Commerce to study the flying field needs of the metropolitan area...

Buckner Gets Job of Sifting Connolly Case

Former U. S. Attorney Is Chosen by Scudder, with Order to Uncover 'Truth Without Fear or Favor'

Defenders Appear For Queens Leader

Mrs. Pratt Rebuked by Alderman; Lawyer Blames Form of Government

Justice Townsend Scudder, designated by Governor Smith to investigate the administration of Maurice E. Connolly, Borough President of Queens, announced yesterday that Emory R. Buckner, former United States Attorney for the Southern District of New York, has accepted the appointment as special counsel for the state...

Mr. Coolidge Asks Halt To Gift of Jackknives

From the Herald Tribune Washington Bureau

WASHINGTON, Dec. 20.—President Coolidge told callers to-day that he had received a surplus of jackknives from admirers who seemed under the impression that when he ceased to be President he would devote his time to whittling...

Acquit Remus As Insane When He Killed Wife

10 Men, 2 Women Find Ex-'RumKing' Not Guilty and Wish Him Merry Christmas; Now Faces Asylum

Special to the Herald Tribune

CINCINNATI, Dec. 20.—A jury to-day acquitted George Remus, master bootlegger, of murdering the wife he admitted killing. The jurors, ten men and two women, deliberated nineteen minutes before deciding that Remus was insane when he shot the woman who was on her way to set in motion legal machinery that she hoped would free her from him...

8,000 Track Boy as Stolen Girl's Slayer

William E. Hickman, 19, Called Kidnaper of Marian Parker, Traced by DrugTheft inLosAngeles

Revenge as Motive; Just Foils Capture

Youth Discharged for Forgery From Bank Where Girl's Father Is Cashier

By The Associated Press

LOS ANGELES, Dec. 20.—Defying capture at the hands of more than 8,000 officers, the greatest force ever assembled for a man hunt in the West, William Edward Hickman, identified as the kidnaper and slayer of Marian Parker, twelve-year-old schoolgirl, was still at large late to-day.

Hickman is a former messenger for the Los Angeles First National Trust and Savings Bank, of which the girl's father, Perry M. Parker, is assistant cashier...

Diver About to Drop Down to Sunken S-4

*Herald Tribune photo—Acme
Thomas Eadie, ear phones in place, ready to descend to sea bottom to hear messages tapped by imprisoned men. He will go down again to-day if the storm abates.*

1 Dead, 4 Hurt in Blast on Langley, Plane Carrier

Gas Explosion, Second in a Year, Cripples Naval Craft, Kills Seaman, Injures 4 Badly at San Diego

Special to the Herald Tribune

SAN DIEGO, Calif., Dec. 20.—James B. Ailsworth, forty-one years old, aviation chief carpenter's mate, is dead as result of an explosion aboard the aircraft carrier Langley here at 9:50 a. m. to-day. Several others are suffering from minor injuries, sustained when they were blown into the bay...

Wilbur Orders Safeguards for Undersea Craft

Strict Patrol To Be Kept in Future Submarine Operations to Prevent Recurrence of the S-4 Disaster

From the Herald Tribune Washington Bureau

WASHINGTON, Dec. 20.—Despair for the fate of the entombed men on the S-4 pervaded the Navy Department to-day but everything was in readiness to save them, Secretary Wilbur declared, if there was even a moment of lull in the weather...

'DoAnything,' Navy Orders; Divers Can't

AdmiralBrumby,Standing Watch Over Submarine Grave, Told All Must Be Dead at 3 This Morning

Wife'sPrayerTapped In Code to Lt. Fitch

Dim Response Received, Hammer Blows Become Incoherent and Cease

By Francis D. Walton
A Staff Correspondent

PROVINCETOWN, Mass., Dec. 20.—Seven indistinct and meaningless taps from the bottom of the sea at 5.25 o'clock this afternoon gave renewed hope that some at least of the six men entombed alive on the submarine S-4 might not yet have succumbed.

The taps, however, only faintly relieved the gloom aboard the naval vessels gathered off Provincetown, for there was no let-up in the turbulent seas which have blocked all rescue efforts since the submarine was rammed and sunk by the destroyer Paulding last Saturday afternoon at 3:37 o'clock.

The crew of the S-4, sister ship of the disabled S-4, which by its oscillator mechanism picked up the latest sounds from the sea, were not even certain that they came from the imprisoned men. They were only sure that seven sounds had been recorded on the instrument of their craft and they hoped they might have come from the sunken vessel.

Rear Admiral Frank H. Brumby, in charge of the rescue operations, expressed doubt than these taps came from the stricken craft, although he reported them to the naval district headquarters in Boston.

Wife's Prayer Tapped Out

The last distinct message from the S-4 came at 6:30 this morning. For hours the oscillator of the S-8 had been repeating this message to Lieutenant Graham Newell Fitch, one of the six men:

"Your wife and mother are praying for you."

Then came a faltering tapping-tapping—indecipherable, but much like the letter "R"—and plainly indicat-

(Continued on page thirteen)
(Continued on last page—page 44)

Women and Children First

The Sinking of the Vestris 1928

New York Times

NEW YORK, TUESDAY, NOVEMBER 13, 1928.

TWO CENTS in Greater New York | THREE CENTS Within 200 Miles | FOUR CENTS Elsewhere in U.S.

339 TAKE TO LIFEBOATS AS LINER VESTRIS SINKS; RESCUE SHIPS AT SCENE FIND NO SIGN OF THEM; DOZEN VESSELS JOIN IN SEARCH OFF VIRGINIA

THE LINER VESTRIS AND POINT OFF VIRGINIA COAST WHERE SHE SANK.

Associated Press Photo.

SEARCHLIGHTS SWEEP SEA

Seven Vessels at Spot 240 Miles Out as Waves Run High.

BATTLESHIP AMONG THEM

Rain and Fog at Night Delay Relief Ships and Dim Hope for Survivors.

TAMPERING CHARGED AT STEWART TRIAL

Venireman Says Stranger Asked Him if He Would "Hold Out" in the Case.

JURORS PICKED, 3 WOMEN

Standard Oil Official Fights Perjury Accusation Over Continental Bonds.

Special to The New York Times.
WASHINGTON, Nov. 12.—When the perjury trial of Robert W. Stewart, Chairman of the board of the Standard Oil Company of Indiana, opened in the District of Columbia Supreme Court this morning the Court was told by Robert V. Caldwell, one of the veniremen called for prospective service on the jury, that he was approached yesterday by a man giving the name of "McGinnis," who asked him if he would "hold out in this case" if he were chosen on the jury.

This development came just after

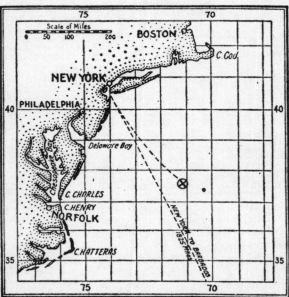

The Scene of the Disaster Was About 240 Miles From Sandy Hook and Virtually the Same Distance From Cape Henry, Va. The Vestris Was Bound for Barbados and South America and Had Been Driven From Her Course by a Storm.

HOW SHIP BEGGED AID RECORDED BY RADIO

Frenzied Calls Broadcast at Intervals Until Order to Take to Lifeboats.

'OH, PLEASE COME!' WAS ONE

Vessel Later Flashed 'Can't Wait Any Longer'—Urged Rescue Ships to Hurry.

The radio told its part in the tragedy of the sea during a short three hours of the day. Starting a little after 10 o'clock yesterday morning with the S O S, the Vestris made frantic efforts to call assistance up to 1:25 in the afternoon. Then there was the despairing, staccato announcement: "We are taking to the lifeboats."

The first message known to have been sent out was received by the Radio Corporation of America at 10:05. It gave the brief announcement:

"S. S. Vestris Lamport and Holt

CAUSE OF WRECK UNKNOWN

Liner Radios Frantic Appeals and Reports Heavy List Before Final 'Good-Bye.'

One of the greatest sea disasters in recent years was feared last night as the result of the sinking of the Lamport & Holt Steamship Vestris, bound from New York to Barbados and South America, about 240 miles off the Virginia Capes yesterday afternoon.

The 129 passengers and 210 officers and crew—339 persons in all, of whom half were women and about 15 children—abandoned the sinking ship in lifeboats at 1:25 o'clock yesterday afternoon. At 3 o'clock this morning, more than twelve hours later, no trace of them had been found by seven rescue ships which reached the scene of the disaster late yesterday afternoon and last night.

The first ship which reached the scene was the San Juan of the Porto Rico line at 5:45 o'clock yesterday afternoon, four hours and twenty minutes after the Vestris had been abandoned. The San Juan reported

---

The events of Monday 12 November 1928, are simply told. The liner *Vestris*, bound for Buenos Aires from New York with 128 passengers and a crew of 210, encountered heavy weather some 240 miles out of port: already shipping water through an ash-ejector and a coal-chute door, she had by dawn on the 12th developed a twenty degree list to starboard that sent deck cargo careering into the forecastle and passengers sliding around their cabins. An attempt to pump out a starboard ballast-tank only worsened the situation, obliging Captain William Carey to send out a CQ (stand-by) call to other ships in the area. That was 8.37am, but by ten o'clock—with the ship pitching at an alarming thirty-two degrees—this was translated into a desperate SOS. As the minutes went by the pleas from the stricken *Vestris*,

picked up at the radio station on Hickory Island N.J., grew ever more urgent. 10.45: 'Rush at all speed!' 11.03: 'Oh, please come at once!' 11.07: 'Ship sinking slowly.' Then at 1.17: 'Can't wait any longer. Going to abandon.' 1.25: 'We are taking to the lifeboats.'

It was the last message from the *Vestris*, but there was some comfort for the rescue ships (three to four hours away) knowing that the storm was abating and that the liner had lifeboats to accommodate twice the number of people on board. Yet the newspapers, that night, had to go to press reporting the tragedy and including the ominous news that rescue ships arriving on the scene had found no trace of survivors. Only at 4.00 the next morning did the SS. *American Shipper* radio that the first lifeboat had been picked up; and in the frantic

daylight hours that followed another seven were reported safe. Gradually, the awful truth came in over the crackling wireless waves. More than three-quarters of the crew had survived—but less than half the passengers. Even worse, out of forty-nine women and children, only eight women had been rescued. Every child had perished.

'Murder', 'Brutal neglect' were some of the violent denunciations hurled at the captain and men of the *Vestris* by passengers as they landed at New York. Captain Carey had criminally delayed sending out an SOS until it was too late, they complained. For twenty-four hours before abandoning ship it had been obvious the liner was in a critical condition. Moreover the ship had been unseaworthy (they said), the lifeboats leaky, and the crew in-

93

A PAGE OF PICTURES OF THE VESTRIS SEA DISASTER—PAGE 11.

"All the News That's Fit to Print."

The New York Times.

THE WEATHER

VOL. LXXVIII....No. 25,863. NEW YORK, THURSDAY, NOVEMBER 15, 1928. TWO CENTS

205 VESTRIS SURVIVORS LAND HERE, CHARGE NEGLIGENCE AND TELL OF SHIPWRECK HORRORS IN STORM-TOSSED SEA; FEDERAL INQUIRY BEGUN OF DISASTER THAT COST 115 LIVES

SECTIONALISM GONE, HOOVER TELLS SOUTH; PRAISES GAIN THERE

He Appeals in Letter for End of All Bitterness in Political Contests.

PLEASED OVER SUPPORT

He Credits Sincerity and Honesty of "Those Who Voted for My Opponent."

PLEDGES AID AS PRESIDENT

Will Seek to Further South's Present Economic Progress, He Informs Baltimore Editor.

Special to The New York Times.

WASHINGTON, Nov. 14.—An appeal to avoid political bitterness and an assurance that in his administration as President of the United States he "shall seek to deal with absolute fairness and justice to every section of our common country," are contained in a letter written by Herbert Hoover to Richard H. Edmonds, editor of the Manufacturers' Record of Baltimore, made public here today. The Hoover letter, written Nov. 7, was in response to a request from Mr. Edmonds, whose periodical is devoted chiefly to the development of Southern resources.

In his letter, Mr. Hoover shows his anxiety to have partisan bitterness ended. He says he "is not at all unmindful of the conditions which for years brought about the political solidarity of the South," an apparent reference to the race question and resentment to the Republican Party's reconstruction policy following the Civil War; but he expresses the belief "that the time has come when in all sections men and women should vote from their convictions as to conditions at the present time and not based on things of former generations."

In calling upon the people of the South to participate in political contests as a duty, Mr. Hoover says:

"I want to make very emphatic that I give full credit to those who voted for my opponent for the sincerity and honesty of their convictions."

He promises the South his fullest cooperation in developing its natural resources and declares especially that the intercoastal canal syztem should extend eventually "all the way from Boston to the end of Texas."

Text of Hoover's Letter.

Mr. Hoover's letter reads as follows:

Palo Alto, Cal., Nov. 7, 1928.

Mr. Richard H. Edmonds, editor Manufacturers' Record, Baltimore, Md.

Dear Mr. Edmonds—I am pro-

SURVIVORS TELL OF HEROES

Negro of Crew Credited With 20 Rescues by Boat He Manned.

SHIP SUCKED MANY DOWN

Men and Women Tell of Fight With Sea After Leaving Liner in Damaged Craft.

FIRST LIFEBOATS CAPSIZED

Those Who Escaped in Overturn Describe Loss of Children—Most Passengers Calm.

In pleasant contrast to the stories of failure and cowardice on the Vestris, other stories were told yesterday when the survivors landed, stories of individual courage and self-sacrifice in rescue work on the part of both passengers and crew.

There was the heroic little negro quartermaster with the picturesque name Lionel Licorish, who crawled into a lifeboat containing an injured fireman and no oars, who again braved the shark-infested seas to swim to a capsized boat for oars, and then rowed back and forth through the wreckage for hours until he had picked up all he could find. Sixteen was his own count of those he saved; others said twenty.

"That little negro did what the officers of the Vestris failed to do," was the eulogy pronounced upon Lionel Licorish by Alfred Ramos, who was in the water fourteen hours before the negro pulled him aboard.

Two of "Pluckiest Survivors."

Then there were Paul A. Dana, the young passenger, and Mrs. Clara Ball, the stewardess, whom Captain Cumings of the rescue ship American Shipper characterized as "two of the pluckiest people I ever met." They spent twenty-two hours tossing about in the heavy seas after Dana pulled Mrs. Ball out of the wreckage of a smashed lifeboat, drifting all one afternoon, all that night in rain, fog and sleet, and all next morning on a piece of grating until the American Shipper picked them up.

Also there were T. E. Mack of Tecla, Wyo., and his companion, O. L. Maxey of Richmond, Va., who swam for two and a half hours past crowded lifeboats without trying to climb in lest they upset the boats and drown the others, until they found a boat with plenty of room.

Second Steward Alfred Duncan showed the same qualities when, after waiting until the last moment on the bridge alongside Captain Carey, he went overboard in a life belt and swam past crowded lifeboats until he reached one that could take him aboard safely.

There was the young Irish radio

Times Wide World Photo.

PICKING UP A SURVIVOR FROM THE SEA.

Picture Made From the Deck of the Berlin as Karl Schmidt of Chicago Was Saved After Twenty-two Hours Afloat.

FRENCH SHIP BRINGS 57 FROM THE VESTRIS

Tanker Myriam Picked Up Three More Survivors Than She Reported by Wireless.

NEW LIGHT ON DISASTER

Woman and Husband, Separated When Ship Sank, Reunited at Brooklyn Pier.

Fifty-seven exhausted passengers and crew of the Vestris landed at Pier 8, at the foot of Clark Street, Brooklyn, at 1:30 o'clock this morning, after being transferred from tseir rescue ship, the French tanker Myriam two hours previously to a waiting tug in Gravesend Bay.

The survivors included eight passengers, six officers, three musicians, seventeen stewards and twenty-three members of the Vestris's engine room crew.

One of the eight passengers was Mrs. Cline Slaughter, who celebrated her twenty-first birthday yesterday in the cabin of the captain of the Myriam, recuperating from the shock of the tragedy, which nearly cost her her life.

Mrs. Slaughter was met at the pier by her husband, who is connected with the International Harvester

TELLS VIVID STORY OF GROWING ALARM

Dr. E. Lehner, Strange to Sea, Felt Only Slowly Portent of Reeling Vestris.

BOAT PATCHED WITH TIN

Graphic Tale of Night Adrift Completed by H. C. Johnson, Who Praises Seamen.

The following graphic account of the sinking of the Vestris and the fate of its passengers was given to THE NEW YORK TIMES *by two of the survivors, Dr. E. Lehner and H. C. Johnston, who were en route for Trinidad, where they are connected with the Trinidad Leaseholds, Ltd., an oil company. The first part of the narrative is by Dr. Lehner, an inexperienced voyager, who became so seasick in the lifeboat that he did not know what happened after that. The story was then picked up by Mr. Johnston, who has traveled 200,000 miles on the sea and was keenly alert to all that went on.*

By DR. E. LEHNER,
Chief Geologist for the Trinidad Leaseholds, Ltd.

When the ship listed to starboard early Sunday afternoon, I did not become afraid because I thought it was due to the wind, which was hitting us broadside. It seemed to me

TRAGEDY TERMED 'MURDER'

Survivors Heap Blame on Captain for Delay in Asking Help.

CALL BOATS UNSEAWORTHY

Former Sea Captain, Charging 'Criminal Neglect,' Asserts One Had Six-Inch Hole.

CREW BITTERLY DENOUNCED

Ignored Pleas, Say Passengers—Allege Ship Was Loaded Improperly and Leaked.

Surviving passengers of the Vestris tragedy who returned to New York yesterday on rescue ships were almost unanimous in bitter criticisms of the Lamport & Holt line and the officers and crew of the lost steamer.

They accused the company of failure to provide adequate safety equipment, the ship's master of inefficiency and vacillation in face of danger, his officers of callous indifference, and the crew as a whole with downright cowardice, panic, desertion and brutal neglect of passengers.

Some of the crew joined in the condemnation of the ship's condition and her officers, and white members of the crew blamed the negro members for the crew's failure to meet the emergency in the proper manner of the sea.

Officials of the line replied to criticisms of the ship itself by saying that the United States Steamboat Inspection Service had examined the Vestris last Wednesday, three days before she sailed, and had passed the ship and lifeboats as seaworthy. This was confirmed by the Steamship Inspection Service. As to the charges against the officers and crew, the company reserved any statement pending investigation. It praised Captain Carey, the master of the Vestris, as "one of our best captains, the Commodore of our fleet." Some of the crew denied the charge that the lifeboats were not in proper condition.

Summary of Charges.

A summary of the charges made by survivors follows:

1. That the Vestris sailed from New York without having been properly inspected, in an unseaworthy condition, with an unclosed coal port, a leaky hold and defective watertight compartments, and with the cargo improperly loaded, so that when she ran into a heavy gale her cargo shifted, tons of water rushed in, and she listed so she could not straighten up.
2. That some of her lifeboats had holes or were leaky, that none was equipped with sufficient oars, axes, lights, provisions and fresh water, and that some of the apparatus for lowering lifeboats was rusty and

Times Wide World Photo.

"THE PLUCKIEST PAIR" RESCUED.

Paul A. Dana, Passenger, and Mrs. Clara Ball, Stewardess, So Described by Captain Cumings of the Rescue Steamer American Shipper.

DRIFTED 22 HOURS WITH WOMAN IN SEA

Paul A. Dana Relates Struggle to Hold to Debris After Huge Waves Destroyed Boat.

FEARED SHARKS ON VIGIL

He Felt Fish Brush Past Many Times, but Kept Companion in Ignorance of Terror.

By PAUL A. DANA,
As Told to Lorena A. Hickok, Associated Press Staff Writer.

Copyright, 1928, by The Associated Press.

Our first night out, Saturday night, the Vestris began to hit rough weather. As the night progressed the storm got worse until, before the night was over, we were in the worst storm I ever saw on the sea.

It was late that night, perhaps a little after midnight, that a thing happened which I believe started the trouble that ended in the tragic sinking of the Vestris.

Two big waves struck her, almost simultaneously, bow and stern. The ship quivered from end to end. You could almost feel her wrenching. The next day she developed a leak: and I believe that started the leak. One of her plates must have been wrenched loose

'VESTRIS WILL SINK,' FRIENDS TOLD QUIROS

Consular Aide Warned Before Sailing, He Says, That Ship Would 'Meet the Mafalda.'

NOTED LIST ON FIRST DAY

Peril Obvious Sunday, He Holds—Asserts Vessel Was on Beam Ends as Boats Put Off.

By CARLOS QUIROS,
Chancellor of the Argentine Consulate in New York.

I took passage on the Vestris to visit my mother, who is in Buenos Aires. I did not reach Buenos Aires, but I will do so. However, next time I will sail on an American ship.

Had I listened to the advice of my friends I would not have gone on the Vestris at all. No less than three persons told me not to go on her. One said, jokingly, I thought, "So you are to sail on the Vestris? Well, be careful, for the Vestris is going to meet the Principessa Mafalda!" He was right. They have met—the Vestris and that other ship that sank off the Brazilian coast. Two other friends, both of them women, warned me that the Vestris had a list. "You will have to walk on one side," they said. But

SURVIVORS ON THREE SHIPS

Report All Children and Most of Women Were Swallowed in Sea.

TELL OF TOWERING WAVES

Victims Menaced by Sharks and Lashed by Tropical Storm—Lifeboats Flooded.

SEVERAL GO TO HOSPITALS

Myriam, With 57 Aboard, Drops Anchor in Lower Bay—21 Bodies Taken From Water.

Storm-tossed and dazed with the burden of their memories, 205 survivors of the Vestris had been returned to the haven of this port today, straight from the grimmest epic of the seas since the Lusitania was sunk.

They came on three ships that had snatched them from the engulfing waves, after hours adrift in the lashing fury of a mountainous sea. The American Shipper and the Berlin brought in 148 persons yesterday, and early this morning the French tanker Myriam arrived with fifty-seven more. The battleship Wyoming was nearing Norfolk with eight rescued. Twenty-one bodies were bound here aboard cutters.

On a background of survivors' tales of individual heroism, of sacrifice and endurance, as the rollers pounded their lifeboats or they clung to bits of wreckage, were painted the ominous outlines of fear, mismanagement and dubious nautical judgment on the part of the captain and crew of the British ship.

84 Are Still Missing.

Of the list of 328 persons who set out from this port on Saturday on the Lamport & Holt liner bound for South American harbors, 84 were missing last night, including most of the women and all of the children. Only five women were among the survivors that reached New York, and one of them the outstanding heroine of the disaster, a stewardess who, with a man passenger, clung to wreckage for twenty-two and a half hours before being picked up.

Through lips blue from her experience, but in a voice she still tried to make strong, Mrs. Clara Ball, a member of the crew, denied that she had felt fear as she and her companion, alone in the raging sea, were beaten by rain or blinded by night. "You can't be afraid," she said, "when you have

competent to lower them. One passenger—who had been a sea-captain himself—Frederick Sorenson, had some particularly harsh words to say about sailors who had refused to pick up survivors and about the captain's 'negligence'. His accusations were reported voluminously by the *New York Sun*, the *Telegram* and *The World* among others. An article bearing his signature appeared in the *New York Herald Tribune*.

Perhaps it was the heat of the moment, because at the American Inquiry a few days later Captain Sorenson was calling the newspapers liars and denying that he had made such disparaging remarks—even to the face of the *New York Sun* reporter who was called upon to produce his shorthand notebook. However a good many disgruntled passengers did stick to their guns: Thomas Mack, a consulting engineer, declared 'the women and children in the boats were murdered as plainly as if they had been hit over the head with a hatchet; the ship's officers waited in sending an SOS just to save a few dollars.' The women and children had died, it was discovered, because they had been bundled into the first two lifeboats on the port side which, because of the listing, had capsized into the sea 'their screams and cries of distress suddenly muffled by the rush of waves.'

As complaint was piled upon complaint, the British Press began to get very restless with the course the Inquiry was taking. As in the wake of the *Titanic* tragedy, Fleet Street was soon assailing 'American methods of trial by a mixture of newspapers stunts, sensation and scandal' as the *Daily News* would have it. 'The bullying, biased, ignorant and inconceivably stupid procedure suggests inevitably a preconceived resolve to condemn and vilify British seamanship' it went on. 'Most of the witnesses are persons who have just escaped from a most shattering ordeal' declared the *Standard*. 'Even if there were against any of them a strong prima facie suspicion of guilt it would still be not only humane but politic to handle them with gentleness and consideration.' Captain Carey, moreover, as *The Star* was quick to point out, had drowned and could not defend himself. 'It is indecent to subject the reputation of this British ship and British captain to this monstrous manhandling.' Britain, as the *New York Times* wryly surmised, believed the truth would only be discovered by its own Board of Trade.

And in due course the Board of Trade had its day. It found the American agents in New York very much at fault for allowing the liner to sail overloaded and with an excess of coal in its bunkers (there was no load-line rule in the USA at that time), and—not very surprisingly—it was much more charitable about the British officers. It thought Captain Carey 'unduly optimistic' in his hopes of saving the boat, and mildly reproved the British owners for recommending that its masters attempt to fight their way unaided to the nearest port. It had been 'unwise' to attempt to lower the port lifeboats and 'imprudent' to have pumped out the starboard ballast tank. Otherwise the Court might have echoed Captain Carey's dying words, as he walked down the side of his abandoned ship and into the water: 'My God, I am not to blame for this!'

A Sacrifice to Improvidence

The R.101 Crash 1930

DAILY SKETCH. MONDAY, OCTOBER 6, 1930.

SURVIVORS' VIVID STORIES OF AIRSHIP DISASTER

DAILY SKETCH

INCORPORATING THE DAILY GRAPHIC

R101 MEMORIAL NUMBER

No. 6,699. [Registered as a newspaper.]   MONDAY, OCTOBER 6, 1930.   ONE PENNY.

THE LAST OF THE GIANT R101: WONDERFUL AIR PICTURE

The Empire was stunned yesterday by the news of the appalling air disaster in which R101 crashed in flames near Beauvais, Northern France, within eight hours of leaving Cardington on a flight to India. Forty-six of the passengers and crew w re killed, there being only eight survivors. Her commander, Flight-Lieut. H. C. Irwin, was last seen "standing at his post quietly giving orders." The Air Minister, Lord Thomson, another of the victims, initiated the construction of R101 and R100 in 1924. He was always a supreme believer in giant airships and lighter than air vessels.

95

ORS SAY
UST BE
ANASPRIN
THE SAFE BRAND

Sunday Express

LAST
LONDON
EDT^N

To-day's Weather: SOME SHOWERS.

NO. 614.   LONDON, OCTOBER 5, 1930.   TWOPENCE.

R 101 DISASTER : 45 DEAD. Afternoon Special.

AIRSHIP CRASHES IN FLAMES.

FAMOUS AIR ACES PERISH.

Lord Thomson And Sir S. Brancker Dead.

LORD THOMSON.

SIR SEFTON BRANCKER.

ONLY EIGHT SAVED: 45 TRAPPED IN AN INFERNO.

R 101 AS LONDONERS SAW HER.

R 101 flying over the huge crowd at Hendon Air Pageant last June, when the airship also flew over London.

SIR DENNIS BURNEY.

Sir Dennis Burney, the designer ... sister ship of the ... said to ...

FULL LIST OF THE DEAD

PIONEERS OF FLYING LOST IN R 101.

LORD THOMSON'S SERVICE TO THE STATE.

GREAT CAREERS.

SIR W. S. BRANCKER AND MAJOR SCOTT.

THE Empire has lost three of her most distinguished pioneers in flying in Lord Thomson, Sir W. S. Brancker, and Major Scott.

Lord Thomson was raised to the peerage and appointed Secretary of State for Air when Mr. Ramsay MacDonald came into power in ... He again held that office in the present Labour Ministry. He had always been an enthusiast for flying. ... from the Army in 1919 ... honorary rank of brigad... after having seen extensive ... many campaigns, including the war and the great w...

"F.E.'s" DOG AT HIS FUNERAL.

MOURNING FOR ITS MASTER.

MR. CHURCHILL'S TEARS.

By JAMES DOUGLAS.

The funeral of Lord Birkenhead at Charlton, near Banbury, in Oxfordshire, yesterday was secret and simple and natural.

It was what his heart would have desired, for he had qualities of heart which the nation that ... in storm and tempest, in the ...

LAT...

The *R.101* was to be more than the biggest, most expensive, most luxurious airship ever built. A conscious symbol of national pride and prestige, she was 250 yards long and kept aloft by 5.5 million cubic feet of hydrogen: the very sight of her ample bulk sailing gracefully over cities would raise the eyes—not to say, the hearts—of men to the skies, as they stood in the lengthening dole queues. Her maiden voyage to Ismailia, and on to India (where the spectre of Gandhi and revolution lurked) would be a demonstration of imperial solidarity more potent than a fleet of gunboats. Such were the hopes, at least, of the Labour Government in 1930 and of its Minister for Air, Lord Thomson, in particular.

But the *R.101* had a rival—the *R.100*, a capitalist venture which was not only ready first but had flown triumphantly to Canada and back almost before the *R.101* was even out of its hangar. Lord Thomson was determined his 'socialist' airship would be even more successful. It must, he insisted, be ready at any cost to fly him to India and back before the Imperial Conference at the end of October. By any standards, that was a tall order for the engineers at Cardington, for on its first public outing in June the *R.101* had flown dangerously 'heavy' and narrowly avoided a premature end. It was also found that its useful lifting capacity was only half what had been projected. A formidable schedule of modifications was embarked on—including splitting the monster in half to insert an extra bay. By the beginning of October the *R.101* had been patched up, after a fashion, but had yet to be tested in flight.

In spite of the protestations of its designer, Sir Sefton Brancker, that the airship was not yet airworthy, Lord Thomson refused to budge an inch from his schedule—even arranging for a 'temporary' Certificate of Airworthiness to be issued (whatever that might have been). So it was that as the gloom gathered in around Cardington airfield on Saturday evening, 4 October 1930, the Air Minister stood beneath the shadow of the *R.101* and offered some words of good cheer to the assembled reporters. 'We are starting off with very great confidence' he announced. 'The conditions are quite satisfactory . . . I have promised the Prime Minister we shall be back on Monday October 20th.' And with that he disappeared into the lift which carried him into the belly of the airship.

His words were to be read at breakfast tables all over the country the next morning. By then, Lord Thomson was dead.

The Air Minister was not alone in his optimism. With its promenade of potted palms, its fire-proof smoking-lounge, its gold-and-white state rooms, the *R.101* exuded all the confidence of the great ocean-liners. Even *The Times*, a little earlier, had bestowed a few words of encouragement in an editorial: 'Face to face with timid misgivings and open prophecies of failure of the airship, engineers and scientists have gone a long way to justify their enthusiastic belief in its possibilities . . .' And on the morning of the *R.101*'s flight the *Daily Herald* was enthusing: 'She is in perfect trim.' It might not have seemed so to more knowledgeable observers, watching her dip sharply on leaving the mast and shed nearly half her entire water ballast just to gain height—but at any rate by 1.50 in the morning of Sunday 5 October the ship had crossed the Channel and Lord Thomson was being wafted across the skies of Northern France and, according to the routine wireless report, 'enjoying several cigars before retiring'.

In a beetroot field just outside Beauvais, at that very moment, Georges Rabouille was poaching rabbits quietly and without interruption. He was naturally startled to hear a loud throbbing sound coming towards him, then even more astonished to see the huge, illuminated sky-palace looming barely a hundred feet above him. He later described what happened next: 'Suddenly there was a violent squall. The airship dipped by the nose several times, and its forepart crashed into the north-west edge of the Bois de Coutumes. There was at once a tremendous explosion, which knocked me down. Soon flames rose into the sky to a great height—perhaps 300 feet. Everything was enveloped by them. I saw human figures running about like madmen in the wreck. Then I lost my head and ran away into the woods.'

Rabouille was the only human being to witness the fatal descent of the *R.101* at close quarters, but for the time being the poacher found it prudent to run to ground himself.

The explosion had been heard in the town, however, and it was 3.05am precisely when the chilling news reached Fleet Street over the wires. At 3.00 in the morning all the Sunday papers—bearing the good tidings of a successful take-off—had long gone to press. But at the *Sunday Express* one newsman, Arthur Christiansen, made a historic decision. He got the presses rolling again and worked through the night to re-make his paper. Belatedly the other Sundays followed suit, grasping whatever fragments of information they could until well into the afternoon. For the dailies it was no less of a testing-time. In 1930 the popular press was locked together in the early paroxysms of a bitter circulation battle. Circulation meant survival in those Depression years. The glittering target: 2 million readers, with every 100,000 a milestone. When times were quiet that meant give-away sets of Dickens or Free Insurance policies (indeed the *Daily Mirror* soon ascertained that at least five of the *R.101*'s victims were 'registered readers' and therefore qualified for its insurance). When the story of the decade broke, it meant saturation coverage.

Of the fifty-four on board six had miraculously survived the holocaust. Two of them, both engineers, had been saved by being drenched by a fractured water-tank. Another, Disley the wireless operator, had literally had to batter his way through the flaming shell. As he explained to the *Daily Sketch*: 'The whole structure of the airship seemed to be cracking up and crashing about my ears . . . I turned this way and that, but there seemed no way out. I beat my hands against the fabric, trying in a wild sort of way to tear it. I kicked at it but I was still a prisoner. It was like a dog must feel when he has a blanket put over him and can't escape from it. But this blanket was burning . . .'

The *Daily Herald* unearthed an Englishman who had happened to be driving a few miles away at the time of the crash. 'We saw one man who was evidently trying to get out of a cabin further along' he recounted, 'but he was terribly burnt, and we saw him fall back helpless into the flames . . .' It was several days before the *Reuters* correspondent tracked down the principal witness, M Rabouille—in a police station.

When reporters reached the scene early on Sunday morning all that remained of the *R.101* was a gigantic burned-out carcass, looking (from the specially chartered aeroplanes that buzzed about) like a stranded whale, and poignant mementoes of the voyage. 'As I clambered through the network of steel wire' cabled back the *Evening Standard*'s correspondent, 'there was evidence on all sides of the

Daily Express

TO-DAY'S WEATHER: Rain at Times.

DAILY EXPRESS, Monday, October 6, 1930.

NO. 9493.   MONDAY, OCTOBER 6, 1930.   ONE PENNY.

The R101 Crashes And Is Destroyed: Lord Thomson, Sir Sefton Brancker And 44 Others Burned To Death.

TO-DAY'S WEATHER: Showers; squally at times.   MONDAY. The Daily Mail OCTOBER 6, 1930.   **13**

MYSTERY OF THE R101 DISASTER:
Graphic Stories.   Wonderful Pictures by Air.

46 BURNED TO DEATH IN WRECK.

STORM, CRASH, EXPLOSION, AND FLAMES.

Daily Herald

No. 4568   ••   MONDAY, OCTOBER 6, 1930   ONE PENNY

R101 CRASHES—EXPLODES—BURNS:
GREAT AIRSHIP DISASTER: PAGES OF PICTURES

MEN PERISH

FRENCH POLICE

Daily Mirror
THE DAILY PICTURE PAPER WITH THE LARGEST NET SALE

No. 8,387   Registered at the G.P.O. as a Newspaper.   MONDAY, OCTOBER 6, 1930   One Penny

R101 MEMORIAL NUMBER

engines after the fire had burned out.

THE TRAGIC END OF R101
AIR MINISTER AND AIRSHIP EXPERTS LOST—46 VICTIMS

Looking along the wreckage of R 101, which ran into a storm, crashed and burst into flames soon after 2 o'clock yesterday morning at Allonne, near ... tempted flight to India. Only ...

·TION MOURNS

TRIBUTES BY THE KING AND PREMIER

The King has sent the following telegram to the Prime Minister:—
" I am horrified to hear of this national disaster. The Queen and I sympathise deeply with the relatives and friends of those who have perished in the service of their country, and also with the injured survivors."

Mr. MacDonald issued the following message from Downing-street :—
" I am grieved beyond words at the loss of so many splendid men, whose sacrifice has been added to that glorious list of Englishmen who on uncharted seas and unexplored lands have gone into the unknown as pioneers and pathfinders, and have met death.

" My most heartfelt sympathy goes out to their families in this hour of their bereavement. Only those who have been associated with Lord Thomson know how much the country has lost. To me no one can now fill his place of genial companionship and friendship."

r the Big Competitions ?

0 IN PRIZES
ALREADY BEEN
THIS YEAR
READERS OF

The ader
AUTHORITY ON ALL COMPETITION MATTERS

every current Picture Puzzle and Crossword cluding those which appeared in the Sunday y—is solved in this morning's issue of THE still three or four days for you to post in is no reason why you should not win your share this year, over 1,700 readers of THE LEADER ng First Prize.

Injured Opera the News to

" Can you hear me? She has gon These words, heard faintly ... first news of the airship disaster They were telephoned by an i ... one of the wireless operators o ...

WIRELESS OPERATOR DISLEY hospital yester

WALKED FLAMII
Englishman Amazing R

A man who walked through t amazing stories of the airship passing over Bea

" I jumped into my car, down and hit the earth with flames sprang up at one end, before they had got a substa

97

RECONSTRUCTED BY FRENCH ARTIST FOR TH

Evening Standard 6 October 1930

Evening Standard

havoc that had been wrought. Here was a burnt folding camera . . . a smell of carbide, a fused jumble of electrical fittings, a tin of bully-beef, a collection of knives and forks. All lay in the debris of mangled steelwork . . .'

Eager to provide their readers with some clue to the mystery, reporters clung like leeches to the tight-lipped experts who arrived to inspect the wreckage. On the Monday they were rewarded. The *Evening Standard*'s front page posed the startling question, 'Did R.101 Crack in Mid-air before Crashing?' The story quoted an announcement by Air-Commodore Holt of the Air Ministry: 'The definite cause of the accident was breakage of the structure, and not motor failure. We have found parts which fell as far as five miles from the scene of the wreck, indicating that something happened at least 5 to 10 miles before the crash.' It was indeed startling, since it appeared flatly to contradict all the evidence of the survivors. And the experts must have thought so too, for the same afternoon *Reuters* published an outright denial: 'Air-Commodore Holt emphatically denies having given any interview or made any statement regarding the cause of the loss of the R.101.' No matter, each paper had its own theory.

The *Daily Express* had some disturbing news. After the crash it felt itself able 'to reveal the complete details of an alarming experience which overtook the R.101 during her flight over Hendon last July . . .' The writer explained that the gas-bags were found to be riddled with thousands of minute holes, probably from rubbing against the steel framework. He added ominously: 'there were elaborate precautions against publication of these facts and until now the secret had been kept successfully'. It looked as if a good many private apprehensions were starting to surface. The *Daily Sketch* devoted many columns to a Naval Architect (named Spanner) who had publicly 'prophesied three years ago' that the *R.101* type of lighter-than-air vessel was lethal.

Then the bodies began their slow journey back from Beauvais. When the authorities announced they were to be laid out in a London mortuary the papers, correctly divining the depths of public emotion, denounced the whole idea. A Lying-in-State in Westminster Hall was hurriedly arranged, to accommodate the tens of thousands who flocked to do homage to the 'heroes' (as they now firmly were in the public mind). From all walks of life they came, or as one reporter—wrestling manfully with his syntax to extract every ounce of pathos—put it: 'Men and women in the flush of vigour, cripples dragging their twisted limbs, the aged, the young, the weary child asleep on a parent's shoulder, the sick, the indulgent, morning and sunset of life rubbing shoulders.' Exactly a week after the catastrophe, the victims of the *R.101* reached their final resting-place, a common grave in Cardington cemetery within sight of 'the very spot where fifty-four men set out on a great and high adventure—to fly to India in the largest, most modern, most perfectly equipped airship that the world has yet seen.'

And for all the sound and fury down in Fleet Street, it had been Cardington's local paper, the *Bedford Record*, that ironically had cut through all the theorizing with a bitter indictment so unanswerable that even the national papers ran it verbatim: 'Why did they let her go? They knew she was dipping at the nose. They knew she had not been tested properly, and they knew that one engine at least was out of order. And yet they let her go. Our brave men and our wonderful ship were sacrificed to improvidence . . . The plain man's story (and until a better one is produced it holds the field) is that the Government were determined at all costs to 'make a demonstration while the Empire Conference was still in session. And they made it: at all costs.'

The report of the Official Inquiry did nothing to mitigate the *Record*'s indictment, surmising that the gas-bags already chafed had sprung

FRANCE'S NOBLE TRIBUTE FOR HOMECOMING OF R 101 VICTIMS—WONDERFUL PICTURES OF THE IMPRESSIVE SCENES

The scene at Beauvais as the coffins of the forty-seven men killed in the R 101—   —were borne in slow procession from the town hall on the start of the journey to England.

Some of the numerous beautiful French official wreaths.

Air Chief Marshal Sir John Salmond.

A to B. M. Tardieu, French Premier, Mr. F. Montague, Under-Secretary of State for Air, and Mr. W. Wedgwood Benn, Secretary of State for India.

Spahis saluting with their flashing sabres as the coffins were carried past.

The muffled drums which were carried in the procession.

M. Laurent-Eynac, the French Minister for Air.

The scene as the procession was leaving the town hall, where the coffins had lain in state. Yesterday was observed as a day of national mourning in France.—("Daily Mirror" photographs.)

leaks, the envelope already skimpily patched up had been torn by buffeting in bad weather, and the airship already overweight had grown heavier as it became more waterlogged. The report ended unequivocably: 'It is impossible to avoid the conclusion that the R.101 would not have started for India on the evening of the 4th October if it had not been that reasons of public policy were considered as making it highly desirable for her to do so if she could.'

The day after the funeral, the *Sunday Pictorial* ran an article written by the *R.101*'s designer, Sir Sefton Brancker. In it he predicted: 'The airship probably has many years of life— perhaps at least fifty.' Had he not written those words before the *R.101* took off, and had he not himself been buried in that common grave at Cardington, might he not now have agreed with the *Express*'s opinion 'in one second the arguments of those who have urged the development of the lighter-than-air machine seem to have been swept away'? Or the *News Chronicle*'s view that it was 'manifestly folly to spend more millions on the development of craft so very expensive and so very speculative in operation'? Or even with the *Daily Mirror*'s final, summary judgement: 'Stop Building the Gas-bags!'

THE LIVING AND THE DEAD
THREE R 101 SURVIVORS IN THE BEAUVAIS CORTEGE

Three of the seven survivors of the R 101 disaster—Messrs. J. H. Binks (light coat), H. J. Leech (centre) and A. V. Bell—in the procession of coffins of the forty-seven victims from Beauvais Town Hall to the railway station yesterday for transport to Boulogne. The French paid the tribute of full military honours. Troops lined the streets, aeroplanes circled overhead and dropped flowers and a salute of 101 guns was fired. At Boulogne the British destroyers, Tempest and Tribune, were waiting to carry the coffins to Dover for London. The above and other "Daily Mirror" photographs in this issue were carried by "Daily Mirror" aeroplanes. See also pages 5, 12, 13, 20 and 24.

Sunday Dispatch

128th Year.   No. 6,728.   **OCTOBER 12, 1930.**   Wireless Programmes in Page 15.   TWOPENCE.   POSTAGE {IN U.K. 2½d. CANADA 2½d. ABROAD 2d.}

**R 101
FUNERAL
NUMBER**

The Journey's End for Gallant Crew of the R 101.

TO THEIR LAST RESTING-PLACE.—Members of the Royal Air Force carrying the coffins, draped with Union Jacks, from the tenders to the common grave at Cardington.

RACE WINNERS EXAMINED.

HOT BUN SURPRISE AT KEMPTON.

HORSES were examined by the official course veterinary surgeons after races at Kempton Park and Haydock yesterday.

The stewards at Kempton Park, without issuing any preliminary warning, ordered Hot Bun to be examined after she had won the rich Duke of York Handicap.

Hot Bun defeated Racedale after a thrilling struggle; and it was her first success this year.

The stewards, of course, have power under the Rules of Racing to order the examination of any horse after it has run in a race, but usually in the past they have announced that they intended to do so.

STEWARDS' NOTICE.

Hot Bun is owned by M. Jacques Wittouck, a well-known Belgian sportsman who races extensively.

Soon after the horses had left the paddock for the Saturday Selling Handicap at Haydock Park, a notice was posted stating that the first three would be examined and that the winner would not be sold until after the next race.

The Saturday Selling Handicap was won by Filibuster, second and third places being filled by Cretan Lassie and Downholme.

LATEST NEWS.

U.S. AND HELIUM.

The U.S. Commerce Department states that nine licensees for export of helium, (the safety gas for airships) have been approved since control was created. Only one had been refused. This information is given owing to the agitation against restrictions following the R 101 disaster.—Exchange.

[It has been definitely asserted that had it 101 been inflated with helium the loss of life would have been greatly minimised.]

DIED WARNING THE CREW.

HERO WHO PERISHED IN THE FLAMES.

'WE ARE DOWN!'

AIR AMBULANCE FOR SURVIVORS.

"SUNDAY DISPATCH" SPECIAL.
BEAUVAIS, Saturday.

DRAMATIC new evidence regarding the last few moments before the R 101 crashed to earth, revealing that one member of the crew was aware that the

Wireless Operator A. Disley.

ship was doomed, has emanated from the investigation.

This statement was furnished by Wireless Operator A. Disley, of Shortstown, one of the survivors of the disaster, who is now in Beauvais Hospital.

A few seconds before the airship plunged to the ground, Disley, who was in bed, was warned that the ship was going down to destruction.

DRAMATIC CALL.

This warning came from one of the men who had been in the control-room of the airship. With no thought of his own safety, this hero dashed into the switch room, in which Disley was in bed, and cried out:—

"*We are down!*"
Then he dashed towards the crew's quarters, which adjoined the switch room, to warn the men there.
He perished in the flames.

Disley attempted to switch off the two generators which furnished electric light for the inside of the airship. His bed, however, was so placed that when the airship's nose went down his feet were in the air.

COMING HOME.

By the time he could get up to reach the switches the airship had struck the ground and the explosion followed.

In this evidence, Wireless Operator Disley admits that the base of R101 struck the ground first.

It is hoped to remove the three survivors by R.A.F. air ambulance to London to-morrow or on Tuesday.

SPECIAL FUNERAL PICTURES in Pages 13 and 24.
LONDON'S FAREWELL on Page 2.

AIRMEN HEROES ARE HOME AGAIN.

200 Relatives and 75,000 People in Last Scene.

In sight of the great hangar that had been the home of the airship R 101, Cardington yesterday took her sons into her arms and laid them gently to sleep.

A week before they had set forth, with cheers ringing around them, on a magic voyage to the East. Now 48 of that crew had reached the end of their journey. Seventy-five thousand people went to the grief-stricken village to pay homage at the grave where they lay undivided in death as in life.

The centre of London was hushed as, earlier in the day, with a whole nation's pageantry and solemn ceremonial, the 48 coffins were taken from the Great Hall of Westminster to Euston Station, where the capital of the Empire bade a sorrowful farewell to her gallant airmen.

UNDIVIDED TO THE LAST.

By IAN HAY, the Famous Author of "THE FIRST HUNDRED THOUSAND."

CARDINGTON, Saturday.

A PERFECT October day. We are waiting here to complete a day of national mourning, of national homage.

Just a week ago to-day 54 men set out from this very spot (you can see the hangar and the big mooring mast just across those fields) on a great and high adventure—to fly to India in the largest, most modern, most perfectly equipped airship that the world has yet seen. Many of those who stand here now—mates, sweethearts, wives—saw them go, and cheered and wept.

To-day they are coming home.

Forty-eight of them for the last time. They come followed by the salutations of France and the homage of England. For a week they have belonged to the nation—two nations. This afternoon they are among their own people.

A MILE OF PEACE.

Cardington is very quiet to-day. Footsteps are all you hear. A police cordon has been drawn round the village, outside which all wheeled traffic must remain. So the church and the graveyard lies in the centre *of a square mile of utter peace.*

Blinds are drawn in every cottage; out in the street or under the trees on the village green people stand talking, in undertones.

They are most numerous on that part of the street which runs between the graveyard and the church, for here the great square grave lies waiting, lined with green

IAN HAY.

turf and chrysanthemum blooms, just inside the churchyard wall.

The cortege must have left Bedford by this time; in due course we shall see it winding down from the north end of the street. All morning spectators have been pouring out of Bedford; the road must be lined by this time from end to end.

On the other side of the road just outside the church lie the wreaths. They come from all parts of the country and from every walk of life, from regimental depots, business houses, schools, associations, and the like.

There is one from the Air Base at Montreal; another from a pierrot troupe in Bedford; and there are scores of wreaths from nearer home, inscribed to a single name and addressed to a single memory.

We take up our positions. Deep silence has fallen now, marred only by the roar of aeroplane engines. A glittering squadron is wheeling in perfect formation high in the sky to the east. They are a

beautiful sight, but somehow one wishes they were not there.

Now it is nearly four o'clock, and the tensity is increased.

The street outside the low graveyard wall is cleared. The villagers are lined on the far side. The Red Cross and the St. John Ambulance men are in their places. Suddenly from up the road to Bedford comes the sound of music, the Royal Air Force Band playing Chopin's Funeral March.

THOSE LEFT.

First a police escort, then, with arms reversed, a picked detachment of the Royal Air Force, magnificent young men in their blue-grey uniforms, then in the place of honour wreaths from the King and Royal Family.

Next the immemorial adjunct to this heart-stirring ceremonial, the firing party and trumpeters.

At last, the central figures of this immemorial pageant, a line of 6-wheeled R.A.F. tenders each with its mournful burden. There are 24 of them, two coffins reposing in each tender. They are followed by the Third Watch of the R 101,

Dauntless Young England.

That the spirit of young England remains undaunted has been abundantly proved by an unprecedented rush of recruits to the R.A.F.

Since the wreck of R 101 the recruiting department in Whitehall has been to-day more crowded than ever.

Immediately the funeral procession had passed the Air Ministry yesterday dozens of young men, some still bareheaded, presented themselves for recruitment.

An official said: "After a disaster men are fired with new enthusiasm. It is the old story of the Englishman's refusal to admit defeat."

TENSION IN SPAIN.

MADRID, Sunday Morning.

Arrests have been made throughout Spain owing to the fear of revolutionary disturbances. The arrest of Commander Franco, the Spanish Atlantic airman, has created a sensation.

All the police of the "Social Brigade" have been mobilised, and the houses of the anti-Monarchial leaders are being closely watched.—B.U.P.

men who were left behind when the airship sailed.

The procession stops, and the band wheels into the graveyard. The clergy appear walking up the road from the church in their white robes and war medals.

One by one in endless succession the flag-draped coffins are unloaded and carried down the ramp into the waiting grave, each by six grey clad Airmen.

Beside the grave stands the firing party with bowed heads. All is silent now, save for the rumble of the tenders as they move into place.

BROTHERHOOD.

Now from another direction a black clothed procession enters the graveyard. They are the relatives of the dead. They take their places at the head of the grave. *There are more than 200 of them.*

All the time the line of flag-covered coffins passes onwards and downwards—the bodies of air chiefs, officers, rankers going in common brotherhood to a common resting place.

Far away down the Bedford road at the other end of the now stationary procession, the band of the Bedford and Hertford Regiment can be heard playing Handel's majestic march from Scipio. It dies away and the R.A.F. band close at hand breaks

Continued in Page 2, Col. 6.

MUST WE ALL BE FATALISTS?

is the title of an arresting article by Bernard Falk in Page 12. It deals with the R 101 disaster in an unusual way.

Other features.—   Page
Did Lord Thomson Have a Premonition?   4
Digs Into the Past With "J.J.B."   8
Our War Babies are Bright Boys.
By Sir Max Pemberton.
Whom Would You Rather Be?
Six Years Tête....   16
Skirts in Eleven Fashions   17
Pioneers Who Died For Empire   19
£500 Picture Puzzle
and £500 Crossword   20
Keystone's Last Word on Centre
article   23
Other News in Pages 3, 5, 7, 9 &....   11
Four Pages of Sport.

TO-DAY'S WEATHER.

A depression centred off the N.W. coasts continues slowly to deepen and to move E. Occasional rain or showers in most districts. FURTHER OUTLOOK.—Showers; bright intervals.

The Earthquake at Hawkes Bay 1931

FOURTH EDITION.

WEEKLY FEATURES.

Monday—Sport and Athletics.
Tuesday—Rifle Notes, Aquatics, Suburban and Junior Grade Cricket.
Wednesday—The Bookshelf, Tennis, Motor Notes, Health Notes, Yachting.
Thursday—Children's Comic Supplement, Music in the Home, Cycling, Housewife's Column.
Friday—Sports Review.
Saturday—The Talking Screen, Drama, Poultry, Rabbits, Gardening.

The Christchurch Star

FIAT LUX

"CHRISTCHURCH STAR" TELEPHONES:

Manager
Advertisements
Editors and Reporters
Publisher
Job Printing

Vol. XLIV. No. 29. ESTABLISHED MAY 14, 1868. CHRISTCHURCH, N.Z.: WEDNESDAY, FEBRUARY 4, 1931. (NINEPENCE A WEEK DELIVERED.) Price Twopence.

Napier Casualties May Reach 1,500

APPEALS MADE FOR FOOD AND BEDDING

1000 LOAVES OF BREAD DISPATCHED TO NAPIER.

The Salvation Army has made arrangements to accommodate refugees at their premises in Palmerston North. The Army also despatched 1000 loaves of bread early this morning.

The St John Ambulance Association and the Red Cross Society are appealing for foodstuffs and blankets, depots being established all over Wellington. It is stated that all food should be cooked, where possible, as there is no water connection and no heat in the majority of the Napier houses.

In Christchurch the Commercial Travellers' and Warehousemen's Association has established a depot at 161, Cashel Street, for the collection of food and clothing. The association members are using their cars to collect donations.

The Canterbury Automobile Association is working in conjunction with the Commercial Travellers' Association, and the two patrol cars are being used to collect food. Calls may be made on members for the use of their cars.

Mr R. B. Clarke, of the Taupo Town Board, has left for Napier by car with provisions. While there he will arrange transport for refugees wishing to go to Taupo, where there is accommodation for 100. There are cottages, food and bedding there.

The Farmers' Union, Wairarapa, are also appealing for assistance, their branches being used as depots.

Nine babies and their mothers from the Salvation Army Maternity Hospital at Napier, have arrived in Palmerston North.

Helping Refugees.

Mr Palliser, proprietor of the Capitol Private Hotel, Otaki Beach, announced through station 2YA, Wellington, that he had accommodation for forty refugees.

"CANNOT EXAGGERATE POSITION AT NAPIER."

PLENTY OF MEDICAL HELP NOW, SAYS DOCTOR.

Per Press Association.

GISBORNE, February 4.

Dr Douglas Muir, who flew to Napier yesterday to render assistance and returned by plane this morning after working all night, reports: "You cannot exaggerate the position at Napier. It is indeed terrible. Plenty of medical help is now available."

Manutuke settlers report that fresh water and sand are gushing from deep fissures in the old riverbed.

A steamer with three doctors and a large party of nurses left Gisborne early this morning for Napier.

A fairly sharp earthquake was experienced here at 12.35 a.m.

WAIROA REPORTS THREE KILLED.

RAILWAY WORKERS ESCAPE FROM TUNNEL.

Per Press Association.

WAIROA, February 4.

Yesterday's was the severest shake in Wairoa's history. No chimneys are left standing. Whole buildings were demolished. All land communications to the south are cut off. Miles of road have been obliterated. The town bridge is all but gone.

Three fatalities are reported. They include:—

Mrs J. O'Malley, wife of a local solicitor.

Lim Kee, a Chinaman.

Many are injured.

The inhabitants have been terrified. Since the main 'quake, severe tremors have been almost continuous.

The Mohaka railway tunnel collapsed and workmen escaped through an eighteen-inch fissure.

The local freezing works are disorganised and 40,000 carcases will rot unless they are shipped on a meat boat within two or three days.

Hundreds of thousands of pounds' worth of damage was done within the town.

Gisborne is not so bad.

H.M.S. Diomede is proceeding to Waikokopu to pick up medical relief for Napier.

DEAD LYING IN NAPIER STREETS.

BUILDINGS CRASH AND FIRES QUICKLY FOLLOW.

Per Press Association.

WELLINGTON, February 3.

"Anyone who was at the war will know what it felt like to be in Napier," said Mr S. Lewis, of Sydney, who arrived in Wellington from Napier this evening.

Row of Taxis is Overwhelmed.

Two-storey buildings, he said, came down like a pack of cards, and in one of the streets two sides met, burying a whole row of taxi cars with their drivers.

Sitting in the lounge of a city hotel, Mr Lewis gave a "Dominion" representative a graphic account of the disaster. "I was sitting in my car outside the Napier post office when the 'quake came," he said. "All of a sudden the car shook violently. I jumped out to see what was wrong, but fell over. On looking up, I saw all the buildings opposite collapsing, and then clouds of dust enveloped the whole place. People were rushing out screaming. No one knew what was going to happen next. Thousands rushed to the beach. They thought that was the

PEOPLE WERE TRAPPED IN FALLING BUILDINGS AT NAPIER.

HOSPITAL COLLAPSES, KILLING NURSES AND PATIENTS; SHOP GIRLS ENTOMBED.

Ever increasing casualty lists were received hourly to-day from the earthquake stricken area at Hawke's Bay. The graphic accounts of survivors show that the devastation was greatest at Napier and Hastings.

Relief measures on a gigantic scale have already been undertaken. Fifty additional doctors and over 100 nurses have been sent to the afflicted towns.

Doctor Muir, of Gisborne, who flew to Napier yesterday, estimates that the total casualties will be in the vicinity of 1500. Many of the bodies of the dead have not yet been extricated from the ruins.

One woman was burned to death in the Napier Cathedral, which, according to an eye-witness, collapsed like a pack of cards.

There were ten deaths at the Greenmeadows Seminary, including that of two priests and several South Island students.

Nine girls are entombed in a shop at Hastings and their fate is unknown. Many of the Napier Technical School pupils are believed to have been killed. Eight nurses and twelve patients are believed to have been killed in the Napier Public Hospital.

An army field hospital capable of handling 200 cases has been sent to Napier. All roads to the area are guarded by the police.

The King has sent a message of sympathy to the relatives of those killed and injured.

The Christchurch City Council made an urgent grant of £1000 this morning and the Lyttelton Harbour Board gave £250.

Casualty List From Napier.

WOMAN BURNED TO DEATH IN CATHEDRAL.

Per Press Association.

WELLINGTON, February 4.

The following [illegible] been transmitted from [illegible] the Press Association [illegible] ings:—

The known dead in Napier are:—

ALFRED BONOR, aged about 56 years, married, with a grown-up family.

MRS T. BARRY, burned to death in St John's Cathedral.

VAL HARRISON, jobbing compositor, aged 18.

NANCY THORNE GEORGE, nurse at Public Hospital.

TWO PRIESTS AND 7 STUDENTS DEAD.

GREENMEADOWS MARIST SEMINARY DESTROYED.

The Greenmeadows Marist Training Seminary, five miles from Napier, on the slopes of a hill, was badly damaged by the earthquake and, according to advice received by the authorities at St Bede's College, two priests and seven students were killed.

They were overwhelmed in the chapel during a retreat.

It is also known that one nun at the Napier Convent has been killed, with the possibility of others being dead. A Christchurch nun recently went to Napier to teach music.

The known dead are:—

Father Gondringer, S.M., M.A.

Father Boyle (Australia).

J. Doogan (Greymouth).

B. Anby (Greymouth).

A. Devonport (Fendalton).

finally professed as a member of the Marist Order on February 11.

Leonard Mangos, of Timaru, aged nineteen years, was a son of Mr and Mrs N. D. Mangos, Craigie Avenue. He was an ex-pupil of the Timaru Boys' High School and St Bede's College. He left St Bede's in 1929. While at school he was a prefect and showed himself to be a brilliant scholar and a fine pianist.

J. Durning, who with Mangos, came from Timaru, was twenty-two years of age. He was very popular while at school and showed himself to be a fine scholar. He also was a prefect while at school.

N[illegible] Rafter (Wellington), an ex-pupil of St Patrick's College, was in his second year.

[illegible] (Waimate) is an ex-pupil [illegible] year of the seminary. He was in the first fifteen and first eleven at school, and left in 1929. He was also a fine runner.

RETREAT WAS HELD AT A SPECIAL TIME.

STUDENTS RETURNED TO

UNEMPLOYED ARE READY TO HELP.

OFFER SENT TO-DAY TO PRIME MINISTER.

Before the ordinary business was broached the meeting of unemployed at the Trades Hall this morning made an offer to assist the victims of the earthquake.

Mr J. Roberts, who presided over a very large attendance, spoke sympathetically of the terrible disaster that had overtaken Napier and the surrounding townships.

Mr E. Hamilton said he was sure they would all wish to express their sympathy with the people in the stricken areas, and he was equally sure they would wish to offer their services if required in the rescue and other work.

The motion was carried unanimously, all those present standing to show their sympathy with the relatives of the killed.

At a later stage in the meeting Mr E. J. Howard, M.P., also addressed the meeting. He said he had just got back from a tour of the whole area that had been overtaken by the disaster, and he was so confused that he hardly knew what to say. He had just heard that Mr C. E. M'Millan, M.P. for Tauranga, with whom he had lunch last Tuesday, had both legs either amputated or badly injured. It was terrible to think that people with whom his party had been laughing and joking a few days ago should have been overtaken by this terrible disaster, and were possibly dead or injured.

Mr Flannery called attention to the offer of volunteers from the unemployed of Christchurch if their services were required at the scene of the disaster.

Mr Howard said he would go straight to the Post Office and telegraph the offer to the Prime Minister. He mentioned that he had offered his own services when in Wellington last night, but the Prime Minister had pointed out that ample help was being sent to Hawke's Bay, and it was useless sending people up indiscriminately.

PROGRESS LEAGUE WILL LEND ITS AID.

READY TO CO-OPERATE WITH OTHER BODIES.

Mr P. R. Climie, organiser of the Canterbury Progress League, stated this morning that as the monthly meeting of the executive of the league would be held to-night the question of rendering assistance to the sufferers by the earthquake would be discussed.

The disaster was of such a magnitude that it was imperative that relief measures should be organised on a comprehensive scale, said Mr Climie. He felt that the league would be only too

COUNCIL GRANTS £1000 FOR RELIEF.

"FIRST INSTALMENT OF A LOCAL RELIEF FUND."

An urgent and special meeting of the council was called at 10.15 o'clock this morning by the Town Clerk on the instructions of the Mayor (the Rev J. K. Archer). Most of the councillors were present, but it was found impossible to get into touch with two or three.

Unanimously the councillors present decided to request the Mayor to notify the Prime Minister (Mr Forbes) that on behalf of the city, the council was at once placing at his disposal the sum of £1000 for immediate relief in the area affected by the earthquake, the method or proportions to be employed in the distribution to be left to his discretion.

It was further decided to ask the Prime Minister to give an assurance that this gift and any other that might be made by public bodies would be validated at the forthcoming session of Parliament.

First Instalment.

The Mayor was requested to regard this contribution as the first instalment of a local relief fund, and the council will be glad if individuals and organisations will as quickly as possible send contributions to the City Treasurer. Contributions have already begun to come in.

As soon as possible after the meeting the Mayor got in touch with the Prime Minister by telephone and also made a statement to the public through 3YA and later through 2ZC.

On behalf of the council and the citizens generally the Mayor has expressed regret to the family of the late Mr A. Rattray and offered them sympathy in their unexpected bereavement.

"It is interesting to notice, too," said the Mayor, "that Christchurch is to be represented on the scene of the disaster by several members of the local branch of Toc H and other people, who, at their own cost, are immediately proceeding to the devastated area to render whatever assistance may be possible."

£250 IS VOTED BY HARBOUR BOARD.

WILL SEND EQUIPMENT AND FURTHER MONEYS.

An immediate grant of £250 for earthquake relief was voted by the Lyttelton Harbour Board this morning, and the Board also decided to place immediately at the disposal of the Napier Harbour Board all equipment that could possibly be spared. The £250 will be probably quadrupled later.

"New Zealand is shocked at the news of the earthquake which caused such serious loss of life and destruc-

To newspaper readers emotionally insulated against the sheer statistics of modern earthquakes, the Hawkes Bay earthquake might seem a minor affair. Yet the three-minute tremor that convulsed this small territory of the north island of New Zealand on the morning of 3 February 1931 obliterated the hearts of Napier and Hastings as surely as its predecessors had destroyed San Francisco and Yokohama. Until that morning in February the highest recorded death-toll in New Zealand had been seventeen, even in a country where such visitations were almost a way of life. In those three minutes 260 people died—in an area that mustered barely 25,000 souls in all—and many hundreds more were injured. In Hastings, twelve miles inland, virtually every concrete building in the commercial centre was destroyed and scarcely a house survived without a gaping hole where the chimney had crashed down. At the port of Napier, the seafront crumbled in a cloud of dust and fires (apparently started by explosions in several chemists' shops) began to converge on the centre of the town, where helpless victims lay trapped in the ruins of numerous buildings: the cathedral, the post-office, nurses' home, public library . . . The rising wind and the drying-up of the mains (the pumping-station had been levelled too) left fire-fighters impotent in the face of the flames. What ultimately saved Napier from extinction was partly the prompt intervention of rescue-parties from naval ships in the harbour but, more significantly, the response of the civilians themselves: communication with the outside world—destroyed completely by the earthquake—was restored after a fashion the same day, and the unhesitating demolition of key buildings brought the conflagration under control that night.

The Christchurch Star

FIAT LUX

WEEKLY FEATURES.

Monday—Sport and Athletics.
Tuesday—Rifle Notes, Aquatics, Suburban and Junior Grade Cricket.
Wednesday—The Bookshelf, Tennis, Motor Notes, Health Notes, Yachting.
Thursday—Children's Corner, Supplement, Music to the House, Cycling.
Friday—Sports Review.
Saturday—The Talking Films, Drama, Poultry, Rabbits.

"CHRISTCHURCH STAR" TELEPHONES:

Manager 34-307
Advertisements 34-900
                    34-909
Editors and Reporters 34-905
                    34-806
Public 34-808
Job Printing 34-807

Vol. XLIV. No. 31.   ESTABLISHED MAY 14, 1868.   CHRISTCHURCH, N.Z.: FRIDAY, FEBRUARY 6, 1931.   (NINEPENCE A WEEK DELIVERED)   Price Twopence.

BUSINESS CENTRE OF NAPIER AFTER EARTHQUAKE AND FIRE.

A panoramic view of Napier with its wrecked business area. On the left is the Municipal Theatre, with the Public Trust right opposite, one of the few undamaged buildings. On the extreme right are the remains of the Fire Brigade Station, opposite which stand the remains of the Provincial Hotel. In the centre of the picture are the remains of the Hawke's Bay Farmers' and Napier Working Men's Club. To the left centre are the ruins of the Central Hotel, at the corner of Dalton and Emmerson Streets. Buildings in the foreground included the Baptist Church, a garage and a number of private residences.

"THERE WILL BE NO NAPIER TO GO BACK TO AGAIN"

Earthquake Refugees Bring Tales Of Suffering And Privation.

CARRYING what little of their belongings they had been able to scrape together, their faces haggard and strained, a party of Napier and Hastings refugees arrived at Lyttelton this morning by the ferry steamer, on their way to friends in the south who would help them in the tremendous task of reconstructing their whole lives.

There were about ten of them, women for the greater part, and several little children added with their very presence to the pathos of the scene.

Their stories were told listlessly, every one of them showing only too plainly the marks of the strain to which they had been subjected.

For the most part, these folk were among those who were in their homes in the suburbs when the shock occurred, and though the damage was not so spectacular there as in the business areas, they tell of incidents of horror which almost pass comprehension.

"Money is what is wanted now," said one woman. "There is plenty of food, and they are doing great things in getting drinking water, but people have no money to leave the

A PHOTOGRAPH showing one of the faults common in all the roads in Napier and Hastings.

ARMED MARINES PROTECT NAPIER AGAINST LOOTING.

More Shakes Experienced Last Night, Menace Of Further Outbreak Of Fire.

(Special to the "Star.")

NAPIER, February 6.

Last night in Napier was the worst night since the earthquake. In addition to a heavy shake about 9 p.m. there was a severe shake shortly after midnight and numerous minor tremors later.

A number of cases of petty theft have been reported, but the presence of armed Marines in the town has had a beneficial effect, and there has been no serious looting.

The town's chief danger now is a renewed outbreak of fire, and the menace was fully realised when soon after midnight a house in Seapoint Road, at the top of Bluff Hill, was discovered burning. It is believed that the owner, Mr J——, had been burning rubbish in a copper and that successive shakes demolished the brickwork and released the burning embers. The burning house menaced

NAPIER PHOTOS.

Special photos of wrecked streets and buildings in Napier appear also on pages 8 and 10 of to-day's issue. They arrived from the north this morning.

The Deciding Factor

The Akron and the Macon 1933 and 1935

"All the News That's Fit to Print."

The New York Times.

5:30 A. M. EDITION

WEATHER—Fair today, tomorrow; little temperature change.

Copyright, 1933, by The New York Times Company.

VOL. LXXXII....No. 27,461. Entered as Second-Class Matter, Postoffice, New York, N. Y. NEW YORK, TUESDAY, APRIL 4, 1933. TWO CENTS In New York City | THREE CENTS Within 200 Miles | FOUR CENTS Elsewhere Except in 7th and 8th Postal Zones

DIRIGIBLE AKRON CRASHES IN LIGHTNING STORM AT SEA; ONLY 4 OF THE 77 MEN ABOARD ARE REPORTED RESCUED; AIRSHIP IS BELIEVED A TOTAL LOSS; WIDE SEARCH ON

THE WEATHER
Today: Fair
Tomorrow: Cloudy followed by rain; little change in temperature
Temperatures yesterday: Max., 48; Min., 40
Detailed Report on Page 32

NEW YORK Herald Tribune

LATE CITY EDITION

VOL. XCII No. 31,552 (Copyright, 1933, New York Tribune Inc.) WEDNESDAY, APRIL 5, 1933 * * * * TWO CENTS In Greater New York | THREE CENTS Within 200 Miles | FOUR CENTS Elsewhere

Hope Ends for Admiral Moffett and 72 on Akron; Survivor Tells of Airship Crash in Storm Vortex; 2 Die in Rescue Blimp; Roosevelt Voices U.S. Grief

Lehman Fails To End Beer Deadlock at New Parley

Hard Feelings Evident as Governor and Legislative Leaders Confer on Dunkel Bill Defeat

Stage Seems Set For Compromise

1 Tax Bill Being Rushed, With an Extra Session Threatened; Mandatory Local Boards Suggested

By Hickman Powell
A Staff Correspondent

ALBANY, April 4.—However much good fellowship beer may bring when it goes on sale Friday under local soft-drink laws, as now appears certain, the beer problem's fermentation in Albany has reached the point of hard feelings.

The long-drawn-out deadlock between Governor Lehman and the Republican legislative leaders, which has been carried on with the most grave patience, continued tonight without change after another conference. The Governor came from the conference using much more crisp language than usual, which aroused the temper of Senator George R. Fearon, Republican leader.

Party Leaders Clash

The Republicans, said the Governor, had offered no new suggestion except one "even more political" than the Republican Dunkel bill, which was defeated by the Democrats in the Senate today on a party vote, 26 to 25. Hearing that, Senator Fearon flared up and accused the Governor of violating an agreement to be non-committal about the conference.

The Governor's remark is believed to have been prompted by a suggestion that the old Raines law holds a precedent for the local control demanded by the Republicans. Under an amendment in 1917 aimed to reduce the number of saloons it was provided that absolute power to accomplish the reduction should be intrusted to local boards in places of less than 55,000 population. In cities these were appointed by the Mayor and in towns by the town boards.

As the Legislature rushes its business in hope of adjourning on Friday or, more probably, on April 14, the threat of an immediate extra session hangs over it unless it adopts a beer bill satisfactory to the Governor.

Governor Insists on Control

"We must have state control of beer," said Mr. Lehman, when asked whether he would call an extra session.

The Governor is understood to be ready to yield temporarily on the issue of state control, however, in order to permit the sale of beer on Friday. Immediate adoption of the Governor's bill for centralized control, as it stands, would shut down on the sale of beer until state licensing machinery could be put into operation, and that is a situation for which hardly any elected official would care to be responsible.

A bill was reported today to be in preparation setting up standards for the temporary issuance of beer licenses by municipalities and fixing license fees that could be charged, in order to tide over the period between Friday and the accomplishment of state control. The adoption of such a measure would make it much easier for the state to take over the licensing after the localities have had their first taste of license money than it would be if the municipalities took possession unrestricted.

Stage Set for Compromise

As matters now stand, the Senate

Urged Big Wisconsin Vote

Herald Tribune photo—Acme
Governor A. G. Schmedeman

Wets Lead 4 to 1 In Wisconsin's Vote on Repeal

Early Returns Show Heavy Anti-Prohibition Ballot; Drys May Not Have Voice

By The Associated Press

MILWAUKEE, April 4.—Sentiment for the repeal of the Eighteenth Amendment—turning thumbs down on prohibition by a margin of about four to one—was sweeping Wisconsin tonight as returns in today's referendum were tabulated.

In 645 of the state's 2,899 precincts repeal pledged delegates were in front by a vote of 129,421 to 31,108.

Town and country alike turned in heavy wet majorities. First returns were from rural districts where drys entertained some hope of gaining support, but even these voters favored repeal by a two-to-one majority.

Then, the cities of the eastern portion of the state, where polls closed late, began piling up the wet lead.

Milwaukee, where breweries are humming to produce the beer which will become legal on Friday, did the expected by going wet, on the basis of early returns, by more than ten to one. In thirty-seven precincts in Milwaukee the vote was: for repeal, 10,937; against, 966. In Racine, Sheboygan and Kenosha it was similar.

On the basis of the present trend, wet leaders were predicting every one of the fifteen delegates to a constitutional amendment convention to be held at Madison on April 25 would be committed to vote for repeal. A bare majority is required to cast the state's vote one way or the other.

Dr. J. J. Seelman, of Milwaukee, chairman of the state branch of the Association Against the Prohibition Amendment, said the apparent result was about what was expected. He expressed belief that a decisive Wisconsin vote for repeal would have a "stimulating effect" in other states which soon are to pass on the repeal proposal.

Wisconsin voters selected fifteen of thirty candidates for delegate to the constitutional convention. The fifteen drys and fifteen wets were listed separately. None of the candidates made a personal campaign and all were committed definitely as to how they would

(Continued on page six)

Crash Inquiry Is Rushed at Washington

Senate and House Will Center Study on Structural Problem; Naval Court Views All Phases

Navy Going Ahead With Macon Plans

President Orders Full Publicity; Swanson Denies Sabotage Reports

From the Herald Tribune Bureau

WASHINGTON, April 4.—Under orders by President Roosevelt to the Navy to permit the freest publicity, the Navy's search for survivors and wreckage of the dirigible Akron went forward tonight, and is to be redoubled throughout tomorrow over a hundred-mile area off the coast of New Jersey and Virginia.

While hope of finding more of the crew waned as darkness overtook the twelve ships and twenty-three aircraft in the rescue fleet, the traditions of the Navy called for continuance of the effort so long as human life might exist in the sea, and the Navy's instructions were to search particularly the northern part of the area. Evidence of wreckage had been sighted there during the day.

The White House order to offer the news of the tragedy without restraint was issued without regard to its possible bearing on contemplated investigations—naval and Congressional—to determine not only what caused the great dirigible to fall into the sea but whether the United States, like Great Britain, should abandon this type of craft in the scheme of national defense.

Even in high Administration circles doubts about having America continue to pioneer in this type of naval craft were in evidence after the President had discussed with his Cabinet the immediate aspects of the catastrophe.

The President previously had voiced the nation's grief and saluted those who perished in the following statement:

"The loss of the Akron with its crew of gallant officers and men is a national disaster. I grieve with the nation and especially with the wives and families of the men who were lost.

"Ships can be replaced, but the nation can ill afford to lose such men as Rear Admiral William A.

(Continued on page thirteen)

Bringing Akron Survivors Ashore at New York Navy Yard

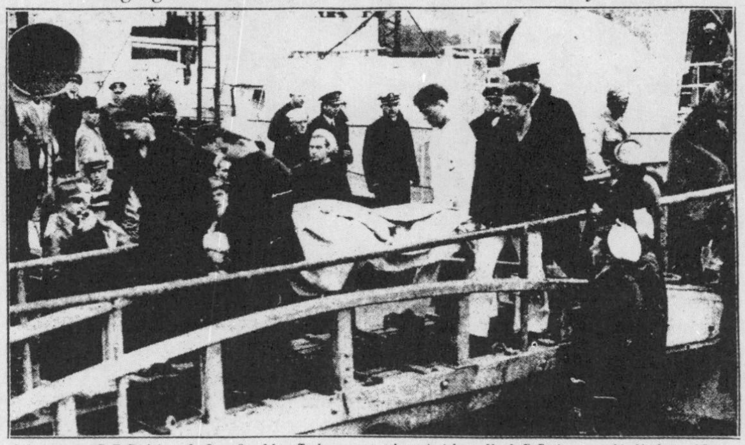

Sailors carrying R. E. Deal from the Coast Guard boat Tucker on a stretcher. At right are Moody E. Erwin, wrapped in blanket, and Lieutenant Commander Herbert V. Wiley, second in command of the dirigible Herald Tribune photo—Frank

Commander Frank Carey McCord, in command of the Akron, lost

Rear Admiral William A. Moffett, chief guest officer, among the missing

Lieut. Commander Herbert V. Wiley, executive officer, saved

Clew Lacking To Cause of Sea Tragedy

Search Fleets and Air Squadrons Find Only Drifting Wreckage at Spot Airliner Vanished

Ship Whirled Down Ringed in Lightning

Radio Man, 1 of 4 Picked Up, Dies; Officer's Body Found 10 Miles Distant

A pictorial history of airship Akron—Page 10.

The crash into the sea of the world's largest airship, the Akron, yesterday morning was reckoned after a day of futile search for survivors as the most costly disaster in the history of aviation. Only three of the seventy-six men who were aboard the ship when she plunged into the waters off the Jersey coast in the midst of an electrical storm at 12:30 a. m. were known to be alive last night.

There was every reason to believe that seventy-three had perished, among them Rear Admiral William A. Moffett, chief of the Navy's Bureau of Aeronautics, and Commander Frank C. McCord, who was in command of the airship.

Two Die in Searching Blimp

During the day two other Navy men, among the thousands who scanned the coast waters from the air and from the armada of searching ships, died in that line of helpful duty. They were aboard the Navy's little blimp J-3, which went out from Lakehurst to look for survivors of the Akron and fell into the water a few hundred yards off the shore at Beach Haven, N. J.

There were life preservers and rubber boats on the Akron, but the dirigible had ridden out storms before, and every man stuck to his post to the last. Engines responded to every command from the control room, and the men of the Akron plunged to death in the dark Atlantic under perfect discipline.

Wreckage of the Akron was found by searching ships at various places from ten to twenty miles away from the spot—twenty miles offshore—where the giant aircraft, unable to resist the buffetings of the storm, fell into the sea. One of her officers and three of her men were picked up within an hour or so after the crash by the German tanker Phoebus, whose captain witnessed the end of the silvery airship. Of these survivors one, Robert W. Copeland, chief radio operator, unconscious when lifted from the sea, died four hours later aboard the ship which rescued him, and the others were brought to the New York Navy Yard, in Brooklyn, aboard a Coast Guard destroyer. They were

Summary of Today's News

AKRON DISASTER

Only three of seventy-six on Akron believed to have survived. Page 1
Search for survivors redoubles today over 100-mile area. Page 1
Navy blimp J-3 crashes on Akron hunt, killing two. Page 1
No disorder aboard ship, says Wiley, executive officer. Page 1
List of officers and men on lost Akron. Page 1
Sea and air craft hunt in vain for survivors of Akron. Page 11
Five New York men, one a Shenandoah survivor, lost. Page 12

CITY AND VICINITY

Beer deadlock continues with growing bitterness at Albany. Page 1
Fireman turns in false alarms to get ride on hook and ladder. Page 3
Mayor O'Brien initiates own charter revision movement. Page 4
Death rate in maternity cases too high, doctors learn. Page 5
Mayor O'Brien lifts city's beer lid Friday. Page 6
Lehman seeks boards to protect mortgage holders. Page 7
Fritz Kreisler asks Toscanini to conduct Wagner festival. Page 17

2 Die as Blimp Seeking Akron Falls Into Sea

N. Y. Police Plane Saves 5; Officials Were Reluctant to Put Old Craft on Duty

The J-3, a semi-rigid Navy blimp dispatched from Lakehurst to aid in the search for survivors of the air cruiser Akron, was blown into the ocean a few hundred feet off Beach Haven, N. J., at 1:30 o'clock yesterday afternoon with the loss of two of the

Akron's Roll of Living and Dead

SURVIVORS

WILEY, LIEUTENANT COMMANDER HERBERT VICTOR, forty-one; executive officer of the Akron; born Wheeling, Mo.; was graduated from Naval Academy in 1915; commander of U. S. S. Radford from 1920 to 1923; became commander of dirigible Los Angeles in 1929. Home, New London, Conn. Married, three children.

DEAL, RICHARD EDWARD, boatswain's mate, second class; wife, Mrs. Gertrude V. Deal. Home, 307 Fourth Street, Lakewood, N. J.

ERWIN, MOODY EUGENE, aviation machinist's mate, second class. Home, 2077 Vinton Street, Memphis. Nearest relative, aunt, Ida M. Davis, Tulsa, Okla.

mental Squadron (U. S. S. Akron). Duty involving flying. Additional duty commanding Naval Air Station, Lakehurst; born in Iowa, enlisted in Navy 1904, commander since 1926. Holder of Navy Cross. Home, San Diego, Calif.

CECIL, COMMANDER HENRY BARTON, forty-five, attached to Bureau of Aeronautics, Washington. Born, Tennessee, graduated Naval Academy, 1910; at sea next ten years. Commissioned commander 1930. Under orders to go to sea in June aboard aircraft carrier Lexington. Married. Home, Washington.

MASURY, LIEUTENANT COLONEL ALFRED F., Ordnance Reserve, U. S. Army; forty-eight. Born Danvers, Mass., graduated Brown University, 1909. In World War, major in

No Fire or Blast As Akron Fell, Wiley Reports

Survivor, in Brooklyn Hospital, Tells Experiences; Praises Crew's Conduct

The men aboard the Akron, according to Lieutenant Commander Herbert Victor Wiley, executive officer, knew perfectly well what was happening to their ship yesterday morning, but they took their places in quiet order when the command went out, "Stand by for

Pictorial History of World's Greatest Dirigible Destroyed in Storm Off Coast

In retrospect, it is easy to appreciate the almost oracular significance of the two leading stories that appeared on the front page of the *New York Times* of 4 April 1933. One recorded the successful attempt of the British Mount Everest expedition to fly over the world's highest peak ('our minds were numbed by the stark vision of beauty as we rose to more than 29,000 feet above the roof of the world' said one of the fliers). The other story touched the very depths of tragedy, retailing the destruction of the US airship *Akron*, forced down into the Atlantic by the cold currents of a storm centre and carrying to their doom seventy-three officers and men, including Rear-Admiral Moffett the architect and 'father' of the American airship programme.

The page might have served as a requiem for the passing of the lighter-than-air machine, except that, as it happened, the *Akron* was not America's last airship. It was intended, in fact, as the pioneer of a long line of dirigibles scheduled for reconnaissance service with the US Navy, and in its chequered career it had shown enough promise to give its advocates considerable hope for the future. One of its most notable achievements was the successful in-flight launching of up to six small 'spider' planes, carried like parasites in their own internal hangar. These one-seater crafts could be propelled and recovered by means of a special 'trapeze' attachment, and obviously offered intriguing possibilities for the airship's use in wartime.

The *Akron* also provided fuel to kindle the arguments of the opponents of lighter-than-air travel. It was vulnerable to attack, they claimed, and unwieldy (it was by far the biggest yet built, 785 feet in length and carrying over 6,750,000 cubic feet of helium). And a series of mishaps throughout its life had given it a very bad press: an attempt to sabotage it by a 'communist' while it was under construction at the Goodyear plant; the discovery that the completed machine was ten per cent heavier than its original specifications; and an accident on the ground in 1932, when part of the stern was ripped off just as a party of Congressmen was about to inspect it. The persistent rumour that the ship was jinxed gained further currency later in 1932 when, on coming in to land before a crowd of 10,000 spectators near San Diego, the *Akron* was suddenly hoisted by an upward current back into the sky, dragging three of the landing crew up with it on the end of their ropes. One of them was hauled into the airship: the other two fell to their deaths.

But Admiral Moffett kept faith with the *Akron*, telling the Press: 'I find there is a general impression in the country that the Akron is a failure . . . To my knowledge she is the best airship that has ever been built.' So it could have been with no misgivings that he took off in it (under the command of Commander McCord) from Lakehurst on 4 April 1933, to take part in fleet manoeuvres over the Atlantic. At 12.30am the next morning the ship was cruising at 1,600 feet above the ocean when they found themselves unexpectedly pitched

into severe turbulence. The ship plunged to within 700 feet of the waves before the dizzy descent was halted, but no sooner had the helmsman regained height than the fickle currents struck again: once more the *Akron* was catapulted from the skies. This time the strain proved too great for the rudder controls, which parted with a chilling crack—now the crew could only wait impotently for the grinding impact with the sea. Within minutes the jealous waves had pounded the airship to pieces.

Only three of the seventy-six on board were picked up alive by searching ships (and two more were added to the casualty-list when the *J.3*, a semi-rigid 'blimp', also crashed into the sea during the search). One of the survivors, Lt Commander Wiley, afterwards told reporters of those final few seconds in the control car: 'Discipline was perfect . . . there was no noise, no confusion of any kind and all orders were given in a low voice and were carried out efficiently', a suitably laconic account that moved the *New York Times* to editorialize on 'The officer standing at his post coolly giving orders, although the heavens open and death stares him in the face . . . they went down into the sea, illuminated in a fitful flash or two, true to the navy's traditions.'

Much of the wreckage of the *Akron* was salvaged in due course, and examination revealed that the structure as a whole had remained intact until hitting the sea—pointing inescapably (so far as the Board of Inquiry was concerned) to the conclusion that Captain

Sunday,
April 23, 1933

The New York Times

Rotogravure
Picture Section
In Two Parts

7

THE U. S. S. MACON READY FOR HER TRIAL FLIGHT:
THE NAVY'S NEWEST AIRSHIP.
Sister Ship of the Akron, in Her Hangar at Akron, Ohio, Where
Both Ships Were Built.
(Times Wide World Photos, Cleveland Bureau.)

THE FUTURE HOME OF THE NAVY'S GIANT AIRSHIP: AN AIRPLANE VIEW
of the Lighter-Than-Air Base at Sunnyvale, Cal., and the Hangar Built to Accommodate the Macon.

CLEARING SPACE FOR A
CAMP IN THE VIRGINIA MOUNTAINS: THE CITIZENS' ARMY.
After Two Weeks at Fort Washington, Md., Starts Work on a New Camp Near Luray,
Va., Where 200 of the Unemployed Were Assembled From the District.
(Times Wide World Photos, Washington Bureau.)

McCord was at fault for not making positive efforts to avoid a storm area, and perhaps for not adjusting the altimeter to allow for a drop in atmospheric pressure. The clean bill of mechanical health thus accorded the *Akron* offered renewed encouragement to the devotees of the airship—encouragement that unexpectedly (in view of the barrage of published criticism the *Akron* had sustained) found echoes in the Press. 'Before anyone had even a vague idea of what had happened' commented the *New York Herald Tribune*, 'newspapers and Congressmen were raising the cheap cry for "investigation", were damning the dirigible as a disaster and a folly, and calling for the abandonment of the whole dirigible programme. The callous cruelty of this proceeding seems to have occurred to no-one. It amounts to telling the men who have devoted their lives to the airships that they were fools and wasters, if not

near-criminals. We do not believe that the sacrifice was in vain . . . that all the work that has gone into the development of the rigid airship has been wasted, or that the type necessarily stands condemned upon its record.'

Such public morale-boosting was opportune, to say the least, in view of the fact that the *Akron*'s sister ship, the *Macon*, stood ready and waiting at that very moment in its hangar in Ohio to begin its trials. These were allowed to take place as scheduled less than a month after the *Akron*'s tragedy. For the next eighteen months the *Macon* worked hard, if unspectacularly, with the Pacific fleet. Then on 13 February 1935, as the airship returned to its base (under the command of none other than Commander Wiley) at Sunnyvale, California, it too was belaboured by severe turbulence: in its earthward swoop the top stabilizing fin was torn away, puncturing three gas bags and

starting a relentless disintegration of the stern. Luckily the sea was relatively calm and all but two of the crew were rescued by nearby warships, minutes before the whole edifice settled into a watery grave (of the two who died one, a wireless operator, unaccountably jumped from the ship while it was still more than a hundred feet above the sea). The end of the *Macon* also marked the end of America's involvement with the rigid airship: it was the deciding factor. Not only were there now no ships left in commission, but every one of the machines built for or by the United States (the *R.38*, the *Shenandoah*, the *Akron* and now the *Macon*) had crashed with loss of precious lives.

105

The Morro Castle Mystery

New Jersey 1934

THE WEATHER
Today: Clearing, little change in temperature
Tomorrow: Generally fair
Temperatures Yesterday: Max. 7?, Min. 64
Detailed Report on Page 31

NEW YORK Herald Tribune

LATE CITY EDITION

Vol. XCIV No. 32,071 | (Copyright, 1934, New York Tribune Inc.) | SUNDAY, SEPTEMBER 9, 1934 | Section One | **** | TEN CENTS Within 200 Miles | TWELVE CENTS Elsewhere

186 Dead, 39 Missing, as Liner Morro Castle Burns; 333 Survivors Tell of Heroic Rescues Off Jersey

Victims Fight Raging Seas On Rafts, Logs

Scene Like Battlefield as Rescuers Jam Beach at Spring Lake to Save Tired Swimmers in Surf

Crowds Seek Kin: Confusion Reigns

Cars Pack Highways as Ambulances and Guard Speed to Aid Injured

By a Staff Correspondent

SPRING LAKE, N. J., Sept. 8.—Soon after dawn this morning the first boatloads of survivors from the flaming Ward liner Morro Castle drew up on the sandy beach in front of the southern bathing pavilion of this seaside resort, and in that instant the village, usually deserted this late in the season, began to assume the aspect of a beleaguered community.

All day long the gray breakers lashed the shore, driven by northeast winds. Through the surf from time to time emerged exhausted swimmers, singly, in pairs and in groups, clinging to logs, rafts and life preservers. The Spring Lake police headquarters became a distributing base from which ambulances dashed off at intervals to hospitals in the vicinity.

Homes Opened to Survivors

Private homes all along the shore took in the sea-battered survivors, put them to bed, and furnished warming drinks until medical aid could arrive. Every available physician and nurse was called into duty, and the National Guard camp at Sea Girt consigned its trucks to ambulance service and sent its orderlies to assist the overcrowded hospital staffs to the north.

As the day wore on the storm increased in violence, yet crowds unceasingly lined the boardwalk, peering out into the torrents of wind-driven rain, searching for bobbing heads upon the waters. Constant streams of automobiles choked the roads as families and friends of those on shipboard hurried down from New York City in the hope that survivors' lists would contain the names of those they sought.

Legion Members Aid Police

So dense did the crush of traffic become that members of the local American Legion were summoned into duty to help police details keep the lines of cars in motion. New Jersey State troopers on motorcycles wove in and out among the sluggish files with sirens screaming, as they convoyed physicians, nurses and ambulances from homes, the ocean front and police headquarters to the hospitals.

It was as though a battle had been fought in the vicinity, what with army trucks, ambulances and motorcycles lurching madly along the tree-lined roads, past the great estates with their flower beds and rolling lawns.

Overhead, airplane motors roared throughout the day as the seaplanes of the United States Coast Guard continued to battle the driving rain and low, scudding clouds in their search for survivors by air. Looming on the horizon could be seen the gray hulls of Coast Guard cutters tossing on the angry sea.

At no time during the day did there seem to be any semblance of order emerging from the frantic confusion. Because of the great stretch of coast-line between Point Pleasant and Long Branch, no one knew at what hospital or even what town the

(Continued on page four)

REAL ESTATE FOR SALE
OFFERED IN TODAY'S CLASSIFIED COLUMNS

Garden City, 8 rooms, 3 baths, 2-car garage, price	$12,000
Bronxville, new Colonial homes, completely modern	17,900
South Berkshires, 2 houses, 135 acres, trout brook	10,000
Florida farm and strawberry land 2½ acres, price	69
Mount Vernon, beautiful Colonial home, 7 rooms, 2 baths	13,800
Bergen County, River Edge Manor, new model home, price	5,250
Lake Mohawk, attractive, 3 bedrooms, cottage, lake view	3,500
Florida orange grove, 4-room bungalow, 5 acres	700
Maryland estate, 720 acres, deep-water frontage, price	35,000
Mount Vernon, 9-room house, 3 baths, double garage, price	35,000
N. J. State highway bungalow, large plot, price	2,500
Clinton, Conn., 10-room modern house, 7½ acres land	2,000

SEE SECTION X

The Morro Castle Being Ravaged by the Flames, and Passengers Fleeing in Lifeboat

Herald Tribune photos—Acme
Aerial view of the ship abandoned six miles off Asbury Park

Lifeboat with rescued passengers approaching the Monarch of Bermuda, one of the rescue ships

Survivors

ADAMS, MISS JANE, 6205 Limekiln Pike, Philadelphia, in hospital at Point Pleasant, N. J.
ANESSOHN, LESTER, no address.
ARNETH, PAUL, Brooklyn.
ATTENS, HERMAN, no address.
ASCHOFF, Mr. and Mrs. THORP, 150-15 Sanford Avenue, Flushing, Queens.
BARNSTEAD, Mr. and Mrs. LLOYD G., 1891 Harrison Avenue, the Bronx.
BARRIOS, ANTIRO, 115 Kane Street, Brooklyn, to Marine Hospital.
BECK, MISS EDNA, Ship's librarian, of 8502 East Seventy-eighth Street Brooklyn, in hospital at Point Pleasant, N. J.
BEHR, CHARLOTTE, 423 Hancock Street, Brooklyn.
BEHR, ETHEL, 423 Hancock Street, Brooklyn.
BIKEN, MISS ROSE, 1521 Spruce Streeet, Philadelphia, in hospital at Point Pleasant, N. J.
BLOODGOOD, MARJORIE, Hillside, N. J.
BLONDIAU, DR. JULES F., 2141 Locust Street, Philadelphia, in hospital at Point Pleasant, N. J.
BLONDIAU, MRS., wife of Dr. Blondiau, same address, in hospital at Point Pleasant, N. J.
BODNER, STEPHEN, 55 Summit Road, Elizabeth, N. J., in hospital at Point Pleasant, N. J.
BODNER, MRS. STEPHEN, same address, in hospital at Point Pleasant, N. J.
BORMAN, HARRY, 352 Roosevelt Avenue, Freeport, L. I.
BORRELL, DR. J. H., Buffalo, N. Y.
BOSSELER, KATHERINE, Brooklyn.
BOSSELER, THEODORE, Brooklyn.
BRADBURY, MARTHA, Wetherly, Pa., immersion, in Fitkin Hospital, Neptune, N. J.
BRADY, MRS. E. J., 7048 Greenhill Road, Overbrook, Philadelphia, in hospital at Point Pleasant, N. J.
BREWER, HARRY, 242 Carleton Avenue, Brooklyn.
BRIDIE, HELEN, at Oak Street Inn, Spring Lake, N. J.
BRIGSTEIN, DR. S. J., 7825 Fourth Avenue, Brooklyn
BRINKMAN, Dr. and Mrs. HARRY, Bellerose, L. I.
BROABT, MRS. E. J., Overbrook Avenue, Philadelphia.
BRODIE, MISS H., of Hartford, Conn
BROWN, FLORENCE, 530 West End Avenue, New York, home. Aunt of Alice Madeline Desvernine.
BROWN, IDA, 30, of 1455 New York Avenue, Brooklyn, in Fitkin Hospital, Neptune, N. J.
BROWN, MRS. HARRIET B., 5304 Rising Sun Avenue, Philadelphia, in hospital at Point Pleasant, N. J.
BUDLONG, MISS MARJORIE.
BURGOS, JUAN, 68 East 114th Street, New York, to Marine Hospital.
BURNE, WALTER E., 330 West Ninety-fifth Street, New York, home.
BUSQUETTE, OPHELIA, at a private home in Spring Lake.
BUTTE, JAMES, 1332 Troy Avenue, Brooklyn.
BYRNE, WALTER E., 370 Bloomfield Avenue, Caldwell, N. J.
CAMPBELL, DANIEL, 86-22 Durgan Avenue, Elmhurst, Queens, to Marine Hospital.
CANAVAN, MISS K., 20 Butler Place, Brooklyn, in hospital at Point Pleasant, N. J.
CANNON, THOMAN, jr., Livingston, N. J., in Fitkin Hospital, Neptune, N. J.
CAPOTE, MRS. RENEE MENDEZ, thirty-two, daughter of the first Vice-President of Cuba.
CAREY, MISS CAROLINE, 6943 Chester Avenue, Philadelphia, in hospital at Point Pleasant, N. J.
CELL, NAT, 104-13 108th Street, Ozone Park, Queens; ship's waiter.
CHESLER, MISS ESTELLE, 500 Van Siclen Avenue, Brooklyn, in hospital at Point Pleasant, N. J.
CARPENTER, MADGE, 41-08 171st Street, Flushing, Queens.
CLARE, FRANK, 156-14 Channel Street, Queens, N. Y.
CLARKE, WILLIAM F., forty-nine, of 156-14 Channel Street, Howard Beach, Queens, burns of eyes and throat, taken to Bellevue Hospital.
COCHRANE, DR. CHARLES STITTS, fifty-five, 70 Eighth Avenue, Brooklyn.
COCHRANE, MISS C. M., 70 Eighth Avenue, Brooklyn.
COHEN, ABRAHAM, department store manager, 11 Kenney Terrace, Hartford, Conn., in hospital at Point Pleasant, N. J.
COHEN, MRS. ABRAHAM, same address, in hospital at Point Pleasant, N. J.
COHN, GERTRUDE, 27, 600 West 165th Street, Manhattan, in Fitkin Hospital, Neptune, N. J.
COLL, Mrs. J. P., care of "Luckenbach."
COLL, MISS DOROTHY, twenty-three, 54 Duncan Avenue, Jersey City, N. J.; sent home.
CONBOY, RUTH.
CONDUICUS, DAN, 38, of 66 Madison Avenue, New York, overcome by smoke, in Fitkin Hospital, Neptune, N. J.
CONROY, CAMILLA E., of 323 West Loraine Avenue, Baltimore.
CONROY, ANNE, 2109 Segal Street, Philadelphia.
CONWAY, MISS ANNA, twenty-nine, nurse, at Jewish Hospital, Brooklyn.
CORTE, ROBERT, 25, member of crew, 202 Ninth Avenue, Manhattan, in Fitkin Hospital, Neptune, N. J.
COTTER, MARGARET B., 34 Pearl Street, Springfield, Mass.
COTTER, MISS MARY V., Springfield, Mass.
CULLEN, UNA, 66 Chauncey Street, Brooklyn.
DAVIS, MRS. MINNIE, sixty-three, of 200 Pine Street, Brooklyn, eyes slightly burned, possible fracture of right shoulder, St. Vincent's Hospital.
DAVIS, ANNE, 200 Pine Street, Brooklyn.
DAVIDSON, DOLLY, 6912 Gerard Avenue, Bronx.
DAVIDSON, SIDNEY, 6912 Gerard Avenue, Bronx.
DAVISON, MISS LILLIAN, 33 Athens Street, Clifton, N. J., in hospital at Point Pleasant, N. J.
DESVERMINE, MADELINE, 291 Marblehead Road, Tuckahoe, N. Y., to Broad Street Hospital.
DASILIDIES, JOHN, 122 Fort George Avenue, New York City.
DESVERMINE, ALICE, 1010 Prospect Place, Jersey City, home.
D'ORN, MRS. ANGELA, of Havana, Cuba.
DIETTMAN, FRANK, 16, of Ninth

(Continued on page two)

Unaccounted For

Following is the list of passengers given out at the Ward Line offices who have not been accounted for:

ALTENBERG, MRS. S.
ATROMEZ, GEORGE
BEHLING, MISS ANN
BERRY, MISS AGNES D., Springfield, Mass.
BORRELL, MRS. J. H., of Buffalo.
BRADY, MISS NANCY.
BREGSTEIN, MASTER M., 7825 Fourth Avenue, Brooklyn.
BRENNON, MISS ELEANOR, New York.
BROWNEY, MISS GEITMER, 73 St. Paul's Place, Brooklyn.
CHALFANT, MR. J. M. 2d.
CLARK, MRS. WILLIAM F., of 156-14 Channel St., Howard Beach, Queens.
DISTLER, ERNEST F., of 56 Lencx Road, Brooklyn.
EGELHOFF, GEORGE T.
ELIAS, CHARLES, of 75 Aycrigg Avenue, Passaic, N. J.
FAULCONER, FRED.
FISH, MISS EVA, New York.
FILTZER, MR. AND MRS. CHARLES, 115-35 Mayfield Road, Jamaica, Queens.
GAMRINGER, MISS L.
GAMRINGER, MRS. DORA
GONZALES, ROBERTO.
GRADY, E. S., of Overbrook, Philadelphia.
GRIES, MRS. A., 2400 Cornelia St., Ridgewood.
GRIMM, WILLIAM.
HAGEDORN, MR. and MRS. HENRY, 356 Euclid Ave., Brooklyn.
HOFFMAN, MISS L.
HOED, FRANCESCO
HOOD, FRANCISCO
KLEIN, MILTON, 122 East Thirty-third Street, Paterson.
KOSBOTHE, MR. and MRS. A.
KRAUSS, MISS R.
KUHN, MISS ANNA, 199 Piccadilly Drive, Lynbrook.
LIONE, MASTER N.
LIONEL, RAYMOND, seven years old.
LIONEL, ANTHONY, father of Raymond.
LISCOMB, HARRY
LISTIG, MR. MILTON, 398 Lake Avenue, Worcester, Mass.
LOFMARK, MRS. D.
LOHSE, MRS. M.
LOHR, MRS. L. C.
LYON, MR. N. M.
MARSHALL, MISS NELLIE
M'ARTHUR, MRS. ALEXANDER, of Philadelphia.
M'CONNELL, LOLA, of Paterson, N. J.
MORAN, MRS. E.
MORAN, MISS M.
NASS, MRS. FRANCIS, Philadelphia.
NATHANSON, MISS Z.
NELEY, F. B., New York.
ONERGENE, MISS L.
POTTBERG, E.
POLLICE, MRS. VIOLA.
PERLMAN, MISS V.
REINEKING, MR. FERDINAND, 205-22 111th Street, Hollis.
RENZ, MRS. MARTIN
SAENZ, MRS. C.
SAENZ, MISS MARTHA
SIVATION, GEORGE, of Upper Darby, Pa.
SPACTOR, MISS F.
STEWART, MR. FRANK, 4568 Spuyten Duyvil Parkway, Bronx.
STRAUCH, DR. H. G.
STRAUCH, MRS. H. G.
SAENZ, MISS MARGARITA
SAENZ, MASTER BRAULIO Jr.
SUAREZ, EDUARDO MURIAS.
TOST, FRANCISCO, New York.
THRONE, MISS S.
VOIGHT, MISS L.
WACKER, MRS. R.
ZIPLINKI, MR. R. F.

Service for Ship's Crew Listed

Memorial services for the members of the Morro Castle's crew who died in the disaster will be held Sunday, September 16, at 8 p. m., in the chapel of the Seamen's Church Institute, 25 South Street, it was announced last night.

Dies in Wife's Arms Just as Help Arrives

Special to the Herald Tribune

POINT PLEASANT, N. J., Sept. 8.—Among the tragic Morro Castle figures was Mrs. E. J. Brady, of 7048 Green Hill Road, Overbrook, Pa., whose husband died in her arms just before help came.

"I jumped from the third deck, followed by my husband," she said, "and we swam for a couple of hours, drifting to the southwest. We had life belts on, but my husband grew exhausted and said to me, 'I can't hold out any longer.' I told him: 'Hold on a few more minutes, here comes a boat,' but he keeled over and died in my arms just before a boat picked us up."

Known Dead

Passengers

HOFFMAN, MISS EVA, twenty-four years old, of 263 Adelaide St., London, Ont., identified by Max Krause, of 147 West Eighty-sixth St., and by Goldie Hoffman, a sister.
BADER, CHARLES, twenty-two, Orange Drive, Baldwin, L. I., identified at Sea Girt, N. J., by Theodore C. Wenzel, of 7175 Orange Avenue, Irvington, N. J., his prospective father-in-law.
BRADY, EDWARD J., of 7048 Greenhill Road, Philadelphia.
BOUGUSON, ELIAS, thirty-one years old, of 42 Eldridge Street.
DILLON, MRS. JAMES, of Fourth Street, Brooklyn, identified by son-in-law, C. R. Murphy, of 495 First Street, Brooklyn.
DISTLER, MRS. ADELAIDE L., fifty-five years old, of 56 Lenox Road, Brooklyn, wife of Ernest F. Distler, retired brewer.
ERIKSON, MISS JERRY, 28, of 41-12 171st Street, Flushing, Queens, identified by W. J. Ardiff, of 41-08 171st Street, Flushing.
FRYMAN, MISS FANNY, of 1247 South Second Street, Philadelphia, identified by brother, Samuel Fryman, of Philadelphia.
GRIESNER, MRS. F., 60-30 Woodbine St., Ridgewood.
HEIMAN, JOSEPH A., of 40 East Eighty-eighth Street.
HOFFMAN, MISS E., twenty-eight years old, of Paterson, N. J., drowned.
HOLDEN, MRS. R. A., of Michigan Avenue, Cincinnati, Ohio, identified by W. J. Lippincott, of Monmouth Hotel, Spring Lake, N. J. Her husband and two sons were rescued.
KENT, JOHN S., twenty-seven years old, of Swarthmore, Pa. Identified by W. M. Fotte, of 540 Ogden Avenue, Swarthmore.
LIKEWISE, JACOB A., of 115 Cleveland Street, Brooklyn.
M'ARTHUR, ALEXANDER, of 2019 Bleich Street, Philadelphia.
OLESON, MRS. LAURA, of 413 College Avenue, Westerleigh, S. I.
POLLICE, LOUIS, of 83 Clermont Avenue, Brooklyn.
PRICE, MRS. WILLIAM F., of 90 Pine Street, Brooklyn, wife of Patrolman W. F. Price, of the General Repair Division of the New York Police Department, at Bellevue Morgue.
VILLAHAFT, IRINEO.
WACHER, HERBERT J., 225 Union Avenue, Roselle Park, N. J.
WECKER, HENRIETTA, Brooklyn.
WILLABACK, IVINS, no address.

(TENTATIVELY IDENTIFIED)

Griesner, Frederick, 60-30 Woodbine Street, Ridgewood, Queens, at Bellevue Morgue.

Unidentified

MAN, about forty-five years old, six feet one inch tall, weighing 200 pounds, with large, drooping mustache.
WOMAN, about twenty-five years old, five feet five inches tall, weighing 120 pounds, with brown hair and gray eyes, wearing a silk lavender slip and a blue coat trimmed with gray fur.
WOMAN, forty-five years old, weighing 170 pounds.
WOMAN, about twenty-three years old, four feet eight inches tall, weighing 100 pounds.
WOMAN, about thirty years old, brunette, weighing 130 pounds.
GIRL, about twenty years old, blonde, weighing 115 pounds, five feet two inches tall.
GIRL, about thirteen years old, wearing pink pajamas, with severe burns on face, arms and hands.

Crew

FARNELL, HAMLET, forty-six, night watchman, 7804 Ninety-fifth Street, Ozone Park, Queens.
KURLAND, ALFRED, musician, 21 Sherman Avenue, New York.
LARRINAGA, NICHOLAS, thirty-two, assistant cook, 48 Cherry Street.
MATARADO, ARTURO, 25 South Street.

3 Relief Ships Bring Many Injured Here

Charred Hulk Beached After Flames, Origin a Mystery, Sweep Liner, Trapping Passengers in Sleep

Tourists, in Panic, Feared To Enter Boats, Crew Says

Disaster Occurs in Storm Off Asbury Park While Captain, Heart Victim, Lies Dead in Cabin; Bodies Strew Jersey Beaches; Emergency Morgue Set Up at Sea Girt

The liner Morro Castle of the Ward Line, bound from Havana to New York with 318 passengers and a crew of 240, burned before dawn yesterday about six miles off Asbury Park with an estimated loss of 186 lives. Early today the wrecked liner lies beached but still burning just off the Asbury Park Convention Hall, which is built on a pier extending 200 feet into the water.

A wet gale, increasing in strength, sent searchers and rescue boats home late last night after a day of cruising the rainswept sea and beach in search for victims and survivors.

225 Dead or Missing, 333 Rescued

A checkup by Ward Line officials showed that 184 passengers and 149 members of the crew had been rescued. There were 558 aboard the vessel. With only 333 accounted for, 225 are dead or missing, according to the company's figures.

The New Jersey National Guard checkup reported an unofficial tabulation of 186 bodies, but it is feared many of the thirty-nine missing were burned to death in their cabins, so rapid was the spread of the flames.

A watchman discovered the fire in the ship's library soon after 2:30 a. m., and forty-five minutes later, with flames raging throughout the vessel, the first S O S went out. Liners, Coast Guard vessels and pleasure and fishing craft responded to the appeal, but high waves and fog and rain hampered their rescue efforts. The Monarch of Bermuda, homeward bound from a vacation cruise, arrived on the scene early in the day and picked up seventy-one survivors from the water; the Andrea F. Luckenbach rescued twenty-two, and the City of Savannah picked up sixty-five, all these being brought to New York. Smaller craft saved others and took them to the Jersey shore. The President Cleveland put out two boats but found no one in the sea.

The cause of the fire remained a mystery, although it was fairly definitely established it had originated in the ship's library. Commodore J. E. Jones, in charge of the Ward Line fleet, said in Havana that it was impossible for lightning to have caused the disaster.

Some Swim Six Miles to Shore

Others from the Morro Castle fought their way four to six miles through the waves to the shore, some by clinging to floating bodies, others with the aid of life belts and a few strong swimmers without any aid.

Back on the ship William F. Warms, who had sailed as first officer, was on the bridge as captain, having had the post forced upon him only a few hours before the fire by the death of Captain Robert R. Willmott, who had been master of the $5,500,000 vessel most of the time since she went into service in 1930 until his death from a heart attack on the bridge at 7:45 p. m. Friday.

Captain Warms remained on the bridge for hours and, as commander of the vessel at the time of the disaster, is the one authentic source of information. No word came from him, however. It was reported that he had collapsed at his post at 2:30 yesterday afternoon and, with other officers and men who had struck by the burning ship, had been transferred to the Coast Guard cutter Tampa. The cutter's radio was out of commission and Captain Warms, even if able to make a report, was unable to do so.

The Tampa was one of several Coast Guard craft which started towing the Morro Castle to New York, where it was hoped that fireboats could quench the blaze within her. The steel liner parted in the northeast gale soon after 7 o'cclock last night, however, and the Morro Castle, still burning fiercely, was driven ashore at Asbury Park at 7:35 p. m.

The apparently dying flames outlined gaping holes in the Morro Castle's hull. On her port side a partly burned lifeboat dangled from a twisted davit cable. She had twelve lifeboats, but only eight were accounted for as having been launched, six from the starboard side and two from the flame-swept port side.

Sixty Bodies Taken to Sea Girt Morgue

Dramatic evidence of the chaos existing aboard the Morro Castle came last night when a checkup showed that only eighty-five persons were saved in five of the eight lifeboats launched. Each lifeboat had places for seventy persons.

The work of collecting the bodies of the Morro Castle victims progressed slowly toward night. Unidentified bodies were being taken to the emergency morgue set up at Sea Girt, N. J. About sixty were at Sea Girt. It was estimated that about 125 other bodies were in undertakers' establishments along the coast of north Jersey.

At the two morgues in Manasquan last night forty-two bodies had been received. Approximately 150 survivors were taken ashore at Spring Lake, Manasquan and Point Pleasant, according to the Guardsmen.

Twenty-seven survivors were treated at Point Pleasant Hospital, ten later being allowed to leave the hospital. Thirty-seven were admitted to Fitkin Hospital, in Neptune. All taken to hospitals were treated for shock, submersion and exhaustion. Few were reported in a serious condition.

New York Red Cross workers, other relief agencies, police trucks and ambulances met each rescue boat to give aid. At midday one hundred coffins were ordered by New York authorities to be sent to the piers, but most of the dead were recovered along the Jersey shore, although the Coast Guard brought in eight bodies to Bellevue morgue last night.

The list as given out by the Ward Line which left 225 persons unaccounted for was carefully checked. Names were placed on the list only after a report had been received from an officer or member of the crew who had been on the ship, or from checks made by the line officials with hospitals.

The Ward Line said the crew list showed that out of 240 employees, 149 had reported to the line office up to 8:30 o'clock.

About twenty public and institutional ambulances and fifteen private

The story of the fire on board the Ward Line cruise ship *Morro Castle*, which led to the deaths of 134 passengers and crew in September 1934, reads today like the most implausible kind of mystery thriller full of raw emotions, human folly, political intrigue and psychological hang-ups. The truth is still not known: in all probability it will remain buried for ever in the complex web of innuendoes, lies, and accusations that surrounded the strange events of 7 to 8 September 1934.

The first strange event that occurred on the last night of the *Morro Castle*'s voyage from Havana to New York was that the captain died. Captain Wilmott had been acting peculiarly for most of the trip, immuring himself in his cabin and communicating with the bridge only by telephone. At supper-time on Friday the 7th he was discovered slumped on the floor of his cabin: his skin was already turning blue. The ship's surgeon diagnosed acute indigestion and heart failure as the cause of death—which seemed to one of the officers present a somewhat peremptory judgement since the captain had only eaten a melon (the same officer later revealed that Wilmott had been convinced that someone was 'out to kill him').

The ship was now under the command of First Officer Warms—who had already twice in his career achieved the rank of captain, and twice been demoted (ironically, on both occasions for lack of attention to fire precautions). He was determined not to squander what would surely be his last chance to redeem himself. With only a few more hours before the *Morro Castle* docked at New York it must have seemed, therefore, like the cruellest mischief fate could devise when a watchman rushed onto the bridge, where Captain Warms was guiding his new command through a light swell off the New Jersey coast, and reported that there was a fire in the library and that smoke was pouring through the portside ventilators. From that moment the *Morro Castle* sailed into the world's headlines.

LINER SET AFIRE, OFFICERS TESTIFY, TELLING OF BLAZE ON MORRO CASTLE
(New York Herald Tribune)

It was Warms' undeviating belief that the fire had been started by a human hand—a conclusion he drew from the suddenness with which it appeared and the speed at which it spread. Within minutes the lounge and the cabins aft were alight: in half an hour the ship was an inferno. On the other hand, much of this was Warms's own doing, since he continued to steam at nineteen knots into a stiff wind which fanned the flames like a giant bellows. Even worse, when it became clear the fire could not be extinguished he turned in towards the shore in the hope of beaching the ship—which merely served to fan the blaze into new parts of the liner and cut off more escape routes for the desperate passengers. In due course the *Morro Castle* was beached: after an attempt to tow it to New York had failed, it drifted of its own accord onto the strand at Asbury Park, a New Jersey holiday resort which earned itself a small fortune from the fees charged for tens of thousands of sightseers to view the smouldering hulk and for journalists to be hoisted aboard in a bosun's chair (for their first-person accounts of the tragedy). Obligingly, the liner landed immediately opposite the studios of the local broadcasting station, making it the first 'live' sea-disaster in radio history.

WHOOPEE PARTIES— GAMES WITH LIGHTED CIGARETTES
(Daily Mail)

One of the great attractions of the *Morro Castle*, in those Prohibition days, was the opportunity outside territorial waters to have as much drink as you liked without any of the furtive manoeuvres that went on ashore. Per-

The Morro Castle, Beached at Asbury Park, and View of Wrecked Interior

MONDAY, SEPTEMBER 10, 1934   ****   TWO CENTS In Greater New York | THREE CENTS Within 200 Miles | FOUR CENTS Elsewhere

U.S. Inquiry in Morro Castle Fire Begins Today; Captain Warms Called to Explain Tragedy at Sea; Death Toll Stands at 164, Many Still Unidentified

Commander Of Death Ship Still in Daze

Chief Officer Who Took Over as Skipper Died Lands With 13 Who Stuck to Morro Castle

Haggard, Shaken, He Greets Family

Forced to Quit Fiery Wreck; Is Praised by Coast Guard as Hero

Acting Captain William F. Warms of the Morro Castle, who rose to the command of that ill-fated liner for only the few hours of her disaster, was brought ashore at 11:30 a. m. yesterday at Stapleton, S. I., by the United States Coast Guard cutter Tampa. He is scheduled as the first witness today at the Department of Commerce investigation into the burning of the vessel. The hearing begins at the Custom House at 10 a. m.

With Captain Warms as he left the cutter were ten of the thirteen officers and sailors aboard the Morro Castle who followed their captain in remaining with their ship until she ran herself into the beach at Asbury Park. Captain Warms was the last man to leave the boat alive, and, according to Lieutenant Commander E. G. Rose of the Tampa, he left only when threatened with force if he tried to stay aboard.

Commander Rose gave high praise to Captain Warms and the little group of seamen who remained beside him. "They are the real heroes of this affair," he said. "I think Captain Warms is a very honest and conscientious man, and a thorough seaman."

Captain Warms, forty-eight years old, a native of Greenwich Village, has been with the Ward Line for thirty years, working up from ordinary seaman.

Captain Warms was in the hands of lawyers for the Ward Line, even before he left the Tampa. One of the lawyers went aboard the cutter from a tug in the harbor. Thereafter they guarded him closely, permitting him to meet reporters only long enough to say that he would tell his story of the disaster at the inquiry and to thank

The liner, close to the Convention Hall and the Boardwalk, viewed by part of the crowd of 250,000 that filled the resort yesterday

At the top of the picture is the ruined framework of the top deck, wrecked by the flames from the interior   Herald Tribune photos—Acme

250,000 View Fiery Wreck, Fast on Beach

Asbury Park Mecca for Curious; Unclaimed Bodies Taken to Mortuary in Jersey City

Conboy to Sit In At Investigation

389 Survivors Listed, 45 Passenger Dead Are Identified; 53 Missing

The counting of the dead and search for the missing in the Morro Castle disaster drew toward the end last night as the Federal government prepared for an inquiry this morning into the reasons for the large loss of life in the fire which swept the $5,500,000 Ward Line vessel before dawn on Saturday.

One hundred and sixty-four persons are believed to have lost their lives in the tragedy, but the lists of the dead and missing and of the survivors are still incomplete and company and relief workers' check-ups are at variance.

250,000 View Wreck

The still smoldering turbo-electric liner, beached in a calm sea just off Convention Hall on the Asbury Park, N. J., boardwalk, yesterday drew a crowd of 250,000 sightseers. The charred Morro Castle had driven deep into the beach sand, and there was little hope that the ship could be floated. Searchers boarded the vessel, brought off one charred body, and then settled down to wait until the still-blazing interior cooled off. Firemen pumped in tons of water.

Dead Taken to Jersey City

The bodies of all unidentified dead—fewer than half of the victims have been claimed—were being concentrated in the undertaking establishment of Bert A. Waters, 48 Brinkerhoff Street, Jersey City. More than sixty bodies were identified yesterday at the National Guard temporary morgue at Sea Girt, N. J., and late last night

New York Herald Tribune

SEPTEMBER 11, 1934.   TWO CENTS In New York City. | THREE CENTS Within 200 Miles | FOUR CENTS Elsewhere Except in 7th and 8th Postal Zones

MORRO CASTLE FIRE WAS INCENDIARY, SHIP OFFICERS TESTIFY AT INQUIRY; LINE PUTS DEAD AT 87, MISSING AT 50

413 ON THE LINER RESCUED

66 Passengers Known to Be Victims, With 28 More Unfound.

GRAND JURY INQUIRY TODAY

Conboy Questions Radio Man and Subpoenas Witnesses at Custom House Hearing.

FIREMAN CRITICIZES CREW

Developments in Morro Castle Disaster As Inquiries Seek to Fix Responsibility

Official inquiry into the burning of the liner Morro Castle, and the efforts of friends and relatives on behalf of the victims and survivors, led yesterday to the following developments:

Acting Captain Warms of the Morro Castle testified at a hearing conducted at the Custom House by the Steamboat Inspection Service that he believed the fire was incendiary. It started in a locker in the writing room, he said, and "got out of control."

United States Attorney Martin Conboy announced that evidence on the disaster would be submitted today to a Federal grand jury. The Department of Justice announced it would help to locate witnesses.

The Ward Line, which operated the destroyed ship, issued a revised list of survivors and casualties, showing a total of 550 persons aboard, with 413 survivors, 87 dead, including the captain, and 50 missing. Funerals for many of the victims who lived in the metropolitan area will be held today and tomorrow.

The City Council of Asbury Park decided to make an effort to keep the hulk of the Morro Castle on the beach near the Board-

SUSPECT OIL WAS SPREAD

Warms and Chief Aides Say Blaze Was Set in Writing Room Locker.

ENGINE CREW LEFT POSTS

Fight Had to Be Abandoned When Smoke Drove Them Out, Acting Captain Declares.

HE DENIES DELAYING SOS

---

haps the parties did get a little abandoned, especially on the last night of the voyage with 'dry' land imminent. Even after Captain Wilmott's demise and the cruise director's appeals to cancel all parties out of respect, quite a number of drunken gatherings materialized. Stewards spoke darkly of wild 'games with lighted cigarettes', no doubt with all sorts of incendiary possibilities, but no concrete accusations were ever made, let alone proved.

MORRO CASTLE WAS BURNT BY THE FIRE BUGS OF HAVANA
(New York Sunday Graphic)

In fact, unknown to her passengers, the *Morro Castle* was leading a double life. She was gun-running. Cruising regularly between New York and Cuba the liner provided the perfect cover for the shipment of arms to the corrupt but pro-American regime in Havana, to help suppress the growing threat of Communist insurgents. Almost certainly in the summer of 1934 this secret had been discovered by the Communists: only a week before the disaster a mysterious fire had been started in the hold, which had quickly been extinguished by the ship's automatic sprinklers. (On the fateful trip these sprinklers had unaccountably been turned off.) Havana's chief of police stated quite categorically that the fire had been the work of Reds, and later dutifully arrested six of them for it.

MORRO CASTLE, A WHITEWASH JOB ON THE WARD LINE
(New York Evening Post)

For a time the sensation of shipboard orgies and Red conspiracies seems to have obscured the possibility that negligence had allowed the fire to start, and inefficiency permitted it to spread. Nevertheless an inquiry established that no proper fire drill had been held and fire doors had not been shut in time. Water pressure in the hoses had been worse than inadequate, and there had been a long delay in even getting them operative—astonishingly, Captain Wilmott had recently ordered all hoses to be stowed away and the operating spanners to be removed (a lady had claimed heavy damages against the Line the previous month after slipping on a deck made wet by unauthorized use of the hoses). The origin of the fire was tracked down to a storage locker in the wall of the library, which at first sight seemed to strengthen the theory of arson. But then it came to light that a funnel passed immediately behind that locker, and added to the evidence of a

steward that flammable cleaning materials had been kept there this was sufficient for the Board of Inquiry to return a verdict of 'spontaneous combustion'. It did not help Captain Warms, though, who was indicted for 'misconduct, negligence and inattention to duty' nor the Chief Engineer, who had been one of the first to flee the burning ship in an almost empty lifeboat. Both were sentenced to prison (though both convictions were quashed on appeal).

ROGERS . . . VAUDEVILLE TURN
(New York World Telegraph)

Then the final mystery. One man emerged from the whole tragedy a national hero, George Rogers, the radio operator who stayed at his post as the new captain failed to give orders for the emergency call, then tapped out the urgent SOS even as the flames licked round the radio-room and the heat blistered the soles of his feet. Rogers later capitalized on his fame by launching himself on a coast-to-coast stage tour, in which he re-enacted his part in the dying hours of the *Morro Castle*. But the radio-operator was not what he appeared: even on that last voyage he was under notice. The Ward Line had discovered that he had a long criminal record and had cabled Wilmott to dismiss him. After his stage-tour Rogers opened a shop in Bayonne, which shortly burnt down, netting for him a large sum in insurance. He then joined the police force, of all things, only to be convicted in 1938 of attempting to murder his superior with a homemade bomb. A few years after his parole in 1942 he was again convicted, this time for the murder of a neighbour. He died four years later in New Jersey State Penitentiary, without making a conclusive statement about the unknown part he had played in the *Morro Castle* fire, but at which he had hinted in his more boastful moments.

THE AFTERMATH OF ONE OF THE WORST SHIPPING DISASTERS OF RECENT YEARS: AN AERIAL VIEW OF THE WRECK OF THE MORRO CASTLE,
Beached at Asbury Park and Still Burning After Fire Had Broken Out a Few Hours Before the Ship Would Have Docked in New York on the Voyage From Havana. More Than 100 of the Passengers and Crew Lost Their Lives.
(© Fairchild Aerial Surveys, Inc.)

A DECK OF THE MORRO CASTLE AFTER THE FIRE HAD SUBSIDED: A NEW JERSEY NATIONAL GUARDSMAN,
the First to Board the Ship After the Disaster, Searches for Bodies in the Charred Wreck of the Liner.
(Times Wide World Photos.)

THE BURNING LINER AS THE RESCUERS SAW IT: THE MORRO CASTLE,
With All but the Bow Swept by Fire and With a High Sea Running, Photographed From the Chester, Which Stood by to Aid in the Rescue Work.
(Times Wide World Photos.)

A CALM SEA FOLLOWS A NIGHT OF HORROR: THE MORRO CASTLE,
Her Decks a Mass of Twisted Metal, Still Burning After She Had Washed Ashore at Asbury Park.
(McLaughlin Aerial Surveys.)

THE RESCUE SHIPS STAND BY AS DAWN BREAKS: THE MORRO CASTLE,
a Blazing Furnace, With the Monarch of Bermuda (Left), Which Rescued Seventy-one Persons, and the Andrea S. Luckenbach, Which Rescued Twenty-one, the First Ships to Reach the Scene of the Disaster.
(Times Wide World Photos.)

THE MORRO CASTLE FOLLOWS THE DEAD TO SHORE: THE STERN OF THE SHIP,
From Which Many of the Survivors Leaped, With the Name Still Visible in Spite of the Intense Heat Which Made a Shambles of the Rest of the Vessel.
(Times Wide World Photos.)

The Gresford Colliery Disaster 1934

REYNOLDS'S ILLUSTRATED NEWS," September 23, 1934.

LATE LONDON EDITION

REYNOLDS'S
ILLUSTRATED NEWS
An Independent Newspaper Outside the Big Combines

No. 4,386   (90TH YEAR.)   LONDON, SUNDAY, SEPTEMBER 23, 1934   PRICE 2d.

RESCUERS PERISH IN BLAZING PIT

LITTLE HOPE for VICTIMS of
WORST DISASTER SINCE the WAR

120 Feared Beyond Aid | Burning Tomb May Be Sealed

IN the worst British pit disaster since the War, 120 miners are trapped in an underground furnace, a mile and a half from the bottom of the pit shaft at Gresford Colliery, near Wrexham, North Wales.

Ravaging fire followed an explosion in the early hours of yesterday morning. More than 300 men reached safety. The rest were cut off by a searing wall of flame.

Deadly fire damp, fallen roofs and, indeed, every conceivable horror of an underground disaster, hampered the heroic efforts of the rescue parties. Many were gassed. Four lost their lives in their efforts to reach their entombed comrades.

After countless hours and ceaseless effort, only 15 bodies were brought to the surface. Fears were expressed that few of the others would be recovered, for it was stated that the pit may have to be sealed to prevent the spread of the all-consuming flames.

Colliery directors made it clear, however, that no such step would be taken until it was absolutely certain that none of the entombed men could be brought out alive.

An aerial view of the Gresford Colliery after the disaster yesterday. The picture shows the sorrowing crowds lining the road and waiting for news.

FURNACE OF DEATH

"REYNOLDS'S" SPECIAL CORRESPONDENT

WREXHAM, Saturday.

DRENCHING rain beat down piteously on the uncovered heads of the multitude that watched and waited by the Gresford pithead this morning.

Tramping feet, squelching through the mire, and the occasional scream of some poor woman, as she collapsed under the ghastly strain, were the only sounds to reach the human ear.

Like a funeral pall, the black clouds hung low overhead. The great, silent crowd stood numbed by the awful knowledge that more than a hundred men—husbands, brothers, sons, and sweethearts—were cut off from the world by a mile and a quarter of unquenchable underground flames.

Such was the scene when I arrived at the pit of death this morning. People were muttering in hushed whispers. "There's no hope," they sobbed. "The pit will be sealed. . . . We shall never see our men again. . ."

But there was a sudden movement in the crowd. A stretcher appeared. Men craned forward to catch a glimpse of the shrouded form it was bearing towards the hastily improvised mortuary.

The heroic rescue parties had found the first body. At agonising intervals, 14 more covered forms appeared. Women fainted, and men cried with grief as the grim procession passed by.

No words are adequate to describe the scenes of horror and heroism as men braved death to save men who, they knew in their hearts, could not be living.

Yet, miracle of miracles, seven men came up alive. Five had escaped the flames, the falling roofs, and the deadly firedamp, without the aid of their fellows.

Two others were found at the pit eye, mangled and scorched, but still breathing.

As party after party of rescuers descended the pit, women fell to their knees in the mud and rain and prayed for the safety of their loved ones.

Scores of doctors and nurses were ready to strain every effort to keep them from the clutches of the Reaper.

To save those two lives two others had to be sacrificed. A rescue party had hurried down the shaft. They found a wall of flame eating its way round the tomb of their fellows.

Epic Heroism in Face of Gas

MEN WHO ARE CUT OFF

Late last night, the Ministry of Mines announced: "Good progress is being made in subduing the fire, and rescue work is being rigorously continued with a view to getting access to the workings where the men are cut off.

"The number of men who were cut off in the pit has not yet been determined exactly, but is believed to be between 100 and 120.

"Unfortunately, in the course of rescue operations, three men of the rescue brigade have lost their lives."

[A fourth rescuer has since been reported missing.]

When the rescuers returned to the surface, three of whom were dead. The features of one, Tom Rance, of Llay, were burned out of recognition.

A fourth rescuer did not come back. He was posted as "missing."

More than 400 men were working underground when the dull thud of the explosion shook the bowels of the earth.

Nearly three-quarters of them were in an unaffected portion of the mine. They reached the surface in safety, and at once volunteered to go down again to search for the men who were trapped.

Mr. Harry Lloyd, chairman of the local miners' lodge, told me that the explosion occurred between 1.30 and 2, when 480 men were down the pit.

"The disaster happened in the Dennis Main Deep, which is one and three-quarter miles from its deepest point.

One of the rescue party said:—

"Three-quarters of a mile down the pit we were met by a ball of fire, which made further progress impossible."

When there was a call for volunteers to help with rescue work, the waiting miners stepped forward almost to a man. Twenty men were asked for; 150 begged to be allowed to go.

James Brewin was working on his back in the pit when the explosion occurred.

"There was a noise like thunder," he told me, "and the roof, only a foot or two above my head, cracked, and large lumps of coal fell upon me.

"I scrambled to my knees and

Continued on page three.

To-day's Weather

Weather will be generally unsettled with strong winds.

All Sea Passages: Sea rough.
Further Outlook: Unsettled.
Sun rises, 6.48; sets, 6.57. Lighting-up time (front and rear lamps), 7.57.

OURSELVES
Building the New "Reynolds's"

A new site has been purchased for "Reynolds's." Within twelve months, a new "Reynolds's" — a giant in journalism—will arise.

THIS announcement was made at Birmingham yesterday by Mr. Alfred Barnes (Chairman of the National Co-operative Publishing Society, Ltd., owners of "Reynolds's" and associated newspapers).

Mr. Barnes was addressing a conference organised by the Midland Sectional Board of the Co-operative Union.

After three or four years of experiment, said Mr. Barnes, the Co-operative Movement had finally determined its policy in relation to the Press.

It was a policy which he forecast with confidence, would place "Reynolds's" in a position to compete on terms of equality with its rivals, and would put it in the forefront of journalism.

Development Scheme

Explaining the development policy, Mr. Barnes said it had been agreed by the directors of the N.C.P.S., in collaboration with various sections of the Co-operative Movement, to create a national advertising pool, to which retail societies would contribute, voluntarily, one farthing per £ of sales.

Already the response to this equitable proposal had been most encouraging.

No fewer than 43 societies, whose joint contributions to the advertising fund would amount to £100,000 in the next three years, had joined the scheme to date; and the number of contributing societies was increasing every week.

Arrangements had been made with the Co-operative Wholesale Society to advance the capital necessary to enable far-reaching development plans to proceed.

A site in Gray's Inn-road, having a

MR. ALFRED BARNES, chairman of the National Co-operative Publishing Society.

frontage of 180 feet, and within easy reach of all London's railway termini, had been bought. Plans for a new building were well in hand.

This great new Co-operative productive venture would be equipped with up-to-date plant and machinery. In addition to producing a new and better "Reynolds's," it would enable the Co-operative Movement to launch a daily newspaper immediately the Movement considered such a proposition desirable.

Strong support for the scheme outlined by Mr. Barnes was expressed by Mr. J. Millington (president) and Mr. Cardinal (director), Birmingham Co-operative Society, and by Mr. W. Rogers, Northampton Co-operative Society.

See pictures on Page 13.

Turn the Pages

GEORGE GODWIN writes of Men of Enterprise ... 4
HAMILTON FYFE on Bathing Belles ... 6
J. JEFFERSON FARJEON and the Cup that Cheers ... 6
H. N. BRAILSFORD and the Socialist Way to Peace ... 12

SAVE THE MOTHERS
See Page 12

SECRET HISTORY ... 12
ELEANOR FARJEON and the Children ... 15
Books and Radio ... 18
£300 Crossword ... 20
SPORT ... 20—24

A Poem Written in Tears Page 8

260 DEAD AND MISSING IN WELSH PIT DISASTER

ALL HOPE ABANDONED LAST NIGHT

Rescue Parties'	Fire Breaks Out
Forty Hours'	Afresh After
Fight in Vain	More Explosions

WORK OF SEALING PIT SHAFT COMMENCED

A responsible official of the colliery company stated late on Sunday night:—" As near as we can say, the total roll of dead and missing in the Gresford Colliery disaster is 260."

FROM OUR SPECIAL CORRESPONDENT

WREXHAM, Sunday.

IT became known late to-night that the disaster in the Dennis Main Deep, Gresford Colliery, near Wrexham, on Saturday, had exceeded in magnitude even the gravest fears, and that 260 men are dead or missing, making it the third biggest

NEARING SOLUTION OF LINDBERGH BABY KIDNAPPING

Mystery of Isadore Fischer

PIT DISASTER.—Left: Waiting for news. Centre: Mrs. Irwin Foulkes, whose son is entombed, being led away from the pit by friends. Right: Anxious wives.

MR. SOPWITH'S AMERICA'S CUP

OPPOSITION ON DAY OF REICHSBISHOP'S ENTHRONEMENT

Pastor Niemoller's Attack

Pastor Niemoller, read an extract from Dr. Koch's protest from his pulpit. He said: " We reproach these misleaders who seek to impose a German National Church on the denomination.

" In doing that, Reichsbishop Mueller, Dr. Jaeger, and all those who follow

---

There were 400 miners working down Gresford Pit in North Wales in the early hours of Saturday 22 September 1934, when the explosion occurred. It was a popular shift—because it gave the men some sort of weekend—and the Dennis Main Deep, a mile and three-quarters below the surface was more crowded than usual. Rescue-parties re-entering the mine soon after the explosion found unquenchable fires raging at the three-quarters of a mile level: there was no way through, no way of knowing the fate of the men working the deeper coal-faces. For forty hours they blindly fought the carbon monoxide fumes and the melting heat, knowing in their hearts the futility of it. Four rescuers were killed by further explosions, and several others injured. Only ten bodies could be recovered from the accessible part of the mine before, at dusk on the Sunday evening, the bitter decision to seal the pit shaft was taken. It was scarcely too soon—the next day a new spasm of explosions racked the mine, blowing off the seal and killing a man nearby. The row upon row of empty pegs at the pithead where the miners stowed their lamps told of the immensity of the disaster at Gresford: 260 men had perished in that deep tomb, more than twice the original estimates. It was, after Hulton and Senghenydd, the country's worst mine disaster of the century, and—if only for a moment—it reminded the whole country of the appalling facts of contemporary mining life: that each year in British mines between 800 and 1,000 men were being killed and as much as five times as many injured. As the *Sunday Times* put it: 'In a sense the men at the coal face are on active service, as soldiers are in time of war. Moreover like soldiers they are directly serving their country.'

DAILY SKETCH

MONDAY, SEPTEMBER 24, 1934. Head Office, 200, Gray's Inn-road, W.C.1. 'Phone: Museum 8641.

Choosing Your New Furs, By Modestina

POIGNANT VIGIL AT PITHEAD
ANGUISHED WOMEN AND CHILDREN WAIT FOR NEWS

Cyril Challenor, who made an amazing escape from the mine by crawling up through a narrow airway for two hours.

A view of the Gresford Colliery, Wrexham, North Wales, with relatives waiting while rescue parties were below fighting to reach the entombed miners.

C. E. Harrison, aged 27, who was a victim.

Mrs. J. Nicholls and her little daughter Doreen waited anxiously for news of her husband and brother.

George Mitchell, aged 22, another victim.

Mrs. Robinson appealing to be let through the barrier when she heard her husband was a victim.

Members of a volunteer rescue party preparing to go down the mine at the call for help.

Printed and Published by The DAILY SKETCH and SUNDAY GRAPHIC, Ltd., 200, Gray's Inn-road, London, W.C.1, and Withy Grove, Manchester, 4.—MONDAY, SEPTEMBER 24, 1934.

STOP PRESS NEWS

The Final Spectacular
Crystal Palace Fire 1936

For eighty-five years it had stood, a landmark of London and the last great Victorian playground. The Crystal Palace had been built by Joseph Paxton (one of the founders of the *Daily News*) to house the Great Exhibition of 1851 in a style and splendour appropriate to Britain's pre-eminence in the world. Not everyone had approved, at the time, of this gaudy, glittering monster of steel and glass but Londoners had got to like it and were pleased when, after the exhibition, it was moved from Hyde Park to a permanent site on Sydenham Hill. Since then its heroic halls had housed every imaginable form of human activity, from displays of Egyptian mummies to demonstrations of television machines.

At the end of 1936, with a Coronation year in sight, Sir Henry Buckland, the general manager, was looking forward to an exciting season. But it was he who, at about 7.30 in the evening of 30 November, first noticed a red glow reflecting somewhere within the kaleidoscope of glass. Summoning the duty firemen at once, he remembered that some thirty members of the Crystal Palace Orchestral Society were still in the building rehearsing, and dispatched his daughter (also called Crystal) to warn them of

the danger. The orchestra fled to safety with their instruments (except the double bass) through the South Door, but the three firemen were helpless against the conflagration that now confronted them. Within twenty minutes the entire ribbed framework, a quarter of a mile long, and the great 1,600-foot centre transept was a furnace.

The entire London fire-brigade was mobilized that night—350 firemen with sixty-five engines. But for all the prayers of women who reportedly fell on their knees in the streets, there was nothing they could do. Red-hot girders tumbled around them and molten glass devoured their hose-pipes: the steel ribs started to writhe and twist like agonized living things, as the flames leapt 500 feet into the air. The blaze was seen as much as fifty miles away on the South Downs, and aeroplane pilots later reported seeing the glow even eighty miles away. Nearby the streets were packed solid with sightseers, with thousands evacuated from their homes, and with cinema audiences who had left their theatres when the news was flashed up on the screen. All over the city people flocked up hills or crowded rooftops to watch the Crystal Palace's final spectacular.

An additional, incongruous touch was added to the display when a stockroom of fireworks exploded, sending up a constellation of coloured stars into the night-sky. Flocks of exotic birds from the aviary were saved in the nick of time by releasing them from their cages: the occupants of the aquarium were not so fortunate. Nor was the Baird Television Company whose precious apparatus—the result of years of dedicated research—was all consumed in the fire, along with the magnificent Palace organ.

By dawn all that remained standing was a solitary tower. The rest of the building was a giant luminous skeleton, in which half-burnt statues and blackened columns were draped with collapsed roofing, and white-hot beams crashed from time to time into pools of liquid glass. No lives were lost in that monumental bonfire (though countless firemen collapsed in the smouldering heat). For London, nevertheless, it was a very personal loss.

THIS WAS THE CRYSTAL PALACE

Daily Herald
Wednesday,   December 2, 1936.

BEHIND THE BLACKENED FRAMEWORK of the wrecked north transept, one of the Crystal Palace towers stood sentinel-like as the smoke drifted away and the flames died down, to reveal a desolate waste. A mass of twisted iron, steel and glass was all there was to be seen when a "Daily Herald" photographer flew over the scene, yesterday, of the once gracefully-arched centre transept.

Daily Herald

No. 6489   TUESDAY, DECEMBER 1, 1936   ONE PENNY

CRYSTAL PALACE BURNED DOWN

Flames Seen Over 8 Counties

MOLTEN GLASS IMPERILS FIREMEN

THE Crystal Palace, most famous landmark south of the Thames, was last night destroyed by the biggest fire London has seen for years. This morning the great exhibition building is a twisted, smouldering ruin.

Firemen saved the two great towers, but the rest of the building, with everything in it, was reduced to ruins.

The entire London Fire Brigade was mobilised soon after the fire started at 7.30 p.m., and 65 engines, with 350 firemen, raced to the spot. Six giant water towers played a ring of water on to the burning mass.

M.P.s Watch Glow From

Windows Of The House

Great flames, leaping nearly 500 feet, were visible over eight counties. They were seen from the Devil's Dyke at Brighton, 50 miles away, and from the Hog's Back, 30 miles away, in Surrey.

Every hill within 20 miles of London was a vantage point for great crowds. M.P.s watched the reflected glow of the flames from committee room windows and the terrace of the Houses of Parliament.

Showers of sparks fell near houses at Beckenham, two miles away. A newspaper could be read in a garden at Norbury, three miles off.

Buses Pushed On Pavement:

Cars Parked In Gardens

By car, on bicycles and on foot great crowds raced to the Palace. They blocked every road for a mile around and an S O S was sent out to the suburbs for more police to help to control them.

They disorganised bus and tramcar traffic. Firemen were hampered by large numbers of buses and cars on the Palace parade; police pushed the buses on to pavements and cars were even run into front gardens.

The crowds were so dense that the B.B.C. broadcast an S O S urging others not to go to the Palace.

Fireworks Explode: Rockets

Shower Stars Above Smoke

The Duke of Kent, with his equerry, motored from the West End to see the fire. Wearing evening dress, he stood in the road gazing up at the blazing North Transept.

Then he walked to a travelling coffee stall where firemen were standing. He had a coffee with them.

An orchestra was rehearsing in the garden hall lobby when the fire started. The players rushed out of

(Continued on Page Two; Crystal Palace in the Past, Page 9; Scenes at the Fire, Page 2.)

FLAMES leaping high in the air shortly after the centre structure had collapsed at the Crystal Palace last night. (Other pictures on Back Page.)

"My Life's Work Is Finished"

— SIR H. BUCKLAND

"MY life's work is finished," said one man as he watched the Crystal Palace blaze and crumble into ruin.

He is Sir Henry Buckland, General Manager of the Palace.

He it was who discovered the fire, and as he watched the flames eating through the famous Alhambra Court he told the "Daily Herald" how he gave the alarm.

"I saw a red glow and raced along to the seat of the fire, shouting for the three firemen who were on duty," he said.

"The firemen and my daughter answered at once. While the firemen attacked the flames, my daughter ran across to the other side of the Palace, where the Palace Orchestra was rehearsing. They got the South doors open and escaped that way.

His daughter's name is Crystal. He named her after the Palace.

"The whole of our enterprise appears to have been destroyed," he went on.

"I was looking forward to a particularly good season in Coronation year. Now everything is destroyed. I feel that my life's work is finished.

"It is heart breaking that in a few short hours this should happen to finish off as far as I am concerned 22 years of work. It is almost beyond my comprehension . . . yet."

"It will never be rebuilt," he added sadly. "In 1854 it cost £1,350,000—just think what that means to-day.

"We have spent £300,000 bringing it up to date. Now it is finished—to live only in memories."

Sir Henry Buckland said his greatest anxiety had been to save the two towers. At the top of each were tanks containing 1,200 tons of water.

"I knew this vast quantity of water could not be emptied," he said. "Every minute I expected to see the girders buckle and these great containers go crashing down into the houses in the near neighbourhood.

"All the contents of the tower were destroyed, but the girders held."

MOLLISON HALF-WAY THERE

THIRTY-ONE hours after leaving Croydon, Jim Mollison and his co-pilot, Corniglion-Molinier, arrived in Khartum at 4.46 p.m. yesterday, having covered about half the distance to the Cape.

They intend to resume the flight after a few hours' rest, and hope to be at Kisumu on Lake Victoria (Kenya) at six o'clock this morning, says Reuter.

Other front page news yesterday:—

SPAIN:—

Labour M.P.s will oppose in the House of Commons to-day the Government's Bill to ban the carrying of arms to Spain in British ships.

(See Page Three)

LORD NUFFIELD:—

Announced gift valued at £2,125,000 to his workers.

(See Page 11)

CRICKET:—

Finances of county cricket clubs were mentioned in the House of Commons yesterday. During the five years before last season, county cricket clubs paid £75,000 in entertainment tax. In the same period their aggregate loss amounted to practically the same figure.

(See Page 11)

COKE FAMINE:—

Thousands of men who might be employed in producing steel are idle because the British steel industry is experiencing a famine in coke.

(See Page 3)

BALLOON IN SEA:—

A highly inflammable Army balloon fell into the sea off Worthing and lifeboats which went out were recalled owing to the danger from gases.

(See Page 11)

THIS GRAPHIC PICTURE shows the extent of the fire. Acres of flame-covered ground as the blaze raged from end to end of the building when the centre transept had fallen in.

The Advancing Crest

Ohio Valley Floods 1937

One moment the talk was all of drought . . . The front page of the *New York Times* for 17 January 1937, was focussed on the crisis in the Mid-West: 'Migration of Farmers Continues while Fear of New Drought rises' the headline ran. 'Barren mid-west land deserted by 15,000 families and those remaining fight for existence.' The story went on to report how farmers by the thousand were quitting the drought-stricken territories of Dakota, Western Kansas and Eastern Montana; how cattle stocks were depleted by half; how the winter snows, which were relied on to provide subsoil moisture had been far below average that year. 'I sometimes wonder' remarked one of the disillusioned farmers philosophically 'if there has been a permanent change in the weather.'

But that was not quite the view from the Ohio Valley that day. A massive thaw, in league with some torrential unseasonal rains, had swollen a number of tributary rivers far beyond their banks: in Cincinnati the Ohio had already climbed to within a few inches of the flood stage.

Flooding had been virtually an annual hazard to the towns of the Ohio Valley, ever since it had first been settled. There were very many people who still recalled with trepidation the disastrous deluge of 1913, when the flood-waters had topped every known record stage by ten to fifteen feet and had reaped 140 million dollars' worth of damage. Some efforts had been made at the time towards a concerted flood-control programme, but the Ohio was a decidedly erratic river at its height and its 1,000-mile valley was a relatively highly urbanized area. In 1937 the problem remained as imminent as ever.

On 18 January the waters continued to rise inexorably, in spite of a brief freeze, spreading alarm from Illinois and Indiana to Ohio, West Virginia and Kentucky. Farmers watched the inundation of their crops in despair, and thousands began an exodus to safer countryside. The next day the Ohio River was in flood along its entire length, for the second time in history. The inhabitants—from the Golden Triangle in downtown Pittsburgh to below Cairo, Ill.—were now prepared for a long siege; but not for what was to transpire. The flood crest simply rose, and rose, and rose not by inches but by feet. On the 20th the citizens of Portsmouth, Ohio, galvanized by the waters lapping the top of their 60-foot concrete wall, prepared to evacuate their homes and sacrifice part of their town by opening the flood-gates, to avert an even greater catastrophe. At Louisville, Ky., a chocolate sea began to seep into the town, unresisted and irresistible.

There was no doubt about it (in the words of the *Chicago Tribune*) 'the Ohio was out to make it the greatest flood America ever has known.'

Within the next few days no less than ten states were in an emergency, some of them under martial law. Complete towns had been engulfed, Wheeling, W. Va., Marietta, Ohio, Covington, Ky.; even Memphis on the Mississippi was awash on a three-mile-wide flood.

No news was heard from Paducah, Ky., for twenty-four hours, so utterly isolated was it from the outside world. By the 24th it was estimated that 400,000 people had been made homeless—a figure that was to be dwarfed in the days to follow.

At the heart of the disaster stood the cities of Louisville and Cincinnati. The situation in Louisville, the greater part of which was totally marooned, became the focus of the nation, largely through the radio broadcasts that were used to direct relief work. The mayor telephoned President Roosevelt personally to inform him of the gravity of the situation. There were 200,000 refugees (at a conservative estimate), food was running out, there was a famine of drinking-water, and power was non-existent. But perhaps Cincinnati, where the floodwaters reached their highest-ever stage (a fraction below eighty feet), suffered the worst horror. There a broken gasoline tank spilled thousands of gallons of highly flammable oil on the turbulent waters, which carried it downstream towards the city's industrial district. A chance spark from a trolley wire had transformed the surface of the water into an inferno, shooting flames 300 feet into the air. Buildings over a three-mile front were destroyed before the blaze was brought under control.

Day after day America read of mounting dramas, some imagined, some very real; of houses collapsing under whole families huddled on the roof, of a dozen convicts killed in fights

---

114

The Times-Picayune

VOLUME CI—NO. 3   Issued Every Work-Day Morning at 601-615 North St. BY THE TIMES-PICAYUNE PUBLISHING CO. Founded January 25, 1837   NEW ORLEANS, WEDNESDAY, JANUARY 27, 1937   Entered N. O. Postoffice as Second-Class Matter Under Act of March 3, 1879   SINGLE COPY 5 CENTS

CITIES ABANDONED; 750,000 ARE HOMELESS

MISS PERKINS AND ROOSEVELT SCOLD GENERAL MOTORS FOR REFUSING BID

Rejection of Secretary's Invitation to Parley Is Called 'Unfortunate Decision' by President

FIVE HURT IN CLASH AT CADILLAC PLANT

Violence Flares in Detroit as Auto Corporation Recalls Thousands of Idle Employes to Jobs

(By The Associated Press)
Washington, Jan. 26—President Roosevelt joined Secretary Perkins today in reprimanding the General Motors Corporation for refusing to accept Miss Perkins' invitation to a peace conference.

Mr. Roosevelt said at his press conference he had told "everybody" today he "was not only disappointed by the refusal of Mr. Sloan to come down here, but I regarded it as a very unfortunate decision on his part."

Previously Miss Perkins had told reporters General Motors "has failed in its public duty," had made a "great mistake," and had disregarded the "moral challenge" resulting from the strike.

Miss Perkins had asked Alfred P. Sloan, Jr., General Motors president, and John L. Lewis, strike generalissimo, to meet her here tomorrow and try to work out an approach to peace negotiations.

Sloan refused to come, saying he...

'Wasn't Doing Anything'
The possibility of the labor department power to subpena witnesses and documents during strikes, to determine causes and to make findings of fact, was one item discussed at these conferences.

Reporters reminded the president that Sloan said last week, when he left Miss Perkins' last series of conferences with union leaders and General Motors officials, that he would be glad to come back if Mr. Roosevelt invited him.

The president said that a representative of the chief executive already had invited Sloan. He referred to Miss Perkins.

Asked whether he intended to do anything "great emphatic," Mr. Roosevelt said he wasn't doing anything.

Police, Pickets Clash at Cadillac Plant

(By International News Service)
Detroit, Mich., Jan. 26—Violence broke out again in the strike-torn Motor City area today as police clashed with pickets in the closed Cadillac plant, scene of yesterday's disorder.

A woman was injured as police officers clubbed strikers away from a company official's car. She was taken to a hospital. Four men picketing suffered head injuries.

"Go ahead, run over them!" an

Continued on Page Two

To the Rescue! Help for Flood Sufferers Rushed on All Sides

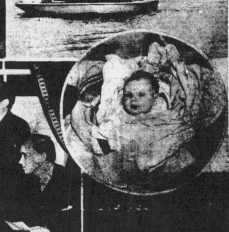

—Photos at top right by The Times-Picayune, others by The Associated Press.
As the tragedy of the great floods increases in intensity and extent, assistance from all areas of the nation is being sped to the stricken. National Guardsmen (top left) help patrol Louisville, Ky., as the Ohio's waters take a heavy toll. From New Orleans go forth to transport supplies Coast Guard vessels (top right) recruited from the Gulf division. In Washington, army, navy, Coast Guard, CCC, WPA and Red Cross officials (left center) gather at the call of the president to plan further aid. They are, left to right, seated, Major-General Malin Craig, army; Robert Fechner, CCC; Harry Hopkins, WPA; and, standing, Admiral W. D. Leahy, navy; Rear Admiral R. R. Waesche, Coast Guard, and Admiral Cary T. Grayson, Red Cross. One of the youngest flood refugees at Charleston, Mo., is Dorothy Sue Hale (right center), two months old. Below, fire blazes high in the Crosley Radio Corporation's electrical refrigerator plant at Cincinnati as the flood attacks the city.

Singer Dies from Wound Given by Stage Dagger in Lawrence Tibbett's Hand

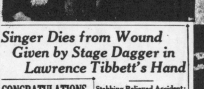

CONGRATULATIONS CONTINUE POURING IN ON CENTENNIAL

The Times-Picayune Deluged With Good Wishes

Congratulations by letter, telegram and word of mouth continued to pour in Tuesday upon executives of The Times-Picayune and the newspaper, concerning both the celebration Monday of the 100th anniversary of its founding, and the quality and exhaustiveness of the edition with which it signalized the event.

Typical messages received Tuesday were:

R. L. Menuet, Acting President of Tulane University—"Tulane university has already expressed in your monumental centennial edition, through the board of administrators

Continued on Page Eleven

Stabbing Believed Accident; Occurred in Rehearsal at Opera House; Victim Was Chorus Basso

(Special to The Times-Picayune)
New York, Jan. 26. — The fatal stabbing of a chorus basso with a dagger reportedly wielded by Lawrence Tibbett, noted operatic and screen star, on the stage of the Metropolitan Opera House during a rehearsal, presented police with a new mystery of "death at the opera" tonight.

The victim, Joseph Sterzini, 50 years old, of Brooklyn died at 5:45 p. m. in Manhattan General hospital.

Continued on Page Four

Army Flashlight Bombs Shake Up City in New York

(By The Associated Press)
Merrick, N. Y., Jan. 26.—This Long Island town was thrown into panic tonight by two terrific blasts which broke windows, cracked plaster and sent hundreds of residents scurrying in fear to places of safety.

Colonel W. H. Frank, commander of the 18th Reconnaissance Squadron at Mitchell Field, said the blasts were apparently set off by two Douglas bombing planes sent aloft tonight to test a recently developed flashlight flare for night photography.

"The device consists of a parachute to which is attached a flashlight bomb," he explained. "It should go off immediately after leaving the ship but atmospheric conditions may have had some other effect and caused them to behave differently."

Police Lieutenant Joseph Stadel, whose office was swamped with telephone calls, said most callers believed either that the army ordnance works at nearby Baldwin had exploded or that Long Island was being bombed by hostile airmen.

Colonel Frank said the photographic device had been tried recently at Rochester, N. Y., and "they had a lot of trouble up there, too."

GIST OF THE NEWS

THE TIMES-PICAYUNE, New Orleans, Wednesday, January 27, 1937.
Cities are evacuated, deaths hit 132 and 750,000 are homeless as Ohio flood sweeps toward Mississippi river.
—Page 1
President Roosevelt and Secretary Perkins reprimand General Motors for refusing to attend peace parley on strike.
—Page 1
An opera chorus singer dies from a wound received during a rehearsal from a dagger in the hands of Lawrence Tibbett.
—Page 1
Martial law is proclaimed in Eastern Arkansas as militia starts task of removing 50,000 to safety.
—Page 7
A member of the House charges that Germans in Nazi uniforms are drilling in the United States.
—Page 9
Senator Ellender attacks American bankers underwriting $25,000,000 Canadian bond issue in maiden speech.
—Page 11
Senator Guffey asks study by Senate of criticism against supreme court made in book.
—Page 15
A cabaret dancer and a waitress are held in connection with death of two from carbon monoxide gas.
—Page 26

An act passed by a special session of the Legislature giving Louisiana's governor power over election boards is attacked in supreme court.
—Page 1
Property owners on South Carrollton and South Claiborne oppose "unzoning" of corners.
—Page 9
Stocks stumble on strike and flood news. Bonds lower. Grains mixed. Cotton higher. Sugar irregular; rice firm; coffee higher.
—Page 20-21

FLOOD DEATH TOLL HITS 132; OHIO CRESTS

Weather Bureau Forecasts Mississippi River Will Reach Peak of 21 Feet Here Late in February

Cincinnati Sees Water Recede from 80 Feet to 78.8; Evansville, Portsmouth Being Evacuated

SPILLWAY TO GIVE PROTECTION TO CITY

Bonnet Carre Floodway to Be Opened If Needed, Says Engineer, Pointing Out No Danger Exists

MISSISSIPPI'S DIKES TO BE BUILT HIGHER

Breaks Threaten in Levees at Helena, Three Other Points; Arkansas Put Under Martial Law

Coincident with a forecast by the United States weather bureau here that the Mississippi river will reach a crest stage of 21 feet at the Carrolton gauge by the latter part of February, Lieutenant-Colonel William F. Tompkins, in charge of the Second New Orleans District, United States Engineers, said Tuesday afternoon that if the river does reach a 21-foot stage he will ask permission of the chief of United States Engineers to open the Bonnet Carre spillway.

At the same time Colonel Tompkins issued a formal statement in which he said "it is my opinion that there is absolutely no danger for the city of New Orleans."

The spillway, which may be opened on authority of the chief of engineers, according to Colonel Tompkins, "will of course be opened long before there is any actual danger to levees in this area."

May Open Spillway
Colonel Tompkins reiterated a statement issued by W. F. McDonald...

Should the gauge at Carrollton reach 20 feet and remain at that point for several days the engineers here would recommend use of the

Continued on Page Two

Status of Record Ohio Valley Flood Briefly Reviewed

(By The Associated Press)
Washington — Admiral Cary T. Grayson, chairman of the Red Cross, reported 750,000 persons were homeless along 1500 miles of flood front. House approved and sent to the Senate $790,000,000 relief bill after President Roosevelt promised every cent would be used for flood victims if necessary. Federal agencies, including 50,000 WPA workers, moved to aid sufferers on wartime basis.

Louisville—Federal troops established military rule. Thirty of city's 40 square miles inundated. Ohio river stationary at 56.9 feet. Some 230,000 homeless.

Cincinnati—Water famine plagues city. Water covered a fifth of urban area. Some 65,000 homeless. Ohio river stood at fraction of an inch below 80 feet.

Memphis—Prediction of a "superflood" on lower Mississippi river sent emergency crews out to heighten levees.

Cairo, Ill.—Mississippi levees dynamited anew to divert flood burden to Missouri lowlands, relieve threat at Cairo.

Little Rock, Ark.—Martial law declared in Eastern Arkansas when Mississippi threatened to burst levees. Troops began evacuation of 50,000 in vicinity of Mellwood, near Helena.

Evansville — Evacuation of territory along the Ohio river in Southern Indiana attains major scale.

Continued on Page Five

CONGRESS TAKES LIGHTNING ACTION ON FLOOD RELIEF

$790,000,000 Fund Gets House Approval; Goes to Senate

(By The Associated Press)
Washington, Jan. 26.—The plight of 750,000 flood refugees brought lightning action in Congress today upon a $790,000,000 relief fund.

Without a record vote, the House approved the huge appropriation and sent it along to the Senate, where administration leaders planned similar fast action.

President Roosevelt promised that every cent of the fund would be used for flood victims if necessary. Originally he had requested it to finance general relief throughout the nation for the next five months.

Amendments Defeated
Administration forces in the House

BLAST CAUSES DEATH OF FOUR IN WATERS
(By International News Service)
Madisonville, Ky., Jan. 26.—Four men were killed today when the Flat Creek Mining Company's powderhouse exploded and threw them from a boat into surging floodwaters. Air pressure due to water pouring into the mine shaft was believed to have caused the explosion. Rescue workers immediately began a search for the bodies.

City's Flood Relief Quota May Be Raised by Tonight, Committee Heads Believe

More Than $8000 Donated Already; Individuals and Firms Will Be Called on for Rest of $35,000

The belief that New Orleans' quota of $35,000 for the flood sufferers will be raised by tonight was expressed at a meeting of an emergency committee which met in the mayor's parlor of the City Hall Tuesday afternoon.

President Roosevelt promised that New Orleans Public Service Inc., was elected chairman of the committee, and Burt W. Henry, attorney, vice-chairman.

In accepting the chairmanship, Mr. Paterson announced that New Or-

Continued on Page Six

STATE'S ELECTION LAW IS ATTACKED IN SUPREME COURT

Act Giving Governor Power Over Boards Called 'Unconstitutional'

The groundwork for testing validity of a 1935 extra session legislative act, which empowers the governor of Louisiana to control the board of election supervisors in each parish.

Continued on Page Fourteen

at Frankfort State Reformatory as prisoners were 'driven to frenzy by the rising water', of armed farmers preventing the cutting of levees. At Cairo, Ill., which stood on a danger-point between the Ohio and Mississippi Rivers, a desperate battle to save the town was in progress. Here a recently completed floodway (a sort of reserve 130,000 acre reservoir) was put to the test for the first time. Some 1,500 people had voluntarily chosen to live and farm the fertile land of this floodway that stretched seventy miles along the west shore of the Mississippi: when the waters began to flow it was reckoned that at least twenty per cent of them had ignored the warning to flee. Most,

though not all, were subsequently rescued. Further down the Mississippi Valley scores of other communities waited anxiously for the Ohio to shed its swollen burden on them, and wondered if their own levees and floodways would hold (by the time the flood crest passed New Orleans on 1 March, most of them were relieved to find that they had).

As the death toll climbed past the hundred mark an unprecedented national rescue operation was mobilized. President Roosevelt—who had himself sampled the miseries of the elements at his inauguration on the 20th, insisting on delivering his address outside as water poured down the pavements like trout streams and then driving in an open car through the beating rain—ordained that relief-work should be put on a war-footing. The Army and Navy were ordered into the disaster zone to perform superhuman tasks—in one case to build a 300-mile wall of sandbags and planks between New Madrid and Louisiana. By the end of January, so far as anyone could tell, a million and a half people had been driven from their homes and 4 billion dollars' worth of damage had been done. But at least the floods had receded, leaving behind their legacy of filth and confusion—and a deep-rooted conviction that nature must not be allowed to run its course again. As the *New York Herald Tribune* expressed the sentiment: 'The rains of the vast Mississippi basin have been rolling down to the sea in great flood waves from time to time since the beginning of history. But only in recent periods have they met populous communities to overwhelm in their course . . . Knowledge at best is scant. Many engineering problems presented in flood control work are difficult of solution. But confronting this recurrence of disaster, it seems obvious that the menace cannot be met piecemeal with those admixtures of haste, politics and logrolling that characterized so many earlier efforts.'

NEW YORK, FRIDAY, JANUARY 22, 1937

'FLOOD-PROOF' CITY TO LET IN THE OHIO TO ESCAPE DELUGE

PORTSMOUTH ACTS

Sirens Warn People to Flee Before Sewers Are Opened

WATERS SWEEP 10 STATES

80,000 Are Made Homeless as New Rains Bring Threat of Higher Floods

KENTUCKIANS RUN TO HILLS

Indiana Town Is Evacuated— Red Cross Masses Aid in Southern Illinois

By The Associated Press
PORTSMOUTH, Ohio, Jan. 21.— Screeching sirens and roaring factory whistles at 11 o'clock tonight gave citizens of Portsmouth four hours to abandon the low-lying business district before sewers were opened to let in the muddy Ohio River flood waters at 3 A. M.

City Manager Frank Sheehan had first decided to give the alarm at midnight, but ten minutes later he moved up the signal an hour, the time for evacuation being cut to four hours instead of the six previously agreed upon.

He estimated that by 5 A. M. the streets along the river front would be several feet deep in water.

The river was lapping around the 3,000 coin and other relief equipment by the only road that gives access to the city, which has 43,000 inhabitants. It was estimated that 15,000 of these would be affected by the flood.

The ferryboat Captain John sank while on refugee work in the Scioto River.

The National Guard rushed in with her leaped into the water, and Sheriff her leaped into the water, and Sheriff Brandell said he believed all reached safety.

Increasing seepage came through the dike protecting the city from the Scioto River.

Hitler Coups Cause Paris To Shut Bourse Saturdays

By The Associated Press
PARIS, Jan. 21.—According to the request of the Paris Brokers Association, the government announced tonight that the Bourse would be closed for the next six Saturdays.

Chancellor Adolf Hitler's habit of making important international pronouncements on that day had been cited by the association as partly responsible for the request.

The newspaper Paris-Midi, pointing out that the Paris market was virtually the only one to remain open on Saturdays, said that "the slightest international incident provokes disorders on the Bourse" and that, as a result, "professional traders are troubled—and sometimes Ministers."

SEAMEN HERE VOTE TO CALL OFF STRIKE

2,000 at Meeting Take Action Conditioned Upon Decision in Other Eastern Ports

PUT FAITH IN LABOR BOARD

Washington Hearings Today —Failing Resources, $10,- 000 Debt Influenced Men

After a five-hour closed meeting at which all outsiders were barred, 2,000 participants in the seamen's strike in this city voted last night to end their walkout if strikers in other Atlantic and Gulf ports would take similar action.

Their action apparently was the first of several moves which it is believed will end the maritime strike that has hampered shipping from Portland, Me., to Goose Creek, Texas, for nearly three months.

The decision of the meeting here has no relation to the strike of seamen on the West Coast. In fact, it was pointed out, that calling off the fight in the East would also be contingent upon assurances that the West Coast unions that it not interfere with their
Final Action

Comparative

FOUNDED 1865

Francisco Chronicle
THE CITY'S ONLY HOME~OWNED NEWSPAPER

SAN FRANCISCO, CAL., MONDAY, JANUARY 25, 1937

DAILY 5 CENTS, SUNDAY 10 CENTS

Weather
Fair, Becoming Unsettled
Complete Weather Report on Page 23

ROOSEVELT COMMANDS WAR-TIME ACTION IN EASTERN DISASTER ZONE; FLOOD AND FLAMES SWEEP CITIES

Employers, I.L.A. Making Progress In Peace Parleys

Accord Appears Within Reach as New Meeting Set Today to Determine Status of Checkers, Clerks

Employers and longshoremen's negotiators took steady steps yesterday in the direction of a settlement—and that accord, if and when reached, promises to be the "break" in the maritime strike.

It may come today—and it may not.

The two groups spent a large portion of yesterday in a discussion of the status of cargo checkers and clerks who are affiliated with the International Longshoremen's Association. They probably will meet again today to
to see how closely they can come
longshoremen on an eight-hour day

Strike Peace Ratified on East Coast

Pacific Maritime Unions Place Approval on Action Ending Walkout

Houston, Jacksonville, Mobile, Providence Oppose Action

NEW YORK, Jan. 24 (UP)—The three-month insurgent seamen's strike on the East and Gulf coast was officially ended tonight when a majority of ports of these sections and the Pacific maritime unions ratified the action.

Termination of the strike was announced at a noisy session of 200 seamen in Stuyvesant High School. All but Stuyvesant, Providence, Jack-

State Offices Face Shakeup After Inquiry

Investigation Expected to Develop Into Drive for Democratic Control

Assembly Committee to Discuss Probe at Meet Today

By EARL C. BEHRENS
SACRAMENTO, Jan. 24—California's State Administration and all of its various agencies and departments face a legislative investigation which may produce political shakeup with many ramifications.

Tomorrow afternoon the new $10,000 Assembly Committee on state governmental organization, consisting of seven Democrats and two

Panic Seizes Louisville

Fire Rages in Cincinnati

Flames, Oil-Fed and Borne on Water, Rage Along Three-Mile Front; Ohio River Climbs Higher

(By Associated Press)
CINCINNATI, Jan. 24—Flames 300 feet high floated through Cincinnati's flooded Mill creek industrial district today and wrought damage estimated at $1,500,000 while the ponderous Ohio river set a new flood mark of 76.2 feet and brought a water shortage to plague this district's 65,000 homeless.

Fire Chief Barney Houston made the damage estimate tonight after announcing the spectacular fire had been brought under control.

At the same time, Chief Houston

Roosevelt Orders Army, Navy Into Stricken Sectors; Fifty Dead, at Least 400,000 Homeless

CHICAGO, Jan. 24 (AP)—The Federal Government's strength was thrown into the fight tonight against suffering and terror in the Ohio valley.

President Roosevelt ordered the army, navy, Coast Guard, Works Progress Administration and Civilian Conservation Corps forces pitted against the flood with virtual war time vigor.

Louisville was a blighted city. The Mayor, expecting power to fail at any moment as darkness added to the flood horror,

At a Glance

Fire in the Sky

The Hindenburg Crash 1937

EXTRA

FIRST PICTURES

Taken at Hindenburg Tragedy Scene

EXTRA

COMPARATIVE TEMPERATURES			
	High Low		High Low
San Francisco 56	49	Denver 70	48
San Jose .. 68	46	New York ... 70	54
Los Angeles.. 64	56	Chicago 58	44
Seattle 76	46	New Orleans. 84	66
Honolulu 76	42	Salt Lake .. 74	52

San Francisco Chronicle

THE CITY'S ONLY HOME-OWNED NEWSPAPER

Weather

Partly Cloudy

Complete Weather
Report on Page 39

FOUNDED 1865 — VOL. CL, NO. 112   CCC   SAN FRANCISCO, CAL., FRIDAY, MAY 7, 1937   DAILY 5 CENTS, SUNDAY 10 CENTS;

HUGE ZEP EXPLODES!
HINDENBURG DESTROYED, 33 DIE

Photodrama

At the exact moment the Hindenburg exploded at Lakehurst last night an Associated Press staff photographer had his camera focussed on the mammoth dirigible and captured one of the most remarkable news photos ever taken.

Here is that picture:

The Zeppelin exploded with a terrific roar over the airport as it neared the mooring mast after a transatlantic journey from Germany.

Murray Becker, an ace cameraman of the New York A. P. staff, had been assigned to cover the arrival and as the ship dropped her lines to be hauled in to the navy mooring mast, was snapping pictures. Thus his camera in a series of pictures recorded one of the most shocking air disasters in recent years

Those pictures are on Page B—a full page!

WIREPHOTO

Crowd Views Holocaust at Lakehurst

LAKEHURST, N. J., May 6 (AP) —Germany's great silver Hindenburg, the world's largest dirigible, was ripped apart by an explosion tonight that sent her crumpling to the naval landing field a flaming wreck with horrible death to about a third of those aboard.

Exactly how many died was still in dispute, as the flames licked clean the twisted, telescoped skeleton of the airship that put out from Germany 76 hours before on its opening trip of the 1937 passenger season.

The American Zeppelin Company, through its press representative, Harry Bruno, placed the toll at 33 of the 97 aboard. The company listed 20 of the 36 passengers and 44 of the 61-man crew as the disaster's survivors.

These figures were at slight variance with unofficial estimates of the number of dead.

In the crowded hospitals in the communities neighboring this hamlet in the pine covered New Jersey coastal plain, many of the survivors were in critical condition, a number suffering from excruciating burns. Some were so gravely injured, among them Captain Ernest Lehman, that the last rites of the Roman Catholic church were administered to them. Lehman, skipper of the ship's 1936 flights, made the ill-fated flight as an observer. He was listed among the injured survivors.

Storms and buffeting headwinds had delayed the slim, graceful ship far behind her schedule for the maiden trip, and she nosed down in the early evening to keep the unexpected rendezvous with disaster.

She had been due to tie up at the mooring mast at 5 a. m. (E.S.T.) but radioed last night that the bad weather had retarded her speed so

much that she would land around sunset.

IN FULL VIEW OF CROWD

After cruising down over New York's crowded streets in the afternoon, she hove into sight at the air station here at 3:12 p. m. but landing conditions were not favorable and she circled around idly in full view of the small crowd of spectators who had assembled for what was to be a routine hurry-up ar-

rival and departure. A rainstorm came up and whipped across the field and Captain Pruss decided to ride it out to make sure of most favorable landing conditions.

Rain was still falling lightly when she headed into the mooring circle shortly after o'clocks, nosing down gracefully and with the nice precision that had marked so many of her arrivals last year.

The ground crew of sailors, sold-

iers and marines moved out onto the field to handle her landing ropes. Lower she nosed, her Diesel motors throttled down. Passengers gaily waving at the crowd, lined the long lounge windows which showed like transparent slits in the great silver belly of the ship.

LANDING ROPES LET OUT

The spider-like web of landing ropes snaked down the little trap doors in the nose. Men of the ground

crew grabbed them at the wooden crossbars.

It was 6:23.

Then came the terrific explosion, and red flames sudenly splashed out toward the stern and the rudder that bore the red-and-black Nazi swastika. The detonation tore the ship in half as if it were made of paper. The tail dropped earthward. The blunt nose bobbed up, hung a moment in the air and then crumpled toward the field, flames running along its sides and its fabric flaking off in big chunks. Passengers and men of the crew were hurled through the walls of the Hindenburg to the sandy loam below. The crowd receded in a panicky surge to the shouts of "run for your lives." Navy men dashed into the flaming debris to make rescues.

ADDITIONAL BLASTS

girders and aluminum beams, the Collapsing in a tangled mass of

ship was torn by a series of additional explosions, lesser in force than the first shattering blast. And the flames roared up in a red and yellow wall to envelope the ship that had seemed so durable and safe a few short minutes before.

Night came down. A steady stream of ambulances carried away the injured. Badly burned bodies were gathered in a hastily improvised morgue and the grim task of identification begun.

As this went on passengers for the homeward trip of the Hindenburg unaware of the destruction which had overtaken the ship, were arriving to embark. Many planned to attend the coronation and the Hindenburg, until tonight, represented the fastest way of getting

(Continued on Page A, Col. 7)

HITLER STUNNED BY TRAGEDY

BERLIN, May 7 (Friday) (U.P.)—Reichsfuehrer Hitler was called from his bed early today to receive news of the worst disaster to German air transportation in history—loss of the proud dirigible Hindenburg.

The dictator apparently was

stunned by the news. He refused formal comment.

A report of the catastrophe was telephoned to the Chancellor and Propaganda Minister Joseph Goebbels. Later, DNB, official Nazi news agency, announced German Zeppelin traffic across the North Atlantic will continue

"unabated."

"A new dirigible, now building at Friedrichshafen, "will continue to carry the German flag across the Atlantic in the Hindenburg's place."

The statement emphasized the previous "safety of German Zeppelins."

THE WEATHER
Today: Fair, little change in temperature
Tomorrow: Fair, little change in temperature
Temperatures yesterday: Max. 71; Min. 54
Detailed Report on Page 35

NEW YORK
Herald ⚜ Tribune

LATE CITY EDITION

Vol. XCVII No. 33,045

(Copyright, 1937, New York Tribune Inc.)

FRIDAY, MAY 7, 1937

TWO CENTS In Greater New York | THREE CENTS Within 300 Miles | FOUR CENTS Elsewhere

Hindenburg Explodes at Lakehurst, 34 Die;
Dirigible, Landing, Falls 500 Feet in Flames

Horror Dazes Field Crowd Unable to Aid

Allen, Herald Tribune Aviation Editor, Pictures Spectacle He Sees as 'Most Terrible' of Air

Storms Kept Ship Drifting 3 Hours

Air Station a Madhouse of Activity as Trucks and Ambulances Race Out to Succor Victims

By C. B. Allen
Herald Tribune Aviation Editor

LAKEHURST, N. J., May 6.—Spectators peering through the light rain at the ground crew walking the Hindenburg to her mooring mast at the air field here tonight froze silent and then cried out in horror when they saw flames flare out from the hulk of the giant airship on the starboard side, a third . . . the way forward from the tail, and spread in a great burst down the length of the ship.

Most of them had waited wearily at the field from the time, 4:15 p. m., when the Hindenburg was first sighted from the Naval Air Station. Through a gusty wind and unsuitable landing conditions the big ship passed over the field, evidently preferring not to attempt a landing, and continued on to the Atlantic seacoast.

Soon after the airship passed over the Naval Air Station, a series of thunderstorms approached from the southwest. These gradually drew nearer the field and blocked any effort by the airship for an attempted landing until a few minutes after 7 o'clock. At this time the storm had passed over the field

Herald Tribune photos—Acme
The Hindenburg exploding above the Lakehurst field

63 Survive in Plunge Of Burning Zeppelin

World's Largest Airship Shattered as She Approaches Mooring Mast at End of Season's First Flight

Static Electricity Theory Is Advanced as a Cause

Commander Pruss and Captain Lehmann Saved; Latter Believed Dying; Ground Crew in Peril; Heat Drives Rescuers Back From Ship

The German dirigible Hindenburg, largest airship ever built, was destroyed by explosions and fire at 7:23 o'clock last night as she swung toward her mooring mast at the Naval Air Station, Lakehurst, N. J. Thirty-four of the ninety-seven persons aboard were known to have lost their lives in the crash of the great airliner. Twenty of the thirty-six passengers and forty-three of the sixty-one officers and members of the crew escaped.

Of the survivors, however, many are expected to die of their injuries suffered as the 804-foot dirigible fell to earth in flames a few seconds from the scheduled end of her first 1937 crossing to the United States.

Among these is Captain Ernst A. Lehmann, former commander of the Hindenburg, who served in an advisory capacity on the flight, the first of eighteen round-trip crossings scheduled for this year. Suffering from third-degree burns, he received the last rites of the Roman Catholic Church in Paul Kimball Hospital, Lakewood, and called for a German interpreter, to whom he dictated his will. Captain Max Pruss, commander of the airliner, also is in Paul Kimball Hospital, but less seriously injured.

The Hindenburg, which sailed from Frankfort, Germany, on Monday night, was destroyed on the first anniversary of her departure on her first voyage to North America from Germany.

Zeppelin Dead And Survivors

Identified Dead

Four hours before the Hindenburg settled to the rain-soaked Lakehurst Field, her 215 tons a smoking mass of twisted metal, she had crossed over New York City majestically, watched by thousands of persons who little reckoned that at dusk the

---

'The *Hindenburg* is floating down like a feather, ladies and gentlemen. The ropes have been dropped and they have been taken hold of by a number of men on the field. Passengers are looking out of the windows waving . . .' Herb Morrison, a radio commentator from station WLS Chicago, began his leisurely account for listeners of the German airship's arrival at Lakehurst Field on its first trip of the 1937 season. Out on the field newsreel crews from Pathe and Paramount, Universal and Fox began turning over their cameras automatically; a few photographers underneath the mast fiddled with their plates, to get some stock shots of the landing. In the Press Room reporters lounged about waiting for the passengers to disembark —a few had even returned to New York after waiting all that day, 6 May, since 8.00am for the airship's delayed arrival. After all, it was hardly news any more—the *Hindenburg* itself had crossed the Atlantic ten times the previous year, and there weren't any outstanding celebrities on board.

'The ship is standing still now' Morrison continued his commentary. 'The back motors of the ship are holding it just enough to keep it . . .' Then his voice took on an agonized tone: 'It's broken into flames. It's flashing! Flashing, it's flashing terribly! It's bursting into flames and falling on the mooring-mast. This is terrible, this is one of the worst catastrophes in the world. Oh, the humanity and all the passengers. I told you . . . it's a mass of smoking wreckage. Honestly, I can hardly breathe . . . I'm going to step inside where I can't see it . . . it's terrible! Folks, I'm going to have to stop for a moment because I've lost my voice. This is the worst thing I've ever witnessed . . .'

As if mesmerized by the flames the cameramen, who were temporarily concentrating on the efforts of the ground-crews, failed to redirect their lenses for several vital moments. Cinema audiences the next day observed the *Hindenburg* already a living pyre, the stern enveloped in flames, the fuselage melting away. It had all happened so fast—thirty-four seconds from the first puff of smoke to the ship's grinding, hideous collapse, an inferno from end to end. Some of the press photographers barely escaped with their lives. Recalled one of them afterwards: 'I'm practically underneath the mooring-mast and I'm shooting pictures every minute when blam! It went up. An explosion like a hollow boom, maybe like an explosion of a firecracker in a monstrous empty can. We saw the flames light out from near the tail . . . It started down nose first. Then another explosion. This one was in the middle of the ship and the Hindenburg went up just like a large ball of oil-soaked cotton waste dipped in flames. It started doubling as it fell . . . I didn't think of the people on it as I watched. I didn't think of the beautiful thing I had looked at a minute before. I only tried to keep my hands from fumbling as I slid the plates in.'

It didn't seem possible that any one of the ninety-seven people aboard could escape. Yet even as horrified spectators watched, they saw frantic passengers fling themselves from the burning hulk fifty feet to the ground. One of them, his face blackened, rushed straight for a hangar demanding to phone his mother in Chicago. Another, trapped in a gondola, was pulled out just before the scorching debris settled on it. Some were not so fortunate, mistiming their leap or being caught as the airship rebounded nearly 100 feet back off the ground. Within seconds would-be rescuers were driven back by the intense heat. A few survivors including Max Pruss, the captain, had to be forcibly restrained from dashing back into the flames to rescue the doomed. Thirty-five people perished in there or died of their appalling burns a few hours later.

The *Hindenburg* was the last of the great passenger airships. This tragedy at Lakehurst ensured that it *was* the last—not simply because of the horrific nature of the disaster, but also because (through the Press and screen) millions of people became eye-witnesses to it. Airships had been falling out of the sky with disturbing regularity in the thirty-seven years since Count Zeppelin's first rigid had taken reluctantly to the air. One by one, nations had abandoned the idea of lighter-than-air flight: France, Italy, Britain after the *R.101*, the United States in the wake of the *Akron* and *Macon*. Now only a devoted band of believers, mostly in Germany, continued to prophesy a commercial future for it. Foremost amongst these was the aging pioneer, Dr Hugo Eckener (sometimes called the 'father of the airship'). When the *New York Times* tracked him down in Austria on the telephone, his immediate reaction to the news was that the *Hindenburg* must have been sabotaged.

Some papers embraced the theory with enthusiasm, and the subsequent discovery of a Luger in the wreckage minus one bullet appeared to lend weight to the idea. So did the revelation that sabotage threats had previously been mailed to the German Embassy in Washington. The embassy itself, however, was the first to denounce the sabotage rumour—appreciating only too well the diplomatic indelicacy of it. Pressure was put on Eckener to recant in a public broadcast, following which he opted for the 'static electricity' explanation. This phenomenon—otherwise known as St Elmo's Fire—had been observed flickering around other airships, and at least one bystander claimed to have witnessed it in this instance. Conflicting evidence was offered by other witnesses who swore that the first flame came from a motor gondola. Perhaps an engine had exploded? Or perhaps an unseen lightning bolt had struck the ship. Or perhaps a passenger had inadvertently struck a match?

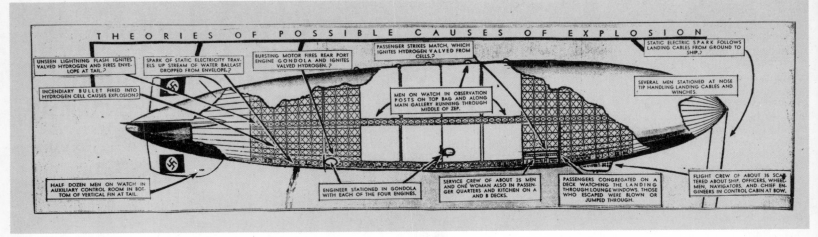

THEORIES OF POSSIBLE CAUSES OF EXPLOSION

UNSEEN LIGHTNING FLASH IGNITES VALVED HYDROGEN AND FIRES ENVELOPE AT TAIL.?

INCENDIARY BULLET FIRED INTO HYDROGEN CELL CAUSES EXPLOSION?

SPARK OF STATIC ELECTRICITY TRAVELS UP STREAM OF WATER BALLAST DROPPED FROM ENVELOPE.?

BURSTING MOTOR FIRES REAR PORT ENGINE GONDOLA AND IGNITES VALVED HYDROGEN.?

PASSENGER STRIKES MATCH, WHICH IGNITES HYDROGEN VALVED FROM CELLS.?

MEN ON WATCH IN OBSERVATION POSTS ON TOP BAG AND ALONG MAIN GALLERY RUNNING THROUGH MIDDLE OF ZEP.

STATIC ELECTRIC SPARK FOLLOWS LANDING CABLES FROM GROUND TO SHIP.?

SEVERAL MEN STATIONED AT NOSE TIP HANDLING LANDING CABLES AND WINCHES.

HALF DOZEN MEN ON WATCH IN AUXILIARY CONTROL ROOM IN BOTTOM OF VERTICAL FIN AT TAIL.

ENGINEER STATIONED IN GONDOLA WITH EACH OF THE FOUR ENGINES.

SERVICE CREW OF ABOUT 25 MEN AND ONE WOMAN ALSO IN PASSENGER QUARTERS AND KITCHEN ON A AND B DECKS.

PASSENGERS CONGREGATED ON A DECK WATCHING THE LANDING THROUGH LOUNGE WINDOWS, THOSE WHO ESCAPED WERE BLOWN OR JUMPED THROUGH.

FLIGHT CREW OF ABOUT 35 SCATTERED ABOUT SHIP, OFFICERS, WHEELMEN, NAVIGATORS, AND CHIEF ENGINEERS IN CONTROL CABIN AT BOW.

Wirephoto Brings Spectacular Pictures of Crash of Dirigible Hindenburg in Which 41 Met Death

The giant dirigible Hindenburg as it burst into flames over the landing field at Lakehurst, N. J., last evening. The nose of the ship is moored to the mast at the lower left. The flames are raging in the rear end. Minutes after this remarkable picture was taken the ship plunged to the ground. This picture and the two below were taken by photographers on hand to see the landing and sent to Chicago by Associated Press Wirephoto.

All these theories were seriously considered and endlessly debated. But all of them presupposed one additional hazard: that somewhere in the ship there was a gas leak. To account for this Eckener suggested that the landing manoeuvres had caused a bracing wire to snap and gash open a gas-cell, and his explanations—though inconclusive—appeared most likely to satisfy the investigating board.

With a fanaticism that seemed endemic to the country at that time, Germany blithely declared it would resume the transatlantic airship service as soon as possible. As well as hastening work on a new edition of the *Graf Zeppelin*, the official Nazi newspaper announced, yet another ship was projected 'for which workers are already contributing generously from their earnings'. This news revived a longstanding bone of contention: America's ban on the export of helium. The *Hindenburg* had originally been designed to carry helium, a non-explosive gas, instead of hydrogen which had more than once proved lethal—but the USA was the world's sole producer of helium and had had no intention of bestowing any on a warmongering dictator, not unreasonably.

The *Hindenburg* disaster offered a powerful argument to the lobby that was pressing for the helium ban to be lifted: if the Germans were dead-set on persevering with these elephantine machines, surely it was inhuman deliberately to allow them to remain floating time-bombs? For a while Congress agreed, and lifted its embargo. Ironically it was Germany herself who signed the airship's death warrant—or more properly, Hitler (whose name the *Hindenburg* would have carried to Lakehurst Field but for the Fuehrer's own ineradicable superstition). In March the following year he invaded a defenceless Austria, dispelling any lingering doubts about his peace-loving protestations. The trickle of helium dried up instantly: eighteen months later Germany's last two airships were pulled to pieces, to make Messerschmidts.

The Hindenburg: Bomb, Bullet, Lightning, Backfire?

ZEPP COMMANDER DIES OF BURNS

Wife's Vain Dash By Air

EXPERTS PROBE SABOTAGE THEORY

TRAGEDY which stalked all day amid the tangled ruins of the burned-out Atlantic Zeppelin Hindenburg, was intensified late last night by the death in hospital at Lakehurst, New Jersey, of Captain Ernst Lehmann, joint commander of the airship, while his wife was flying from Berlin to Cherbourg to sail to his bedside.

Four official inquiries, 24 hours after the crash, were already under way, and Dr. Hugo Eckener, the airship's designer, will sail from Cherbourg to-day with a commission which includes German Air Ministry chiefs to co-operate with the United States Authorities.

Sensational evidence is likely when the inquiries are completed, for here is what those in closest touch with the disaster had to say about its causes:

SABOTAGE.—Mr. D. C. Roper (U.S. Secretary of Commerce): Every phase will be investigated. Sabotage is one of them.

Dr. Eckener: I have repeatedly received anonymous letters warning the Hindenburg not to land at Lakehurst. . . . I do not rule out the possibility of a bomb in the mail. . . .

Some New Jersey aviation officials suggest: "Someone may have fired an incendiary bullet." The German Ambassador says there is no sign of this.

BACKFIRE.—This is the view most widely held by scientists, who believe that, since hydrogen was being released from the airship as she sank to moor, a spark from the exhaust of the throttled-down engines ignited this gas.

LIGHTNING.—Dr. Eckener, in a later statement, said he had received news from the United States which showed him there was little to support the sabotage theory, and added: "It is possible that lightning was the cause."

Herr von Meister (vice-president, American Zeppelin Co.): "The explosion may have been due to static conditions after the thunderstorm."

Of all the eye-witness stories of the disaster, none is more poignant than that of a mother, who (as described in Page 10), threw her two children from the blazing dirigible before she leapt for life herself.

Death Roll of 32

From Our Own Correspondent

NEW YORK, Friday.

The latest figures in the Hindenburg disaster are:

32 dead.

65 survivors.

Twenty-nine of the bodies have been identified. One of the three missing, presumed to have been consumed in the fire, is Mr. Charles Seymour Higgins, of London.

Twelve passengers, 19 crew, and one member of the ground staff comprise the dead.

Germany's faith in Zeppelins remains unshaken. Herr Hitler is expected to open a national fund for the building of a successor.

A striking radio picture of the Zeppelin Hindenburg crashing in flames at Lakehurst. Blazing débris dropping from the sky, and the vivid light from the fiercely burning envelope combine to make an awesome spectacle. Left: Dr. Hugo Eckener (right) at Vienna yesterday before he flew to Berlin on his way to New York to investigate the disaster.

'Something Strange' —*An Expert*

From Our Special Correspondent, LIONEL G. SHORT

LAKEHURST, New Jersey, Friday Nigh

WAS the destruction of the Hindenburg due to sabotage?

This startling possibility was put forward as four separate inquiries into the disaster of which the whole world is talking began here to-day.

Mr. D. H. Roper (United States Secretary of Commerce), announcing that every phase must be examined, states The question of sabotage will be one. I have instructed Mr. Harold Hartney to find out about that.

Senator Copeland (chairman of the Senate Committee investigating air safety): Evidence will be sought by the committee as to whether anti-Nazis are responsible

Mr. G. R. Wilson (Aviation Director of New Jersey) There was something very strange about the explosion. The Hindenburg had stopped completely and was preparing to moor when the flames broke out at the back

German Consulate officials, who also rushed to Lakehurst, declared: We cannot believe that the disaster was an "Act of God."

Count Zeppelin, nephew of the great inventor, when he learned of the disaster in Chicago, surmised that sabotage might be the cause.

Turning to possible scientific explanations, the most generally accepted among experts is that hydrogen, which was being released from the back of the airship, was ignited by sparks from the exhausts as the great engines were throttled down.

Herr F. W. von Meister, vice-president of the American Zeppelin Company, also surmises that the fire might have been caused by static conditions

The German Ambassador, who flew from Washington, remarked: "It must not cause us to lose faith in dirigibles, because the Graf Zeppelin has operated safely and efficiently for eight years."

The Goodyear Zeppelin Company states that it will continue building its £1,500,000 dirigible intended for European trade. The company has two on order, but their use over the Atlantic is dependent on obtaining the Government mail contract.

Suggestions of sabotage recall an incident in New Jersey last Wednesday, when someone fired a bullet through the tank of a flying aeroplane.

One theory is that if the Hindenburg were sabotaged a similar happening might have been the cause.

General Friedrich Bötticher, Air Attaché at the German Embassy, after exhaustive inquiries at Lakehurst, reported to the Embassy that there seemed little likelihood that the Hindenburg could have been destroyed by an incendiary bullet.

"Has the Airship Any Future?" by Captain Norman Macmillan, in Page 8.

CAPTAIN DIES CRYING 'WATER!'

From Our Special Correspondent

LAKEHURST, New Jersey, Friday Night.

CAPTAIN LEHMANN, commander of the Hindenburg, died in hospital here this evening.

Terribly burned, he had been lying staring at the ceiling all day crying "Water, water."

With his clothes ablaze he had staggered from the wreckage soon after the dirigible crashed last night, and his last coherent words were: "I can't understand it . . . I can't undrestand it . . ."

As he lay in agony the Last Sacrament was administered to him.

Now he is dead—and Capt. Max Pruss, the other commander of the Zeppelin, is stated to be very critically ill.

A LONDON RAIDER

Captain Lehmann was for nearly a quarter of a century with the Zeppelin Company, which he joined about a year and a half before the war started.

He had flown the Atlantic more than 100 times, in the Los Angeles, when it was delivered to the United States in 1924, in the Graf Zeppelin, and the Hindenburg.

Early in the war he bombed the fortifications of Antwerp. Later he was on the eastern front with an airship. In March 1917 he set out to bomb London but was beaten by fog and crashed at Maubeuge. On one occasion when flying the LZ 98 his airship was struck by lightning.

Wife's Air Dash

From Our Own Correspondent

FRANKFURT-ON-MAIN, Saturday Morning.

Shortly before news of Captain Lehmann's death reached here, Frau Lehmann, his wife, lef by aeroplane for Cherbourg, where she planned to board the Europa to sail to the United States to be with him.

German universities have been forbidden to grant the degree of "Doctor"—equivalent to that of Master of Arts—to Jews who are German subjects.

The Queen Mary's Bid For Record

By MICHAEL KILLANIN

(BY RADIO TELEPHONE)

A HINT that the Queen Mary may dock at Southampton to-morrow night in time to regain the Blue Riband of the Atlantic from the French liner Normandie was given to me last night when I spoke by radio telephone to Sir Victor Wilson, president of the Motion Picture Distributors of Australia, who is one of the passengers coming here for the Coronation.

Rushing through a calm Atlantic the Queen Mary is bringing nearly 2,000 visitors from the United States, Canada, and Australia.

"The ship's speed has been kept a secret from the passengers," Sir Victor said, "but I have been told that we may reach England on Sunday night—some hours before we are scheduled to arrive on Monday.

"I understand that we have been averaging well over 30 knots since passing the Ambrose Lightship, in New York Harbour.

"You cannot imagine what the excitement about the Coronation is like on board. The ship is just crammed. Women seem to be in the majority.

"There are scores of well-known people aboard—representative of the stage, business, and every profession.

RICHEST GIRL

"Gertrude Lawrence, who has been playing in New York, is a passenger. She is a centre of admiration. Then there are Mr. and Mrs. Jimmy Cromwell. Mrs. Cromwell is better known as Miss Doris Dukes—the richest girl in the States."

The Blue Riband is awarded for the highest average speed across the Atlantic from the Ambrose Light to the Bishop Rock, Scilly Isles.

The Normandie gained the trophy with an average speed of 30.31 knots on March 28. In August last year the Queen Mary won it with a speed of 30.63 knots.

U.S. to Allow Export of Helium

NEW YORK, Friday.

Shocked by the catastrophe to the Hindenburg, the Senate Military Affairs Committee to-day approved a Bill to liberalise the commercial sale and export "in quantities not of military importance," of helium, the non-inflammable lighter-than-air gas, of which the United States has a monopoly.—Reuter.

Use of helium instead of hydrogen would, it is believed by those who favour lighter-than-air craft, make airships safe at least from fire.

Bus Strike Decision To-day

By An Industrial Correspondent

THERE was good news last night in all the labour disputes, except that of the miners, where there is a fresh deadlock.

Mr. Ernest Brown, the Minister of Labour, will meet both sides in the London bus dispute to-day, and it is expected that a decision will be reached about noon.

It is hoped that the men will return to work on Monday.

Some of the provincial busmen have agreed to resume work this morning. They struck without authority, and agreed last night to accept the advice of their leaders in the Transport and General Workers' Union to go back on the terms which existed when they ceased work, provided that there is no victimisation. Others are still holding out—without union sanction.

In the case of the London bus

Continued in Page 10, Col. 5

"MY CORSICAN LOVER LIED FOR VENGEANCE"

From Our Special Correspondent

NICE, Friday.

"IN a flat of Mme. Arbel was found a ticket giving her weight. This weight, added to that of the trunk when empty, corresponds exactly with the weight of the heavy trunk you registered at the railway station."

In slow, measured tones the chief judge at the Assize Court addressed these words to the handsome 27-years-old gigolo, Robert Egender, central figure in the "murder trial without a body," which opened here to-day.

Egender is charged with murdering Mme. Renée Arbel, wealthy widow of 50, with whom he had been on intimate terms. It is alleged that he killed her in her luxurious flat in the Avenue Felix-Faure at Nice, and took her body in a trunk to his mother's home at Viviers, many miles distant.

A human trunk was found in a river near the home of Egender's mother, but pathologists were unable to determine whether it was Mme. Arbel's or even whether it was that of a man or woman.

Love Affair at 15

Egender was smartly — almost flashily—dressed when he stepped into the dock. His sleek hair was brushed back, and he wore a red bow tie with white spots, blue shirt and double-breasted waistcoat.

The court was told that from an early age he was a dissolute character

"At the age of 15 you had an affair with a married woman which led to her divorce," stated the prosecutor, Maitre Dalesme. "You have associated with innumerable women in your life."

Egender denied again and again that he murdered Mme. Arbel, or that he knew where she was.

"You became her lover," declared Maitre Dalesme. "How long did this liaison last?"

"A month," was the reply.

Missing Witness

Egender added that the affair ended when Mme. Arbel told him she was going for a holiday, and asked him to buy her a large trunk—the trunk in which he is believed to have removed her body.

The most important witness, the raven-haired Corsican, Thérèse Buttafoghi, once passionately in love with Egender, was missing to-day. It was she who informed the police that Egender had told her he had murdered Mme. Arbel and buried her in his mother's garden.

The judge ordered that a telegram should be sent to Bastia, in Corsica, ordering that Thérèse should travel to Nice by aeroplane at once.

Egender claimed that his former sweetheart had made false statements for vengeance. "Once she said to me, 'I am Corsican. Sooner or later I will have revenge,'" he said.

A list of objects found by the police in their search in the garden of Egender's mother was read, and it did not include a pink chemise said to have been found at the time of the tragedy.

This discrepancy was commented on by the defending counsel.

The trial was adjourned.

LATEST NEWS

NO MORE HANGING IN CALIFORNIA

San Francisco, Friday.

Governor Merriam to-day signed a Bill abolishing hanging as the death penalty in California and substituting for it the lethal gas chamber.—Exchange.

3

STORM EXTRA! — LIST OF VICTIMS ON PAGE 11

Boston Evening Globe

Reg. U. S. Pat. Off.

Copyright, 1938, by the Globe Newspaper Co.

LATEST NEWS
and SPORTS

CLOSING PRICES

7:30 FINAL COMPLETE

VOL. CXXXIV   NO. 74   Entered as second class mail matter at Boston, Mass. under the act of March 3, 1879—242 Washington St.

BOSTON, THURSDAY EVENING, SEPTEMBER 22, 1938—28 PAGES—2 CENTS

HURRICANE DEAD 275

Will the Hurricane Return?

There is no reason to anticipate that the New England hurricane will make a return visit, G. Harold Noyes, chief of the United States Weather Bureau here, said this afternoon. Yesterday's big wind has petered out, he said, somewhere in the wilds of Quebec. All is serene on the weather map and sunny skies are in prospect.

SUMMARY OF HAVOC

10,000 evacuated from homes in Springfield as flood crest is awaited at 10 o'clock tonight.

New Haven train rolled over at Stonington, Conn.

Western Express, Chicago to Boston on B. and A. marooned since 9 yesterday morning at West Brookfield.

Tidal wave at Buzzard's Bay.

CAMBRIDGE—Man killed by falling debris. Many hurt. Trees down. Church cupola blown off. Cambridge Post, A. L. does storm duty.

SOMERVILLE—Part of church roof collapses. All Police, Fire and Highway Department employees called out.

BROOKLINE—Damage at least $150,000.

DEDHAM—Headstones flattened in cemetery. All call firemen, off-platoon men and police reserves called.

BEVERLY—Yachts ashore. Heavy damage. A. L. Post helps clear trees from streets and local Boy Scouts give their aid.

EVERETT—Man fatally injured when struck by piazza roof torn off by wind. National Guard called out.

CONCORD—Part of 30-foot Concord Reformatory wall blown down, prison officials not alarmed. Roofs crushed by falling trees in several sections. Falling chimneys hurt several.

HINGHAM—More than 20 boats sunk in the harbor. Many more ashore.

LEXINGTON—Tree crashes

Summary
Continued on Page 10

VIEW OF RUINS OF FIRST UNITARIAN CHURCH ON MAIN ST., WORCESTER

Tidal Wave, Fire, Flood Follow Gale -- Many Areas Still Isolated

By JOHN BARRY

Death and devastation in the wake of the hurricane which veered from its seaward course to lash Boston and all New England last night left great areas of the East virtually paralyzed today.

In the work of reconstruction, clearing the debris of thousands of trees, wrecked homes, fallen wires, poles, washed-out roadbeds and tracks, thousands were engaged today. The W. P. A. in Massachusetts suspended all projects on orders of Administrator John J. McDonough to throw 80,000 workers into the breach and speed the clean up.

Transportation and communication facilities were at a standstill. Bridges are gone, rivers have climbed their banks to create inland flood conditions as menacing as the great flood of 1936. And along the sea, where a tidal wave of typhoon proportions smashed its way 1000 feet inland with a frightful toll of lives and property, the shores were strewn with dead bodies this morning.

Fear Death List Will Exceed 275

The mounting roster of the dead is expected to exceed the horrifying total of 275. Late today there were 243 known dead as a result of the tornado-like gale. Of that number 209 were in New England. New York, also hard hit, had 32 dead and in Jersey and Canada two were killed.

The toll of the hurricane in Massachusetts was 77 dead. In Rhode Island there were 87 bodies recovered from the sea and the floods. Connecticut had 31 known dead. In New Hampshire 13 died. In Vermont one person was dead.

Today the threat of disease hung over many New England cities. Water supplies had become polluted. Chlorinators were being put into use and anti-typhus serums were being flown by the National Guard to threatened areas.

Twenty-three different communities saw National Guardsmen patrolling their streets where the hurricane in its mad fury had left the thoroughfares as desolate as the shelled cities

Storm
Continued on Page 12

Chicago Daily Tribune
THE WORLD'S GREATEST NEWSPAPER

2 CENTS PAY NO MORE!

FINAL ★★

VOLUME XCVII.—NO. 227 C [REG. U.S. PAT. OFFICE COPYRIGHT 1938 BY THE CHICAGO TRIBUNE.] THURSDAY, SEPTEMBER 22, 1938.—36 PAGES [THIS PAPER CONSISTS OF TWO SECTIONS SECTION ONE] PRICE TWO CENTS [IN CHICAGO AND SUBURBS] [ELSEWHERE THREE CENTS]

115 DIE; HURRICANE RIPS EAST

The eyes of the world, in September 1938, were set anxiously on Germany. Herr Hitler was once again straining the fragile peace of Europe, demanding of Czechoslovakia the return of German-speaking Sudetenland to its 'rightful' owner (him). Observing the ineffectual diplomatic toings and froings of the Allies from across the Atlantic the *Chicago Tribune* concluded on **19 September**: 'Czechs Sacrificed to Hitler.' The preoccupations of the *New York Times* were similar—only a very small front page paragraph warned of more urgent headlines to come: 'Hurricane in Atlantic heads towards Florida.' A tropical disturbance of dangerous proportions, it warned, was roaring westward over the Atlantic Ocean. From then on both events moved on inexorably to their disastrous climax.

20 September. 'Czechs invade Germany' reported the *San Francisco Chronicle* (a little hastily); 'Hurricane Veering from Florida' announced the *New York Times*, 'Curving Path May Keep it at Sea.' The Bahamas had been spared, but Miami was still boarded up. The liner *Carinthia* was directly in the danger zone.

21 September. 'Give Up Allies Tell Czechs' was the *Chicago Tribune*'s lead; 'Loss Heavy As Rains Lash East' you would have found deep in your *New York Times* that morning, and probably wouldn't have worried until, further down—'Tropical Hurricane Rushing North, Is Expected to Hit Jersey Coast by Tonight.' And so it did, toppling Hitler's brinkmanship out of the headlines even on west coast papers.

22 September. It is self-evident from the Press this morning that a major disaster has occurred, even if its scale is still a little vague. Seven states from New Jersey to Vermont have been desolated by a freak of nature. Long Island has been struck by a tidal wave that has carried away holiday homes on the coast wholesale: in the midst of torrential flooding and total power failure, casualties cannot even be estimated—they are believed enormous. New York has been brought to a standstill by full gale-force winds that have caused the Empire State Building to sway. Throughout the state towers and radio masts have been blown down and houses, by the thousand, splintered to matchwood. Providence is under water and quite cut off from the world. Coastguards estimate literally hundreds of boats along the east coast have been battered to pulp. The *New York Times* tells of the strange adventures of Mr and Mrs Livingston Gibson of Westhampton Beach. Having climbed onto their roof for safety as the advancing sea surrounded their home, they suddenly found themselves (and their roof) swirled out to sea—along with a small snake and three rats who had also taken refuge there. The menagerie went sailing across Moriches Bay, finally to pile up on the Westhampton golf course. Mr and Mrs Gibson, the snake and the three rats all survived without injury. Almost the only concession to the hurricane made by Boston's *Christian Science Monitor* is the cryptic headline 'Flood Blocks Music Critic so Pianist Plays in Taxi.' However we do learn that the British Prime Minister is hoping personally to intervene with Hitler.

23 September. The storm-toll has exceeded anyone's imaginings: more than 400 dead, over 200 of these in the inundated city of Providence. The still-rising Connecticut River threatens

Storm Death Toll Near 600; Fear 130 Lost at Watch Hill; 36 Missing Hunted on L. I.

8 States Survey Losses of $200,000,000 and Care of 60,000 Homeless; Relief Is Rushed

New England Towns Get Typhoid Serum

Danger of Serious Floods Believed Past; Map of Coastline Is Changed by Chunks Torn by Surf

A death toll that may rise above 600, a total of at least 60,000 persons homeless and property damage exceeding $200,000,000 created a terrifying picture of desolation in New England, New York and New Jersey yesterday as the full force of Wednesday's hurricane and tidal wave was revealed. The force of wind and water so ripped away

Prof. Renshaw and Wife Killed In 19-Story Fall at Tudor City

Dr. Raemer Rex Renshaw, fifty-eight-year-old chemistry professor at New York University and former president of the New York Section of the American Chemical Society, and his wife, Mrs. Mary Wallace Renshaw, fifty, were killed shortly before midnight last night in a nineteen-story plunge, apparently hand in hand, from their apartment in Prospect Tower, 45 Prospect Place, Tudor City. Passersby said that the two bodies landed simultaneously six feet apart in a grassy courtyard on the Forty-third Street side of the building.

Detective Tony Fater, of the East Fifty-first Street police station, listed the deaths as double suicide, although no notes were found in the apartment.

A French window in the couple's three-room apartment on the nine-

research work at the university on Wednesday, with the beginning of the fall term. Dr. Hill, who could not suggest any motive for suicide, said that his associate's death would be a great loss both to the university and chemical research.

Dr. Renshaw's specialty was organic chemistry, in particular the chemical functioning of the blood and the endrocine glands of human beings. In September, 1937, in a paper which he read before the American Chemical Society in Rochester, N. Y., he described a drug, acetylcholine, which, he said, might cause a whole army to faint by lowering the blood pressure of the soldiers.

During the brief period of unconsciousness after shells containing acetylcholine had burst, the troops who were affected could be easily

Springfield and Hartford, forcing thousands to flee their homes. Along the south shore of Long Island, which had borne the brunt of the attack, thousands of houses have been levelled by the devastating 100mph gale, 'a raging screeching demon gone mad'. More than a hundred people are reported killed in Boston and Massachusetts, where bridges, roads and railways have disappeared en bloc. One express train at New Haven was marooned by the trespassing sea: before its 300 passengers could be evacuated the track had started to give way—initiating a panic-stricken stampede into the water. There is considerable concern for the safety of James Cagney, who was believed to be at his home on Martha's Vineyard when the storm struck: his studios have been unable to reach him. 'Chamberlain Sees Hitler, Urges Calm' reports the *New York Herald Tribune*.

24 September. The European crisis regains pride of place the further west you go today: 'France Begins to Mobilize' is the ominous news in the *Chicago Tribune*. But the hurricane news is worse too. Estimates by *Associated Press* and other sources indicate a death roll of 500 to 700, the higher figure including a putative one to two hundred believed swept out to sea by a huge wave at Watch Hill, R.I. as they stood watching the huge breakers pound the beach. Sixty thousand people are homeless, and President Roosevelt from his sickbed (with a cold) has initiated a vast federal relief programme—a little late for the *Chicago Tribune*: 'Part of the disaster might have been averted if the Roosevelt administration had not delayed construction of a much-needed flood control system. For three years plans and methods of

dealing with the waters in New England have been political footballs' it grumbles. An item from Providence reports that women (refugees) have been admitted to the exclusive Hope Club for the first time in its history. 'The oldsters at the club didn't like it' it went on. 'They said no good would come of it.' Martial law is in force in parts of Rhode Island, and National Guards have been shooting at looters in Cape Cod. On the Stock Exchange both the storm and the European crisis are blamed for a severe fall in trading.

Both Hitler and the hurricane had their way, though the after-effects in Europe took rather longer to remedy. In New England, however, the final account was staggering enough: over 600 people dead; 1,000 boats destroyed or damaged; 57,000 houses razed or shattered. But in the attendant welter of statistics one, above all, was almost impossible to comprehend. The *New York Times* summed it up a few weeks later: 'In the forests of Vermont, New Hampshire and N. Massachusetts the trees have been slaughtered as if by a mile-high giant plunging crazily through them and slashing with a half-mile scythe . . . Today the place is a grotesque waste of prostrate broken trunks, green tops and upturned roots flung about in wild confusion with perhaps a single battered tree still standing amid the ruins. That picture multiplied by 25,000, the estimated number of wood lots destroyed, gives some notion of the extent of the ravages the forests of New England suffered. The loss is officially put at 5,000,000,000 board feet.'

Forty-eight Hours on the Thetis

The Sinking of the Thetis 1939

Daily Express

WORLD'S LARGEST DAILY SALE

No. 12,179   Saturday, June 3, 1939   One Penny

ADMIRALTY LATEST: 'Regret hope of saving any further lives is now diminishing'

GAS CHOKING MEN IN SUBMARINE

HOW THETIS FOUNDERED

Nazis expel Poles

Daily Express Staff Reporter

BERLIN, Friday.

ANGERED by the stalemate over Danzig, Germany tonight revived her systematic expulsion of Polish Jews,

LATEST
CENTRAL 8000

Weather fair (see Page 11)

dropped last October after thousands of refugees had been stranded in a no-man's-land.

Notices to quit the Reich before July 1 were delivered to thousands of Polish Jews by German police officials.

It is estimated that 16,000 are affected.

Survivor tells of heroes' last hours

RESCUERS CARRY ON BY SEARCHLIGHT

86 trapped : 5 saved

TEN MINUTES AFTER MIDNIGHT TODAY AN OFFICIAL OF CAMMELL LAIRD'S, BUILDERS OF THE THETIS, SAID IN A BROKEN VOICE TO A HUSHED CROWD CLUSTERED ROUND THE GATES OF THE SHIPYARD IN BIRKENHEAD: "I AM SORRY BUT THERE IS NO HOPE FOR THE MEN REMAINING IN THE SUBMARINE."

It was stated that the vessel, lying on the mud in Liverpool Bay, had turned turtle while efforts were being made to raise her, preventing all chance of her being raised in time to cut into her hull.

Women wept at the news. Eighty-seven on board had been stated in the afternoon to be still alive.

Four escaped in the morning. Three more, it was reported in the evening, were dead.

Two of these were said to have made a desperate attempt to shoot themselves out of the conning tower and to have been drowned. One was Stoker W. T. Hole, of Plymouth; the name of the other is not yet known.

TAP SIGNALS CEASE

The third, according to one of the survivors, Mr. F. Shaw, went mad in the ship and died. When he escaped, said Mr. Shaw, the gas in the submarine was getting worse, and men were lying sprawled about the compartments, though there was no panic.

Then, at 12.35 a.m., news was received in Liverpool that one more had been rescued. Within a few moments ambulances sped to the landing stage to await the destroyer bringing him in. A green beacon was raised to guide the boat to her berth.

At ten o'clock the Admiralty had announced:

"The stern of the Thetis did not reappear as anticipated when the tide slackened about 6 p.m. and an attempt is now being made to lift the stern with pontoons. The Admiralty regret to state, however, that hope of saving any further lives is now diminishing.

As "zero hour" drew near today, rescue efforts were intensified. It had been calculated that by 1.40 a.m. the supply of air on board would be exhausted.

An officer in one of the destroyers on the spot, asked what were the chances of the men being saved, shook his head silently and walked away.

Anxiety had grown when, during the afternoon, no answering signals came to divers tapping on the hull. The last message came just after 3 p.m.; it was so faint as to be almost indecipherable. The Thetis, after having been partially raised several times yester-

▶ PAGE TWO, COLUMN FOUR

TORPEDO VALVES OPEN?

SUBMARINE experts last night formed this theory about the Thetis:

She was probably trapped by the flooding of the forward torpedo compartment. Only the forward torpedo compartment can be flooded if the commander reported, on reaching the surface, that all his men were safe.

Water might have entered through torpedo tube valves accidentally open, either during diving or testing.

In the event of flooding of the torpedo flat, the crew would at once blow compressed air into the water-filled forward ballast tanks.

This would have brought Thetis to the surface on an even keel had her bow not been held fast in the mud.

Wife told, "He died trying to escape"

Mrs. Caroline Hole, of Plymouth, wife of Stoker Hole, one of the men who died trying to escape from the Thetis, received this telegram last night: "Regret to inform you that Stoker Hole is believed to have died while endeavouring to escape from submarine Thetis. This will be confirmed when definite news is received. Submarines, Gosport."

Mrs. Hole was to have celebrated her first wedding anniversary today. The telegram was sent by the Commander, Submarines, Depot-ship Dolphin, Gosport.

180 FT WATER

A—Oil fuel storage tanks.
B—Engines.
C—Water release valves.
D—Air bottles.
E—Control room.
F—Conning tower.
G—Periscopes.
H—Batteries.
J—Escape chamber from which men using Davis escape apparatus emerge.
K—Torpedoes.

65 FT MUD

Stern of the Thetis was at one time above water; Daily Express diagram completes the picture; shows how the submarine was stuck in the mud. Here is the key to the diagram:—

Survivor says 'SUFFERED FROM GAS, BUT TALKED OF SPORT'

Daily Express Staff Reporter

LIVERPOOL, Friday Night.

LYING in a cabin of the tug Grebe Cock coming down the Mersey tonight from the sunken submarine Thetis, Mr. Frank Shaw, last to be rescued, said: "There is little hope for the other chaps."

Mr. Shaw rose to the surface at 10 a.m. today by the Davis escape apparatus and was picked up semi-conscious.

He had been gassed, and was apparently one of the strongest of the men trapped in various compartments of the Thetis.

'IT WAS AWFUL'

To Mr. Arthur Mawson, second engineer of the Grebe Cock, Mr. Shaw said: "It was awful last night. Two men tried to escape through the conning tower. They were both drowned. Another man lost his reason. He went mad and died also.

"When I left, the gas was getting worse. Men were lying sprawled in compartments. It seemed as if they were doomed to die, but there was no panic."

Mr. Mawson, with others in the tug, left Cammell Laird's yard with the Thetis on Thursday morning. Out in Liverpool Bay a lieutenant and a signaller were perched on the tug's bow. The Thetis was a mile away.

A signal passed between the submarine commander and the lieutenant on the tug.

It was one word: "Diving."

A minute later the Thetis settled

▶ PAGE TWO, COLUMN ONE

Capt. Oram was human buoy

CAPTAIN H. P. K. ORAM, Commander of the Fifth Submarine Flotilla for which the Thetis was intended, offered himself as the human buoy to mark the spot where the submarine sank.

The extraordinary revelation was made last night that the crew of the submarine were unaware that salvage operations were going on overhead.

Consequently Captain Oram volunteered to risk his life by delivering dead or alive news of the vessel's whereabouts.

Full story on Page Two. Other stories and pictures Pages Five, Six, Twenty.

COUNTESS SENT BACK

COUNTESS SCHULENBURG, daughter of a German general, was ordered out of Britain as soon as she landed at Croydon Airport yesterday.

See Page ELEVEN.

300,000 MEN will register for military training this afternoon.
Page NINE

GOLFING JUDGE sympathises with young general but gave judgment against him.
Page NINE

MP INVITED to attend mass protest meeting against higher fares.
Page SEVEN

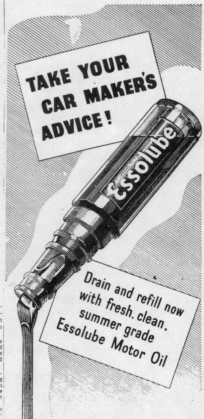

Evening Standard

To-morrow's Weather—
Little change.
See PAGE THREE.

Lighting-up Time
To-day 10.7 p.m.

No. 35,803   LONDON, SATURDAY, JUNE 3, 1939   ONE PENNY

HOPE IS FAINT NOW

Cammell Laird Believe Gas Escaped in Thetis; "Rumours" Answered

LATE THIS AFTERNOON IT WAS OFFICIALLY STATED BY MESSRS. CAMMELL LAIRD, BUILDERS OF THE SUBMARINE THETIS, THAT THERE WAS NOW NO HOPE OF SAVING ANY MORE OF THE MEN. THE ADMIRALTY, HOWEVER, STATED THAT THERE WAS STILL, IN THEIR VIEW, SLIGHT HOPE.

Rescue boats standing by near the scene of the disaster.

WHILE RESCUE EFFORTS CONTINUED UNABATED IN LIVERPOOL BAY, AN OFFICIAL OF MESSRS. CAMMELL LAIRD SAID: "WE HAVE NOW NO HOPE OF SAVING FURTHER LIVES."

He denied that there was any truth in the statement that they were contemplating blowing the vessel up. Now that there was no hope of saving life they would attempt to save the vessel.

"WE CONSIDER THAT THE MEN DIED FROM CHLORINE GAS," HE ADDED. "THE SHIP CARRIED A LARGE QUANTITY OF CHLORINE WHICH WE THINK WOULD ESCAPE OWING TO THE ANGLE AT WHICH SHE LAID."

On Page Twelve allegations about delay and the rescue methods employed are answered by the Admiralty and Cammell Laird.

Attempts were being made to get the Thetis into a horizontal position with the aid of "camels"—compressed air chambers—three of which were taken to the scene yesterday.

When the submarine is again on an even keel, it is likely that

(Continued on PAGE TWO)

Low's Topical Budget 7   Radio 16
Amusements Guide .... 8 & 9   Weekly Sports Guide 20

125

What happened in the Thetis: Last survivor tells
Daily Express the first full story

"THREE DIED, THEN I WAS TOLD TO GO"

Jokes, a jolt, drama on the sea bed

"Close all the doors!"

Men panic in escape chamber

One is pulled back, whispers 'The hatch won't open'

The air grew bad

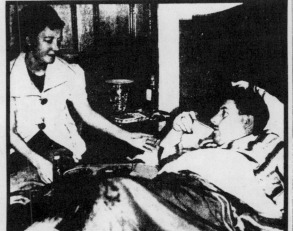

WIVES' PENSIONS FROM £180 TO £27

THE Admiralty, asked last night what provision will be made for the dependants—probably more than 400—of members of the Navy in the Thetis disaster, replied:—

"Rates are laid down in the case of dependants of members of the Royal Navy. They range from £180 a year in the case of a commander to 10s. 6d. a week for the widow of a seaman without eligible children."

"Pensions are at the discretion of the Admiralty, and the regulation rates could be altered if thought fit."

The case of civilians does not come within the Admiralty's consideration, but Cammell Laird's have announced that they will look after dependants of their employees.

Half million go back to work

Unemployment fell last month by 152,112—the largest April to May reduction on record—making the total fall this year 547,900, a record for the five-month period also.

There are now 1,492,282 registered as unemployed, and there are 12,687,000 insured workers in jobs.

Full story—Page Eleven. See also Page Fifteen.

Schacht says : "There will be no war"

Daily Express Correspondent

COLOMBO (Ceylon), Monday.—When he arrived here today during his tour of India, Dr. Schacht, ex-president of the Reichsbank, said:—

"There will be no war. I know Hitler's mind better than most. His one wish is to be friendly with Britain."

'WATER ROSE OVER MY HEAD . . . MY MIND WAS GOING'

By F Shaw

as told to O. D. Gallagher
(World copyright reserved)

Jowitt may head public inquiry

MR. CHAMBERLAIN, announcing in the House of Commons yesterday a full public inquiry into the loss of the Thetis, said it was caused by two forward compartments being flooded through one of the torpedo tubes.

The Daily Express Political Correspondent writes:—

The decision that there must be a searching public inquiry was taken by the Prime Minister himself.

I understand the inquiry will be made by a tribunal with powers of the High Court.

There will include the taking of evidence on oath, the power to order the production of documents and to compel any one to give evidence, and the authority to commit to prison for contempt of court any one who obstructs the inquiry.

Secret evidence

Normally, the inquiry will be in public, but the tribunal will have the right to sit in secret if the nature of the evidence to be given makes this course necessary in the public interest.

An eminent lawyer or a judge will preside, and in political circles last night the names of Lord Fairfield (formerly Lord Justice Greer) and Lord Macmillan (one of the Lords of Appeal) were being mentioned.

The name of Sir William Jowitt, K.C., former Socialist Attorney-General, has been submitted by the Opposition.

IT WAS A FINE MORNING WHEN WE LEFT CAMMELL LAIRD'S AT BIRKENHEAD ON THURSDAY IN THE THETIS FOR THE SUBMARINE TO DO HER ACCEPTANCE TRIALS IN LIVERPOOL BAY. THE SEA WAS VERY SMOOTH.

I was in the control room when the order was given to dive. I didn't think much about it: the ship had been down before.

But I did have an idea she began to dip a bit steeply, and soon the angle was very steep. Then we hit the bottom. There was a heavy jolt—not a crash or anything—but it sent every one flying off his feet. We fell against the forward bulkhead and had to catch hold of something to try to stand up.

The deck was cocked at about 45degs. Tools and binoculars and all sorts of loose gear came crashing down. Orders were given by shouts and by phone through the ship to shut all the watertight doors. We had to clamber about like monkeys because of the angle of the ship.

There was suddenly silence. All the machinery stopped—not because of the bump, but on orders from the control room. It was so quiet that you could hear men moving about. I looked at the men near me, and they looked at me. I suppose they realised, too, that something had gone wrong.

I helped to close our watertight doors. Though we were

FRANK SHAW, engine fitter to Cammell Laird's, and last man to see alive any of the ninety-nine victims of the Thetis disaster, lies in bed in his home in Ivydale-road, Birkenhead. His wife sits beside him.

Every window and door in the house is wide open. Shaw is ill from shock; if the doors and windows are closed he cries that he is trapped, he dreams he is back in the submarine.

On his cheeks and chin is the stubble of a beard that began to grow when disaster overtook the submarine. He is tired; his breathing is laboured.

His story is told slowly, four or five sentences at a time.

Abbey service?
The Dean telephones the Admiralty

LAST night the Daily Express suggested to the Dean of Westminster, Dr. Paul de Labilliere, that Westminster Abbey should hold a national service of remembrance for the men of the Thetis.

It was suggested that the service should coincide with the memorial services to be held tomorrow at Chatham, Portsmouth, and Devonport, on Merseyside, and near the buoy-marked waters where the submarine was last seen.

Westminster Abbey would hold more than 4,000 people for a service of remembrance.

The dean said later: "I want to do what is most fitting, and what will meet the wishes of all concerned. I have telephoned the Admiralty and put forward the suggestion.

"I am not bound by the other services have been arranged, and I want to see how the situation develops.

"But I would be ready, of course, to hold a service if the public feel that there should be one."

QUEEN MARY WILL DRIVE OUT AGAIN

QUEEN MARY has almost completely recovered from her car accident, says a bulletin by her doctors last night. She hopes to attend the Trooping of the Colour on Thursday.

The official statement adds:

"Her Majesty will proceed to the Horse Guards Parade by motor-car."

News Summary

M. TITULESCU, exiled Rumanian .)

On 1 June 1939, the British submarine *Thetis* sailed out into Liverpool Bay on her first—and last—voyage. For this auspicious occasion, the first of her diving trials, there were over a hundred people on board, officers from other submarines, Admiralty officials, and engineers from the shipyard, in addition to her regular crew. The weather was clear, calm and sunny and, at midday, from its station a mile away the escort tug *Grebecock* watched the submarine prepare for its first dive.

Thursday 1.40pm: the awaited signal came, just one word 'Diving'. Observers on the tug watched the *Thetis* submerge—at a rather steeper angle than anticipated since this dive was only supposed to be at periscope depth. Nevertheless, according to instructions the *Grebecock* steamed off on her pre-arranged course, expecting her ward to re-appear at any moment. But minutes turned into hours. By four o'clock she still had not surfaced: yet there were no distress signals coming through, nor could the tug find any trace of a marker buoy. But there *was* a marker buoy, far astern of the *Grebecock*'s position. It marked where the *Thetis* lay helpless, gripped tight by her prow in the mud.

Thursday 6.15pm: a message from the *Grebecock* has arrived at naval headquarters in Portsmouth, by the strangely pedestrian route of the Post Office. 'The *Thetis* has not surfaced.' At once an air-sea search operation was mounted, but it was another three hours before the first ship could reach the area, and by then it was dark.

Friday 7.30am: in the early morning mists the destroyer *Brazen* reported sighting the stern of the submarine—just eighteen feet of it—protruding above the water. Within minutes two heads appeared near the sub. Two of the trapped men had successfully used the new Davis escape apparatus: Captain Oram, commander of the flotilla which the *Thetis* would have joined, and a crew-member, Lieutenant Woods. When he had sufficiently recovered Woods described what happened in the fateful minutes after the dive. It seemed that the ship's buoyancy had not gone down as expected, and he

had been detailed to investigate nos 5 and 6 torpedo tubes, to check that they had been flooded as required. For some inexplicable reason the bow door to no.5 tube had not been closed, so that when its rear door was opened the sea poured in irresistibly, flooding the first two watertight compartments before its on-slaught could be checked. The ballast tanks had been duly blown, without the slightest effect on the sub which now lay nose-down in 180 feet of water. Breathing was difficult when he left the sub, he added, and conditions were 'rather serious'.

Friday 10.00am: the Admiralty has said that there was thirty-six hours of oxygen supply inside the stricken vessel, but that did not take into account the fact that there were twice the usual number of people aboard. The true estimate was more like eighteen hours—and that deadline had passed. That the atmosphere had already become lethal was confirmed shortly after ten o'clock when two more escapers bobbed up to the surface, Stoker Arnold and a civilian, Frank Shaw. What they had to report sharpened the edge of desperation among the rescuers: four men had entered the escape chamber before them (instead of the normal two, because of the length of time the operation took), but they had been unable to shift the escape hatch, had panicked and three had died. Everyone on board by then was in bad shape, many on the point of expiring.

Friday 12.00am: The situation has changed from bad—to hopeless. It had been planned to cut a hole in the pressure hull as an escape route for the trapped men. But at the crucial moment the sub lurched, breaking the line that was attempting to keep it steady, and sinking beneath the waves. No more of the victims had yet escaped.

Friday 10.00pm: the stern of the *Thetis* had not re-appeared, as hoped, when the tide slackened at six o'clock. Hope, the Admiralty announced, was now 'diminishing', although pontoons were assembling for a final effort to raise the vessel off the sea-bed. Two hours later the builders of the *Thetis* (Cammell Laird) more realistically admitted that all chance of survival had vanished.

Already the Press was asking some very pertinent questions about how ninety-nine men could have perished in a brand-new submarine, equipped with escape apparatus, in home waters. Why were there so many personnel aboard? How did the alarm take so long to reach headquarters? Why did the navy commit so few resources to the rescue operation until it was too late? The answer to one question—how the *Thetis* had come to be flooded in the first place—was found when the submarine was eventually salvaged: the valve-hole on no. 5 torpedo tube had been painted over! It never was discovered why the bow door had been left open, however. To add to the public disquiet over the fate of the *Thetis*, it had only been a week before that the news-papers had been full of the successful rescue of the crew of the US submarine *Squalus*, which had sunk on 23 May in uncannily similar circumstances (by flooding through an open valve, also on her diving trials). On that occasion thirty-three men had survived the accident. The craft had settled on the sea-bed some forty fathoms down but, using for the first time the new McCann rescue bell, every one of the crew had been brought up alive. The comparison was as inevitable as it was embarrassing.

WAITING...

One hundred and thirty feet below these rolling waters, fifteen miles off Great Ormes Head, North Wales, a company of men, sailors and civilians in the submarine Thetis are waiting....

Hoping....

For Rescue.

   ✦ ✦ ✦

For twelve hours they had been there when this picture was taken—for the greater part of the time in darkness, because light supply does not last for long in a submarine.

They were clinging to supports because the decks of the submarine are at an angle of forty-five degrees.

They can neither sit down, nor lie down; on that sliding surface their muscles are in ceaseless strain.

Cramping strain.

   ✦ ✦ ✦

When this picture was taken air was getting short in the submarine interior, adding anxiety to the men in the boats striving to save their comrades.

Four men who were aboard when the submarine dived were with these rescuers.

They had been shot from the submarine, with the Davis Life-Saving apparatus, and had come to the surface—the second time that men from a British submarine have been saved this way.

   ✦ ✦ ✦

Submarines, by Admiralty instructions, must carry Davis apparatus for every member of the crew.

Why only four men have used the apparatus is a mystery.

For more than five hours when the photographer obtained this picture, eighteen feet of the stern of the submarine has been above the surface of the sea....

With the heroic company still inside.

You can see that stern sticking out of the water in this picture; men in boats round it.

   ✦ ✦ ✦

There are devices for burning a hole through steel plates, through which men can crawl.

Why, five hours after that stern has been above water in a ship costing £350,000, had not that hole been made?

In the darkness, on their sliding death-trap, men must be wondering why....

And hoping....

...HOPING

Evening Standard

To-morrow's Weather—
Fine ; very warm.
See PAGE THREE.

Lighting-up Time
To-day 10.9 p.m.

No. 35.804   LONDON, MONDAY, JUNE 5, 1939   ONE PENNY

Premier Promises Full Public Inquiry : Thetis Revelations

MARKER BUOY AND SMOKE FLOATS WERE NOT SEEN

Signal System Destroyed When Submarine Struck

THE PRIME MINISTER MADE A FULL STATEMENT IN THE HOUSE OF COMMONS THIS EVENING ABOUT THE SINKING OF THE SUBMARINE THETIS.

He revealed that it was caused by the flooding of two forward compartments through the rear door of one of the bow torpedo tubes being open.

This confirmed a statement made earlier by Mr. R. S. Johnson, managing director of Cammell Laird's, builders of the submarine, who described what happened inside the Thetis. Mr. Johnson's statement is given in full on PAGE FOURTEEN.

Mr. Chamberlain promised that a full public inquiry will be held.

He said he would give a full account, so far as was at present known, of "this lamentable disaster."

Her Acceptance Trials

On June 2 the Thetis was carrying out acceptance trials in Liverpool Bay. She was accompanied by a tug carrying a naval submarine officer.

They Watched and Waited

A section of the crowd outside the Admiralty to-day while the Board of Admiralty were in session.

Princesses Visit Queen Mary

Princess Elizabeth and Princess Margaret to-day drove from Buckingham Palace to Marlborough House to visit Queen Mary.

It was the first time they had seen their grandmother since the motorcar accident

Lord Rosebery Lost a Dog

MAN WHO FOUND IT SUMMONED

1939-1960

SEA INVASION DISASTER

...over the East Coast, brings... hundreds

This was the Canvey...

138 di...
Holla...
floo...

BRITAIN
HELICOPT...

THREE centur...
have been...
olland by f...
ashed their...
dikes yester...
Zeeland P...

THE GREAT CALAMITY

A GREAT disaster has come to England. Storm and flood have, in a few hours, wrought destruction along the east coast such as has not been known for centuries.

The whole...

FEARED DROWN...

Tens of t...

'DEATH PASSED 50ft. ABOVE M... HEAD'

By the man who took explosion pictures

MR. LEONARD ALSFORD, the photographer who took these dramatic rescue pictures on this page and Page 1, tells his story of the awful moment when disaster struck from the sky.

This is his story...

I was watching the DH 110 when suddenly I saw two puffs of white smoke, and then a silver-looking dart diving down towards the airfield.

There were two sharp cracks as the plane went through the sound barrier. Then it leve...ed out and came down past ...sident's tent.

The DH...
banked ...
aerodro...

Sudd...
explosi...
up, ...
and ...
stra...
ma...
be...

THE DAILY MIRROR

Tragedy that sha...

THIS IS IT, RAY—AND...

By ELIZAB...

A MONG the ... at Farnboro... the air-minded ... rigger at Croy... Hilda, and Ra... old "mad-abo...

Now they are... was one of the ... wreckage of te... plane showere...

And for lo... Lord thought...

The Lords ... with a party ... ton, Walling... very happy ... citement, sa... of Bedding... them when ...

Ted sai... back fro... oranges. ... had torn... plane di... father. ... Derry...

He pu... the top ... to get a ... excited ... he said.

Sude... were sp... didn't a... all.

I fe... top of ... yelled ... wasn'... leg b... bular... hill.

... aroun... hit ...

Public may be told the cause

MR. Duncan Sandys, Minister of Supply, and Lord de L'Isle and Dudley, Air Minister, are expected to tell Cabinet Ministers today that because of the deaths of onlookers in the Farnborough jet crash, there ought to be a public statement on the causes of the accident.

The statement would follow the official inquiry opened at Farnborough yesterday by Sir Vernon Brown, Inspector of Accidents, Ministry of Civil Aviation.

'Precedent'

The jet the DH110, is still top-secret.

But a precedent may be set on instructions from the Government that some details as to the cause of the disaster be given in a way that would not affect national security.

Even if a secret part of the plane were found to have caused the crash, a statement will probably be made without naming it.

You...
Cor...
feel...

Suffering

BUT they ... patient cl... turns and re... pened at ... year. Now ... peated on a ... The hurricane... was at the heig... —leapt like a ... upon the people ... of the North Sea ...

This morning fam... and well-know... haunts from the ... to Kent find th... battered and torn.

But the low-lying plac... Canvey Island in the ... Estuary and villages ... the coast of Lincoln ... have suffered even mo... ribly. Canvey was lit... overwhelmed.

The story of that isla... agony through a long n... of remorseless terror ... heart-rending.

Destruction

THE loss of the Princess Victoria between Stranraer and Larne was the first horror of this tragic weekend. In itself it was a major catastrophe, but now it has become one more incident in a national calamity.

Along hundreds of miles of coast houses have been battered and swept away, sea walls torn down, piers and promenades broken, boats sunk, cattle drowned, land flooded, and villages isolated. Even a lighthouse has been destroyed.

Once again we are reminded that Nature is more powerful in her wrath than the worst engines of destruction invented by man. One earthquake, one tidal wave can be more death-dealing than an atom bomb.

The week-end's inundations were caused by north to north-westerly winds swooping down on the spring tides which follow a full moon.

Sympathy

THE water is not driven in front of the wind but to the right of it. Thus a north-westerly wind lashes vast masses of water into the southern part of the North Sea, as into a narrowing funnel. Hence the toll taken, also, in Belgium and Holland.

Such tempests as this were not unusual from the 11th to the 15th centuries. They submerged great areas of this country and flooded a large part of Holland, to form the Zuider Zee.

The death-roll was often enormous. In this one, also, it is sadly large. Normal expressions of sympathy seem pitifully inadequate against such a disaster.

Bodies of ... been recovered ... posted "missing... to London has ... boil all drinking ... Sea water has fi...

Only three of ... and-a-half-mile be... hours' rescue work ... waves, 15ft. high.

American airme... 40 families trapped ... upper rooms and on bungalow roofs. A r-sea rescue craft, walkie-talkie sets, jeeps, and searchlights used.

...ong a 30-mile stretch of the Lincolnshire coast sea walls were ripped away at ten points. At least 15 people died as the floods surged in ; and 6,000 lost their homes. About 20,000 acres of land are flooded.

The whole of Mablethorpe is under water to a depth of several feet. Last night 300 people were still marooned in the "ghost town " and neighbouring Sutton-on-Sea. Army trucks and coaches took the rest of the population—about 3,000—to rest centres inland. At midnight, with a howling wind blowing in from the sea, rescue work was suspended.

Some villages are believed to be under 20ft. of water. There has been no word from them since the sea burst in. Telephone communications are almost all gone and rescue work is ...

...etcher cases are carried to waiting ...es who may be among the victims.

... man ...verside factories ...oed. A night watchma... drowned.

... smashing ...

2½d
FICH
R WITH AN
VERY DAY
ERUARY 8, 1958
the Daily Sketch

BRAVE WIFE'S PLANE HALTED ON HOSPITAL DASH

MRS BUSBY DRAMA

IN GREAT SNOW

SECOND EDITION

September 8, 1952

ppy family

SHOUTED
UP HILL
OF DEATH

The New

Telephone 34-490

AUCKLA

New Zealand's Heaviest

156 MISSING

Express Plunges Into
Flooded River

BRIDGE TORN AWAY

(From Our Special Reporters)

OHAKUNE. Friday

At least 31 people are dead and 125 missing, feared dead, in the most terrible train smash in New Zealand history.

Christmas Eve's 3 p.m. express from Wellington to Auckland plunged through a weakened bridge at 10.21 p.m. into a roaring torrent of floodwater sweeping down the Wangaehu River—known locally as Sulphur Creek—10 miles south of Ohakune and about the same distance north of Waiouru military camp.

The Prime Minister, Mr Holland, gave these provisional figures in a broadcast tonight:—

Passengers and crew in the train at the time of the disaster	
Known to be safe	270
Total death roll feared	114
	156

Eight passengers were put down at Waiouru, the last stop before the smash.

The Prime Minister added that it might be some time before some of the bodies were found, and it was feared that some victims might have been carried out to sea, more than 100 miles away.

Carriages Torn to Pieces

The first six carriages of the express and one first class—wer

NAMES OF THOSE
INJURED
AND SURVIVORS

(P.A.)

WANGANUI. Friday

The following names of survivors and those injured in the disaster are subject to correction regarding spelling and initials.

In Waimarino Hospital, Raetihi, suffering from fractures, abrasions and shock:—

Ivan Rowe, Palmerston N

James Kite

YOU
... his bag of or

"I went back t the arm. I thoug family but I did then. Back at th said, . They're g

"I didn't sa back staring a morning when wif was all grand kid. Ted added designer

1939–1960

Black Friday
The Bush Fires of Victoria 1939

The Fire at the Coconut Grove 1942

The Panic at Bolton Wanderers 1946

The Texas City Explosions 1947

Death Dive
Farnborough Air Crash 1952

The Ransom of Progress
The Comet Disasters 1953–4

Invasion by Sea
North Sea Floods 1953

The Christmas Eve Rail Crash
Tangiwai, New Zealand 1953

The Rough Law of Sport
Le Mans Disaster 1955

The Day a Team Died
The Munich Air Crash 1958

Black Friday

The Bush Fires of Victoria 1939

FORECAST: Fine. Map, Page 18.

COUNTRY NEWS: Page 19.

The Courier-Mail

GREATEST DAILY SALE IN QUEENSLAND

No. 1674. (Registered at the General Post Office, Brisbane, for transmission by post as a newspaper.)   BRISBANE, THURSDAY, JANUARY 12, 1939.   'Phone B-0111.   22 PAGES—TWOPENCE

21 DEAD, 20 OTHERS MISSING

DIED IN FLAMES

AUSTRALIA AFTER CHINA?

Next Move If Japan Wins

Courier-Mail Special Service

LONDON, January 11. — If Japan succeeds in dominating China further aggression to the southwards and to Australia will be not merely a possibility but a virtual certainty, because the prize would be most valuable.

This is one of the hitherto unpublished conclusions of the Commonwealth Relations Conference which was held in Australia in September.

It appears in the record of the proceedings, "The British Commonwealth and the Future," edited by Mr. R. V. Hodson, with a foreword by Sir Thomas Bavin.

The record points out that there is not merely proof of the weakness of western diplomacy, without active American support, than the United States isolation and Australia's own isolation, in the Manchurian affair of 1931. America and Australia were unwilling to do anything, or to apply sanctions, yet everything that has occurred in the last seven years has sprung from the aggression in Manchuria.

Britain realises, as a world Power, that if she sacrificed an outlying part of her Dominions her ability to defend the remainder would be endangered, hence war in practically any part of the world threatens British interests.

The most urgent British defence problem is in the air, and unless she overcomes the threat of a war that the Empire it will be most difficult for her to send forces to outlying parts of the Empire.

Few air squadrons could be spared to reinforce distant threatened territories in the event of a European war.

"Australia Anxious"

Forty per cent. of the British Army is already stationed abroad, including Palestine, hence many months would elapse before Britain could send the territorial army to the Continent.

Britain's local defence is of supreme importance to the Dominions, because the destruction of Britain would result in the destruction of the whole Empire except Canada, which, because of its isolated outlook, and its resentment of some aspects of recent British foreign policy, might remain neutral.

No British capital ship is stationed east of Suez, nor is one likely to be before 1940. Australia's lonely position makes her anxious that Britain should not become entangled in European complications. Even the Mediterranean is not regarded as vital, while a strong section of Australian opinion favours Japanese aggression in China, believing—possibly mistakenly—that it will mean less suffering from hostilities, and that Egypt would be spared.

It is probable that all the Dominions will concentrate on supplying material, rather than man power, in the event of becoming involved in war.

BUSH FIRES SWEEP ON

Little Hope For Party of 18

GRAPHIC STORIES OF SURVIVORS

THE charred bodies of 19 more bushfire victims were found to-day, bringing the death roll to 21 in the most disastrous fires in Victoria within living memory.

At least 20 other people are missing, and the list of dead may yet exceed that of February, 1926, when 31 persons lost their lives.

When the flames die down sufficiently to allow search parties to break into the danger zone the fire in the Rubicon Forest, out from Alexandra, may be found to be the worst the State has ever known. Many of 18 men who are missing in the lower part of the Rubicon Valley are almost certainly dead.

The bodies of 12 men were discovered this morning in Rubicon Forest, where four mills have been wiped out.

On the Acheron Way, east of Narbethong, seven people, including a woman and a six-year-old girl, were burned to death while fleeing from their disabled cars.

Four of the Rubicon victims—West, Johnstone, Murdoch, and Neason—lost their lives because of one man's affection for his dog.

The seven lost on the Acheron Way would have been safe had they not tried to flee from the fire which menaced Feiglan's Mill, where six men were employed.

Kenneth Kerslake, with his wife, their little daughter, and Frank Edwards, Mrs. Kerslake's brother, sought safety in a last-minute dash towards Narbethong.

Their car, however, crashed into a tree which had fallen across the fire-swept road, and they were forced to flee on foot. They had gone barely 60 yards, when they collapsed, and the flames swept over them.

Had they stayed in the river where they first sheltered with seven of their comrades they would have been safe. Instead they took the first chance of escaping by car. Fifteen minutes later they were dead.

The other seven men, all of whom were saved, told a graphic story of how throughout last night they lay in the river while the flames roared above them.

The seven other Rubicon victims were completely cut off by the flames, and had no chance of escape. When they were discovered by a party which forced its way through the smouldering bush three were lying in a dugout. They had been roasted to death. The other four bodies, burned almost beyond recognition, were found lying along a track which, had it been possible to follow it, would have led to safety.

Dash For Dog Cost 4 Lives

ONE of to-day's most tragic stories is that of the four men whose lives were lost at Rubicon because one dashed back to save his dog.

Jack King, one of the eight men who escaped, told a dramatic story of their race against death.

"We were making a road from No 3 mill to the Rubicon power station," he said. "Late yesterday afternoon the fire swelled up into the bush around us. We were working until a telephone message warned us to leave everything behind and run for our lives. Another ten seconds and we would not have needed any warning.

"There was a great mass of flame blazing fiercely around Erica, in the Walhalla district.

"Then we saw a great wall of flame sweeping down on us, leaping the tops of trees and devouring everything in its way. We all started to run, but one man stopped suddenly and dashed back to get his dog. Four others waited for him. They were well behind as we raced down the track.

"Walls of flame 100ft. high bounded us on each side, and the flames were meeting above our heads.

"Suddenly the flames swirled round and cut in behind us. The other five men were about 100 yards back.

"Bill Cherry, who is a fast runner, put his head down and dashed through the flames to join us. By then the other four were completely cut off, and we never saw them again.

"We would have gone back for them, but no human being could have lived in that hell.

"We were not out of danger ourselves," King continued. "We had a two-mile run between giant walls of flames that threatened to sweep on to us at any minute just as they swept on to our mates. I count myself one of the luckiest men in the world to have got out of that inferno alive."

Many of the 18 men missing in the lower part of Rubicon Valley are almost certainly dead.

On 200-mile Front

TO-NIGHT the fire area may be defined roughly as an oblong bounded on the north by a broken line of fires which begins about 40 miles north of Melbourne and extends approximately 50 miles farther north.

This 50-mile strip extends eastward for more than 200 miles, gradually narrowing to a rough peak east of Omeo. However, the smoke is so

TWO men who used this car were burned to death in the bush fires near Glendale (V.). They were trapped by the flames, while driving along a bush track.

Left: Child refugees from the forest fire areas near Erica, quartered in the Erica Town Hall. While they rested after their ordeal, their fathers were still out in the forest fighting the flames.

Cheering Crowds Greet Mr. Chamberlain In Italy

Australian Associated Press

LONDON, January 11. — Shouts of "Viva, Chamberlain," "God save Chamberlain," and "God bless your country," greeted the British delegation on its arrival at Genoa this morning, when Mr. Chamberlain for the first time walked on Italian soil.

Stepping from the train—without his umbrella—on to the flower-bedecked station, the Prime Minister was enthusiastically welcomed by a large crowd, which sang "For he's a jolly good fellow."

Mr. Chamberlain was met by the Acting British Ambassador (Sir Noel Charles) and the local Italian authorities. He reviewed detachments of infantry and Fascist youth, and then, after the band had played the British National Anthem, he boarded a special train for Rome, where he is expected at 4.20 p.m. (2.20 a.m. Thursday, Brisbane time).

As the train drew out he stood at a window smiling and waving his hat in response to the cheers of the crowd, in which women predominated.

Interest In Cairo

Sydney Morning Herald Service

The outcome of the British Ministers' visit to Rome is being awaited with keenest interest in Cairo, because it is felt that the visit will give a very

valuable pointer to developments in the international situations during the coming year, also to the frame of mind in which Italy may be expected to enter upon negotiations with Egypt consequent on the Anglo-Italian agreement.

The Cairo correspondent of The Times understands that Egypt has demanded that London should permit the last word regarding any Italian claim to a seat on the board of the Suez Canal to rest with Egypt, which firmly rejects Italy's claims.

A recent suggestion in a Wafdist newspaper, that Mr. Chamberlain had been authorised to champion the Egyptian viewpoint in Rome, drew a notably strong official dementi, which declared that Egypt would speak for herself.

At the same time the vigour of the French reaction to Italian pretensions is admired and applauded, and is held to have strengthened the British resistance to any blandishments calculated to impair further the status quo in the Mediterranean.

"Desperation" Bowler Won Match

Tried in desperation by Bradman when the recognised bowlers had failed to rise to the occasion, Ken Ridings, the 19-year-old South Australian cricketer, caused a Queensland collapse in the Shield match at the Brisbane cricket ground yesterday.

Ridings is in the team for his batting, and has not bowled even in a club game for two years. A grin however, he had, at one stage, taken four wickets, Brown, Baker, Cook, and Dixon, for 11 runs. Ridings scored 122 in South Australia's first innings.

Queensland was dismissed in the second innings for 283, and was beaten by 10 wickets.

Don Tallon, who has an injured hand, did not bat for Queensland, and G. Cook, who was suffering from tonsilitis, went to the wickets only when it was seen that the side was hard pressed to avoid outright defeat.

Waite and Whitington did not field for South Australia. Both had tonsilitis, but should be able to leave with the team for Sydney to-day.
(See Page 12)

IN OTHER PAGES

Science Congress	Mr. Kemp's Job	
Pictures	Poor Water	
Camera	Supply	
Irritation	Air Defence	
Strikes	Muddle	
Big Store	Fear of War	
Merger	Rome Talks	

HOSTILE RECEPTION TO MR. MENZIES

Failure At Wollongong To Settle Pig Iron Dispute

SYDNEY, Wednesday.—The Federal Attorney-General (Mr. Menzies) was given a hostile reception when he visited Wollongong to-day to discuss with union officials the pig iron dispute. Mr. Menzies attended the conference at the invitation of the local member, Mr. Lazzarini, M.H.R., but he was jeered at upon arrival, and counted out upon his departure from the township.

All South Coast lines, with one exception, declared a one-day strike to mark Mr. Menzies' visit. The conference failed to reach any settlement.

As a result 4000 employees at Port Kembla steel works will continue to remain idle, and the plant will continue to operate on the Port Kembla waterfront, which has been practically closed to shipping for several weeks.

Mr. Menzies emphasised at the conference, which was attended by Sydney and local union officials, that the Commonwealth Government could not accept dictation from the Port Kembla waterside workers concerning national policy or external affairs.

He promised, however, that if the Port Kembla waterside workers loaded the present contract for the export of about 20,000 tons of pig iron to Japan the Federal Government would reconsider its policy concerning the export of iron to aggressor nations, and would also consider the withdrawal of licences from the Port Kembla waterfront.

Shortly after Mr. Menzies arrival at Wollongong officials were taken to the hall that he intended to address only a conference, instead of a public meeting.

CHALLENGE ACCEPTED

Mr. Menzies replied that he was not prepared to address a public meeting in Wollongong during the afternoon, but he would also address a meeting of the Port Kembla waterside workers if desired, however, whether the unions directed him to do so.

It was announced from the South to-night that the union had declined to ask him to debate in public the pig iron dispute at Wollongong.

"I agree with you that there should be complete embargo by all unions on the export of goods to aggressor nations," said Mr. Menzies, "when applied upon him after he had concluded his conference with union officials.

"But I put it to you that this should not be a mad, mad export of pig iron to Japan, but it should also ban that export of wool and wheat to Japan, but we ask me to do that.

"You select pig iron, because you feel that the waterside workers at Mile 21 Lassell were taken to the Brisbane General Hospital in a manufacturing plant to reach down the Chinese pig iron but must realise that the manufactured soldiers need clothing and

MIGHT LEAD TO WAR

"Might I not suggest that we these?" asked Mr. Menzies. "I pointed out that waterside workers should load wool and wheat for Japan in the West after dust storms.

"If you refuse to load pig iron because you feel that it is something which is going to be manufactured against those who would reach down the Chinese pig iron but must realise that the manufactured soldiers need clothing and

Mr. Menzies added that it would be unfair for Australia to take the unions. Such action is provocative, and might actually lead to war.

TWO DEATHS IN SMASH

Daughter And Mother

A mother and daughter were killed, another daughter was seriously injured, and a man slightly injured, when a car crashed into a tree near Coomera, yesterday.

The victims were:—

DEAD

Mrs. Jessie Lassell, widow of the late Nathaniel Lassell, 76, of John Street, Clayfield, head injuries. Died after removal to Brisbane General Hospital.

Miss Irene Barbara Lassell, 43, of the same address, daughter of Mrs. Jessie Lassell, fracture of base of skull. Killed instantly.

INJURED

Miss Harriett Jessie Lassell, 35, fracture of left thigh near knee, lacerated scalp wound, injury to left leg, and severe shock.

Eric Napper, 21, Welsh Street, Southport, driver of the car, slight injury to chest and abrasions on nose.

The accident happened at the foot of a steep hill on the Pacific Highway, half a mile on the Brisbane side of the overhead railway bridge near Coomera.

When the impact occurred the occupants of the car were thrown forward violently, but not out.

The Beenleigh Ambulance, in conjunction with the Southport Ambulance, gave first aid. Mrs. Lassell and Miss H. J. Lassell were taken to the Brisbane General Hospital in the Beenleigh car. Mrs. Lassell died four and a half hours after the accident occurred.

Mrs. Jessie Lassell was a sister of the late Rev. Edward Griffith, of the Congregational Church, and a sister of the late Sir Samuel Griffith, former Chief Justice of Australia.

Colourful Sunset

Brisbane witnessed a colourful sunset last night. Such scenes are uncommon in the city but are frequent in the West after dust storms.

Weather Bureau officials explained that the "tints" in the sunset were caused by impurities in the air, such as smoke and haze from bush fires in the outlying portions of the city.

FOUR DIE IN HEAT

The heat wave in New South Wales yesterday caused four deaths.

Eleven men collapsed from the heat when cutting a trench at Lidcombe. Two were taken to hospital for treatment.

Although a mild southerly change brought temporary relief to Melbourne the heat wave continued unabated in most inland districts. Sharp cyclonic storms caused havoc in several country districts.

After five consecutive centuries, the temperature did not reach the century at Adelaide.

The temperature at Thargomindah yesterday was 115 degrees. This was the 27th consecutive day on which the century mark was passed. At Charleville, 106 degrees was recorded.

The maximum temperature in Brisbane yesterday was 85.5 degrees, which is only .1 degree above normal. The minimum reading was 71 degrees—2.1 above normal.

Terrifying sight at Erica, centre of some of the disastrous fires, now sweeping Victoria. This great tree trunk blazed from end to end, turning the darkness of night into dazzling light.

Map showing areas most devastated by the bush fires in Victoria. The heaviest death roll has occurred in the Rubicon Forest, bordering the Rubicon River.

HEAVIEST DEATH ROLL MANY MISSING

SEVEN FOUND DEAD

A SCORCHING WIND and a record shade temperature in Adelaide of 117.7 degrees revived the bush fire peril in the hills yesterday. Fresh outbreaks occurred at Mount Osmond, Crafers, Bridgewater, and Bull's Creek, and homes were again menaced. ABOVE—A terrific blaze on the Mount Barker road, about a mile past the Eagle-on-Hill Hotel. TOP CENTRE—A St. John Ambulance man treating burns on fire-fighters near the danger zone. TOP RIGHT—A fire-fighter running for help on Measday's Pinch. Flames licking the fence along the road. BOTTOM CENTRE—A mass of scrub ablaze at Bridgewater. RIGHT—A carpet of flame running up the hillside towards Mount Osmond. The golf clubhouse was in danger at one stage.

Black Sunday, the *Melbourne Argus* called 8 January 1939, not knowing what the rest of the week was to bring. Ever since Christmas isolated bush fires had been breaking out in the state of Victoria: it had been one of the hottest, driest summers in Australia that anyone could remember. That Sunday the cities sweltered in temperatures ranging from 103°F (39°C) in Adelaide to over 109°F (43°C) in Melbourne—at Sea Lake (Victoria) the mercury topped 116°F (47°C). Creeks baked dry, and forests crackled like tinder-wood under the relentless sun. Then the wind blew up: small fires that had been smouldering—apparently well under control—were fanned together into galloping conflagrations, sweeping through homes, orchards, haystacks, and vast tracts of timber and grass lands. Menaced by the worst bush fire in its history the community around Haunted Hills and Yallourn was saved from destruction only by the united efforts of a thousand fire-fighters. Dromana was not so lucky. The wind drove the flames along the foot of Arthur's Seat till they descended on the little township, devouring everything in their path and driving inhabitants to flee for safety to the beach. Two forestry men had miraculous escapes. Cut off by flames, they spent the afternoon in all that remained of a river—six inches of water—dousing each other as the blaze roared above them.

When Monday dawned there was a trail of destruction across thousands of square miles of Victoria, and no respite from the flames. Seventeen women and twenty-five children had spent a terrifying night in a dug-out on the slopes of Mount Erica, expecting the advancing wall of fire to overwhelm them at any moment, as it already had several mills and dozens of homes near Buxton. By Tuesday—as the thermometer crept inexorably up to 120°F (49°C)—practically the whole mountain country of Victoria was ablaze. A pall of smoke covered nearly the whole state, spreading out over the Bass Strait and Tasman Sea. Out of towns hemmed in by the inferno, Erica, Powelltown, Healesville, a mass evacuation was taking place (or more of a motorized stampede trying to weave its way through fronts of fire often ten miles long). In the cities at least seven people died, just from the heat; no-one could even guess what the casualties were in the countryside.

On Wednesday and Thursday the figures

began to come in: in the Rubicon district the bodies of eleven men were found in the ashes of a mill they had been fighting to save. In the Acheron Valley the charred remnants of two cars were found in a forest where the fire had cut off their escape: their seven occupants (including an entire family) were found suffocated nearby. Thursday, which had offered some prospect that the worst was over, gave way to Friday which dashed these hopes utterly. A blistering seventy mile an hour gale sprang up, driving the huge tongues of flame faster than a man could run. It began to look as if the whole of Victoria would be consumed: 100 buildings at Warrandyte were razed to the ground; settlements at Hillend, Knott's Siding, Pomonal, and Warburton were reported wiped out. Unceasingly news flooded in of more tragedies, of amazing escapes and epic heroism. At two mills in the Matlock forest sixteen more bodies were discovered, some of them beneath a large heap of sawdust where they had crawled to try and escape the searing heat. The inhabitants of Noojee left their township on the local train just as the first flames began to eat into their homes and embarked on a nightmare race against time, with the fires scorching the outside of their carriages and devouring bridges only minutes after they had crossed. And all Australia was soon to learn the name of Gladys McIntosh, the postmistress, who stayed at her

post until the very last moment warning outlying farms of the impending danger (she was later awarded the OBE).

That weekend new fires began raging in New South Wales and in the Canberra district plans for evacuating Government House were even considered at one stage, when a sudden bushfire threatened the outskirts of the capital. Only on Monday 16th did the weather finally break and the fires recede. They left behind them a landscape littered with the blackened corpses of thousands of cattle, sheep and native animals. Across millions of acres the charcoal stubble of once-beautiful timber-forests was the heart-breaking legacy of that terrible week. It took years for the fertile soil to recover from its roasting, and for the economy of the region to re-establish itself. The memory of it is still strong among Victorians: they cannot perhaps prevent bush-fires entirely, but they will not be caught unawares again.

The Fire at the Coconut Grove 1942

Official List of Night Club Dead and Injured—Page 8

Rain Today
Boston and vicinity—Rain today becoming colder in the afternoon.
High tide, 5:10 A. M.; 5:22 P. M. Low tide, 11:19 A. M.; 11:47 P. M.
Full report on page 2.

THE BOSTON HERALD

LATE CITY EDITION

VOL. CLXXXIII, NO. 153 · Boston (Copyright, 1942) Herald-Traveler Corporation · BOSTON, MONDAY, NOVEMBER 30, 1942—FORTY PAGES · ★★★★ · THREE CENTS

BUS BOY'S MATCH SET BLAZE, COCOANUT GROVE DEATHS 440, 289 IDENTIFIED, 181 INJURED

Entire Families Wiped Out in Holocaust, Bereaved Kin Throng Hospitals, Morgues

SEEKS MISSING SON—An unidentified elderly lady seeking her son, stands bewildered and apart from the crowd of anxious people seeking admittance to North Mortuary. (AP Photo)

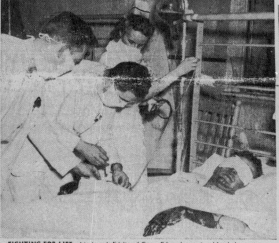

FIGHTING FOR LIFE—Lt. Joseph Edelin of Camp Edwards, receives blood plasma transfusion at City Hospital. Treating him are Dr. Karlin, Dr. Sexton and Nurse Dorothy Monahan.

By LAWRENCE DAME

Loss of at least 440 lives and injuries to 181 persons in Boston's worst disaster—the Cocoanut Grove holocaust—yesterday was traced to the fumbling of a 16-year-old bus boy who accidentally touched a match to flimsy decorations.

An imitation palm tree burst into flames in the night club's basement bar shortly after 10 P. M. Saturday as the dread tocsin of disaster which deprived scores of children of their parents, in some cases wiped out entire families, brought death to service men and prominent citizens and overtaxed the emergency facilities of a great city.

Panic, that might have been avoided had there been calmer heads, accounted for most of the casualties that cast a pall of horror over Greater Boston and that last night found more than half of the terribly mutilated bodies identified.

A total of 289 victims were claimed by sorrowing friends and relatives as new death names were added to hospital lists and many injured faced imminent extinction.

Prank, Careless Match Causes of Disaster
Police investigation of the catastrophe that transformed a gay "hot spot" into an oven of doom led to Stanley P.

Churchill Urges Italians Quit· FIREMEN TELL Death Houses Echo

---

With its silk drapes, artificial palm-trees, Melody lounge, bars, restaurant and floorshow, the Coconut Grove night club was just the place for servicemen on leave to forget the rigours of war, or for disconsolate football fans to put out of their minds the trouncing Boston had just received in a match that afternoon, 28 November 1942. Sure enough that evening the club was packed beyond capacity, nearly 1,000 diners and dancers on two floors built to accommodate some 600. By ten o'clock the evening was going with a swing: upstairs the show was just beginning, in the lounge below one customer took it upon himself to make the twilit room even more romantic—by removing one of the light bulbs. A young assistant—working there part-time to earn pocket-money—was ordered to replace it and, groping to find the socket, lit a match. In an instant the mock foliage, highly flammable, was alight and spreading the flames through the room like a forest fire. Horrified, the crowd could see only one exit, the narrow stairs up to the foyer, and stampeded for it. Few even got that far. Upstairs, as the flames licked through the floor, there was the same dilemma: the only way out appeared to be through the swing doors at the front, and these almost immediately jammed with the weight of people trying to force their way through. In fact, there were a number of exist to the street at the back and at the side, but none had signs or were in any way obvious. There were windows, too, but most of them were boarded over—to enhance the cosy atmosphere of the club. Those who did escape were the lucky ones near the front, or those who clambered up onto the roof and jumped the short distance to the ground. A few survived by locking themselves in the basement refrigeration room. The panic lasted perhaps twelve minutes, but in that time 492 people died or were so badly burned they died later, and nearly 200 were injured. When firemen succeeded in extinguishing the blaze an hour later they found people still seated at their tables, asphyxiated before they could move. In spite of an inspector's protestations that he had himself tested the decorations of the club ten days before and found them non-flammable, the courts later judged that the Coconut Grove had violated a whole catalogue of building and fire-precaution regulations, and sentenced the manager and several city officials to prison. That such a calamity could have followed another fatal blaze in a Boston night club just two weeks earlier was, as the *Christian Science Monitor* bluntly declared, another demonstration of 'the chaotic conditions of Boston's building laws, incompetent enforcement and careless management'.

TODAY'S FEATURES INDEX

Amusements	14	Financial	23-24
Classified	26-29	Radio	29
Comic Page	15	Sports	16-17
Editorial	12	Society	21-22
Fiction	10	Woman's Page	20

The Times-Picayune

U. S. WEATHER REPORT
Louisiana, little temperature change, except colder in southeast portion.

106th YEAR—NO. 310 | Exclusive Pictures by AP WIREPHOTO Associated Press News | NEW ORLEANS, MONDAY, NOVEMBER 30, 1942 | Entered N. O. Postoffice as Second-Class Matter Under Act of March 3, 1879 | SINGLE COPY 5 CENTS

431 DEAD IN BOSTON NIGHT CLUB FIRE

★ ★ ★ ★ ★ ★ ★ ★ ★ ★ ★ ★ ★ ★ ★ ★ ★ ★

Allies Cut Tunis-Bizerte Link in Africa

REDS CONTINUE TO ADVANCE AND WIPE OUT NAZIS

(The Associated Press)

Allied forces fought their way to within 12 miles of Tunis Sunday, driving a steel wedge between that Axis stronghold and Bizerte as Winston Churchill told the world by radio that the Germans and Italians "soon" would be expelled from their last foothold in North Africa.

When that has been done, the British leader warned in a chilling message to the Italian people, Italy will be put under a "prolonged, scientific and shattering air attack" from across the Mediterranean and the weight of the war brought home with a vengeance to the Fascist nation.

"It is for the Italian people, 40,000,000 of them, to say whether they want this terrible thing to happen to them or not," he added in an obvious offer of clemency if Italy should abandon its Axis partner.

The plight of the 20,000 to 23,000 German and Italian troops cornered in Tunisia became increasingly apparent with the announcement that the Amercans, British and French of Lieutenant General K. A. N. Anderson's British First Army had captured the rail junction of Djedeida, only 12 miles northwest of Tunis, severing communication between that city and Bizerte except by air or along a coastal road.

To Divide Garrisons

The Allied plan, possibly perfected at a meetng several days ago of top American and British commanders with Lieutenant General Dwight D. Eisenhower, plainly was to split the Tunis and Bizerte garrisons and then to destroy them separately. With the capture of Djedeida, the Allied spearhead had only about another dozen miles to go to reach the sea and complete the twin encirclement of the Axis ports.

The fact that British and American aerial commanders flew from Egypt to participate in the two-day war council with Lieutenant General Eisenhower indicated that the great Allied air armada strung across North Africa would play a vital role in the final assault on Tunis and Bizerte.

With the Axis crushed finally in Tunisia, the big Allied force of perhaps 150,000 would be free to swing down into Tripolitania, strike Marshal Erwin Rommel's depleted Africa corps from the rear and complete the job begun by the British at El Alemein over a month ago.

Rip German Lines

Fighting in their own element—bitter cold and deep snow—the Russians continued to rip yawning breaches in the German defenses west of Moscow and to send the Nazis reeling back upon Stalingrad in the south as their twin offensives roared unchecked through another day.

In the last 10 days, the Soviets reported, they have slaughtered 100,000 Germans, and the newspaper Pravda said portentously:

"The Germans have not yet felt the full force of the Red army; even heavier blows are in store for them."

The Red army's offensive on the central front, which began some days ago but was disclosed by the Russians in a triumphant announcement only Saturday night, was declared already to have thrown the Nazis back to within 90 miles of the old Latvian border and to have recaptured hundreds of towns and villages. The action extended from the region of Rzhev, 130 miles northwest of Moscow, westward to Velikie Luki.

Deep Snows Aid Reds

The Russians were converting the deep snows in that area to their own uses against the shivering Nazis. They dragged their big guns forward on skis, their tanks were specially fitted to plow through the drifts and their planes took off and landed on skis.

Dispatches from the front said German prisoners (of whom there were very few in comparison to the number killed) "don't look any better than last year's. They are ragged, frozen and vermin-covered."

On the Stalingrad front the Russians announced that their onrushing forces had broken a new German defense line on the east bank of the Don and that they had taken 66,000 prisoners since they opened their big offensive to lift the siege of Stalingrad 10 days ago.

The Russians previously had reported that the last of the Germans had been thrown back across the Don eastward toward Stalingrad by the Soviet army looping in from the west and northwest. The latest communique apparently disclosed that the pursuing Soviets had themselves crossed the Don and were fast closing the "escape corridor" for the 300,000 Nazis estimated to be in the Stalingrad area.

Japs Occupy Attu

That the Japanese had again occupied little Attu Island in the Aleutians was disclosed in a naval communique which told of the sinking of an enemy cargo vessel by American bombers off the island and the strafing of Jap antiaircraft installations there. Since October 7 the navy previously had seen no signs of life on Attu, which lies about 160 miles northwest of the main Japanese Aleutian base of Kiska.

That the Japs had reoccupied Attu was considered significant, possibly indicating that they had found Kiska too hot to handle under constant attacks from American bombers and were in process of retreating out of point-blank range of the Flying Fortresses. The continuous pounding has made Kiska practically useless to the Japanese as an aerial base.

From a United States air base in China came the report that American bombers had sunk a 10,000-ton ship and destroyed 19 Japanese fighters and a transport plane in a raid on Canton on Friday.

GIST OF THE NEWS

Allies drive wedge between Tunis and Bizerte in move to encircle both places and wipe out Axis in Africa. —Page 1

Churchill offers Italy chance to quit before nation is shattered. —Page 1

Ouster of Laval hinted as Nazis try to fix blame for Toulon. —Page 4

Italian generals reported plotting for separate peace as Mussolini sinks into illness, dscouragement. —Page 5

Failure of Hitler attempt to bribe Daladier to make statement against President Roosevelt revealed. —Page 5

Turin given terrific hammering for eighth time by R. A. F. bombers. —Page 9

Allies dividing Axis forces in Tunisia as generals from Libya arrive to help plan final campaign. —Page 9

All men in Greece between 20 and 30 years are being mobilized for forced labor, reports Ankara, Turkey. —Page 10

Russians report 100,000 Germans killed in 10 days of fighting, gain anew in two offensives. —Page 11

* * * * * * * * *

Navy announcement of enemy ship sunk discloses Japs again at Attu. —Page 1

Eleven United Nations merchantmen were destroyed by Axis U-boats in Western Atlantic last week, says navy. —Page 1

Landing of submarine-borne Jap reinforcements at beleaguered Buna is indicated. —Page 13

Remnant of Florida winter colony arrives in Palm Beach ahead of usual time to avoid transportation jam. —Page 20

Establishment of north flank production at Vinton oil field Calcasieu parish, is announced. —Page 29

Wickard tells farmers that responsibility for feeding United Nations rests on U. S. —Page 29

* * * * * * * * *

Tolerance and consideration urged as ration nears for gasoline and coffee. —Page 1

W. S. Farish, president of Standard Oil Company and war council member, dies of heart attack. —Page 1

Army War Show puts forth its realistic display of American military might at City Park Stadium. —Page 14

Longshoremen's rally hears naval officer appeal for recruits for [illegible] battalions of Seabees. —Page 19

Steve Quarles, Fred C. Pieper accept joint chairmanship of United Community and War Chest's labor committee. —Page 19

Back Entrance to Night Club Where Over 400 Perished in Boston Fire

—WIREPHOTO by The Associated Press.

City police and firemen watched Sunday over the rear entrance to the "Melody Lounge" section of the Cocoanut Grove night club in Boston, Mass., where the death toll from the fire which broke out Saturday night mounted to over 400. Debris from broken chairs, tables and personal effects of some of the guests in the club when the fire started litters the sidewalk and gutter.

W. S. FARISH, OIL EXECUTIVE, DIES OF HEART ATTACK

Standard President Also Spent Much Time on War Council

(The Associated Press)

New York, Nov. 29.—W. S. Farish, president of the Standard Oil Company (New Jersey), died unexpectedly Sunday of a heart attack at Millbrook, N. Y., where he was visiting friends. He was 64 years old.

He was a pioneer in developing the first important oil pool in Texas. He was an organizer and leader of the national petroleum war service committee which handled all oil supplies for the Allies in the first world war and was an organizer and later president of the American Petroleum Institute.

Farish was born in Mayersville, Miss., on February 23, 1881, and helped finance his way through college as a school teacher. Graduated from the University of Mississippi with a law degree in 1900, he practiced law for three months in Clarksdale, Miss.

When oil was discovered in Beaumont, Tex., in 1901, Farish went to the boom town, where he later founded the Brown-Farish Oil Company. In 1915 he became president of the Gulf Coast Producers' Association and subsequently was named president of the Texas-Louisiana Oil & Gas Association.

Helped Found Humble

He was a founder in 1917 of the Humble Oil and Refining Company, serving as its vice-president. The Jersey Standard Oil Company bought a substantial stock interest in Humble and supplied the necessary capital to enable Farish and his associates to carry out their plans for building refineries and pipe lines.

Farish became chairman of the

Continued on Page 2, Column 5

Put Christmas Savings in War Bonds, Is Plea

Members of the city's Christmas savings clubs were urged Sunday by Joseph M. Rault, chairman of the Orleans parish war savings staff, to invest their checks in war bonds and stamps.

"Since the retail merchants of New Orleans are suggesting the purchase of war bonds and stamps as Christmas presents, it seems timely to propose that these specific checks be converted by their holders into war bonds and stamps," Mr. Rault said.

"Turn your Christmas savings check into war bonds and stamps on December 7—remember Pearl Harbor," was Mr. Rault's suggestion to the members of these clubs who are to receive their Christmas savings checks early in December.

The Whitney National Bank of New Orleans and the Louisiana Savings Bank and Trust Company, which have sponsored such clubs, announced that with the mailing of this year's checks the clubs will be discontinued for the duration. They also urged club members to continue the saving habit and buy war bonds and stamps with the money they would have deposited in Christmas savings clubs.

Churchill Offers Italians Chance to Overthrow Leaders Before Nation Is Shattered

Victory [illegible] With Warning of Long, Hard War to Follow Recent Successes

(The Associated Press)

London, Nov. 29.—Prime Minister Churchill tonight advised the Italian people to break with Mussolini and their German partners and sue for peace before their nation is brought "under prolonged, scientific and shattering air attack" from Allied North African bases.

Broadcasting to the world on the eve of his 68th birthday, the prime minister declared that "now at this moment the First British Army is striking hard at the last remaining footholds of the Germans and Italians in Tunisia" and "before long" they will be expelled and the war will be carried to Italy "in a manner not hitherto dreamed of by its guilty leaders."

"It is for the Italian people, 40,000,000 of them, to say whether they want this terrible thing to happen to them or not," he said.

Emphasizing the Allied peace offensive that was being directed toward Rome, the British Broadcasting Corporation this afternoon preceded the prime minister's 30-minute speech with broadcast appeals to the Italian people to make a separate peace.

During the next 24 hours Churchill's speech will be broadcast in full to Italy, Germany and France four or five times by the BBC, and the high points of the address will be broadcast to the same countries throughout next week.

Sees Long War

It was a victory speech that the war leader made in a strong, firm and confident voice, but he warned his people and their Allies against dreaming their successes in North Africa, Russia and elsewhere had removed expectation of anything but a long war.

Somberly, he concluded, "The dawn of 1943 will soon loom red before us, and we must brace ourselves to cope with the trials and problems of what must be a stern and terrible year."

"But we are becoming ever

Continued on Page 2, Column 1

NAVY ANNOUNCES ELEVEN SINKINGS IN ATLANTIC AREA

Week's Toll of Merchantmen Is Highest Reported in Month

(The Associated Press)

Eleven United Nations' merchantmen were destroyed by Axis U-boats in Western Atlantic waters, the navy announced last week, the highest number of sinkings to be reported for that area over a seven-day period in three months. At least 150 crew members were dead or missing, but 342 others were saved.

Majority of the attacks occurred off the northern coast of South America, where a concentration of Axis submarines appeared to be operating. Reports in recent weeks have placed most torpedo attacks against United Nations cargo vessels in that sector.

Allied acquisition of the French naval base at Dakar, some 1600 miles from the South American "bulge," removed possibility that the port might be used for Axis raiders. Additionally, Dakar provides the United Nations with a vital base for South Atlantic operations.

Canada's Navy Minister Angus MacDonald, disclosing early last week that only 20 ships had been sunk by undersea craft in the St. Lawrence area this year, squelched rumors which had placed the number of losses as high as 40 vessels. However, MacDonald's statement pictured the North Atlantic as a region where the submarine threat still was grave.

Five vessels were lost in the Caribbean, three off South America and three off the United States. Area losses since Pearl Harbor were tabulated as follows: Off the United States, 189; off Canada, 49; in the Caribbean, 174; in the Gulf of Mexico, 46; off South America, 85. Total reported lost in the Western Atlantic since Pearl Harbor, 543.

TOLERANCE URGED AS RATION NEARS FOR GAS, COFFEE

Conservative Buying and Judicious Use of Commodities Advised

[illegible] for others was [illegible] of buyers of gasoline and coffee Sunday as the rationing of these commodities approached.

Coffee drinkers, who will start buying the rationed bean today, were asked by R. L. Simpson, executive chairman of the Orleans parish rationing board, not to purchase their allotment right away if they have a large enough supply on hand to last a while. He said there was enough for everyone if all didn't insist on buying at once.

Gasoline rationing will begin Tuesday. Robert H. Fine of New Orleans, president of the Service Station Association of Louisiana, said that members of the association had been very busy Saturday and Sunday serving motorists who wanted to get the tankful of gasoline they are allowed to have when rationing begins.

"We expect to be even busier Monday," he said, "and we should like to ask the customers to bear with us. I expect we won't have much time to do anything but put gasoline in tanks. We'll have the rest of the week to wash windshields and put air in tires and give the other usual services."

U. S. Goodman of Baton Rouge, director of the state office of the office of price administration, in a telephone conversation Sunday informed the office of war information in New Orleans that preparations were complete throughout the state for gasoline rationing.

Remarking that there had been some speculation that rationing would throw an increased burden on public transportation systems, he said that this need not be so.

"If the public will use their gasoline rations for essential purposes only," he said, "rationing should not throw a great additional burden on transportation systems. In fact, if many automobile owners will take advantage of the opportunity to get B books by forming car-sharing clubs, it might even relieve streetcars and busses."

Man With Goodness of Heart to Give Will Find Doll, Toy Fund Ideal Agent

A man looks at a gift catalogue realizing how many things there are to give; how many there are to give to. He realizes, too, how little he has to buy with.

Besides his family there are others whom he knows should be cared for. In his heart is the spirit of giving, for in his soul is the incarnate word of the one who gave so much to humanity, that Christmas so long ago.

For such men there is a method of "passing the buck." And at this season, there is an institution which gladly accepts the shifted responsibility and receives the buck. The Times-Picayune Doll and Toy Fund and Christmas Gift Fund are means by which a man may give only a dollar, but that dollar will be added to an aggregate of dollars which will buy more and better toys for the many to whom he thought he could not give.

Contribution received Sunday follows:

DOLL AND TOY FUND
November 28, 1942

Previously acknowledged	$2439.93
In Memory of Ed; M. Gueydan	1.00
Total	$1.00
Grand total	$2440.93

START OF GRIM FLAMES TRACED TO LONE MATCH

Horror of Panic in Trapped Throng Described; Many Service Men Are Victims; Over 200 Injured With Some Near Death

(The Associated Press)

Boston, Nov. 29.—A terrific "flash fire" that caused more than 600 casualties among a thousand suddenly panic-stricken merrymakers in Boston's Cocoanut Grove—the nation's worst night club holocaust—was traced tonight to a tiny match flame in the hands of a 16-year-old busboy.

While Deputy Police Superintendent James R. Claflin quoted the youngster as saying he had accidentally ignited a paper palm tree to start the lightninglike blaze, the Boston Committee on Public Safety reported the death toll alone at 431.

The horror scenes at the fire that started late last night and those that followed today never had been duplicated in Boston. Tonight fewer than 250 of the bodies had been identified. Some were so terribly burned that final identification may never be possible.

Long lines of relatives and friends stood outside the city's two principal morgues, waiting to be taken inside two by two to see if they could identify the bodies lined up row on row.

Hospitals throughout Greater Boston were jammed with injured, some of them on the danger list. An unofficial estimate placed the injured at about 200. Blood plasma was rushed here from Washington and a supply of sulfa drugs from Newark, N. J. Specialists in treating burns were flown in from other cities.

Some Victims Prominent

Among the hundreds trapped in the inferno were:

Charles "Buck" Jones, Van Nuys, Cal., cowboy star of motion pictures, critically burned.

Scott R. Dunlap, also of Van Nuys, motion picture producer, injured and in a hospital.

Edward [illegible], Brookline, president of the [illegible] state Theatre Corporation and treasurer of a [illegible] textile firm, dead.

Norine H. Welch, student-daughter of Vincent S. Welch of Port Washington, N. Y., vice-president of the Equitable Life Assurance Society, dead.

Joseph A. Boratyn, star fullback at Holy Cross college last year, dead.

Katherine Woods, 22, daughter of Carl F. Woods, prominent Boston manufacturer, president-treasurer of the Crosby Steam Gauge Company, dead.

Missing was Mary Ellen McCormack, niece of Representative John W. McCormack, House majority leader.

Grace McDermott, New York, entertainer at the club — known under the stage name of "Vaughn," dead.

Robert Beverly Charles, 28, of Winchester, Mass., son of Mr. and Mrs. W. R. Charles of Oak Park, Ill., and Eastern manager for a Chicago candy company.

Inquest Is Opened

While the death list grew slowly, name by name, grim-visaged fire officials opened an inquest attended also by two United States Navy captains—there were many service men among the dead—and by two representatives of the federal bureau of investigation.

A transcript of the testimony will be forwarded to District Attorney William J. Foley.

Deputy Fire Chief John F. McDonough testified that one door of the night club was equipped with a panic lock, which would open under pressure, but that this was out of order and the door was secured by another lock. He added, however, that although he found a number of bodies piled near this door, none was nearer than 10 feet.

District Chief William J. Mahoney said he had found bodies tangled and piled four or five deep, most of them frightfully burned, and that there was definite evidence that the crowd had been thrown into a fighting, clawing panic. Chairs and tables were tipped and scattered among the bodies.

The inquest will be resumed tomorrow, with testimony by survivors and police.

Busboy Tells Story

The youngster who reported he started the fire in the Melody Room of the club, a new addition opened within the last two weeks, was identified by Deputy Police Superintendent Claflin as Stanley V. Tomaszewski, of [illegible], Mass.

[illegible]

"A patron came into the place and unscrewed a bulb in the ceiling. This made the room too dark. One of the waiters came to me and asked me to screw the bulb back in.

"I stood on a chair to do it. I lighted a match and held it while I screwed the bulb in with the other hand.

"The match set fire to a palm tree. That is how the fire started."

Blaze Raced Swiftly

Thus the flame of a match started a blaze that raced so swiftly and so fiercely through the night club that many bodies were burned beyond recognition.

Many of the victims were "terribly burned" after death, asserted Medical Examiner Timothy Leary after examining bodies at the Southern mortuary.

Most of the deaths of those he examined were due to carbon monoxide poisoning, inhalation of smoke and holocaust, he said.

The orchestra leader had raised his baton to signal for the national anthem as a prelude to last night's floor show, then—

There was a puff of smoke; a thin finger of flame raced among the decorations; a girl cried, "Fire," and within seconds the crowded night club was a bedlam.

Scores are Injured

The rising list of dead reached 431 today and there were uncounted scores of injured being treated in hospitals throughout Greater Boston.

By daybreak all the bodies had been taken from the one and one-half-story stucco building that squatted among taller structures on a narrow Back Bay street.

Soon after dawn a handful of youthful scavengers was scut-

Continued on Page 3, Column 3

Japanese Reoccupy Attu Island; Kiska Aleutian Base 'Too Hot'

(The Associated Press)

Washington, Nov. 29. — Renewed Japanese occupation of Attu Island in the Aleutians was disclosed today by the navy which reported that a small enemy cargo vessel had been bombed, set afire and apparently sunk off the island.

A communique containing this information also reported new aircraft attacks in the South Pacific against the Japanese-held Munda bay area of the New Georgia islands in the Solomons.

Japanese destroyers have shelled native villages in the western islands of the New Georgia group, the communique said.

The report of Japanese anti-aircraft installations on Attu, westernmost of the Aleutians, was the first definite evidence that the enemy had thrown land forces into the island again following his withdrawal last September.

The navy announced October 7 that aerial reconnaissance had disclosed no signs of life on either Attu or Agattu.

These two small, bleak islands lie about 160 miles northwest of the main enemy Aleutians base of Kiska where the Japanese have maintained a foothold continuously since they first moved into the Aleutians last June.

Their withdrawal from Attu and Agattu, according to the best judgment of authoritative sources here, was prompted by a desire to concentrate their forces on Kiska, which offers not only facilities for a land base but also an excellent harbor for both surface ship and seaplane operation.

Kiska, however, was under very heavy attack by American planes throughout the fall. The attacks increased in frequency and intensity after the army opened an air base in the Andreanof Islands close by.

The attacks from the Andreanoffs have made Kiska useless to the Japanese so far as aerial operations are concerned and have driven them underground except for the operation of infrequent planes and supply ships and their anti-aircraft installations.

Military experts have expressed the belief that it was the consistent pounding of Kiska which had compelled the Japs to resort to the use of Attu as a base once more.

Allied Bombers Blast Two More Jap Destroyers

(The Associated Press)

Allied Headquarters in Australia, Monday, Nov. 30.—Two Japanese destroyers, part of a naval force maneuvering off New Guinea, are believed to have been sunk by Allied bombers, the Allied high command reported today.

Enemy naval forces were reported Sunday maneuvering off the coast near the Buna-Gona area where American and Australian trops, under the personal direction of General Douglas MacArthur, have the Japanese pinned against the sea.

Allied naval forces, the communique continued, intercepted a German auxiliary ship of 8000 tons. The craft was pounded so fiercely by Allied gunfire that the crew scuttled the ship. Seventy-eight Germans were captured.

The Panic at Bolton Wanderers 1946

With English football leagues beginning to return to normal after the chaos of the war years, officials at Bolton Wanderers were expecting a big gate for the Cup tie against Stoke on 9 March 1946. But they weren't prepared for the huge mass of humanity that converged on the Bolton ground: half an hour before kick-off there were more than 65,000 on the terraces and another 15,000 still fighting to get in. Too late the gates were closed on the over-crowded stadium and in vain did the police attempt to repel the additional thousands that climbed over fences or forced their way in through an unlocked gate. By the time the two teams kicked off, scores of spectators were fainting in the suffocating crush and being manhandled over the heads of the crowd to waiting stretchers. Then twelve minutes into the match the inevitable happened—under the relentless pressure two crush barriers at the railway end collapsed. Surging waves of spectators rushed downwards, bulldozing hundreds to the ground then trampling them underfoot in the panic to get free. Fans pouring out of the fatal enclosure and onto the pitch brought the game to a belated halt. By then thirty-three people, including a woman, were dead and 500 injured. Astonishingly, even as ambulancemen and police carried the dead and injured away, the match was re-started—and finished (without further interruption) in a hollow victory for Bolton.

Sunday Dispatch 10 March 1946 (inset)

The Texas City Explosions 1947

"All the News That's Fit to Print"

The New York Times.

LATE CITY EDITION
Clearing and cooler today.
Fair and warmer tomorrow.
Temperatures Yesterday—Max., 55; Min., 44
Sunrise today, 5:16 A. M.; Sunset, 6:36 P. M.
Full U. S. Weather Bureau Report, Page 55

VOL. XCVI....No. 32,590. Entered as Second-Class Matter, Postoffice, New York, N. Y. NEW YORK, THURSDAY, APRIL 17, 1947. THREE CENTS IN NEW YORK CITY

BLASTS AND FIRES WRECK TEXAS CITY OF 15,000; 1,200 FEARED DEAD; THOUSANDS HURT, HOMELESS; WIDE COAST AREA ROCKED, DAMAGE IN MILLIONS

VISIT BY MARSHALL TO STALIN IS TERMED NO KEY TO IMPASSE

Basic Differences on German Settlement Are Expected to Continue in Big Four

COUNCIL TAKES UP AUSTRIA

Vienna Is Said to Plan Appeal to U. N. if Ministers Fail to Agree on Treaty

By DREW MIDDLETON
Special to The New York Times.

MOSCOW, April 16—No break in the deadlock in the Council of Foreign Ministers on a German settlement is indicated, despite the conference last night between Secretary of State Marshall and Premier Stalin.

This is the opinion of reliable United States sources here. They do not, however, exclude the possibility of a conciliatory move by the Russians on minor points for propaganda purposes before the conference ends. But these sources do not expect that the Russians will take any other alternative to their present position on the major German question—reparations from current production.

Today the Council began consideration of the Austrian treaty. It agreed to listen tomorrow to a Yugoslav presentation of Marshal Tito's claim to part of Carinthia, and it accepted some of the Austrian treaty articles that already had been agreed upon by the Foreign Ministers' duputies.

Pessimism Regarding Pact

However, there was pessimism regarding the chances for obtaining an Austrian treaty at this session. And high Austrian sources disclosed that Vienna was planning to take the issue to the United Nations Security Council, or to ask one of the Allies to present it there.

The Austrians, it was said, take the view that if a treaty is not produced here in Moscow, and the occupation of Austria by foreign troops continues, the resulting situation will be a threat to world peace.

Regarding the general Soviet-United States deadlock in the Council, one American indicated today that it was not too late for the Russians to change their tactics, bu. the general advice was not to "expect too much" as a result of the conversation between Premier Stalin and Secretary Marshall.

If Soviet Foreign Minister Molotov, before the present Council session ends, makes a frank plea for reparations from current production based on the needs of the Soviet Union and the failure of the removal program in Germany to fulfill those needs, some accommodation might be worked out.

Position of U. S. Is Firm

But the United States will not give way on the question of reparations, any more than Secretary Marshall already has, so long as the Russians make reparations from current production the "absolute condition" of the economic unity of Germany.

Meanwhile, it is clear that the Russians hope that their present "grinding" tactics in the Council will in the end wear down the United States and British opposition to the Soviet policy for Germany. Following this theory, the Russians believe that some sort of adjustment can be made here or at the next meeting of the Foreign Ministers.

There is nothing to support the idea that any adjustments or concessions were made by either party during last night's meeting in the Kremlin, which lasted for one and a half hours.

Secretary Marshall had taken the initiative in arranging the visit, since Premier Stalin is chief of the Soviet Government. The Secretary of State's delay in seeking the interview is explained by his reluctance to talk with the Premier until he felt that problems warranted it.

[Secretary Marshall asked for

Continued on Page 4, Column 5

China Urges Big 4 To Act on Korea

Special to The New York Times.

NANKING, April 16—Chinese Foreign Minister Wang Shih-chieh today dispatched a letter to Secretary Marshall urging the establishment of an independent government for a united Korea without further delay.

Dr. Wang said that if the occupying powers could not reach an agreement soon on Korean unity and independence, a "full consultation" should take place among the United States, Russia, Great Britain and China as parties to the Moscow Agreement of December, 1945.

The Minister's letter is in response to Secretary Marshall's note of April 8 to Foreign Minister Molotov. Dr. Wang sent copies of his letter to Mr. Molotov and to British Foreign Secretary Ernest Bevin.

Regret was expressed that no Korean Government had as yet been set up.

HOUSE GROUP VOTES MID-EAST AID BILL

Senate Action Due Tuesday—Vandenberg Warns Opponents We Must Defy Russia

By C. P. TRUSSELL
Special to The New York Times.

WASHINGTON, April 16 — The $400,000,000 Greek-Turkish aid bill was approved formally by the House Foreign Affairs Committee today.

Twelve members voted "aye." Three members — Representatives Helen Gahagan Douglas of California and Mike Mansfield of Montana, Democrats, and Jacob K. Javits, Republican, of New York—voted "present." This maneuver, they explained, was not in complete disapproval of the program, but to reserve the right to criticize and seek to revise it.

The action came, after several weeks of committee hearings and deliberations, as the Senate in night session agreed to vote without further debate on its own Greek-Turkish aid measure at 4 P. M. next Tuesday.

Vote Accepted as Binding

Before coming to this decision, the Senators had plunged into their first sustained crossfire debate on the bill. Not all members, particularly those of the opposition, joined the bipartisan leadership push to let a prompt Senate vote be its "answer" to attacks on the Truman Doctrine by former Vice President Henry A. Wallace in Europe.

Not all members, particularly those of the opposition, joined the bipartisan leadership push to let a prompt Senate vote be its "answer" to attacks on the Truman Doctrine by former Vice President Henry A. Wallace in Europe.

Although ten members of the House Foreign Affairs group were absent when the test was made, the vote was accepted as final and binding. The reorganization act requires a vote of a committee majority. Thirteen of the twenty-five

Continued on Page 12, Column 3

BARUCH ASKS WORK FOR 44-HOUR WEEK TO STOP INFLATION

Proposes No Strikes, Layoffs Before 1949 to Maintain Production, Jobs and Buying

AIDING WORLD'S ECONOMY

At South Carolina Unveiling of His Portrait He Calls on America to Lead the Way

Text of Baruch's appeal for increased production, Page 21.

By The Associated Press.

COLUMBIA, S. C., April 16—Bernard M. Baruch said here today that the world "can get going only if men work" and that "if we accept the challenge to preserve civilization, it means greater effort than that exerted during the war."

Asserting that "we cannot achieve our purpose with the present hours and limitations on work," he urged a five-and-one-half-day week of forty-four hours, "with no strikes or layoff, to Jan. 1, 1949" to increase production.

"The result would be electrifying," he said.

Mr. Baruch spoke at the unveiling of his portrait in the hall of the State House of Representatives. The portrait, painted in 1928 by Oswald Birley, an English artist, was unveiled by Mr. Baruch's daughter, Belle. It was a gift from Mr. Baruch, made after $4,000 was authorized to be spent for a new painting.

New Outlook for Security

The native South Carolinian said that if his work proposal were adopted "production would flow smoothly, a sense of security would return to worker and employer; and the reaction upon the economy of the world would be deep and lasting."

"Until we have unity, until we straighten out and solve our own problems of production, and have internal stability, there is no basis on which the world can renew itself physically or spiritually," he added.

"Upon this change in our material outlook, there would follow a change in our sense of security. Make no mistake: our military lines are no stronger than the industry behind them.

"Unless we work, we shall see a vast inflation. Unless we work, we shall not be able to maintain our claim to power. That would be the greatest blow we could receive, for it would strip us of our strength to preserve our way of life."

He declared that such a program would meet the needs of other nations, asserting:

"There is no place left to which to turn for regeneration except to America. We must answer that call or we shall fail civilization in its most tragic moment, and thus ourselves.

"We cannot do it by loans, grants, subsidies, bonuses or pious

Continued on Page 21, Column 1

British Alert for Palestine Reprisal; Time Bomb Found in London Office

By CLIFTON DANIEL
Special to The New York Times.

JERUSALEM, April 16—All of Great Britain's forces in this tumultuous country were alerted tonight against reprisals by the Jewish underground for the hanging of four convicted terrorists at Acre today. By a new decree, military justice was made supreme in the land.

Half the country's 700,000 Jews were confined indoors all day today as a precaution against popular demonstrations and terrorist retaliation.

The first furtive acts of defiance to the house curfew imposed on Jewish urban centers occurred in Tel Aviv, where dummy road mines were strewn and road blocks erected tonight. Near one of the

Continued on Page 13, Column 1

By CHARLES E. EGAN
Special to The New York Times.

LONDON, April 16—A crudely made time bomb believed to be the work of Jewish terrorists was found in the Dover House offices of the Colonial Office shortly after 6 A. M. today. Dover House in Whitehall is within 200 yards of 10 Downing Street, official residence of Prime Minister Attlee.

Later in the day, an anonymous telephone call warned police that the War Office in Whitehall would be blown up at 4 P. M. Police cleared the building and searched it thoroughly without result.

Although they dismissed the telephone call as a hoax, Scotland Yard officials were working on the

Continued on Page 14, Column 3

TEXAS CITY BURNING AFTER IT WAS ROCKED BY EXPLOSION

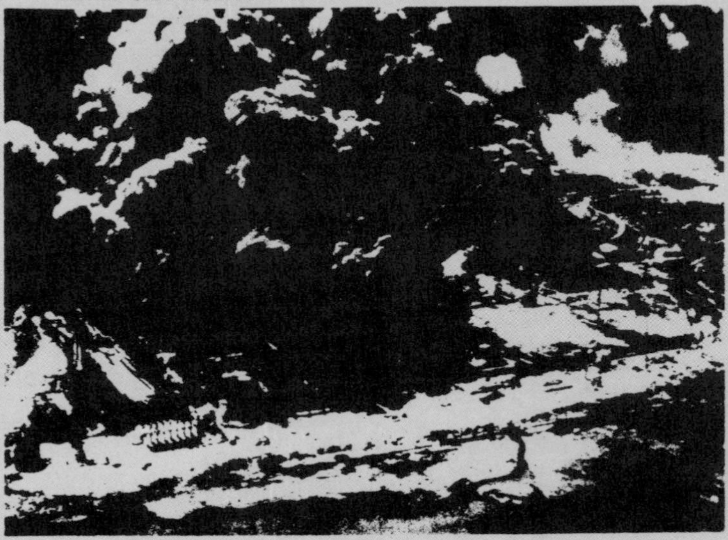

Air view of the industrial plants following the blast. In left center foreground is the sprawling Monsanto Chemical Company
Associated Press Wirephoto

PAY-AS-YOU-GO SET BY DEWEY AS POLICY

Reviewing Legislative Record, He Says Present Generation Should Not Mortgage Next

Dewey's radio review of the legislative session, Page 20.

By LEO EGAN
Special to The New York Times.

ALBANY, April 16—Governor Dewey, in a review of this year's legislative record, emphasized tonight that his administration was committed to the pay-as-you-go policy with respect to public expenditures and believed that local

Continued on Page 20, Column 2

Doctors, Clergy Brave Fires And Fumes to Help Injured

By ROBERT E. BROWN
United Press Staff Correspondent.

TEXAS CITY, Tex., April 16—I flew over the Texas City disaster area today—over waves of black smoke which hid all but five huge clusters of licking flame. A rectangle roughly a mile long and a half mile wide along the waterfront was a mass of twisted steel structures and charred debris.

Clouds of smoke erased the sun. Fires were burning at the ruined plant of the Monsanto Chemical Company and in two oil refineries. Every few minutes another explosion spewed more flame and smoke into the sky.

Wading through the destruction area were doctors and nurses—grimy, sweaty and with blood on

Continued on Page 18, Column 8

PHONE UNION INSISTS ON PAY RISE OFFER

Beirne Says 'Pattern' Is Set—Arbitration Would Bring Wage 'Hodge-Podge,' He Holds

By LOUIS STARK
Special to The New York Times.

WASHINGTON, April 16—The National Federation of Telephone Workers insists on a wage increase now because "millions of workers" have received such increases in recent months, according to Joseph A. Beirne, president of the federation. The "pattern" has been set in industry, he said.

In a broadcast tonight over the American Broadcasting Company network the union president defended his organization's rejection of the arbitration proposal made by Lewis B. Schwellenbach, Secretary of Labor.

The setback suffered by the Secretary of Labor when both the union and the American Telephone and Telegraph Company and asso-

Continued on Page 19, Column 1

RED CROSS SPEEDS AID TO TEXAS CITY

Allocates $250,000 and Flies Disaster Experts, Medical Supplies to Stricken Port

Special to The New York Times.

WASHINGTON, April 16 — The American Red Cross made an initial appropriation of $250,000 today to aid victims of the Texas City explosion.

Basil O'Connor, chairman, indicated that the sum might be enlarged after a survey of the area.

Meanwhile, twenty trained disaster workers of the Red Cross are being rushed to the scene of the blast to assist and relieve volunteer workers from local chapters.

The organization has been forced to withdraw some of its trained disaster workers from duty at the scene of the recent Oklahoma-Texas Panhandle tornado, which also had a $250,000 allocation.

Three disaster specialists were flown from headquarters here to Texas City in a Navy plane. Another special plane left St. Louis with five Red Cross experts. Doctors and nurses are also on the way from a 100-mile radius of the scene.

Medical supplies, blood plasma and wholeblood, tetanus and gas gangrene antitoxin are being flown from the St. Louis office of the Red Cross.

Galveston Red Cross is prepared to take in all refugees from Texas

Continued on Page 18, Column 7

World News Summarized

THURSDAY, APRIL 17, 1947

A nitrate-laden ship exploded in the Gulf port of Texas City, Tex., yesterday, killing probably 1,200 persons and injuring more than 1,000 others. The city of 15,000 was almost completely destroyed by a series of blasts that followed the ship explosion and fires. Poisonous gases hampered rescue work. [1:8.]

Experts said the reconverting ammonium nitrate from wartime explosives to fertilizers was so delicate that similar blasts elsewhere might be expected. [19:3.]

The country's economic situation was widely discussed. Bernard M. Baruch said that to avoid inflation there must be a forty-four-hour week and no strikes through 1948. [1:3.] Congress was told that tax cuts and volume production had done more than price increases to raise profits last year [22:4], and a joint Congressional committee decided to seek civilian advice on price and related problems. [23:4.] General Motors Chairman Sloan said that business could not slash profits and simultaneously cut prices and increase wages. [22:2.]

General Motors offered its factory workers the same 15-cent hourly increase accepted by its electrical workers; the union demanded 23½ cents. [24:5.]

Striking telephone workers must receive a pay increase before they return to work, their leader said in Washington. [1:6.]

The House Foreign Affairs Committee, without a negative vote, favorably reported the Greek-Turkish aid bill with the Vandenberg amendment. [1:2.]

Former Premier Herriot denied that he had been asked to sign the "non-partisan" invitation to Henry A. Wallace to visit France although he was listed among the signers. Mr. Wallace delivered his final speech in Britain before an all-party meeting in the Commons. [9:1.]

General Marshall's talk with Generalissimo Stalin is not expected to close the gap between the American and Russian views on Germany. Austria was reported considering an appeal to the United Nations should the Foreign Ministers Council fail to agree on a treaty. [1:1.]

Armand D. Willis, former attaché to the United States Embassy in Moscow, is on his way home after having accused some members of the staff of being "anti-Soviet." Washington said he was being dismissed. [6:3.]

British forces in Palestine have been alerted for trouble following the execution of Dov Gruner and three other Zionist underground terrorists. An attempt was made to bomb a building of the Colonial Office in London. [1:2-3.]

Agreement was reached in China for a coalition government, with Gen. Chang Chun the Premier. [3:5.]

Russia has nominated Senator Georg Branting, Swedish Social Democrat, for Governor of the Free Territory of Trieste. [15:1.]

The Board of Estimate endorsed a contract leasing all city airports for fifty years to the Port of New York Authority, which will finance all improvements. [29:8.]

U. S. Calls on Lewis and Operators To Meet for Talks on Bargaining

By JOSEPH A. LOFTUS
Special to The New York Times.

WASHINGTON, April 16 — The Government moved today to bring together operators and miners in the soft coal industry in a resumption of collective bargaining.

Capt. N. H. Collisson, Federal Coal Mines Administrator, invited officials of the United Mine Workers and spokesmen for the forty-six coal operators' associations to meet here April 29. The suggested date is about two months before the end of Government possession of the mines.

"The purpose of the meeting," Capt. Collisson stated, "is to discuss the means by which a resumption of collective bargaining between the UMW and the coal operators may most effectively and expeditiously be accomplished."

The operators and the miners have not met face to face since early last fall, when attempts at negotiations failed to make progress.

The meeting was called as the National Labor Relations Board ruled that, despite Government operation, the mine employes still work for the private owners of the mines for purposes of the Wagner Act. The board said that the Supreme Court's decision in the contempt case against John L. Lewis and the UMW, of which he is president, did not alter that relationship.

The NLRB dismissed the peti-

Continued on Page 24, Column 3

SHIP STARTS HAVOC

Nitrate Vessel Blows Up and Sets Off Chain of Explosions Ashore

OIL TANKS EXPLODE

Huge Monsanto Plant Razed—Fires Prevent Rescue of Injured

By The Associated Press.

TEXAS CITY, Tex., April 16—A chain of explosions set off by the blowing up of a nitrate-laden ship smote this Gulf port today, killing hundreds and injuring more than 1,000. It was the worst American disaster in ten years.

Much of the boom industrial city of 15,000 population was destroyed or damaged. Property loss will run into millions of dollars.

Fires followed the blasts. Poisonous gas from exploding chemicals was reported to be filtering through the area.

Estimates of the fatalities ranged from 1,200 down to 450.

Mayor J. C. Trahan said he knew of 300 dead. G. B. Finley, State highway commission official, said at Austin that officials at the scene had indicated the toll would reach 1,200. Wiley Whatley, Houston police sergeant at the disaster scene, estimated that the death total would be between 450 and 500.

Exodus Is Reported

Midwestern headquarters of the Red Cross at St. Louis reported that 500 bodies had been brought out of the explosion area late today and that more bodies were being found constantly.

Gen. Jonathan M. Wainwright, hero of Bataan, visited the scene and said:

"I have never seen a greater tragedy in all my experiences. I have come here to offer this stricken community every facility that the Army can place at its disposal."

He is now Commanding General of the Fourth Army.

A report to The Houston Post said that residents were evacuating the city tonight because of a feared new explosion of a nitroglycerine ship at the docks. It declared that residents were racing to get out of town.

It stated also that chlorine gas had saturated the dock area and was feared to be moving toward the city's residential and business sections.

Mayor Trahan, who wears the Purple Heart for buzz bomb wounds received in Belgium, said that "no buzz bomb could ever compare with what happened here today."

"It is such a teerrific tragedy that the people have not been able to realize what happened," he added.

Crew of Forty Killed

The chain of explosions was set off by the blowing up of the French freighter, Grandcamp, at 9:12 A. M. The ship was obliterated and its crew of forty perished.

Subsequent blasts wiped out the huge-war-built plant of the Monsanto Chemical Company. Thirty-five employes were reported hopelessly trapped in the burning ruins late today.

The blasts rocked the surrounding region for 150 miles.

Mr. Finley said: "Rescue parties bringing out casualties from the blast area estimated that about one out of every three persons had been killed, which would indicate around 1,200 dead."

He referred to the dock area, where the principal damage occurred and where there were about 3,500 persons when the explosions began.

A reporter flying over the scene likened it to bomb destruction of European cities in the recent war. The mushrooming cloud of smoke that arose was described as resembling the aftermath of the atom bombing of Hiroshima.

The first eye-witnesses to move into the area after the explosion

Continued on Page 18, Column 1

BLASTED TEXAS CITY WINNING FIGHT TO CHECK FIRES AND NEW EXPLOSIONS; DEATHS NOW EXPECTED TO TOTAL 400

SMOKE STILL TOWERING OVER TEXAS CITY

FLAMES STILL RAGE

Giant Pillars of Smoke From 9 Conflagrations Cast Intense Heat

190 BODIES IN GYMNASIUM

Total of Injured Is Estimated at 2,000—'In Good Shape Now,' Says Rescue Chief

By JOHN N. POPHAM
Special to THE NEW YORK TIMES.

TEXAS CITY, Tex., April 17—Under a sky blackened with gigantic pillars of dense smoke from nine separate fires that cast a withering heat over a large area, the residents of this war-boom town claimed late today a costly victory over the catastrophic forces that brought them untold dead and injured. Property damage has mounted into millions of dollars.

[According to The Associated Press, a fresh fire posed a new threat to Texas City, ravaged by a death-dealing chain of explosions and conflagrations that have taken an estimated 450 lives and injured at least 2,000 in the last twenty-four hours. The latest outbreak was in the Humble Refinery area. Officials asked for more fire trucks from Baytown to help combat the flames. The chain of explosions which caused such devastation began at 9:12 A. M. Wednesday when the Grandcamp exploded shortly after fire had broken out. Almost immediately a second explosion occurred, this one at the Monsanto Chemical Corporation plant. Balls of hemp twine stored in the hold of the Grandcamp were hurled over town, flaming and causing new fires.

The devastated dock area, completely barren of ships, burning on the second day
Associated Press Wirephoto

AIRPORT CONTRACT SIGNED BY MAYOR

Port Authority Leases 3 Fields for 50 Years From June 1— Terms Favorable to City

By PAUL CROWELL

The Port of New York Authority will take over the city's three major airports on June 1 under a 50-year lease contract signed yesterday afternoon at City Hall by Mayor O'Dwyer and Howard S. Cullman, chairman of the bi-state

Texas City Is a Ghost Town In Shadow of Raging Fires

By LUCY GREENBAUM
Special to THE NEW YORK TIMES.

TEXAS CITY, Tex., April 17—Terror-stricken Texas City was a gray ghost town today. House after house stood in splintered silence, deserted in destruction. In the shadow of the raging fires a lone cow munched away at scrubby grass, no one to care for her milk. The only other moving thing in that torn land was a red apron that waved on a wash-line in an abandoned backyard.

Billboards, a few blocks away from the inferno, were blown to bits, their colored pieces lying on the ground like a giant jigsaw

TRUMAN PROMISES ALL FEDERAL AID

French Embassy Maps Inquiry

New York Times 18 April 1947

Shortly after 9.00am on 16 April 1947, the French freighter *Grandcamp*, taking on a heavy cargo of ammonium nitrate, exploded in the harbour of Texas City on the Gulf of Mexico. The blast was heard quite clearly more than a hundred miles away: that explosion alone would have ranked as a major disaster of the twentieth century. But to compound the tragedy, the *Grandcamp* at that moment was lying alongside another tanker loaded with ammonium nitrate and opposite the great Monsanto chemical works, itself flanked by oil refineries and sulphur warehouses. Within minutes the whole harbour was a living holocaust, racked by repeated explosions, and whole tracts of Texas City lay in ruins, smothered by black acrid smoke and deadly fumes. A *Houston Chronicle* reporter who flew over the scene of devastation some hours later declared the smoke was rising to 4,000 feet: 'One oil tank, about a thousand feet away from the blaze, was

crumpled like a piece of tinfoil' he wrote. 'An industrial section close to the bay was afire with the biggest blaze. Smoke was pouring from the tanks and buildings. A refinery west of the tracks also was burning. Several oil tanks were blazing brightly, a few were crumpled by the force of the blast. A heavy cloud of smoke hung over the scene, shot with flashes of flame from the fires that still raged along the waterfront.' They continued to rage for forty-eight hours: the town looked, said one press photographer, 'as if a flight of B-29 Superfortresses had bombed it.' It was also reckoned something of a miracle that, although Texas City suffered considerably more material damage than did Halifax in 1917 (see page 72), the actual death-toll did not exceed 450. Perhaps the furies were not satisfied with that: the same week a fierce tornado swept through the Texas Panhandle, adding another 132 lives to the toll.

Death Dive
Farnborough Air Crash 1952

WHITES WHITER with
Tintex
Dye-white
THE AMAZING
NEW WHITE DYE
Made by Tintex Dyes

SUNDAY GRAPHIC

No. 1,952. September 7, 1952.   C   A Kemsley Newspaper 2½d.

HOLLAND
TOFFEE
Best on Earth

This was test-pilot John Derry's DH110 jet fighter a few seconds before it blew up in the air over Farnborough air show yesterday. Derry (left) and his observer were killed in the explosion, just after breaking the sound barrier. Twenty-five spectators died and more than 60 were injured when wreckage fell on the crowd.

JET DISASTER

"Derry's engine ploughed a red furrow of death through the spectators on either side of me."

"'Mummy, look out!' and a dark object whistled past our faces and crashed into the crowd."

"Police and ambulances came and soon there were shrouds on the Farnborough hillside."

"There was a moment of deathly silence, and then we heard the screams."

FULL STORY PAGE THREE

Last picture of John Derry with his wife at Farnborough. Mrs. Derry was watching from the pilots' tent when the 700-m.p.h. DH110 exploded in mid-air.

A young victim, hit by wreckage from the jet explosion, being carried to an ambulance.

MORE RESCUE PICTURES ON MIDDLE PAGES

Only the most insensitive reader of the British Press in 1952 could have failed to note a distinctly optimistic edge to its scribblings that summer. The country had—if the leader-writers were to be believed—embarked on the New Elizabethan age, with the accession of a young and attractive Queen whose very name and promise recalled one of the glorious reigns in history. She would be the symbol, if not the instrument of national regeneration. The years of war, rationing, and austerity were in the past: now would be the time to emulate the deeds of Drake and Raleigh.

High on any roll-call of 'New Elizabethans' (a tireless newspaper pastime) would invariably come the test-pilots, men like John Derry, Neville Duke, and 'Cats-Eyes' Cunningham, whose names were as familiar as football-players or pop-stars are today. These were the pioneers whose hair-raising dives through the

sound-barrier magnetized hundreds of thousands of spectators, and whose steel nerves were establishing Britain as a world leader in civil aviation. And if proof were needed of the industry's 'workmanship that rivals ancient Chinese craftsmanship at its best, and engineering skill brought to a pitch that would bring respect and approval from Leonardo da Vinci himself' (the *Daily Mirror*), you had only to peer in at the great shop-window of the Farnborough Air Show.

There 'you will see beauty and naked force tearing and screaming through the skies' the *Mirror* continued lyrically on the eve of the 1952 Show. 'You will see unimaginable power locked up in jet engines that are little bigger than a pillar-box.' You would also witness Duke's high-speed, grass-cutting runs over the airfield and Derry's spectacular vertical banked turns. One of these was promised for Saturday

4 September, a public day at the Show and, as it happened, the fourth anniversary of Derry's first supersonic flight.

A crowd of 120,000 was packed into Farnborough that afternoon, waiting, squinting to catch sight of Derry's De Havilland 110 as it dived from 40,000 feet, gathering speed to break through the sound barrier. The sonic booms reached the spectators first, three of them, then two puffs of smoke, then the 110 thundered into view levelling out over the crowd. Derry swept round into a huge turn until he was pointing directly at the President's tent.

And then the plane disintegrated, crumpling and throwing out its parts in the same instant. The two engines sailed on under their own momentum, one of them tearing sickeningly straight at 'The Hill' where a mass of spectators was jammed. A *Daily Express* reporter was among them: 'an engine hurtled towards us in a glowing arc . . . it seemed a lifetime before it blotted out the sky . . . red hot scraps of machinery sprayed onto men, women and children. Then everything was still . . .' he wrote the next morning. Around him the scene was like a battlefield, thirty people dead or dying, scores more injured, a mile and a half from the spot where Derry and his observer had lost their lives.

What had happened? Well, the Press was never told, since the official enquiry was in secret (the De Havilland being a military plane). It was generally agreed that structural failure of some kind had occurred—the *Daily Telegraph* suggested Derry's 'acrobatics' had caused it, without much foundation. The *Daily Express* was sure Derry had known he was in trouble and had fought to clear the crowd. The *Mirror* the next day quoted Ground Control, to prove Derry had had no warning whatsoever.

But in one respect there was no disagreement. Fleet Street firmly closed its ranks against any suggestion that this catastrophe should in any way reflect on Britain's growing pre-eminence in the air. Test pilots (as the *News Chronicle* pointed out) were 'pioneers who die in the cause of discovery in this modern age.' 'This is the Jet Age' maintained the *Sunday Express*. 'The work must go on.' And so it did, with Neville Duke the next day jumping straight into another plane and breaking the sound barrier once more. And on The Hill, which had been twenty-four hours earlier a scene of utter carnage, an even greater crowd turned up to watch him.

One of the few notes of caution was struck by *The Times*. 'The doubt suggested by Farnborough's first grim casualty list is of the wisdom of such pioneering displays over the heads of densely packed crowds, until the hazards which face the brave flyers are better understood.' Its words were heeded, for never again were such spectacular stunts permitted at Farnborough.

DAILY EXPRESS

No. 16,291 — MONDAY SEPTEMBER 8 1952 — CONTROLLING SHAREHOLDER LORD BEAVERBROOK — Weather: Mainly cloudy, showers

NEGUIB Forms a 'purge' Cabinet — **MOSSADEG** Speeds new oil strike — **SHIP** Navy boards freighter after SOS call — **PLANE** Inquiry opens on jet disaster

14-SECOND CRASH DRAMA

THIRTY SECONDS BEFORE TEARING APART THE DH 110 STREAKS OVER THE FIELD, SHROUDED IN A STRANGE VAPOUR GLOW.—Daily Express exclusive picture.

Derry fought to clear crowd as jet burst

By GROUP CAPTAIN HUGH DUNDAS and CYRIL AYNSLEY

THE de Havilland jet which killed test pilot John Derry, his observer, and 25 civilians on Saturday began to break up two miles before it flew over the heads of the crowd at Farnborough air show, it was officially said last night.

And if John Derry knew what was happening, he had 14 seconds—at around 500 miles an hour—to swing his plane away from the airfield and out of danger to the 130,000 spectators there.

And it seems that he *did* know and *did* try to swing off course.

For many eye-witnesses say that his plane was turning away from the crowds as its twin-boomed tail, barrel-like engines, and some eight other pieces fell on to spectators.

The 14-second drama was one of the reports put before an official inquiry into the disaster which opened at Farnborough yesterday.

Every available piece of the jet—the prototype DH 110, which had topped the speed of sound more than 100 times—will be examined.

Confident

From them, experts confidently expect to discover the cause of the crash.

And while they worked and theorised yesterday, just as many people drove and walked to Farnborough for the last day of the show as did on Saturday.

Some 140,000 it was estimated turned up. And, as before, the ... pilots gave of their best.

Under a hanging curtain of mist every plane and pilot on the programme took off and performed—except only the giant ten-engined Princess flying-boat, which could hardly have fitted its huge wingspan between cloud and ground.

The speed-of-sound boys showed their unshaken belief in British wings at the show which marks the first year of the Elizabethan jet age.

Even the eight-day-old Avro Delta four-engined bomber cavorted below the cloud like a handy fighter.

Duke again

And Neville Duke, the man who flew through the sound barrier on Saturday after John Derry died?

He did it again yesterday—not only passing the speed of sound, but reaching, in his Hawker Hunter, the highest speed he has yet recorded at this show.

He first went through the overcast sky to 40,000ft. Then, aiming by radar, he dived towards the airfield.

The crowd tensed. The voice of the air show announcer came over the airfield amplifiers: "He is just beginning to dive. He is well over Mach 1"—speed of sound at sea level, 760 miles an hour.

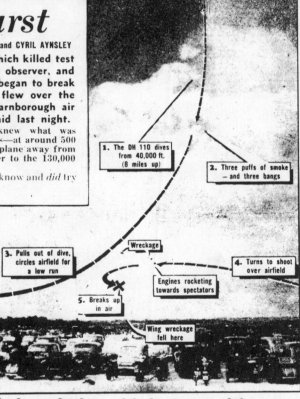

1. The DH 110 dives from 40,000 ft. (8 miles up)
2. Three puffs of smoke—and three bangs
3. Pulls out of dive, circles airfield for a low run
4. Turns to shoot over airfield
5. Breaks up in air
Wreckage
Engines rocketing towards spectators
Wing wreckage fell here

He's bought it, said the man-with-a-mac

By PETER DRAKE

SUDDENLY the man with a raincoat standing next to me pointed and shouted "There she is."

And high above—just a pinhead to a crowd standing shoulder to shoulder on a hillock 200 yards from the main enclosure at Farnborough—was John Derry.

In his 700 miles an hour DH 110 he dived. It seemed only a second before there were three bangs: Derry and his 24-year-old observer, Anthony Richards, were through the speed of sound and swinging out of sight again.

PUFFS OF 'CLOUD'

The heads of the crowd turned like a Wimbledon crowd—only this time upwards as well as sideways.

The grey, twin-engined fighter jet did a sweeping arc and came low over the airfield. I looked [...]wards, reminding me of a wind-born seed pod from a sycamore tree.

Then an engine hurtled towards us in a glowing arc.

I could not move. The engine no longer seemed to be hurtling.

Slowly, timelessly it fell. It seemed a lifetime before it blotted out the sky.

After that, the first impression was noise:—

A dull thud as the engine dug into the grassy slope;

The crowd scattering as best it could;

Red hot scraps of machinery sprayed on to men, women and children.

Then everyone was still. There was silence again. Grass was smouldering. I was sitting—fell that way I suppose—at the edge of a circle of people lying huddled or flat.

[...] inches away a splintered pair of horn-rimmed spectacles;

Over an elderly woman, a man and woman bent; he held her hand; the younger woman wept;

A young boy in cycling shorts, killed instantly, was lying with his leg twisted under him, his hand still clutching a brightly coloured programme;

A handful of soldiers—too young to know death even in the last war—carried stretchers.

A little girl of about five, in a pink gingham dress, ran around crying: "Mummy, I want my mummy." A sailor picked her up and carried her away.

So it went on.

CRACK-CRACK

Several hundreds went home immediately. Those who waited heard the twin-cracks as Neville Duke dived again through the sound barrier in a Hawker Hunter.

It was then that a man in a Royal Flying Corps tie of the First World War turned and

MAHER OUT, NEGUIB NOW DICTATOR

From THOMAS CLAYTON: Cairo, Sunday

GENERAL NEGUIB is dictator of Egypt tonight, after a day in which he arrested nearly every prominent politician outside the Government.

Two ex-premiers, two princes, millionaires, and editors are among the 52 held.

They include men suspected of major parts in the Palestine arms scandal. All who surrounded Farouk are also now under arrest or out of Egypt.

In the middle of the round-up Prime Minister Aly Maher resigned. General Neguib took on the job. He also becomes War Minister and retains his title of Commander-in-Chief Armed Forces.

His new Cabinet of 14 sworn in by the Regency Council tonight, includes anti-British Fathy Radwan as Propaganda Minister. But there are also moderates and some first-class men whose names are untainted by graft allegations.

Neguib, the almost unknown army officer of a couple of months ago, carried out today's purge with the same ease that he toppled Farouk off his throne on July 26.

Arrests at dance

His first arrest was made while Cairo society was dancing on the Semiramis' rooftop. It was done so quietly that no one noticed the two army officers who went and sat with an Egyptian in tropical dinner dress. The band was playing "Jezebel," and Doris Duke, the tobacco heiress, had been present a few tables away.

Many were arrested at home and the last reported seizure tonight was a man living in a Nile houseboat.

Not a shot was fired, not a revolver drawn. Armoured cars patrol the streets of Cairo and Alexandria, but these great cities are as quiet as an English market town on early closing day.

Among the arrested are El Hilaly, Premier until July 23, Ibrahim Abdel Hadi, Premier in 1948, Prince Abbas Halim, Prince Said Halim, Mustapha Sadek, ex-Queen Narriman's uncle, Serag ed-Din, the powerful Wafd (Nationalist) Party Secretary-General, his millionaire brother-in-law Abdel Aziz Badrawi, Ahmed Mortada el Maraghi, former Minister of Interior, and Hafez Afifi, who was Farouk's chief of the Royal Cabinet.

Triple-chinned, 18 stone Serag ed-Din was Minister of the Interior at the time of the "Black Saturday" riots in January.

415 rescued, then liner sinks

TORONTO, Sunday.—The Canadian luxury cruise liner Princess Kathleen (6,000 tons) ran aground on a reef off Alaska today. The 300 passengers and crew of 115 were saved. Then the ship sank.—Express News Service.

TROOPS STAND BY ALL NIGHT ON LYN

Express Staff Reporter: Lynmouth, Sunday

VIOLENT thunderstorms again hit the devastated Lynmouth valley and the hilltop town of Lynton twice this week-end.

The first storm, late last night, lasted two hours.

Lightning struck electric cables plunging both Lynmouth and Lynton into darkness, cutting off electricity and telephones.

The levels of the East and West Lyn Rivers rose as the water poured down from the 1,000-feet high Exmoor watershed.

Workmen taking their first week-end off since Lynmouth was shattered by floods three weeks ago were recalled.

Royal Engineers with walkie-talkies kept watch on danger spots all night.

Troops who moved out of Dulverton yesterday were warned tonight to be prepared to return from their camps on Salisbury Plain and at Taunton if necessary.

Two houses in Bridgewood-road, Worcester Park, Surrey, were struck by lightning. Three people were treated for shock.

Streets in Portsmouth were flooded by torrential rain.

Cold note:—Yesterday was the coldest early-September day in London for 81 years—53 degrees between 9 and 10 a.m.

HOLIDAY YOUTHS FIND URANIUM AMONG TIN

SIX young men on holiday say they have found uranium in an old tin mine.

The place: in the Wheal Edward mine, near Kenidjack Castle, Cornwall — four miles from Land's End.

The six: Worksop, Notts, College students who belong to a geological society.

They are combining a month's holiday with their research, and they claim to have dug out 18cwt. of ore containing 25 per cent. uranium oxide.

Mr. M. A. Piasecki, aged 20, of Lilford, Oundle, Northants, who is supervising the geological survey, said the students are volunteer workers for a North London mining and electronic engineer.

Chapman Pincher writes: The Supply Ministry would certainly buy this ore if it proved to have a uranium oxide content of more than 10 per cent.

Never-win horse wins at 20–1

Express Staff Reporter

NINE-YEAR-OLD racehorse Island Tale has broken his own peculiar record. He has won a race.

In 29 outings he did no better than finish second twice. And on one of those occasions was disqualified. The other was a two-horse race.

Since May he had not raced until Saturday's 3.30 at Southwell's jumping meeting.

Six runners—and in came Island Tale—by six lengths, at 20—1.

Said his owner Mr. William Selby, a timber merchant, of Bulwell, Notts: "Yes, I had a nice bet—got 33's.

"But that's not important. The big thing is that Malcolm, my 18-year-old son who rode Island Tale, is back on top again."

Last October Island Tale fell in a race and Malcolm, a former boy jumping champion, was badly hurt.

THE VOICE —in Georgian

NEW YORK, Sunday.—A floating radio station built to pierce Soviet "jamming" will broadcast "Voice of America" news tomorrow in Georgian, language of Stalin's home province.

The station is in a U.S. coastguard cutter anchored off the Greek island of Rhodes.—Express News Service.

21 volunteers defy curfew

DURBAN, Sunday.—Twenty-one Africans were arrested in Durban tonight for being out after curfew without passes. They were volunteers in the passive resistance campaign against the racial segregation laws, and in the afternoon

MOSSADEG PINS HOPE ON NEW WELLS

Express Staff Reporter: Washington, Sunday

MOSSADEG is pinning high hopes on a brand new oilfield which is now being actively "proved" by American experts for the Persian Government at Qum, 100 miles south of Teheran.

The new field has aroused tremendous enthusiasm in the capital because if it should give a good yield Mossadeg will be able to snap his fingers at Britain's sanctions, by offering for sale oil that never came from a well owned by the Anglo-Iranian Oil Company.

All urgency in getting a settlement with the company would disappear as far as the Persians were concerned.

Orders have gone out that new wells must be sunk at top priority and no effort or expense spared.

First reports about the new field reached Washington secretly six weeks ago. It was discovered by a "field team" of the firm of Drill Exco, an American concern.

A State Department expert said tonight: "Our understanding is that the strike was a modest one. The full possibilities are not yet known, but it is certainly promising."

And what role is Alton Jones, multi-millionaire boss of the £350 million Cities Service Company of America, playing?

Jones's role

A top oil-man said tonight: "It was Jones who was called in by the United States Government during the war to build pipelines

The most amazing picture of the year

Daily Mail

THREE HALFPENCE

TUESDAY, JANUARY 27, 1953

STANDING ONLY 25 YARDS AWAY AN AMATEUR PHOTOGRAPHER RISKED HIS LIFE TO TAKE THIS AS JOHN DERRY'S DH 110 EXPLODED AT FARNBOROUGH

THIS astonishing picture was taken by a *Daily Mail* reader. He took it at the Farnborough Air Display last September. Mr. John Derry was breaking the sound barrier in his DH 110 before 100,000 people. Suddenly his plane began to break up. The twin engines tore away from the fuselage, the tail fell off—then this happened. The main part of the plane has just struck the ground and is breaking up into a thousand pieces.

Some components can be identified—the windscreen (top right); part of the seat and part of a hatch (centre, right); part of the engine

took the picture, Mr. H. H. J. Orr, explain : " I was in the 10s. enclosure about 25 to 30 yards from the actual impact, but as most people had ducked I had an unimpeded view. At the time it was given out that the authorities would be glad to have any pictures of the crash for the purposes of an inquiry. I developed and printed mine on the Sunday and handed them in on the Monday morning. I only recently received the negative back, so I have not been able to offer this picture for publication until now."

The *Daily Mail* now reproduces it as the most dramatic news picture submitted to this newspaper by a reader this year. Mr. Herbert Henry James Orr, who had the courage to stand up and obtain it with evident risk

The Ransom of Progress

The Comet Disasters 1953-4

Sunday Pictorial 3 May 1953

COMET LOST

B.O.A.C.'s Comet. Just a year ago a new era of air transport began.

And among the passengers there are

10 WOMEN, 2 CHILDREN

The Comet was more than an airliner in Britain in the early 1950s, it was a national hero. A quarter of a century later—in which we have seen spacecraft land on the moon and airliners cruising at supersonic speeds—it is easy to forget the ordinary man's enthusiasm and pride of those heady years. 'It makes me feel so British and proud of it that I want to sing out loud' one Fleet Street correspondent in 1953 wrote about the Comet, an emotional endorsement that would sit most embarrassingly in today's columns. Yet, then, it no more than reflected the country's renewed hopes and aspirations to leadership in the air. It was the Comet, the world's first-ever turbo-jet airliner, which was the key to those ambitions. To build it the De Havilland company had broached new frontiers of design and technology, and in 1952, its first year of service, it had triumphantly fulfilled all expectations. The world's airlines were clamouring for it: for every model that came off the production line, there were five customers waiting to buy.

Saturday 2 May, four weeks to the Coronation. A team of British climbers were preparing for an historic assault on Everest. Stanley Matthews was playing in what would probably be his last

Cup Final. At Dum Dum airport in Calcutta Comet *Yoke Victor* was taking off, bound for London. The control tower received the routine wireless message 'climbing on course'—then silence. Six minutes after that call and still climbing on course, one must imagine, the airliner disintegrated. Most of the wreckage fell around the remote village of Jugalgari, though parts of the wings were later found as much as eight miles away. Everyone on board was killed.

As the Minister of Transport pointed out, this was the first fatal BOAC accident for nearly five years: but that it should have happened to one of the new Comets was a stunning blow. The Press's first reaction was to argue that the Comet was no ordinary plane; it must have been some extraordinary circumstances that caused it to crash. Examining the weather reports from Calcutta, the *Daily Express* came to the conclusion that *Yoke Victor* had encountered a 'Killer Cloud' striking 'an up-draught and a down-draught almost simultaneously', which would have been an impact of enormous violence. Such conditions being an accepted hazard of flying, the paper proceeded to set the public's mind at rest. 'Fly on, fly on to glory' trumpeted its editorial. 'The *Titanic* was not a

bad ship because she ran into a berg . . . it added elsewhere.

The other papers agreed. 'Unless the enquiry brings to light some factor at present unsuspected' suggested the *Daily Telegraph*, 'the Comet will continue to hold its place as the pride of the world's air fleets'. The optimism was not unreasonable. Only the subsequent drumbeating sounded a little desperate: two days later the *Express*'s front page was exuberant. 'Comet II beats record' was its banner-headline. 'London to Cairo cut 30 minutes.' Then just three days later: 'Twice as High as Everest! 15-stone pilot cracks jet record no. 2 in week.' Even the Duke of Edinburgh landing at Buckingham Palace by helicopter later that month was 'A boost for British aviation'. Normally such stories would hardly have led any front page, but things weren't normal and the *Express*'s proprietor, Lord Beaverbrook, had a personal interest in Britain's reputation in the air, having been Minister for Aircraft Production during the war.

For eight months nothing more untoward occurred to disturb public confidence—indeed, the Comet was surely flying on to glory when a new service to Johannesburg was opened and the travelling time cut by a third. Then on 11 January 1954 an Italian fisherman at Castiglione, walking out with his wife in their Sunday best, caught sight of a silver jet high in the blue sky. Suddenly he saw a plume of black smoke where the Comet had been, then watched in horror as the stream arrowed down to meet the sea and a column of smoke rose momentarily, like a passing monument, from the water. Comet *Yoke Peter*, en route from Singapore to London, was twenty minutes out of Rome airport when it fell from the sky, silently and for no discernible reason. The weather was perfect and no radio distress signal had been sent. The clue, if any, to the riddle lay deep in the Mediterranean south of the island of Elba.

Now the editorials took on a questioning tone. 'We are left wondering whether we know all we think we know about the jet' remarked the *Daily Mail*. 'Are there things still hidden from us?' Even the *Daily Express* wondered 'Can the Comet's glory fade?' Meanwhile BOAC had taken the drastic step of grounding all its operational Comets, while its experts treated them to every imaginable indignity, including pouring paraffin on one of the red-hot engines. 'It still would not ignite' one of them told the *Daily Sketch*. 'We treated the plane like a tank, but it came out 100 per cent.' After ten weeks of fruitless search the Comets were returned to service.

At the same time the inquest in Elba had produced more mysteries. On the bodies picked up from the sea, the *News Chronicle* reported, 'the facial expressions showed no fear or pain. There was no sign of burning or scorching . . . Severe head injuries showed they had either been flung forward or struck by something hard with great force.' The only hope lay in the epic salvage operation then being conducted by the Royal Navy: it was truly like combing a haystack for a needle, trying to locate the wreckage 500 feet below the surface somewhere in an area of several hundred square miles. For the first time ever an underwater television camera was used, in conjunction with sophisticated grabs which had to set to work with pinpoint accuracy, when a single inch out either way meant failure.

As it turned out the operation was an out-

DAILY HERALD

No. 11800 (D)   MONDAY, JANUARY 11, 1954   PRICE 1½D

35 KILLED IN COMET CRASH

Ten children in plane lost at Point Calamity

HERALD REPORTER   **ROME, Sunday**

A LONDON-BOUND Comet of BOAC plunged into the sea from four miles up today killing all 29 passengers and the crew of six.

HOLIDAY END FOR A FAMILY

PASSENGERS aboard the doomed Comet, in addition to Mr. Chester Wilmot, were:

Capt. R. V. Wolfson, one of BOAC's senior men, who joined the plane at Beirut. He was general manager of BOAC subsidiaries overseas and a member of the Corporation's management panel.

Mrs. R. K. Geldard, who was travelling to London with her two children, a boy and a girl, on holiday. She was the wife of a BOAC man at Beirut.

Master J. M. Bunyan and Miss A. Bunyan (both children) and an infant named Bunyan. They were travelling from Bahrein, in the Persian Gulf.

Miss R. Khedouri, aged 13, and Miss N. Khedouri, 23 (from Bahrein).

BEA PILOT

Capt. Charles Livingstone, a BEA pilot, who joined the plane as a passenger at Rome.

Miss R. Sawyer-Snelling, aged 24 (From Bangkok).

Miss L. Yateem, aged 17; Mr. B. Butler; Mr. J. B. Crilly and B. Crilly (a child) and someone named Israel — all from Bahrein.

Mr. F. J. Greenhouse (Bangkok); Mr. J. P. Hill (Singapore) BOAC Far East representative; Miss E. Fairbrother; Mr. T. Moore; Mr. H. E. Schuchmann, Mrs. D. Baker (all joined the plane at Karachi).

Mr. John Steel, aged 52, of Redcar, Yorks, a constructional engineer in Borneo. He served in the Scots Guards for 23 years. He was Army welterweight champion for three years. He became boxing instructor at Harrow School. None of his relatives knew he was on his way home.

D. Leavet (a child); Mr. S. F. Saamin, Mr. E. S. Maehlachlan, J. V. (or J. Y.) Ramsden, A. Vrias—all travelling from Beirut.

CREW

The six crew were:

Captain Alan Gibson, D.F.C., 31 of Highcliffe, Hants. Married with two children. He went to BOAC from the RAF in 1946 and joined the Comet fleet last June. He had 5,800 flying hours.

First Officer William John Bury, 33, of Gosport, Hants. He had over 3,000 flying hours. Ex-RAF man who joined BOAC in 1947. Married with two children.

Engineer Officer Francis Charles MacDonald, 27, of Yateley, Hants. Married with two children. Ex-RAF man and joined BOAC last year.

Radio Officer Luke Patrick McMahon, 32 of Omagh, Northern Ireland.

Steward Frank Leonard Saunders, 34 of Dover.

Stewardess Jean Evelyn Clark, 21, of Buckingham. A S.R.N. registered nurse, she joined BOAC last May. Made her first trip as a stewardess to Rome 1 August.

GUN-BOY ROBS WOMAN

A schoolboy, with a gun in his pocket, held up a woman cashier in a... [text obscured]

IT was due in London by midday yesterday. But G-ALYP, the crashed Comet, with flying log of 3,500 hours, had disappeared into the sea.

Among the passengers were a girl of 17, a baby in arms, and nine other children, some of whom were returning to school in England after Christmas visits to parents in the Far East.

Adult passengers who died included Mr. Chester Wilmot, the 42-year-old war correspondent and broadcaster, and six BOAC staff members coming back from holiday.

The 36-seater Comet was on the last lap of an extra service from Singapore which it left on Saturday morning, flying via Bangkok, Rangoon, Calcutta, Karachi, the Bahrein Islands and Beirut.

DID IT BLOW UP?

It left Ciampino Airport here at 9.31 this morning. Some 30 minutes later it was flying at eight miles a minute high above the island of Elba. At 10.10, trailing flames and plumes of smoke, the Comet fell into the sea —10 miles off Point Calamity, Elba's southernmost tip.

Italian fishermen declare the jet airliner blew up with a series of explosions before it fell. But Mr. David Craig, who is chief of British European Airways in Italy, said tonight that he doubted the fishermen's report because they also reported seeing parachutes open beneath the plane and there was no parachute aboard.

The big mystery is that no distress signal from the Comet was picked up. Weather conditions were good and whatever happened must have occurred suddenly. The last routine message was received shortly before 10 a.m.

ALL-NIGHT SEARCH

From Elba and the nearby island of Monte Cristo, came a fleet of Italian motor fishing vessels to join in an all-night hunt by the searchlights of Italian Naval units, including minesweepers and torpedo-boats, from the ports of La Spezia, Viareggio and Leghorn.

British, U.S., Italian and French planes also scoured a wide area until dark and reported the positions of wreckage and bodies.

A four-nation rescue service which went into immediate operation has recovered 15 bodies so far. Eight picked up dead by one Italian vessel, the Pericha, were burned. Identification of the bodies was extremely difficult. Among them was the stewardess, Miss Jean Evelyn Clark, a young Indian woman and two children. Miss Clark had changed planes with the regular stewardess, Miss Elaine Baker at Karachi because Miss Baker had ear trouble.

Wreckage recovered includes a bag of mail, coats, two life-jackets — and a jagged piece of metal bearing the BOAC insignia.

Flash from the clouds

THE 15 bodies—two children, 17-year-old Miss L. Yateem and six men and six women—were brought into Porto Azzuro, Elba, by local fishermen and carried to the tiny, whitewashed chapel of the cemetery.

Tiny fishing boats, painted in faded blues and reds, had lowered flags to half-mast as they arrived in port just after dark with the bodies laid on the foredecks and covered with blankets from the fishermen's bunks says *Reuter's Correspondent by radio-telephone from Porto Azzuro.*

A priest came to the quayside and gave a benediction as the bodies, laid on planks, were transferred ashore. Then the fishermen walked to the candle-lit cemetery chapel where flowers had been placed by village children. At the cemetery gates stands a civic guard of honour.

HEARD THREE EXPLOSIONS

A fisherman, 39-year-old Giovanni di Marco who first reported the crash to the island authorities. I was fishing when I heard the whine of the plane above the clouds.

"Then I heard three explosions, one after the other.

★ CONTINUED ON PAGE TWO

CHESTER WILMOT, broadcasting as a BBC war correspondent. Below: George McCarthy of the *Daily Herald*, who covered the war fronts with Wilmot, tells of their meeting in Rome yesterday.

Australia ease-up will help Britain

AUSTRALIA will relax her remaining import controls in April, *Reuter* reports from Sydney.

Imports of most types of British goods will go back to the 1951 level before controls were imposed. China, textile and engineering exporters will benefit, but a degree of restriction is expected to stay on strictly luxury goods when the licensing year begins on April 1.

Although details have not yet been completed it is estimated Britain will be allowed to send Australia goods worth £40 million.

Drain death riddle

A MAN reported missing on Saturday was found dead yesterday in about 15 inches of water in a drainage ditch near Great Salterns golf course, Portsmouth.

He was Mr. Albert Russell, a 36-year-old married dockyard worker of Montague-road, North End, Portsmouth.

Police investigating at the spot said that the possibility of foul play had not been ruled out.

MP'S DAUGHTER FINDS HOME RANSACKED

An M.P.'s daughter, 15-year-old Lenette Bromley-Davenport, returned last night to find that thieves had climbed a 100-ft pipe to ransack her top-flat home at Westminster-gardens, S.W.

Lieut.-Col. Walter Bromley-Davenport, Tory M.P. for Knutsford, Cheshire, is out of London.

Cars race to save bomb boy

A RELAY team of three police cars speeded across London last night with a packet of drugs to save the life of a boy.

The boy is 14-year-old John Jesty, who blew himself up with a bomb he was making from a chemistry set given to him for Christmas.

John, son of Police constable Robert Jesty, of Stoneleigh, Surrey, became seriously ill in Epsom Hospital yesterday. An SOS for anti-tetanus drugs was sent to Scotland Yard.

A police car collected the packet from a Piccadilly all-night chemist shop and drove to Chelsea Bridge. There the packet was transferred to an "L" Division car and taken to Tooting Broadway. And from there a "W" Division car took it to the hospital.

The drugs arrived 43 minutes after the SOS went out. Total distance: nearly 20 miles.

Boy No. 2 gets wrong serum

VIENNA, Sunday.—A serum flown specially to the Atlantic by American Army planes to save an Austrian boy was found to be the wrong one when it reached Innsbruck.

The correct package was at an airfield in Massachusetts. Tonight it was flown across the Atlantic.

The boy, eight-year-old Gottfried Eider, is being kept alive by transfusions. He suffers from haemophilia. Its victims are liable to bleed to death even from a scratch.—Reuter, A.P.

LORD SIMON

The condition of Lord Simon, 80-year-old former Lord Chancellor, was last night "giving some cause for anxiety," it was said at Westminster Hospital.

HE NEARLY CHANGED TO SLOW PLANE

By George McCarthy

CHESTER WILMOT nearly changed planes at Rome yesterday. When the Singapore Comet stopped to refuel there he met a group of his friends. I was one of them.

We, too, were heading home to London on a slower aircraft. We had heard the Comet arrive, with its own whine and roar, and were delighted and surprised to see Chester walk off.

Out for TV

He had been abroad for months—in Australia and Japan —gathering material for a TV programme.

There was much news to exchange and we were eager to hear Chester tell his own high tales of peace and war and friends at home and abroad.

He seriously considered switching to our aircraft although it would delay him three hours.

But before he could make arrangements the loudspeakers summoned us aboard and he decided to go back to his seat in the Comet, due to leave 20 minutes later.

In the air, we heard that the Comet had exchanged signals with us as it raced past and above us over the coast of Italy, where the mountain snows glistened in the sun.

Last message

It must have been almost its last message. And Chester Wilmot had gone on his last assignment.

He had been on many. He was, I think, the best, certainly the best-informed of all the correspondents who covered the Western campaign of the war.

He landed in Normandy on D-Day with airborne troops. For the rest of the war he wore the brave beret of these men like a red badge of courage.

His pleasant Australian voice, familiar to millions of wartime radio listeners, seldom told colourful stories of the campaign.

He was a factual, rather quiet reporter, intent on giving the whole picture of the war as it swayed, paused and advanced.

Because, perhaps, of that painstaking accuracy and his wise understatements, those who campaigned with him often felt that he was underrated by those who listened.

If that were true, he found his true place in renown a year ago when his book, "The Struggle For Europe," was published telling with vivid detail the first full and brilliant account of the war in the west.

Chester Wilmot was born in Melbourne in 1911. He joined the BBC after serving as a war correspondent with the Australian forces in New Guinea and North Africa.

STEWARDESS Jean Clark. She was not due to fly in the Comet, but took the place of her friend, Elaine Baker, who became ill.

COMET CRASHED 10 MILES SOUTH OF ELBA 10·10 G.M.T.

The Woman Cashier

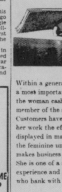

NEWS CHRONICLE

No. 33,646 | FRIDAY, APRIL 9, 1954 | PRICE 1½d.

ANOTHER COMET MISSING

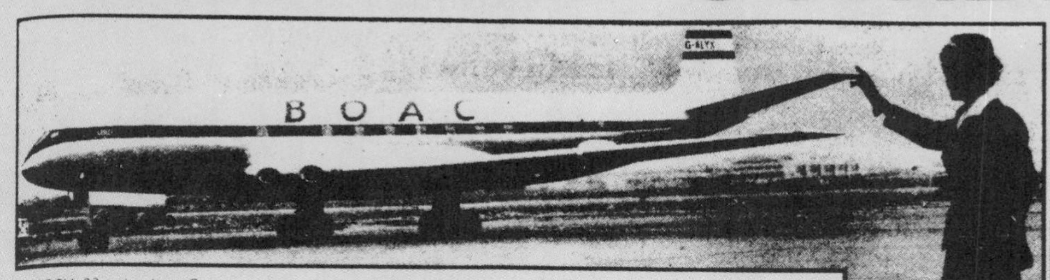

MARCH 23—the first Comet to go back into service after the crash off Elba takes off from London Airport

BOAC chief grounds all the others

21 IN PLANE LOST ON ROME RUN

NEWS CHRONICLE REPORTER

A BRITISH COMET JET AIRLINER WITH 14 PASSENGERS AND CREW OF SEVEN WAS THIS MORNING REPORTED MISSING.

First news came from Frankfurt, where radio operators intercepted messages listing the plane as overdue between Rome and Cairo.

Other planes were asked to keep a look-out, but a first search was fruitless.

Later B.O.A.C. confirmed that the plane, G-ALYY, which was on loan to South African Airways, is overdue.

The last message

This was quickly followed by an order from Sir Miles Thomas, B.O.A.C. chairman, suspending all B.O.A.C. Comet services throughout the world pending further information.

The plane—"Yoke-Yoke"—was on a flight to Johannesburg from London via Rome and Cairo as part of the thrice-weekly service operated by B.O.A.C. and South African Airways on a pool system. Her crew are all South Africans.

She left London Airport at 3 p.m. on Wednesday.

In Rome she was delayed for nearly 24 hours with technical trouble. She finally took off from there at 6.25 last night—with 14 passengers—and was due in Cairo at 11.26 p.m. She had fuel to last till 12.23 a.m.

THE LAST MESSAGE FROM HER RECEIVED AT NAPLES AIRPORT SAID: "OVER NAPLES—STILL CLIMBING."

That was shortly after 8 p.m. She was due to contact Catanzaro later, but did not.

Air, sea search

When Yoke-Yoke became overdue planes from the R.A.F. in Malta and the Italian air-sea rescue squadron went in search. Ships are also keeping a look-out. The air hunt will be resumed today.

It is estimated that the plane should be somewhere within the zone between Naples and the heel of Italy.

An official of B.O.A.C. said: "All we know is that the Comet is missing and has not arrived at its destination."

"Yoke-Yoke" narrowly escaped disaster on July 16 last year when she made an emergency landing at the Juhu airport at Bombay. The pilot had to jam on his brakes to avoid overrunning into a water-filled ditch. He blew out all eight tyres on his landing-gear, but the 13 persons aboard escaped injury.

The B.O.A.C. Comet fleet, grounded after the crash off Elba on January 10 last, in which 35 people were killed, only began flying again with passengers on March 23. The first service to be resumed was to Johannesburg.

Tests, inch by inch, to detect any possible flaw went on day and night. None was discovered. During the minute examination 60 modifications were made but none affected airworthiness.

They included the improving of ventilation of the electric battery compartments, installing extra fire-warning devices in the fuel-tank zones, and fitting armour plate guards round the inboard engines.

The mystery remains

The examination convinced B.O.A.C.'s investigators that there were no mechanical defects. The loss of Yoke Peter remained a mystery.

Warships were switched to the scene of the crash to search for wreckage. That search is still continuing and only a few days ago the control cabin was recovered almost intact. Underwater TV cameras were used.

Parts already flown to this country include one engine found without its 83-bladed turbine disc.

B.O.A.C. have been using 36-seater Comets, the world's first jet liner, since May 2, 1952. Three of the original fleet have been lost.

There were no casualties in the first accident, which occurred on October 26, 1952, while one was taking off from Ciampino Airport, Rome. But all 43 on board were killed on May 3, 1953, when another crashed a few minutes after taking off from Calcutta on the Singapore-London route. (Yoke Peter was also flying from Singapore to London.)

Later a Canadian Pacific Airlines Comet crashed, killing all the 11 crew and technicians aboard, at Karachi on March 3, 1953, while on a delivery flight from the U.K. to Sydney.

The first three of the Series II Comets, a larger version, are due to be delivered to B.O.A.C. in about two months' time. A still larger version, the Comet III, is being built by de Havillands and the prototype is scheduled to begin flying tests this year.

A new Mediterranean search starts for a missing Comet while the examination continues in Britain of pieces of the broken Comet Yoke Peter salvaged from the sea-bed ten miles south of the Island of Elba. After Yoke Peter crashed on January 10, B.O.A.C. grounded its Comet fleet and brought them home for detailed examination. They began to fly again on March 23

ATOMIC PACT SECRET OUT

Truman agreed to consult Attlee

By GEOFFREY COX

MR. ATTLEE and President Truman made a personal and secret agreement in 1948 to continue, as far as was practicable, the war-time pact under which America would not drop an atom bomb without British consent.

This information reached me last night from a reliable source.

The disclosure fills in a gap in the dispute over H-bomb control in last Monday's Commons debate.

The Prime Minister then accused Mr. Attlee of allowing to lapse promises of consultation made to Sir Winston by President Roosevelt at Quebec in 1943.

But it is now clear that Mr. Truman's undertaking was still in force up to Labour's leaving office in 1951. The undertaking was to maintain the spirit of the Quebec Agreement so far as the President's Constitutional position would allow.

But whether the 1948 secret pact still operates remains a mystery.

THE H-BOMB

In the light of Sir Winston's anger about the lapse of the Quebec pact, it seems possible, if not probable, that the U.S. regards the Truman - Attlee arrangements as binding only on the two men concerned, and therefore no longer in force.

It is uncertain how far the H-bomb, detonated by an atomic bomb, can be regarded as simply a development of the atomic bomb, and therefore covered by the Attlee-Truman agreement.

The Quebec pact was kept secret by Sir Winston Churchill in 1943 even from his colleagues in the War Cabinet. This fact was revealed in the Commons yesterday by Mr. Herbert Morrison.

The sequence of events is:

In 1945, when Mr. Attlee came to office, he learned for the first time the details of atomic development and of the Quebec pact.

He quickly took two steps—started Britain's own atomic development plans and gave orders for an atom bomb to be made as soon as possible.

LEGALITY DOUBT

He flew to Washington in November to sort out with President Truman and Mr. Mackenzie King of Canada the future relationships of the three countries in the atomic field.

The future of the Quebec Agreement was vital, but the peacetime legal position was obscure.

President Truman, to meet this uncertainty, gave Mr. Attlee an assurance that his administration would continue to act in the spirit of Quebec. The agreement itself remained in force.

In 1946 came the McMahon Act, which forbade the United States to share its atomic secrets with others. This cut across arrangements for sharing some information.

Sir Winston Churchill argued last Monday that Mr. Attlee, to halt the McMahon Act, should have published the Quebec Agreement, whose existence was unknown to Senator McMahon.

Mr Attlee retorted that he left that to President Truman, who decided against such a course.

But meanwhile, Alan Nunn

Turn Page Two, Col. 1

Cut down that tree—it's eerie

A TENANT who says a tree in his garden makes eerie noises in the night, frightening his wife, has been offered another home by Belper Urban Council, Derbyshire.

But Mr. Keith Hitchcock has just spent £50 on decorating the house. "We can't afford to move, and we like the house," he said yesterday. "It seems we shall have to put up with the tree.

"It makes noises, blocks the light and dirties the washing. Its roots stop us growing anything in the garden and its leaves stop the drains."

Mr. Hitchcock wanted the council to cut down the tree, but his neighbours, Mr. and Mrs. Harold Boswell objected. "We *love* trees," they said.

BBC urged: Ban Amos and Andy

New York, Thursday.—America's National Association for the Advancement of Coloured People asked the B.B.C. tonight to reconsider its decision to buy "Amos and Andy" for TV. The association called the show "a gross caricature of the negro."—A.P.

Brother, sister hurt on zebra

Twelve-year-old Pauline Brackett and her nine-year-old brother David, of Glen Park Road, Finchley, were injured at a zebra crossing in Ballards Lane, near Finchley Central Station last night. They are in hospital.

Crashing buses injure 19

Nineteen people, including eight women and two children, were injured last night when two double-deck buses collided head-on at Rusthall, near Tunbridge Wells. Women tore up sheets to bandage the injured.

Radar net ready

Washington, Thursday.—Mr. Charles Wilson, American Secretary of Defence, said today that the setting-up of a joint Canadian-American radar warning network in the far north is well advanced.—B.U.P.

Helicopter finds 'lost' Leopold

News Chronicle Reporter

NEW YORK, Thursday.

LEOPOLD, ex-King of the Belgians, is safe tonight after reports that he was missing in the Panama jungle.

A searching helicopter landed on a river bank and met a member of the royal explorer's party who confirmed that Leopold is well.

His 43-year-old wife, Princess Liliane de Rethy, explained the "mystery" tonight in Panama City.

She had sent a plane to drop a message to her adventure-loving husband, telling him of the death of his sister-in-law, Crown Princess Martha of Norway.

The pilot was unable to find the party and returned with the message undelivered.

So General Horace McBride, commander of the American air base in the Panama Canal Zone sent out a helicopter.

Indian guides

Its pilot sighted a lagging member of Leopold's expedition and touched down to meet him.

The explorer, Santiago Quantana, said that the others, slightly behind their time-table, had pushed on towards the Atlantic coast.

The 52-year-old ex-king and five companions, with a band of Indian guides, set out on March 28 to trace in reverse the sixteenth-century route taken by the Spanish explorer Vasco de Balboa when he "discovered" the Pacific.

37 die in crash

Montreal, Thursday.—Thirty-seven people died today in a crash between a trans-Canada airliner and a military training plane over Moose Jaw, Saskatchewan.—News Chronicle

Bunyan's clock, 15s.

A grandfather clock which belonged to John Bunyan was auctioned for 15s. at Leek, Staffordshire, yesterday.

DULLES FLIES TO LONDON

Britain, France will be urged: Warn China

By WILLIAM FORREST

AMERICA'S Secretary of State, John Foster Dulles, whose call for "united action" on Indo-China had a mixed reception this side of the Atlantic, is flying to London and Paris before the Far East conference at Geneva, diplomats said in Washington last night.

He is expected to have two days of conversation with Sir Winston Churchill and Mr. Anthony Eden, the Foreign Secretary.

Two more days' discussion will follow in Paris with Premier Joseph Laniel and other leaders.

His tentative plan is to return and report to President Eisenhower by the end of the week.

Earlier forecasts of the flight by State Department officials were followed by this warning from Senator Knowland, Republican leader in the Senate:

"Congress may withhold a decision on foreign aid until America's allies have decided how to respond to Mr. Dulles's call.

"Some nations have suggested waiting till after the Geneva conference before deciding how to respond to Mr. Dulles.

Ten-nation call

"I find a growing sentiment in Congress that it should delay until after Geneva before deciding on appropriations for NATO countries."

This applied particularly to countries "that have dragged their feet as far as the European Army is concerned," he added.

France and Italy are the only European Army nations that have not yet ratified the Treaty.

Mr. Dulles wants "united action" on Indo-China by ten nations—U.S., Britain, France, Australia, New Zealand, Siam, the Philippines and the three associated Indo-Chinese States of Vietnam, Cambodia and Laos.

Alive to danger

As a first step Mr. Dulles suggests a joint declaration, warning Communist China to keep out of the war, which the French have been waging for seven years against the Communist-led Viet-minh.

Britain and above all France are alive to the danger of Chinese intervention in the war, but they shrink from action which, in the words of the French Foreign Ministry spokesman, "might compromise the chances of success at Geneva."

The French Government moreover has pledged itself before Parliament to seek a negotiated settlement of the war at Geneva.

Premier Laniel will make another statement to Parliament today.

Elisabeth Mackenzie cables from Rome: A wave of strikes to stop Italy ratifying the European Defence Community treaty was forecast last night by Giuseppe di Vittorio, Communist leader of Italy's biggest labour federation.

Cambodia mobilises

Paris, Thursday.—General mobilisation was decreed tonight in the Indo-Chinese kingdom of Cambodia, invaded by Communist rebels. An appeal is to go to the United Nations.

AGA KHAN SLASHES RACING INTERESTS

From JOHN TOMICHE: Paris, Thursday

THE Aga Khan, winner of five Derbies, announced in Cannes today that he is severely cutting his racing activities. He is selling in England and the U.S. "all my Irish-bred yearling colts without exception and a large number of my high-class brood mares."

LEADING IN THE WINNER
Mahmoud, 1936 Derby

The Aga said he was doing this "in view of growing responsibilities. His son and partner, Prince Aly Khan, also had new responsibilities," he added.

The sale in autumn from his five studs in Ireland means that by 1956 he will have only a few horses from his three French studs racing in English classics.

Smaller scale

Two years ago the Aga Khan decided to stop buying horses. Only last month he said he did not know how many he owned.

At his Cannes villa, the Aga's secretary refused to say what the new responsibilities were.

The Aga *will* continue to breed horses, on a very much smaller scale.

Since 1922, when he had his first winner, the Aga's horses have won nearly a million pounds.

He sold all his Derby winners, the most recent, Tulyar, going to the Irish National Stud for a record price of £250,000.

Horses bred by the Aga Khan in Ireland and raced in England last year won 24 races worth £17,752.

Throughout the world, his Irish-bred horses won more than 80 races, worth £39,699.

Tap-wires Bill gets approval

Washington, Thursday.—The House of Representatives voted 377 to 10 today to empower the Attorney-General to tap telephone wires and use the information as evidence in the prosecution of spies and saboteurs, subject to court approval. The Bill was sent to the Senate.—A.P.

Their big day

The Royal yacht Britannia, with Prince Charles and Princess Anne on board, will sail from Portsmouth on Wednesday for the Mediterranean.

Work from Moscow

Kiel, Thursday.—Kiel shipyards are negotiating a £2 million contract in Moscow to overhaul 25 Russian cargo ships.

M.P.s may get expenses

BUT NO RISE

Political Correspondent

THE Government has decided against a £500-a-year pay rise and pensions for M.P.s.

Sir Winston Churchill broke this news to the Tory back-bench 1922 Committee last night.

But Ministers will support some form of expense allowance, particularly for M.P.s who must keep a home in London and in their constituencies. Details will be announced to the Commons on Tuesday.

Labour M.P.s were warned at their party meeting last night that they must not react angrily when the decision against a rise is announced to the House.

But it will anger many Labour M.P.s; some have only £5 a week to live on from their £1,000-a-year salary after they have paid what they consider official expenses — secretarial help, hotel expenses, postage, and so on.

Book this date

THE Duke of Edinburgh will be at the White City Stadium on Saturday, July 17, to see Britain's finest athletes competing in the British Amateur Athletic Board's international tournament sponsored by the News Chronicle.

It will be the final test for the British Empire Games team which leaves for Vancouver a few days later.

Teams from the Gold Coast, Kenya, Nigeria and possibly Pakistan—in London on their way to the Games—will also be competing.

Another attack will be made on the men's 4 x 1,500 metres relay world record set at 15 minutes 27.2 seconds by Britain last September.

There will also be special invitation events for women.

American Reds to escape call-up

Washington, Thursday.—Known Communists will not be conscripted into the United States forces in future; doubtful cases will be kept in the forces on the lowest possible pay while they are investigated, the Senate Armed Services Committee was told today.—Reuter.

LATE NEWS

COMET: ITALY SENDS WARSHIPS

Two Italian naval vessels have been sent to search the Gulf of Naples for the missing Comet.—B.U.P.

A plane has reported seeing floating lights in the Tyrrhenian Sea.

CENTRAL 5000

Labour holds Edinburgh E

Labour held Edinburgh East in yesterday's by-election. Voting:

E. G. Willis (Lab.)	18,950
W. Grant (Con.)	13,922
Labour majority	5,028

The by-election was caused by the elevation of the Labour member, Mr. John Wheatley (now Lord Wheatley) to the Scottish Bench.

Figures at the 1951 general election were: Wheatley 25,201, Grant 21,400. Labour majority 3,801.

Labour's percentage of votes rose from 54 to 57.6.

Evening Standard

CLOSING CITY PRICES

Mekay SHIRTS
MEKAY, LONDON, N.1
40,407

FRIDAY, APRIL 9, 1954 ●● Three-halfpence

FINAL NIGHT EXTRA

bear brand SUPERFINE STOCKINGS

Search planes find wreckage in sea

COMET: 'WARSHIP PICKS UP BODIES'

Miles Thomas bans passenger flights

'UNTIL CAUSE OF TRAGEDIES HAS BEEN FOUND AND PUT RIGHT'

British and Italian aircraft searching for the lost Comet jet airliner, G-ALYY, today reported finding bodies floating in the sea off the west coast of Italy.

The Italian corvette Ibis, part of a five-nation sea and air team hunting for the Comet, radioed to shore headquarters saying that bodies were being taken aboard. A British search airplane was reported circling over the spot.

Another search airplane reported sighting orange-coloured boxes and "white fabrics" in the sea.

FAMOUS HORSEMAN IS MISSING

7 Britons in list of passengers

Seven Britons are named as passengers in the Comet in a list issued by British Overseas Airways.

One of them is Captain "Tony" Collings, the horseman who trained Britain's team for the Helsinki Olympic Games.

The list is:

PASSENGERS FROM LONDON TO CAIRO: Mr. O. L. Anderson (American), of American Fort, Utah; Mr. and Mrs. A. Basil Brooks, of Layer Marney, Colchester; Miss Diana Eady, a British schoolgirl living in Cairo; Mr. E. H. Harbison (Ameri-

Couple were Cairo bound

DAILY SKETCH

AND DAILY GRAPHIC

2d

SATURDAY, APRIL 10, 1954

Bodies found in the sea

IS THIS THE END OF THE COMET?

Daily Sketch Reporter

B.O.A.C. will not use Comet jet airliners again until the cause of three "inexplicable tragedies" has been discovered and put right by the makers.

This decision was announced by B.O.A.C. chief Sir Miles Thomas yesterday as news reached London of the finding of bodies from Yoke Yoke, the Comet which crashed earlier in the sea off the south

ing up bodies from amid floating wreckage and oil patches 70 miles south of Naples.

Aircraft among the ships and planes of many nations searching the area radioed that they had seen more bodies.

No survivors have been found.

The last message from Yoke Yoke, which left Rome at 6.25 p.m. on Thursday, was: "Over Naples, still climbing."

A certain pattern

This message was pinpointed by Sir Miles Thomas's statement

The clue to two disasters

Daily Mirror

FORWARD WITH THE PEOPLE

1½d No. 15,678

MON APR. 12 1954

'CAT'S EYES' TO COPY COMET DEATH CLIMB

DAILY MIRROR REPORTER

TEST-pilot "Cat's Eyes" Cunningham is to copy, during the next few days, the death flights of the two Comets that crashed into the Mediterranean.

Time after time he will take another Comet airliner into a screaming full-throttle climb to 26,000ft.—to see what happens.

Cunningham, thirty-six-year-old bachelor and chief test-pilot for De Havilland, the

makers, will be seeking the reason for the two mystery Comet crashes that cost fifty-six lives:

● THE COMET that crashed into the

Mediterranean in January, and
● THE COMET that met disaster, also in the Mediterranean, last Thursday. In both cases,

sudden and mysterious disaster overtook the liners as they reached 26,000 ft. at full power after leaving Rome.

No Seeks Secret

Five Miles Up

Cunningham's task is to find out: WHY?

He will fly an ordinary service Comet under conditions as near as possible to the known conditions under which the other two crashed.

What unknown factors may he meet when he gets five miles up from the De Havilland airfield at Hatfield, Herts?

Telling me last night about the tests, he said: "Am I apprehensive? Not a bit.

They Will Fly

Comets have been going up under similar conditions every day and have not

proximate the conditions as exactly as possible—load, height, rate of climb, and speed.

Other test pilots will accompany him to check his observations.

With Him

An Open Letter to A VERY IMPORTANT VISITOR

Dear Mr. Dulles:

WELCOME to Britain. Welcome to Europe.

You arrive at a crucial moment in the affairs of the great Western alliance. For recent events have caused misgivings here about the way America is shaping Western policy without consulting her partners.

Last month Russia sent the West a Note on collective security. She indicated she was prepared to discuss joining NATO (the North Atlantic Treaty Organisation). Within a few hours of receiving Molotov's Note your own State

A WEEK OF WONDERFUL PICTURES

—Starts today in the Centre Pages

POLICE HUNT GANG

---

standing success, as the *Daily Telegraph* commented on 9 April: 'four-fifths of the Comet airliner wrecked off Elba have now been recovered . . . The Royal Navy has achieved an outstanding success against what at the outset might have appeared hopeless odds.' That morning, however, before the reader reached the editorial page he would have been confronted on page one with another chillingly familiar headline: 'BOAC Comet is overdue today'. Comet *Yoke Yoke*, it was confirmed the next day, bound for Cairo, had also vanished over the Mediterranean, with twenty-one on board.

The circumstances of this crash were distressingly similar: no Mayday wireless message, and once again less than half an hour out of Rome airport. It was too much of a coincidence for some papers: 'Was it sabotage at airport?' asked the *Daily Sketch*. 'Sabotage hint by Comet test pilot' confided the *Daily Herald*. The *New York Times* even proposed an intriguing theory as to how a bomb could have been fiendishly linked to the plane's radio transmitter. The Italian papers stormed back that sabotage at one of their airports was impossible.

This time the Government stepped in and withdrew the whole fleet's certificate of airworthiness. The dream was shattered, under the impact of three crushing—and inexplicable—blows. The newspapers' response to each succeeding tragedy had shifted from determination to doubt, and now from doubt to disillusion. 'Is this the end of the Comet?' asked the *Daily Sketch*, the question hardly anyone dared put into words. At the Royal Aircraft Establishment at Farnborough it was a question they were working day and night to answer. With meticulous patience experts were rebuilding the stricken *Yoke Peter* as the sea, with daunting reluctance, yielded up its parts. Every minute scrap of salvage was carefully analysed to build up a picture of what happened in the moments before the crash, every button, screw and piece of paintwork. One Comet was flown with radioactive fuel in its tanks to try to discover fuel leaks. Another was stripped, filled with hundreds of delicate instruments and literally thrown about the skies. Yet another was cocooned in an iron sheet to fathom the effects of pressurization.

It was this Comet that finally surrendered the key to the riddle. By pumping water in between the plane and its casing, and by flapping the wings on hydraulic jacks, the experts had invented a means of simulating thousands of hours of flying-time in a matter of days. On 24 June, after the Comet had 'flown' nearly 9,000 hours, the gauges of the pressure tank dramatically dropped to zero. Hurriedly the tank was emptied. There it was. A split in the skin of the cabin eight feet long. On any plane that would have resulted in decompression with the force of an explosion. Metal fatigue. But was this what had happened to *Yoke Peter* 35,000 feet above the Mediterranean? Only two months later, as the search for wreckage off Elba was nearing its end, the amazing discovery of a similar torn piece of metal confirmed that it had.

So what *was* the answer to the *Sketch's* question? Was it the end of the Comet? In one sense, it wasn't, for in death the Comet I had bequeathed to its successors—indeed to every plane that has flown ever since—a vital piece of information. But as a symbol, as a dream even, it was indeed the end. The obituary which the columnist Cassandra of the *Daily Mirror* had penned two days after the final crash summed it all up. 'The poor dead are hauled from the warm Mediterranean' he wrote. 'A few melancholy bits of wreckage are fished out of the Tyrrhenian sea—a sodden mailbag, a broken seat, a strip of fabric, a waterlogged suitcase . . . There ended a brave and brilliant chapter in British aviation—the attempt by the Comet aircraft to seize the leadership of the aerial trunk lines of the world. The blow that has been struck at our hopes is as tremendous as it is tragic.'

Invasion by Sea

North Sea Floods 1953

SUNDAY EXPRESS

FEBRUARY 1 1953 Lighting-up Time 5.19 p.m. to 7.8 a.m. (Mon.). Founded by LORD BEAVERBROOK Moon Rises 7.48 p.m. Sets 8.33 a.m. (Mon.). PRICE 2½d.

IRISH SEA DISASTER: 'From a plane I watched this nightmare in the gale-swept channel'

128 LOST: 49 SAFE

Not a woman or child among those so far rescued

FROM SUNDAY EXPRESS AIRPLANE

Picture taken by William Johnston flying 200ft. above the sea.

CAPTAIN JAMES FERGUSON

Wallowing in the trough of a deepening wave, in wild, churning seas. . . . A lifeboat, packed with life-jacketed survivors from the Princess Victoria, has put out a sea-anchor—attempting to keep headed into the wind. . . . Right: Two survivors, Fusilier Walter Baker and L/Corporal Albert Dickie, in Belfast, last night.

By IAN FORBES

ONE HUNDRED AND TWENTY-EIGHT people are believed to have been drowned when the British Railways ship Princess Victoria, one of the Irish Sea ferries, sank barely five miles from the Irish coast yesterday during an 80-mile-an-hour gale. It is the worst disaster in British waters for more than a hundred years.

Early today only 49 of the 177 passengers and crew had been accounted for. Of these 33 were rescued by the Donaghadee (Northern Ireland) lifeboat, eight by the destroyer Contest, four by a trawler, two by the Port Patrick lifeboat.

Rescue ships which have not yet reached port may bring more in. *But among those so far landed there is not one woman or child.*

People cling to wreckage

One of the ship's boats, it is known, capsized in the raging sea. This, it is feared, was the one containing the women and children.

FROM MY PLANE AS I FLEW OVER THE RESCUE SCENE I SAW PEOPLE SPRAWLED ACROSS PIECES OF DRIFTING WRECKAGE. I SAW A LIFEBOAT PACKED WITH SURVIVORS, AND ANOTHER WITH ONE MAN IN IT. I SAW RAFTS, LIFEJACKETS, AND BODIES FLOATING ON THE WATER.

As dusk fell airplanes dropped flares into the sea to guide the rescue ships and people were still being snatched from the raging seas. The whole rescue was carried out in a blizzard.

Shortly before 6 p.m. the search was called off. The coxswain of a lifeboat said: "We have been right through the wreckage all over the area and there is no sign of life. I don't think anyone could have survived long in such a terrible sea."

Searchlights swept the scene—overturned ship's boats, floating life-jackets, empty rafts—but not one living thing. The rescuers, it was thought, could do no more.

But six hours later, long after the Donaghadee lifeboat had landed her first party, there came the message: "More survivors sighted." At once the lifeboat put out again.

When the 2,694-ton Princess Victoria, a motor vessel, left Stranraer yesterday morning it was just a routine crossing. She is the link with the overnight train from Euston. Her passengers should have been at Larne for lunch.

Fears for an M.P.

They are believed to include Major J. Maynard Sinclair, Northern Ireland Minister of Finance, and Sir Walter Smiles, Unionist M.P. for County Down. Their names are not in any list of survivors.

Among the passengers were a group of 40 men employed by Short Bros. and Harland, aircraft engineers, who were returning from the Stranraer district for the week-end to Ireland. With this party was Mr. Victor Large, who was accompanied by his five children, all aged under eight.

Outside Loch Ryan, the ship met the full force of the gale in the Irish Sea.

Terse radio messages gave news of her plight; and of the rescue operation:

9.47 A.M.—Hove to off mouth of Loch Ryan. Vessel not under control. Urgent assistance of tug required.

PAGE FIVE, COL. FOUR

HOW DID IT HAPPEN?

● *What was the cause of the disaster? Survivors gave a clue in interviews with the Sunday Express.*

● The ship was a car ferry. At her stern were doors which open into her car hold. And from survivors' accounts it seems that the key to the disaster is the fact that these doors were forced open by a gigantic wave which flooded the car deck.

● Angus Mackay, a seaman in the Princess Victoria, had this to say: "After 35 minutes' sailing we had nosed out into the Irish Sea, and that is where the trouble started.

A freak wave

"The ferry doors, which are built below the passenger deck, but above the water-line for the loading of motor-cars, were stove in by a freak wave in the heart of a heavy sea.

"The ship flooded quickly. We coped with it at the time. By eight o'clock we had a ten-degree list. An hour later that list had gone to 45 degrees."

● The ship was only six miles from the Scottish coast when first in difficulties. But the bow rudder was jammed by the storm preventing any attempt to turn the ship towards the shore. Helpless, she drifted across the Irish Channel.

● Fusilier Robert Baker, whose home is in Rochdale, gave support to the view that the opening of the car-deck doors was the origin of the disaster.

He said: "After we left Loch Ryan we were hit by a tremendous sea. The water burst open doors at the back of the ship and water poured in."

Red secrets 'given away'

MOSCOW, Saturday.—Soviet State secrets have been "leaked" to British, American, and French spies, said Pravda today.

The newspaper named "careless" officials in four Ministries, and said they played into the hands of the spies. One of them, A. I. Orlov was said to have tried to pass a secret document to a foreign Power.—Reuter.

Two youths maim woman of 76

Two youths attacked 76-year-old Mrs. Lou Hamilton, of Hammersmith-grove, Hammersmith, last night, throwing her on to the pavement and stealing a bag containing £10. She is seriously ill in hospital with a broken thigh.

HUNDREDS FLEE 5ft. FLOODS

AS the great gale swept across the country yesterday there were reports of wholesale damage and flooding.

At Bacton, on the Norfolk coast, two cottages were swept into the sea. There was nobody in them.

At King's Lynn hundreds of people were evacuated from their homes when the River Ouse burst its banks and flooded streets to a depth of 5ft. Electricity and phones were cut off.

Later the water began to subside. But with the gale still raging the town faces a further flood this morning on the new high tide.

At Hunstanton 40 families, mainly Americans, were trapped in their bungalows when the sea broke inland for half a mile.

The American authorities at Sculthorpe, 14 miles away, immediately rushed in a force of 100 men with radios, amphibians, and sea-rescue craft to help the trapped families.

Thames warning

At Whitstable the sea swept over the new sea wall and the town had its worst flood for 50 years.

In Margate there were two and a half feet of water in the main streets.

A flood warning was issued for the Thames and police loud-speaker cars warned people in the old fishing town of Leigh-on-Sea to barricade their houses.

Reginald Dines, 36, of The Avenue, Lowestoft, was killed when the gale blew his motor-cycle into a tree.

The Fleetwood trawler Michael Griffiths, with a crew of 15 aboard, vanished off Barra Head in the Hebrides.

For seven hours a lifeboat, another trawler, and an aircraft searched the sea in a blizzard but could find no trace of the missing vessel.

U.S. counts its gold

WASHINGTON, Saturday.—The U.S. Treasury is to count its gold hoard at Fort Knox, Kentucky, uncounted since the Democrats came to power 20 years ago.

B.B.C.'s licence crisis: The 'Home' may end

By GERALD SCHEFF

THE B.B.C.'s Home Service in its present form may vanish after the Coronation. This is one of two moves to make more cash available for better and longer TV programmes.

The financial crisis is severe. I learned yesterday that the B.B.C. has asked the Government to restore cuts in its income of nearly £2,000,000 a year because of "money difficulties."

This is the sum which the B.B.C. is losing annually through the Exchequer's 15 per cent. levy on revenue from radio and TV licences.

From reserves

I can reveal that unless the B.B.C. gets more money it cannot continue to meet expenses on their present scale without drawing on reserves before the end of this year.

A formal application asking the Government to abandon the raid on licence funds has been sent to the Treasury by the B.B.C. through the Postmaster-General.

If the Treasury refuses, an increase in licence fees may be inevitable to provide the B.B.C. with more money.

It is believed that the way has been paved for a £1 increase in the combined TV-radio licence fee—from £2 to £3.

Biggest drop

But restoring to the B.B.C. the 15 per cent. of licence money now seized by the Treasury may avert the need for this move.

If the Home Service as we know it is scrapped its variety shows may go over to the Light Programme. And the Third may take the heavier talks and features.

The Home Service has been losing popularity steadily. Audience research has found that a number of the programmes have suffered the biggest drop in listenership. Already budgets for feature programmes are being closely examined.

MORE SHOCKS

IT was a Cup-tie day of sensations, with the biggest by amateurs Walthamstow Avenue.

They drew 1—1 with League champions Manchester United—thanks to Stan Gerula, their 33-year-old Polish goalkeeper.

Once he had defied a 40-minute continuous barrage. He described it in his halting English: "I was lucky. I punch and I punch."

Said Manchester manager, Matt Busby: "It was amazing." And George Burchell, Avenue's team manager: "A miracle."

Hero No. 2: Walthamstow's centre forward Jim Lewis. He was chosen only ten minutes before the match because of an injured ankle. But he got the equalising goal.

Afterwards the team celebrated with bottles of pop.

Tonic wine ended the boy's fight

Fourteen-year-old Brian Treleaven was disqualified in the Southern Counties Schools boxing championships at Aylesford, Kent, last night because, said the referee, "his seconds gave him something stronger than water." It is believed that Brian had a sip of tonic wine.

'Set up Europe army now'

ROME, Saturday.—Mr. John Foster Dulles, United States Secretary of State, opened his fact-finding tour of Western Europe today by pleading with Italy's Premier de Gasperi to help set up the European Defence Community quickly.

In Washington, reports say Mr. Dulles will suggest that Britain should agree to co-operate closely with the European Defence Community on military and technical matters.

Sir David asked about Bentley

Sir David Maxwell Fyfe, Home Secretary, was asked "What about the Bentley case?" at a meeting at Bangor, North Wales, last night.

He replied that it was neither practice nor custom for the Home Secretary to disclose or discuss the grounds of his decision with the public. There were cheers and the questioner came up to the platform, bowed, and said: "I would like to bow to that."

Ballinalee off the wires

The new postmistress of Ballinalee, Co. Longford, Mrs. Norah Mannix, yesterday had no telephone, no telegraph, no windows to her shop, and no customers.

Incensed by the closing of the old post office, men cut down 28 telephone poles and stoned Post Office men who tried to repair the damage. There were 125 policemen in the village, which has a population of 141.

Truman's peace prize?

ATHENS, Saturday.—Marshal Papagos, Prime Minister of Greece, has proposed ex-President Truman for the Nobel Peace Prize for his work in promoting the Pacific Pact.—Exchange.

Mozart gets 2nd prize—from the B.B.C.

MOZART, who died in 1791, has won *second* prize in a TV musical composition contest for children. The B.B.C. admitted this last night in the Children's Hour television programme, "Whirligig."

And musician Steve Race announced a revised list of winners in the competition for the best original tune for the recorder.

TV chiefs had discovered that an entry submitted by an 11-year-old girl from Yorkshire, to whom they awarded second prize a fortnight ago, was in reality a Mozart minuet—"slightly changed and given a new title."

Lime Grove last night refused to give her name, saying: "It would not be fair."

The prize, a book token, was not sent to her. It now goes to Brenda Wicks of London, S.E., who was originally placed third. The winner is Joyce Moore, of Aldershot.

A B.B.C. spokesman said last night: "More than 600 entries had to be sorted out by musician Steve Race in a few days. We think he did a brilliant job in picking out the Mozart tune at all."

Ike is asked for loyalty files

WASHINGTON, Saturday.—President Eisenhower was asked by the Senate Foreign Relations Committee today to hand over secret loyalty files, especially testimony given by General Bedell Smith, to a loyalty review board. Mr. Truman had refused a similar request.

'Chinese atom plant'

CALCUTTA, Saturday.—The newspaper Amrita Bazar Patrika says the Chinese Communist Government has established an atom bomb plant in Sinkiang, north of Tibet.—B.U.P.

TODAY'S WEATHER Strong winds, slowly moderating. Showers of rain, sleet, or snow, some bright periods. Further outlook: cold.

ON PAGE 2

THE MAN WHO NEVER WAS

And another exclusive:

THE SUNDAY EXPRESS today makes the first announcement of a notable event in the history of post-war publishing.

Through this newspaper a document of immense historical importance is to be brought for the first time to the British public.

It is:—

Hitler's Table Talk

Already the Sunday Express has told the inside story of the outstanding military figures of the war: Eisenhower . . . Rommel . . . Roosevelt . . . Hopkins . . . Mountbatten. . . .

And, of course, many other men of achievement have told their story, too.

★ ★ ★

But Hitler?

What, during those breathless years, was he confiding in off-the-record moments with those in his closest private circle?

The Sunday Express has already reported how a screened-off stenographer took down every word Hitler spoke at his top-level wartime dinner parties. Hitler on his enemies . . . on his friends . . . on his ambitions, his failures, his secret dreams.

These fascinating notebooks have now been collated. It has been a complicated task—and one requiring great care—for, of course, they add up to a work more impressive in historical significance than even "Mein Kampf" itself.

They present the unique exploration of the 20th century's most shattering personality.

They will be published exclusively in the Sunday Express. The date will be announced shortly.

Latest news

HIGH STREET FLOODED

Sea poured over the sea wall at Deal, flooding the High-street to a depth of 4ft.

TELEPHONE London CEntral 8000

Famous for
fine Quality
"Nell Gwyn"
Marmalade

NEWS CHRONICLE

Sharps
the word for TOFFEE

No. 33,279   MONDAY, FEBRUARY 2, 1953   PRICE 1½d.

300 DIE IN TIDAL FLOOD

Thousands are left homeless: island cleared

ROWBOAT RESCUE FLEET SAVES MAROONED STORM VICTIMS

G.I. FAMILIES MISSING

MORE than 300 men, women and children—162 in England and 150 on the Continent—are known to have died over the week-end, when high tides burst sea defences and caused one of the worst flood disasters on record.

Many more are feared dead in England, because the counting of casualties is slow and the list of missing in one of the badly hit spots—Canvey Island, in the Thames Estuary—is far from complete. It may be days before the final list is issued.

THE DEATH ROLL

KENT
Be'vedere Marshes ...... 4 dead

ESSEX
Great Wakering .... 6 dead
Southend .... 4 dead
Jaywick .... 10 dead
Harwich .... 1 dead, 1 missing
Canvey Island .... 20 dead
Wallasea Island .... 1 dead

LINCOLNSHIRE
Skegness area .... 20 dead
Mablethorpe area .... 16 dead

SUFFOLK
Felixstowe .... 21 dead
Southwold .... 1 dead

NORFOLK
Hunstanton
    12 dead, 25-30 missing
Snettisham ..5 dead, 25 missing
Heacham ....10 dead, 20 missing
King's Lynn .... 15 dead
Sea Palling .... 7 dead
Gt. Yarmouth .... 6 dead
C'ev .... 1 dead

LONDON AREA
Barnes .... 1 dead
Total: 162 killed, 71-76 missing

It began with a cyclone

THE cause of it all was —a cyclone.
It started west of Scotland, then moved to the North Sea.
There, with gusts up to 113 m.p.h.—highest on record in Britain — it drove huge masses of the sea southwards. The wind-driven sea got behind the high tides normal at the present lunar phase and smashed into the bottleneck between the East and South-East coasts of England and the Dutch coast

The floods—whipped up by the same hurricane that sank the Princess Victoria in the Irish Sea on Saturday—poured inland over the Norfolk bulge; surged over the sea defences of Lincolnshire; hit Essex and Kent; submerged a submarine in Sheerness dockyard; and raced up the Thames—past Gravesend, London's docks, to Richmond and Kingston-on-Thames.

This is the state of the flood areas this morning:

THE EAST COAST OF ENGLAND is covered by mile after mile of grey flood waters; streets are running rivers; vast areas of farmland are one great lake; roads and railways are submerged.

A CALL for help has gone to the Services from almost every local authority affected. Men, heavy breakdown equipment, lorries, amphibious vehicles, sandbags, searchlights, helicopters, rubber dinghies, blankets, food are wanted.

That help is flowing in—with the Americans doing all they can as well. From their air force base at Sculthorpe, Norfolk, they sent dinghies, doctors, rescue teams.

FOULNESS ISLAND, off Southend: No news from 250 on island since yesterday morning. Navy helicopters due to take off at dawn.

CANVEY ISLAND: 12,000 were ordered to be evacuated. Three-quarters were off by dark; more were evacuated during the night; many were taken to London.

TILBURY: Call for help sent to Southern Command. Ships asked to help take people from rooftops at water's edge. Hundreds rescued from top floors.

LONDON: Dockside areas hit; 3,000 may be homeless in West Ham; appeal sent to Thames police for boats.

HARWICH: Three thousand people being evacuated.

JAYWICK: bungalow holiday town next door to Clacton: Only a line of roofs to be seen.

MABLETHORPE, Lincolnshire: Whole population

One light burns on cut-off island

STANLEY BARON last night flew over Foulness Island, cut off between the Thames and Crouch estuaries. There had been no news from the 250 islanders since the telephone failed 24 hours before.

He reports: It was almost impossible in the moonlight to tell which was sea and which land.

In one big isolated farmhouse, a light burned in the window. The building stood half in the water, on the edge of an island of mud 70 yards across.

the 100 yards of water that normally cuts off Foulness has swollen to six miles.

Troops in amphibious "ducks" made several attempts to cross the water. Mud and floating trees forced them back.

Early this morning the Southend lifeboat, towing two small boats, was standing by Foulness, waiting for a chance to close in.

This morning, too, fishermen from the east coast will make a mass attempt to reach the island in small boats—many of which were at the Dunkirk evacuation.

A score of other mud islands were separated by sheets of ruffled water.

The great floods hit a holiday town . . . trim houses are half hidden by water . . . road signs bring out survivors. . . . In this picture is summed up the story of Britain's week-end disaster. . . . The holiday spot? Jaywick, next door to Clacton

Boat goes in church to save children

REPORTS OF DAMAGE SENT TO CHURCHILL

By DOUGLAS BROWN

A GOVERNMENT statement on the floods will be made in the Commons this afternoon—probably by Mr. Churchill.

Reports of damage and loss of life were sent to the Prime Minister at his home at Chartwell yesterday.

Other Ministers, whose departments are affected kept in close touch with events.

Mr. Harold Macmillan, Minister of Housing, was perhaps the busiest. He was in constant telephonic contact with his top officials.

He has arranged for the best

LATE NEWS

CENTRAL 5000

The headlines in all the papers that Sunday, 1 February 1953, were concerned with a disaster in the Irish Sea. A car-ferry, the *Princess Victoria*, bound for Belfast from Stranraer, had foundered a few miles off the entrance to Belfast Lough. The ferry's stern doors, it appeared, had burst under the impact of a huge freak wave whipped up by the gale that was pounding the whole coastline of Britain. Rescue ships, battling through the violent seas, reached the *Princess Victoria*'s last position an hour and a half after she had gone down: they found only three lifeboats and forty-three survivors—every woman and child aboard had perished.

It was the worst disaster in home waters for over a century. Yet even as the Sunday papers were going to press with the news of it, the overture to a greater calamity was already under way. On the other side of Britain the North Sea was renewing its ancient struggle with the lands that had been reclaimed from it patiently over the centuries. Readers of the *Sunday Express*, the *Observer*, or the *Sunday Times* could have gleaned an inkling of impending disaster from smaller news items: sea defences at Mablethorpe in Lincolnshire had burst, families were being evacuated from their homes in King's Lynn, Norfolk, and in nearby Hunstanton bungalows half a mile inland were marooned. At 6.00pm on the Saturday this was all the news available, but to anyone familiar with the behaviour of North Sea tides it was ominous enough; high tide along the vulnerable Essex marshes and Thames estuary would be several hours later.

By the time the Sunday papers were delivered,

of course, the full tragedy had unfolded—from Mablethorpe to Whitstable in Kent the highest tide in history had battered its way inland, swamping hundreds of thousands of acres and devastating towns and villages. The suddenness was almost as shocking as the destruction. Said the *Daily Mail* the next day: 'Most of us have seen, incredulously, pictures of ruin wrought by some hurricane roaring out of Florida and sweeping, perhaps, across New England. Such things we have thought comfortably do not happen in Old England. But they do. This mild, patient climate sometimes turns and rends us.' But never like this. As disjointed reports filtered through from isolated areas the scale of the disaster was brought home. At least 50,000 were homeless, deaths were numbered in hundreds. Herds grazing on the succulent marshlands had been slaughtered wholesale, houses had been swept out to sea like so much driftwood and boats swept onto land and pounded into fragments. The sea's offensive had broken through Britain's sea-walls in over a thousand places, and whole islands were submerged.

Being a Sunday ('The Sea, it seems, Keeps no Sabbath' was the *Daily Express*'s indignant headline), mobilizing emergency services and local authorities was an even more formidable task than usual, but with daybreak an armada of small boats was launched on what the papers dubbed a 'second Dunkirk mission'. In some villages like Jaywick, Essex, they found only rooftops poking out of the muddy waters and families huddled frozen on them. Snettisham in

Norfolk, a village of holiday bungalows, had been transformed into a lake of debris that claimed twenty-five lives. At Hunstanton forty American servicemen or their families had died when their seafront houses had crumpled into the sea. An *Eastern Daily Press* reporter flying over the shattered coast declared Salthouse looked 'as if it had been hit by high explosive'. The Thames, up to Kew, flowed greyly through the streets of London, inundating countless basements.

But the worst horror was reserved for Canvey Island in the Thames Estuary. This one-time stretch of marsh had been prized back from the sea over the years and fortified with a complex system of walls and drainage dykes. Inside their defences a thriving community of city commuters, retired people and weekenders had grown up in what had quickly become a popular tourist spot. When their sea-walls surrendered to the importunate tide, the waters flowed over the length and breadth of the island at alarming speed and in the lowest section—with good reason called the Sunken Marsh—it descended with the force of a tidal wave, trapping and overwhelming families in their bedrooms before they had barely had time to wake. Rescue teams moving in to the stricken island found (the *Evening Standard* reported): 'People lay dead on rooftops, with the water lapping at their feet. Others were entangled in trees, into which they had been flung by the mighty waves which engulfed the island. Children were among the victims.'

Canvey's final toll of fifty-eight was less than

No. 16,416 Price 1½d. TUESDAY FEBRUARY 3 1953

DAILY EXPRESS

CONTROLLING SHAREHOLDER LORD BEAVERBROOK

Weather: Some snow

MORE PICTURES: PAGE 3 PAGE 5 PAGE 8

DAY TWO OF THE GREAT DELUGE—R.A.F. and Army go in

BATTLE OF THE GAPS

Coast breached in 280 places

H.Q. WORKS BY CANDLELIGHT

Express Staff Reporters

SIR THOMAS DUGDALE, Minister of Agriculture, in telling the Commons last night that more than a quarter of a million acres have been flooded, said this: "Rebuilding the sea defences will present one of the greatest civil engineering problems we have ever had to face."

● And all yesterday, as the count of victims went grimly on, there were "war tempo" attempts to repair the gaps in the sea walls of the East Coast. There are 280 breaches in Essex alone, said Sir Thomas Dugdale.

● Late last night there were 287 *known* dead and still hundreds missing. The most-stricken area—Canvey Island—yielded up 60 bodies, and the total for Canvey may reach 100.

● Here was the list of dead, area by area, as compiled late last night. It takes no account of speculations.

LINCS

SKEGNESS	9
MABLETHORPE	21
SALTFLEET	4
INGOLDMELLS	10
TRUSTHORPE	1

ESSEX

CANVEY	60
JAYWICK	21
POINT CLEAR	2
WALLASEA ISLAND	6
FOULNESS ISLAND	5
GT. WAKERING	6
SOUTHEND	7
HARWICH	7

KENT

BELVEDERE	3

NORFOLK

KING'S LYNN	15
HUNSTANTON	22
SEA PALLING	7
GREAT YARMOUTH	7
SNETTISHAM	25
HEACHAM	12
SALTHOUSE	2
WIVETON	1
DERSINGHAM	1
CLEY	1

SUFFOLK

FELIXSTOWE	28
SOUTHWOLD	1

THAMES

PUTNEY	1
WOOLWICH	1
TILBURY	1

● The battle of the gaps yesterday was an operation in which local groups were helped at all points by the Army and R.A.F. It was a fight against time—the time of high tides.

● R.A.F. freighters were helping trains and Army lorries to deliver 4,000,000 sandbags. These were *all* to be at the trouble spots by dawn.

● Engineers and surveyors met by candlelight in offices on Canvey Island to plan defence works.

● Yesterday 500 airmen, soldiers, and civilians, were sandbagging the sea wall. Sleet whipped down, but the floods did not increase.

● *Military police took over traffic control. Mobile generators provided electric light. The Red Cow, a popular inn, became military headquarters. All bars were closed.*

● In spite of urgent police warnings 3,800 of the 13,000 population of Canvey refuse to leave the island. Some are in peril, the water lapping their window-sills, furniture afloat.

● A man who tried to rescue an aged couple was told "Come back later, please. We haven't had our dinner yet."

● *And last night the alarm sounded again at Great Yarmouth. The town with 6,000 homeless and a growing list of missing is in danger from a vast wall of water from the tidal basin of Breydon Water.*

● Twenty thousand sandbags are being rushed to Yarmouth from London.

● All day, too, the work of mercy went on along the battered coast. R.A.F. fighters were called in to help rescuers. They patrolled—searching for life.

● A hoverplane took off Mr. Edmund Lambert, a manufacturing chemist, of Hyde Park Mansions, W., from the cut-off Isle of Sheppey. He must fly today with urgent medical supplies for similarly stricken Holland.

● Three hundred people were rescued from Foulness Island in the mouth of the River Crouch—and 50 people, including "resisters," will be taken off today.

● *Foulness Island, richly fertile two days ago, will be 12 square miles of salt-water wilderness for at least seven years.*

● Cases of explosives have been washed to sea from the I.C.I. factory at Bramble Island, near Walton-on-Naze, and may come ashore. The public are warned: "Don't handle them."

DAILY EXPRESS £1,000 FOR FLOOD FUND

MR. CHURCHILL announced in the House of Commons yesterday that the Lord Mayor of London is opening a National Distress Fund for flood victims.

A cheque for £1,000 will be sent today by the Daily Express to the Lord Mayor's Fund.

A cheque for a similar amount is being sent by the Daily Mail.

The Mayor of Wimbledon in South-west London telegraphed the Lord Mayor last night that he was forwarding £1,000 on account "anticipating Wimbledon's support."

At the Mansion House last night an official said that the Lord Mayor expected to make a statement today about his fund.

TIDES EARLY —BY 2 HOURS

SIR THOMAS DUGDALE, Minister of Agriculture, told the Commons last night:—

"The Saturday evening tide came two hours earlier than predicted and maintained itself at a high level for several hours.

"At all places along the East Coast it was 6ft. above the predicted level with strong winds and heavy wave action. Sea defences along the Essex coast had been maintained above the record flood level of 1949.

"The tides were from one to two feet above this level and disaster was inevitable. As a result of these unprecedented conditions, the sea defences on a great length of the coastline were overtopped and breached in many places and the sea penetrated far inland.

"It was abundantly clear that the disaster was far beyond the scope of first aid measures."

PROBLEM OF CLAIMS

By Frederick Ellis, City Editor

THE big insurance companies yesterday put into action emergency operations to deal with flood claims. Hundreds have already been lodged.

On life policies the insurance companies are paying out at once, without demanding death certificates.

Holders of comprehensive household policies—rate 5s. a £100 of goods—are fully covered for damage or loss of the home's contents. These policies also cover damage to the actual house from storm and tempest—but not from flood unless special risks have been accepted.

At the Lynmouth disaster the insurance companies paid out for damaged property, although they were not liable. It is too early to say if they will repeat the gesture on the East Coast.

State flood chief switched

Sir David Maxwell Fyfe, the Home Secretary was appointed chairman of the flood committee of Ministers last night in place of Mr. Harold Macmillan, the Housing Minister who was Mr Churchill's first choice.

The change was made because so many Government departments are involved that it was considered necessary to have the senior Secretary of State in charge.

THE QUEEN—LIKE SUN AFTER A STORM

AMONG THE FIELD KITCHENS

THE QUEEN, visiting the flood disaster areas yesterday, walks with the Duke of Edinburgh—talking to the girl in uniform — and Duke of Gloucester among field kitchens set up in a street at King's Lynn.

At a reception centre in the town a woman lying on a stretcher smiled for the first time in 24 hours as the Queen walked in.

"It's like the sun breaking through after a storm," she said.

At Hunstanton the Queen was "extremely distressed and upset" when she was told how children had been lost.

She spoke to an American Serviceman. "I understand you people have suffered badly," she said.

Replied the American: "That's true, madam, but it's always good to have you British around when there's any suffering going on."

AND AMONG THE CHILDREN

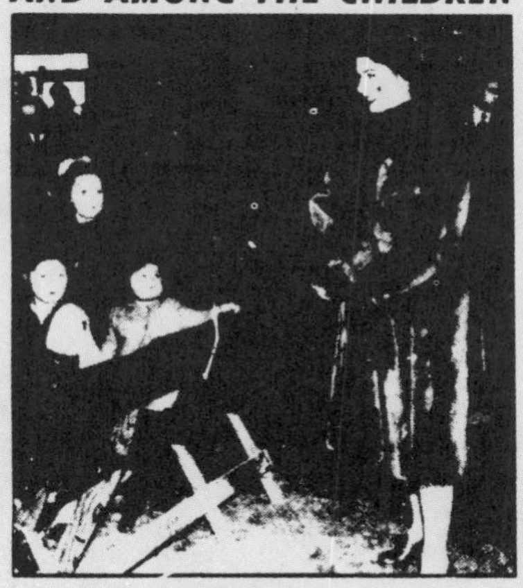

Children in the King's Lynn centre turn in surprise and delight as the Queen walks in, smiling. The Duke—in the background—chats with one of the women workers.

FLOODS CARRY OUT TINS OF DEATH

TEN round grey tins, each filled with enough poison gas—hydrogen cyanide—to kill anyone who opens the lid, are missing in the back streets of London's dockland.

They were swept by the floods out of a fumigating firm's store into the thickly populated area bordering Victoria Dock-road.

Twenty tins—they are gallon-sized—were missed. But police found ten. Some were under kitchen windows, others in gardens where children had begun to play again.

And last night patrols in knee-boots continued to search in flooded bomb-sites and derelict buildings.

In the Royal Albert Dock: A diver went down last night to help a heavy rescue unit try to recover 200 tons of lead ingots, worth about £19,000, which sank with a barge in the flood tide.

Seize houses? Yes—No

Requisitioning notices were pinned on 20 empty houses in Erith, Kent, last night, but they cannot be enforced.

The Housing Ministry authorised the requisitioning yesterday—to house flood refugees—then, five hours later, cancelled the order. A Ministry spokesman said: "The Minister wants empty houses used for refugees, but does not want them requisitioned, except in emergency. It is too expensive."

Mr. Norman Dodds (Soc., Dartford) told the Commons last night the cancellation had made his constituents angry.

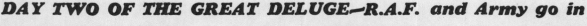

Troops start the great task of closing the gaps in Canvey sea wall.

M.P.s TO PROTEST OVER FORMOSA

Express Political Correspondent DEREK MARKS

SOCIALIST M.P.s are planning a vigorous demonstration in the Commons this afternoon when Mr. Eden explains the British Government's attitude to the new U.S. policy on Formosa, General Chiang Kai-shek's stronghold.

In his Message to Congress yesterday President Eisenhower said that the U.S. 7th Fleet will no longer be used to restrain Chinese Nationalists attacking the mainland from Formosa.

This caused violent alarm among Socialist M.P.s, and in the Commons yesterday **Mr. Desmond Donnelly** (Soc., Pembroke) tried unsuccessfully to move the adjournment in an attempt to force an immediate debate on Formosa (*as William Berkley reports on Page Two*).

It is certain that a similar attempt will be made today, probably with the full support of the Opposition Front Bench.

Mr. Eden will be able to do little to stave off this Socialist attack. He will have to tell the House that the British Government was not consulted before the U.S. decision was taken.

SILENT

It was not until last Friday that the Government was first advised by the American administration of the impending change in the Formosa policy.

A Foreign Office spokesman declined to say last night whether or not Britain has made any representations to America.

Mr. John Foster Dulles, the new U.S. Secretary of State, arrives in London this afternoon, accompanied by Mr. Harold Stassen, the Mutual Security administrator.

Mr Dulles will have his first talks with Mr. Eden this evening unless an immediate debate on Formosa keeps the Foreign Secretary at the Commons.

Americans object too

WASHINGTON, Monday.—Confirmation by President Eisenhower (*his speech is on Page 4*) that Chiang Kai-shek's Formosa troops are now free to attack Red China was criticised by Congressmen tonight.

Senator Wayne Morse, a Republican, said it was "most unfortunate that Eisenhower didn't first discuss his decision with the allies."

A Democrat, Senator John Sparkman said the world was entitled to know to what extent the U.S. was willing to help an assault by Chiang.

A State Department spokesman said the President's decision did not need allied approval because the order to prevent action by Chiang, given to the U.S. Navy by President Truman in 1950 was the responsibility of America alone.

IN FORMOSA Chiang's officials said for a few months the biggest action would probably be only raids.

IN PARIS Mr. Dulles, U.S. Secretary of State, is reported to have said that the U.S. will not support Chiang in any "reckless" action.—Express News Service and Agency Cables.

A straight fight

Nominations for the Canterbury (Kent) by-election on February 12 closed yesterday. Only candidates: Mr Leslie Montagu Thomas (Tory), son of the late Mr J. H. ("Jimmy") Thomas, and Mr John Albert Evan Jones (Soc.). Tory majority in three cornered fight at General Election was 14,089.

13 children lost over ocean

A York plane carrying ten soldiers, their wives, and 13 children, and a crew of six vanished over the Atlantic yesterday on a flight from England to Jamaica.

The pilot, Captain D. Nicholls, began to send out an SOS 320 miles from Gander, Newfoundland. Then silence. Canadian planes have found no trace.

Eisenhower message

WASHINGTON, Monday.—President Eisenhower today sent a message of sympathy from the U.S. to the Queen for the suffering caused by the floods in Britain.

4.30 a.m. LATEST

CREW WALK ASHORE

The Grimsby trawler Roder ran aground on Donna Nook, Lincolnshire, at the entrance to the Humber, last night. The crew walked ashore.

CENtral 8000

Daily Mail

DIEU ET MON DROIT

LONDON EDITION

NO. 17,691 THREE HALFPENCE — FOR QUEEN AND COMMONWEALTH — THURSDAY, FEBRUARY 5, 1953

THE SEA BREAKS IN AGAIN

Smashes new defences, floods back into a town's drying streets

Comment

THURSDAY, FEB. 5, 1953.

LET US BE FAIR

FROM some quarters comes the cry that people in the flooded areas should have been warned of impending catastrophe. Various authorities are being blamed for failing in their duty to the public.

These charges may be the sequel to strain and exhaustion. They are understandable but unfair. Perhaps in calmer moments they would not have been made.

One parish council in Suffolk, for example, has deplored "the extreme negligence of the Government Department concerned." The fact is that such a Department does not exist, because there is no warning system.

As Sir David Maxwell Fyfe said yesterday, no Government in this century had thought it necessary to organise such a thing because in that time the British people have not suffered this kind of ordeal.

Warning

BUT even had there been a system it is hard to see how it could have predicted the unpredictable. The tide came two hours before it was expected, and was 1ft. to 2ft. above the record high level.

The Meteorological Office did warn certain scheduled authorities of exceptionally strong winds over the North Sea. Among these was the Great Ouse Catchment Board, who said they did not receive the message.

But an official of the Board is reported to have said: "There have been six such warnings in the past three months. Ninety-nine times out of 100 nothing happens, so we don't warn the population."

That is the danger of warnings. If they are too frequent they come to have as little effect as the boy who cried "Wolf!"

The announcements of the B.B.C. have also been unfavourably compared with the efficiency of the Dutch radio station Hilversum.

Experience

HEARTBREAK HOUR—AFTER RADIO WARNS

WHOLE COAST OF NEW GALE PERIL

CANVEY NIGHT OF FEAR

From Daily Mail Reporter: Mablethorpe, Lincolnshire, Thursday Morning

THE sea, carried on the fringe of a North Sea gale, broke through the temporary sea defences in part of the Lincolnshire coast late last night. Flood waters rushed again into the streets of the evacuated towns of Mablethorpe and Sutton.

Two days' work by 1,000 troops and bulldozers to bridge the great 300-yard gap in the sea wall, was dashed away by the waves.

I waded thigh-high down streets here which were dry half an hour earlier. In a few minutes at high tide by the light of a police inspector's torch I saw 30ft. of a great sandbank thrown up by the bulldozers washed away. The sea crashed through.

It came through in several other places. At Sutton-on-Sea, where work on the breaches has only just begun, the flood waters poured in unchecked.

FAMILIES MOVE UP TO THEIR TOP ROOMS

Daily Mail Reporting Corps

AT other places along the battered and flooded East coast the gale danger came—and passed. As high tide approached homes were issued with sandbags to seal doorways. People took to their top rooms. And police radio cars warned families to be prepared for trouble.

But early today only Canvey Island's hour of peril was to come. Stay-put islanders were visited by police and Servicemen in boats and lorries and warned to listen for two maroons. Watchers on the sea wall were ready to fire the maroons if the sea went over an agreed danger point.

Four hours before high tide the waters were 2ft. above normal at Southend pier head. It was a quiet night in the Thames estuary and the wind had dropped. A building inspector at Canvey said: "If the walls hold tonight we can definitely say we are winning."

Duchess walks the plank

Before high tide at Great Yarmouth last night the town's seven cinemas put the Home Office gale warning on their screens. The mayor called his public utility, health, engineering, and administrative staffs to emergency stations.

Amphibious cars nosed their way by searchlight to carry more supplies of sandbags and rubble to men still at work filling the embankment's culverts. The north-westerly wind brought with it driving snow.

But then Mr. C. F. Jecliff, Chief Constable, reported that danger had passed. A police spokesman said: "Now Great Yarmouth can get down to the business of living again. Only the fringe of the gale struck us."

At 9.30 p.m. what was officially described as "a major breach" in

THE BRAVE DON'T CRY

For 4 days and nights she waited in the dark, without food or water

From T. F. THOMPSON: Canvey Island, Wednesday.

IN the gloom of one of the drowned bungalows here today rescue workers saw a slight movement by the far wall. They thought it was a cat. Then a calm voice said, weakly, "I'm glad you've come. I could not hold out much longer."

The rescuers pushed their boat's prow into the room and there saw old-age pensioner Mrs. Rosemary Allen sitting on the top shelf of her dining room sideboard.

She had sat there for four days and nights without food, without water, without light and without heat.

Her home in Newlands Park was in one of the worst flooded areas and she had been missed time after time by rescue workers. She was taken to hospital in a weak condition.

In another place the rescue crew heard somebody call "Have you got a match?"

The voice came from a bungalow attic. There they found Charles Fowler and his sister Margaret, both in their eighties, and both suffering from exposure. They, too, had been waiting, without food, water or light or heat for four days. And they didn't want to leave their home.

But the rescue men lifted them out gently and took them into the boat, then to hospital on the mainland.

Old Miss Fowler did not cry. She had not cried. Even in this moment of incredible relief at her rescue she did not cry.

Below, you see this very brave old lady, in the police car with the cat which never left her.

MANACLED MAN DIVES OUT WINDOW

Daily Mail Reporter

A MAN in handcuffs dived through the window of a private bus in Glasgow yesterday and escaped through the traffic, with blood pouring from cuts on his face and hands.

Sweet rationing ends —and the rush begins

MIDNIGHT RULING BRINGS CHAOS

Daily Mail Reporter

ALL sweets are off the ration today—and they are off for good. Official price control is also ended. The announcement was made by the Food Minister, Major

EXIT *the costly, vanishing* FARTHING

Daily Mail Reporter MONTAGUE SMITH

NO more farthings will be struck, an official of the Royal Mint told me last night.

When no more are in circulation—and they are fast disappearing—this will force a revision of prices such as those of bread, petrol, and drapery goods sold at so many shillings "and 11¾d. a yard."

The decision has been taken for two reasons: First, because it costs nearly a halfpenny to make every farthing, and second, because farthings seem to vanish as soon as the Mint sends them to the banks for issue.

Hoard and forget

This mystery is referred to in the annual report of the Royal Mint for 1950, published today. In that year 10,324,800 farthings were issued in response to the demand from the banks—more even than in pre-war years.

Men, the official suggested, throw them away, and housewives hoard and then forget them. And hundreds of thousands have been going to the United States to be made into women's bracelets and similar ornaments.

The report also tells why the Mint refuses to make a 1½d. piece—to allow free circulation there would have to be an issue of not fewer than 400,000,000, equal to the Mint's output of all other coins in a normal year.

JORDAN SEEKS BRITISH AID

Against the Jews

JERUSALEM, Wednesday.—Jordan has invoked the 1948 Anglo-Jordan Defence Treaty, appealing to Britain for help to defend her frontiers against alleged attacks by Israeli forces.

Jordan claims Israel has been making "organised army attacks" that cannot pass as patrol operations. Officials claimed that two Israeli attacks last night were repulsed.—*A.P.*

June Haver 'may enter convent'

HOLLYWOOD, Wednesday.—June Haver, the dancing star, today refused to confirm or deny a statement by a Roman Catholic official that she had decided to enter a convent.—*B.U.P.*

SEVEN MEN SET A TRAP

And catch 28 Mau Mau

NAIROBI, Wednesday.—Four young Europeans of the Kenya Regiment with rifles and three Africans with spears and bows and arrows tracked an armed Mau Mau gang of 28 for three days and cornered them in a copse thousands of feet up in the Aberdare Mountains in North Kenya.

A spotting plane, which was hit by Mau Mau rifle fire, called up reinforcements, who attacked, killing eight of the Mau Mau and capturing the remainder, including 15 women.—*D.M. Reporter.*

EDEN AND BUTLER FOR U.S. IN MARCH

From WILSON BROADBENT: Washington, Wednesday

MR. EDEN, Foreign Secretary, and Mr. Butler, Chancellor of the Exchequer, are to confer here in the first week in March with Mr. Dulles, U.S. Secretary of State, and Mr. Humphrey, U.S. Secretary to the Treasury.

They will discuss financial and economic problems.

The arrangement was made before Mr. Dulles left on his European tour.

Mr. Eden and Mr. Butler will be accompanied by officials for what will be full-scale talks in which policies agreed on at the November Commonwealth talks in London will be examined.

Meanwhile jet-fighter deliveries to Chiang Kai-shek's forces on Formosa under existing military-aid programmes of the United States will begin soon. Nationalist Chinese pilots have been training at Williams Air Force Base, Arizona, for this purpose.

The number of machines and men involved is not revealed. It is thought to be small.

Secret decision

But high-ranking military spokesmen were quoted today asserting that increased military aid to Formosa and Indo-China must be accepted as a natural sequel to President Eisenhower's decision on Formosa.

There is general agreement among experts and commentators here that Chiang Kai-shek's relief from Mr. Truman's 1950 neutrality Order cannot have any effect for a long time. One authority said that it would be six or nine months.

According to reports, President Eisenhower did not consult the Defence Department before making his decision, which confirms that it was essentially political.

There is every indication, however, that the President has not really settled the lines of his foreign policy. Mr. Eden's quick and forceful public protest and the conferences in London may have a profound effect.

Daily Mail Diplomatic Correspondent PERCY CATER

MR. JOHN FOSTER DULLES, U.S. Secretary of State, in protracted talks with the British Government in London yesterday.

Turn to Page 2, Col. 3

DAILY MAIL: CENTRAL 6000

TANKER SOS SAVES MATE

Ambulance men and doctor answered SOS from tanker Sideling Hill (10,000 tons) moored in the Mersey late last night. Norwegian third mate, Rolf Rismussen, 34, had collapsed from oil fumes. He revived after being given artificial respiration and oxygen for an hour.

3

had been feared initially, but it remained a distressing percentage of the east coast's overall casualties of more than three hundred. And even this figure was eclipsed by the appalling carnage that had taken place in Holland. Almost 1,800 died in the country's worst deluge in memory. Whole islands, like Overflakkee where 433 drowned, were given back to the sea: renewed gales hampered the work of evacuation so that thousands were exposed to the bitter cold for three or four days, clinging to roofs, trees and broken dykes. Many gave up the struggle. 'The people cannot bury their dead' reported the *News Chronicle*'s correspondent, 'for there is neither space nor soil for burial. The dry area is for the living and the dead are being left to their fate.' It was nine months before Holland's last breach was filled.

In England, alongside the search and rescue operations, a frantic battle against time was being fought to plug the gaps in the sea-defences. Each new high tide would bring fresh dangers to those who could not—or would not—be evacuated. ('Come back later, please', one old couple told rescuers even as waves lapped at their window. 'We haven't had our dinner yet'.) Thousands of troops and firemen, undergraduates and housewives worked round the clock in the effort to pile four million sandbags in the breaches along 300 miles of coastline. Throughout Monday and Tuesday, in sleet and biting wind, they toiled. Forecasts of a new north-westerly gale the following day added the impetus of desperation to their work.

On Wednesday night the danger returned: anxious watchers saw the waters creeping nearer and nearer the top of their emergency barriers. At Mablethorpe the sea once again mocked their labours, crashing through the defences and returning to familiar streets. Elsewhere the crisis came, and passed. But the work of rescuing still went on—one old lady on Canvey was only discovered after four days and nights, which she had spent immobile on top of her sideboard without food or water, heat or light.

With the easing of tension came the inevitable question, why was there no warning? The epic disaster had exposed the painful fact that Britain had virtually no system of early flood-warning. As the *Daily Express* put it: 'The attack had been building up since morning. And its advance was observed. Every consequence was foreseen, as the meteorologists plotted the southbound swoop of gale-force winds . . . What did the men and women who went calmly to bed along the battle line know of all this? Only if they had stayed awake listening to the BBC until midnight would they have heard what was upon them. And by that time the sea was at their doors.' The paper recalled that the Inquiry into the 1928 London floods had called for public warnings of exceptional tides. Britain, it pointed out, had built up a radar system to give warning of the approach of enemy bombers—'is there not cause for bewilderment now when a nation which has built up a splendid meteorological service fails to prepare its people for bombardment by wind and tide?'

The BBC responded smartly with the reminder that 'it cannot itself initiate warnings and instructions.' The Government for its part explained that the conditions had been 'unprecedented', the disaster 'inevitable' and anyway the tide had arrived two hours earlier than anticipated. And the *Daily Mail* sympathized: 'Let us be fair' it suggested. 'Various authorities are being blamed for failing in their duty to the public. These charges . . . are understandable but unfair. No people in the world know more about flood prevention than the Dutch, and if they could not stop a disaster it is hard to know how we could either . . . Even had there been a system it is hard to see how it could have predicted the unpredictable.'

Eastern Daily Press

5 a.m. Edition

No. 25,570   NORWICH, MONDAY, FEBRUARY 2, 1953   Price 2d.

NORFOLK GALE DISASTER

100 MISSING AND DEAD

Seas' Wild Rush into Towns and Villages

AT LEAST 100 PEOPLE ARE REPORTED MISSING OR DEAD IN FLOODS ALONG THE NORFOLK COAST, WHICH STARTED WITH SATURDAY NIGHT'S GALES AND HIGH SEAS. MANY HAVE BEEN RENDERED HOMELESS. THESE ARE THE WORST FLOODS WITHIN LIVING MEMORY IN THIS PART OF THE COUNTRY. BY LAST NIGHT 39 BODIES HAD BEEN RECOVERED ALONG THE COAST BETWEEN KING'S LYNN AND HUNSTANTON.

The worst flood centres are:—

HUNSTANTON.—It was reported unofficially this morning that 40 people, including many Americans, might have been drowned. Twelve bodies have been recovered, including those of three Americans and a child. Most of the bungalows between Hunstanton and Heacham, principally occupied by American families, were swept away. Salt water entered the town's water mains and the supply was cut off. It was also stated unofficially today that 20 might have been killed at Snettisham.

KING'S LYNN.—Fifteen bodies have been recovered. Between 1000 and 1500 people have been evacuated from South Lynn housing estate, where the houses are standing in several feet of water. Part of the town's electricity supply has been cut off.

SEA PALLING.—The sea broke through a 100-yard gap in the dunes, washing away houses and causing the deaths of seven people, including three children. Some of the inhabitants in the bungalows were still refusing to leave their homes.

YARMOUTH.—Six are known to have been killed, others are missing or injured. There is extensive damage to the sea front and the Southtown and Cobholm districts. The police station and power station are flooded.

SOUTHWOLD.—Five people, including three women and a child, are missing, and the body of a woman has been recovered. Seven Americans were rescued from the roof of a house by boat and a rescue ambulance was overturned.

THE QUEEN SEES FLOODED AREA

AFTER morning service at Sandringham Church the Queen and the Duke of Edinburgh motored to Wolferton to view the floods. There the water had come across the marshes to within a comparatively short distance of the station.

Several emergency council meetings were held in the coastal towns yesterday and councillors inspected the damage. Cromer Urban District sent a request to the Minister of Housing and Local Government to pay a personal visit to the North Norfolk coast.

"Food Flying Squads"

On Saturday night and again yesterday the Mayor and Mayoress of King's Lynn (Mr. and Mrs. C. A. Freestone) visited the scenes of the flooding. Yesterday Comdr. R. Scott-Miller, M.P., visited South Lynn. Practically the whole of the South Lynn housing estate was affected and by last night some 2060 people had been evacuated, mostly from homes still standing in several feet of water. Many found accommodation with friends and relatives in the town but a number were sent to rest centres.

The Regional Food Officer at Cambridge yesterday sent out two "food flying squads," one from Cambridge to King's Lynn and one from Watford to the 13,000 homeless from Canvey Island, where at least 40 are believed to have been drowned. Staffed mostly by members of the W.V.S., they are intended to supplement local Civil Defence organisations with emergency feeding services in stricken areas.

Seas, regarded by older fishermen in North Norfolk as more violent than any they have ever seen, whipped by a gale which reached over 110 miles an hour, brought havoc and destruction to one of the most picturesque and popular holiday strips of coastline.

Light or moderate north-easterly winds, fresh in places on East Coast, are forecast for today.

Between Cromer and Walcot. Along this strip sea walls were breached, holiday bungalows were blown down, blown out to sea or torn to pieces and strewn over a wide area. At Bacton three houses at least disappeared over the cliff and at Walcot a number of bungalows, possibly as many as a dozen, have disappeared or been destroyed. At Walcot also, the coast road, for the protection of which a temporary sea wall was built recently, was washed away.

The Automobile Association reported last night that many roads on and near the coast in Lincolnshire, Norfolk, Essex and Kent are impassable.

Danger at Palling Past

Seven people, including three children, are believed to have lost their lives after the sea smashed through a gap in the dunes at Sea Palling carrying away four houses, a café, a general store and bakery and severely damaging the Lifeboat public-house.

The names of the dead were given as Mrs. Doris May Fox, aged 42, of the Longshore Café, Stephen Wilmott, aged 13, Merle Wilmott, aged eight (two children of Mrs. Fox's first marriage); Mr. William Hamblin, aged 87, and his wife, Mrs. Isabella Hamblin (80), and Mrs. Sarah Ellen Clarke (68), widow of Cranbury Cottages. The bodies of Hamblin, Mrs. Fox and the children, Stephen and Merle, were recovered last night. A third child of Mrs. Fox, a baby, Edwin Eric Fox, is missing.

Late last night the winds had moderated and the sea had begun to ebb. Word was then passed round that all was safe and with great relief villagers began to trickle back to the homes they had been warned to be ready to evacuate. Watch was again being maintained all night. At midnight further emergency equipment arrived by lorry at Sea Palling.

It was also stated that though the position at Bacton and Horsey Gap had caused great anxiety for over three hours, there had been no further serious inroads by the sea.

Electricity Breakdown

Strong winds and high seas were still lashing the stretch of coast between Sea Palling, Bacton and Horsey Gap late last night, however. The inhabitants had been warned to be ready to leave their homes at the first sign of any break through of the sea. Sea Palling itself was a village in darkness owing to the breakdown of electricity and also of deep mourning.

As the hour of high tide approached P/Sgt. F. Stevenson and a posse of constables who had established their headquarters in a shop, went in rubber boats to Beach Road and waded through three feet of water towards the gap where the sea broke through the previous night. They ventured within 75 yards of the gap and saw the sea lapping through it strongly. The water

Continued on Page 5, Column 3

Rescue Work by American Service Men

American Service men, who took a big part in rescue work in the Hunstanton area and elsewhere, bring in a casualty from a Hunstanton bungalow overturned in the gale.

Norfolk coastline inland at Cley, the photograph.

Evening Standard

40,040   MONDAY, FEBRUARY 2, 1953   Three-halfpence

CANVEY: 100 DEAD AND 400 UNTRACED

Four new breaches in Thames banks this afternoon

Canvey Island this afternoon—Servicemen are trying to repair a breach in the sea wall.—Air picture

500 ARE TAKEN TO HOSPITAL

Evening Standard Reporters

AT least 100 bodies were counted in flood-devastated Canvey Island, in the Thames Estuary, to-day. More have been seen floating on the water. Five hundred people from the island have gone to hospitals, and another 400 to 500 are untraced.

This new evidence of the flood's toll was brought to first-aid and reception centres as the immense rescue operation gathered force. It made the island the worst-hit of the stricken areas.

Total number of known dead in all the floods-swept areas or Southern and Eastern England is above 280. Last night it was the new extensive flooding. But with this afternoon's tide the Thames made four new breaches in its banks before Crayford Ness and Dartford Ore.

PEOPLE LIE DEAD ON ROOFS

Watch a lot of people I'd stayed on Canvey Island to escape from the flood taking refuge in various ways... To-day police advised nearly all to leave new flooding, but there was a few homes...

Some persons refusing to be evacuated...

WINSTON ON THE FLOODS

Our hearts go out to Canvey

Evening Standard Parliamentary Reporter

THE Lord Mayor of London is opening a Distress Fund immediately, Mr. Churchill told the Commons this afternoon.

He said that the Government would contribute to the fund on a scale to be announced when the magnitude of the disaster had been assessed.

...Parliament...

Plane missing —39 aboard

A four-engined York airliner with 33 Servicemen and six crew on board was...

The Christmas Eve Rail Crash

Tangiwai, New Zealand 1953

— The Dominion —

SATURDAY, DECEMBER 26, 1953.

ALL NEW ZEALAND MOURNS TODAY

At a time when otherwise there would have been much happiness and rejoicing, all New Zealanders have been shocked and saddened by the grievous disaster which befell the Main Trunk express near Waiouru on Christmas Eve. This catastrophe, one of the worst of its kind in the history of this or any other country, has bereaved many homes, and all fortunate people in this grieving Dominion will feel the deepest sympathy for the relatives of those who have lost their lives and for the injured.

This appalling disaster is another reminder that no man is master of his own soul or of his own destiny. Here were hundreds of travellers looking forward to the joys of home-coming or reunions on this Christmas Day, most of them no doubt, for the time being at least, without a care in the world. Yet it was so ordained that their train should be approaching the bridge at the very instant when, through some freak of nature, a gigantic wall of water was sweeping down upon it to send no fewer—by the latest sombre accounting as the Prime Minister has told the country—than one hundred and sixty-six people, it is profoundly regretted, to their death.

Everyone will have been deeply touched by the manner in which the sympathy of the whole nation with the relatives of the victims was expressed by our beloved Queen and the Duke of Edinburgh who had a message broadcast sharing the people's sorrow. Here was yet another example of how closely knit with the people are the Sovereign and her husband. They came to share our joys and remain to mourn with us.

So also did the Governor-General and Lady Norrie ask that the Prime Minister convey to the people their Excellencies' heartfelt sympathy. All New Zealand, irrespective of party politics, will feel gratitude to the Prime Minister, who at an instant made haste to the scene of the disaster and there played a notable part in organising emergency measures and reported to the country with dignity, restraint and accuracy, as manifestly befitted his position, the tragic tidings. Mr. Holland told the story calmly, yet anguish was to be discerned in his words as he recorded the third greatest disaster since European settlement in this country, the earlier visitations of more serious proportions being the Orpheus wreck and the Hawke's Bay earthquake.

His was a narrative which not only stunned New Zealand by the magnitude of the toll it revealed—a great disaster for a country of such small population—but was such as to move peoples of other nations. A flood of messages of sympathy and offers of assistance has come from all parts of the world, and we may reflect once again how in misfortune truly all humankind are kin.

As Mr. Holland has stated, no praise can be too high for those who shared in the rescue work. The stories by survivors and others which we publish this morning, of how more fortunate travellers fought to free their trapped fellow passengers, and similar incidents, tell of heroism of the highest order. These courageous efforts, and the fact that there was an absence of panic, stand out to illumine one of the darkest accounts of any happening in this country.

Meanwhile everything in human power is being done in the emergency, with all resources mobilised for recovery of the missing victims, identification and other work. In this sad task the authorities will receive the utmost co-operation wherever this is required of individuals or organisations, and those whose homes have been afflicted by this dreadful tragedy will be very much in the thoughts of all their countrymen, for this is a national calamity.

The Queen's Inspiration

Christmas 1953 was beginning to look like a washout for Cyril Ellis, his wife, and his mother-in-law. It was already 10.00pm on Christmas Eve and their prospects of reaching Rangitau—where they were supposed to be spending the holiday with his folks—seemed to be dim. Ahead of them, the waters of the Whangaehu River were sweeping clear over the road bridge—and over the rail bridge about fifty yards away. Just then he saw a light behind them: at first he thought it was another car, and he walked down the road with his torch to warn the driver. Then, to his horror, he realised it was the Wellington-Auckland express heading towards imminent danger at fifty miles an hour. Frantically he raced down the track, waving his feeble light.

It will never be known if the train-driver saw him. One witness later said the train was slowing down as it reached the fatal bridge. Perhaps the driver caught sight of the freak twenty-foot wall of water (the offspring of an eruption of Mount Ruapehu that towered over the Whangaehu) which was at that very instant roaring down the river valley. Even if he did, it was too late. The flood and the train reached the bridge at the same moment: beneath the weight of the train and the impact of this huge surge of water, the massive concrete piers and steel girders crumpled. With a shattering explosion the locomotive crashed into the opposite bank, wrenched away from its coaches—five of which were sent swirling away in the cascading waters. The sixth, miraculously, stayed poised perilously on the brink of the torrent.

In that moment of frozen suspense Cyril Ellis leapt into the coach, and yelled at the dazed passengers to jump for their lives. But before any of them could move, there was a sickening snap as the coupling parted and the coach (with Ellis in it) lurched into the flood. Once again fortune was on their side: it seemed to roll over three times in the water, then settled on one side. Somehow as the water poured through the carriage Ellis contrived to smash some windows, climb out—with the aid of another passenger—pull out many of those trapped inside. Between them they saved twenty-six people, and were both awarded the George Medal. He recalled afterwards seeing the other five coaches swept downstream, the lights still burning in them: but there were no sounds from within, and wreckage from some of them was found the next day two and a half miles from the bridge.

Some 131 people were known to have died that evening, though the true death-toll may in fact have exceeded 150 since twenty people were never accounted for. One of the saddest aspects of the tragedy was that the train was more crowded even than for a normal Christmas for the Queen was visiting Auckland that day. 'The very last thing that New Zealand would have wished was that a disaster should have occurred when our beloved Queen and her husband were with us on their so eagerly awaited visit' lamented the *Auckland Star*. But as the people of New Zealand heard the Queen sharing their grief in her broadcast Christmas message to the Commonwealth 'in a special kind of way' the *Star* went on, 'she had become more than ever one of us.'

Scene Of New Zealand's Greatest Railway Disaster

A VIEW FROM THE NORTH BANK of the Whangaehu River showing the scene of the train crash. In the foreground the engine's boiler and cab lie cheek by jowl with a 25-foot section of the broken off bridge and a section of one of the carriages. The engine's tender finished 50 yards downstream.

BODIES OF 26 VICTIMS OF TANGIWAI DISASTER TAKEN FROM RIVER

By last night the bodies of 26 victims of the Main Trunk railway disaster at Tangiwai had been recovered.

Of these 21 are at Waiouru and three of them have been identified, but the emergency committee has decided not to publish the names of the identified bodies till the next-of-kin have been advised by the police.

Either four or five bodies have been found on the lower reaches of the river and are in Wanganui.

To help next-of-kin it is thought advisable to have one identification point and the bodies are being taken from Wanganui to Waiouru.

The main problem with which the emergency committee has to deal is immediately is that of identification.

Everything indicates a death-roll of 166. The difficulty is that there is no list of persons who were on the train—only the numbers are known.

Another major difficulty is that the force of the floodwaters has destroyed a good deal of evidence, such as correspondence and other papers that would have assisted materially.

Washed Down Stream

According to a Press Association message from Wanganui bodies are being washed all the way down the Whangaehu River. So far 25 have been located about Mangamahu, less than 30 miles from Wanganui, and the Wanganui police have boats at the mouth of the river, believing that some will be found washed out to sea.

The 25 bodies found are being brought to Wanganui as fast as the available police transport can carry them. Descriptions of the bodies are being taken and every effort to identify them will be made.

Offices of both were flowing into the Wanganui central police station last night as private cars were held for the thorough combing of the river from dawn today. It is proposed to divide the river into sections and arrange for a concentrated search in each section.

The search may start from the mouth and work inland, and every effort will be made to cover every yard of the swiftly-flowing isolated reaches in the Karioi region.

Two fishing launches and a host of dinghies were used on the river yesterday as debris reached the lower reaches, carrying with it some of the bodies.

Toys Among Debris

Onlookers watched with awe a litter of shattered timberwork, items of apparel, and even children's toys, that floated past on the swollen stream.

Late last night the police conquered floodlights at Whangaehu to maintain the vigil, and every effort is being made to prevent the bodies reaching the sea.

Woman Describes Passengers' Ordeal

The ordeal of passengers in the carriage which halted, overhanging the precipitous drop into the river, was graphically described by a woman survivor.

"I had just finished an orange and was dozing when it all happened," she said. "The brakes went on violently, the carriage bucked like a mad thing, there was a series of crashes from the front of the train and then I heard the screams of people and a roaring of water in the darkness. The carriage hung at an acute angle, passengers and baggage were flung about in confusion. Mercifully the lights stayed on. I think I must have fainted.

"I have vague memories of someone helping me up the bank. I looked down into the dark, rushing water. To my horror I saw lights actually in the river and realised it was a carriage under the water. It was all so horrible it seemed like some ghastly nightmare."

NINE CARRIAGES IN ILL-FATED TRAIN

The ill-fated train which left Wellington for Auckland at 3 p.m. on Thursday comprised a Ka-class engine, five second-class and four first-class carriages, a guard's van and a postal van.

The train crew were the engine driver, a fireman and the guard. It is possible that a sleeping car attendant was aboard, though the train had no sleeping cars.

Searchers say that many of the bodies found were almost completely devoid of clothing. Such was the force of the torrent that even footwear was torn off.

The Post and Telegraph Department set up special toll lines to the central station and the Wanganui courthouse today, where a big flow of telephone enquiries was being received from all parts of New Zealand. The Wanganui courthouse staff worked the full day to help out the police.

Work Of Identification

The Prime Minister, Mr. Holland, in a broadcast address last night, asked those who could assist in identifying passengers in the wrecked train to go immediately to Waiouru Camp.

Though not compulsory persons going to Waiouru should limit themselves to two in each case. Where they could not arrange their own transport, persons should apply to the nearest police station which, with the Railways Department, will make necessary arrangements.

Any person who was on the train and who left the scene of the disaster by private transport should immediately advise the nearest police station so that checks may be completed.

To assist, persons should give full names of passengers, their sex, age, height, weight, hair and eye colours and identifying marks or peculiarities.

Local police would give this information to police headquarters at Waiouru Camp and this would enable identification and save unnecessary viewing of bodies.

Mr. Holland said an adequate service of coroners to conduct inquests and other necessary procedure had been arranged.

"I am very sorry to say it appears that many of the victims may not be recovered very soon, in fact such was the force of the floodwaters that it is feared some victims may have been carried out to sea, 20 or so miles away. Some recoveries have already been made some miles from the scene of the disaster."

CREWS TO WORK ROUND CLOCK ON NEW BRIDGE

Railway repair crews will work round the clock for the next few days, building a new bridge to replace the one destroyed on Thursday night.

It is estimated that if wooden piles instead of steel piles can be driven there is every possibility that the line will be open in three or four days. If steel piles have to be driven, however, the line may just be open for perhaps a week. It is not yet known which type of pile will be used.

Yesterday almost all the equipment for the work was on the site. Huge cranes and bulldozers have been clearing the wreckage and preparing the ground throughout the day, the men working in shifts.

Works Department engineers were busy yesterday preparing to erect a Bailey bridge next to the road bridge which was also damaged. This bridge, if work goes according to plan, will be ready for traffic today.

Racing Fixtures

December 26—Dunedin J.C.
December 26—Taranaki J.C.
December 26—Manawatu R.C.
December 26—Auckland R.C.
December 26—Dunedin J.C.
December 28—Taranaki J.C.
December 28—Manawatu R.C.
December 28—South Canterbury J.C.
December 28—Auckland R.C.
January 1—Ashburton R.C.
January 1—Stratford R.C.
January 4—Wairarapa R.C.
January 2—Hutton J.C.

A RAILWAY LINESMAN working on the south end of the bridge at the site of the train crash on Thursday explains to a companion how the engine and six carriages hurtled into the raging torrent below. When this picture was taken the river had subsided to only a foot or two above its normal level.

WELLINGTON SHIELD XI DISAPPOINT

An excellent spell of bowling late in the afternoon by H. B. Cave, the Central Districts captain, placed his side in a strong position in the Plunket Shield match at the Basin Reserve yesterday against Wellington. Wellington at the close of the first day's play had lost seven wickets for 88 runs.

Cave finished with four wickets for 22 runs. This experienced player, in his first season as captain of Central Districts, did particularly well as the one of the toss meant fielding in a cold wind with occasional showers to handicap the bowlers.

After the excellent spring and early summer weather, the dismal conditions which marked this evening of Plunket Shield season at the Basin Reserve came as a great disappointment. Only a small crowd attended.

Wellington should have done much better. Though rain had slowed up the fielding, the pitch looked easy and the occasional drizzle was not against the bowlers.

This was noticeable early after R. Cave had won the toss and opened Wellington's innings with D. W. Crowe. In five minutes 12 runs were scored and a heavy drizzle then caused a hold-up of 32 minutes. At the tea adjournment the score was 55 without a further 40 minutes' batting. Vance 37 and Crowe 13.

Light Deteriorates

The light deteriorated after the reception and this may have accounted for some of the batsmen getting themselves out. Crowe gave a chance to mid-off in the same over as he was bowled, caught by the wicketkeeper, who had previously given two chances, one off a rising ball to slip and the other to leg slip off the bowling of Cave. Snell's duck was a hell from D. D. Beard and was caught at first slip.

After the early settlers with two bowlers down for 45, Wellington adequately recovered. K. Tyson and F. E. Fisher put on useful contributions, with Smith in the first Plunket Shield game. He did well behind all his and was unlucky in being dismissed with a ball which kept low. He was the only delivery by Cave that could not be said to have defeated a worker. Those which deceived Fisher and McMahon were full of life and moved sharply off the pitch.

The game will be resumed at 11 with this morning. The umpires were Messrs. L. G. Clark and R. Curlewis-Scores:—

WELLINGTON.

First Innings

(scores illegible)

BOWLING

(scores illegible)

Ordeal Of Man Aged 77

Mr. John Hamer, aged 77, of Christchurch, was in a carriage near the front of the train and now is feeling the pain of a cigarette.

"The next thing I knew I was under water. The next thing was dark. The next thing two men pulled me out. The water was cold. That's all I know."

Mr. Hamer, who was in bed at the Waiouru Hospital yesterday afternoon, was feeling quite well.

SALVATION ARMY LEADER'S MESSAGE

The following telegram was sent today morning to the Prime Minister, Mr. Holland, by the Territorial Commander of the Salvation Army, Commissioner B. Hoggard:

"On behalf of the Salvation Army I extend to the Government deepest sympathy and assurance of prayers in this hour of national tragedy and disaster.

"Our entire organising including for the children, for the aged, and all is any kind of need are gladly at the disposal of the Government. Early this morning all our men throughout the North Island are directed to visit the homes of the bereaved to offer spiritual comfort and practical help.

"We are eager to serve and await their direction."

All Blacks Play At Twickenham Today

The All Blacks will play their seventh match of the present tour at Twickenham, home of English rugby, at their next Combined Services game.

The earliest visit to this famous ground was on November 7, when they beat London Counties 11-0. The third match at Twickenham will be against Ireland on January 30.

The 1924 All Blacks beat a Combined Services team 25-3, but the 1935 side by a close tussle, winning 24-6. The 1951 Springboks beat Combined Services 24-8.

The All Blacks' record to date is: Played 11, won 12, lost two, drawn two. Points for 254, against 55. Their next match is against Combined Services at Twickenham today.

MORE UNIVERSITY EXAM. RESULTS

(illegible)

Canterbury Lose Six Wickets For 140 Runs

CHRISTCHURCH, December (P.A.)—A miserable lack of initiative on the part of the Canterbury batsmen allowed the Auckland bowlers to gain ascendancy when the two provinces met in their first Plunket Shield match of the season at Lancaster Park today.

On a wicket which was easy at time Canterbury threw away countless chances of notching a good score and at stumps had made only 140 for the loss of six wickets.

It was dour uninteresting cricket for a fair crowd and at no time was the scoring competing with the clock.

Though he made a chanceless 57, J. G. Legget failed to get on top of the bowling and for most of the time was content with easy singles.

The only time a little dash was added to the innings was when P. Harris teamed with Legget. For a while Harris rattled the runs, but also slipped into slow gear towards the end of his innings.

With the aid of a fairly stiff north-easterly breeze E. Child managed to move the ball very consistently through the air and much of the credit for Canterbury's small score must go to him. C. J. Hanbrook, bowling of swingers, was another who helped to keep down the score.

The Auckland fielding, except one or two small patches, was excellent.

CANTERBURY.

First Innings

J. G. Legget, c. Hanbrook, b. Child		57
G. Miller, b. Hanbrook		4
R. Snell, b. Child		5
B. Howarth, b. Burke		12
E. A. Harris, lbw. b. Child		14
S. C. Collins, c. Petti, b. Child		5
I. Sinclair, not out		6
G. Gearie, not out		6
Extras		

Total for six wickets 140

Bowling

	O	M	R	W
D. F. Clarke	18	5	35	1
E. Child	23	8	43	3
T. Hanbrook	15	6	21	1
C. J. Burke	15	2	23	1
R. Carrington	2	1	5	0

Tragic Flotsam Along River

Passengers' belongings, including suitcases, clothing and shoes, are strewn for miles down the course of the Whangaehu River. This grim evidence of the disaster could be seen yesterday from a Dominion plane which followed the winding course of the stream.

Evidence of the height of the flood was provided by a woman's hat caught in the branches of a tree some 20ft. above the surface of the water.

Royal Tour Staff Diverted To Train Disaster

AUCKLAND, December 25 (P.A.)—In the space of a telephone message the closely integrated Royal tour organisation in Auckland was diverted early this morning almost exclusively to the Tangiwai disaster. The fact that so many key men were together in Auckland meant that orders to administration could be arranged speedily and completely.

Exhausted after the Christmas Eve tour programme, regarded as the busiest day of the entire Royal visit, members of the Royal tour staff were either preparing for bed or had settled down to sleep when they were alerted. They carried on without sleep till this afternoon or tonight.

The Prime Minister, Mr. Holland, was awakened at the Grand Hotel. The Royal tour director, Mr. A. Harper, Mr. C. H. Williams, Press and public relations officer, Mr. H. Hildreth, communications officer, Mr. W. Yates, Director of Broadcasting, and Mr. E. H. Compton, Commissioner of Police, and their staffs, were among the groups which met immediately to make decisions.

Mr. Holland and his private secretary, Mr. K. M. Sheighs, left by car for the scene and with the Prime Minister who spearheaded of the dead group.

Awakened at the Station Hotel, the Leader of the Opposition, Mr. Nash, joined the administrative groups of the Grand Hotel.

Throughout the day the Royal tour staff spent more work on the disaster than on any other arrangements.

Governor-General's Message To P.M.

AUCKLAND, December 25 (P.A.)—A telegram was sent to the Prime Minister, Mr. Holland, at Waiouru today by the Governor-General, Sir Willoughby Norrie. It stated:

"My wife and I were most distressed to learn early this morning of the railway disaster near Waiouru and the tragic loss of life involved. We join with the people of New Zealand in mourning the loss of so many valuable lives and would be grateful if you would convey to the relatives those concerned our heartfelt sympathy in their great loss.

"We sincerely hope that those injured in the accident will soon be restored to health."

LONDON SENDS CONDOLENCES

London has expressed its sympathy with the relatives of the railway disaster victims through the Lord Mayor of that city, Sir Noel Bowater, as has cabled the Mayor of Wellington, Mr. Macalister, as follows:

"I have just heard of the tragedy which has brought so much sorrow to so many homes in your city and in North Island at this time when we in London hoped you would have nothing but great rejoicing. On behalf of citizens of London and on my own part please accept our very sincere sympathy for the bereaved and the injured."

Christmas Concert

The Eastbourne Lyric Singers, directed by Mr. R. H. Radford, gave their Christmas concert to a filled house on Tuesday night. They sang songs, madrigals and Christmas carols, almost all unaccompanied. Soloists were Kitty Petrie, who sang "Joys" and "The Magic of Your Presence" (Roger Quilter), "Oh, Thank Me" (Sung My Songs) (Clarke), and Ruth Macaulay, who sang "Ah the Moon" (this Love Song) (Abrams) and "I Passed (lines illegible) company last week.

William Davey, conductor, was joined by forty show-dancers who gave a present or class. Finally the Keister's Beagles (illegible).

The Rough Law of Sport

Le Mans Disaster 1955

Le Mans 24-hour race at 6.30 in the evening. The thirty-sixth lap. Precisely what made TV cameraman Jean-Jacques Rebuffat train his camera on the pits at that exact moment, he couldn't afterwards explain.

Into the view-finder comes the leader, Mike Hawthorn, slowing down to make a pit stop. Behind him another British driver, Lance Macklin, swerves to pass him. On his tail the Frenchman Pierre Levegh raises his arm to indicate he is going to overtake Macklin. And behind Levegh, Fangio responds by decelerating. In an instant—no more than a few frames on a cine-camera—Levegh's machine has brushed Macklin's, and somersaulted into the air, hurtling at over 150mph towards a barrier crowded with spectators. As it plunges through, an axle swathes through the mass of people, the car explodes like a bomb, igniting the straw barriers and illuminating the daylight like a magnesium flare.

That is what French viewers saw, a few hours later, on their television screens. The next morning the world read of its consequences in their papers: seventy dead, probably more, and at least a hundred injured. And even as they digested the news, the race was continuing

with Mike Hawthorn battling his way to a cheerless victory. 'The most callous sport event ever' reckoned the *Sunday Dispatch*, marvelling that officials had not abandoned the race. And *Franc-Tireur*'s question was echoed by much of the French press: 'when a race becomes a race with death, must it then imitate war which no tragedy can stop?'

The official in question, Charles Faroux, defended his decision not to stop the race with the blunt excuse that 'too many interests were involved in any sudden cancellation'—referring to the compensation the big car firms might have demanded. He also pointed out, for the benefit of Fleet Street, that the 1952 Farnborough Air Display was not called off after Derry's plane had ploughed into the crowd. Which was exactly the reason proffered by the *News Chronicle* for embarking on a splashy series about racing drivers by Stirling Moss ('in no way connected with Saturday's tragedy') the next day.

Levegh's own team, Mercedes, would have pulled their remaining cars out hours before they actually did, but for the organizers' pleas that a quarter of a million people streaming home would impede rescue work. As it was, it

was a minute and silent crowd that stayed to watch Hawthorn cross the finishing-line— only then to be faced with a barrage of innuendo that it was his braking that had caused the accident. Interviewed by *Paris-Presse* he could only mumble: 'I don't know, I just don't know.' As the final death-roll climbed to eighty-three, the same newspaper emphasized the discrepancy between the 'theory' of the 24-Hours as an endurance test and its reality as a speed-race, and the inevitable risk to spectators on an unsuitable track. It was a point that motor-racing—eventually—took to heart, conceding that even if the sport was 'a battle', as M. Faroux maintained, there was no need to put the spectators in the front line.

NEWS OF THE WORLD

LATE LONDON EDITION

No. 5,822 [Estab. 1843]   SUNDAY, JUNE 12, 1955   PRICE 2½d.

Telephone: Central 3038   Telegrams: Worldly, Fleet, London

LE MANS CAR MOWS 70 TO DEATH

The Scene Was Like A Battlefield

MISSING GIRL SENSATION THIS MORNING

From NORMAN RAE

Coventry, Sunday.

EARLY this morning detectives and uniformed police were rushed to Corley Woods, five miles north of here, where they believe the body of 10-year-old Evelyn Patricia Higgins, the missing Coventry schoolgirl, may be buried.

The decision to search the woods followed a statement made by a car owner an hour or two earlier.

I understand that a man indicated Evelyn had been strangled and afterwards buried in some undergrowth in the woods.

In heavy rain police began a search by the light of torches. Earlier bloodhounds had been used in the woods without result.

Meanwhile Professor James Webster, the Home Office pathologist, has been called from Birmingham by Mr. E. W. C. Pendleton, the Chief Constable of Coventry, and in gum boots and heavy mackintosh is at the police headquarters for a message that may say the search goes on.

As I telephone the search goes on. I understand the police has indicated an area on which the officers are now concentrating.

Two Liners Beat The Strike

WEEK-END OF RAIL DOUBTS

BRITAIN faced up to its third week of rail doubt and anxiety when yesterday's peace talks at the Ministry of Labour were adjourned until 11 a.m. to-morrow.

Mr. Jim Baty, the strikers' leader, rejected the latest proposals of the British Transport Commission. "They are unacceptable. . . . the strike is still on," he said. He did, however, emphasise that the whole situation was under review and that the Commission's document containing the settlement proposals "could be amended considerably to meet our point."

The adjournment of the talks and the publication of the proposals—put forward on Friday—followed a session at which the Associated Society of Locomotive Engineers and Firemen executive met the Commission in the presence of the Minister of Labour, Sir Walter Monckton.

It was the only joint meeting of a dramatic, peace-at-all-costs day which, it was hoped, would find representatives of all three parties concerned at the same conference table. The parties are the Transport Commission, the A.S.L.E.F. and the National Union of Railwaymen.

During the morning all three organisations had occupied separate rooms at the Ministry of Labour whose Chief Industrial Commissioner, Sir Wilfred Neden, consulted them in turn as reached at the earliest possible moment. Although we have been standing by we have expressed our willingness to give any assistance which may lead to an honourable settlement.

NO ROYAL ASCOT THIS WEEK

The Stewards of the Jockey Club announced last night that as a result of the further adjournment of the railway talks they have decided to postpone the Royal Ascot meeting.

A meeting of the Stewards will take place to-morrow when an announcement about the new date for the meeting is expected. "It should be within a month," an official told the "News of the World."

Jim Campbell, the general secretary.

The Commission's latest proposals include:

*After the cancellation of the strike negotiations should open with both unions.

It accepted the principle there should be higher awards for special skill where not already given.

The Commission was prepared to examine basic wages in the driver grade, particularly in respect of the highest-rated drivers and motormen.

Application of the higher rewards clause to other than footplate staffs should not justify a further upward revision of the settlement for footplate staffs.

As soon as the proposals were made known, Mr. Baty made his statement that the Commission's document "did not prove acceptable."

Then the N.U.R. issued a statement.

"True to the undertaking we gave to the T.U.C., the N.U.R. have stood aside to enable the A.S.L.E.F to resolve their immediate difficulties with the Transport Commission. Unfortunately, it appears that a series of meetings since Wednesday has not yet achieved their purpose.

"Having regard to the effect of this dispute on the industry and the country, it is our sincere hope that a settlement will be

THE RACE WENT ON

FROM OUR SPECIAL CORRESPONDENT   LE MANS, Sunday Morning.

A RACING car cut a swath of death through tightly-packed spectators here yesterday when it overturned at over 100 m.p.h. and exploded in flames against a grandstand. Seventy people were killed and 100 injured. The death roll was still growing this morning.

Eye-witnesses said the car, a powerful Mercedes, blew up "like a magnesium bomb." Its rear axle rocketed towards the embankment by the stand, tearing into the men, women and children lining the route and, like the whirling blade of a helicopter, sliced off the heads of some of them. The driver, Frenchman Pierre Levegh, was killed.

The blazing wreck of the car itself leaped into the air and landed only 10 yards from where

Minutes after the crash this was the tragic scene. Bodies lie right and left of the priest as he goes about his task of ministering to the dying.—Picture radioed from Le Mans last night.

dead girl friend in his blood-stained arms, walked away from the carnage desperately murmuring endearments in her ear.

A mother, one arm dripping blood, screamed hysterically and

inquiries were received from anxious relatives and friends in all parts of Britain.

An hour and 40 minutes after the accident five badly battered bodies still remained at the scene. They were partly covered with blood-stained newspapers, and a four-foot pile of clothing and shoes lay nearby

MURDER IN THE SMALL BACK ROOM

THE shopkeeper whom neighbours called the happiest man in the road was found stabbed to death last night.

Police who broke into the newsagent's and tobacconist's shop which he managed at Hillside, Stonebridge Park, London, discovered his body in a little back room.

He was 45-year-old Herbert Blades—"Buster" to his friends —whose home was at Balmoral gardens, Ealing.

There were lights in the shop early to-day as Mr. R. Ressler, the proprietor, checked how much money ha- been stolen by the murderer.

"I think about £50 is missing from a tobacco jar in the back room," he said. "Mr. Blades had a number of concealed crevices and compartments for storing money. We devised the arrangement in case there was ever an intruder. That is what makes it so difficult to discover exactly how much money from other parts of the shop is missing.

Detectives headed by Chief Supt. Gus Mahon of Scotland Yard, believe that Buster Blades died because he wanted to oblige a customer while the shop was closed for his lunch break.

Knock At The Door

He probably answered a tap at the door, said Mr. Ressler. "He always tried to please his customers—and I think he must have opened the door for the intruder without being suspicious.

"In the circumstances the front door could have been locked as the customer stepped inside the little shop."

Police were told that "Buster" might even have known his last caller. They are convinced there was no break-in—otherwise a burglar alarm system would have functioned.

Neighbours who became alarmed when they found the shop shut late in the afternoon called the police. When the detectives entered, they discovered the fish and chips that would have been "Buster's" lunch still warm under an electric fire. A glass of light ale was untouched.

BIG BANG, BIG SIGH OF RELIEF

Ike's Atoms

Sunday Dispatch

154th Year. No. 8,010.   2½d.   JUNE 12, 1955.   TV & Radio Page 6.

The Most Callous Sports Event Ever

70 DIE IN RACE HORROR

But The Le Mans Twenty-Four Hour Car Contest Is Still Continuing

AT least 70 spectators, including many women and children, were killed and 75 injured last night when one of the cars in the Le Mans 24-hour race crashed into the crowd lining the track and burst into flames. But, despite the disaster, the race is still continuing. It will end this afternoon.

The car, a Mercedes driven by Pierre Levegh, who was killed, tried to pass an Austin Healey with 35-year-old Londoner Lance Macklin at the wheel. The cars touched, and the Mercedes heeled across the track and smashed into the protective barrier in front of the stands. Macklin escaped with minor injuries.

The engine and back axle of the Mercedes sliced like a razor through the packed spectators. Some were decapitated, and for 100 yards along the straight the scene was like a bloodstained battlefield.

Some of the dead and injured inside the enclosure.

Wailing men and women tried frantically to find out whether their friends or relations were among the victims.

Police, doctors, nurses, and first-aid men took nearly two hours to remove the dead and injured.

Spectators Faint

Women's screams rose above the roar of the cars as they continued round the course.

A mother screamed hysterically as she clasped the mangled body of her small son from where it lay beside that of her dead husband.

Spectators fainted at the scene of carnage.

Within 15 minutes another accident occurred some two miles away near the Muisanne curve, when the British driver R. Jacobs, in an M.G., crashed in flames.

He was rushed to hospital with serious injuries.

Thrilling Duel

As a shuttle service of ambulances carried the injured to nearby hospitals officials appealed over loudspeakers to the crowd for blood donors.

Until the disaster the race had been a thrilling duel between a British Jaguar driven by Mike Hawthorn and a Mercedes with the Argentine world champion, Juan Manuel Fangio, at the wheel.

Then, a Mercedes spokesman said, Jaguar officials called Hawthorn into the pits. He roared in and as he pulled in Macklin, who was right behind him, also braked sharply.

Levegh, close to Macklin's tail, hit the back of the Austin Healey.

The Austin Healey spun round, stopped, and Macklin climbed out unaided.

Terrible Injuries

An eye-witness said the Mercedes exploded "like a magnesium bomb" in a burst of white-hot sparks.

The elaborate barrier did not protect the crowd. It consisted of one wooden barrier, a sandpit, and then another wooden barrier.

Flying pieces of hot metal caused terrible injuries. A police inspector told of two children who were decapitated. Their parents, senseless with grief, took the bodies away without informing the police.

Among the first of the dead identified was a man from London, whose name was given as Jack Diamond, aged 24.

Race officials described the accident as the most murderous catastrophe in motor-racing history.

'Impossible' Race

The Automobile Club De L'Ouest, the organisers of the race, issued a communiqué expressing to the families of the dead its "deepest grief at this cruel accident."

John Fitch, the team-mate of Levegh, the driver who was killed, said early today that the race should have been stopped immediately after the accident. He revealed that Mercedes officials had asked the race organisers moments after the accident to stop the race or let the Mercedes team withdraw.

He claimed that the officials refused both requests.

Fitch said that Levegh and Fangio and he all agreed before the race that it was becoming an impossible competition and that the track was not large enough for the mixture of powerful cars.

Fangio's partner, Stirling Moss, of Britain, said: "I believe the race ought to have been stopped."

Moss said: "I cannot understand how people can go on singing, drinking and having fun at the side of the track while some 60 or other spectators are lying dead."

Moss said that Mike Hawthorn, the British Jaguar ace, during a brief interval in the pits, told him: "I wish, Stirling, that I did not have to race in this damn thing any more. This is too much for me."

Early this morning a Mercedes, driven in turn by Juan Fangio and Stirling Moss, was leading a lap in front of a Jaguar driven by Mike Hawthorn. A Mercedes was third, and Jaguars were lying fourth and fifth.

'Buster' Stabbed To Death In Back Room Of His Shop

MANAGER of a lock-up tobacconist's and newsagent's shop in Hillside, Stonebridge Park, Willesden, affectionately known by children and almost everyone else as "Buster," was found stabbed to death in a small back room at the shop yesterday.

The man, Herbert S. Blades, aged 65, who lived at Balmoral-gardens, Ealing, W., had managed the shop for more than 20 years.

Mr. Eric Reynolds, proprietor of a grocer's shop across the road, noticed that the newsagent's was still closed at four o'clock. Mr. Reynolds went to see what was wrong.

He found a bundle of evening papers lying on the step outside the door.

Police were called. They broke into the shop through a window.

It is believed that only about £40 was stolen, though several hundred pounds were handled by Mr. Blades each week; he hid the money in various places in the shop.

Fierce Struggle

Detectives last night were working on a theory that Mr. Blades was about to close for lunch when the last customer tapped at the door-window.

While he was letting him in and as it was so near to lunchtime, shut the door.

Police believe he was attending to the customer when he was attacked. There was a fierce struggle.

ASCOT OFF

ASCOT has been postponed because of the rail strike.

The meeting was to have taken place next Tuesday to Friday. New dates will be announced tomorrow.

The Ascot Heath meeting arranged for Saturday will be transferred to Newbury.

The Garter ceremonies at Windsor Castle tomorrow — at which Sir Anthony Eden and Lord Iveagh were to have been installed—will not now take place this year.

Lighting-Up Time (London)

JUNE 12-13 (B.S.T.)
Lights up. 10.16 p.m.
Lights out. 3.43 a.m.

The scene of desolation after the crash.

The remains of Levegh's Mercedes.

UNION DELEGATES TO MEET AGAIN

THE delegate conference of the striking "blue card" union in the docks adjourned yesterday—20th day of the strike—and will meet again on Tuesday.

The delegates, leaders of the National Amalgamated Stevedores and Dockers' Union, had before them at their meeting in London two letters, one from the T.U.C. and one from the National Association of Port Employers.

The T.U.C. letter stated that the complaint about the publication in pamphlet form by the Transport and General Workers' Union of the terms of a T.U.C. letter to N.A.S.D.U. before the stevedores' executive had seen the letter, was still being investigated.

BABY'S BODY IN CARDBOARD BOX

WHEN the parents of a dead baby asked for the body to be sent home from the hospital it travelled the 40-mile rail journey wrapped in cotton wool in a cardboard box, it was disclosed yesterday.

The father, Mr. Robert Donaldson, went to the station at Fintona, Co. Tyrone, with the local undertaker.

He was handed a brown paper parcel with a stick-on label.

The label said: "For immediate delivery" and "Carriage forward." He was asked to pay £1 18s. 11d. carriage.

"It was a great shock for me to find the body in a parcel," said Mr. Donaldson.

BANNISTER WEDS HIS 'DREAM GIRL'

FIRST man to run a mile in under four minutes, Dr. Roger Bannister, was married at Basle, Switzerland, yesterday to Miss Moyra Jacobson, 26-year-old daughter of a Swedish economist. In a speech at the reception he called her his "dream girl."

Governors of the banks of 12 nations, including Mr. Cameron Cobbold, of the Bank of England, were among the guests. The church ceremony will be televised by the B.B.C. today. After it the bridegroom threw toffees to children in the crowd outside.

Miss Finland Wins—In Finland

THERE was a surprise in Helsinki yesterday when Miss Finland was declared the winner of a "Miss Europe" beauty contest, although, according to Associated Press, she is round-faced and has heavy dark eyebrows.

Miss Turkey was second, and Miss France was third.

When the result was announced Margaret Rowe, 19-year-old beauty from Britain, burst into tears and fled from the stage. She rushed away to dress and left to return to the stage. She was still weeping when she left the hall.

Miss Rowe had been loudly cheered when she paraded before the audience. Miss Germany first, Miss Turkey second, and Miss Britain third.

Babies Escape In Crash

A hundred day trippers, including dozens of children and babies, escaped injury when two coaches, returning to Stevenage New Town, Hertfordshire, collided at Eastern-avenue, Arterial - road, Ilford, Essex, last night.

Big Diamond Found

Measuring 1in. long, 1in. thick, and 1¼in. wide, a 572½-carat diamond has been found at Jagersfontein Mine, Johannesburg.

Today's Weather

Cloudy, rain at times. Brighter weather spread up from northwest; showers, generally cool.

Outlook: Changeable, bright periods.

The Day a Team Died

The Munich Air Crash 1958

DAILY MIRROR, Friday, February 7, 1958   PAGE 13

E VERY one a star! These are the eleven players who have made Manchester United League Champions for two years. This is what happened to them in yesterday's tragic crash:
DUNCAN EDWARDS. Left Half. He has broken his right thigh and fractured his ribs. He is also suffering from shock.

BILL FOULKES. Right Back. Escaped with slight injuries.
MARK JONES. Centre Half. Dead.
RAY WOOD. Reserve goalkeeper. Seriously injured.
EDDIE COLMAN. Right Half. Dead.
DAVID PEGG. Reserve Outside Left. Dead.

JOHN BERRY. Outside Right. Eye injury.
BILL WHELAN. Inside Forward and Eire international. Dead.
ROGER BYRNE. England Left Back and Captain of United. Dead.
TOMMY TAYLOR. England Centre Forward. Dead.
DENIS VIOLLET. Inside Left. Head injuries.

BUSBY 'little chance'
Matt Busby, the great manager who brought Manchester United world fame, was "doing badly" last night. A doctor said he had "little chance."

SCANLON head injuries
Bert Scanlon, the local Manchester boy who made good, has head injuries. He recently established himself in the League side and was showing promise.

CHARLTON head injuries
Bobby Charlton, who is doing his Army call-up, has head injuries. Bobby is a nephew of famous former Newcastle forward Jackie Milburn.

GREGG slight injuries
Harry Gregg, the world's most expensive goalkeeper, was recently bought from Doncaster Rovers for £23,000. The crowds thought him worth it.

BENT dead
Geoffrey Bent, reserve full back, is dead. He was one of Busby's bright young men. He was all set to become a big star of the future.

BLANCHFLOWER broken pelvis
Jackie Blanchflower, Irish international centre half, has broken pelvis, rib injuries. He is a brother of Spurs' Danny Blanchflower.

MORGANS injured
Ken Morgans, Welsh outside right from Swansea. He has only just established himself in the League side—another Busby new boy of promise.

Busby's Babes, the Press liked to call them, a tribute to their youth and skill and to the manager, Matt Busby, who had fashioned a football team that had commanded the heights of English soccer for two seasons. In 1958 Manchester United were poised to take Europe by storm: for the second successive year they had reached the semi-finals of the European Cup, this time by beating the formidable Red Star of Belgrade 5-4 on aggregate. It was a notable achievement to have held the Yugoslavian side to a 3-3 draw on their home ground, and the team was tired but elated as it boarded its chartered BEA Elizabethan in Belgrade the next morning, Thursday 6 February.

It was a rare combination of talent, of seasoned internationals like England stars Roger Byrne, Tommy Taylor and Duncan Edwards, Irish centre-half Jackie Blanchflower, and brilliant newcomers like Denis Viollet and Bobby Charlton (whose two goals in Belgrade had been an inspiration). Flying back to Manchester with them were four club officials, including Busby, and a contingent of journalists representing most of the Fleet Street dailies and three local papers. Six other passengers and six crew members made up the complement of forty-four on board.

Munich, where the plane landed just after 1.00pm to refuel, was hardly an inspiring place in which to kill time, slushy underfoot but with a distinct nip in the air. But the passengers made the best of it, combing the duty-free shops, and were back in the plane shortly after two o'clock. As the Elizabethan accelerated down the runway the co-pilot noticed fluctuations in the pressure gauges: the take-off was abandoned and the plane juddered to a halt. A second time the airliner was given clearance and picked up speed down the tarmac: a second time the engine pressure leaped. This time the captain decided to return to the airport buildings, to consult the station engineer.

This 'power surging', the engineer explained, was not uncommon at Munich's altitude, and a third take-off was agreed. It was by now just after three o'clock, below freezing and starting to snow. The plane's wheels sprayed up grey clouds of slush as it gathered momentum yet again down the runway. Anxiously the passengers watched the ground speed by them—but the plane wasn't lifting off!

The end of the runway was in sight, then the wooden perimeter fence, then a few hundred yards further on—a house. The plane plunged into the building, lurched on like a reeling monster, tore through a hut, and finally skidded to a halt, a crumpled wreck enveloped in flames yet uncannily quiet. Twenty-one died in those nightmare seconds, seven players: Roger Byrne, Tommy Taylor, Eddie Colman, Mark Jones, Billy Whelan, David Pegg and Geoff Bent; and eight journalists including the ex-England footballer Frank Swift. Others were critically injured, like Edwards and Busby. Of those who could scramble out of the wreckage some, like goalkeeper Harry Gregg and Bill Foulkes, rushed back into the flames to help others out.

An hour or so later one of the survivors, photographer Peter Howard of the *Daily Mail*, stumbled to a telephone and brokenly recounted the bare details to his paper. His words appeared on several front pages the next morning: 'The plane suddenly appeared to be breaking up. Seats started to crumble up. Everything seemed to be falling to pieces. It was a rolling sensation and all sorts of stuff started

News Chronicle

AND
Daily Dispatch

No. 34,813 © NEWS CHRONICLE LTD., 1958 FRIDAY, FEBRUARY 7, 1958 PRICE 2½d.

SEVEN MANCHESTER UNITED STARS AMONG 21 DEAD

ROGER BYRNE

TOMMY TAYLOR

EDDIE COLMAN

MARK JONES

BILLY WHELAN

DAVID PEGG

GEOFF BENT

SOCCER PLANE DISASTER

EIGHT JOURNALISTS DIE, TOO

Take-off crash after Europe Cup game

By News Chronicle Reporters in Munich, Manchester and London

SEVEN players and three officials of Manchester United, Britain's star Soccer team, died last night when their airliner crashed in a snowstorm near Munich.

Twenty-one of the 44 people in the plane were killed. Eight British journalists are among the dead. They include big Frank Swift, ex-England and Manchester City goalkeeper, who had been covering United's match against Yugoslav Red Star in Belgrade.

Manager Matt Busby, who built United into the most famous football team in the world, is one of the survivors. But he is gravely injured.

The dead players were: Eddie Colman, Roger Byrne, Mark Jones, Bill Whelan, Tommy Taylor, Geoff Bent and David Pegg. Trainer Tom Currie, coach Bert Whalley and secretary Walter Crickmer were killed.

The chartered twin-engined Elizabethan airliner crashed on take-off after refuelling at Munich's Riem Airport. The Manchester team were on the way home after their 3—3 draw with Red Star team had put them through to the European Cup semi-finals.

United were riding the crest of the wave when the crash came. It was the second year in succession that they had reached the semi-finals of the European Cup. They are English League champions and favourites for the F.A. Cup.

Of the 17 players with the party 10 are internationals. They are known as the Busby Babes because of their manager's habit of developing young players.

Made two false starts

Peter Howard, a Daily Mail cameraman flying with the team, went back into the burning wreckage to do all he could in rescue attempts.

This is his story: "I was sitting in the front row of seats on the starboard side. When the pilot tried to take off there seemed to be some kind of slight fault with the engines. He stopped.

"Then he tried a second take-off. That did not seem satisfactory so he taxied back to the apron to get things checked up.

"It was on the third take-off that we crashed. I think we were about the end of the runway only a bit above the ground.

"The plane suddenly appeared to be breaking up. Seats started to crumble up. Everything seemed to be falling to pieces.

No screams—just silence

"It was a rolling sensation and all sorts of stuff started coming down on top of us. There wasn't time to think. No one cried out. No one spoke—just a deadly silence for what could only have been seconds.

"I can't remember whether there was a bang or not. Everything stopped all at once. I was so dazed I just scrambled about. Then I found a hole in the wreckage and crawled out on hands and knees.

"It looked as though those who had been sitting in the forward part of the plane were the lucky ones who got out.

"Part of the engines had gone 150 yards and hit a small house, which burst into flames."

The Elizabethan crashed into a shed stacked with petrol and oil. The plane itself did not explode. But the shed and its contents became a raging inferno.

Bonds of death

Rescue workers said that many of the victims died still strapped in their seats. "As the fire spread, the safety straps became bonds of death," said one.

Burning debris was scattered for about 300 yards around, setting several houses on fire.

News of the disaster shocked Soccer officials all over Europe

The Manchester United match with Wolves due to be played tomorrow was cancelled. It was announced that before each League match there would be a two-minute silence and flags would be flown at half-mast Players will wear black armbands.

The board of directors of Wolverhampton Wanderers ordered their club flag to be flown at half-mast yesterday in memory of the victims of the crash.

United are due to meet Sheffield Wednesday at

CONTINUED ON THE BACK PAGE

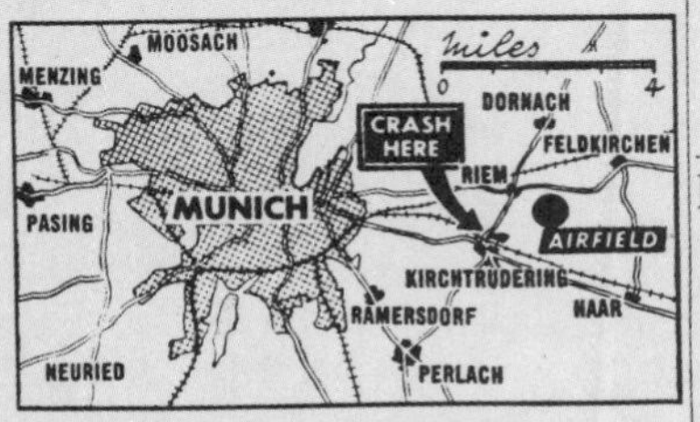
MOOSACH
miles
0
4
MENZING
DORNACH
CRASH HERE
FELDKIRCHEN
RIEM
MUNICH
PASING
AIRFIELD
KIRCHTRUDERING
RAMERSDORF
NAAR
NEURIED
PERLACH

Matt Busby —critical

MATT BUSBY
Last night his condition was serious and reported to be growing worse

The dead and injured

THE 21 dead were officially named early today as:

PLAYERS: Roger **Byrne** (captain), Mark Jones (centre-half), Billy **Whelan** (inside-right), Eddie **Colman** (right-half), Tommy **Taylor** (centre-forward), Geoff **Bent** (left-back), David **Pegg** (outside-left), Walter **Crickmer** (club secretary), Bert **Whalley** (coach), Tom **Currie** trainer).

JOURNALISTS: Frank **Swift** (News of the World), Tom **Jackson** (Manchester Evening News), Archie **Ledbrooke** (Daily Mirror), H. D. **Davies** (Manchester Guardian), Eric **Thompson** (Daily Mail), Henry **Rose** (Daily Express), George **Follows** (Daily Herald), Alf **Clarke** (Manchester Evening Chronicle).

OTHERS: W. T. **Cable** (steward), of Farnham Common, Bucks. B. P. **Miklos** (travel agent), W. **Satinoff** (wealthy businessman and racehorse owner).

They survived

The injured:

Players: Harry **Gregg**, Ray **Wood**, William **Foulkes**, Jackie **Blanchflower**, Dennis **Viollet**, John **Berry**, Ken **Morgans**, Bobby **Charlton**, Bert **Scanlon**, Duncan **Edwards** and manager Matt **Busby**.

Blanchflower is reported to have complicated fractures of the arm, shock, broken ribs, fractured pelvis and internal injuries.

JOURNALISTS: Peter **Howard** (Daily Mail), Edward **Ellyard** (Daily Mail), Frank **Taylor** (News Chronicle)

OTHERS: Mrs. Nebojsha **Tomasevsic** (Yugoslav Consular Department), Eleanor **Miklos**, Mme Vera **Lukic** (wife of Yugoslav Military Attache in London) and her baby

CREW: James **Thain** (captain), of Winkfield, Berkshire; K. G. **Rayment** (First Officer), of Billingshurst, Sussex. G. W. **Rodgers** (Senior Radio Officer), of Harlington, Middlesex, Rosemary **Cheverton** (stewardess), Margaret **Bellis** (stewardess)

Allowed to leave hospital: Foulkes, Gregg, Howard, Ellyard, Thain, Miss Bellis, Miss Cheverton.

The tail and a wing of the plane are silhouetted against the flames from the building which it struck

Rescue workers use levers as they break into the wrecked airliner's fuselage to get at the trapped players

TODAY'S WEATHER

A NORTHERLY airstream will probably maintain cold weather over most of Britain.

Forecast: Becoming cloudy with chance of sleet or snow. Cold

Outlook: Mainly cold.

Sun rises 7.32 a.m. sets 4.58 p.m. Moon rises 9.45 p.m. sets 9.01 a.m. tomorrow. Lights 5.30 p.m.-6.57 a.m. tomorrow. High water at London Bridge 3.38 a.m., 4.07 p.m.; at Dover 12.49 a.m., 1.13 p.m.

Fuchs in trouble

Dr. Fuchs ran into trouble yesterday when two of his vehicles plunged into crevasses only 28 miles from Depot 700.

Both were recovered but one had its steering broken. Dr. Fuchs also reported that he was off the course mapped out for him by Sir Edmund Hillary.

Sir Alexander weds

Sir Alexander Maxwell, former head of the British Travel and Holiday Association and wartime tobacco controller, was married recently to a young New Zealand actress, Miss Angela Hargreaves, it was learned in London last night.

INSIDE

PAGE 3. — John London sees the Thorneycrofts move out of No. 11—biscuits and all.

PAGE 5.—Driver tells his story of the Dagenham rail crash. . . . Former model says: "I was millionaire's mistress."

PAGE 7.—"I like the simple life," says Brighton club man's wife. . . . Breadlines form again in America.

PAGES 8 and 9.—SPORT.

£100 fines for dark smoke

From June 1 it will be an offence, punishable by fines up to £100, to allow dark smoke to issue from chimneys.

The new regulation applies equally to factories, private homes — although house chimneys rarely produce "dark smoke"—shops, offices, railway engines and ships.

TITO MESSAGE: I AM DEEPLY MOVED

PRESIDENT TITO of Yugoslavia has sent this message to Mr. Macmillan: "I am deeply moved by the news of the aeroplane disaster which severely struck British sport and the English people. Allow me to express my profound condolences."

At home the feelings of many people echoed the secretary of the Football Association, **Sir Stanley Rous**, who said: "What can I say except that I am absolutely shocked by the news."

He was in Edinburgh for a dinner, but cancelled his engagement and flew back to London. "The loss of such a magnificent team to Manchester, to England and the world cannot be measured," he said.

"The game will go on, but our hopes and plans will be overshadowed for a long time."

Mr. Joe Richards, Football League president: "This is a most terrible day in the history of English football. My heart is full of grief"

Mr. Alan Hardaker, Football League secretary: "This appalling tragedy will be felt everywhere football is played."

Mr. A. H. Oakley, Wolves director and former president of the Football League: "It is a staggering loss, and I am heartbroken."

Old friends

Mr. Stan Cullis, Wolves's manager, said: "I feel the loss tremendously in view of my great respect for Manchester United, including my old friend and opponent, Matt Busby."

Mr. Alan Douglas, chairman of Manchester City Football Club: "I am absolutely staggered. I am very sorry to hear about all my friends who have died."

Stanley Matthews: "It is a great blow to English football."

Of the journalists who died, **Mr. H. J. Bradley**, general secretary of the National Union of Journalists, said: 'The disaster has just about swept the North of England, and Manchester in particular, of its leading sports writers. I cannot recall a greater disaster to journalism."

'1958 champions'

Tributes flowed in from abroad.

The directors of the **Red Star (Belgrade)** team propose that Manchester United be awarded the honorary title of 1958 European champions

Red Star captain, Rajko Mitic, said they were "wonderful fellows, and great sportsmen."

Milan Football Club: "We had been hoping to meet Manchester They were the pride of British Soccer."

Torino and **Juventus** also sent their condolences

World's loss

Danish Football Federation president Ebbe Schwartz: "This is too sad for us even to speak of it. It is a blow to the entire world of Soccer. Manchester were one of the two best teams in Europe."

A **West German** spokesman expressed his Government's deepest regrets at the disaster.

Spanish Football Federation: "The team has always been a fine and most respected opponent."

From **Zurich** the International Football Association cabled "deepest sympathy" to the Football Association.

In **Paris**, organisers of the European Football Cup expressed their greatest sympathy.

Two players went back to help

GOALKEEPER Harry Gregg struggled out of the wreckage, dazed. Then he ran back.

"I helped out some of the people who were in a worse way than me," he said last night.

"The plane had caught fire at the back where it hit the farmhouse, and some of us were stopped from going into the wreckage there.

Gregg was in the front of the plane where the casualties were lightest. So were right-back Bill Foulkes and inside-right Bobby Charlton.

Blacked out

Foulkes said: "I got a bang on the head and blacked out. When I came to, I heard one of the crew shout, 'Get clear, run.'

"I unstrapped myself and ran like hell. I stopped 50 or 60 yards away, turned and saw the wreck for the first time.

"I went back. I jumped over wreckage and some things which looked like bodies.

"I saw Mr. Busby. He was conscious. I helped rescue workers get him out. They shunted me off too.

"All I got was a bump on the back of my head and a scraped nose."

Said Charlton, describing the take-off: "The trouble was we never left the floor.

"But we three were all right. We helped to get Matt Busby into an ambulance."

LATE NEWS

COURSE CORRESPONDENT'S late wire. Best at Hurst Park: King (2.45, nap) and Look (4.15)

FLEet Street 5000

Manchester Evening News, Tuesday, February 11, 1958, reporting on the Munich air disaster.

coming down on top of us. There wasn't time to think. No-one cried out. No-one spoke. Just a deadly silence for what could only have been seconds. Everything stopped all at once . . .' It was, as the *Daily Mirror* put it, 'Sport's blackest day': it was also, as *The Times* headline pointed out, 'A Blow to Journalism'. This time the Press was having to report on its own tragedy.

Mourning descended on Manchester like a shroud. Tearful crowds kept silent vigil in the streets, shop windows were transformed into flower-decked tributes to the dead, all football matches the next day began with two minutes' silence. Messages of sympathy poured in from all over the world—from Yugoslavia coming the suggestion that Manchester United be made honorary European Champions for the season. But the question as the first shock of loss subsided, was would there *be* a Manchester United? To many the club was Matt Busby, and he was battling on the verge of life and death in an oxygen tent in a Munich hospital. On the Saturday the *News Chronicle* and *The Star* both published a photograph of the patient in his tent, with a German nurse leaning solicitously over him.

There was an immediate outcry. Letters showered on both papers denouncing them for their 'bad taste' and 'intrusion of privacy', and complaints were aired on television and even in Parliament. On the 11th the controversy was further sharpened by a letter to *The Times* from BEA's Chief Executive, Anthony Milward, who had been at the hospital the day after the disaster: 'The German doctors and nurses were working with devotion to care for our critically injured countrymen—how great a contrast with the horde of British cameramen waiting for a chance to photograph the victims in the wards . . . I hope I may be spared from seeing

again the flash of camera bulbs from six or more photographers at a time as they walked into a ward in which three men were fighting for their lives, in order to photograph an unconscious man lying in a critical condition in an oxygen tent.' The *News Chronicle* responded with an editorial on the front page, dissociating its photographer (Bill Beck) entirely from the scenes described by Mr Milward. 'The *News Chronicle* decided to publish the picture' it went on 'having first obtained assurances that there had been no intrusion and that the picture had been taken with the full co-operation of the hospital authorities . . . It believes the British public has a right to hear about and see for itself what is being done in such tragic circumstances.'

The Star, too remained unrepentant after being publicly attacked by a member of Parliament. It maintained the photographers in question had been German ones and, anyway, 'the photographs, far from offending against human dignity revealed the efficiency, the tenderness and the compassion of the German hospital authorities. *The Star* is proud of being *The Star* . . .' The fuss was soon overshadowed by the happy news that Matt Busby, against all odds, was beginning to pull through and by the growing fears that Duncan Edwards (regarded by many as one of the best footballers in the world) would not.

He died, of internal injuries, nearly two weeks after the crash—the same day that Manchester United played their first match since the disaster. It was an intensely emotional occasion for the 60,000 that packed into the Old Trafford ground that day, to watch a side that (apart from Gregg and Foulkes) was unrecognizable as Busby's Babes—inueed in hospital at Munich their manager was told nothing about the game since he was not yet judged strong enough to be informed of the cruel extent of the casualties. Amazingly Manchester United won the game 3-0: even more amazingly, carried on the same tide of emotion, these reserves took the team to the Cup Final at Wembley. Manchester United *would* live, and so would Matt Busby.

Meanwhile another drama was unwinding. At a press conference the plane's captain, James Thain, revealed to the Press that the man at the controls at the fatal moment had been his co-pilot, Captain Rayment (who was then in a coma and who later died without regaining consciousness). Captain Thain explained about the 'power surging' on the first two runs but declined to answer questions about the third take-off attempt, for fear of prejudicing the German Inquiry already in progress. From his remarks many papers ascribed the accident to engine failure (the German papers at the same time were asking some very pointed questions as to why a house came to be built in the take-off path only 300 yards from the end of the runway). It came as a shock, then, when the German Inquiry made public its preliminary findings with almost indecent haste—just three days after the accident—and reported that the Elizabethan 'probably failed to leave the ground because the wings were iced up'. It came as a shock to Captain Thain too, since he had repeatedly denied there was any icing on the wings. Suspended indefinitely he now revealed that on the last run the plane had reached 117 knots, then inexplicably lost speed, making it impossible either to stop or to take off. It was his opinion that slush on the runway had caused this—the responsibility of the airport authorities. It was small consolation for his lost career that ten years later (when the drag effects of even small amounts of slush were better known) a British Inquiry found he was very likely right.

News Chronicle
AND
Daily Dispatch
*

No. 34,814   © NEWS CHRONICLE LTD., 1958   SATURDAY, FEBRUARY 8, 1958   PRICE 2½d.

Plane engine twice was 'not normal'   ●   What happened the third time?

CRASH TAKE-OFF RIDDLE

HOW THE INJURED ARE DOING

THESE were the conditions late last night of the 13 injured :

Matt Busby
Shock, fractured right foot, chest injuries. Critical.

John Berry
Outside-right. Shock, cut head, broken cheekbone. Critical, but a little better.

Duncan Edwards
Left-half. Shock, broken ribs, compound fracture of the right leg. Critical.

Dennis Viollet
Inside-left. Concussion and cut head. Condition good.

Ray Wood
Goalkeeper. Bruises and flesh wounds. Condition good.

Ken Morgans
Outside - right. Concussion and shock. Condition good.

Bobbie Charlton
Inside-right. Wounds and shock. Condition good.

Albert Scanlon
Outside-left. Shock, fractured skull, head wounds. Satisfactory.

J. Blanchflower
Centre - half. Right arm broken, stomach injuries, shock. A little worse.

Frank Taylor
News Chronicle sports writer. Compound fracture of the right lower leg, compound fracture of the left upper arm, bruises, broken rib on right side. Critical.

Kenneth Rayment
Co-pilot. Broken legs, suspected internal injuries, lacerated left leg, concussion. Critical.

Mrs. Eleanor Miklos
Travel agent's wife. Cuts on legs and arms, chest bruises. A little better.

Mr. Tomasevic
Yugoslav Embassy, London. Wounds to legs and face. Condition good.

Councils get brainwave

Members of seven borough councils in South-East London last night watched a film about an electronic brain.

They discussed whether they should get together to buy their own, possibly for £100,000, and are recommending their councils to set up a working party to go into it.

Already Greenwich council reckons to save £83 a week from April 1, by having its payroll worked out on an electronic computer belonging to a catering firm. The council is paying an initial £3,000 for adjustments to the programme.

A rise ? Gaitskell limit is 10s.

A wage increase of 5s. to 10s. a week would be permissible, said Mr. Hugh Gaitskell last night, but if you go beyond that level, inflation is sure to follow.

Mr. Gaitskell told undergraduates at Cambridge : "A Government must persuade trade union leaders that restraint should apply not only to wages but also to salaries, dividends, and all forms of income."

TODAY'S WEATHER

MID-DAY FORECAST CHART

Captain tells of yellow glow

From GEORGE VINE : Munich, Friday

THE commander of the Manchester United airliner today revealed that the port engine was not running normally just before the take-off crash that killed 21

It was giving full power but it had a varying note. "There was a surge of power," explained 37-year-old Captain James Thain.

Twice he taxied out to take off. Twice he turned back because of the engine.

But after B.E.A.'s British station engineer at Munich airport had reported it to be completely satisfactory Thain gave the order for the third and fatal take-off attempt.

The last few seconds

How was the engine this time ? Captain Thain declined to answer this question. B.E.A. director "Jimmy" James said no answers could be given that might prejudice the official German investigation that began today.

The young commander also declined to say whether he felt any adverse effects of slushy snow that covered the runway.

But his description of the last few seconds on take-off appear to confirm that it was a failure of one of the Elizabethan's two engines that was responsible for the snow-storm crash

[Angus Macpherson, the Air Correspondent, writes: Thain's reference to "a surge of power" might mean the engine was racing.

That could be caused by a propeller slipping out of pitch and starting to act as a brake.

If this happened it would explain why the aircraft, which can normally climb with full load on one engine, was barely able to get off the ground.]

Mr. Anthony Milward, B.E.A.'s chief executive, repeated today that there was no question of sabotage

Thain was not at the controls when the plane crashed. The take-off was made by Captain Kenneth Rayment. He volunteered to deputise for the airliner's regular co-pilot, who was on leave.

PILOT THAIN
Port engine worried him

Thain said the plane tore off the roof of a gardener's house a few hundred yards from the end of the runway.

Then it spun round, hit a hut and a stationary lorry loaded with inflammable liquid, setting it on fire.

He added : "A second or two before we came to rest I was conscious of a large yellow glow on the port side. I could not see the flames through the windscreen, which was covered with snow. When we suddenly stopped the glow disappeared.

"The crew scrambled out of the aircraft. The belly of the plane was only a few inches from the ground. Captain Rayment was trapped in his seat with his foot jammed in the controls and the debris of the crushed nose of the aircraft.

We rescued passengers

"When the crew had got clear we came back and started to rescue passengers

"There were small fires in both wings. We grabbed fire extinguishers and tried to put them out."

The plane broke in half. The 20 passengers sitting in the forward half of the plane had backward facing seats. Most of them survived. Those in the rear section who were in forward facing seats suffered worst.

Co-pilot Rayment was on the danger list tonight with a skull fracture and leg injuries.

Four surgical teams have performed 20 operations on the injured in the Munich hospital where they were taken.

Doctors were fighting for the lives of United

Turn Page Two, Col. 7

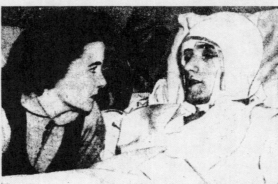

Picture by News Chronicle staff photographer BILL BECK

A NURSE TENDS MATT BUSBY

Under the plastic oxygen tent in a Munich hospital Matt Busby fights for his life. And into the tent goes a German nurse . . . to bring comfort to the critically injured man who has so much to live for. Below : In the same hospital last night Albert Scanlon and his wife Jane are reunited. Mrs. Scanlon had flown to Munich from Manchester

Wives fly out to their husbands in hospital

THE wives of Manchester United's injured players flew to Munich yesterday to see their husbands in hospital. With them went Mrs. Jean Busby, wife of manager Matt Busby. His condition worsened slightly last night.

Mrs. Busby, her face wet with tears, sobbed and leaned on her son Sandy and the assistant team manager, Mr. Jim Murphy, as she gazed at her husband.

Matt Busby lay in a transparent oxygen tent, breathing heavily under sleeping drugs. He did not know his wife was there. She could not approach him closely. Mr. and Mrs. Busby's daughter, Mrs. Sheena Gibson, stood at the foot of the bed in tears.

They had both been told before entering the ward : "You must smile."

There was little to smile at. Matt Busby was desperately ill.

He had earlier been given the last rites by a Catholic priest.

Mrs. Busby left her husband's ward to visit some of the injured players.

Her face was white ; she
fair-haired, was helped from the ward, sobbing and near collapse after being taken in to see her husband, John, the most badly hurt of the Manchester party.

Berry is with Duncan Edwards, also critically ill, in a room next to Mr. Busby.

JOHN CAMKIN and

ICE AND SNOW HIT ALL BRITAIN

SNOW was still falling over much of Britain late last night.

There was not a single county in England, Scotland and Wales not affected by snow and ice—and more snow is expected today in many areas.

Worst hit were South Wales and the West Country, where drifts up to five feet deep and snowfalls of seven inches to a foot were reported.

Ploughs out

Many Dartmoor roads were impassable, but rain in the South-West later turned the snow to slush.

Very lights were fired at Exeter so that a plane carrying Mr. G. R. H. Nugent, Parliamentary Secretary to the Ministry of Transport, could land in a blizzard

Birmingham had its heaviest fall of the winter—several inches in the afternoon, and it was still snowing last night.

Roads in the city became treacherous and there were long traffic hold - ups after accidents.

In Derbyshire 160 snow ploughs, some radio-controlled, were standing by, and motorists were warned, to avoid moorland routes in the Peak District.

Slippery

A three - mile queue of vehicles was held up in Staffordshire on the main road north from Newcastle-under-Lyme.

In Norfolk, snow ploughs were working at Northrepps, near Cromer.

Last night the A.A. stated that although afternoon snowfalls melted on many roads, severe icing followed a drop in temperature.

All parts of Britain except the South-West were freezing this morning, and roads in London and the Home Counties were very slippery and in places dangerous.

U.S. rocket blows up

Cape Canaveral, Florida, Friday.—The U.S. Air Force fired a huge Atlas inter-continental missile—100 tons of potential destruction—today and then announced that it "destroyed itself shortly after completion of the powered phase of its flight."

This was the fifth testing of an Atlas. The first two exploded shortly after launching.

It was announced today that the first Atlas rocket would be in the hands of a U.S. unit by December, 1959.—Agencies.

Strangled spinster was taken by car

News Chronicle Reporter

POLICE were hunting last night for the man who strangled 52-year-old Lilian Chubb.

Miss Chubb was found dead yesterday in undergrowth near the house in Broadstairs, Kent, where she lived with her brother and his wife.

But detectives do not think she was killed at that spot. They believe she died elsewhere and was taken there by car.

Bus journeys

Until a few weeks ago Miss Chubb, buyer in the hosiery department of a Margate store, travelled to work by bus each morning.

It is thought, however, that for some time she has been getting lifts by car into Margate.

The police would like to see the driver of this car and have appealed for him to come forward

They also want to trace Miss Chubb's movements from the

LATE NEWS

... s ...bbed
in fight

time she left home at 8.40 on Thursday morning.

She did not turn up for work that day but her employers were not surprised as she had a bad cold.

The police say there is nothing to link the strangling with the death of Anne Noblett, victim of the Hertfordshire deep-freeze murder.

Pruned

The 11,820 employees of the Forestry Commission have had their working hours cut from 47 to 46 a week after asking for 44.

Trouble Cooking

1960-1976

...save flood victims

Comment

Wrap it up

"WE WANT to stabilise the industry," said the British Egg Marketing Bo... at the beginning of th... Then added, " b... rather higher level...

And in case y... realise what th... yesterday's an... must have ma... clear. The pr... to be raised b... from next we...

The station o... at London W. Usher... this week... craft ma... than air... era. "... of a di... said.

It is to be presumed... one present actually wan... a tool for digging, paring or cutting ground, turf, etc., now usually consisting of a flattish, rectangular iron blade (yawn) socketed on a wooden handle which has a grip or cross-piece at the upper end, the whole (yawn, yawn) being adapted for grasping with both hands while the blade is pressed into the ground with the foot to be called a spade. Do they?

Guild

CERTAINLY NOT MR. DENIS NORDEN, who was quite prepared to contort himself out of all recognisable shape — also this week—in explaining that a closed guild was not a closed shop.

"We are working towards a guild shop," he had said. "Anyone who wants to opt out—to them we say the guild shop will apply."

Coming out with it straight is the last thing we expect of our fellow mortals.

We don't want the plain, unvarnished truth. Look how mad we got a few weeks ago when the Southern Gas Board, vetoing the sale of any more gas fir... spring, explained use a lot of gas."

Guided

AND CERTAINLY Douglas Houghton never have got in th... he did for mentionin... dreaded phrase "dir... of labour" if, as som... suggested the other da... had adopted a suitable sonian euphemism "guided redeployment."

The truth is harsh. Save from it. Nothing was mo... unwelcomely frank tha... the letter written to Th... Times this week by Dr Joseph Trueta, the brilliant surgeon who pioneered the development in Britain of power-controlled artificial limbs for thalidomide children.

After 27 years in Oxford Dr. Trueta is going back home to Barcelona. There was an immediate brouhaha about the brain drain to Spain. Dr. Trueta wrote to say he just wanted to be among his family for his last years (he is 68).

And then this nice old man...

From RONALD SINGLETON Rome, Friday

FIFTY-THOUSAND rescue workers tonight toiled through thunderstorms and 100 m.p.h. winds to reach victims of Italy's worst floods for centuries.

From the Alps to Sicily some ...00 square miles lies under water ...ds of mud. No region has ...n fury of 40 hours ...mest.

Boats save art treasures in killer floods

From LESLIE CHILDE, ROME, Friday

AN ARMADA of small boats sailed the floodedy streets of Florence tonight rescuing priceless art treasures threatened by muddy water swirling through historic buildings.

In a radio broadcast Mayor Piero Bargellini declared a state of emergency and gave the "mournful news" that floodwater had entered Florence Cathedral and bre, Giotto's Bell Tower.

Paintings were being removed to safety from gineers ca the famous Uffizi art nent to' rail gallery.

Police commandeered all boats to salvage the art treasures and rescue hundreds of people marooned in their bedrooms in a city cut off from the rest of the country by floods.

...nd trail. 21 people have ...20ft. in 20 ...carried in all Italy this ...century.

more are missing ...e passenger ...in Tuscany.

Newspaper Design Award for 1966

SEE PAGE SEVEN

Rebels back d... on school

A threatened revo... Labour back-bench th... out in the Common... when they with... opposition to the... Bill, which gives r... ment aid to churc...

Mr. Hugh Ro... for Hornsey, said... were "a very h... attack on th...

...RBARA MURRAY : "She is out "

ANNIE ROSS : I don't know

Beatles miss Aberfan show

By BRIAN DEAN

BEATLES' manager Brian Epstein has turned down an invitation for the group to app... special two-hour television ... the Aberfan Dis...

Beat...

Frost in TV row ov... Viet sh...

IN PARIS ... London ... DAILY MAIL REPORTING TEAM

TELEVI... Frost s...of the charit... casu... draw...

No...gr...t...

show, ...
Mr. Frost...
Larry Adler, Annie...
Johnny Dankworth, Barbara...
Roy Hudd were due to appear in...
concert at the Royal Court Theatre in London on November 13.

The concert has been arranged by the Medical Aid for Vietnam Committee.

Mr. Frost told viewers: "I assumed it was for all the suffering in Vietnam, but quite the reverse.

...found today that it ...lusively to the North ...se or the Vietcong ...South Vietnam. ...look at the poster ...Aid for Vietnam, ...charity concert, ...bleeding.' No ...t all for what."

...said that it was ...Aid Committee ...the decision to ...the Communist ...y penny goes to ...not a single ...to Saigon. ...nese peasant ...Ame. ...ans the ...help him. If ...'the Vietcong

...ted

...ing on that ...that fact. ...hat, on the ...dley and I ...er artists, ...rc too." ...at of the ...Barbara ...udd had ...w, and ...with...vidence ...would

Larry ...drlaw ...aigh ...eater ...Ross ...don't know if I am ...prepared to withdraw."

Dudley Moore and David Frost did not indicate whether they would withdraw or not.

Mr. Frost asked the secretary of the committee, Dr. Joan MacMichael, to answer the allegations.

She said: "The main purpose of the committee has been to supply aid where the need was greatest, where the casualty rate is highest and the war has been going on the longest.

"We don't send supplies to

Why the committee sat on the amorous ducks

By Daily Mail Reporter

THE SEXUAL habits of the mallard are playing ducks and drakes with the Ministry of Public Building and Works.

And the Ministry of Public Building and Works has no option but to lump it.

The trouble in the London parks stems from two things.

First, there are something like 2½ drakes to every duck. ...d. towards the end of ...season in Kensing... ...many extra ...n that

Did Arab bom... jumbo nightm...

THE NIGHTMARE of the jumbo jet generation came true yesterday...345 people were literally ripped apart as a giant Turkish Airlines DC-10 crashed into a French forest.

Tiny fragments of the £9 million jet were strewn across miles of woodland along with the gruesome remains of the passengers.

At least 250 of them British...

...jacket lying in...

STAIRWAY WHICH LED TO DISASTER

...Day of drama in the air...

The stairway leading to Cairnlea Drive from the Copland Road end of Ibrox Stadium where 66 fans died. On the left is the Rangers Pools Club.

...Fifteen seconds from time...

...spring...
...ore than 50,000 toys have been sent in reply to Princess Margaret's appeal for Aberfan, and she has asked that those left over should go to children's hospitals, orphanages and other deserving causes in Wales.

Chain of circumstance

Russia...

NEW YORK : Russia...104th veto to kill a ...Nations resolution aimed ...ending the border trouble between Israel and Syria.

Prince at shoot

Prince Philip and five companions yesterday bagged 247 pheasants in the first shoot of the season at Sandringham.

t 2/-

...en implemented ...eze day for 50 ...yard men. ...be claimed in ...vening News, ...the decision

£600,000 order

A £600,000 order for 15 high-

The New Zealand Herald

Telephones: Classified Advertising - 34-460
Other Departments - 34-400

AUCKLAND, THURSDAY, APRIL 11, 1968

Price 4c Air Freight 5c

N·Z·I
FIRST in insurance

WAHINE TOLL 45 AND RISING

Grim Night Watch On Shore

Staff Reporter   Wellington

Fears of a huge death roll from the wreck of the interisland ferry Wahine were growing in Wellington last night as searchlights played across the subsiding harbour seas.

By 12.30 a.m. today 45 deaths had been confirmed. But more than 100 of the 724 passengers and crew have not yet been _____ for.

_____ harbour shore, a grim watch for _____ was continuing through

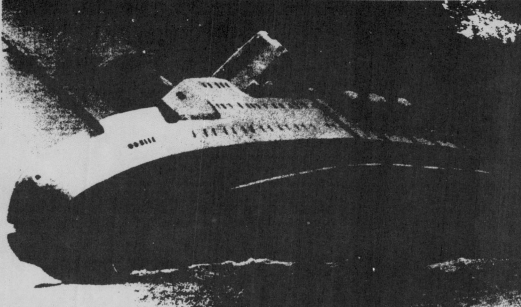

The stricken Wahine rolling over on her side off Worser Bay. Other pictures are on page 2, page 3 and the back page.

WELLINGTON
BAY EASTBOURNE
WORSER
BAY
_PLE

ON BOARD THE STRICKEN VESSEL

Tedium That Turned Into Nightmare

By IAIN MACDONALD,
A New Zealand Herald reporter who was a passenger in the Wahine.

My first reaction to the stewards' shouts of "Lifebelts on and muster aft" was incredulity.

This was either one of those boring lifeboat drills (but surely not on the interisland ferry) or something that happened only to other people.

But the steward seemed all too serious. And it was certainly nobody else's face that looked back at me from the shaving mirror in Cabin B261 of the Wahine at 6.30 yesterday morning.

My second reaction was surprise at some people's order of priorities.

Parents of course were snatching up babies and children plus blankets _____

hoped that both had survived the night's buffeting.

A nervous-looking girl near me refused my offer of a seat and rejected any suggestion that she at least loosen her lifejacket. At the time she seemed a one-girl minority, tension and distress that bored ____

counted for many of the broken limbs.

Some of us—passengers, crew together—ferries through

CITY EDITION

Thank God I missed seeing it capsize a few minutes later. From the shattered comments _____ and me I gathered it had _____ were pretty hopeless to try _____ anything any more boats. An _____ confirm this the Wahine _____ another lurch and the _____ gas washing round up _____ I stood against the

able (so-called) rub-_____ by wallowing _____ ship came _____ the dying cabins _____ projection, came _____ side down, _____ on Page 2.

Other clippings

The Petrified Forest... devastation like a war scene from Vietnam

_____een the smoke rises from the shattered fuselage of the DC-10 as a refuse column _____ along the track which the blazing airliner burned through Ermenonville Forest

_____ the victims: A Rugby _____er for the big match

_____ were
_____ by the fren-
_____ked Up
_____ of the survivors who _____ the boats, or were snatched _____ up by small craft _____ ashore at Seatoun Manly _____ were on liferafts were _____ by wind and tide _____ the harbour mouth to _____ astbourne side of the _____
_____red who came ashore _____ eastern shore were _____ ies landed at Seatoun _____ admitted to Wellington _____al
_____ Minister of Marine, Mr _____ announced last night _____ a preliminary depart-_____l inquiry into the dis-_____ would begin immedi-
_____6½ million ferry _____ began service in

Heathrow strike made passengers switch to DC-10

Wahine many lives _____
Passengers had been in-structed to go to the star-board side of the ship, but many, not knowing port from starboard ended up on the wrong side. Survivors said the ship's broadcast system finally told passengers how to distinguish port from starboard.

Hundreds of volunteers joined police, ambulance men military and civil defence staff rushing to the Seatoun shoreline. Roads in the area were sealed off to ordinary traffic as emergency vehicles, sirens howling, made

literal _____
capsiz_____
the ship w_____
This complica_____
Authorities remained _____ of exactly how many pas-sengers and crew the Wahine carried on her fateful trip how many had reached the shore safely.
Police broadcasts were made throughout the late afternoon and evening for survivors who had not already done so to report to the police. Until all survivors do so, there will be uncertainty about the number who died.

ne dead _____ the night's _____ that _____ positively _____ identified _____ were being into_____.d.
Because of lack of informa-tion of actual deaths in the disaster the only news avail-able was of survivors.
Frequently people sought news of two or more friends or relatives and most times they were told they were safe and well.
The Leader of the Opposi-

THE GUARDIAN
Manchester Saturday November 5 1966   Price 5d

North Sea gas key to cheap steel
By MARK ARNOLD-FORSTER

Floods threat to Florentine art treasures

Widespread disruption in Central Italy

From GEORGE ARMSTRONG

_____
The Italian best was raising _____ Americans, whose rescue large parts of Central Italy _____ which carrying large parts of the art treasures _____ Florence today _____ being brought under _____ water

_____
_____ dead _____ Bi_____ and_____ me_____

Three heart valves replaced
By GEOFFREY BOWKER

Rhodesia replies to Britain

Bill will force out boardroom secrets

Magistrates wrong to take TV set

HIGH SCHOOL HEAD SHOT DEAD
Press Assn   New Plymouth

The headmaster of Inglewood High School, Mr Alexander Stuart Black, was shot dead at the school soon after 2 p.m. yesterday.

A youth was located two hours later after the armed offenders squad surrounded a farmhouse at Inglewood. The youth offered no resistance. He was later arrested and will appear in the Magistrate's Court at New Plymouth to-

Nibbling a cheese sandwich and half dozing, I spared a moment's thought for my car and contents below decks and

crazily _____
deck of the _____
_____
Most of us slid and crashed from port to star-board. This must have ac-
_____e're using _____India against deck

1960–1976

The Last Avalanche
Vaiont Dam Disaster 1963

The Fire on the *Lakonia* 1963

The Sinking of the *Thresher* 1963

The Black Mountain
The Aberfan Disaster 1966

Lost Heritage
The Florence Floods 1966

Oil on Troubled Waters
The Sinking of the *Torrey Canyon* 1967

The Apollo Fire 1967

The Sinking of the *Wahine* 1968

An Improper Balance
The Yarra Bridge Collapse 1970

What Happened at Ibrox?
The Glasgow Panic 1971

Paris Air Show Disaster 1973

The D.C.10 Crash at Ermenonville 1974

The Destruction of Darwin 1974

The Udine Earthquake 1976

The Last Avalanche

Vaiont Dam Disaster 1963

'MACMILLAN GLAND REMOVED: CONDITION EXCELLENT'—PAGE SEVENTEEN

DAM HORROR
THOUSANDS PERISH

After the deluge in the dark night of horror rescue workers scrabble in the mud. The scene is grimly reminiscent of an early film epic. But here the flood story is true.

Cataract wipes out Italian town and six villages

Evening Standard Reporter: Rome, Thursday

It was like hurling a stone into a cup of coffee. But the stone was a mountain. And just before midnight it plunged into the 873ft. concrete Vaiont dam to spill over its side a 150-million ton liquid cataract of death.

A waterfall of horror that is estimated to have cost up to 4000 lives in a town and six villages.

For the sleeping families in the Piave River Valley were engulfed. Their homes, their churches, their village halls were pulped into a mass of rubble.

Longarone, a town famous for its green pastures and sparkling red wine, does not exist any more. "Bodies are stacked up like cordwood," said one of an army of rescuers.

To add to the terror, barrels of cyanide potassium have been swept into the river - so even a drink can mean death.

IN FAE almost nothing remains. Where the central square of the village had been . . . there is now an enormous hole.

IN PIRAGO there is the bell tower of the church, part of the altar, a chapel and one house.

IN VILLANOVA : Just one house remains.

Now from the waters of the Piave, hundreds of bodies of men, women and children have begun to emerge, most of them stripped of clothing by the force of the water that hit them.

Italy mourns . . . its television is silent; its radio only flashes out news items; theatres and opera houses are closed; and a glittering Rome premiere of Elizabeth Taylor's Cleopatra is called off.

Full story—PAGE SIXTEEN.

WEATHER—Sunny.—See Page SEVENTEEN

They knew part of the mountain might one day fall into the waters of Vaiont Dam. The engineers knew it in 1960 when they completed this Olympian 870-foot cradle of water that curved gently around the side of Mount Toc. The authorities knew it, when they hesitated to fill the reservoir until 1962. The surveyors knew it, when they reported that the mountain did move —if very gradually. The Mayor of Erto knew it, when, after minor landslips in the autumn of 1963, he posted a warning to inhabitants not to venture near the shore of the lake. And the people of the Piave Valley in Northern Italy knew in their hearts that all the time they were living in the shadow of a disaster. But, like the citizens of Johnstown in 1889, they just hoped for the best.

When a whole face of Mount Toc finally *did* crumble into the lake, just before midnight on 9 October 1963, there was virtually no warning for the 4,000 or so inhabitants of the valley. One survivor talked of hearing a sinister and terrible roaring—and knowing instinctively what had happened—then a strange and sudden wind. A precipice of water, displaced by a quarter of a billion cubic metres of soil and rock, hurtled over the lip of the dam onto the villages below: first onto Longarone, where all but the highest houses were obliterated, then inexorably on over Pirago, Rivalta, Villanova, Fae—all were extinguished as if they had never been. The path of the flood was transformed into a flattened wilderness of mud and rubble. Literally everything, trees and pylons, squares and railway lines were ripped from the earth and carried for miles. At first it seemed as if no living thing in that valley could have survived, but the next day huddled groups were rescued from the mountainsides, where they had fled—by some miraculous reflex action—at the moment of danger. Even the official estimate of the dead, 1,900, could only be approximate since all local records had been washed away.

Astonishingly, the vast dam-wall remained intact—though it no longer shielded a burden of water, but a landscape of new-born hills and crevices. The building of it, an Inquiry later decided, had put unusual pressures on a mountain that was geologically unsuited to tolerating them. The dam, in other words, should never have been built on that site at all, the blame for which was unequivocally laid upon the national electricity authority. One astounding fact that emerged was that, even as deluge and death came to the Piave Valley, reports and analyses on the suitability of the dam's siting were still in progress!

THE HORROR OF VAIONT DAM.. where death came down the mountain as 4,000 slept

From JOHN CHECKLEY and HOWARD JOHNSON
Belluno, Italian Alps, Thursday Night

WE have seen Death Valley . . . the wilderness which has been called today "one huge mortuary beneath a sea of mud."

A wilderness in a once-beautiful valley—where five villages were first savagely ripped apart by floods and then submerged under mud and rubble.

In these villages, it is feared tonight, at least 4,000 died. Most of them still lie buried where they were trapped—in their beds. For it was just before midnight when death came.

Earth and Rock

Somewhere high up on 6,000ft. Mount Toc, towering above the Piave valley, a huge mass of earth and rock began to slip.

It roared down the mountainside and hurtled—hundreds of thousands of tons of it—into the waters of the vast Vaiont Dam, one of the world's biggest.

The great mass plunging into the dam raised a wave more than 300ft. high.

The wave dashed against the wall of the dam. The wall stood firm, but the water poured over the top.

Down the valley . . . raging and roaring. Towards Longarone, where about 4,500 people slept.

The sound of the landslide—the "sinister roar" as municipal official Mario Laveder called it today—warned many of the people in time and they fled for higher ground.

Only the quick and the strong made it. Most of the people died in their beds under the mud fall brought by the floods.

Children

Chief victims were old people, wives and children. For about half the able-bodied population were away—some following their traditional trade of ice-cream sellers in Switzerland, Germany, France and Belgium.

In Longarone, the police chief and all five of his men died.

The main hotel vanished —with all its occupants. Of thirty people watching television in one house, only seven are now alive.

Only three houses remain standing today in the village.

Six American helicopters picked up eighteen survivors from nearby mountainsides.

The pilots reported that no one else was left where Longarone once stood.

Tonight more than 600 bodies had been recovered there.

So Longarone died. "It has disappeared almost as if it never existed," Francesco Belisario, a State welfare director, said tonight.

Wind

After wiping out Longarone, the flood swept on. It roared through little Villanova and tore it apart. It ripped through Rivalta, Pirago and Fai.

In Villanova, 20-year-old Mario Fami heard a terrible wind saw water pouring in through the windows of his home and felt like "a mouse in a trap."

He and his father and brother jumped out of the back window and raced up the mountainside.

The wind plucked at them. "Our pyjamas were torn off," said Mario today. The floodwater snatched at them. But they gained safety.

The water scene of one of the worst floods disasters of modern times,

ONE HUGE MORTUARY BENEATH A SEA OF MUD

Men from the Mirror see Death Valley

is now the centre of world-wide sympathy.

Messages of condolence —including one from the Queen—and promises of help are pouring in tonight from all over the world.

The Swiss TV service put out a revolutionary "Give now—pay later" aid programme.

Bill

Viewers were told to ring the Swiss Post Office information office and simply state their name and the amount they wished to give.

The amount will be added to the telephone bill for October.

Today comes the reckoning. Was anyone to blame for the fantastic loss of life? Could the tragedy have been avoided?

Mirror man PETER HARRIS reports from Rome:

A big row is likely to open in the Italian Parliament today.

It is likely to develop into a three - cornered battle between the Ministry of Public Works, who are responsible for the dam; the Ministry of Agriculture and Forestry, who are responsible for dealing with landslides; and the Ministry of the Interior, which has the power to take emergency measures.

Danger

It had been known for some time that there was danger of a landslide, but survivors had reported that its movement was very slow.

The mayor of the little village of Erto E Casso—stricken in the dam disaster—saw danger coming ten days ago.

He is reported to have posted notices all over the village advising people to evacuate their homes.

But nothing was done to provide them with alternative accommodation.

Joy amid the desolation . . . as survivors embrace in the valley of horror where 4,000 died

DISASTER SPOT

The 873ft.-high Vaiont Dam pictured before its waters spilled death into hundreds of homes strung along the valley.

SAVING

Two men gently raise a little girl from her shattered home. A beam of light from a rescuer's torch shows that she is alive.

SEEKING

Workers search the debris hoping for a sign of life. They listen for a cry for help and hope they are in time to bring the victim out safely.

The Fire on the Lakonia 1963

The cruise ship *Lakonia* emerged from its compulsory service as a troopship through six years of war unbattered and unbowed—which may or may not have been what inspired its new owners in 1963 to advertise its Christmas cruise to Las Palmas as 'a holiday with all the risks removed'. In the light of events it was an unfortunate phrase, but one that persuaded 646 passengers (nearly all British) to sail from Southampton on 19 December in search of the sun. With the liner just refitted by the Greek Line at a cost of £500,000, it should have been a perfect holiday but on the fourth day at sea it turned into a horror-story. On the evening of the 22nd fire broke out in the hairdressing salon—it seemed controllable, but as midnight approached it had taken an unshakable grip on the liner. Yet it was not the fire that claimed any of the 128 lives lost that night, but the haphazard launching of the lifeboats, some of which

had to be axed from their davits while others proved to leak like sieves. One up-ended on its way down, another capsized on contact with the water—both hurling their terrified occupants into the sea. When all launchable boats had gone, more than a hundred people still remained on the burning decks—only some of them were still alive in the water at dawn to clamber into life-rafts dropped by the US Air-Sea Rescue Squadron in the Azores. Several of the survivors later spoke bitterly of panic among the crew; others more charitably put it down to differences of language and temperament between British passengers and the Greek and Cypriot crew.

24 dead, 135 missing as the rescue ships race for port

THE OCEAN INFERNO

877 saved from liner blaze

From HERALD REPORTERS: MADRID, Monday

FIVE ships of different nations were sailing for port tonight with 877 survivors of the burned-out Christmas cruise liner Lakonia.

Twenty-four bodies had also been picked up, leaving 135 people missing. Search for them was still going on in the disaster area—180 miles from Madeira in the Atlantic.

Meanwhile the 20,300-ton Lakonia drifted, deserted and smouldering. There were gaping holes in her sides, presumably caused by boiler explosions.

Around her, tossed on the waves, were Christmas gifts—many of them toys for the 30 or so children who were on board.

'BODIES FLOATING'

A Casablanca radio report said bodies floating in life jackets were still being recovered by rescue crews.

There were 1,036 people on board the Lakonia—651 passengers and 385 crew. Most of the passengers were Britons, who boarded the liner at Southampton last Thursday for a sunshine cruise.

Names of only 2 survivors were issued tonight. They included the Lakonia's master, Greek-born Captain M. N. Zarbis, who is in his middle fifties.

A number of the 877 survivors are injured.

Two rescue ships, including the British motor vessel Montcalm, which is carrying 240 survivors and 14 dead, will steam into Casablanca, Morocco, tomorrow. Survivors on these ships will be flown to Britain.

Her sides battered by the explosion the Lakonia drifts helplessly in the Atlantic

TOYS DRIFT IN THE SEA OF TRAGEDY

the Straits of Gibraltar on her way to Britain from Australia.

Tonight, here in Madrid, the crews of American Air Force rescue planes told their stories of the Atlantic drama.

They arrived over the burning Lakonia as dawn was breaking.

Captain Don Spencer, 33-year-old pilot, said: "I spotted the glow of the Lakonia from about 15 miles away. After our first look we all wanted to get down and help.

spotted a man sprawled on a plank of wood. He waved, and we dropped another life-raft within 10ft. of him. You can't get closer than that.

"But he would not get in. Nothing was going to persuade him to leave his little plank."

Flight mechanic David Berger said: "I saw a baby lying alone in a life-saver made for a plank. She was dead, and I felt sick.

TOGETHER . .

"Then the next minute someone started waving to us from the water, and I cheered up and felt.

FAMILIES WAIT FOR NEWS

THE first list of Lakonia survivors reached London last night and was released to relatives who had been waiting anxiously all day.

Names of 28 passengers and crew who were picked up by the Pakistan steamer Mehdi were given. The Mehdi also has three dead passengers aboard.

News of the survivors was announced from the offices of Ormos Shipping—London agents of the Greek Line—at

THE FIRST SURVIVORS NAMED

THE 28 survivors picked up

Peace bid fails at steel works

By GODFREY FRANCIS

ATTEMPTS to stop Europe's biggest steel works from closing down indefinitely failed yesterday.

Talks began in Cardiff between union leaders and employers shortly after the Steel Company

British soldier shot by Cyprus gunmen

By FRANCIS MOIR
Herald Diplomatic Correspondent

A BLAST of machine-gun fire seriously wounded a British soldier yesterday as he went on a mercy mission in a Cyprus town.

The soldier—as yet unnamed—was trying to reach a Greek family stranded in the Turkish quarter of Lanarca, South Cyprus.

A British patrol went to rescue him, but were driven back by a hail of bullets.

Later they returned and carried the wounded man to safety. He was "dangerously ill" in hospital last night.

Another British soldier was slightly wounded, but managed to crawl to safety.

The shooting came after three days of riots between Greek and Turkish Cypriots about proposals by the Cyprus President, Archbishop Makarios, to streamline the island's constitution.

These proposals are strongly opposed by the Turkish minority.

RIOTS

President Makarios and Vice-President Kutchuk both made radio broadcasts appealing to Greek to Turkish Cypriots to refrain from violence.

They promised a full investigation into the causes of the strife which has so far cost 14 lives, according to the latest police figures.

Last night Britain took urgent action over the mounting crisis in Cyprus—a member of the Commonwealth.

The Foreign Secretary, Mr. Butler, issued a statement expressing the British Government's "grave concern over a breakdown of law and order on the island."

He told the Greek and Turkish Foreign Ministers that he was ready to join them in a peacemaking approach to Archbishop Makarios.

Because of the Cyprus crisis, Mr. Butler and Mr. Duncan Sandys, the Commonwealth Relations Minister, will both stay in Whitehall today instead of starting their Christmas holidays.

BACK ON FRIDAY

Like other national dailies, the Daily Herald will not be published on Christmas Day or Boxing Day. Our next issue will be on Friday.

The Sinking of the Thresher 1963

FINAL ★★ 5c

WEATHER: Mostly sunny and not so cool. High in 50s.

New York Mirror

Vol. 38, No. 176   THURSDAY, APRIL 11, 1963   CO

EXTRA!

ATOM SUB MISSING IN ATLANTIC, 130 ABOARD

WASHINGTON, April 10 (UPI) — The U.S. nuclear powered submarine Thresher is "overdue and presumed missing" in the Atlantic 220 miles east of Boston with 130 men on board, the Navy announced tonight.

The announcement said the Thresher was conducting routine tests in water 8,400 feet deep in the Atlantic and had been submerged since shortly after 9 a.m. (EST) today.

There has been no communication with the atomic submarine since it submerged, the Navy said.

A massive search and rescue operation, involving ships, aircraft and other subs, has been set in motion, the Navy said. Extremely unfavorable weather and seas were reported in the search area.

The Thresher is the first of a class of nuclear-powered subs which are considered the world's fastest and deepest-ranging underwater craft.

No other nuclear sub has ever been lost, the Navy said.

The Navy announcement said there was a "possibility" that a communications failure accounted for the Thresher's failure to report its position.

The USS Skylark, a submarine rescue vessel, was accompanying the Thresher during its routine tests—a normal procedure when submarines undergo tests and trials after overhaul.

The Skylark first reported the Thresher's failure to communicate after it submerged this morning.

The Navy said that next-of-kin of the crew were being notified "that the ship is overdue and presumed missing."

No names or addresses of the crew will be released, the Navy said, until after the notifications.

(See later Editions for Complete Details)

The US submarine *Thresher* was a mystery from the start, a top-secret capsule of sophisticated equipment with a speed, range, armament and diving power that outclassed anything in the world. Launched in 1960, she was the prototype of a whole new class of nuclear submarines that were to extend American influence into hitherto unattainable reaches of the ocean. For such high ambitions, the prodigy's first years were not too encouraging: deep-diving tests were not completed on schedule, and then she was accidentally rammed and was forced to spend a year in dry dock. On 10 April 1963, however she was back at sea once more, 220 miles off Cape Cod and ready to resume her diving trials. On board were ninety-five officers and men and thirty-four naval and civilian observers.

At almost 8.00am on the 10th the *Thresher* reported to its escort vessel (the *Skylark*) that she was making a routine dive. At twelve minutes past nine another message was received—there was a 'minor problem', the sub was tilting and the crew were attempting to blow up the ballast tanks. The *Skylark*'s inquiries as to the ship's course and position elicited no reply, only five minutes later an indecipherable jumble of words—then silence. For two frantic hours the *Skylark* tried every means to re-establish contact with its protégé, until forced to acknowledge a disaster had struck. A massive—but forlorn—search was mounted immediately, forlorn because the depth of the sea at the place where the *Thresher* dived was 8,400 feet. The pressure at that depth approached 4,000lb per square inch, more than sufficient to crush the submarine into oblivion: indeed at anything much lower than a thousand feet she was doomed.

At least for friends and relatives the agony of waiting was short-lived. No-one really harboured the illusion that the *Thresher* had simply lost communication temporarily, and on the 11th the Navy announced positively that no hope remained, at the same time assuring reporters that an explosion of the nuclear reactor could be ruled out. In truth, of course, there was no way of knowing what *had* happened in the silent depths of the Atlantic, but it was certain that in the frontiers of ocean that the *Thresher* had hoped to breach the smallest error of design, the slightest defect of welding, would have proved fatal. Several months later the wreckage of the sub was located by the deep-diving vessel *Trieste* and photographed from its bathyscope. Although the official court of inquiry surmised that a piping system had failed in the engine room, the broken mound of metal on the seabed really offered no clues as to the cause of the tragedy. The *Thresher* even in death kept her mystery.

FINAL ★★ **5c**

WEATHER: Variable cloudiness, occasional sprinkles. High in 50s.

New York Mirror

Vol. 38, No. 177   FRIDAY, APRIL 12, 1963   CO

No Hope

How Could It Happen?

By GERALD DUNCAN

Was it the machine? Or was it man?

Those were the questions yesterday after disappearance of the mighty Thresher at sea with its 129 officers, crew and civilians.

The best opinion was that the atomic submarine sank after filling with water—by springing a massive leak barring operation of water-tight compartments, or by flooding because somebody neglected to close a valve.

Explosion of the nuclear reactor, as many laymen surmise, was definitely ruled out by authorities. Sabotage wasn't, but it was regarded as unlikely.

Fire? Possibly, which would account for the lack of communication with surface vessels.

Jamming of diving controls? Highly unlikely.

A welding flaw in the hull during the Thresher's overhaul might have been responsible, Adm. George W. Anderson, Chief of Naval Operations, conceded. Or, he said, the steel might not have been strong enough to resist the sea pressure.

Thus, enlightened speculation of the cause centered around flooding by tons of water, pouring into the submarine with such speed and force that the Thresher plummeted 8,400 feet into muck and eternity.

Such an eventuality would explain the absence of debris afloat in the Atlantic. The Thresher would be in one piece because the water inside would equalize the pressure outside, and there would be no immediate break-up.

If the sub had been forced to the bottom suddenly, without being flooded, it would have been crushed like a steamroller going over a cracker. Mattresses, wooden equipment, bodies would have been catapulted to the surface.

The pressure of sea water increases a half pound for every foot depth, and at 300 feet this means about 11 tons per square foot.

"The most logical explanation would be that of springing a leak," Dr. John R. Dunning, Dean of Engineering at Columbia University and a leading nuclear physicist, said.

"An explosion in the nuclear reactor is almost impossible. The Navy, under severe tests, could not make it explode. The reactor is buttoned up tight in strong cells that can withstand anything that the ocean has to offer."

"Atomic equipment is an added safety feature," said Rear Adm. Edward N. Ellsberg, USN (ret.), a salvage expert who won the Distinguished Service Medal for raising the submarine S-51 after it sank off Block Island in 1925.

It was Ellsberg who suggested the possibility of man-failure. The Squalus was lost off the New Hampshire coast in 1939, he said, because a crewman neglected to notice an open valve when the diving signal was given.

Capt. William R. Anderson, USN (ret.), who piloted the Nautilus on the first voyage under the North Pole, concurred in the flooding conjecture.

"It could conceivably have been a major seam leak, but it's more likely that a rupture caused flooding and put the ship out of control," he said.

Adm. Anderson, also ruling out an explosion, doubted sabotage as the cause, but he said:

"That is probably a remote possibility, but something that the court of inquiry would certainly have to consider."

Threat of Contamination

By ROBERT JONES

Radioactive contamination in the Atlantic was regarded as a possibility yesterday as an aftermath of the sinking of the Thresher—but not for years, and there was some expert opinion for optimism.

Dr. Bostwick Ketchum, famed biologist and associate director of Woods Hole Oceanographic Institution on Cape Cod, expressed the fear.

"It seems certain," he said, "that there will be high-level radioactivity added to the ocean in that area.

"I would not expect it to reach George's Bank or other fishing grounds in the near future. There would be some isolation at the location indicated.

"It would be diluted in deep waters before reaching the surface. It could take a good number of years to reach the surface in any detectable quantity."

Vice Adm. Hyman G. Rickover, often called the father of the atomic submarine, was positive in his optimism.

"I CAN ASSURE YOU there is no radioactive hazard as a result of this unfortunate accident," he said.

"The reactor can remain submerged indefinitely in sea water without creating any hazard."

Dr. Joseph Liebeman, top nuclear safety expert with the Atomic Energy Commission, agreed. Even under the

Log of the Thresher...Tragedy

The zebra-striped, deep-diving research submarine Trieste will probe Atlantic floor for the hapless nuclear sub Thresher. The bathyscape is being rushed here from San Diego by rail.

(AP WIREphoto)

Partial list of the small rescue armada rushed to the Thresher sinking site, 220 miles off Boston, is posted by Lt. (jg) Walter Hyde at the Portsmouth Yard.

(AP WIREphoto)

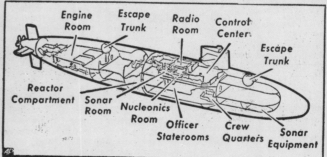

The apparent loss of the Thresher ironically coincided with observation of Submarine Week, annual tribute to other undersea heroes who died in service. Here, a wreath is dropped into water from the sub Hake at Philly Naval Yard.

(AP WIREphoto)

Cutaway drawing, from material supplied reporters on a cruise last year, details interior layout of the lost $45,000,000 A-sub.

(AP WIREphoto Diagram)

New York Mirror 12 April 1963

THE GUARDIAN

37,414

Saturday October 22 1966

Price 5d

150 feared lost as landslip hits school

Aberfan : above, the roof of Pantglas School protrudes from the rubble ; below, the path of the mountain that slipped, photographed by *Frank Martin*

83 bodies found as rescuers dig on

From DENIS FROST

Aberfan, Saturday

More than 150 people, including a whole generation of schoolchildren, are missing or dead after yesterday's landslip disaster here. Early today the bodies of 75 children and eight adults had been found ; more than 60 children were missing.

The tragedy happened when an avalanche of pit waste slid down a mountainside to engulf a school and houses in this mining village six miles from Merthyr Tydfil. It is feared that more bodies will be found in a row of cottages which was also engulfed. The Chief Constable of Merthyr Tydfil, Mr Tom Griffiths, who earlier said that there could be 200 fatalities, has declared the whole zone a disaster area.

The Prime Minister and the Chancellor of the Exchequer, Mr Callaghan, arrived here last night to join Mr Cledwyn Hughes and Mr George Thomas, Secretary and Minister of State for Wales. Mr Wilson has promised " the most high level independent inquiry."

Lord Snowdon arrived here early today. The Duke of Edinburgh is due later this morning. Messages of sympathy have been received from the Queen, the Prince of Wales, and President de Gaulle. The Pope has asked the apostolic delegation in London to express his condolences.

It was 9.15 yesterday morning when, with a roar likened to the explosion of a crashing plane millions of tons of mine waste, boulders, rock, sludge and water crumbled down the Aberfan mountain from a 50-year-old coal tip. It took less than half a minute to reach Pantglas junior school, just 500 yards away. The children—there are 254 on the register—had just finished prayers. They were due to start their week's half-term holiday at noon.

Fifty-six children and two teachers were saved, and it is certain that many more children never reached school at all. Fog delayed a bus load of 50 seniors and juniors from the nearby village of Mount Pleasant. Some decided to walk—and arrived late enough to miss the landfall.

' Flying round '

A description of the school disaster was given by Dilys Pope, aged 10. She told me how her class was waiting for the calling of the register. " We heard a noise and we saw all stuff flying about. The room seemed to be flying around. The desks were falling over and the children were shouting and screaming. Children were lying all over the place. The teacher, Mr Williams, was also on the floor. His leg was caught. He managed to free himself and smashed the window with a stone. I climbed out and went round through the hall and out through the window. I opened the classroom window and some of the children came out that way. There were stones everywhere. The teacher got some of the children out and told us to go home."

Pantglas secondary school—a senior school with 200 pupils—is only 100 yards or so from the junior building, but it was hardly touched. A row of six cottages between the schools was buried, however, and a farmhouse further

through tons of slurry which had swept part of the school away.

Mr Griffiths said the main problem was getting rescue and earth-moving equipment through Merthyr to the cul-de-sac disaster site. He was operating a one-way traffic system through the town and diverting traffic, and a police cordon had been thrown

More pictures and reports, back page

around Merthyr, with three checkpoints keeping all but essential traffic out of Aberfan.

The mountain, Mr Griffiths confirmed, was still moving. " There is a grave possibility of its moving in on us. It is a fight to stop the sludge sliding down off the mountain.

Merthyr's borough engineer is leading a team of men trying to cut the landslide off. Mr Griffiths

Turn to back page, col. 1

Rescuers hurt at the scene

A report that a small boy had been taken alive from the debris was discounted when it was discovered that this casualty, like a number of other live casualties of the disaster, was a young rescue worker. Earlier an injured fireman had been taken to hospital.

up the mountain was swept away. Minutes before, the woman who lived there had taken her five children into Mountain Ash on a shopping trip.

But possibly 15 adults died in the row of cottages and in another terrace of seven houses, a post office, and sweet shop in Moy Road, just across the street.

In nearby streets, threatened houses were evacuated. People carried their furniture and personal belongings to the homes of neighbours.

At one stage, more than 3,000 people were at work among the rubble and debris.

Pantglas means "green hollow," but now it is a grey and bitter place. A place, too, without water, for the Cardiff water main cracked in the landslip, and water and sludge turned the streets of Aberfan into a scene not unlike a First World War battleground. Supplies of water to the entire Rhymney Valley, Cardiff, and Barry were cut off.

Grim rollcall

Last night the parents of every schoolchild in Aberfan, Merthyr Vale, and Mount Pleasant met at Merthyr Vale school to hold a grim and final rollcall of the

'Absolute power' for action

By our own Reporters

The Prime Minister, Mr Wilson, has given the Secretary of State for Wales, Mr Cledwyn Hughes, " absolute military powers " to take any action he deems necessary to cope with the disaster in South Wales. He has instructed that no question of statutory limitations or financial expenditure must inhibit the operation.

Mr Wilson flew to St Athan, South Wales, from Speke Airport, Liverpool, last night in an RAF aircraft which had been standing by for most of the day.

After visiting Aberfan Mr Wilson said : " I don't think any of us can find words to describe this tragedy today. I am here to make absolutely sure that the Secretary of State had all the backing he needed to make certain that everything which had to be done is being done."

Mr Wilson said that the top priority now must be given to rescue, to work at the school and to caring for the relatives of the bereaved. He went on : " But I can assure you that there will be the most high-level, independent inquiry that it is possible to mount into this tragedy. We shall have to consider the details when we reach the right time."

Rest of the news

CBI walk out in protest

CBI leaders, " provoked " by the Government's action in statutorily freezing laundry and dry cleaning prices (page 12) staged a virtual walkout at a meeting with Mr Stewart, Minister of Economic Affairs, whom they accused of breaking faith in not consulting them.   Page 3

*   *   *

COMMON MARKET : An official report believed to conclude that membership of the Common Market would on balance be in the British interest will be before Ministers meeting at Chequers this weekend. *Page 4*

*   *   *

MR GUNTER, the Minister of Labour, hopes that the country's position will improve " by late spring or summer."   *Page 3.*

*   *   *

THE CAR DELIVERY dispute continues. Drivers' representatives yesterday voted to continue the strike.   *Page 3*

*   *   *

WEST GERMANY is thinking of replacing its ill-fated Starfighter aircraft with Phantoms, reports Clare Hollingworth from Bonn. If these were fitted with Rolls-Royce Spey engines it would go far to offsetting support costs of Rhine Army.   *Page 9*

*   *   *

MR RODERIC BOWEN, QC, former Liberal MP, is going to Aden at Mr George Brown's request to investigate the treatment of suspected terrorists by British security forces.

*   *   *

RHODESIA : The UN General Assembly meets in extraordinary session today to debate an emergency resolution on the Rhodesia question.

*   *   *

DR HEWLETT JOHNSON, the former Dean of Canterbury, is gravely ill in Kent and Canterbury Hospital, after a fall.

On other pages

Crossword 13
Finance and Industry 11, 12
Gardening 7
Harry Whewell 2
Home News 3, 4, 12, 14
Leaders and letters 8
Obituary 9
Overseas news 9
Sports report 10
Stanley Reynolds 2
TV and radio 2
Travel 4, 5
Weather forecast 14

Classified advertising

Appointments :
Senior and executive 12
Full index 12

Anyone returning to the Valleys knew he was home when the slag-heaps came in sight. These towering cones of black slurry were not a prepossessing part of the landscape, lending an angular ugliness to the soft contours of the hills, but they were a fact of life. Generations of mining families in Wales had lived with them and watched them encroach on their hillsides and creep nearer their villages as ton after ton of coal-waste, year in and year out, was poured onto them. Aberfan, a small mining community in the Merthyr Vale, was no different from other villages in this respect, except that perhaps it had more than its fair share: seven tips, the oldest already sprouting patches of grass but the newest still rising less than half a mile from the village and dominating the view from the classrooms of Pantglass school.

On the morning of Friday 21 October 1966, though, you'd not have known it was there for a thick mist covered the mountainside. And the only warning the people of Aberfan had that the black mountain was on the move was a vibrating crescendo of noise, like thunder some said afterwards, like a low-flying plane others thought. Gathering speed the avalanche of sludge and liquid coal roared down the hill and over the old railway embankment, rearing thirty feet high, till it reached the village. The first building it encountered was the junior school, battering through its walls and windows; then it plunged on, cutting a swathe through the row of houses down Moy Road, and on till it came to a precarious halt against the very roofs of the houses fronting Aberfan Road.

It was 9.15am. On the far side of the monstrous finger of the landslide the senior school had not yet started lessons, but the juniors began half an hour earlier and some 240 children, aged from $4\frac{1}{2}$ to 11, were already at their desks when the mountain struck. At lunchtime that day they were due to start their half-term holiday.

The first outside help, the fire brigade, that arrived at 9.30 faced an unimaginable and overwhelming scene. Water-mains torn apart by the avalanche were flooding the already waterlogged coal with hundreds of gallons more water, threatening at any time to start new slides. Smoke from fires in the debris of wrecked houses seeped through the oozing slurry. Neighbours were already tearing with their bare hands at the rubble, fearful that their efforts would only bring down more masonry. Within an hour help was converging from all quarters, police, civil defence, and miners coming off their shifts at nearby mines and beginning what for some of them would be another ten hours of uninterrupted digging. A BBC newsflash at 10.30 brought in volunteers by the thousand, until all roads into Aberfan were clogged with vehicles and the area round the school seethed with well-intentioned but ill-directed humanity.

No-one knew how many children or adults lay entombed in that black grave. Some had escaped in those last vital seconds; a few had not gone to school that morning. The most pessimistic estimate put the toll at 200, but for the rescuers the only way to drive the horrific thought from their minds was by sheer unrelenting effort. Long bucket-chains formed to shift the squelching debris away, while others tunnelled into the mass. Every now and then a policeman would blow his whistle and a silence would fall—in the wild hope that a cry or a scratching might be detected from within. After 11.00 that morning no body was brought out alive.

By the glare of gas arclights, clouded by the smoke from fires, the diggers toiled on through the day and into the night even when all hope was gone. By 10.00 in the evening sixty bodies had been recovered: some of the children had tried to scramble under their desks, one teacher had attempted to shield the bodies of five children with his own. Added to the ever-present danger was the problem of concealing (usually with blankets) the delicate exhumations from the eyes of curious sightseers—and sometimes from the television cameras. For what was, in effect, the first time in its history television mounted full-scale 'live' coverage of a major disaster. With a few unintentional exceptions its outside broadcasts from Aberfan were conducted with scrupulous sensitivity. But the very presence of cameras at the site—and this went for press photographers as well—inevitably created the occasional outburst of resentment.

But the deepest well of resentment was reserved for the National Coal Board, whose tip it was. Officials claimed that the coal-waste had become inundated with water from a spring that had unexpectedly risen beneath the tip, an explanation the coal chief, Lord Robens, repeated publicly for the benefit of the Press. Reporters on the spot, however, had already begun hearing rumours that this 'new' spring, on the contrary, had been known locally for years—long before the tip was started. A report in the *Merthyr Express* back in January 1964 was unearthed and widely quoted: 'We had a lot of trouble from slurry causing flooding' Councillor Gwyneth Williams had warned. 'If the tip moved it could threaten the whole school.' In fact the slag-heap *had* moved twice, in 1959 and in 1964, and it was recalled that before the war, further down the valley, another tip had slipped bodily a third of a mile and diverted the river Taff from its course.

'Coal Board were warned of danger' ran a headline in Saturday's *Sun*, the article listing a string of 'warnings' over the years from local residents, teachers and councillors. In the next day's *Sunday Mirror* a letter from the Bishop of Llandaff urged everyone to write to their MPs to have all coal-tips inspected and prevent another Aberfan (the NCB did a very quick check on some 500 tips in Wales—and found more than a hundred of them in dangerous condition). Nevertheless the Coal Board, in the face of some searching inquiries from newsmen, persisted in its denial of responsibility for the present tragedy: 'we *don't* build tips on top of springs' claimed one spokesman. Another reminded them that all tips were regularly inspected. On the Tuesday (the 25th) the Prime Minister announced the setting up of a Tribunal to investigate the cause of the disaster—a rare instrument of investigation with much more solidly-based powers than a simple Inquiry.

The previous evening the '24 Hours' current events programme on BBC television had run an interview with the chargehand who had supervised tipping on the fatal mountain. In it he revealed that he and his men had long known of the existence of the spring: 'we've sent men

THE OBSERVER

London, Sunday, 23 October 1966

ESTABLISHED 1791 No. 9,146 PRICE 8d.

'YOU GO COLD . . . YOU JUST GO ON BRINGING THE BODIES OUT'

Miners silhouetted against the smoke of burning slag by the arc-lights that enabled rescue work to go on all night.

Photographs by DAVID NEWELL SMITH

Bishop of Woolwich: Abortion not a crime

by a Staff Reporter

ABORTION should be regarded like suicide, as something each individual must decide for himself, the Bishop of Woolwich, Dr John Robinson, said yesterday. It should not be treated as a crime.

The Bishop was speaking at the annual meeting of the Abortion Law Reform Association in London.

The present law was 'manifestly unenforceable,' and there was 'a great deal of evidence of police toleration,' he said.

Ideally what the law should do was to 'enhance and protect the freedom to decide, which must lie ultimately, if it is to be a moral decision, with the mother herself.'

Scientific advances, such as an effective abortifacient pill, might cause fundamental changes in our attitude to abortion. In addition, we should aim to abolish the need for abortion by making contraception totally efficient and fully available.

The Bishop's lecture: Page 10

Conscience call by Catholics

A demand that doctors, nurses and others who may be affected by changes in the abortion law 'shall not be asked to act against their own conscience' was made yesterday by the Roman Catholic Hierarchy of England and Wales.

In a statement about the Medical Termination of Pregnancy Bill, they said: 'Certain clauses of the proposed Bill are contrary to the ethical code hitherto accepted not only by Catholics but by all who hold life sacred. These clauses have already been contested in Parliament. We are confident that MPs of all creeds will support appropriate amendments.'

New slip feared as Aberfan hopes fade

from ERIC CLARK and ALAN ROAD: Aberfan, 22 October

OFTEN tottering with exhaustion but hoping desperately for miracles, an army of nearly 2,000 volunteers went on burrowing today into the avalanche of slag which engulfed the school and 17 houses here on Friday.

But no miracles came. As time passed the whistles which stopped all work and silenced the bulldozers, so that rescuers could listen for any sign of life under the black morass, became less frequent. By this afternoon 116 bodies had been recovered, about nine of them adults, and 85 had been identified. The Chief Constable of Merthyr, Mr Thomas Griffiths, said that there were between 58 and 60 bodies still to be recovered.

Though parents and relatives still stand immovably at the site and the digging goes on with a weary determination, hope is rapidly dwindling. No one has been recovered alive since Friday morning. At one time during the night bodies were being taken from the school wreckage at the rate of one every two minutes.

The rain which precipitated the landslide returned this afternoon and made rescue operations even more difficult.

Work may stop

The medical centre and houses near the school were evacuated because of the danger of another landslip. There were fears that all the work, all the sandbags, all the irrigation channels, may not stop the hill from sliding again. A klaxon will tell the town that it has. Many of the men in the ruins had been working for 30 hours. As the pace began to tell some were taken to hospital for treatment for exhaustion.

One ambulance worker said he had helped to carry 30 bodies to his ambulance. He thought there was little hope of anyone being alive in the school now. 'This stuff leaves no gaps,' he said, gesturing at the mountain of wet coal-dust. 'You go cold after a while. You stop feeling anything. You just go on bringing the bodies out.'

One of the bodies recovered today was that of the headmistress, Miss Ann Jennings, 64, who was due to retire next year. She had been wrongly reported saved and taken to hospital yesterday.

It was learned at Buckingham Palace that the Queen, who had made provisional arrangements to visit Aberfan tomorrow, had decided to defer her visit for some days as she did not wish her presence to interrupt the rescue work.

Rumours—the sort that kept hope alive—continued to circulate. One nurse was said to have gone up to a weeping mother to console her. 'I am weeping for joy,' she had said. 'My child came out alive.' But no one could trace the mother today.

There are signs that the numbness created by the disaster will soon be replaced by anger. The woman who says, 'I blame the Coal Board,' is still a lonely voice. But tomorrow many more may join her.

Bishop's call

The hope among many here is that this anger will be channelled into a campaign to see that the hundreds of old slag tips in South Wales are removed or made safe. The Bishop of Llandaff said today: 'I call upon all to support me by every means in their power to have this terrible problem faced at once.'

The Prime Minister is personally supervising the preparation for the independent committee of inquiry which he promised during his brief visit to Aberfan on Friday night.

(Continued on page 3)

Wilson will talk shop to stewards

by DAVID HAWORTH our Industrial Reporter

THE Prime Minister is planning to hold a one-day meeting in London with about 600 shop stewards representing the whole of industry.

In what is described as a 'one-man teach-in,' Mr Wilson will tell his audience how he sees their role in industry, and will answer questions about the Government's industrial and economic policy. He has suggested that the event, which will probably be held early next year, should be televised.

The Prime Minister sees the event as a parallel development to his National Productivity Conference held a month ago and proclaimed as a forerunner to a possible 'parliament of industry.' But it was in Brighton during the Labour Party conference, after the Prime Minister was lobbied in his hotel by angry BMC shop stewards complaining about redundancies, that he decided to plan the London conference.

There is no precedent for a gathering of so many shop stewards from all the unions.

Chequers meeting

Key members of the Cabinet were called to Chequers yesterday to examine how far and how fast Britain should move towards joining the Common Market.

The Cabinet is known to be sharply divided but among those at Chequers there were at least twice as many committed 'Europeans' as declared antagonists.

Getting Wilson to Market: Page 11

Heaviest rainfall on record

Many areas of southern Wales have had the heaviest rainfall on record this month. Cardiff, about 17 miles from Aberfan, has had 4.65 in., against a monthly average of 3.94.

More than 2 in. of rain fell last Wednesday, half of this within three hours.

VALLEY OF LOST CHILDREN

100 missing after Black Avalanche

SATURDAY · ·   OCTOBER 22 1966   FOURPENCE   No. 653

SUN

THE INDEPENDENT DAILY NEWSPAPER

PAGE 3
Diary of a boy called Paul

PAGES 6, 7
Death of a generation

BACK PAGE
The girl who came back

Killed by the mountain their fathers made

From JON AKASS
ABERFAN, Friday

THIS THING is unspeakable. One hundred and fifty little children, perhaps more, crushed in a terrible mountain of filth.

I have just been to Pant Glas junior school. The place is awful, unthinkable.

It swarms with life, light, people. And there are men and women everywhere digging, scraping, tugging beams and concrete slabs. Anything rather than have to stop and look at the dirt and think.

The foul piles of slag are everywhere. One part of the school, where the youngest children were, is smashed and broken by it. The rest of the school still stands, but the evil stuff is piled in every classroom.

BLACKNESS

The slag heap is still moving, still dangerous, almost invisible now against the blackness of the sky, a hole in the night where there are no stars.

Below it, at the school, there is the glare of the emergency lights and the din of bulldozers and shouting men. Occasionally a policeman blows a whistle and there is silence.

They listen.

We wait for perhaps two minutes for the sound of scratching, the voice of a child. And then, hearing nothing, they look at each other and continue working.

At intervals there is a shout for space, room to move, and two men come through the crush carrying a stretcher upon which is a small bundle wrapped in a grey blanket.

So far, 72 bodies have been taken to the sombre and austere little chapel, a quarter of a mile away.

They pass through dim streets, cluttered by the vehicles of rescue, where women huddle under yellow sodium lights, not speaking.

APARTNESS

The enormity of what has happened here has not, could not, fully register, although they are accustomed in these valleys to sudden and cruel deaths.

Children are different. The death of a child, even one child, is too awful to contemplate. There is not grief enough for it. One hundred and fifty children . . .

This evening there was a meeting at Merthyr Vale school, where there was to be a roll call, the reading of a dreadful school register.

The parents came, mostly the mothers, with their neighbours holding their arms.

● **CONTINUED ON PAGE SEVEN**

And still they search . . inside the tomb of a school deluged by an avalanche.

And still they wait . . for news of their children.

WILSON TOURS THE STRICKEN VILLAGE

THE PRIME MINISTER arrived at the disaster scene last night after flying from Liverpool.

His R A F plane landed at St. Athan and he was driven to the emergency headquarters at Merthyr police station.

After a 30-minute conference there, Mr. Wilson toured the stricken village of Aberfan.

Mr. Wilson walked through thick mud to the main entrance of the school just after the 64th body had been found.

Later he said: "I don't think any of us can find words to describe the tragedy.

"I am concerned to ensure that if steps can be taken even now to save just one life, that will be done."

Mr. Wilson, who was visiting Lancashire development areas yesterday, was at a civic lunch in Wigan when he heard of the disaster.

He immediately arranged for the Secretary for Wales, Mr. Cledwyn Hughes, to be flown to the scene, and asked for reports every half-hour.

Mr. Hughes, who was opening a reservoir in Anglesey, cancelled a State visit to Ireland, due to start on Monday, and flew to Aberfan by R A F helicopter.

He was given "military-type powers" to deal with the disaster.

Mr. Wilson told him by telephone to take whatever action he thought necessary, and to err on the side of action rather than caution.

Also at the scene were the Chancellor of the Exchequer, Mr. James Callaghan, the Minister of Power, Mr. Richard Marsh, and the Minister for Wales, Mr. George Thomas.

Prince Philip will fly there today.

The Queen and Prince Charles sent messages of sympathy.

Mr. Heath, who went to a Conservative ball in Bexley last night, suggested that the proceeds should be sent to the Mayor of Merthyr.

From **GODFREY FRANCIS** and **ALAN ROGERS**
ABERFAN, Glamorgan, Friday

GRIEF-STRICKEN parents assembled tonight in a school-room to hear the death toll of the Black Avalanche of Aberfan.

It may or may not be the final toll. Rescue teams, working by floodlight, are still tearing their way into the black tomb which only this morning was a village school. While they work there is still some hope.

HOPE AND FEAR

The death roll of schoolchildren, teachers and families in nearby houses was once estimated at 200. Now, with more than 60 known to be dead, it seems the total may be less than 150. Eighty-five children and about 20 others are still missing.

All day, parents of children at the school have lived through an ordeal of hope and fear. Tonight they assembled in a school two miles from the disaster for a "roll call" of the casualties.

Mr. Thomas Griffiths, Chief Constable of nearby Merthyr Tydfil, took charge. Nearly all the parents stood weeping, unable to speak. As Mr. Griffiths stood up to address them there were cries of: "How many are alive? How many are alive?"

Mr. Griffiths held out his hands and calmed them. Then he read out a list of names — the names of children known to be alive.

COMFORTERS

He could hardly be heard above the sobs. Nurses moved among the parents to comfort them.

The parents then filed into another room where teams of girls were waiting to take names of missing children. As the parents left the school Mr. Griffiths, a tall burly man with a moustache, tried to comfort them.

He placed his arm round the shoulders of a father who was weeping openly and told him: "I know you think it is easy for me to say it — but don't despair. There must be some hope left."

Rescue workers tonight found the body of the deputy head teacher at the stricken Pant Glas school—Mr. David Beynon.

One man in the rescue party said: "He was clutching five little children in his arms as if he had been protecting them.

"He and the five children died clinging to each other."

Today's disaster has numbed the minds and chilled the hearts of people as no pit tragedy has ever done in a Welsh valley.

Mr. George Thomas, Minister of State for Wales, said sombrely: "A generation of children in this village has been wiped out."

ENGULFED

And the danger is not yet over. The mountain of rain-soaked slag and coal-dust which crashed on Aberfan this morning is still moving.

Today started just like any other day for the 5,000 people of Aberfan, four miles from Merthyr Tydfil.

There was no sign or danger from the 800ft. heap of slag towering above the village. But heavy rains in the past three days had built up to set the mountain slowly on the move.

Just after the children had dispersed from prayers at Pant Glas junior and infants' school it happened—suddenly and incredibly.

Two million tons of wet slag, dust and earth slid into the village. The school,

CONTINUED ON PAGE SIX

Coal Board 'were warned of danger'

By BARRIE FRASER

MR. GEORGE THOMAS, Minister of State for Wales, last night promised "a most searching inquiry" into the disaster.

He said: "A generation of children in Aberfan have been wiped out. South Wales has an abundance of tips and it is essential that such a disaster is not repeated."

Last night in Aberfan there were bitter comments about the long - standing danger of the tip. Mr.

Stephen Davies, Labour M P for Merthyr Tydfil, said: "I and others have been very concerned about this tip. We had a dread that sooner or later it would give way.

"Debris from a local colliery was still being emptied on to the tip when it collapsed this morning."

PROTESTS

For years Aberfan people have protested and signed petitions about the danger of the coal tips overhanging the village.

Twice before tips have slid towards the village, once blocking a road.

But the Coal Board have done little to make the tips safer, said villagers.

Mr. Tom Davies, aged 49, who saw yesterday's disaster, said: "The Coal Board were told two weeks ago that the tip was on the move. They did not even stop tipping there."

Mr. Ronald Scriven, 55-year-old local Labour Party official, added: "Action should have been taken years ago. The Coal Board are to blame, because I believe this tragedy could have been averted."

Councillor Sam Edwards, aged 64, of Merthyr Council, said: "The Coal Board should not put tips so near to houses and schools."

Villagers recalled that the previous headmaster of the school, Mr. W. J. Williams, who died in March, had often said: "One day we shall all be buried."

Another forecast of the disaster came in January, 1964, from Councillor Mrs. Gwyneth Williams, who is now dead.

She told Merthyr Council planning committee: "If the tip moves it could threaten the whole school."

RAINFALL

Last night the Coal Board said in a statement: "Preliminary investigations suggest that the recent abnormal rainfall had so permeated the tip that internal water pressure reached a strength which burst the base of the tip and movement down the mountain took place most suddenly."

A Coal Board spokesman in Cardiff said routine inspections of coal tips were carried out daily.

THE SORROW AND THE ANGER

Slagheap workers say: We gave 90 minutes' warning

From KEN GARDNER and a team of 'People' reporters.

ABERFAN, Saturday.

THE giant killer slagheap of Aberfan moved again as torrential rain fell over the tragic village tonight. Some of the rescue workers halted their search for victims to build a barricade of sandbags to keep out the creeping mountain.

They died at Aberfan... children on the nation's conscience

Police cars toured the valley calling all men to return to the disaster area. Teams with klaxon horns stood by to sound the alarm if the creeping became an avalanche.

So far 117 bodies have been found—most of them of children engulfed in the infants' school in Friday's slip. A further 65 children are missing. Mingled with the grief of toiling rescue workers and weeping mothers is a growing anger. . . .

Everyone is asking: *Why was this horror allowed to happen?*

Warnings have been made for over three years. And some villagers allege that the Merthyr Vale Colliery was alerted **NINETY MINUTES BEFORE FRIDAY'S DISASTER** that the tip was on the move.

REPORT TO OFFICE

The man who gave that warning was 47-year-old Les Davies, a deputy chargehand in charge of a gang which went to work on the top of the tip at 7.45 a.m. Friday.

He said last night: "I knew the tip was sinking so I went to tell my mechanic at the colliery. He told me to return and draw back the crane we were working with.

"But by the time I got back to the top of the tip it had got worse."

Mr. Davies added: "No one could have foreseen there would have been such disastrous results. The

KAY BOWNS
She died—aged ten

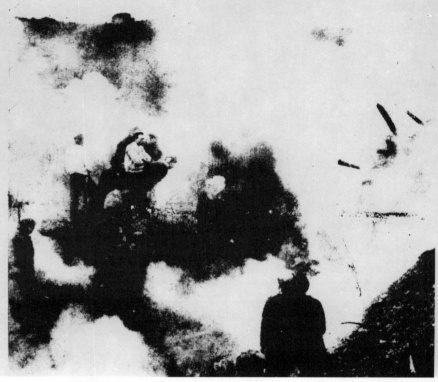

down there to fill our cans with water to boil tea down in that spring he said. He also stated that, in all the time he had worked on the tip, he had not known of an inspection made by anyone qualified. The interview ended with a barbed reference by the interviewer to previous Inquiries, and previous 'exercises in official whitewashing'. Perhaps as a result of this interview and the coverage it got in the papers (and perhaps not), a feeling soon developed in the Government that the media were beginning to conduct their own trial in anticipation of the Tribunal. The Attorney-General immediately announced that any further comments by television or the Press would be tantamount to contempt of court. In other words he was imposing, as the *Daily Sketch*'s indignant headline put it, 'a gag'.

Fleet Street was outraged. 'Here potentially is a weapon that could be employed to censor the Press and television, in what no doubt would be called "the national interest" ' insisted *The Times*, 'but would in practice become a means of stifling embarrassment and criticism.' The fact that a nationalized industry was involved, thundered the *Daily Express*, was 'no reason to attempt to threaten the Press in a statement issued under the wig and gown of a

senior law officer.' In the event the fears—if not the indignation—of the papers were assuaged by the conduct of the Tribunal under Lord Justice Edmund Davies (who had himself been born in a neighbouring valley). It was the longest Inquiry in British history, lasting 76 days, and its findings were quite specific. The blame for Aberfan rested squarely on the shoulders of the National Coal Board: 'it was [said the report] a terrifying tale of bungling ineptitude by many men charged with tasks for which they were totally unfitted, a failure to heed warnings, and a total lack of direction from above.

It was claimed, in one complaint submitted to the Press Council after the disaster, that the Press had devoted a disproportionate amount of space to Aberfan. The point, quite rightly, was never pursued and plenty of respected voices were raised in defence of journalists who had performed very responsibly under harrowing circumstances. In fact the degree of exposure, in both Press and TV, given to the tragedy was indeed heavy, yet it no more than reflected the extraordinary distress and emotion felt at large about the fate of the 144 victims (116 children and 28 adults): it undoubtedly contributed to the overwhelming public response to the Aberfan Disaster Fund—which reached over

£1,600,000 before it was closed. The fund in its ultimate administration created unforeseen problems, and of course never compensated the bereaved families or the village for their loss. The scars of Aberfan no longer disfigure the mountainside—the remaining tips were removed in due course: the scars are deep within those who survived.

Lost Heritage
The Florence Floods 1966

Mark Twain was desperately disappointed with the Arno when he first made its acquaintance in Florence, a lethargic trickle he considered a disgrace to its magnificent Renaissance setting. He would certainly have revised his verdict had he seen it on 3 November 1966, a foaming torrent that butted the piers of the Ponte Vecchio and swirled within a few feet of the embankment protecting the old fourteenth-century quarter of the city. The rains, all over Italy, had been exceptional throughout October. November looked like offering little respite, but the Florentines trudging home through the interminable rain that evening were not unduly worried. The Arno had not flooded Florence for 120 years, and tomorrow was a feast day, anyway.

There were to be no celebrations, as it turned out. In the early hours of Friday 4th, while most of the city still slept, the river rose unregarded up to flood levels, choking the ancient drains, creeping insidiously into cellars and short-circuiting power supplies. Florence awoke to find the water rushing pell-mell down the Lungarno and through the narrow streets, pausing only to fill up a venerable piazza before finding some unexplored outlet. By lunchtime the flood had tugged huge segments out of the medieval shops on the Ponte Vecchio and threatened to topple the precious bridge itself. Churches with their incalculable store of frescoes and statuary—Santa Croce, the Spanish Chapel, Sanctissima Annunziata, the Medici Chapel—were all inundated. The lower floors of the world-famous Uffizi Galleries, the National Library, Dante's House, the Piazza del Duomo and scores of other precious monu-

ments all disappeared beneath a muddy turbulent lake.

For eighteen hours the waters preyed on Florence, spinning thousands of cars into grotesque traffic-jams, despoiling shops regardless of their status—delicate leatherwork and jewellery from the Tornabuoni were as surely ruined as cheap souvenirs from the Straw Market—and forcing families up to their top floors (or even roofs). By Saturday 6 November the flood had receded, but for those who dared to venture out into the streets it had left an even more terrible legacy: a vast expanse of mud mixed with oil and naphtha (from broken heating systems in basements), as thick as molasses and two or more feet deep in places. Half a million tons—it was later estimated—had been deposited like an obscene carpet in every corner of the old city. Ugly black tidemarks, sometimes fifteen feet above street-level, on outside walls were fearful omens of the desolation within. In shop after shop the owners, their entire livelihoods gone, stoically shovelled at the sludge, willing it not to resume its former position. Others just stared in disbelief at this *finimondo*—the end of their world.

By their prodigious efforts on the Friday, as the flood-waters advanced, the staff of the Uffizi had saved many priceless works of art—by Giotto, Botticelli, Masaccio and others—by manhandling them to upper floors. But they could only rescue a fraction of what had been stored below ground or stacked in the laboratories (much of it from other countries) awaiting restoration. The casualties among rare books, manuscripts and old documents from the National Library ran to over a million, many of

them damaged beyond hope of repair. Frescoes, panels and wall-carvings suffered piteously—the worst perhaps being the great Paradise Door of the Baptistry, where a number of Ghiberti's famous gilded plaques had been torn off by the force of the torrent. Santa Croce with its tombs of Galileo, Michelangelo and Machiavelli, was a devastation. Giotto's frescoes, which had escaped the scum of oil by inches, were now in imminent danger from the rising damp. Worst of all, its most precious possession was lost for all time. The correspondent of the *Daily Mail* observed a heart-rending sight: 'A broken-hearted professor walked crying through the alleyways in knee-deep mud and carried the remains of a carved and painted wooden crucifix. He was followed in line by workmen, students and friars . . . the cross was part of the Crucifixion by Giovanni Cimabue (1240-1302) the greatest artist of his time. This crucifix was considered to be the most beautiful in Italy. Now it is ruined. It is covered with oil and mud and hopelessly scratched.'

The fate of these inestimable treasures brought forth a stirring response from art-lovers all over the world—including an international corps of student volunteers who converged on Florence, rolled up their sleeves and set to work to rescue whatever was rescuable ('the angels of the mud' they were nicknamed by the Florentines). Perhaps inevitably, with so much of Europe's cultural heritage at stake, the plight of human beings was sadly overlooked. Yet in fact the floods—the worst in memory—affected a third of Italy and claimed over 170 lives. Venice and Pisa were disaster areas, and some 800 smaller communities besides. Only

The Evening News
and STAR

No. 26,383   LONDON SATURDAY NOVEMBER 5 1966   PRICE 4d.

Storm havoc spreads to Austria and Switzerland

EUROPE'S TRAIL OF DISASTER

Floods and avalanches kill 70

The River Arno, turned into a raging torrent by the floods, is anxiously watched by technicians in the town of Figline, 18 miles south-east of Florence.

PATERNITY CLAIM AGAINST ACTOR

Actor Michael Crawford—"Byron" of "Not so much a Programme"—has been served with a paternity summons.

Confirming this today a solicitor for Mr. Crawford, who is at present filming in Spain, said the summons would be heard at South Western magistrates' court next week.

Acclaimed

The summons has been taken

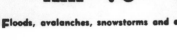

Floods, avalanches, snowstorms and a

HUNDREDS MISSING AS FLOOD WATERS RISE

Rescuers help women through floods at Bologna in Northern Italy.

SKETCH FOREIGN SERVICE

AT least 16 people died as rising flood waters continued to threaten Italy last night. Hundreds more are missing, injured or homeless.

The floods, the worst for 20 years, cut the country in two.

In Florence art treasures worth millions of pounds were threatened by swirling waters.

They lapped at Cellini's bronze statue of Perseus, which stands outdoors in the main square.

• EVACUATED

They invaded St. Mark's monastery, where Fra Angelico painted frescoes.

They poured into the ground floors of the Uffizi gallery, which houses works by Raphael and Botticelli.

And they threatened to sweep into the Duomo, Florence's cathedral.

Lightning hit the city as terrified householders, many carrying their children, fled to upper floors.

Others evacuated their homes. Bridges over the River Arno were in danger of col-

belatedly did the true scale of the calamity dawn on other countries. The *Sunday Times* later explained the reason: 'The Italian floods are an international disaster. This has been recognized late for the reason that a developed country like Italy is commonly expected to be able to provide the immediate response to disaster on its own. Foreign aid would normally be channelled into the relief network set up by the domestic government. In Italy this pattern has been shattered and meanwhile there are people dying, families homeless, animals rotting in the streets, cities without water, buildings without foundations and the finest fruits of the Italian Renaissance decomposing in the mud.

Why, the people of Florence would like to have known too, did day after day pass without any signs of assistance from their Government? It must have known, for by 6 November coverage by the Italian and foreign Press left no doubts about the gravity of the situation— yet the first bulldozers, trucks and tractors did not reach Florence for a week! 'In Rome incredibly' explained the *Sunday Times* 'the flood has become party politics. The Renaissance produced not only paintings but city states. As the art has gone down in the mud the politics have risen from it . . . The extent of the catastrophe was assessed too late. Its national implications were clouded over and the measures to meet it are still totally inadequate. Rome's *Il Messaggero* accused the politicians of making an exhibition of themselves, boasting of what their party had done and what other parties hadn't done. In Milan the *Corriere Della Sera* said the Italian Government couldn't be blamed for the rainfall—but it *could* be blamed for rivers which overflowed too easily, for the scarcity of hydraulic maintenance and the lack of forests which aggravates flood damage. A perfect example of centralized apathy occurred five days after the flood, when Rome radio blithely reported that things were returning to normal in Florence. 'What Normality?' the city's paper, *La Nazione*, bitterly bannered its front page the next day, contemplating the black quagmire that blanketed the streets, almost untouched.

A sense of urgency was slow to communicate itself to foreign governments as well. A fortnight after the disaster *The Times* felt obliged to run a sternly sarcastic editorial: 'Giving a vigorous and dramatic lead to match the country's mood the Government have sent out 6,000 blankets, twenty large marquee tents, quantities of vaccine and are thinking about sending some breeding cattle. This is one of the occasions when it would have been better to have kept quiet. What Italy is facing is not a rained-out picnic but the greatest calamity to hit it since the war . . .' A month later it was still pointing out that the Italian flood fund had barely reached one-fifth of that subscribed for Aberfan, not from lack of generosity (it added) 'rather a lack of any single clear channel through which to address gifts.' Meanwhile in Italy facts were emerging to heap yet more embarrassment on the authorities. It seemed that on the evening of 3 November the Electricity Authority had been forced to open the flood-gates of the Levane Dam, thirty-five miles up-river from Florence. This had made it certain the city would be flooded, and formal warning had been passed on to the city engineers. As a conscious decision, that warning was not made public—for fear of the chaos that might ensue from everyone trying to flee in their cars. The final irony was that *La Nazione* had somehow learnt the news and carried it in its last edition. By the time is should have been on sale on the streets, there were no streets left.

BURTON

Evening Standard

44,289 FRIDAY, NOVEMBER 11, 1966 ●●● 4d. 5

SYDNEY EDWARDS cables from Italy:

'Why Richard Burton's friend told him to stay away from Florence'

THE CITY THAT CRIES FOR HELP

FLORENCE, Friday

A pale Tuscan dawn took over from the searchlights in Florence this morning, the Renaissance buildings still submerged in water and mud.

There is still no power or water in the city, and the army searchlights, pointed into the sky, provided the only means of lights for the work of reclamation that went on through the night.

Hundreds of soldiers and civilians will have attempted the seemingly impossible task of turning the tide of mud that followed the disastrous flood in the city last weekend.

The enormity of the damage done by the flood is only now beginning to be seen as the flood waters recede.

A sad sight

At dawn today a queue for food was beginning to form under the shadow of Michelangelo's David outside the Palazzo Vecchio. This was being used as one of the main food distribution points.

In other parts of the city you can see army buses distributing bread and salami and milk to Florentines.

Michaelangelo's tomb in the Santa Croce is submerged in mud. So is Dante's monument. And the tomb of Rossini.

Santa Croce is one of the saddest sights. It is one of the best known churches and the most famous and beautiful of the Franciscan order. Many of Italy's great men lie buried here.

The interior is like a muddy battlefield. Some frescoes on the walls have been badly damaged by flood waters, but fortunately, the Giotto frescoes up are undamaged.

£60 million damage

In the cloisters, late last night David was standing in 3ft. of water giving emergency aid to damaged paintings. They were working in total darkness with only one hand lamp for each cloister and the occasional candle.

This lack of power is one of the most tragic aspects of the disaster. Also the stench from the water makes one wonder how people keep away. The drains and sewers are still blocked.

Altogether the damage to the city of Florence is estimated at £60m. Many buildings have been damaged, and the famous Cimabue is completely ruined.

More than 1000 manuscripts and ancient books have been partly destroyed.

Many paintings and tapestries are still being saved from the basements and cellars of churches and galleries. They are being carried, shoulder-high like corpses, by parties of six men up to the Uffizi Gallery. There, among the Botticellis, they are laid out.

The long top gallery resembles a mortuary with the sodden, wrecked paintings from the 13th, 14th and 15th centuries laid out in lines like decomposed bodies.

From the Uffizi one can look out over Florence's most famous bridge, the Ponte Vecchio.

THE SUNDAY TIMES, 13 NOVEMBER 1966

THE ORDEAL OF FLORENCE

Uffizi masterpieces on the way to the Pitti Gallery for cleaning

The Cimabue destroyed by water and heating oil

Crucifixion by Cimabue (c. 1280).

An agonising accounting in the Florence galleries

A preliminary assessment of the losses in Florence by John Shearman, Senior Lecturer on Renaissance Art, Courtauld Institute

DAWN ADDAMS'S

Car men decide

Aid from Britain increasing

By Jeremy Bugler

Oil on Troubled Waters

The Sinking of the Torrey Canyon 1967

When one of the largest ships in the world ran aground on the formidable Seven Stones reef, to the north of the Scilly Isles, just after 9.00am on 18 March 1967 it was news—but not spectacular news. The next day both the *Observer* and the *Sunday Times* printed pictures on their front page, but neither report communicated any sense of urgency: neither photograph, come to that, showed the ominous trickle of black oil seeping from the guts of the stricken supertanker. There appeared to be no cause for alarm. There were no casualties, and the Dutch salvage team that had won the usual scramble for prize-money was standing by to tow the *Torrey Canyon* off the rocks on the next high tide. As for the oil—in 1967 the prophets of ecology with their woe-begotten predictions were still voices crying in the wilderness. The fact that in less than ten years this attitude has been reversed, and that the Press has become an equally earnest watchdog of potential assaults on our environment, is due in large measure to the events of Easter Week 1967.

On the other hand, even that Saturday there were omens of the impending disaster if anyone cared to regard them. Local fishermen would have told you that, of the numberless vessels driven onto those rocks in the past 150 years, not a dozen had ever been refloated, let alone a 120,000-ton tanker brimful of crude oil. The prevailing tide and rapidly freshening wind was already carrying thousands of tons towards the south coast of England, even as the *Torrey Canyon*'s master, Captain Pastrengo Rugiato, pumped yet more thousands of tons out of the tanks in an effort to lighten the ship. It was well into Sunday before it was fully realized that Britain had a potential catastrophe on its hands. The navy, sailing out of Devonport dockyard, had been spraying the truant oil with all available detergent since Saturday evening: it had had no effect whatsoever. It was, *The Times* described these initial efforts, 'like trying to mop up Kensington Round Pond dry with a sponge.'

The Prime Minister (whose holiday home on the Scilly Isles gave him more than a professional interest in the tanker's fate) decided on the Sunday afternoon that the situation warranted the presence of a Minister on the scene, and chose Maurice Foley, the Under-Secretary for the Navy. When he arrived that night, armed with a mandate to cut through all red tape, the oil slick was already covering more than forty square miles. Two proposals were immediately put forward: empty the *Torrey Canyon*, or salvage her. The first expedient was soon discarded—quite apart from the risk of explosion it would have taken an estimated three to four weeks to pump her dry with the equipment available. And Tuesday was to prove that salvaging was fraught with danger.

By the morning of the 21st compressed air pumped into the tanks had corrected the list partially, and hopes were rising that the coming spring tides would unpin the ship. But the concentration of gas from the oil was also rising: at midday a huge explosion in the engine room ripped through the belly of the ship, scything through three decks and the swimming-pool. To the papers and everyone else it was a 'mystery blast' (and the reason for it never was discovered) that injured seven salvagemen, Captain Stahl the salvage chief fatally. In spite of this tragic setback the Dutch salvage team insisted they would persevere with their operation.

As early as Tuesday the *Guardian* had questioned whether salvage would succeed, and was proposing a somewhat radical solution: 'Napalm for once could be used effectively for a decent and useful purpose . . . It is an operation which may need to be done, perhaps today.' But as Mr Foley told the Press, 'until the owners (Union Oil Company) have declared the ship a total loss, there can be no question of destroying it'—so that was that. It was a point of view that, in retrospect, the newspapers were to find wanting. 'The government should have been ready to take the law into its own hands. Outrage, piracy on the high seas, an act of aggression against Liberia [where the *Torrey Canyon* was registered]? Possibly, but it would have saved the English coast from a noisome pollution', *The Times* argued later. Yet as long as there remained a hope of extricating the ship, it would have been a brave government indeed that unhesitatingly rode roughshod over the rights of the ship's owners, the international insurance companies, the underwriters and the salvage operators.

So, now abandoned by her captain and crew, the tanker continued to roll and grind on the reef and the sludgy oil continued to pour into the sea. By Friday night the giant oil slick measured 260 square miles. On Saturday morning its advance guard landed on the beaches of Lizard Point and Sennen Cove in Cornwall, wave upon wave of ugly, evil-smelling blackness. The gallant armada of little ships, and the 30,000 gallons of detergent a day they had poured on the blanket of oil, had succeeded only in breaking the slick up into huge sections. Each day hundreds of ideas for alternatives to detergent were pouring into the Navy's 'good ideas department' in Plymouth. The more practical were even tried: blotting-paper blankets to protect oyster beds, and sinking patches of oil with layers of powdered chalk (which proved moderately successful on the French coast). A farmer from Northampton, the *Daily Telegraph* reported, had found straw very handy for mopping up oil; someone else suggested solidifying the oil with iron filings and sweeping it up with a magnet. Notions of filling the *Torrey Canyon* with tennis balls, ping pong balls and even toy balloons were all put forward.

The sights that greeted residents that Easter Saturday were heart-rending—birds and shellfish suffocating in the oily slime, seafronts coated and harbours clogged with oozing layers. A sixty-mile front of oil, from St Ives to Marazion, had already beached, disfiguring

The Daily Telegraph
and Morning Post
4 a.m.

No. 34810. LONDON, TUESDAY, MARCH 28, 1967.   Printed in LONDON and MANCHESTER.   4d.

5 MINISTERS TO FIGHT OIL

'Greatest peace-time menace to Britain'

10 MILES A DAY FLOW ON SUSSEX & KENT

Torrey Canyon in her death throes in the creaming seas at high tide last night.
[Other pictures—P16; Map—Back Page]

2 COLONELS IN PLANE FOR SIERRA LEONE

MUDDLE OVER CHOICE TO HEAD JUNTA

33 TEENAGERS INJURED IN BLAZING COACH

CHINESE TRAP RUSSIANS FOR 7hrs IN CAR

Ford robbed of safari win by buck

COAL FIND IN CITY CENTRE

CASSIUS CLAY'S CALL-UP DELAY

Wilson calls a 'beach battle' Cabinet

The "beach battle" Cabinet. From the left: Mr. Maurice Foley, Sir Elwyn Jones, Mr. Roy Jenkins, Mr. Harold Wilson, Mr. Anthony Greenwood and Mr. Gerry Reynolds.

DAILY MIRROR

4d. Monday, March 27, 1967 • No. 19,673

SHATTERED TANKER BREAKS UP IN GALE

Thousands of tons of oil is spewing from her tanks

By KENELM JENOUR, EDWARD VALE and WILLIAM WOLFF

THE grounded oil tanker Torrey Canyon began to break up last night. The ship's back split in two, and the bow and stern sank under water.

A Royal Navy helicopter pilot said: "My guess is that neither part will be there tomorrow morning. They will both have sunk."

The captain of the salvage tug Utrecht radioed that the Torrey Canyon must be considered lost.

Oil began spewing from the tanker faster than at any time since a week last Saturday, when the ship crashed on to the Seven Stones reef, twenty miles from Land's End.

Ten of the tanker's eighteen oil tanks are now gushing out oil. By late last night the ship had lost about three-quarters of its 120,000-ton load—most of it since the break-up began.

The menace to Britain's South Coast beaches, already suffocated by oil over a sixty-mile stretch, is now graver than ever.

The new mass of oil may prove to be virtually indestructible.

The helicopter pilot, Lieutenant Commander Mike Fournel, flew around the tanker after taking Prime Minister Harold Wilson to the Scilly Isles from a "mini-Cabinet" called to discuss the crisis.

The commander said later:

● On the second circuit I thought I noticed a bend in the hull. She was sagging at both ends. During the next few minutes it became further pronounced, until there was a most positive bend — a hump in the middle.

The well decks were awash, and oil was coming out in great quantities. I have never seen so much coming out on previous occasions that I have flown over her.

When I got there two tugs were connected with wires. Just before I left they were free. The two tugs had been cast off.

The tanker was being battered by high seas whipped up by a strong gale.

Split

The destroyer H.M.S. [...]

DAILY MIRROR

4d. Tuesday, March 28, 1967 • No. 19,674

Now the sea comes in for the kill

This was the Torrey Canyon yesterday. Almost vanished under the waves. Breaking up fast. And still holding 60,000 tons of oil.

VAST OIL THREAT TO THE SOUTH

THE wrecked tanker Torrey Canyon, pounded by gales, split in three last night. Half the ship's 120,000-ton cargo of thick, black oil had poured into the sea.

And a westerly gale was driving the vast oil patch slowly up the English Channel — menacing the whole South coast.

An expert forecast that in eleven to sixteen days, the black tide will have reached Brighton 300 miles from the wreck, on a reef near Land's End, Cornwall.

About a week after that —according to the expert, Captain Graham Denton of Plymouth School of Navigation—the oil will have travelled another 100 [...]

By Mirror Reporting Team
ARTHUR SMITH, BARRY STANLEY, EDWARD VALE and KENELM JENOUR

blackened beaches at favourite holiday spots including Torquay, Weymouth, Bournemouth and Isle of Wight resorts.

One thread of hope remains for the southern resorts: a long spell of easterly winds which would drive the oil out into the Atlantic Ocean.

escaping into the Channel. The boom was made during Easter, at Liverpool. The ship which carried it south was held up to raise for two days.

Today, the boom will probably be assembled on the beach at Newlyn, Cornwall and towed out to surround the Torrey Canyon ... if the ship is still on the reef.

Winds

---

some of the most beautiful tourist spots in Britain, Mounts Bay, Porthleven, Priests Cove, Prah Sands and dozens of others. Gazing out at the eternity of oil waiting to be washed in on the highest tides for years the *Sunday Telegraph* next day feared the whole of Britain's south coast was threatened, and at this rate it would reach Dover by midsummer. But the present disaster was enough for the people of Cornwall, whose very livelihoods depended on the holiday trade. A Dunkirk spirit gripped the disaster zone, as hundreds of volunteers stood shoulder to shoulder with the Army that had been drafted into the area—fishermen, housewives with watering-cans, children with plastic buckets, all scrubbing and shovelling, spraying and scraping. At first their efforts looked futile as succeeding tides deposited yet more black lumps ashore. 'Like whistling against the wind' complained one volunteer to the *Daily Mirror*. But try they did, and took most unkindly to Sunday's front-page headline in the *People*: 'They Pray in the Streets as 50 Miles of Beaches are Hit.' The newsmen from London, they thought, were sensationalizing the situation and guaranteeing a flood of cancelled bookings. 'People get the impression that the whole of Cornwall is being engulfed by volcanic lava' grumbled one hotelier to the *Daily Telegraph*.

If the men of Cornwall were incensed by repeated stories of tainted fish and permanently polluted beaches, then perhaps their spirits were slightly raised later in the week by the *Sun*'s front page which quoted the Prime Minister as 'putting it on record that I have booked my holiday for August in the Scillies. I was trying to book rooms for one or two friends to come down and play golf with me, but I found there were no bedrooms and no cancellations.' However, over the Bank Holiday the outlook *was* bleak. Salvage attempts had failed and gales were buffeting the ship unmercifully. On Easter Sunday the *Torrey Canyon* gave up the struggle and split in two, threatening to unleash the remaining 40,000 tons of oil in her tanks. At last the salvage team conceded she was a total loss and abandoned her to her fate.

On Monday the Prime Minister's 'beach-battle' Cabinet determined the time had now come to bomb the stubborn tanker out of existence, in the hope of igniting the oil before it dispersed. To the delight of reporters circling above in naval reconnaissance planes on Tuesday, wave after wave of Buccaneers and Hunters screamed in over the wreck and pounded the helpless hulk with 1,000lb bombs and thousands of gallons of kerosene. It was almost beautiful, according to the *Guardian*: 'Buccaneers . . . like tiny birds against the background of the huge smoke pillar, glinting silver in the sun . . . The fires eased their way towards each other and became one creeping orange circle of flame.' It was also a failure: the next day the black shroud of oil lay there as impenetrable as ever. More sorties were launched on Wednesday, more explosives, petrol bombs, even rockets and napalm yet still, as Thursday's papers gleefully pointed out, the *Torrey Canyon* refused to die (obliging the frustrated authorities to explain that the object had been to fire the oil not sink the ship).

In all the supertanker resisted three days of concerted air-strikes and more than 160,000lb of explosives—though there was good reason to suppose that most of its oil if not all had, in fact, been disposed of. On the beach front a week of prodigious effort was beginning to show heartening results, though local complaints persisted that Fleet Street was more concerned with mock warfare than with reporting clean beaches. In spite of that the Cornish holiday season, though dented, was not damaged beyond repair. The worst sufferer perhaps turned out to be the fishing industry— too late it was discovered that detergent (and 2.5 million gallons of it were ultimately used) proved to be incomparably more lethal to marine life than the oil. The toll amongst birds was even more visibly tragic: at least 25,000 razorbills and guillemots were victims of the environmental disaster.

Through the whims of wind and current the rest of the south coast was spared—at the expense of Brittany where (in spite of *Le Monde*'s optimistic prediction that France had nine chances in ten of being spared) the oil landed on 9 April, and a new saga of rescue and recriminations was set in train. The last casualty was the *Torrey Canyon*'s master, Captain Rugiato himself, who was officially held responsible for the loss of his ship. In Britain he had appeared as a dignified, if silent, figure: on his return to Italy, oppressed by the relentless attentions of the *papperazzi*, he suffered a complete nervous breakdown. The final indignity was to suffer his photograph syndicated all over the world—crawling beneath his bed in an effort to escape.

The Daily Telegraph and Morning Post

4 a.m.

No. 34811. LONDON, WEDNESDAY, MARCH 29, 1967. Printed in LONDON and MANCHESTER. 4d.

NIGHT TIDE PUTS OUT TANKER FIRE

ATTACK TODAY WITH INCENDIARIES

NAPALM BOMBS READY IF NECESSARY

HIGH tides last night extinguished the blaze in the wreck of the tanker Torrey Canyon on Seven Stones reef, off Land's End, after it had been bombed by Navy Buccaneer jets and sprayed with jet fuel by R A F fighters.

The Buccaneers are standing by to bomb the tanker again today, and Sir Solly Zuckermann, the Government's Chief Scientific Adviser, said there would be "continuous operations with incendiaries." Stocks of "large and small" napalm bombs were being held ready for use if necessary.

A vast black cloud of smoke, 10,000ft high, began drifting over southern Cornwall within a few minutes of the dropping of the first bombs yesterday afternoon. The Torrey Canyon and oil-covered sea up to two miles from her were ablaze.

Mr. Jenkins, Home Secretary, said last night that the tanker's American owners, the Barracuda Tanker Corporation, a subsidiary of the Union Oil Company of California, were told but not consulted when the Government decided on Monday that she would have to be destroyed. Union Oil said in New York they had officially abandoned the Torrey Canyon and would have endorsed the Government's action if asked.

The seas ablaze near the Torrey Canyon.
[Other pictures—P18.]

BUCCANEERS' 42 BOMBS

By JOHN OWEN

A HOME OFFICE statement said last night: "We have been informed officially that the fire in the wreckage of the Torrey Canyon is out. Mr. Jenkins, Home Secretary, has been informed. We cannot say at this stage what the next step will be."

Prisoners save birds; Threat to holidays; and Towns put out booms—P22
Smoke rose to 10,000ft; and Heath holds Wilson to account—Back Page
Pictures—P18
London Day by Day—P14

Naval Buccaneer bombers from Lossiemouth had dropped 42 1,000lb bombs, quickly reinforced by R A F Hunter jets with drop-cans of aviation fuel, on the shattered wreck of the tanker on Seven Stones reef.

Coastguards said the spring tides had put out the flames. Those of the last two days have been particularly high.

Mr. Maurice Foley, Under Secretary of State for the Navy, said in Plymouth late last night: "The bombing strike was successful. Our action now depends on the result of aerial reconnaissance at first light tomorrow."

This will be carried out by Naval helicopters from Culdrose and St. Mawgan.

Naval officers with whom I talked held the view that phosphorous shells fired into the hull close to the water line might generate the intense heat needed to restart the fire in partially submerged tanks.

Yesterday's fire burned for four-and-a-half hours, with flames and smoke enveloping the wreckage and the oil-covered sea for up to two miles around.

BLACK CLOUD
Engulfed by flames

Within four minutes of the dropping of the first bomb on the tanker, aground on the Seven Stones reef off Land's End for 11 days, flames engulfed the wreckage. A black cloud, ten miles across, billowed 10,000ft into the sky.

A few minutes later 26 R A F Hunter jets flew in to jettison 5,200 gallons of aviation fuel on to the wreck and oil-covered sea to feed the flames.

The last of the eight Buccaneers taking part in the bombing raids, made their strike at 7.30 last night, and all of them returned to Scotland.

But a Navy spokesman at Ply-

'WARTIME' AGAIN AT AIR STATION

DAILY TELEGRAPH REPORTER

IT was "wartime" all over again last night at the Royal Naval air station, Lossiemouth.

In the gathering dusk, aircraft of two squadrons from the Navy's front line station flew in from operation "mop-up," the bombing of the Torrey Canyon.

But the pilots, instead of debriefing, gave a Press conference. The spokesman was Lt.-Cdr. David Howard, the commanding officer of 736 Squadron, who led the operation.

"We had been told the vessel was in three parts, but it was only visible to us as two main sections, the stern, our main target, and the forward section. We decided that the best line of attack was from the direction of the Isles of Scilly.

Failed to explode

"I went down first and did one attack, one of my two bombs striking the starboard side, but failing to explode. I was followed in by Lt.-Cdr. David Mears, senior pilot of 800 Sqoadron, who scored two direct hits in the middle of the rear section.

Owners told but not consulted

DAILY TELEGRAPH POLITICAL STAFF

THE decision to bomb the Torrey Canyon was taken on Monday night by the Emergency Committee without consulting the owners.

Mr. Jenkins, Home Secretary, said at a Press conference last night that success could not be guaranteed because there was still a danger that the ship would be destroyed but not the bulk of the 40,000 tons of oil still in it.

It was not until the tanker split on Sunday night, giving rise to a new situation, that bombing and firing the oil could be decided on.

"So long as there was a reasonable chance of getting the ship off the rocks, towing her away and sinking her well away from our coasts, we had a better and more complete chance of getting rid of the source of the pollution."

CLIMAX REACHED
Risk justified

But once the tanker broke up, the owners were told what action would be taken and the operation went ahead without concern for legal or financial repercussions, said Mr. Jenkins.

He said previous experience of trying to fire a tanker in the Persian Gulf had not been encouraging, but scientists had been working on the problem and their experiments "reached a climax" over the weekend.

"When the situation changed over Sunday night we were justified in taking a bigger risk and today's operation followed."

Mr. Jenkins said there had been a change in the Ministerial command in the "field." Mr. Greenwood, Minister of Housing and Local Government, was now in

Continued on Back Page, Col. 6

'NOT SURPRISED,' SAYS REYNOLDS

Daily Telegraph Reporter

Mr Reynolds, Minister of Defence (Administration), said late last night after learning that the Torrey Canyon fire had gone out: "I am not entirely surprised. The fact that it has gone out confirms the views we had about this type of operation and the prospects of its success.

"People have been saying that we should have done this seven days ago. At that time, the best course was to try to get the tanker off the rocks. The general position at Plymouth is that they

STRIKE-BOUND FACTORY CHIEF QUITS JOB

'REDUNDANCIES' WARNING

DAILY TELEGRAPH REPORTER

AFTER 138 days of bitter industrial strife at the American-owned textile machinery factory of Roberts-Arundel at Stockport the company announced yesterday that Mr. John E. Cox has "relinquished his position as managing director."

A statement issued from the headquarters of the parent company at Sanford, North Carolina yesterday, said that machining operations are being discontinued at the plant. A "substantial number" of workers and supervising and technical staff would be made redundant.

Mr. Cox, who has managed the company since 1965, has been appointed vice-chairman of Roberts Europe of Bruges, Belgium, and Roberts International of Sanford.

Nearly 150 workers who went on strike after the company took on five women to work on the machines were dismissed by the firm in December. Later police were called to deal with disturbances near the factory.

"Rioting and damage"

The statement was made by Mr. Robert Pomeranz, chairman of the company, who sent a letter to Mr. Gunter, Minister of Labour, saying that "gains in productivity we have been making are constantly diluted by the rioting, blacking, harassment and damage to our plant.

"There appears little reason to manufacture in Stockport, for export to other Roberts' plants, machines and components which can be produced at lower cost elsewhere."

'No sympathy'

Mr. John Tocher, Stockport district secretary of the A E U, said last night that he had no sympathy with some people who would lose their jobs "They have stolen the jobs of our members and it is poetic justice."

The unions would not be satisfied for the plant to become a design and assembly shop. They wanted a return to the status quo basis.

"We intend to remain in dispute until either the company negotiates a just settlement or it leaves Stockport."

Industrial News—P22

U.S. ACCEPTS NEW

'BLITZ' ON LORRIES BY MINISTRY

Daily Telegraph Motoring Staff

MINISTRY OF TRANSPORT traffic examiners are to conduct "blitzes" against lorry drivers and operators contravening Hours and Records Regulations and committing other offences.

Between April 3 and April 5 a countrywide network of road checkpoints will be set up. Vehicle examiners will also be on duty at some points to check on the mechanical condition of lorries.

Each lorry driver will be given a personal message from Mrs. Castle, Minister of Transport, stressing the need for road safety.

"It is important that there should be no slackening in the campaign against drivers who work round the clock and their unscrupulous employers" the Ministry said last night.

Motoring—P12

BEAUMONT TO SUCCEED BYERS

Daily Telegraph Political Staff

The Rev. Timothy Beaumont, 38, will succeed Lord Byers as chairman of the Liberal party, it was announced last night. Lord Byers was elected leader of the Liberal Peers earlier this month.

Mr. Beaumont has been treasurer of the party and is also a former head of the party organisation. He will co-ordinate the work of various sections of the party

South Africa bans former Tory MP

DAILY TELEGRAPH REPORTER

MR. HUMPHRY BERKELEY, former Conservative M P for Lancaster, said yesterday that he had been declared a prohibited immigrant to the Republic of South Africa.

A letter from the South African Ministry of the Interior informed him that his Commonwealth right to enter the country without an alien's temporary permit had been withdrawn.

For some years in the forefront of the anti-apartheid movement, he was barred from visiting Rhodesia in January to collect material for a Royal Institute of International Affairs book on the effect of sanctions.

Previous visit

Mr. Berkeley, 41, spent two days in Johannesburg where the British Consulate General arranged for him to meet Afrikaner Nationalists, editors, politicians and businessmen.

"I did nothing to break the law or in any way embarrass the South African Government.

"I regard this prohibition as just another illustration of the fact that South Africa is becoming a country where freedom to express views contrary to those of the Government is increasingly difficult and where known critics of apartheid are to be excluded on political grounds. This is all too much reminiscent of pre-war Germany under the Nazis."

WAGE DISPUTE HALTS ITV COLOUR

Daily Telegraph Television Staff

Production on three colour television programmes for the American market was brought to a halt last night when pay talks between I T V and the Association of Cinematograph and Television Technicians broke down.

The technicians are demanding more money for working on colour programmes which are being produced for overseas.

They are a special Morecambe and Wise programme, a drama, Dr. Jekyll and Mr. Hyde, and the life of Chekhov.

If the dispute continues the programmes will still be made in black and white for this country. I T V have told the union they

BAZOOKAS FIRED AT S. ARABIAN HOMES

ERIC DOWNTON
Daily Telegraph Staff Correspondent

ADEN, Tuesday.

BAZOOKA attacks were launched early today in Al Ittihad, capital of the South Arabian Federation, on the homes of Mr. Abdul Girgirah, Federal Minister of Information, and Mr. Sukta Bin Ali, Defence Minister.

A dusk-to-dawn curfew was imposed on Aqrabi sheikhdom in which the capital lies.

No one was hurt in the attack. It was the second in a week on Mr. Girgirah's home.

He said that he was asleep when three bazookas opened fire from a village near by and slightly damaged his house.

Escaped injury

John Handers, a British officer serving with the Federal Army, escaped injury in Crater, Aden, when a hand grenade exploded in his parked Land-Rover.

A grenade was thrown at a Federal Regular Army vehicle in Crater, causing slight damage but no casualties. Federal National Guards got a taste of terrorism when a grenade bounced on their Rover, wounding two.

Terrorists confused

Aden's terrorist groups, who are in confusion tonight over developments around the United Nations mission's visit, are awaiting new instructions from Cairo.

The visit to Cairo of Mr. Gromyko, Russian Foreign Minister, is interpreted in Aden as Moscow trying to persuade Cairo to tone down terrorism in South Arabia during the mission's visit.

Reports that the mission may after all be received in Republican Yemen are also confusing extremists.

U.N. Round Table Proposal—P21
Editorial Comment—P14

Daily Mirror

Navy jets blast stricken tanker and set the sea on fire.. now one question remains

4d. Wednesday, March 29, 1967 • No. 19,675

The first bomb lands on target . . . seen from the Scilly Isles.

IS IT WORKING?

The flames die down.. plan to try napalm bombs today

By BARRY STANLEY, EDWARD VALE, DON COOLICAN and VICTOR KNIGHT

FLAMES still spurted from the bomb-blasted oil tanker Torrey Canyon late last night after intensive "raids" by dozens of war-planes.

But the evening's high tide seemed to have put out most of the huge blaze started yesterday by Navy and R A F planes with bombs and tanks of jet fuel.

And the big question was:

Has the great fire operation succeeded in burning away most of the 40,000 tons of crude oil left in the wrecked tanker, twenty miles from Land's End?

Stocks

If the plan has failed, napalm fire-bombs will be used today to start the blaze again.

This was announced in London last night by Home Secretary Roy Jenkins. The announcement involved the first admission by a Government Minister that Britain holds stocks of napalm—the jellied-petrol killer used by the Americans in Vietnam.

Mr. Jenkins said it was not clear until Sunday night—when the tanker began breaking into three parts—that the ship could not be saved.

About the decision to try setting fire to the wreck, to stop further oil pollution of Britain's South Coast resorts. Mr. Jenkins said:

"This was bound to be an extremely difficult operation, the success of which could by no means be guaranteed.

"The danger was, and still remains, that the ship would be des-

Continued on Back Page

the bombs Torrey Canyon's stern still juts defiantly above the waves.

The Apollo Fire 1967

 DAILY NEWS
NEW YORK'S PICTURE NEWSPAPER ®

FINAL

7¢ 10¢ OUTSIDE L.I. AND SUBURBS

Vol. 48. No. 186 Copr. 1967 News Syndicate Co. Inc. New York, N.Y. 10017, Saturday, January 28, 1967★ WEATHER: Partly cloudy, windy, cold.

3 ASTROS DIE IN CAPSULE FIRE

Grissom... White... Chaffee Lost in First Space Tragedy

Trapped in Moonship. America's first three Apollo astronauts, Virgil (Gus) Grissom, 40, Edward White, 36, and Roger Chaffee, 31, (l. to r.), are shown together in recent foto at Cape Kennedy. Last nigh , all three were killed when a flash fire trapped them in their moonship during a launch pad test at the Cape. (UPI Telefoto)

Stories and Pictures Pages 2 to 7 and Centerfold

In 1967 the United States space programme entered a new and exciting phase. In the previous six years sixteen manned space flights had been made, under the Mercury and Gemini projects, if not without minor mishaps, then at least without a single loss of life. It augured well for the new Apollo project, which would blast off in February and was scheduled to culminate in an epoch-making landing on the moon in 1969. On 27 January 1967 the first 'prime' Apollo crew, veterans Gus Grissom and Ed White along with newcomer Roger Chaffee, clambered in their silvery space-suits into their capsule atop a 200-foot rocket, for a practice countdown. Ten minutes short of the simulated lift-off the monitors in the control room went blank, and horrified ground crew spotted smoke coming from the capsule. By the time rescuers could reach the top of the launching-pad in the elevator, it was far too late: one after another they were driven back by the lung-piercing smoke. All three astronauts died 'in a flash' (the papers said) when the capsule burst with the heat—though it was later revealed that for some seconds before that they had been aware of a fire (from some electrical wiring) but had failed to complete the emergency escape drill in time. As promised at the time the Apollo programme went right on ahead, with the will to beat the Russians at their own game un-dimmed—though with regard for the safety of future astronauts sharpened by the forthright criticism of the official inquiry.

The Sinking of the Wahine 1968

At first the inhabitants of Wellington were told that the *Wahine* had been 'held up' near the harbour entrance by an overnight storm. It was only as freak winds continued to buffet the city all day—and there was still no news of the *Wahine*—that doubts set in. In fact, the almost-new ferry boat had sailed straight into the centre of a cyclone with 734 people aboard. At first light on 10 April 1968 a huge wave hit the ship: a few minutes later she was stuck fast on Barrett's Reef, almost within the western harbour. Passengers aboard believed they were safe: the next day newspaper readers learned of the third worst tragedy in New Zealand's history.

HEAVY DEATH TOLL MOUNTS AS SEARCH CONTINUES FOR SURVIVORS OF WAHINE

More than 200 could have died

FIFTY-ONE people are dead and an unknown number are missing in what could be New Zealand's worst maritime disaster.

It is feared that the death toll could exceed 200.

The interisland ferry Wahine carrying 614 passengers and 130 crew foundered yesterday morning in raging seas in Wellington harbour off Seatoun.

TOP: A lifeboat from the stricken Wahine hits the shore at Seatoun yesterday as rescuers rush into boiling surf to help survivors ashore.

ABOVE: An empty rubber life raft floats among other debris a few yards from the Wahine.

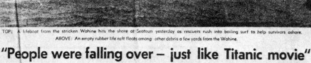

"People were falling over — just like Titanic movie"

WHOSE BABIES ARE THESE?

TRAPPED IN AIR POCKET

• Dead and missing, P.3.
• From reef to ruin, P.3.
• Pictures, P.6, P.7.

An Improper Balance

The Yarra Bridge Collapse 1970

THE AUSTRALIAN

NUMBER 1953   FRIDAY OCTOBER 16 1970   SEVEN CENTS

Registered for posting as a newspaper: Category "B"

| BOLTE ORDERS ROYAL COMMISSION | UNION PUTS BLACK BAN ON BRIDGE | SICKENING ROAR AS SPAN SPLITS |

'IT FELL LIKE A TOY'

30 known to be dead; search for 10 to 15 missing

The Victorian Government yesterday ordered a royal commission into the collapse of a section of the Westgate Yarra Bridge crossing in which 30 men are known to have died.

Between 10 and 15 more are feared dead, buried under the 367ft-long, 2000-ton steel span which crashed 140ft into the river at Footscray.

Another 19 men were injured — at least six of them critically.

The steel span split in the centre and a 134ft high concrete supporting column carrying the outer edge disintegrated. Another inside column at the edge of the river remained intact.

LATE NEWS

Last night, under the eerie glow of iodine lights, rescue workers toiled in the twisted metal and workmen used blow torches to cut through the steel sections while cranes and skindivers stood by.

Officials were unable to say exactly how many workmen were on the span at the time of its collapse because record cards were destroyed. One engineer said it would take weeks to clear the wreckage.

The span collapsed with "a sickening roar" at 11.55 am. One witness said: "It fell like a toy."

Sixty-eight men were working on the span at the time. At least eight are known to have escaped unhurt.

About 10 of the men who were injured rode the steel span down and were thrown clear into the river.

BRIDGE DEATHS

Police late last night said the toll in the bridge collapse stood at 30 dead — of which 20 are identified — 2 believed dead, 4 missing, 12 uninjured,

A MASS of steel and concrete lying in the river mud is all that remains of the mid-section of the bridge. As the 367ft long span collapsed it tore down the 134ft high concrete pylon on which it had rested in mid-river. A second pylon (right) at the river's edge remains intact. Workmen's huts, which were perched on top of the centre span before the collapse, landed on top of the span.

Jack Hindshaw, a resident engineer on the embryo West Gate bridge that was already beginning its first strides across the lower waters of the Yarra River, was returning from the telephone. Certainly he must have been anxious about the bridge, for he had just phoned the senior advisor of the contractors suggesting the workmen might be moved off it. Six weeks earlier a buckle had developed in a plate on the span under construction at the west end of the bridge: until that day, 15 October 1970, nothing had been done about it. But that morning the bolts that held the crippled plate had been removed in an effort to straighten out the buckle. The immediate result was to extend the buckle all along the section. Hurriedly Hindshaw ordered the bolts to be replaced, and went off to phone the contractors for advice. It was as he was returning from the telephone that the 1,200-ton, 360-foot span gave a shuddering lurch, then collapsed with a roar like thunder into the mud of the river bank. Jack Hindshaw died later in hospital of multiple injuries.

And with him died thirty-four workmen, some of whom had been working aloft on the structure while others had just assembled at the foot of the pier to take their lunch-break. One worker who escaped with injuries told *The Advertiser* how he had fallen with the bridge 160 feet into the water, and survived: 'I felt it shaking, but thought it was my imagination and kept on working . . . then the whole damn thing sagged in the middle. I could see daylight through the enormous cracks in the concrete . . . As I tried to scramble out the whole world seemed to go into a massive slide.' Another sixteen of his workmates were badly injured, either by falling debris or in the fire that broke out immediately from some spilled diesel oil.

The Yarra bridge was being constructed on the so-called 'box-girder' system, an economical means of bridge-building that made use of pre-fabricated boxes of steel girders which had to be slid out and then attached to the loose end of the bridge. The engineering complexities and inherent dangers of this method had already been demonstrated by the recent collapse of a bridge in Vienna over the Danube (1969) and of another at Milford Haven earlier in 1970, which had cost four lives (the following year, yet another, over the Rhine, collapsed killing nine). That was not to say that box-girder bridges were impracticable, rather that they required a degree of organization on site and a margin of safety, both of which were conspicuously lacking on the Yarra. A Royal Commission later found literally everyone involved in the building to blame to a greater or lesser extent: the authority in charge of the project 'for failing to define areas of responsibility' between the various design and construction firms; the original contractors—a Dutch firm that had had to pull out—'whose performance fell far short of ordinary competence'; the new Australian contractors for their neglect of the buckle after it first appeared; the labour force and the unions 'for their behaviour on the contract'; the local (joint) consulting engineers for their assurance that the design was fully adequate; but, above all, it blamed the designers, an old-established British firm, for their disorganized approach, lack of guidance to the engineers, and errors of calculation. If any disaster can be said to have a good side, in this case it was that the rebukes of the Commission were heeded by the industry, which has adopted new standards, new procedures and a great deal more research to replace the empirical methods of not very long ago.

THE AGE

Sir Henry Bolte promises Royal Commission into disaster

32 men die—how many more?

Search of ruin resumes at first light

The West Gate bridge disaster death toll stands at 32.

Nobody knows how many men still lie under the tangled mess of concrete and rubble.

Two bodies can be seen among the wreckage and at least 12 and possibly 17 are unaccounted for. Eighteen men are injured, eight of them seriously.

Sixty rescue workers, using heavy cranes, oxy-acetylene torches, shovels and crowbars worked under a flood of lights until 11.30 last night searching for the missing men.

The search will resume at first light.

The Premier (Sir Henry Bolte) said late yesterday that a Royal Commission would investigate the disaster "without loss of time."

Sixty eight men were working on a 384 ft. long section of Melbourne's new $42 million bridge yesterday when disaster struck at 11.50 a.m.

The 2000-ton span collapsed without warning, crashing on to the western Yarra bank.

Many of the victims rode to their death on the 384-foot section which fell from a height of 155 feet. Most were working inside a hollow tunnel inside the falling span.

Casualties

Killed

Ian Miller, project engineer, of Vandilla Street, Balwyn.
Victor Garrada, of Waters Drive, Altona.
George Pram, of New Street, Kingsville
Cyril Carmichael, of Queens Parade, North Fitzroy.
John Little, Dongala Road, West Footscray.
Dennis Anthony O'Brien, Meddings Court, East Geelong.
Vincent Barbita, Ford Street, Newport.
Alfonso Soares, Nicholson Street, Fitzroy.
Edgar Frederick Upstell, Romawi Street, Altona.
Jouzaf Oselis, Cooper Avenue, North Altona.
Jack Henshaw, 43, head engineer

The names of the others killed were being withheld until relatives are notified or the men are identified.

Chaos, horror

Injured

Mr. Ashmore, Derby Street, Kingsville
Angus Seagrin, Gardiner Street, Richmond.
Jesse Ason, Victoria Parade, Fitzroy.
Bozo Seika, Chirnside Street, Footscray
Frank Plemarina, Ethel Avenue, Lalor
David Ward, Tranmere Avenue, Carnegie.
Peter Merola, Kookaburra Street, Altona.
John Boyle, Paywitt Street, Preston.
Thomas Greenwood, Ballarat Road, Braybrook.
W. M. Tracey, Snowden Drive, Cheltenham
Nijo Genia, Killop Street, Northcote.
Charles Santos, Errington Street, St. Albans.
John Thwaites, Frank Street, Box Hill.
Vincent Rosewarne, Stony Street, Hastings.
Nick Caroso, Cardigan Place Albert Park.
George Stassonlakos, Mason Street, Northcote
Des Gibson, Derby Street,

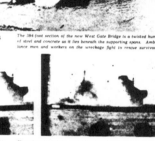

12.30 — Hunt for survivors of a disaster

The 384-foot section of the new West Gate Bridge is a twisted hump of steel and concrete as it lies beneath the supporting spans. Ambulance men and workers on the wreckage fight to rescue survivors.

11.55 — Moment of tragedy as bridge crashes

What Happened at Ibrox?

The Glasgow Panic 1971

SUNDAY EXPRESS

JANUARY 3 1971   Lighting up Time 3.34 p.m. to 8.36 a.m. (Mon.)   Founded by LORD BEAVERBROOK   Moon: Rises 11.55 a.m. Sets 1.19 a.m. (Mon.)   PRICE 9d

HOW DEATH CAME TO THE BIG MATCH

Soccer violence, from fighting on the terraces to hooliganism on the streets and vandalism on the railways, was a much-exercised theme in the British Press by the time 1970 came to an end. It had been a record year by any standards, finally giving birth to an official Government Committee under Sir John Lang, to report on crowd control at football matches. Traditionally one of the most violent clashes of the soccer year was the New Year clash between old Glasgow rivals, Rangers and Celtic. Often dozens, sometimes hundreds of brawling fans had been arrested in the past. On 2 January 1971, there were no less than 350 policemen on duty in Ibrox Stadium prepared for any eventuality.

So it was a pleasant surprise when, within sight of the final whistle, there had been only two arrests out of a crowd of 80,000. Celtic were one goal in the lead, and some Rangers fans were already quietly on their way out. Then, with only seconds to go, Colin Stein, the Rangers centre-forward slammed in a dramatic equalizer from the edge of the penalty area. The stadium erupted, and those leaving the ground sprinted back up the long stairway at the east end of the ground, to find out what had happened.

Suddenly the milling crowd had crumpled like a deck of cards, crush barriers buckled hideously as an avalanche of humanity swept down the stairway. Grown men and small boys alike were crushed beneath the tide, six or eight deep, that flowed inexorably downward impelled by the pressure of the thousands behind. Sixty-six people died in those few nightmare

minutes, and 145 were injured. It was the worst sports disaster ever in Britain.

Yet it was by no means the first such disaster Ibrox had seen. Two years before, to the day, a metal handrail on a different exit had given way as the huge crowd swarmed out: in the resulting panic twenty-five men and boys had been injured. Ten years before the tragedy on stairway 13, in September 1961, at exactly the same spot two men had fallen in the path of the surging crowd, so that it spilled down the steep concrete steps uprooting handrails and fences in its fall. Fifty people had been injured on that occasion, two of them mortally. But the worst previous accident had happened on 5 April 1902 during an England-Scotland international. The south-west terraces were jammed to overflowing: without warning, ten minutes into the match, part of the top of the stand snapped, plunging hundreds of spectators forty feet, twenty-five of them to their deaths. In panic, spectators rushed onto the pitch, stopping the game. When order was restored the match continued, even as doctors battled to attend to the 380 injured.

What had happened at Ibrox to cause this latest, and most numbing tragedy? Like the *Sunday Express*, most papers the next morning accepted the police explanation that the surge of returning spectators meeting the mass of people at the top turned into a rout. But by the next day reporters had unearthed an eyewitness, a housewife who had been standing at the window of her home directly opposite the stairway. She had quite clearly seen, she said,

two exuberant youngsters coming down with the crowd. 'One was sitting on the shoulders of the other and waving his scarf at the top of the steps. They started to come down . . . then the teenagers seemed to disappear completely' she told the *Glasgow Herald*. 'And the rest of the crowd behind them caved in like a pack of cards. It was as if all of them were falling into a huge hole.'

Certainly, those who had been involved and escaped with their lives had little idea of how it had happened. 'I tried to hold myself back' said one, 'but nothing could have stopped the crowd. I remember going down and under. People were flailing their arms and screaming hysterically . . . but all they ended up doing was sinking down with the rest of us. I came to lying near the bottom of the stairs, having been hauled out by the police . . . I looked straight into the face of a dead man lying alongside me.' It was one of fate's cruellest ironies that the very fixture whose wanton violence in the past had been the major cause of national concern over the protection of crowds should once again have become the innocent instrument of directing official attention to new dangers.

THE GLASGOW HERALD

188th Year — No. 292 MONDAY, JANUARY 4, 1971 Ninepence (4p)

Inquiry to be held into deaths of 66 in Ibrox disaster

CAMPBELL TO SEE PREMIER TO-DAY

The stairway at Ibrox Stadium where 66 football fans were killed. In the group which visited the scene yesterday are Sir Donald Liddle, Lord Provost of Glasgow, Sir James Robertson, chief constable, and Mr Alick Buchanan-Smith, Under-Secretary of State for Home Affairs, Scottish Office.

Tributes paid to police and rescue workers

BY IAN IMRIE

An inquiry to be held into the disaster at Ibrox Stadium on Saturday, in which 66 persons died and 145 were injured, could have world-wide repercussions.

Mr Edward Heath, the Prime Minister, will to-day receive a personal report from Mr Gordon Campbell, Secretary of State for Scotland, who is flying to London to tell Ministers of what he learned during his visit yesterday to Glasgow.

Mr Campbell flew on a special military flight from Lossiemouth. Neither he, Mr Alick Buchanan-Smith, Under-Secretary of State for Home Affairs and Agriculture, Scottish Office, Sir Donald Liddle, Lord Provost of Glasgow, nor Sir James Robertson, the city's chief constable, would comment at news conferences on the cause of the disaster. They visited survivors in hospital and the Rangers F.C. ground.

One theory is that supporters leaving the park after Celtic scored the first goal of the match 60 seconds from the end turned back when they heard the roar after Rangers' equaliser. They collided with a wall of people coming downstairs at the Copland Road end of the ground.

Pressure buildup

But Mr Campbell said:—"Appalling as this disaster was it could have been considerably worse if pressure on those who did not know what was happening had not been held and siphoned off elsewhere.

"I believe the police, with the aid of their walkie-talkie instruments, were able in no time to start a physical cordon and divert people, which prevented a build-up of pressure from behind."

Sir James confirmed that ambulances had been delayed getting to the ground because of crowds leaving. He said the match ended at 4.46 p.m. and the disaster occurred after the final whistle. An official of St Andrew's Ambulance Service in Glasgow said that they received the first emergency call at 5.2 p.m.

Mr Campbell said that Mr Heath, naturally, wanted a full inquiry into this disaster of appalling dimensions. Consideration would be given to the best form of inquiry. There could be more than one in this case.

The fatal accidents inquiry was part of the Scottish law, but it could be that some further inquiry would be necessary as well.

Mr Campbell was responsible for home affairs in Scotland, so the decision would be his. He would receive a full report to-day from the department of the Lord Advocate on what courses were open.

Mr Campbell said there could be implications for Britain and other countries, who had had similar misfortunes in recent years, from the Ibrox inquiry.

"There is no doubt that this is a major problem with crowds of this size at sporting events, particularly football," he added.

Conflicting views

"We are concerned with an inquiry into this episode and recommendations for the future. Clearly it could have implications beyond the borders of Scotland."

It would be weeks rather than days before an inquiry got under way.

Speaking of the disaster, Mr Campbell paid tribute to police, rescue workers, and Salvation Army officers. He continued:—"I have in my mind a very clear picture of the way something like this could happen. I can also see there might be conflicting views on what is the action to stop it.

"I don't know of any simple panacea which could avoid this kind of unusual accident. I hear from all sides that this was a very good-natured crowd."

There were signs that all the good work which had gone into promoting good feelings between supporters (there were only three arrests at the game) were succeeding so clearly that the accident had not been caused by rivalry.

Flags in Glasgow will fly at half-mast to-day, Sir Donald announced. He said it was hoped to arrange an inter-denominational service in Glasgow Cathedral on Saturday at 10.30 a.m.

National concern

Sir Donald expected that many people in Scotland, other parts of Britain, and even abroad, would want to show their sympathy in a practical form by donating money to the Ibrox Disaster Fund he had started. He had received one telegram offering 100 guineas.

Sir Donald, who was at the

and the fact that Mr Campbell had come to Glasgow was an indication of the thought, concern, and sympathy not only of the Government but nationally.

Expressing sympathy, Mr Buchanan-Smith said:—"At a time like this words are totally inadequate." He hoped that those who were suffering would find strength from the prayers of the whole country for them.

He paid tribute to all those involved in the rescue operations. "I have been very, very deeply impressed by what I have seen." Mr Buchanan-Smith said.

He had been in touch with Mr Norman Wylie, Q.C., Lord Advocate.

Mr Wylie had asked for a report as a matter of urgency. The police were now working on the information which would be submitted first to the procurator-fiscal. He anticipated that getting the report would only be a matter of days.

80,000 limit

The attendance at the all-ticket game had been fixed at 80,000, and the ground was not filled to capacity (118,000 have attended a game at Ibrox). Sir James, commenting on the three arrests, said:—"This was really amazing."

There had been about 350 policemen in and around the ground.

Sir James said the emergency accident procedure which went into operation after the disaster was the biggest ever mounted in Glasgow. Ambulances were called out, hospitals alerted to stand by

(Continued on Back Page)

Lang to attend meeting

The implications of the Ibrox Stadium disaster will be discussed to-day in London at a meeting called by Mr Eldon Griffiths, Minister responsible for sport.

It will be attended by Sir John Lang, the Government's principal adviser and author of the recent report on hooliganism and crowd control at football matches, and Mr Walter Winterbottom, director of the sports council.

A statement in the House of Commons by Mr Gordon Campbell, Secretary of State for Scotland, is expected a week on Wednesday.

LATE NEWS

DEAD MAN NAMED

A 17-year-old farmer's son who died in a two-car crash on the **Dumfries-Glencaple road** just before midnight on Saturday was named as William Drummond, of Panteth Hill, Mouswald, Dumfriesshire.

Television and Radio Programmes —See Back Page.

Postage: HOME 6d. OVERSEAS 6d.

Housewife saw teenagers celebrating—then disaster

By CHARLES GILLIES and ERNEST PURDY

A theory that the disaster may have been caused by two exuberant young fans was put forward last night by an eye-witness of the disaster, Mrs Maureen Oswell.

Mrs Oswell, aged 33, was standing at the window of her top-storey home at 18 Carnlea Drive — immediately opposite the stairway.

"My husband was listening to the game on the radio and I was watching the corwd coming out. Just as Rangers scored their goal the terracing seemed to erupt.

"I saw two teenagers, one sitting on the shoulders of the other, and waving his scarf at the top of the steps, they started to come down along with the crowd and I said to my husband, 'Something is going to happen.'

"Then the teenagers seemed to disappear completely, and the rest of the crowd behind them caved in like a pack of cards. It was as if all of them were falling into a huge hole."

Discounted

Mrs Oswell discounted the view that the disaster was caused after thousands of supporters swarmed back up the steps when Rangers scored and been met by those leaving the ground.

"I was watching the crowd at the top of the steps all the time. There was certainly a tremendous mass of people at the top of the steps waiting on the final whistle.

"I would not like to blame thes etwo youngesters for causing such a tragedy, but it certainly seemed to me that when they toppled over the rest just fell on top of them. They were like ants falling all over the place."

they tried to uproot the wooden fence at the side of the steps."

Mrs Oswell's 37-year-old husband, Robert, said: — "There was a crowd about four or five deep trying to break down the wooden fence to allow those who were trapped to get free but they just could not move it.

Mass of bodies

"The rescuers pulled scores of trapped people out of the mass of bodies and lifted them over the fence into bushes.

"One young boy managed to stagger down the embankment holding his stomach and I thought he had escaped, but he just flopped down at the foot of the wmbankment and later I learned he had died."

Mr Norman Campbell, Mrs Oswell's brother-in-law, was a spectator at the game. He said: — "I was going to come out by the steps where the disaster occured, then I heard that a barrier had broken so I went to the Emiston Drive exit.

"At a previous Rangers-Celtic game I came down those steps and was spun around like a top in the crowd all the way down. After that I decided in future to wait until most of the crowd had dispersed."Mr Campbell criticised the practice of making fans consume their drinks before entering the ground.

"Some of these young lads are told that they cannot take drink into the ground, so they immediately consume perhaps a five-gill bottle of wine very rapidly to allow them into the game.

"By the time they get in they are in no fit state to watch football. Yesterday there were scores of them littered around the perimeter of the ground completely drunk."

Pulled clear

Mr Desmond O'Donnell, aged 23, of 725 Bilsland Drive, Glasgow, who was injured and is detained in the Victoria In firmary, said last night:—"There was a rush of people and I was pushed down on top of others ahead of me.

"As I fell flat out, I felt some one grabbing me and pulling me aside to safety. I have no idea who did that, but whoever he was I'm quite sure he saved my life."

Also in the ward is Mr Stuart McMillan, aged 25, who is on holiday from St Catherine, Canada. He is being treated for injuries he suffered when he was pushed down at the foot of the stairway.

He said:—"I was visiting relatives and went to the matck with my brother Colin, aged 19. We were just coming away when we were pushed down from behind.

"My brother escaped injury, because he was cought by people crawding round him and carrying him bodily past the danger area.

"I could do nothing to help myself and fell down on top of the other people who had been front of me. I'm not sure how I was taken away, but I think I'm very lucky to be in this bed right now."

James Logan, aged 15, of

(Continued on Back Page)

Special prayer at royal service

There was a special prayer for those who mourned for the fictims of the Ibrox Stadium disaster at a service yesterday attended by the royal family today at Sandringham Parish Church.

With the Queen at the service were the Duke of Edinburgh, the Prince of Wales, Princess Anne, Prince Andrew, Prince Edward, the Queen Mother, Princess Margaret's children — Viscount Linley and Lady Sarah Armstrong-Jones — and Prince Richard of Gloucester.

The Queen and Mr Edward Heath, the Prime Minister, have sent messages of sympathy.

The Right Rev Dr Hugh O. Douglas, Moderator of the sympathy of the Church of Scotland to the people of Glasgow. Our prayer is that those who have been bereaved may be given comfort and that those who are injured may be granted healing. May God sustain and strengthen them all in their time of need."

The congregation at the morning service in Glasgow Cathedral stood in silent remembrance. Offering prayers for the bereaved and injured, the Rev. Dr William Morris said:—

"At such a time, words are powerless and superfluous to the needs of those who sorrow. Like children, we seek the assurance and shelter of a strong Father's love. Tragedy is doubly poignant expressing his sympathy for relatives of those who died or were injured in the disaster.

The telegram, which came through Cardinal Villot, Secretary of State, said: — "Learned with deepest distress of the disaster which has plunged Glasgow into mourning. The Holy Father, through your Grace, expresses his sincerest sympathy with the families of the victims, invoking upon them in their sorrow the assistance and consolation of the Lord."

In Rome, the Pope called on Christians to pray for peace and comfort for the bereaved. Addressing crowds in St Peter's Square, in his Sunday blessing, he said: — "We have present in our hearts the dead and injured Roman Catholics to give generously to the Lord Provost's disaster fund.

Prayers for the dead and injured were said in Roman Catholic churches throughout Scotland. A special Requiem Mass is to be held in St Andrew's Cathedral at noon tomorrow.

Cardinal Gordon Joseph Gray, chairman of the Scottish hierarchy and Archbishop of St Andrews and Edinburgh, sent a telegram to Sir Donald Liddle expressing deepest sympathy and stating he would "remember them in his prayers."

President Giuseppe Saragat of Italy sent a telegram to the

Paris Air Show Disaster 1973

15 die, 28 hurt near Paris

RUSSIAN JET IN FRENCH CRASH

Supersonic airliner plunges on houses

By ANNE SINGTON in Paris

A RUSSIAN Tupolev-144 supersonic airliner crashed on a town six miles from Le Bourget Airport yesterday during a display at the Paris International Air Show. Its crew of six died as it exploded and at least 9 people were killed and 28 injured on the ground.

The Soviet TU-144 awaiting its turn to fly as Concorde took off at the Paris Air Show.

The TU-144—the Russian rival to the Anglo-French Concorde — is the world's first supersonic airliner to crash.

Wreckage was scattered for a mile around the town of Goussainville. A nursery school, which was empty, was smashed by one of the plane's four engines.

The crash, watched by 300,000 people, happened at the end of a 10-minute display by the TU-144.

Michael Kozlov, the pilot, appeared to be coming in for an easy "G" landing in which the plane touches its wheels on the runway and then takes off again without pausing.

He changed his mind and started to climb again.

Lost height

The Tupolev was seen to be vibrating then it suddenly lost height and started to dive. Pieces of metal fell from the fuselage. The left wing broke off followed immediately by the right.

It exploded and burst into flames and a pall of black smoke engulfed the area as it hit the ground.

Soviet officials at the show immediately rushed by helicopter to the scene. Among them was the Tupolev's designer Alexei Tupolev.

Police cordoned off the area and all the helicopters at the show were ordered to help in the rescue operations.

Fifteen houses were totally destroyed and a hundred more damaged. Pieces of fabric from the plane's interior were draped over telephone lines and small bits of metal shimmered on rooftops.

"I just ran"

Mme Marvelle Coulange, 52, said she was standing outside her home watching the plane when it exploded.

"I saw the plane shooting towards me. That image will remain in my mind all my life. I just ran. The wreckage hit my house.

"I ran inside and my daughter in law and her baby were miraculously all right."

First comments by experts at Le Bourget suggested that pilot error was the cause of the accident. It was considered that the aircraft, which was losing speed while climbing steeply, was not able to meet the demands made on it by its pilot.

The angle flight caused one or two of the jets to lose power. The pilot, they believe, attempted to remedy this by stepping up the fuel injection, and this may have caused the explosion.

Very shaken

M. Yves Guena, French Minister of Transport, who visited the scene of the disaster with Mr Vasili Kasakov, Soviet Deputy Transport Minister, said: "It is a miracle that there are not d... ens and dozens of dead." He said the Russians were very shaken by the occurrence.

"It's understandable" he added, "just imagine how we would feel if it had happened to Concorde. I told them we were pathised in their bereavement."

Soviet sources said last night that a committee of inquiry would be put in hand and a communique would be published until it had completed its work.

M. Andre Turcat, Franch chief Concorde test pilot, later that he had asked if could join yesterday's T... demonstration flight as a ...senger, but he was refuse...

The blue-and-white TU-1... been the centre of attrac...

Blow to Russian Pride

Picture—Back Pa...

Pilot caught out by design defects

By Air Cdre. E. M. DONALDSON, Air Correspondent

THE TU-144 crash confirms that the plane is still not quite right, in spite of an almost complete re-design since the Paris Air show two years ago.

The TU-144's performance was suspect at slow speeds and the Russians fitted canards—small wings just behind the cockpit—to give it better stability.

It seems that yesterday the Russian pilot was trying to emu late the show put up by the Anglo-French Concorde, putting th. TU-144 into a steep climb but finding himself too slow at the top.

A supersonic aircraft is not easy to get out of a stall condition and the plane started down, with the Russian pilot applying full power with the after-burner to gain speed.

Then he was faced with having to pull out of the descent rather abruptly and it is possible the speed but with a big load at "G" (gravity).

There was no chance of recovering from this condition and it looks as though "G" loading caused some kind of structural failure. For something was seen to fall off the aircraft at this time.

Many problems

The TU-144 has suffered many technical problems and been the subject of almost continual modification since it first flew in December, 1968.

When the Paris show opened last week Mr Kazakov, the Soviet Deputy Minister for Aeronautics, said the plane would enter service in 1975. But he admitted there were "one or two serious problems" to be resolved.

If yesterday's crash is prov... to be due to pilot error, and the evidence points to something of this sort, it will have no effect on the TU-144's test programme. But if the aircraft is still delicate to handle at slow speeds, then there will have to be more modifications.

This will have no effect on Concorde's development programme, and in fact could enhance its sale prospects.

The two aircraft have very similar performances, both capable of flying 2·25 times the speed of sound but the range of the TU-144 is slightly smaller, carrying 108 passengers compared to the TU-144's 140.

CRASH TOWN FEARED AIR SHOWS

By Guy Rais in Goussainville

THE mayor of Goussainville where the Russian supersonic airliner Tupolev-144 crashed said last night: "I was sure something like this might happen one day."

As he surveyed the wreckage M. Roger Garton, the mayor, said that the municipality, which represents 24,000 people living in the town, has protested several times to the French Government about the danger of holding an international air show at Le Bourget, less than six miles away.

"We are always afraid at this time of the year when the air show is on," said Mr Hughes De Touche, 59, who works for the municipality. "Several years ago, in 1962, an American plane taking part in the show, crashed between our town and another village.

Thrown off feet

M. Bernard Malfois, was walking towards his fiancée's when the force of the explosion threw him on to the road, bruising his shoulder.

"I had heard this noise of a plane, and almost immediately there was a tremendous explosion in the air. The force threw me off my feet, and when I recovered from the blast, houses around me had almost disintegrated.

"For a few seconds there was an uncanny silence. Then people came running from everywhere. Many of them had miraculous escapes as they crawled out of the wrecked houses. Some were bleeding from their wounds and I saw one man with his right arm dangling by his side. It seemed to have been almost severed."

MOON BUGGY ENDS

Russia's moon buggy, Lunokhod-2, has completed its scientific and technical research on the lunar surface. Tass news agency said yesterday. It was sent to the moon's surface on Jan. 16. Tass did not say what had happened to it.—Reuter.

PERON TO GO BACK HOME ON JUNE 21

By Our Staff Correspondent in Madrid

The 18-year-old exile of Gen. Juan Peron, ex-dictator of the Argentine, will end on June 21 when he will return to Buenos Aires, it was announced in Madrid yesterday.

Señor Peron, 76, who ruled Argentina for nine years before being ousted in a military revolt, may become prime minister to President Campora who led the Peronist National Liberation Front in the March elections.

Sources in Madrid, where Señor Peron has been living, said the embalmed body of his second wife, Eva, who died of cancer in 1952, may also be returned to Argentina.

The TU-144 exploding in mid-air over Goussainville, near Le Bourget Airport.

Dean acc... of aidin...

By RICHARD

PRESIDENT NIX... Dean, is reporte... that he discussed p... gate scandal with ... on at least 35 occa...

On one occasio... much more money paid out—would ... £400,000 would ... quired, Mr Nix... that that wou... problem...

These charges, most serious ever ... member of th... immediately deni... House spokesma... two newspapers. ... Post and the N ... who reported ... tions.

'Campaign ...

From The Press ... Gerald Wa... napers of att... the Presiden ... inuendo...

Dean is ... testify un... Watergate... Nixon w... the cons ... ledge of ... the sil ... conspir ... offers ... his na ...

The ... that ... or w ... no...

LAMBTON

...TON ...ding by ...hich ...nitted ...photo ... two

... about it. ... home in ... St. John's

... said at the ...had no com... ... about the ...old article ... e seeing my ... w to discuss it."

...ry call

...er's admission of ... affair brought a ...John Goret. Con... ... Hendon North, ...ocal inquiry into ... of the newspaper ...tures of Mr Lamb... ...flat of Mrs Nora

...called for an inquiry ...nduct of the Sunda... ...ich reported yester... ...e paid an undisclosed ... ...ate Levy and her hus... ...secure their evidence ... Levy took pictures of ...bton to the newspaper's ...

Russia orders inquiry into why three cosmonauts died

Soyuz systems under suspicion

AIRPORT ROCKETS

By Our Belfast Staff

...wo rockets were fired at ...lergrove airport, Belfast, last ...ght, but failed to explode after ...itting an oil tanker and an ...fice block. No one was hurt.

Other Ulster news—P2

Today's Weather

(Midnight forecast)

GENERAL SITUATION: W. airstream will cover British Isles. Weak trough will move into W.
LONDON, S.E., E., N.E., CENT. S., CENT. N. and N.W. ENGLAND, E. ANGLIA, MIDLANDS: Mostly dry, sunny spells. Wind W. light. Max. 64F (18C).
CHANNEL ISLANDS, S.W. ENGLAND: Cloudy. A little rain. Wind W. or variable light. Max. 61F (16C).
S. WALES: Mostly dry, sunny spells, cloudy later. Wind W. light or moderate. Max. 61F (16C).
N. WALES, N. ENGLISH CHANNEL, STRAIT of DOVER E.: Wind variable becoming N.E. Force 2-3 light to gentle breeze. Sea smooth.
ORTOOL: Dry and warm, with sunny periods.
Weather Maps—P30

HUMIDITY FORECAST

	Noon	6 p.m.
London	..55/80	..85/75
Birmingham	..60/85	..90/55
Manchester	..60/85	..90/55
Newcastle	..60/75	..95/55

Saturday's readings in brackets

INDEX TO

Home News 2, 5, 6.
Foreign News 5
Arts Notices ....
Births, Marriages ....
Careers Information ....
City News 18, 19, 20 and 21
Classified Advt Index 2
Entertainments Guide 3
Farmer's Diary 3
Leader Page 16
TV and Radio ....
Wine ....
Woman's Page 18

...amo, ... took ...mam ... in ... Police ...vote—...

...SCE
...ight.
...ated
...4

...programmes ...ent Guide ...ck Page

Russia orders inquiry into why three cosmonauts died

Daily Telegraph 4 June 1973

The Times 1 July 1971 (inset)

The West has always suspected the Soviet Union of minimizing—if not actually suppressing—reports of its domestic disasters. True or not, Russia's entry into the cut-throat world of international space and supersonic travel in the 1960s inevitably subjected their galloping technology to relentless scrutiny, and certainly in the late sixties not everything appeared to be well with their manned spacecraft programme. One of their astronauts died on landing in his Soyuz I in 1967, and in the following three years there were suggestions that several other space flights had misfired. But there was no disguising the tragedy of 30 June 1971 when three of their cosmonauts, Volkov, Patsayev and Dobrovolsky were found dead in their capsule after a record-breaking orbital flight in Soyuz II. They had died, almost instantly, through decompression as their space-vehicle re-entered the earth's atmosphere (Moscow claimed they had failed to close their hatch properly): but the dictates of the 'space-race' between Russia and America demanded only posthumous awards for the dead cosmonauts and no deviation whatsoever from the planned Soyuz programme. It was this same burning competitiveness, very probably, that urged them to push ahead development of their Tupolev-144 supersonic airliner in the early 1970s—at what many observers considered breakneck speed. Its performance at the 1971 Paris Air Show obviously called for fundamental re-design, and two years later on 3 June 1973 it was back at Le Bourget to show its paces to the world, and with a promise that it would be in service by the end of 1975 (so beating the Anglo-Concorde by a year). Precisely what happened, as 300,000 people watched it prepare for landing after its ten-minute display, is still not clear, but an eye-witness saw the aircraft shudder, then begin to lose height as parts of the fuselage snapped off it. It fell, with a shattering explosion, on the nearby town of Goussainville killing ten inhabitants as well as the crew of six. One theory was that the pilot had attempted a manoeuvre completed by Concorde earlier in the afternoon, and in doing so had put strains upon the aircraft which it was not designed to sustain. At all events it was a grim (and perhaps timely) warning to all countries that prestige in the air is a fragile achievement.

The D.C.10 Crash at Ermenonville 1974

It was, as *The Times* put it, the disaster the whole aircraft industry had feared. On 3 March 1974, a Turkish airlines DC10 crashed with 346 people on board, shortly after taking off from Orly airport for London. There were no survivors. The scene of the crash, when rescuers reached it three hours later, resembled a petrified forest with trees scythed to the ground and smouldering fragments of the plane hanging from charred trunks. By dusk only one body that could be identified had been found. It was the first major disaster to have overtaken this new generation of 'jumbo' airliners since scheduled services had begun four years before, and the casualty-list confirmed everyone's worst fears: the death-toll was more than double that of the worst, known crash (in 1973). The initial reaction from the Press was that this horror was the work of an Arab terrorist bomb— a not inconceivable hypothesis in the train of the hi-jacking epidemic that had plagued the world's airlines for the past twelve months, and one fortified by the news later in the day that guerrillas had forced a British Airways VC10 to land at Amsterdam and there set it on fire. But the subsequent discovery of a cargo-hatch cover some distance away from the main wreckage opened up an even more disturbing line of inquiry. Just under two years earlier a similar DC10 belonging to American Airlines had shed its cargo-door over Canada, and had only escaped disintegration by decompression through the brilliant piloting of the captain. In the wake of that near-tragedy it had been found that the plane's cargo-door incorporated a defective locking mechanism (which gave every sign of being locked, even when it was not). Yet instead of a directive from America's Federal Aviation Administration that these cargo doors *must* be modified (there were over 120 DC10s in service throughout the world), all that was ever issued were a number of bulletins from the makers, McDonnell Douglas, 'requesting' operating airlines to make changes. Even more incomprehensible was the fact, later revealed, that the Turkish airlines' plane had been delivered from the makers with the cargo-door unmodified! It took 346 lives for the FAA finally to issue a directive.

Daily Mail 1 March 1974

● There was just a tearing and crashing and ripping and I ran as hard as I could ●   **PHOTONEWS**

Where the wind of death blows through the treetops

AFTER the explosion, the grim silence of death. Beneath the petrified trees only the hushed, stunned shuffle of would-be rescuers moving through a landscape more pitiful than the shell-torn wastes of the Somme.

High in a tree, budding with the first green promise of spring, the remains of a jacket stirs in the icy March breeze, flapping its unmistakable message—no survivors.

Graveyard

Here, in this instant graveyard, lies all that remains of a Turkish Airline DC10 jumbo jet—and its 345 passengers.

The comparison with the gruesome carnage of the First World War is immediate. Except that then, at least, some came home to tell the tale.

"When we got here," says a fireman, "we started looking for survivors. Then I said to myself : 'Forget it.' It took only a second to realise that no one could have lived through that."

Sirens blaring

The ambulances that shrieked into the Forest of Ermenonville, their sirens blaring, rode back silent and empty at a funereal 10 miles an hour.

There remained only the task of clearing the wreckage ; identifying the dead.

A policeman, told that his unit would have to move among the still smoking trees to collect what was left of the bodies, moaned : "Oh, Mother of God."

As night fell, drawing a veil over the horrifying landscape, rescue workers were still putting together the shredded evidence of the holiday that ended in abrupt, unexplained disaster—a yellow dress, lovingly packed, now stripped into rags ; magazines, bought to while away the homeward journey, scattered like a shower of pulp across the scorched earth.

And everywhere the smell of burning and death.

'Ball of fire'

First witness of the disaster was airport worker Maurice Lhote, taking his dog for a walk in the woods. "I heard no explosion on board before the accident," he said. "It was going down very fast. Then there was this big ball of fire.

Another witness at a nearby golf club said : "I saw the plane plunge into the forest. After two or three seconds came the explosion. Immediately there was a terrible blast of air."

And then the silence of the grave—345 lives had just been extinguished in a puff of woodland smoke.

The grim winter foliage of a French wood . . . clothing flaps pitifully among the branches

All that is left is the debris of life . . .

Like a scene from the Somme . . . the dead are carried away

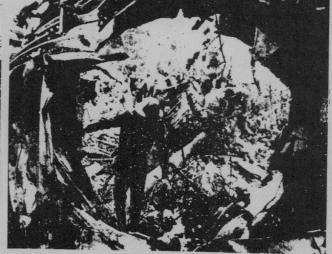

Silhouetted in the fuselage wreck . . . a searcher works on

186

The Destruction of Darwin 1974

Of all days, it was Christmas Day 1974 that a vicious 100 mile an hour cyclone chose to descend upon the Australian city of Darwin, the capital of the Northern Territory. It was the worst one ever experienced on the continent and, in view of the fact that most families were in their homes when it struck, it was a miracle that only forty-eight people died and another sixty-five were posted missing. The city itself was almost entirely destroyed, and plans to rebuild it from scratch were estimated to cost A$600 million.

The Advertiser

Incorporating "The Register"   Television, Page 9

CITY WEATHER
Cool change. Est. max., 26C.
Yesterday's temperatures: Min., 12.4C; max., 25.8C.
December 26 last year: Min., 17.4C; max., 33C.
Weather Map, Page 25.

Vol. 117, No. 36,238   26 Pages 8c   ADELAIDE, FRIDAY, DECEMBER 27, 1974   Phone 51 0421. Classified only 51 0261

'It reminds me of a place I saw in 1945 — Hiroshima'

This was the scene in Darwin yesterday following the city's mauling by a 160 kph (100 mph) cyclone early on Wednesday. About 30,000 are homeless as a result of the devastation.

Cyclone-devastated city will be rebuilt — Cairns

Page 5—Communications failed; city in centre of storm; Editorial.

Page 6—Australia's greatest mercy operation.

Page 7—Story and pictures of the disaster.

Whitlam will fly back

LONDON, Thursday— The Prime Minister (Mr. Whitlam) is returning to Australia today to take charge of the relief organisation for cyclone-devastated Darwin.

He was due to leave London's Heathrow Airport on a commercial flight for Australia about 11 p.m. SA time last night.

Mr. Whitlam may return to Europe in the New Year. Until then the Special Minister of State (Mr. Bowen) will lead the Australian delegation on the rest of its European tour.—AAP.

From BERNARD BOUCHER

DARWIN — The city of Darwin would be entirely rebuilt, the Acting Prime Minister (Dr. Cairns) said last night after a tour of the cyclone-devastated area.

"I doubt whether any city of this size has suffered such destruction in so short a time, even in the most intensive bombing," he told a Press conference in the city's disaster headquarters.

"The result of people's work over many years has gone overnight and all they can do now is search among the rubble to save what they can."

Dr. Cairns said the disaster was of the first magnitude, the cost of which would be shared by the people of Australia.

He said he had just conferred with the Leader of the Opposition (Mr. Snedden), who also flew to Darwin yesterday, and they were in complete agreement.

"There is not a house in the whole area that has not been torn apart," he said.

"People outside can imagine it only if they think of the devastation after the atomic bombs in Japan in 1945.

"The destruction here is almost as complete as that. There is not a home that is not completely liveable.

"We believe that those who choose to go so that their health can be safeguarded should be accommodated by the Commonwealth Government or by voluntary organisations in the States.

"They will be flown from Darwin to their chosen destinations at no cost to themselves.

"On their arrival we want them to be received by people who will be able to record their needs, attend to their requirements and provide them with financial assistance as soon as possible.

"We want the reception depots set up at each airport to involve not only Governments and organisations but also people who can help.

"This tragic situation demands a national responsibility."

Dr. Cairns said the rebuilding of Darwin was not something that could be done overnight.

He also wanted to ensure that those who stayed — the breadwinners — would have satisfactory temporary accommodation.

"We will fly in what they need," he said.

Death toll fear

Firemen are still searching the rubble of Darwin for bodies and authorities believe the final death toll could reach close to 100.

At the moment it stands at 44, but many people will have relatives and friends missing.

Ninety-two people have been

However, all are now accommodated in the hospital's 450 beds.

Dr. Cairns said the first thing was to ensure that the health of the city was looked after, which meant that perhaps the majority of Darwin's 53,000 population would have to be moved.

"Darwin is to be dispersed

Mrs. R. Sabey, of Elizabeth, carrying her two-year-old daughter Mellanie, is greeted at the Adelaide Airport last night by her mother Mrs. A. Harris, also of Elizabeth. They were among 114 survivors of the cyclone to arrive from Darwin.

10,000 to leave in giant airlift

From our Canberra Bureau

CANBERRA — A massive airlift of at least 10,000 people has begun from Darwin.

The Minister for Defence (Mr. Barnard) ordered the evacuation after he had made contact with officials at the cyclone-devastated town.

Among the first planes out was a Fokker Friendship which flew to Brisbane via Mount Isa. It carried 58 evacuees, including 23 pregnant women.

Other planes which flew out of Darwin last night included a Qantas 707, to Sydney, and three Boeing 727s — two from TAA and one Ansett Airlines.

The 727s flew to Adelaide, Brisbane and Sydney.

The director of the Natural Disasters Organisation (Maj.-Gen. A. B. Stretton) advised the evacuation after making an on-the-spot assessment.

He told Mr. Barnard on the first open telephone line established since the cyclone struck early on Christmas morning that a large-scale reduction of the Darwin population was absolutely necessary.

He recommended that at least 10,000 people be flown out, but it is believed this figure may be doubled in the next few days.

Mr. Barnard told a Press conference yesterday that the Federal Government would provide whatever financial aid was necessary.

"Ninety per cent of the town has been hit and badly hit," he said.

"We will concern ourselves with

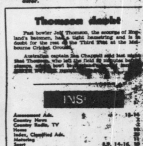

The Udine Earthquake 1976

The Friuli district of Italy, on the northern tip of the Adriatic, has had a curious history of earthquakes. Between 1909 and 1936 it suffered no less than eleven: since then there has been only one—until May 8, 1976 when, at nine o'clock in the evening, a series of tremors struck, the greatest of which reached force 7 on the Richter scale and was felt across half Europe. At its centre the ancient towns of Gemona, Osoppo and Buia—and scores of neighbouring villages—were utterly devastated. The death-toll slowly mounted to 1,000, but volunteers continued to dig yet more bodies from beneath the ruins of medieval buildings and some communities deep in the mountains near the Yugoslav border were still cut off from the outside world for over a week after the disaster had occurred.

UDINE, Italy, Friday.
AN EARTHQUAKE that jolted most of Europe carved a trail of death and destruction through north-east Italy.

Today it was known that 138 were dead, but the final toll is expected to be higher—up to 300. More than 1000 others were injured.

Some 160 people were reported trapped and rescuers heard many of them crying for help.

The quake, which destroyed hundreds of homes in 19 towns and villages with a combined population of 80,000, was felt in France, West Germany, Austria, Czechoslovakia and Yugoslavia.

Three shocks

In Venice, buildings wavered and a few chimneys fell. But there was no visible damage to the frail structures of the famed landmarks in the Lagoon City. Scenic St Mark's Square filled with panic-stricken people who then moved, fearing the collapse of the 325ft. renaissance bell tower which collapsed in 1902 and was rebuilt 10 years later.

In Munich, on the other side of the Alps, houses swayed and families rushed into the streets in fright.

At Nancy, 300 miles north-east of Paris, newly-built houses split at the building seams.

And in the western Yugoslav states of Slovenia and Croatia people quit their homes which were slightly damaged.

Cause of the disaster was attributed by Rome Seismological Institute to a settlement of bedrock 12 miles below the earth's surface.

Three main shocks rocked Italy. The first lasted just 14 seconds.

It acted as a warning, sending people streaming into the streets. Then, a minute later

Cont. Back Page, Col. 2

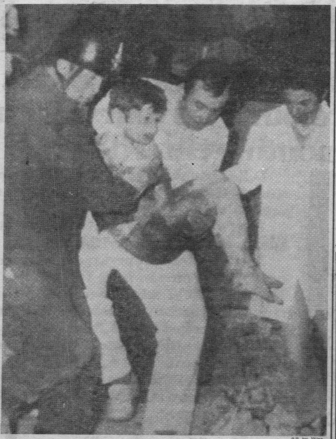

AP by Wire

A YOUNG BOY is carried from the ruins of his home in Buia, Northern Italy, after being buried for four hours.

INSIDE YOUR STANDARD

Town Halls go Tory
THE TORIES chalked up a substantial victory in the local elections yesterday. Overnight figures gave them a net gain of more than 1000 seats with Labour's net loss topping 840.
● Details, results: Page 6

Fifth fire hits Fiat factory
Page 6

Tonight out in London
Page 10

'Vigilantes' to patrol market
Page 8

Stroll in the park to cost 15p?
Page 5

Weekend TV, radio
Pages 2 and 3.

Warmer today—'79 F'
LONDON can look forward to a warm weekend. It may not be quite as hot as today—expected to be 79F—but temperatures could still be around 79F. The May average is 59F.
● Forecast. Back Page.

Revie demands men with guts
Page 42

Hopes and fears of The Marathon Men
Michael Hart—Page 43

Weekend Plus
begins on Page 17
● Sam White's Paris—11. Londoner's Diary —16. Letters —27, Katina, Jumbo Crossword—29, Mind and Matter —35.

Entertainment — 24

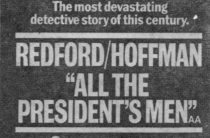

THE TIMES

DAILY MIRROR, Saturday, May

HORROR OF THE QUAKE IN WHICH 500 ARE FEARED DEAD

'It was just like the end of the world'

SCARRED: Remains of the church at Majano, where rescuers are digging for survivors.

From MADELON DIMONT in Rome

RESCUE teams were last night frantically digging with shovels, picks and bare hands for survivors of the earthquake which devastated part of northern Italy.

Fourteen towns and countless villages and hamlets from Venice to the Yugoslav border were badly hit—some of them reduced to rubble.

The death toll at the moment is pure guess-work.

Officially, it is put at about 500. But some sources believe it will rise even higher.

Search

The killer earthquake struck on Thursday night, sending out nine violent tremors, some of which were felt across half of Europe.

One survivor said later: "It was just like the end of the world."

Within minutes, thousands of shocked Italians found their homes had gone and—in many cases—their families had vanished.

More than 7,000 people were recruited in the area to search for survivors.

They included troops, firemen, police, scouts and even those who had been made homeless by the earthquake.

Trapped

A police officer in a small village of Maj... near the city of Ud... said: "We've really... how many peo... are trapped. It co... take a week before... find out."

Among Majano's... lima were forty pe... who were buried in... roadside restaurant... holding a celebra...

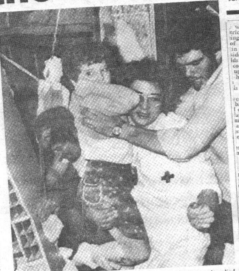

SAFE: A little girl is pulled from the rubble at Gemona. Her mother died.

40 victims at a party

In London, doctors and nurses were ringing the British Red Cross H Q offering to join the relief teams.

Some of the Britons who were on holiday in

An aerial view of Venzone, one of the northern Italian towns wrecked by the earthquake. Another photograph, page 5.

1,000 lives feared lost in Italian earthquake

From Peter Nichols
Udine, May 7

A heavy atmosphere of impending storm still hangs over the areas of Friuli which last night fell victim to an earthquake cosing hundreds of lives—the official figure of 628 is recognized to be far from all of the tragic total—and this sense of foreboding grows increasingly appropriate as the size of the disaster becomes clear.

Signor Natale Labia, Government spokesman in the Udine Prefeca's office, said tonight

that?" The host replied: "Well, I'm rather afraid it must be an earthquake."

Then, despite the heat, what appeared to be a snowstorm began. It turned out to be flakes of plaster falling from the ceiling. The group eventually spent the night in the garden with apprehension and a bottle of whisky to keep up their spirits.

The scenes are bad enough for the outside observer. But local inhabitants keep saying that only if you live here can you understand just how incredible it is in so solid a society as that of Friuli to see

having vanished. In a damaged army barracks, 40 young soldiers are still missing. Outside Gemona, there are signs inviting tourists to visit the town and, as its main attraction, there is a picture of its castle. What remains of the castle after the earthquake is pitifully visible, a shattered wreck of what the picture shows.

Families are camping in tents by the road. Even those with homes still standing are not inclined to go back to them until the tremors are forgotten.

Ambulances and rescue workers have come from all over northern Italy. Units of the ... stationed in the Venito ... been called in to help ... is a certain feeling ... of incredulity has passed, ... ally this out. I not to ... hampened to them. The ... season was just begin ... nd promised well because ... devaluation of the lira ... hey have been struck by ... orst calamity since the ... in earthquake of January,

Continued on page 5, col 3

EARTHQUAKE 1: INSIDE THE STRICKEN VILLAGES

THE SUNDAY TIMES, MAY 9 1976

For thirty hours the old man waited beside the rubble that held his son

Anthony Holden reports from Udine

One man's tomb at Osoppo

THE LITTLE north Italian towns of Buia, Gemona and Osoppo, with a population of some 10,000 between them, each mourns nearly a hundred of its citizens this weekend. At the epicentre of last Thursday's earthquake, these three farming communities took the brunt of the sudden horror.

Miraculously, some say, the ancient bell tower of Buia's Church of the Madonna still stands, veined with ... tilting and swaying ... The twelfth century ... of Gemona lies in ... noble cupola buried ... walls. But in Osoppo, ... yesterday's sunrise, ... sight far more moving ... fall of any great cathed ... more than 30 hours of ... defiant old man finally ... for sure that his only ... dead.

Since Thursday evening ... the main 55-second tre ... duced his son's home ... of Osoppo to rubble ... man had—against all the ... kept alive some hope. ... hung on to it at first ... yesterday, when summon ... soldiers clearing the ru ... the home. But protrudin ... the rubble they had fou ... outstretched hand.

Soldiers wept with him

As the troops picked stone by stone, the old man peered in, weeping, but refusing to face the ... Gradually a shape emerged. The final, brutal thrust ... bulldozer revealed his ... able loss. With a long wai ... broke down, and a few of ... soldiers, young enough to be ... grandchildren, wept with ... The son's body was one ...

50 already recovered from what remains of Osoppo. At least as many more are thought to be still hidden beneath the mountainous debris, which will take perhaps another week to clear. In a circular area north of Udine, covering some 40 square miles, as many as 500 people may have died in those 55 seconds. Those who survived, the thousands ...

Mixing the mortar as the dust settles

From GEORGE ARMSTRONG: Udine, May 9

THE FRUILANI people of this land are known to the Italians for being hard-working. When there has not been enough work for them here, they have found work abroad.

Today, and for some years to come, there will be plenty of work for them here, rebuilding the 20 villages which were totally destroyed or damaged by the earthquake last Thursday night.

Those who are working now in foreign countries are said to be planning to return to help their brothers and cousins put in place. There is no shortage of stones in this plain at the foothills of the Carinthian Mountains. Bricks, however, cost money.

While the bulldozers and steam shovels were removing layers of rubble from what once was a three-storey ... pausing whenever a new room was about to be excavated in case there was tills someone alive in that sealed room — there would be another member of the family trying to recover the few sound ... were put in a

deposited it with other rubble na waiting lorry.

The local prefect said this ... that the official number of dead in the entire stricken area was 755, and that 1,500 are listed injured. There may be as many as another 300 people missing. When entire families vanish in a matter of seconds, it is difficult to say what became of them. Some may have fled, but probably most are dead.

An 84-year-old man was freed last night and, after brushing himself off asked for a cigarette. But time is running out for such miracles. The death toll is bound to be close to 1,000.

The Fruilani were fortunate in having so many of Italy's crack Alpine troops stationed nearby. The Alpini soldiers were relatively fortunate in that most of them were in the base's cinema when the earthquake happened, as two-thirds of their barracks was demolished, leaving, so far, only six dead.

Some of the troops stayed back to dig with their hands to free other comrades trapped inside, but most of them went to the aid of the civilian vil...

Index

tries in bold refer to
individual newspapers. Page
numbers in italic refer to
illustrations of newspapers.

Aberfan 167–70
Abersychan 64
Acheron Valley 132
Adelaide 132
Advertiser 181; *132, 187*
Age 181
Akron 103–5, 120
American Shipper 93
Amsterdam 187
Annapolis 86
Asbury Park 106
Associated Press 26, 33, 40, 61, 85, 123
Atami 82
Auckland 150
Auckland Star 150
Australian 180
Ava 88

Baltic 60
Baltimore 75
Baltimore News 92
Beauvais 96
Belfast 146
Belford Record 98
Birmingham 74
Boston 88, 123, 133–4
Boston American 62
Boston Evening Globe *122*
Boston Herald *133*
Brazen 126
Bridgend 64
Buffalo Commercial 52
Buia 188
Buxton 132

Cairo 114
Calcutta 141
Californian 62
Cambria City 24
Canberra 132
Canvey Island 146
Cape Cod 90, 164
Cape Race 60
Cape Town 75
Cardington 96
Caronia 60
Carpathia 60, 62
Castiglione 141
Chicago 13–16, 44–6, 74
Chicago Daily Tribune 14, 16, 42, 46, 86, 114, 123; *45, 46, 86, 87, 114, 120, 123*
Chicago Record 52
Chicago Sunday Tribune *44*
Christchurch Star *101, 102*
Christian Science Monitor 123, 133–4
Cincinatti 114
Colombo 75
Conemaugh 24
Connecticut 123
Corriere Della Sera 172
Courier Mail *131*
Covington 114
Cuba 28
Cuba 85

Daily Express 98, 138, 141, 146, 148, 170; *61, 97, 124, 126, 139, 147, 186*
Daily Graphic *60, 62, 71, 85*

Daily Herald 60, 96, 144; *59, 97, 112, 113, 142, 163*
Daily Mail 40, 80, 141, 146, 148, 154, 171; *40, 66, 68, 70, 89, 97, 121, 140, 148, 185*
Daily Mirror 80, 96, 99, 138, 154, 175; *57, 58, 79, 80, 82, 97, 99, 127, 144, 154, 162, 175, 177, 189*
Daily News 20, 62, 80, 94, 112; *59, 83, 178*
Daily Sketch 96, 98, 141, 144, 170; *95, 111, 144, 172*
Daily Telegraph 20, 80, 138, 141, 174; *55, 69, 174, 176, 184*
Darwin 187
Desoto 86
Detroit 88
Dixmude 80
Dominion *150, 151, 179*
Dromana 132
Dundee 18
Dundee Advertiser 18

Eastern Daily Press 146; *149*
Ebbw Vale 64
Elba 141
Empress of Ireland 66-9
Erica 132
Ermenonville 185
Essen 74
Evening News *66, 171*
Evening News and Evening Mail *40*
Evening Standard 98, 146; *98, 125, 127, 144, 161, 173, 188*
Evening Star 19

Fae 151
Farnborough 138
Florence 171-3
Fort de France 40
Franc-Tireur 152
Franklin 24

Galveston 32-5
Galveston Daily News *33*
Geelong Advertiser *132*
Gemona 188
General Slocum 47-9
Glasgow 182-3
Glasgow Herald 182; *183*
Globe 73
Goussainville 184
Grandcamp 137
Grebecock 126
Gresford 110-1
Guardian 174, 175; *167*

Halifax 72-3
Harper's Weekly *22, 23, 27, 32, 50*
Hartford 123
Hastings 101
Havana 28, 106, 107
Hawkes Bay 101-2
Healesville 132
Hillend 132
Hindenburg 117-21
Houston Chronicle 137
Hull 80
Hulton 111
Humber 80
Hunstanton 146

Illustrated London News *17, 19, 21*
Il Messaggero 172
Imo 72
Indianapolis News *119*

Jawick 146
Johnstown 24-7

Kansas City Star 44, 48
King's Lynn 146
Knott's Siding 132

Lakehurst 104, 118
Lakonia 163
La Nazione 172
La Soufière 40
Le Mans 152
Le Monde 175
Les Colonies 40
Liverpool Bay 126
Lloyd's Weekly News 64; *63*
London 74, 75, 112
Longarone 154
Long Island 123
Los Angeles 88
Louisville 114

Mablethorpe 146
Macon 104-5, 120
Maine 28-31
Manchester 154
Manchester Evening News 156
Marazion 174
Marietta 114
Martha's Vineyard 123
Martinique 39-43
Melbourne 132
Melbourne Argus 75, 123
Memphis 114
Memphis Commercial 33
Merthyr Express 168
Messina 57
Mineral Point 24
Minneapolis 88
Missouri Republican 16
Mont Blanc 72
Mont Pelée 40
Montreal 75
Montreal Daily Star 56, 72; *67, 72*
Montreal Gazette 56
Morning Post 18, 62
Morrelville 24
Morro Castle 106-9
Mount Toc 161
Munich 154
Murphysboro 86

Napier 101
Newcastle Daily Journal 20; *20, 31*
New Florence 24
New Haven 123
New Madrid 116
New Orleans 116
New Orleans Daily Picayune 33; *25, 34*
New Orleans Times-Picayune *115, 134*
News Chronicle 99, 138, 141, 148, 152, 154; *143, 146, 155, 157*
News of the World 152
New South Wales 132
New York 22-3, 48, 74-5, 106

New York American 62
New York Evening Post 14, 16, 26, 30
New York Herald 14, 16, 22, 23, 33, 40, 42, 44, 48, 52; *13, 14, 15, 23, 35, 39, 41, 48, 52*
New York Herald Tribune 92, 94, 104, 116, 123; *90, 91, 92, 103, 104, 106, 107, 118, 123*
New York Journal 28, 40, 42
New York Mirror *164, 165, 166*
New York Sun 24, 28, 61, 94
New York Telegram 94
New York Times 26, 44, 61, 62, 74, 75, 94, 104, 114, 120, 123, 144; *74, 75, 93, 94, 105, 108, 109, 116, 136, 137*
New York Tribune 26, 30, 33
New York World 13, 26, 28, 30, 40, 48, 62, 94; *14, 15, 28, 30, 42, 43, 47, 49, 54, 88, 89*
Ninevah 24
Noojee 132

Oakland Tribune 51
Observer 80, 146, 174; *168*
Ohio Valley 114-16
Osaka 85
Osoppo 188
Overflakkee 148
Overland Monthly 14

Paducah 114
Pall Mall Gazette 18, 62
Paris 184
Paris-Presse 152
Paulding 90, 92
Penygraig 64
People 174; *170*
Philadelphia Inquirer 44
Philadelphia Public Ledger 26; *25*
Piave Valley 161
Pirago 161
Pisa 171
Pittsburgh 114
Pittsburgh Gazette 44, 48
Pomonal 132
Pompeii 40
Portsmouth 114
Powelltown 132
Princess Victoria 138
Pulham 80

Quebec 56
Quebec Daily Telegraph 56, 62, 66; *55*
Quintinshill 70

R.38 79-80, 105
R.100 96
R.101 95-100, 120
Reuters 30, 62, 66, 96
Reynolds's News 18; *18, 110*
Rivalta 151
Roma 80
Rubicon 132

S.4 90-2
St Ives 174
St James's Gazette 30
St Lawrence 56
St Louis 88

St Louis Globe-Democrat 26; *24, 25*
St Louis Post-Dispatch *53*
St Lucia 40
St Pierre 39-43
San Diego 104
San Francisco 50-4, 75, 85
San Francisco Call 51
San Francisco Chronicle 26, 51, 123; *51, 81, 84, 116, 117*
San Francisco Daily News 51
San Francisco Examiner 51
Sang Hollow 24
Santa Barbara 85
Scilly Isles 174
Scotsman, The 70
Seattle Post-Intelligencer 52
Senghenydd 63-5, 111
Shenandoah 80, 88-9, 105
Sierra Leone 75
Skylark 164
Snettisham 146
Soyuz I 184
Soyuz II 184
Springfield 123
Squalus 126
Standard 18, 20, 94
Star, The 94, 154, 156
Steel Seafarer 85
Storstad 66
Sun 168, 175; *169*
Sunday Dispatch 152; *100, 153*
Sunday Empire News *135*
Sunday Express 96, 138, 146, 182; *96, 145, 182*
Sunday Graphic *138*
Sunday Mirror 168
Sunday Pictorial 99; *141*
Sunday Telegraph 175
Sunday Times 111, 146, 171, 174; *173, 189*
Sunderland 20-1
Sydney 75

Tangiers 75
Tay Bridge 17-19
Texas 85
Texas City 137
Thetis 124-7
Thresher 164-6
Times, The 40, 74, 75, 96, 138, 154, 170, 172, 174, 185; *189*
Titanic 58-62, 66, 94
Tokyo 81-5
Torrey Canyon 174-7
Troy Times 52

Udine 188-9

Vaiont 161
Venice 181
Vestris 93-4
Vesuvius 40
Vienna 181
Villanova 151
Virginian 60

Wahine 179
Warburton 132
Warrandyte 132
Washington 74
Washington Post 48
Wellington 179
Western Mail *64, 65, 111*
West Frankfort 86

Whagaehu 150
Wheeling 114
Whitstable 146

Yarra 181
Yoke Peter 141, 144
Yoke Victor 141
Yoke Yoke 141, 144
Yokohama 82, 85

THE TIMES

DAILY MIRROR, Saturday, May

HORROR OF THE QUAKE IN WHICH 500 ARE FEARED DEAD

'It was just like the end of the world'

From MADELON DIMONT
in Rome

R ESCUE teams were last night frantically digging with shovels, picks and bare hands for survivors of the earthquake which devastated part of northern Italy.

Fourteen towns and countless villages and hamlets from Venice to the Yugoslav border were badly hit—some of them reduced to rubble.

The death toll at the moment is pure guess-work.

Officials it is put at about 500. But some sources believe it will rise even higher.

Search

The killer earthquake struck on Thursday night, sending out nine violent tremors some of which were felt across half of Europe.

One survivor said later: "It was just like the end of the world."

Within minutes, thousands of shocked Italians found their homes had gone and—in many cases—their families had vanished.

More than 7,000 people were recruited in the area to search for survivors.

They included police, firemen, police scouts and even those who had been made homeless by the earthquake.

Trapped

A police officer in a small village at Majano near the city of Udine said: "We've really no idea how many people are trapped. It could take a week before we find out.

Among Majano's victims were forty people who were buried when a roadside restaurant, holding a celebration..."

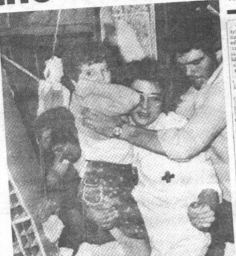

SAFE: A little girl is pulled from the rubble at Gemona. Her mother died.

40 victims at a party

SCARRED: Remains of the church at Majano, where rescuers are digging for survivors.

An aerial view of Venzone, one of the northern Italian towns wrecked by the earthquake. Another photograph, page 5.

1,000 lives feared lost in Italian earthquake

From Peter Nichols
Udine, May 7

A heavy atmosphere of impending storm still hangs over the areas of Friuli which last night fell victim to an earthquake costing hundreds of lives—the official figure of 628 is recognized to be far from all of the tragic total—and this sense of foreboding grows increasingly appropriate as the size of the disaster becomes clear.

Signor Natale Labia, Government spokesman in the Udine Prefect's office, said tonight

that?" The host replied: "Well, I'm rather afraid it must be an earthquake."

Then, despite the heat, what appeared to be a snowstorm began. It turned out to be flakes of plaster falling from the ceiling. The group eventually spent the night in the garden with apprehension and a bottle of whisky to keep up their spirits.

The scenes are bad enough for the outside observer. But with homes still standing are not inclined to go back so them until the tremors are forgotten.

having vanished. In a damaged army barracks, 40 young soldiers are still missing. Outside Gemona, there are signs inviting tourists to visit the town and, as its main attraction, there is a picture of its castle. What remains of the castle after the earthquake is pitifully visible, a shattered wreck of what the picture shows.

Families are camping in tents by the road. Even those

Ambulances and rescue workers have come from all over northern Italy. Units of the army are stationed in the Veneto been called in to help.

There is a certain feeling among the inhabitants, once the first shock of incredulity has passed, that greatly this out, it not so happened to them. The season was just beginning and promised well because the elevation of the lire.

They have been struck by the worst calamity since the Sicilian earthquake of January.

Signor Bursa writes from Udine: The worst-hit area is single measuring about 37 by 25 miles with its centres at Udine, Gemona and Fagagna, but the shock was felt in France, West Germany, Austria, Czechoslovakia, Poland and Yugoslavia. The epicentre was located between Carnia and Gezzo.

Other centres severely hit include Trasaghis, Forgaria, Osoppo, Fagagna and San Daniele.

Continued on page 5, col 3

THE SUNDAY TIMES, MAY 9 1976

EARTHQUAKE 1: INSIDE THE STRICKEN VILLAGES

Bryan Wharton

For thirty hours the old man waited beside the rubble that held his son

Anthony Holden reports from Udine

One man's tomb at Osoppo.

THE LITTLE north Italian towns of Buia, Gemona and Osoppo, with a population of some 10,000 between them, each mourns nearly a hundred of its citizens this weekend. At the epicentre of last Thursday's earthquake, these three farming communities took the brunt of the sudden horror.

Miraculously, some say, the ancient bell tower of Buia's Church of the Madonna still stands, veined with tilting and swaying. The twelfth century of Gemona lies in utter noble cupola buried beneath walls. But in Osoppo, yesterday's sunrise, the sight far more moving fall of any great cathedral more than 30 hours of defiant old man finally for sure that his only dead.

Since Thursday evening the main 55-second tremor duced his son's home at Osoppo to rubble, man had—against all the kept alive some hope. He hung on to a first yesterday, when summoned soldiers clearing the rubble the home. But protruding the rubble they had found outstretched hand.

Soldiers wept with him

As the troops picked stone by stone, the old man peered in, weeping, but refusing to face the Gradually a shape emerged, the final, brutal thrust bulldozer revealed his inexorable loss. With a long wail broke down, and a few of soldiers, young enough to be grandchildren, wept with him.

The son's body was one

50 already recovered from what remains of Osoppo. At least as many more are thought to be still hidden beneath the mountainous debris, which will take perhaps another week to clear. In a circular area north of Udine, covering some 40 square miles, as many as 500 people may have died in those 55 seconds. Those who survived, the thousands of...

Mixing the mortar as the dust settles

From GEORGE ARMSTRONG: Udine, May 9

THE FRUILANI people of this land are known to the Italians for being hard-working. When there has not been enough work for them here, they have found work abroad.

Today, and for some years to come, there will be plenty of work for them here, rebuilding the 20 villages which were totally destroyed or damaged by the earthquake last Thursday night.

Those who are working now in foreign countries are said to be planning to return to help their brothers and cousins put the bricks and the stones back in place. There is no shortage of stones in this plain at the foothills of the Carinthian Mountains. Bricks, however, cost money.

While the bulldozers and steam shovels were removing layers of rubble from what once was a three-storey house, pausing whenever a new room was about to be excavated in case there was still someone alive in that sealed room there would be another member of the family trying to recover the few sound

deposited it with other rubble on a waiting lorry.

The local prefect said this morning that the official number of dead in the entire stricken area was 755, and that 1,500 are listed injured. There may be as many as another 300 people missing. When entire families vanish in a matter of seconds, it is difficult to say what became of them. Some may have fled, but probably most are dead.

An 84-year-old man was freed last night and, after brushing himself off asked for a cigarette. But time is running out for such miracles. The death toll is bound to be close to 1,000.

The Fruilani were fortunate in having so many of Italy's crack Alpine troops stationed nearby. The Alpini soldiers were relatively fortunate in that most of them were in the area when the earthquake happened, as two-thirds of their barracks was demolished, leaving, so far, only six dead.

Some of the troops stayed back to dig with their hands to free other comrades trapped inside, but most of them went to the aid of the civilian vil-

---

(left column fragments)

O
a
$1
B
ra

By
B
ria
volv
ing
nate
drill

Th
the
Geise
impo
Briti
equip
Brazil

The
to 56
two p
randu
signed
Feder
Generi
schild
and se
ing Be
Redmo
estimat

Senh
dent o
organis
working
group o
a furthe
earmark
of the "
plement
Anothe

Tw

bor

From Ch
Belfast

Army p
incursion
Republic
less than
members
vice Regist
Northern I
manded of
bail by th
Court in Du
after crossi

It becam
that the Art
the British
soldiers, bo
and ordinar
their conduct in the sensitive border areas. No details have been given, but it is understood that the matter was discussed at an emergency meeting between Mr Rees, Secretary of State for Northern Ireland, and the GOC, Sir David House.

The latest incursions aroused anger in government circles in both sides of the border; in Dublin because of the breach of territorial rights and in Belfast because of the way, senior officials say privately, that the Irish government has made political capital out of relatively minor incidents.

However, the British side is determined to try so prevent the clash between military and political objectives leading to a deterioration in cross-border cooperation. That has improved greatly since 1974 and is regarded as one of the most significant developments in the struggle against the Provisional IRA.

Government g
dispute over c

By Our Political Staff

The Government has given way in the Commons dispute about the composition of standing committees on Bills. In a motion on yesterday's order paper Mr Foot, Leader of the House, recommends that in Committee of Selection, which decides the party balance on Bill committees, should work to the rule that "only an overall majority in the composition of the House should guarantee a majority in each standing committee".

The rule will apply only to Bills that have not entered the committee stage. But that important for the Conservative opposition, because it means there will be party parity on the committee stage of the Finance Bill, except for clauses to be taken on the floor of the House.

Earlier in the week, Mr H

Guernsey w

A state of emergency is pected to be declared in Guernsey in the next few days that more severe restrictions the use of water may be introduced.

Mr Roger Berry, president of the Guernsey water board, said yesterday that if the present drought continued the island could run out of water by early July.

The board has already imposed the maximum legal restrictions and is to approach the island government's emergency council for powers to try to avoid cutting off household supplies and erecting standpipes. One measure planned is the tapping of water

(right column fragments)

won control trict councils ting contested. of the metro in the large side London ids all six of county coun up for election hold on the I weakened. Is 18 and the res fulfilled big counterbalance of the seats far exceeded metropolitan a very bad in the new elected, but size of the is this week mistic party

Party said results the gains tions were test results local polls units were 1968, when early 1,600

time we .500 gains councils ".

controlled gest non before st five; ster, Notipton. ointed at un-metro in the ey were

taken as a Labour m.

Some of the Britons who were on holiday in

In London doctors and nurses were ringing the British Red Cross H Q offering to join the relief teams.

blocked roads and rail-

räu:

st exclusive

ve beer.

Index

tries in bold refer to
ndividual newspapers. Page
numbers in italic refer to
illustrations of newspapers.

Aberfan 167–70
Abersychan 64
Acheron Valley 132
Adelaide 132
Advertiser 181; *132, 187*
Age *181*
Akron *103–5, 120*
American Shipper *93*
Amsterdam 187
Annapolis 86
Asbury Park 106
Associated Press 26, 33, 40,
   61, 85, 123
Atami 82
Auckland 150
Auckland Star 150
Australian *180*
Ava 88

Baltic *60*
Baltimore 75
Baltimore News 92
Beauvais 96
Belfast 146
Belford Record 98
Birmingham 74
Boston 88, 123, 133–4
Boston American 62
Boston Evening Globe *122*
Boston Herald *133*
Brazen *126*
Bridgend 64
Buffalo Commercial 52
Buia 188
Buxton 132

Cairo 114
Calcutta 141
Californian *62*
Cambria City 24
Canberra 132
Canvey Island 146
Cape Cod 90, 164
Cape Race 60
Cape Town 75
Cardington 96
Caronia *60*
Carpathia *60, 62*
Castiglione 141
Chicago 13–16, 44–6, 74
Chicago Daily Tribune 14,
   16, 42, 46, 86, 114,
   123; *45, 46, 86, 87,
   114, 120, 123*
Chicago Record 52
Chicago Sunday Tribune *44*
Christchurch Star *101, 102*
Christian Science Monitor
   123, 133–4
Cincinatti 114
Colombo 75
Conemaugh 24
Connecticut 123
Corriere Della Sera *172*
Courier Mail *131*
Covington 114
Cuba 28
Cuba *85*

Daily Express 98, 138, 141,
   146, 148, 170; *61, 97,
   124, 126, 139, 147, 186*
Daily Graphic *60, 62, 71, 85*

Daily Herald 60, 96, 144; *59,
   97, 112, 113, 142, 163*
Daily Mail 40, 80, 141, 146,
   148, 154, 171; *40, 66, 68,
   70, 89, 97, 121, 140,
   148, 185*
Daily Mirror 80, 96, 99, 138,
   154, 175; *57, 58, 79, 80,
   82, 97, 99, 127, 144, 154,
   162, 175, 177, 189*
Daily News 20, 62, 80, 94,
   112; *59, 83, 178*
Daily Sketch 96, 98, 141,
   144, 170; *95, 111, 144,
   172*
Daily Telegraph 20, 80, 138,
   141, 174; *55, 69, 174,
   176, 184*
Darwin 187
Desoto 86
Detroit 88
Dixmude *80*
Dominion *150, 151, 179*
Dromana 132
Dundee 18
Dundee Advertiser 18

Eastern Daily Press 146; *149*
Ebbw Vale 64
Elba 141
Empress of Ireland *66-9*
Erica 132
Ermenonville 185
Essen 74
Evening News *66, 171*
Evening News and Evening
   Mail *40*
Evening Standard 98, 146;
   *98, 125, 127, 144, 161,
   173, 188*
Evening Star 19

Fae 151
Farnborough 138
Florence 171-3
Fort de France 40
Franc-Tireur 152
Franklin 24

Galveston 32-5
Galveston Daily News *33*
Geelong Advertiser *132*
Gemona 188
General Slocum *47-9*
Glasgow 182-3
Glasgow Herald 182; *183*
Globe *73*
Goussainville 184
Grandcamp *137*
Grebecock *126*
Gresford 110-1
Guardian 174, 175; *167*

Halifax 72-3
Harper's Weekly *22, 23, 27,
   32, 50*
Hartford 123
Hastings 101
Havana 28, 106, 107
Hawkes Bay 101-2
Healesville 132
Hillend 132
Hindenburg *117-21*
Houston Chronicle 137
Hull 80
Hulton 111
Humber 80
Hunstanton 146

Illustrated London News *17,
   19, 21*
Il Messaggero *172*
Imo *72*
Indianapolis News *119*

Jawick 146
Johnstown 24-7

Kansas City Star 44, 48
King's Lynn 146
Knott's Siding 132

Lakehurst 104, 118
Lakonia *163*
La Nazione *172*
La Soufière 40
Le Mans 152
Le Monde 175
Les Colonies 40
Liverpool Bay 126
Lloyd's Weekly News 64; *63*
London 74, 75, 112
Longarone 154
Long Island 123
Los Angeles 88
Louisville 114

Mablethorpe 146
Macon *104-5, 120*
Maine *28-31*
Manchester 154
Manchester Evening News
   156
Marazion 174
Marietta 114
Martha's Vineyard 123
Martinique 39-43
Melbourne 132
Melbourne Argus 75, 123
Memphis 114
Memphis Commercial 33
Merthyr Express 168
Messina 57
Mineral Point 24
Minneapolis 88
Missouri Republican 16
Mont Blanc *72*
Mont Pelée 40
Montreal 75
Montreal Daily Star 56, 72;
   67, 72
Montreal Gazette 56
Morning Post 18, 62
Morrelville 24
Morro Castle *106-9*
Mount Toc 161
Munich 154
Murphysboro 86

Napier 101
Newcastle Daily Journal 20;
   20, 31
New Florence 24
New Haven 123
New Madrid 116
New Orleans 116
New Orleans Daily Picayune
   33; *25, 34*
New Orleans Times-Picayune
   115, 134
News Chronicle 99, 138,
   141, 148, 152, 154; *143,
   146, 155, 157*
News of the World 152
New South Wales 132
New York 22-3, 48, 74-5,
   106

New York American 62
New York Evening Post 14,
   16, 26, 30
New York Herald 14, 16, 22,
   23, 33, 40, 42, 44, 48, 52;
   *13, 14, 15, 23, 35, 39, 41,
   48, 52*
New York Herald Tribune 92,
   94, 104, 116, 123; *90, 91,
   92, 103, 104, 106, 107,
   118, 123*
New York Journal 28, 40, 42
New York Mirror *164, 165;
   166*
New York Sun 24, 28, 61, 94
New York Telegram 94
New York Times 26, 44, 61,
   62, 74, 75, 94, 104, 114,
   120, 123, 144; *74, 75, 93,
   94, 105, 108, 109, 116,
   136, 137*
New York Tribune 26, 30, 33
New York World 13, 26, 28,
   30, 40, 48, 62, 94; *14, 15,
   28, 30, 42, 43, 47, 49, 54,
   88, 89*
Ninevah 24
Noojee 132

Oakland Tribune 51
Observer 80, 146, 174; *168*
Ohio Valley 114-16
Osaka 85
Osoppo 188
Overflakkee 148
Overland Monthly 14

Paducah 114
Pall Mall Gazette 18, 62
Paris 184
Paris-Presse 152
Paulding *90, 92*
Penygraig 64
People 174; *170*
Philadelphia Inquirer 44
Philadelphia Public Ledger
   26; *25*
Piave Valley 161
Pirago 161
Pisa 171
Pittsburgh 114
Pittsburgh Gazette 44, 48
Pomonal 132
Pompeii 40
Portsmouth 114
Powelltown 132
Princess Victoria *138*
Pulham 80

Quebec 56
Quebec Daily Telegraph 56,
   62, 66; *55*
Quintinshill 70

R.38 79-80, 105
R.100 96
R.101 95-100, 120
Reuters 30, 62, 66, 96
Reynolds's News 18; *18, 110*
Rivalta 151
Roma *80*
Rubicon 132

S.4 90-2
St Ives 174
St James's Gazette 30
St Lawrence 56
St Louis 88

St Louis Globe-Democrat 26; *24, 25*
St Louis Post-Dispatch *53*
St Lucia 40
St Pierre 39-43
San Diego 104
San Francisco 50-4, 75, 85
San Francisco Call 51
San Francisco Chronicle 26, 51, 123; *51, 81, 84, 116, 117*
San Francisco Daily News 51
San Francisco Examiner 51
Sang Hollow 24
Santa Barbara 85
Scilly Isles 174
Scotsman, The 70
Seattle Post-Intelligencer 52
Senghenydd 63-5, 111
Shenandoah 80, 88-9, 105
Sierra Leone 75
Skylark 164
Snettisham 146
Soyuz I 184
Soyuz II 184
Springfield 123
Squalus 126
Standard 18, 20, 94
Star, The 94, 154, 156
Steel Seafarer 85
Storstad 66
Sun 168, 175; *169*
Sunday Dispatch 152; *100, 153*
Sunday Empire News *135*
Sunday Express 96, 138, 146, 182; *96, 145, 182*
Sunday Graphic *138*
Sunday Mirror 168
Sunday Pictorial 99; *141*
Sunday Telegraph 175
Sunday Times 111, 146, 171, 174; *173, 189*
Sunderland 20-1
Sydney 75

Tangiers 75
Tay Bridge 17-19
Texas 85
Texas City 137
Thetis 124-7
Thresher 164-6
Times, The 40, 74, 75, 96, 138, 154, 170, 172, 174, 185; *189*
Titanic 58-62, 66, 94
Tokyo 81-5
Torrey Canyon 174-7
Troy Times 52

Udine 188-9

Vaiont 161
Venice 181
Vestris 93-4
Vesuvius 40
Vienna 181
Villanova 151
Virginian 60

Wahine 179
Warburton 132
Warrandyte 132
Washington 74
Washington Post 48
Wellington 179
Western Mail *64, 65, 111*
West Frankfort 86

Whagaehu 150
Wheeling 114
Whitstable 146

Yarra 181
Yoke Peter 141, 144
Yoke Victor 141
Yoke Yoke 141, 144
Yokohama 82, 85